MARKETING RESEARCH

Concepts, Practices, and Cases

SUNANDA EASWARAN

Dean, ICFAI Business School
Mumbai

SHARMILA J. SINGH

National Qualitative Head and Director
Mode Modellers Pvt Ltd, Mumbai

OXFORD

UNIVERSITY PRESS

OXFORD
UNIVERSITY PRESS

YMCA Library Building, Jai Singh Road, New Delhi 110001

Oxford University Press is a department of the University of Oxford.
It furthers the University's objective of excellence in research, scholarship,
and education by publishing worldwide in

Oxford   New York
Auckland   Cape Town   Dar es Salaam   Hong Kong   Karachi
Kuala Lumpur   Madrid   Melbourne   Mexico City   Nairobi
New Delhi   Shanghai   Taipei   Toronto

With offices in
Argentina   Austria   Brazil   Chile   Czech Republic   France   Greece
Guatemala   Hungary   Italy   Japan   Poland   Portugal   Singapore
South Korea   Switzerland   Thailand   Turkey   Ukraine   Vietnam

Oxford is a registered trade mark of Oxford University Press
in the UK and in certain other countries.

Published in India
by Oxford University Press

ISBN-13: 978-0-19-567696-9
ISBN-10: 0-19-567696-3

Typeset in Baskerville
by Starcompugraphics, Delhi
Printed in India by Saurabh Printers Pvt. Ltd, Noida 201301
and published by Oxford University Press
YMCA Library Building, Jai Singh Road, New Delhi 110001

Preface

In today's competitive business environment, information about the customer, competition, and environment is essential for survival and growth in any business activity. In this regard, marketing research, which is an essential component of marketing, plays a crucial role. Marketing refers to the complete process of identifying customer needs and devising profitable ways of satisfying those better than other players in the market. In this process, marketing research involves the specific identification of these needs, sometimes unstated or undefined. It aims at determining what would satisfy them best, and later assessing the extent to which they have been satisfied. It is thus a means of minimizing financial and marketing risk in an uncertain, competitive environment.

Marketing research is vital for the survival and growth of an organization. The need for marketing research arises out of an organization's need to optimize opportunity and minimize risk. It is commonly believed that marketing research refers to data, but in reality formalized marketing research goes beyond mere data or information. Data merely state facts, but do not by themselves provide pointers to a decision. Often, information may not even be data based but only a reporting of perceptions and impressions. Marketing research is a systematic, data-based, formal enquiry into the views, behaviour, and intentions of the consumer at all levels—corporate, intermediary, and individual. The more competitive the market, the greater the importance of marketing research to understand the consumers and profitably fit in with their needs ahead of competition. It is thus essential for any student of marketing to understand and develop an ability to use marketing research, all the while understanding that *marketing research* is distinct from *marketing* in that it only recommends; it does not take a decision. Students and practitioners of marketing research need to always keep this dividing line in view.

Till a few decades ago, marketing research was largely regarded as a 'large-company activity', limited in scope primarily to problem-solving. Relatively smaller organizations, and sometimes even the larger ones, tended to regard it as a time-consuming and often expensive exercise, its major competitor being the ubiquitous 'gut-feel'. Traditional marketing research also tended to concentrate on *ex-post-facto* enquiry. Over the last few decades, marketing research has developed into a full-fledged, independent discipline, considered to be useful by large as well as small-to-medium corporate organizations alike for opportunity identification as much as for problem solution.

Marketing research has always been essentially a multidisciplinary approach to assisting marketing decision-making, drawing from disciplines as diverse as statistics, psychology, sociology, and management. The Internet has been a major contributor to its growth in the past two decades. Computers have made it possible to extend the scale and complexity of data collection. Developments in information technology have also helped devise complex, extensive techniques of analysis, which have placed marketing research in a position to provide speedy answers to involved, complex queries. This, in addition to the increase in competition, has enhanced the importance of marketing research multifold, and hence the relevance of marketing research as a discipline to be taught in business schools to all those majoring in marketing.

About the Book

Marketing research has today matured into an independent, dynamic career. Even for those who do not intend to choose a career in this field, it has today become essential to possess a good understanding of marketing research, in order to develop insights into an organization's marketing mix, identify viable opportunities, and to minimize the risk associated with wrong decisions. This book aims at providing such understanding to management students and to all marketing professionals. It attempts to examine issues from the perspective of the researcher as well as that of the user of research. As such, it will be useful not only for management students, who form the primary audience, but also for researchers and marketing managers.

As marketing in the country has become progressively professional, Indian writing on marketing research has also developed significantly and has come a long way in the past fifteen years or so. Most of them, like this volume, are today able to base the explanations of concepts on Indian examples. Where this book aims to be different is in its explicit address to the researcher (e.g., Chapter 3: Practical Tips to the Researcher) and its detailed discussion on qualitative research. Qualitative marketing research has grown into an independent area of study, and is being used increasingly by practitioners, who realize that probing the psyche of the respondent is extremely important in order to develop good consumer insights; and both qualitative and quantitative aspects of research have to be understood and learnt well to understand the consumer. This book therefore does not take a position on either side of the 'great quantitative-qualitative divide', but discusses both aspects of marketing research.

Coverage and Structure

This book has been divided into five parts. Part I, *Introduction to Marketing Research,* defines marketing research, discusses its role in marketing, and provides some preliminary guidelines to the researcher for dealing with the marketer and for providing effective and actionable research.

The second part, *Planning for Marketing Research,* includes eight chapters that discuss the complete structure of planning for research. The part begins with a discussion on the starting point of research, that is, defining the research problem and understanding the marketer's perspective. The chapters go on to discuss the formulation of testable hypotheses, various types and techniques of research, the bases of choice of the appropriate research technique, and sampling, that is, methods of identifying the appropriate respondents.

Part III, *Implementing Research: Quantitative Surveys,* takes the discussion to the next stage, that is, the implementation of research plans. The three chapters in this part deal with the ground realities of conducting research studies—data collection, editing, tabulation, and analysis, including the major parametric and non-parametric tests of hypotheses. This part restricts itself to quantitative and computer-based techniques of marketing research.

Part IV, *Qualitative Research and its Implementation,* discusses in detail the fundamentals and application of qualitative research and its methodology. This part begins with a detailed understanding of qualitative research, its nature and scope, its basic modalities, the skills required to be a 'good qualitative researcher', and its position vis-à-vis quantitative research. The chapters go on to discuss the methodology of qualitative research, with due focus on the understanding and application of the projective methodology, which is a core part of qualitative research. The last chapter on qualitative research, *Analysis and Interpretation of Qualitative Research Data*, discusses the analysis and interpretation of qualitative data.

The fifth and final part of the book, *Getting Meaning Out of Data and its Applications*, deals with issues of marketing relevance, that is, the interpretation and presentation of research data. It is concerned with factors that make marketing research relevant to marketing, by providing answers to the original marketing questions for which research is employed in the first place. It includes chapters on writing and presenting marketing research reports, and provides suggestions to the marketer on how to base decisions on research findings. The chapter on applications provides some examples of the major areas of use of marketing research.

Pedagogical Features

Each chapter of the book begins with learning objectives, and ends with a summary of the discussions contained in the chapter. Each chapter includes three types of exercises at the end—concept review questions which test the reader's understanding of the concepts discussed in the chapter, critical thinking exercises which aim at developing teamwork skills and assessing the reader's ability to apply concepts to practical situations, and project assignments.

The book has used a large number of real and hypothetical examples to explain various concepts. Effort has been made to keep the examples current so that their relevance may be comprehensible to the reader. These examples are supplemented by illustrations and tables that attempt to highlight the major points of these discussions, and also to break the monotony. The book contains cases relating to the issues discussed in each part. Some of these are real cases, printed with the permission of the authors' clients. Other cases, though live, had to be masked as they formed part of proprietary research conducted for clients. For example, the three cases included in the first part, dealing with the need for and role of research, have all been masked in order to preserve the client's identity. The case 'The Daily Reporter' in Chapter 10 is based on the actual introduction of a new daily newspaper in the city of Mumbai.

The book is also accompanied by an instructor's manual that will help instructors in the effective use of the book in the classroom. The manual is available on demand and includes outlines of solutions to the exercises given in the book.

Sunanda Easwaran
Sharmila Singh

Acknowledgements

During the period it has been in the writing, this book has drawn on the support and goodwill of many people, to whom the authors are indebted. It was begun when the first author (SE) was the Dean of Narsee Monjee Institute of Management Studies, Mumbai, teaching marketing research. The first debt of gratitude is therefore owed to all her students, especially those in the marketing research class, whose queries and support helped improve the clarity of concepts that find a place in this book, and who willingly submitted themselves to class-testing of the cases included here. Some of their class assignments provided a basis for examples and exercises in various chapters. The same holds true for her students at ICFAI Business School, Mumbai.

Thanks are also due to Amrita Mani, the first author's student, who helped out with some parts of this book. The efforts made by her inspite of the responsibilities of tending to a baby are really appreciated.

We gratefully acknowledge the contribution of the three anonymous reviewers who, through their learned criticism, contributed substantially to improving the content and the structure of this book. Informed criticism always helps, and it is particularly helpful when it is unbiased.

We are thankful to all those corporate personalities who wish to remain unnamed, for their permission to include the cases relating to their organizations, to Mr Saurabh Mukherjee, the CMD of Anjali Mukherjee Health Total (AMHT) for permission to include the case relating to AMHT, and to Mr Mateti Raghavender, Consultant, for permission to include the case on Tatamida on behalf of his client Rallis India Ltd. Thanks are also due to Dr Rajendra Nargundkar for readily agreeing to let us reproduce the SPSS commands from his book on marketing research, and to Mr Narendra Ambwani, Managing Director, Johnson & Johnson India Ltd, for permission to quote examples from the various research studies conducted during the first author's stint with the company.

The second author (SS), especially, would like to profusely thank Mr Sanjeev Goyle (Vice President, Marketing) and Mr G. Sastry (Senior Manager, Market Research) from Mahindra & Mahindra (Tractor Division); Ms Hemangi Desai (Assistant Manager, Market Research), Mr Sumer Dheri (General Manager, Biologicals), Mr Umesh Sidhra (Senior Marketing Manager, Biologicals), and Ms Pramila Naik (Senior Marketing Manager) from Glaxo Smithkline (Pharma Division); and Ms Sheetal Choksi (Customer Care Associate and General Manager, Marketing and Communication) from Shoppers' Stop for their unflinching support and trust in letting us use their respective company and brand names for the purpose of explaining certain core aspects and dimensions of qualitative research.

This gesture of thanks would be incomplete without the mention of Ms Raka Sinha (Brand Manager, Marico Industries) and Ms Seema Arora (Senior Manager, Learning & Development, McDonald's, India), who played an important role in this endeavour by extending their warm support. Last but not the least, Ms Geetika Singh (Senior Project Director, Mode-QQuorum) and Mr Amit Garde (Senior Project Director, Mode-QQuorum) have been two strong arms of the second author and deserve more than thanks for being the pillars of support to the author during the writing of this book as well as during all times in the author's professional and personal endeavours. We must thank the editors at Oxford University Press for their patience, support, encouragement, constant good cheer, and persistence in keeping our noses to the grindstone.

SUNANDA EASWARAN
SHARMILA SINGH

Contents

Preface   *v*
Acknowledgements   *viii*

PART ONE
Introduction to Marketing Research

1. Nature and Scope of Marketing Research
Introduction   3
Marketing Research   4
Marketing Decision-making   8
Scope of Marketing Research   10
Case Studies   19

2. The Role of Research in Marketing
Introduction   26
Problem-solving Vs Opportunity   27
   Definition Research
Quality of Research   31
The Decision-making Perspective   34
Case Study   43

3. Practical Tips for Researchers
Introduction   46
Manager–Researcher Dialogue   47
Defining the Boundaries of Marketing Research   50
Marketing Intelligence and Marketing Research   52
Actionable Research   53

PART TWO
Planning for Marketing Research

4. Stages in Planning Marketing Research
Introduction   59
The Marketing Research Brief   59
Defining the Marketing Research Problem   61
Hypotheses Generation   63
The Marketing Research Proposal   66
The Sample   68

5. Types of Research
Introduction   73
Research Approaches   74
Research Approaches for   82
   Marketing Decision Stages

6. Types and Sources of Data
Introduction   91
Classification of Data   91
Methods of Data Collection   93
Errors in Data Collection   97
Annexure 6.1   108

7. Experimentation
Introduction   110

Causality   111
Experiments in Marketing Research   112
Validity in Experiments   113
Types of Experimental Designs   115
The Limitations of Experiments   126

8. Interview Techniques
Introduction   130
The Choice of Respondents   131
Survey Techniques   132
The Appropriate Interview Method   138

9. Sampling
Introduction   147
Sampling   148
Sampling Techniques   154
Probability Sampling Techniques   155
Non-probability Sampling   160
Determining the Sample Size   161

10. Designing Questionnaries and
    Interview Guides
Introduction   171
Designing a Questionnaire   172
Errors in Questionnaire Design and   176
   the Flow Chart
Questionnaires for Telephone and   182
   Internet Surveys
Projective Techniques and Interview Guides   183
Reproduction of the Questionnaire   185

11. Building Attitude Exploration into
    Questionnaires
Introduction   191
Measurement of Data   192
Types of Attitude Scales   197
Reliability and Validity of Scales   214
Considerations in Scale Construction   218
Case Studies   225

PART THREE
Implementing Research: Quantitative Surveys

12. Fieldwork, Data Editing, Tabulation, and the
    Basic Concepts of Analysis
Introduction   239
Fieldwork   239
Coding and Editing of Data   245
Tabulation of Data   249
Preliminary Analysis of Data   253
Other Measures of Association   262
SPSS Commands   274

13. Specific Techniques for Analysis of Data

Introduction	291
Parametric and Non-parametric Tests	292
Parametric Tests	293
Non-parametric Tests	300

14. Computer Based Techniques of Data Analysis

Introduction	314
Reduction and Grouping of Data	314
Discriminant Analysis	316
Factor Analysis	325
Cluster Analysis	331
Multidimensional Scaling	346
Conjoint Analysis	360
The Influence of Data Analysis on Research Design	369
Case Studies	376
Annexure 14.1	386
Annexure 14.2	390
Annexure 14.3	399
Annexure 14.4	410

PART FOUR
Qualitative Research and its Implementation

15. Qualitative Research

Introduction	415
Qualitative Research	416
Skills Required in a Qualitative Researcher	426
Client–Researcher Relationship	428
Forte of Qualitative Research	429
Qualitative Research vs Quantitative research	429
Relationship between Qualitative and Quantitative Research	431
Strengths and Limitations of Qualitative Research	434
Commencement of the Qualitative Research Study	437
Case Study	447
Annexure 15.1	452
Annexure 15.2	455
Annexure 15.3	459

16. Qualitative Research Methodology

Introduction	463
Methodological Frameworks of Qualitative Research	464
Focus Group Discussions	464
Organization in Focus Group Discussions	466
In-depth Interview	472
Flow of Communication in In-depth Interviews	473
Variations in Qualitative Research Methodology	477
Role, Demeanour, and Skills of a Moderator	478
Guidelines for Effective Moderation	479
Moderation of Focus Group Discussions	486
Projective Techniques	487
Types of Projective Techniques	488
Specific Projective Techniques	491
The Innovative Methodologies of Qualitative Research	495
Case Study	505

17. Analysis and Interpretation of Qualitative Research Data

Introduction	511
Qualitative Research Analysis	512
Process of Qualitative Research Analysis	518
Content Analysis of the Transcripts and Video Tapes	519
Analysis Approach for Qualitative Research	524
Customized Analysis of Qualitative Data	527
Data Interpretation in Qualitative Research Analysis	533
Presentation of Qualitative Analysis Findings	536
Analysis and Interpretation	539
Case Study	542

PART FIVE
Getting Meaning Out of Data and its Application

18. Report Writing and Presentation

Introduction	549
A Marketing Research Report	549
Presentation of a Marketing Research Report	557
Ethical Issues in Marketing Research Report Writing	558

19. Interpretation of Marketing Research Reports

Introduction	562
The Marketing Research Report	562
Using Marketing Research	566

20. Applications of Marketing Research

Introduction	572
Marketing Research for Specific Market Situations	573
Marketing Research During Various Product Life Cycle Stages	579
Market Research Models for Effective Marketing Mix	583
Other Applications of Marketing Research	586
Marketing Research and Brand Positioning	587
Research for Market Segmentation	591
Research for Market Forecasting	592
Research for Developing and Evaluating Marketing Strategies	595

Index	602

PART ONE

Introduction to Marketing Research

- Nature and Scope of Marketing Research
- The Role of Research in Marketing
- Practical Tips for Researchers

1 Nature and Scope of Marketing Research

INTRODUCTION

The concept of marketing is relevant only in a competitive environment. In a controlled or monopolistic market, with limited options for the satisfaction of a consumer's need, the marketer has little or no incentive to understand this need or to find the 'best' means of satisfying it. It is enough to be present in the market, and sometimes not even that—the customer has no choice but to wait for the market to change. As competition grows, the consumer is presented with alternative means of need satisfaction and marketing comes into its own. In order to garner a share of the consumer's purse, it becomes imperative for each player in the market to try and offer the consumer a means of satisfying the need that is demonstrably better than what the competitors offer.

Examples of such changed market circumstances abound in all economies. There is the case of the first commercially marketed automobile, the Model 'T' Ford. The story has gone down in marketing history as the prime example of marketing arrogance in the absence of competition, since Mr Henry Ford decreed that customers could have the car in any colour, 'as long as it was black'. Today, if a company wants to sell more cars, it is not only the colour of the car that is governed by consumer choice, but just about every aspect of the vehicle.

The Indian economy offers an endless list of such examples from the 'pre-liberalization era' till today. One such famous instance is the manner in which the Indian market for domestic air travel has changed from the time Indian Airlines (now called 'Indian') ruled the Indian skies in solitary splendour to the crowded skies of today, where Jet Airways, Air Sahara, and now Air Deccan, all vie for an ever-increasing share of the same business. Under these changed circumstances, it has become imperative to spend time and effort trying to understand consumer requirements in order to stay ahead of other players in the game and succeed in any venture.

As the market gets more competitive, at times it becomes more crucial to not merely understand but even anticipate consumer requirements. Concepts of marketing as well as commonsense thus tell us that success in business is greatly dependent on identifying stated or latent customer needs and satisfying them better than the competition. Briefly put, marketing research is this process of identifying customer needs and determining how best to satisfy them.

The need for marketing research has grown in the past few decades with growth in the quantum and sophistication of competition on the one hand, and the consumer's ability, with rising incomes, to use choice criteria other than the lowest price on the other hand. Marketing research is no longer regarded as merely a 'large company activity', but is increasingly being seen as an essential tool for corporate survival. The relevance of marketing research in Indian markets will increase multifold as the economy opens up in the coming decades. As markets evolve and competition intensifies, marketing research will be needed more than ever for effective and speedy decision-making, in order to

(a) reduce the cost of wrong decisions,

(b) reduce time-to-market when getting there ahead of the competition is critical for survival and growth, and

(c) find ways of keeping the customer.

The sections that follow in this chapter discuss these issues in greater detail. First, we look at the concept of marketing research and its role in marketing decision-making. Then we distinguish marketing research from data and information. This distinction is an important one in marketing decision-making. Both data and information are essential components of research, but will not always suffice by themselves for decision-making.

MARKETING RESEARCH

An organization may adopt four distinct routes when introducing a new market-offering (be it products, services, or ideas):

(a) utilization of existing physical resources

(b) utilization of skills and knowledge available within the organization

(c) identification of a gap in the market, i.e., identified or latent consumer dissatisfaction with the current means of need satisfaction

(d) identification of an unmet need

The first two are internal methods, i.e., based on the organization's strengths, while the third and the fourth are external, owing their origin to identification of opportunities in the market environment. Similarly, long-term strategies for organizational survival and growth may adopt any of these four routes.

Companies may often develop and introduce new market-offerings/marketing strategies on the strength of their resources and skills rather than on any detailed study of anticipated consumer needs or market opportunities. However, developing a product or a strategy on the basis of an organization's strengths without considering consumer requirements involves the inherent risk that there may not be much demand for what has been developed, or that the strategy may have been devised without taking all relevant environmental factors into account and may, therefore, fail to deliver the objectives it aims at.

The Need for Marketing Research

Can we assume that there can be no success in business without identification of consumer needs and developing the means of satisfying them, i.e., without marketing research? Organizations and individuals have been running businesses ever since humans can remember, and success has been achieved at least as often as failure. This success has not always been based on formal marketing research, which is a relatively new discipline. Thus, marketing research is not essential to business in the sense that production and finance are.

Why and when is marketing research needed? The basic function of all information is to reduce risk, and marketing research in particular serves to reduce marketing risk embedded in the 'consumer need identification' activity mentioned earlier. The greater the understanding of consumer needs, the higher are the chances of the organization

---

Sony's Walkman

The Sony walkman is today counted among those new products of the twentieth century that changed the definition of what a 'new product' meant—to the consumers and to the manufacturers. In the dictionary of new product development, it is treated as a classic example of what 'discontinuous innovation' means. It changed forever the way consumers listened to music and extended the definitions of 'privacy', 'mobility', and 'convenience' in the context of listening to music. How did the product originate? This is what Akio Morita, the founder of Sony, has to say: 'Our plan is to lead the public with new products rather than ask them what kind of products they want. The public does not know what is possible, but we do. So instead of doing a lot of market research, we refine our thinking on a product and its use and try to create a market for it by educating and communicating with the public... I knew from my own experience at home that young people cannot seem to live without music. Almost everybody has a stereo at home and in the car. In New York, even in Tokyo, I had seen people with big tape players and radios perched on their shoulders blaring out music... Ibuka's complaint set me into motion. I ordered our engineers to take one of our reliable small cassette tape recorders we called Pressman, strip out the recording circuit and the speaker, and replace them with a stereo amplifier. I outlined the other details I wanted, which included very lightweight headphones that turned out to be one of the most difficult parts of the Walkman project... The idea took hold and from the very beginning the Walkman was a runaway success.' Marketing research seems to have had no role to play in the development and marketing of an innovation of this kind.

being able to develop a market-offering that answers these needs accurately and substantially, assuming of course that the organization has the competencies to develop and market such an offering.

This will lower various risks, such as customer dissatisfaction, product failure, inventory pile-ups, and the resultant increase in costs. The greater the uncertainty involved in marketing decisions, for example, new product category decisions, the greater the need for information relating to an understanding of customer behaviour and the environment, or what may broadly be termed marketing research.

The Indian market has evolved to such levels only in the last few decades. As competition has grown, companies have become increasingly wary of entering the market without first acquiring an understanding of it. In the 1970s, the Indian soft drink major, Parle, first launched the tetra pack Mango Frooti, a fruit juice-based soft drink that has since gone on to set benchmarks for marketing performance of drinks of that genre. The launch was preceded by extensive marketing research, and the brand was test-marketed in Pune for a reasonably long period.

Even so, for a long time, marketing research was regarded as a 'large company activity', undertaken by MNCs and large Indian corporates, and confined primarily to high-value items or decisions crucial to corporate image, such as pre-tests of advertisements. Today, it is not unusual for an FMCG giant like Hindustan Lever to research an every-day, low-ticket item like a toothbrush before launching a new brand, or for a consumer durables/industrial products company like Godrej & Boyce to research the drivers for consumer purchase of their steel cupboard, Storewel.

Information, Data, and Research

Over the last few decades, marketers have increasingly come to understand the need for data-based decisions. What constitutes 'data'? The *Pocket Oxford Dictionary* (1996) defines data as 'known facts used for inference or in reckoning'. In everyday management jargon, it usually refers to figures and measurable facts that can be verified and are supplied by the personnel of the organization, channel members, competitors, government sources, media, or relevant agencies. Managers always need to base their decisions on such facts.

Information   'Information' differs from 'data' in that it may not always be measurable or even verifiable. It includes 'data' as a subset, but may also be an expression of opinions, perceptions, or beliefs, provided through formal or informal, written or oral communication. In order to provide an accurate basis for decisions and actions, information needs to be data-based and its veracity needs to be confirmed.

Data   The most frequent kind of information sought is the opinion of other people, obtained either through personal interaction or from secondary sources such as print or audio-visual media. Data, or known facts based on recorded experience from a large group, must be clearly differentiated from unrecorded opinions or value judgements of a single individual or a small group of people.

Bias in Sample Selection

When a leading land developer and builder wanted to test the market feasibility of an Indian version of 'Home Depot', i.e., a mall providing items for home maintenance and home décor, they decided that their target customers were likely to be restricted to households belonging to the upper-middle and middle income groups. This kind of pre-selection based on the company's biased and subjective judgement excluded the upper income groups totally from the samples selected for the study, despite the fact that this group is as likely, if not more, as the other two groups, to be interested in and informed about home décor and maintenance. Such bias in sample selection would certainly lead to an under-estimation of the market potential of the mall.

Recording assists in verification of information over long intervals of time, and the large size of the group ensures that most variations in opinion have been taken into account and the resultant information may, therefore, be treated as universally representative. Consider, for example, collection of data to determine the relative consumer preference for the three major brands of aerated soft drinks, Coca-Cola, Pepsi, and Thums Up, in the Indian market.

Data obtained from a small group of about ten students from a college might indicate more or less equally distributed preferences as Coca-Cola–3, Pepsi–4, and Thums Up–3. This data, when projected to the national level, would indicate more or less equal market shares for the three brands, an erroneous conclusion. Is data collected from ten students enough to draw conclusions about the preference patterns of a billion people? On the other hand, data collected from a large group of 10,000 respondents might yield a totally different preference pattern.

Since enough people would have been contacted to record all possible variations in preference, the data from this group may be accepted with a greater degree of credibility as representative of the true preference pattern. Again, similar data from the same group, obtained three months later, will make it possible to compare any shifts in preference patterns and draw conclusions about the impact of strategies, if the information has been recorded on both occasions and is not based on memory or impressions.

The criticality of data for managerial decisions makes it imperative that the quality of data be totally reliable. To begin with, out-of-date data could lead to inadequate and, at times, even wrong decisions, embedded as they are in a wrong context. Other limitations of data that could lead to erroneous decisions are bias and lack of objectivity. Biases could occur either in selection or interpretation of data. It is not unheard of for data to be quoted out of context or fitted to support opinions that have been arrived at in advance.

Research Marketing research, as distinct from mere data and information, is in addition the systematic collection and analysis-based interpretation of all data focused on a specific marketing issue (Fig. 1.1). We may, thus, define marketing research as the systematic, objective, and unbiased collection, analysis, and interpretation of recorded data obtained from a large sample in order to provide support to decisions on a specific marketing issue.

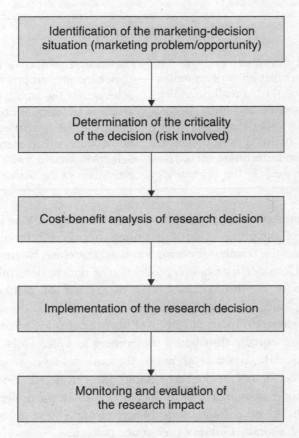

Fig. 1.1   Role of Marketing Research in Marketing Programme Development

As the Sony Walkman case cited earlier suggests, consumers are not always consciously aware of their needs or even of dissatisfaction with the available modes of
satisfying certain needs. It is then left to a savvy marketer to anticipate non-trivial improvements in these current modes of need-satisfaction. Equally important, the marketer
must ensure that the market-offerings incorporating these improvements are perceived
by the consumer as unique, innovative, and relevant. Everett Rogers' theory of product
innovation and diffusion puts most completely 'new-to-the-world' product/service concepts in this category. The very novelty of these ideas implies that they carry a higher
than usual risk, and need to be tested out through marketing research. Otherwise, the
success of one Sony Walkman may come at the expense of a large number of other
failed ideas.

MARKETING DECISION-MAKING

The discussion so far delineates three kinds of decision situations in marketing, which
have been discussed here. Whether aimed at consumers or industries, each carries a
certain amount of risk. The risk arises from a lack of adequate understanding of

consumers' purchase motivations and satisfaction levels with the status quo. Research as a means of risk reduction is, thus, needed to enhance the efficacy of marketing decisions at three increasing levels of complexity.

(a) To identify need-gaps or conscious dissatisfactions with existing ways of satisfying needs. This is the least complex of situations demanding research, as the consumer is already aware of the kind of problems with current market-offerings and is, therefore, well able to define expectations from a better product.

Research into satisfaction levels with anti-allergic drugs, for example, may reveal that all the brands currently available in the market suffer from a major limitation of inducing drowsiness, thereby making it impractical to take them during the day. This would obviously interfere with treatment patterns by encouraging patients to have less than the required dosage, would reduce the efficacy of the treatment, and might even lead to unanticipated side-effects like building up resistance to the drug. The opportunity for a new anti-allergic drug which would either not cause drowsiness or require only night-time consumption, thus, gets defined easily.

(b) To identify opportunities for offering a 'product-plus' in situations when the consumer has latent but not articulated dissatisfactions with existing ways of satisfying needs. Most advances in product categories, or what Everett Rogers (1995) refers to as 'dynamic continuous innovations', occur as a result of research of this kind.

Toilet soaps as a product category do not usually experience much stated consumer dissatisfaction. However, when Dove soap was introduced by Hindustan Lever as '25% moisturizing cream', it was adopted enthusiastically by users as an improved brand, since it brought home to the user the fact that most soaps dry the skin.

Research of this nature, which would usually reveal latent and unmet consumer expectations, is needed not just for protecting or growing an incumbent's market share, as in the case of Johnson & Johnson. It is also particularly useful

---

Johnson & Johnson's Band-Aid

When Johnson & Johnson's introduced the 'wash and dry' plastic version of their Band-Aid adhesive bandages, the original version of the brand had held sway in the market for a very long time, with no apparent user dissatisfaction, and market shares in the region of 80% and above. However, research revealed that for a middle-class housewife who was often getting her hands wet doing household chores and for children who often get cuts and scratches that require covering for two or three days at a stretch and who could not be expected to keep their wounds dry, the brand did suffer from the limitation that it frayed frequently and came off when it got wet. A plastic Band-Aid with better adhesion and better aesthetics was the company's solution to the problem that had not yet been articulated by the users.

Concorde: Too Costly to Fly

Consider the withdrawal from the skies of Concorde, one of the most technologically innovative and expensive means of air travel introduced in the world to date. Proper and detailed marketing research would perhaps have pointed out in advance that the exorbitant cost of travelling by the Concorde and the noise it made far outweighed in the user's mind the benefits of speedy travel it offered and that, as a result, it was likely to remain an uneconomical, if delightful, mode of travel for all but the very rich. Given the size of the aircraft, this would mean mostly vacant seats and, thus, lack of economic viability. Prior research into such situations is critical for the success of an innovation.

---

for late entrants in a growing product category, where every brand has its loyal adherents, offering the opportunity to enter the market with an 'augmented product'.

(c) To determine consumer acceptance of new-to-the-world ideas. The failure rate of new products is phenomenally high. Estimates vary from 60% to 73% and this includes new brands with little product differentiation, augmented products, as also completely new product concepts that require a change in consumer lifestyles—those that Rogers refers to as 'discontinuous innovations'.

Introduction of new marketing channels is fraught with the same risk. When Amway first introduced the concept of multi-level marketing, it was hailed in the Western world as a major advance in distribution strategy. However, attempts to introduce the same concept in India have met with only limited success in spite of all apparent advantages. Some post-facto research conducted by independent agencies suggests three reasons for this: (a) the dependence of the success of the channel on the personality of the 'distributor', who must be a gregarious and extroverted person, (b) the opportunity to choose between a variety of brands that the dealer outlet offers—this is very important in purchase of the large array of low-involvement, low-differentiation items, and (c) the relationship that develops between the dealer and the buyer, where the dealer is seen not only as a supplier of goods, but also as a source of information and an adviser on the best brands to buy. Because of the long-standing relationship, the dealer comes to understand the buying motives and the preferences of the buyer, and the buyer develops a sense of loyalty to the outlet even more than to the brand. This is reinforced by the existence of the large unbranded market in India.

SCOPE OF MARKETING RESEARCH

In a September 2003 article in *Strategic Marketing*, Muder Chiba said, 'The chances of making an error in judgement is mainly because of dealing with consumers who(m) the marketer doesn't know, in places he has never seen, in situations he's never been.

MR then is to be used to reduce the chances of making an error.... And the decision to research or not would depend on the likely cost of the error.'

Parameters Governing Complexity and Nature of Research

In the preceding section, we have discussed the need for marketing research for marketing decision-making at three increasing levels of complexity. Chiba (2003) sums up the need for and scope of research quite comprehensively in his article. Whatever the level of complexity of marketing issues for which research is required, the scope of all research is dependent on certain variables that define its framework. These variables have been discussed below.

Objectives of the decision

Green and Tull (1978) have identified six kinds of management decisions requiring data, namely,

- recognition and definition of problems,
- prioritization and selection of problems,
- solution of the selected problem,
- implementation of the solution,
- modification of the solution based on observation of results, and
- establishing policy.

Marketing Experiment

Mr Saxena, the brand manager for Company A's largest selling brand of detergents 'Bright', is faced with the problem of falling brand sales in the first two quarters of the current year. He is aware that this situation has arisen because of acute shortage of soda ash, one of the major ingredients of the product, at the beginning of the financial year. The shortage had continued for almost the entire first quarter due to a strike in a major supplier's factory. The decline in sales has not been uniform across all states. He needs to decide what kind of marketing support to provide to the brand in order to make up for lost sales, now that the soda ash problem has been solved. In order to decide on the quantum of support required by various states, he needs to determine the state-wise loss in sales of Bright. Let us now assume that Mr Saxena has received data on the state-wise pattern of decline in sales of Bright and is planning a strategy to pro-vide support to marketing effort through one of three methods: sales-promotion drive, stepped-up media advertising, or door-to-door marketing. Because of a limited budget, he has to choose one of the three. Since the brand is not new, the major purpose of the exercise is not to increase aware-ness, but to increase demand. This is a situation requiring marketing research or, more specifically, a marketing experiment, which is one method of research in marketing. He would need to choose three matched regions, try one of the three alter-native methods in each simultaneously for a de-fined period of time, and compare the increase in sales in the three regions in order to decide the most effective method.

These may also be treated as six stages in decision-making, each requiring information inputs of different types. In the marketing context, some, and only some, of these decisions need to be based on marketing research.

Routine marketing information is usually available as brand-wise and state-wise sales analysis within the organization, with the sales administration department or some equivalent function. Though the decision required relates to the brand's marketing mix, and will be dependent on market data, it should not need marketing research. Marketing problems whose solutions are based on routine information, in other words, do not need marketing research. Also, as Aaker et al (1999) suggest, 'Research should not be conducted to satisfy curiosity or confirm the wisdom of previous decisions.' Such research has no relevance to decision-making.

Therefore, marketing research is essential for new information needed for strategic decisions, though not usually for routine decisions. The need for marketing research in decisions that have a combination of routine and strategic elements has to be decided on a case-to-case basis.

Time schedules

Marketing decisions are usually time-bound and if research has to play a role in influencing these decisions, the results must be made available in time for decisions to be based on research.

No matter how well-structured and comprehensive a research study may be, it is not useful if its results are made available after the deadline for marketing decisions has gone by. If a decision has to be taken within too brief a time frame to allow for extensive research, e.g., as a response to competitive activity or in relation to modification in the marketing mix of a seasonal product, it is better to take the risk of going ahead without pre-decision research and conduct a post-facto research to examine the impact of the decision later.

This may, at times, result in wrong or expensive decisions, but that cost will have to be compared with the cost of prior research. This issue will be discussed in detail in Chapter 2, where the Bayesian decision theory in the context of marketing has been explained.

Resources

The financial cost of research is linked to the time available for research. Delayed research often results in opportunity loss because of delayed decision-making or through wrong decisions, as mentioned earlier. Another factor that normally affects the decision about the scope and especially the nature of research, is the availability of monetary and human resources.

In the example of marketing experiment for Bright detergent, conducting the experiment in three matched regions would involve three times the budget required for any one of the proposed research strategies. If the budget is limited, Mr Saxena is left with the options of reducing the sample size substantially, conducting all the experiments in one region, taking recourse to the market-simulation method instead of a full-scale experiment, or exercising his judgement in the choice of the strategy to be adopted.

None of these four methods may provide information as exhaustive or reliable as a full-scale experiment, but it is necessary to undertake a cost-benefit analysis of expensive research methods.

Experienced and knowledgeable analysts

An important issue is the availability of analysts with adequate knowledge of suitable research techniques. Sophisticated research methodologies also require a higher degree of expertise on the part of the researcher. Understanding and interpreting qualitative research data can only be done well by a trained researcher, preferably with a background in sociology or psychology. For example, the science of semiotics can contribute a great deal to a sophisticated understanding of how consumers interpret and relate to colours, symbols, etc. and relate to brands.

Unless the analyst has some degree of experience and understanding of the techniques, it is quite easy to misinterpret this data. Even older methods such as brand-personification exercises require interpretation based on an understanding of the way human consciousness works. Usage of such methodology by a non-expert may result in erroneous conclusions, leading to wrong decisions.

Similarly, in quantitative research, it is essential to have not only a knowledge of sophisticated analytical techniques, including those based on modern computer software, but also an understanding of their scope and applications.

To cite some simple examples, a researcher must have a complete understanding of the assumptions under which the association between two variables may be measured rather than correlation, or the information that a Likert scale provides vis-à-vis a semantic differential scale. In the absence of such knowledge, it is safer to use basic statistical tools of analysis and extract accurate though relatively limited conclusions, rather than to run the risk of drawing wrong inferences using unsuitable, if sophisticated, analytical techniques. Availability of knowledgeable human resources is thus another critical parameter determining the kind of research that may be safely undertaken.

The relationship between marketing mix and marketing research

Decisions relating to the marketing mix and, hence, the required marketing research vary with the life-cycle stages of the market-offering. Table 1.1 illustrates some of these requirements.

The table gives an illustrative list. Individual research requirements may vary depending upon the nature of the product, the extent of competition, environmental factors, and consumer behaviour.

The research requirements discussed in Table 1.1 would be necessary for developing marketing programmes. In addition, marketing research plays a critical role in strategic decision-making.

Role of Marketing Research in Strategic Decision-Making

Some strategic decisions are taken after detailed market research. Some such decision areas have been discussed in this section.

Table 1.1 Marketing Research Requirements During the Life of a Market Offering

Research Area	Product Life-Cycle Stages				
	Pre-launch	Introduction	Growth	Maturity	Decline
Environment	Industry structure, size, and growth; government policies			Environmental trends; changes in technology and consumer tastes; development of new markets	Growth of substitutes
Consumer	Market segments; dissatisfaction with current options; market potential of proposed option	Size/profile of innovator/early adopter groups; motivations for brand adoption	Size/profile of early adopters/early majority; relationship with the brand; motivations for brand adoption; attitudes towards the brand	Brand-response of different segments; size/profile of late majority/ laggards; relationship with the brand	Consumer attitudes towards the brand; reasons for discontinuance
Product/ Service	Acceptability of product concept; positioning; benefit expectations; patterns of product use	Trial/repeat purchase/ adoption rates; brand switch; initial experience; brand opinion vis-à-vis competition	Repeat purchase; brand image and identity; brand loyalty; patterns of brand use	Brand loyalty levels; scope for and acceptance of brand extensions; brand identity	Scope for repositioning and selective promotion
Price	Acceptability of proposed price	Response to price; 'value-for-money'	Opportunity for price modification	Influence of price on brand image; purchase and loyalty; response to price variants	Opportunity of brand-sustenance through price discounts
Promotion		Brand awareness; brand knowledge; initial brand image; appropriate promotion channels	Efficacy of promotion media vis-à-vis brand objectives	Impact of sales promotion; opportunities for repositioning the brand; impact of advertising strategies	

(Continued)

(Table 1.1 Contd.)

Research Area	Product Life-Cycle Stages				
	Pre-launch	Introduction	Growth	Maturity	Decline
Distribution		Availability; dealer acceptance; dealer support to brand	Availability; dealer acceptance; dealer support to brand; dealer network extension opportunity	Degree of reach and penetration; dealer support to brand; opportunities for and potential of new channels	Reasons for dealer discontinuance of the brand
Competition	Substitutes; direct competition; major players; segments dominated; competitive strategies	Early competitive response to brand	Competitive response to brand; development of the market	Market consolidation; competition growth; competitive response to brand	

Project feasibility studies

Market feasibility exploration forms an essential part of any new project feasibility analysis. Such exploration would help define the most suitable target segment, identify consumer expectations, identify competition, influence the marketing mix, and project sales over the long term, thereby providing the needed marketing inputs for the project idea.

Branding and positioning

The need for branding; the most suitable branding platform; branding strategies; positioning strategies; the need for and direction of repositioning strategies—these and all similar decisions are required to be based on marketing research in order to reduce the inherent risk.

Allen Solly

When Allen Solly considered launching women's western wear, they needed to answer all these questions: should they target the product at women executives who have already adopted western wear or should they try to change the taste of women who currently wear salwar-kameez to work? Which age group, income group, and educational background should be targetted? What brand characteristics should they emphasize? What positioning would be most suitable? Should they make it available through the Allen Solly retail showrooms, or place it in multi-brand department stores? How often were women consumers likely to buy such garments? All these, and a host of similar questions essential to determining the market feasibility of the brand, could only be answered through research.

Diversification

Whether and where to diversify? The choice between market development, product development, and diversification strategies has to be based on an understanding of the marketing environment and the company's relationship with it.

When companies like Hindustan Lever Limited start looking at growth avenues, this is a very real issue. Is it better to launch yet another soap or shampoo, where their reputation and experience would help quick consumer acceptance and speedier penetration, or is it better for them to enter the branded commodities market like *atta* (wheat flour), which is a nascent market with little competition and would provide synergies with their bought-out brands like Modern bread?

Once this information has been obtained through marketing research that marries the environment to company capabilities, further decisions about the direction in which the organization needs to move within the framework of any of these strategies will again be dependent on marketing research that measures the company's chances of success in any of these areas. Research would also help a company like The Times of India group to make a similar decision and to foray into 'infotainment' brands like Planet M.

Market development

Market research helps decisions regarding which markets or market segments to develop for future growth. Amul's decision to expand into dairy products other than milk with yogurt and cheese is a case in point, and so is Johnson & Johnson's extension of the baby soap, earlier aimed at the infant below one year, to the three-year plus child.

Measurement and forecast of market trends

Though this field is often treated as the preserve of economic analysis at the macro level, at the company level marketing research is required to relate this information to the organization's growth prospects.

This would often be the precursor to market-entry choices. Most pharmaceutical and FMCG companies, for example, keep track of market trends with the help of ORG-Marg's retail audit, a syndicated market research service providing monthly measures of the market, sales, market shares, and growth patterns of participating companies,

---

Johnson's Baby Lotion

Johnson & Johnson had positioned their Johnson's Baby Lotion brand for teenagers, on the assumption that girls were most likely to be concerned about their appearances at that age and would, therefore, be the most suitable target for a skin-care product. Research, however, revealed that the concept of 'good looks' varies with age: in her teens, with a young skin, a girl is more concerned with treatment of blemishes like pimples and with enhancement of appearance with cosmetics, rather than with preservation of young-looking skin with moisturizers. The thirty-plus woman, on the other hand, becomes aware of the effects of aging and is certainly interested in skin-care products like moisturizers. The result was the repositioning of the brand towards the thirty-plus woman.

brands, and packs. With the help of retail audit, industry players are not only able to keep track of the attractiveness of the various markets, the data also provides a basis for forecasting future growth of the market, the product category, and the major competitors. Using this market research data, companies considering entry into a certain industry are in addition able to identify prospective competition and plan strategies to be employed in case they enter the market.

Customer satisfaction surveys

As in the case of market trends, market research is also needed to focus this environment-related input on the firm and the industry in order to identify opportunity areas. *The Wall Street Journal* in the USA regularly publishes findings of the customer satisfaction index for the US economy, prepared by the University of Michigan.

The customer satisfaction index is constructed on the basis of detailed qualitative and quantitative marketing research data, collected every quarter. It is used by the US industry as well as the government as 'a uniform and independent measure of household consumption experience', which 'tracks trends in customer satisfaction and provides valuable benchmarking insights of the consumer economy for companies, industry trade associations, and government agencies'. *The Economic Times* in India has recently begun reporting a 'customer confidence index', which provides similar measures of customer confidence in the economy.

SUMMARY

Marketing research is required in business to reduce the risk in marketing decision-making. The need for research, therefore, increases with the degree of uncertainty in the environment and the extent of risk inherent in the marketing decision under consideration. It is needed at the product level, the brand level, and also at the strategic level. Research, as distinct from routine marketing information, is systematic, objective, and unbiased data collected from a large sample in order to arrive at answers to a specific marketing issue, which will strategically impact the organization's performance in the long run. All marketing decisions, therefore, do not require marketing research. Major factors that affect the nature of marketing research are the marketing decision areas being investigated, and the life-cycle stage of the product, service, or idea being studied.

KEY WORDS

Market-offering is a product, service, or concept introduced in the market by an organization or entrepreneur.

Information refers to items of knowledge; news.

Data refers to facts and figures that may be used in decision-making.

Efficacy of marketing decision is the ability of a marketing decision to favourably impact the performance and the output of the organization.

Marketing mix refers to the particular combination in which an organization's monetary, knowledge, and human resources are deployed at a point in time.

Strategic decision is one that will have a long-term and major impact on the direction and results of organizational activity.

Pre-decision research is research undertaken prior to decision-making in order to gauge the potential impact of alternative decisions.

Post-decision research is research undertaken after the decision has been taken, to compare actual performance with benchmarks set before the decision and study the impact of the decision on organizational performance.

Market simulation method is a market-experimentation technique in which a market-like situation is created within the confines of a room or a hall, and the marketing element under study is tested out under these simulated market conditions with the target group, usually selected at random from the street.

CONCEPT REVIEW QUESTIONS

1. What role does marketing research play in reducing marketing risk? What factors must be taken into account while weighing the decision to undertake marketing research?

2. Research can be used for help in strategy development as well as for developing marketing programmes. How will the two be different? Give two examples of each.

3. All movies made within the country are screened by the Censor Board before they are released for public viewing. Is it possible to use the views of the Censor Board as equivalent to a marketing research study to predict whether or not a movie would be successful? Why?

4. Indian and Air India have announced a tie-up under which they will extend each other's routes and reduce competition with each other. This is a major decision that will have significant strategic impact on the profitability and operations of both companies. Do you think they should have undertaken a marketing research study before taking such a decision? Give reasons for your answer.

5. The ABC Institute of Management believes that demand exists for a competency-building diploma course in shipping management aimed at senior members of the industry who might, after a few years of service at senior levels on ships, look for opportunities in shore jobs. They are considering conducting a survey to define the nature and size of this demand. What factors should they consider before conducting such marketing research? What are the possible pitfalls they must seek to avoid while conducting the study?

6. Marketing of rural products often fails because of inadequate or poor quality research. In what way would the planning of research for rural products be different from that of urban products? What differences between the two sets of products and consumers should be kept in mind while planning such research?

PROJECT ASSIGNMENTS

1. In what areas, if any, could the following use marketing research?

   (a) SPIC-MACAY, Society for the Promotion of Indian Classical Music and Culture Amongst Youth.
   (b) A new business school opening in your city
   (c) Crossroads, the mall in Mumbai

   Select any one of the three and suggest how the marketing research carried out by it for a marketing issue faced by it might differ from the marketing research conducted by a manufacturing company. Design the research study for any one such marketing issue.

2. Company X, the leader in the market for biscuits, has been losing sales on one of its major brands over the past two years. The marketing department in the company claims that the sales people are not doing their job properly, since the biscuit market seems to be growing. The sales management team on the other hand accuses the marketing group of setting impossible targets, without taking into account the fact that no brand can keep growing at an increasing or even a constant rate for ever. Should a marketing research study be undertaken to provide the answer? Why? Compile a detailed list of other information that should be collected prior to the research, if it is to be undertaken at all.

3. Aditya Gupta has recently taken charge of Fairever, his company's brand of fairness cream. While going through the documentation on the brand, he comes across a marketing research study commissioned by his predecessor on the possible brand extensions for Fairever. The study had been carried out six months ago, and indicated that at this stage in the life of the brand, brand extensions would detract from its equity. Aditya believes that market conditions have changed somewhat since the study was carried out, and decides to commission another study for the same purpose. Do you agree with his decision? Give reasons for your answer and also prepare the brief that Aditya Gupta would give to the marketing research agency through which he is commissioning the study.

4. Choose a major FMCG brand that has been showing stagnating sales for the past few months. Prepare a research plan to assess the brand's need for growth through market development. Discuss it with the company and compile a list of their comments.

CASE STUDIES

1. The Tale of Subbu and The Target

The folders distributed at the Regional Sales Manager's (RSM) conference contained, among other things, photocopies of an article entitled 'Strategic Planning is a Dynamic Exercise' by Walter Vieira, the well-known management consultant. Sitting in one of the middle rows in the Head Office conference hall as the speaker went interminably on with his presentation, Ravi Subramanyam, the South Zone RSM of Bharat Agro Products Ltd, Subbu to his colleagues, idly turned its pages, scepticism writ all over his face. One paragraph had been highlighted for attention, and he ran his eyes over it. 'The company equivalent of a prepared mind is market foresight. Specifically, market foresight relies on identifying changing customer values and needs, monitoring the evolving competitive field, and anticipating which capabilities within the entire supply chain may become the basis for improved competitive advantage. A company with the capability of market foresight establishes practices for gathering and making sense of such information on a regular basis. Fortune will favour such efforts with breakthrough innovations and superior results.' Subbu broke off at that point. He knew all that. 'The same old theorization. When will these ivory tower academicians realize that no one knows the customer better than us guys in the field? What kind of morons do they take us for? Don't we know our competition? Why don't some of them come and work in the field? They are the ones who need to understand the consumer,' he muttered irritably to Srikant Bhattacharya, the East Zone RSM, who was sitting next to him. They shuffled out as the presentation finally came to an end. By long-standing tradition, the RSMs' conference was also the time for individual RSMs to meet with the General Manager—Sales, the Marketing Manager, and other marketing staff. Subbu headed for the cabin of Shirish Shukla, General Manager—Sales. 'Lambs to the slaughter,' he grinned over his shoulder at Bhattacharya, who was going to see Manikutty, the Marketing Manager. That trite remark notwithstanding, he was quite pleased with the performance of his region that quarter, and was fairly certain that he would be in the running for the 'best performer' trophy awarded every quarter. The trophy was to be announced the next day, and there had been strong indications that Subbu's region was a strong contender.

His discussions with Shukla appeared to confirm this further. So when Shukla raised the subject of 'Agriguard', the company's new herbicide, Subbu was taken aback (Table 1.2). Granted that the brand had not met its target in his region, but it was a

Table 1.2 Sales Growth of Herbicides Market and Major Brands

(Rs in million)

Market and Major Brands	1996		1997			1998		
	Rs Sales	Mkt Share (in %)	Rs Sales	Growth % over 1996*	Mkt Share (in %)	Rs Sales	Growth % over 1997*	Mkt Share (in %)
Total Herbicides Market for Wheat	923.0	100.0	1100.7	19.3	100.0	1349.3	22.6	100.0
Arelon	180.2	19.5	158.2	−12.2	14.4	123.4	−22.0	9.1
Marklon	135.2	14.8	181.7	34.4	16.5	169.7	−6.6	12.6
Agriguard	80.2	8.7	102.4	27.6	9.3	160.6	56.8	11.9
Others	527.4	57.0	658.4	24.8	59.8	895.6	36.0	66.4

Note: * The table provides comparative data for the years 1996, 1997, and 1998. The growth columns provide a comparison of growth in 1997 to 1996 and growth in 1998 to 1997. Similar growth rates for 1996 over 1995 have not been included since the discussion in restricted to these three years.

relatively small brand and, on the whole, his region had over-shot the target by as much as 12%. Compared with the major competing insecticide brand 'Agrifan', Agriguard was small fry. But Shukla was talking facts and figures. 'Look, Subbu, I know you have done well on the whole. But the point is, these herbicides are a growing market. Look at this data sent out by market research,' Shukla spread a sheet out on his table. Subbu had no choice but to look at the figures, which are shown in Table 1.2.

'These are the all-India figures,' Shukla resumed. 'As you can see, herbicides are a fast-growing market, and not so small, either. And during the period that Agriguard has been growing faster than the market and is set to become the largest brand, it has been doing badly in your region.' 'But that is not true, Shirish, and you know that,' Subbu was furious. 'I don't care what these figures say, but these are not the figures for my region. And everyone knows that Agriguard is the largest seller in the South right now even though it hasn't met the target set by guys who don't know better than to sit in their air-conditioned cabins and churn out data from thin air. You have worked my market! You know nobody is doing as well as we are! Do you believe these figures? Besides, this is comparing apples with potatoes! How can anyone compare growth in market share with achievement of targets?' 'Subbu, you know that we are all expected to adhere to the targets once they have been finalized. You are consulted before finalization,' Shukla was firm.

'Look, Shirish, I have been doing my best. But a company cannot set targets on the basis of guesstimates like these and then expect managers to stick with them,' Subbu shot back. Shirish Shukla looked at Subbu for a while. There was a lot of truth in what his RSM was saying. Unlike pharmaceuticals and consumer goods, there was no independent retail-audit panel in the agrochemicals industry. The all-India figures were arrived at through mutual agreement between the companies, and different companies employed a variety of methods for calculating their final turnover figures. The financial year also varied for many companies. And for the regions, these all-India figures were used as a mere guideline. He thought for a long time. Subbu had cooled down somewhat after his outburst. He realized it was only Shukla's sense of fair play that had let him get away with such arguments and such language, though he believed his arguments were valid.

Shukla spoke after a while, 'Subbu, this problem keeps coming up every once in a while. You say you do not accept these figures. But you know that figures talk louder, longer, and more firmly than mere emotions. Why don't *you* collect figures for your region and send them to me and to Market Research? They are hampered by the lack of reliable figures. And as you can see, it will be useful to everyone, including yourself.' 'It is *their* job,' was Subbu's first, instinctive reaction. 'We field people have better things to do than go around collecting data. Besides, do you expect me to do this every month?' Shukla grinned. Subbu's last question indicated that even as he was talking, he had seen the benefit to his region of Shukla's suggestion.

'Try to do it at least once a quarter,' he told Subbu. 'Your field people, with their long-term relationship with the distributors, are more likely to be able to collect such information from them than Mukerjee s (the Market Research Manager's) team.'[1]

---

[1] Quoted from a published article by Walter Vieira (2000).

Questions

1. According to you, whose stand do you think the figures support—Subbu's or Shukla's? Why?

2. What kind of information should Subbu collect in order to check whether his stand was right?

3. What kind of information should be collected for setting sales targets for a region, so that the people involved will have an idea about the performance of their brand vis-à-vis other brands? Who should collect this information? Why? Will it improve their decisions? How?

2. Helping Hands

Urmi Patel looked at her husband with defeated eyes. She found it difficult to accept the conclusion that he had reached and that he was trying to make her see the logic of—that her business was not going to take off. There seemed no reason for it not to. Everyone had said at the time that it was a great idea, even her husband. 'I do not deny that, Urmi. We all thought so, at the time. Perhaps we should have checked out the market,' said her husband, Ratan. It pained him to see the disappointment on her face. But there was nothing for it. The mistake had to be accepted.

Urmi was thinking about the time, five months earlier, when the idea had first come to her. For years now, she had lived in Ghatkopar, a Gujarati-dominated area of Mumbai. The second of three children, she had been born and brought up in East Africa, where her father had been running a thriving business in textiles. She came to India after her marriage twenty-eight years ago, and about fifteen years ago, her parents had also retired to Mumbai, when her two brothers decided to emigrate to the UK. They lived not far from Urmi, and she had been taking care of them all this while. Now that her own children were grown up, she found more time on her hands, and had been helping her husband out with his business, too. Her knowledge of computers came in handy in that work.

Talking to her neighbours and the neighbours of her parents gradually made her aware of one fact: it had become common among Gujarati families for children to go off to the USA or UK after they grew up. Parents looked upon the phenomenon with pride, and getting their daughters married to 'boys in America' was something of a status symbol. One major impact of this new trend was that parents were usually left behind to fend for themselves. In a country like India, where the joint family system has not disappeared completely even now, and where it was the norm for sons to look after aged parents, this socio-economic change was striking at the roots of social and emotional security, specially in communities like the Gujaratis, where the number of emigrants was high. Societal structure was still not geared to cope with this change, and there were not many governmental or voluntary organizations around to take care of old people in an organized manner. Increasing life-expectancy had made the problem more acute. Urmi Patel saw her parents facing this problem and trying to find ways to come to terms with it. That she was around to lend a hand helped. This set her thinking. What about people who did not have any children living nearby? Specially those who were really old and not capable of handling the responsibilities of day-to-day living? She herself had been asked by some neighbours and friends of her parents on many occasions to help out with chores like paying the telephone bill, booking the gas, and calling in the plumber to repair a leaky faucet.

She began to realize that here was the opportunity for an innovative business. She could offer to take care of these tasks for old people in her neighbourhood, at a price. She discussed the idea with her husband and a few trustworthy friends. They agreed that it could be a very profitable business idea, though, of course, like any business idea, it needed to be worked upon. Urmi felt that in this way, she would be providing a much-needed service to the community and, at the same time, making some money. She sat down and made a list of the various tasks she usually had to perform for her parents and their neighbours on a regular basis, and the frequency of each task. She estimated the time she had to spend on each task. Working out the cost of each task was a bit difficult, till her husband suggested that she could follow one of two approaches: either ask various artisans how much they would charge for each such task and cost it accordingly, or estimate the cost of her time on the basis of the salary she would expect to get per month for a full time, eight-hour-a-day job. She opted for the second method, since it was not possible to get correct estimates from others for all the tasks on her list. Having calculated the costs on this basis, she now had the list of services she could offer, the frequency with which she would offer them, and the prices she would charge. She was now all set to make a beginning. She decided that she would offer her services at $100 per month, in American currency, for a standard set of services (Table 1.3).

This would cover most of the routine requirements, and the $100 charge would provide her a tidy profit. Additional services, such as banking, were optional and would be charged extra on a pro-rata basis. She would visit each subscribing household once a week to check up on their requirements. In addition, she was always available on call, and arranging for medical aid would be on a priority basis, any time of the day. Urmi decided that she would approach the children settled abroad for subscription to her

Table 1.3 List of Services Offered

Service	Frequency
• Shopping for provisions	— once a fortnight
• Shopping for vegetables	— once a week
• Other shopping	— once a month
• Payment of electricity and telephone bills	— once a month
• Plumbing/electrical repairs and carpentry work	— once a fortnight
• Booking of gas	— once a month
• Outing for the couple (to temples, etc.)	— once a month
• Group outing/picnic for all clients	— once in three months

services for their parents. On the basis of her experience with her own parents and their friends, she was quite sure that there was a good market for her services, which she decided to name 'Helping Hands'. Given the financial position of most of the Gujaratis abroad, and the peace of mind her services would provide, she was confident that the $100 charge would not be found excessive. She estimated that in the first year, she would be able to obtain at least 30 such subscriptions, which would give her a monthly profit of about Rs 2,000 per subscribing household on an average. She got 500 copies of an attractive brochure printed at a cost of Rs 15,000, and mailed them to her brothers for distribution. Even though she found the printing costs rather high, she realized it was important for the brochures to be eye-catching and classy looking. She also devised an attractive advertisement in the form of an open letter, and advertised in *India Abroad* and two other similar magazines with NRIs as the target audience. She then sat down to wait for the response she was sure would follow.

Nothing happened for two months. Urmi was beginning to despair, when the phone rang one morning. A Mrs Shah was on the line from London, enquiring about details relating to Helping Hands. A friend who had come across the advertisement in *India Abroad* had told her about it. Enthusiastically, Urmi told her about it, and offered to send her the brochure. Mrs Shah was interested, but thought that $100 per month, or its equivalent in pounds sterling, was a bit on the high side for such a service. She asked Urmi to send a copy of her brochure. She would discuss it with her husband and get back to Urmi within ten days, if they were interested in subscribing. That was the only call she ever received, till the younger of her brothers had called that morning. He had inquired with some friends, he said, people he thought would be interested. But he had come up against an unexpected difficulty. People were not very willing to let strangers walk into a house inhabited by just old people. He had tried reassuring them, saying it was his sister offering the service, so there was no risk. But a friend of his had asked right out how she could guarantee the reliability of the people she would have to employ—the plumbers, the electricians, etc. Urmi was aghast. The possibility had never occurred to her. 'Can you not explain to them that that would be my responsibility?' she asked her brother. 'After all, such services are fairly common in the West.' 'I did try, Urmilben. But to tell you the truth, I would feel the same concern for our parents, about letting some unknown workers into the house, if you were not around to supervise, along with Ratanbhai or Rakesh,' he said, referring to her husband and son. 'It is different out here because most of these services are provided by the borough councils, which are official bodies.' And that was that. If acquaintances had that fear, she had no hope in the world of being able to guarantee reliability to unknown people. That was perhaps why nobody had subscribed. She mentioned the conversation to her husband in the evening and, as she had been dreading, he agreed with her brother. 'You should have surveyed the market,' he said. Despite the disappointment, Urmi knew he was right. All the effort, the planning, and the expenditure on promotion, had been in vain. As things stood, there was no market for her idea.

Questions

1. Given the amount of information Urmi Patel had collected before launching her business, do you agree with her husband's view that she should have conducted a survey before launching the enterprise? Why? List the specific benefits that would accrue from such a study.

2. If Urmi Patel has to conduct a survey, how should it be designed?

3. How could the data from the study be utilized in developing the business plan for Helping Hands?

REFERENCES

Aaker D., V. Kumar, and G.S. Day 1999, *Marketing Research*, Sixth Edition, Wiley, p. 11.

Chiba, M. 2003, 'To Research or Not?', *Strategic Marketing,* September–October, Vol. 2, Issue 4, pp. 9–11.

Green, P.E. and D.S. Tull 1978, *Research for Marketing Decisions*, Prentice Hall, Englewood Cliffs, New Jersey, pp. 21–23.

Morita, A. 1988, *Made in Japan*, Signet p. 87.

Rogers, Everett, M. 1995, *Diffusion of Innovations,* Free Press, New York.

Vieira, Walter 2000, *Strategic Planning is a Dynamic Exercise*, The Institute of Management Consultants of India, Mumbai.

2

The Role of Research in Marketing

INTRODUCTION

The previous chapter discussed the idea of research essentially as a means of solving the managerial dilemma: whether or not to capitalize on an opportunity; and understanding the possible causes of an observed marketing phenomenon; the likely impact of environmental change; the likely result(s) of a marketing decision; and so on. A manager is forever faced with the need to make such decisions and would usually prefer to have some estimate of the results of the decision in advance of the actual decision itself. Hence, the need for research. The decision to undertake research itself involves the consideration of some issues.

- Is it possible to take a decision without research?
- What kind of research needs to be undertaken?
- How long will the research take? Can the marketing decision await the results of research?
- What will be the costs of carrying out the research?
- Will research add net value in terms of reduced risk to the decision? In other words, would the gains in information, measured as net gain in revenue, be greater than the cost of research?

This chapter discusses these issues in detail. It first examines the organizational, competitive, and environmental compulsions influencing decisions about undertaking research at all. It studies the broad categories of marketing decisions required over the life of a product/organization and identifies the research suitable to marketing decisions that is relevant and required at that stage. The latter part of the chapter takes this analysis further and examines the issue of whether or not to undertake research in the framework of a cost-benefit analysis based on the Bayesian decision theory.

PROBLEM-SOLVING VS OPPORTUNITY DEFINITION RESEARCH

Managers usually have to make decisions under situations of uncertainty. As discussed in Chapter 1, the more uncharted the waters, the greater the uncertainty and the related risk. Compare the decision by Reliance Infocomm to launch Reliance Mobile, using the CDMA technology for the first time in India, with Hindustan Lever launching 'New Wheel', an extension of their well-accepted mass market detergent 'Wheel'. Which of the two carried a greater risk?

The decision theory framework identifies three levels of uncertainty, or doubt. A manager usually needs to make decisions at any of these levels:

- *Certainty* A situation where the possible outcomes of various courses of action or decision are completely known, so that it is possible to estimate the value of each decision. Mathematical models may still be required to arrive at this value if the number of possible courses of action is very large.
- *Risk* A situation where each of many possible outcomes of the different courses of action have a known, but less than one hundred per cent, probability of occurrence. For example, while playing cards, the chance of a player throwing down a spade would be 25 per cent. The lower the probability, the higher the risk.
- *Uncertainty* A situation where the probability of occurrence of any one of many possible outcomes of the different courses of action is not known. For example, if a household durables company launches a vacuum cleaner, the chances of its success or failure are not known in advance. The chances of it acquiring a certain market share in the first year of its life are also not known in advance.

Whatever the level of uncertainty, the primary role of marketing research is to provide decision rules that would reduce this risk by reducing uncertainty.

Internal and External Risk Factors

Figure 2.1 outlines the primary sources of risk in marketing decisions. Risks can broadly be divided into two categories: internal and external. *Internal risks* may arise from a variety of organizational sources relating to uncertainty about requisite knowledge, skills, or human and monetary resources for a decision. These would influence the adequacy of the quantity and quality of inputs required for successful implementation of a marketing decision.

The major *external sources of risk* are the extent and nature of competition in the market, unfamiliarity with the market, and the pace and nature of change in the market. These external sources, in turn, govern concerns about organizational competencies and influence the deployment of internal resources. The most pervasive uncertainty driving the Indian pharmaceutical industry today, for example, is the likely impact of the implementation of the WTO regulations. This will determine the kind of research and development efforts companies undertake, the products they introduce, the choice

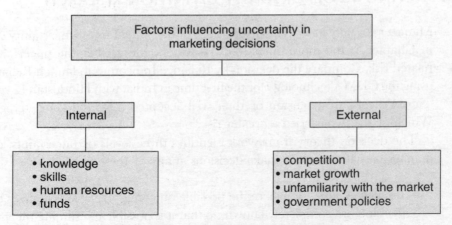

Fig. 2.1 Factors Influencing Uncertainty in Marketing Decision-making

between generics and brands, the pace of introduction, the markets selected, and even the channels of distribution.

The frequency and impact of each of these sources of uncertainty varies with the various stages in the life cycle of a product and an organization. With established products or organizations operating in known markets, i.e., in the growth and maturity stages of the product life cycle (PLC), most uncertainty results either from competitive strategies or doubts regarding the match between consumer requirements and the organization's market-offering. Some examples of such queries have been given below.

- Do consumers perceive my brand as sufficiently differentiated from the competition? Which one do they prefer? Why?
- Has the recent advertisement campaign for my brand of hair oil had any impact on consumer awareness of the brand?
- How will distributing my range of cosmetics through direct marketing, in addition to the conventional channel, influence its consumer perception and sales?
- What are the reasons for the dissatisfaction of my key account customer in the telecom industry with the project team that is dealing with its business?

In the case of new products or new markets, i.e., in the introductory stage of the PLC, unfamiliarity with the market is the primary source of risk and uncertainty. For example, consider the following issues:

- The market for nutraceuticals and herbal drugs is growing very rapidly. Given our strength in related fields like toiletries and processed foods, should we enter this market?

- Should we extend our brand of suitings, currently positioned as premium office wear for the male executive, as Western office wear for the female executive as well?
- If we were to diversify from our current FMCG stable into the market for over-the-counter drugs, what would be the consumer acceptance for our brands?
- The government has reduced the customs duty on imported cars. Should we have a relook at our plans to diversify into the domestic small car market?
- What is the level of dissatisfaction with current brands in the market for flat screen televisions that we are interested in entering?
- Of the three candidates for diversification, viz, readymade garments, industrial cloth, and small tools that we are interested in, which is the most attractive and most suitable for us?

It is to be noted that research relating to the internal category pertains to marketing issues, or 'problems' that a manager faces in the markets currently operated in. The external category refers to research aimed at defining an opportunity and assessing its size and attractiveness, so that the organization may decide whether or not to capitalize on it and what revenues to expect from it. Decisions relating to the appropriate marketing strategy and assessment of customer satisfaction at various stages of the firm's life extend over both these stages. Table 1.1, in Chapter 1, illustrates some situations from both categories.

Components of the Managerial Dilemma

Research required to reduce uncertainty also varies in these two risk categories, namely, internal and external. In both cases, however, it is essential to first understand what Green and Tull (1978) refer to as the components of the managerial dilemma.

The decision maker(s) and objectives

Who is involved in the decision? What is the objective behind the decision that needs to be taken? If there is more than one decision-maker, what is the degree of agreement among them on the stated or perceived objectives?

If, for example, the sales manager, the finance manager, and the quality assurance head are all involved in a decision about transportation of a company's products to the branches, the sales manager's objective may be to minimize stock-outs by ensuring that goods leave the factory immediately after production and are transported by the shortest and the quickest possible route. The quality assessment manager may be interested in ensuring continuing quality by subjecting every batch to quality tests, even if that means some delay in shipment, whereas the finance manager might be more concerned with choosing a mode of transportation that minimizes the cost, than with opting for one that ensures quickest delivery.

Even when there is only one decision-maker, prioritizing objectives relating to a product category or a brand over the short and the long term is important. In a slow-growing market where a company's brand enjoys substantial market share, for example, it is important to decide whether marketing activity should concentrate in the short term on 'milking' the brand, i.e., further strengthening brand position to maximize revenue and repositioning it for a different market in the long term, or exiting the current, stagnating market immediately. Research is required to help the manager to choose between these alternatives.

The context of the problem

The environment within which the company or the product operates will influence marketing decisions. For example, information relating to the size and growth of the market, the number of players and competitive strategies, government policies, usual marketing channels, average margins, the characteristics of target consumers, or their expectations and decision processes will all influence the marketer's decision to enter or not enter a new market.

For an established player, critical environmental data includes the sales, growth rates, market shares, consumer perceptions of their brand versus competing brands, and influencing marketing brand strategy. In the example of the decision regarding transportation of goods to the branches, the costs of transportation by various modes, availability of suitable transporters, rates quoted by them, the urgency of demand for stocks at the branches, extent of competition for the company's brands in the region, the degree of consumer loyalty for the company's brands, etc., will all influence the decision.

Alternative courses of action

Most managerial activity is concerned with decisions regarding what action to take in given circumstances, and when. Again, the action being considered may vary in terms of complexity.

For example, a manager may be faced with the choice between introducing or not introducing a product. 'Not introducing a product' is a course of action by itself. If the action to be taken is 'introducing a product', it may be preceded by choosing between alternative courses of action such as 'making the product', 'buying the product', or 'licensing the product', and the processes involved in each. The manager may not always have enough information to be able to identify all possible courses of action available to him/her in a given situation.

There is also the question of time and place: when and where to introduce a product. For an established product in a cluttered product category, there could similarly be the question of whether or not to reduce prices in the wake of a reduction in the price of a competing brand.

Consequences of alternative courses of action

It has been discussed earlier that a marketer usually operates in an environment of incomplete information, and is rarely in a position to know the complete impact of a decision. The marketer usually has to estimate, or, worse still, guess the consequences of the action taken by the organization.

It is, thus, apparent that the more information that can be obtained about these four components of a problem, the better the decision a manager will be able to take.

This impacts the decision regarding whether to undertake marketing research to look for answers and about how detailed that research should be—the components and the structure of the research problem.

Another major decision is concerned with the appropriate design for research. Opportunity research typically tends to be a lot less structured than problem research. As we will see in Chapter 5, it utilizes a great deal of what is called 'exploratory' research, exploring the respondent's mind, the space occupied by the need, the various satisfiers of that need in the respondent's mental, emotional, and life space, and the respondent's experiences and relationships with these need-satisfiers.

Research at this stage is needed to come to certain assumptions or hypotheses, which may be later checked out through more structured research formats. Of course, in many cases of opportunity research, it may be necessary to use a much more sharply defined framework and model. Sethi and Chandrasekhar (1993) have developed a research method called 'Strategic Cube Analysis' for finding answers to questions such as 'What is the level of dissatisfaction with current brands in the market for flat screen televisions that we are interested in entering?'

In the case of opportunity research as well as problem-solution research, it is important to define the research issues, or what is usually referred to as 'the research problem', clearly. In other words, all components of the research problem on which information is required, as well as their inter-relationships, should be spelt out in detail. This will be discussed more completely in Chapter 4.

QUALITY OF RESEARCH

The question of the quality of research is one that requires a detailed understanding of all the various stages of the marketing decision process. Cooper and Schindler (1999) have discussed the managerial dimensions of the subject in detail. The minutiae of issues that distinguish good research from indifferent or outright bad research extend from planning and implementation to the analysis and interpretation stages. The requirements of good research at various stages are briefly discussed in the paragraphs that follow. These stages are outlined in Fig. 2.2 and will be discussed in detail in subsequent chapters of the book.

Defining the research requirements

It is essential, from the very beginning of an interaction, to understand in detail the research requirements of the client. It might be necessary to have more than one discussion to completely understand the marketing problem and the decisions that will be based on the study. The researcher must keep in mind that the client may not have examined all dimensions of the issue and may have, therefore, not explored all alternatives.

It should, therefore, not be assumed that information not being forwarded by the client has been examined and found irrelevant. It is the researcher's responsibility to query the client and ensure that all aspects of the marketing problem have been considered and all likely decisions have been taken into account.

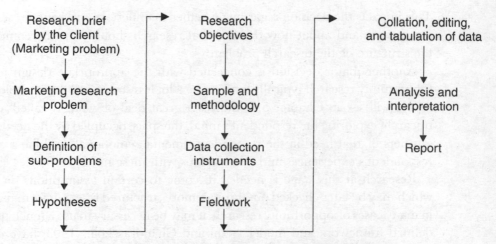

Fig. 2.2 Stages in Marketing Research Studies

Research objectives

Once the marketing research problem has been identified and all associated sub-problems have been defined, the assumptions or hypotheses related to these sub-problems have to be spelt out. The areas of inquiry, or information required to verify these hypotheses, are the research objectives. Good research requires that research objectives in a particular study not exceed a limited number—usually ten or twelve, not more.

It is also necessary to define in detail the variables that each objective would examine. For example, if one of the objectives of a study to determine the market potential of a new product is to define the product's consumer profile, all the variables constituting 'consumer profile' that the study will examine should be defined: age, education, income, family size and structure, occupation, psychographics (if needed), etc. This will ensure that no unnecessary variables are included in the process of data collection and that none of the required variables are missed out.

Research method

The objectives of the study, once defined, and the amount of information already available with the client and the researchers, will influence the research design and the method of data collection to be employed.

In the initial stages, when the need is to establish the various dimensions of the research issue, descriptive research is required if the objectives call for definition of the market variabes. If the relationship between these variables is to be identified, causal research must be undertaken.

Sample and methodology

The choice of appropriate sampling techniques and the size depends on many factors, such as the size of the population, heterogeneity in the population, degree of accuracy required, level of aggregation at which results are required, degree of non-response expected, as well as time and budget available for the study. Research methodology has to be tailored to the life-cycle stage of the concept or the product under study and the objectives of the study.

For example, an exploratory study is not very useful if the objective of the exercise is to determine the linkage between an increase in the sales of the company's brand and a rise in the price of the major competitor's brand; such a marketing problem would need a causal study. Market experimentation may be an effective methodology to study behaviour, but not attitudes; focus groups are usually appropriate at the stage of formation of research hypotheses, but they are not often used for testing hypotheses.

The decision about the appropriate respondent is an equally important one. For example, in a study to determine consumer loyalty to a brand of tea, interviewing retailers will provide only superficial information, since retailers in India generally do not maintain a database of consumer purchase patterns. It will be necessary in this case to talk to housewives.

Data collection instruments and fieldwork

These two stages in research can make or mar the utility of a research study, regardless of the degree of accuracy in planning the research up to this stage. To begin with, it is essential to choose the right means of data collection. For example, if the purpose of a study is to determine the reasons for the consumer's choice of a brand, mere observation (or experimentation, as mentioned earlier) will not provide the required details; the consumer has to be queried using either a structured questionnaire or, preferably, in-depth interview techniques or projective techniques.

These techniques will be discussed in Chapter 16, but the point to be noted here is that data collection instruments have to be developed with the purpose of the study in mind.

The quality of fieldwork is not always regarded in a serious light by most researchers. It is, however, a fact that the quality (and quantity) of data gathered determine the utility of the entire study. Inaccurate, incomplete, or false data does not merely lower the reliability of the findings, but often completely defeats the purpose of the entire exercise.

Analysis and interpretation

This stage provides the information that is most useful for the client, as it aims at answers to the marketing problem being studied. Details and creativity in analysis are needed for the richness of information that can be culled from data. Application of the appropriate analytical techniques is an essential first step for providing this rich analysis. At the same time, the choice of the methods of analysis should be made keeping in mind the client's needs and the level of sophistication required. Application of complex techniques merely for the satisfaction of the researcher would tend to alienate the client.

Report

The final report presented to the client must contain actionable recommendations based on the findings of the study. This means that (a) good research should make

Table 2.1 Characteristics of Good Marketing Research

Stage	Characteristics of Good Research
Defining research requirements	Detailed dialogue with client; understanding of the marketing problem and marketing decisions based on research
Research objectives	Clear linkage between research hypotheses and objectives; objectives covering all aspects of the marketing problem; variables to be studied for each objective clearly defined; number of objectives to be limited to a manageable level
Research process/methodology	Appropriate research method (exploratory, descriptive, or causal) identified based on the nature of information required and availability of prior information about the marketing problem and the respondent; exploratory procedures identified and all relevant constructs defined
Sampling methodology	Based on details of information required; related to sample size, population size, and cost of sampling; rational methods of sample selection applied
Data collection instruments and field work	Appropriate to the information needs; adequately tested before being administered in the field
Analysis and interpretation	Adequate analysis for the client's needs; sufficiently detailed and providing unambiguous, actionable information relating to all research objectives
Report	Data-based conclusions linked to analysis

specific recommendations about the action(s) the client can take on the basis of the report, and (b) the recommendations should be based on the actual findings of the study, and not on the researcher's opinions and assumptions.

Limitations

Every study, no matter how carefully planned, will suffer from some limitations, primarily due to time and budget constraints. It is important to mention these clearly in the report, so that the client may have the right perspective regarding the recommendations made in the study.

Table 2.1 lists the various dimensions requiring attention for generating good quality research that have been discussed earlier.

THE DECISION-MAKING PERSPECTIVE

Given the uncertainty of the market environment and the need for additional information, managers are forever faced with the decision about marketing research: should they go for it or not? As discussed earlier, the decision is based primarily on two criteria: the time and cost of research. In a competitive environment, the time taken for research could mean the postponement of a decision and might result in the loss of revenue, and sometimes, even loss of market opportunity. The costs involved in research may also deter managers from undertaking the activity. However, as we have seen earlier, the more uncertain and volatile the environment, the greater the risk involved in decision-making.

The cost of marketing research should, therefore, be evaluated against the net gain from availability of additional information that would reduce the risk of a wrong decision. It is logical to conclude that research should be undertaken only if the gain in revenue from it exceeds its cost.

Bayesian Decision Theory

The Bayesian decision theory, so called because it is based on the Bayes theorem, is one such tool that helps evaluate the benefits of marketing research against its cost. The theory uses the four concepts of prior analysis, conditional probability, marginal probability, and posterior analysis. The example discussed below explains the method.

Let us consider the FMCG giant Company X's examination of the detergent market, with a view to introducing their brand in this cluttered field. Mr Khanna, the marketing manager, has been entrusted with the task of making a 'go'/'no-go' decision. He has three options.

Option 1   On the basis of his long experience in the FMCG business, Mr Khanna is aware that the chances of his success (of achieving a market share that will optimize his profits) are less than one hundred per cent. In fact, he thinks he can predict the chances he has of obtaining different market-share levels, and calculate the profits at each market-share level (Table 2.2).

Table 2.2   Profits at Market-share Levels

Sl No.	Market-share (MS) %	Chances (P) of Achieving MS %	Profit at Market-share Level (in Rs Lakh)
1	15	0.30 (P_1)	20 (S_1)
2	5	0.50 (P_2)	5 (S_2)
3*	1	0.20 (P_3)	−10 (S_3)

*In the third case, the company is likely to end up losing money, because at 1% market share, the revenue generated will be less than the amount spent on the launch.

Since he believes these are the only three relevant options if the brand has to be launched, he estimates his possible profit on launching as Rs 6.5 lakh.

$$(0.3 \times 20) + (0.5 \times 5) + \{0.2 \times (-10)\} = Rs\ 6.5\ lakh$$

The expected profit on not launching the brand is, of course, zero.

Mr Khanna, thus, has the choice of earning a maximum profit of Rs 6.5 lakh if he launches the brand, or making no profit/no loss if he decides not to launch it. We must note that this method of analysis bases its conclusions on possible quantitative results in the current situation alone; it does not explicitly quantify the long-term impact of launching/not launching under different market-growth conditions, nor does it attempt to quantify the impact of its absence from a large, mass market on the company's image. Moreover, it is based totally on Mr Khanna's judgement alone, and does not take into account any hard data. This method of estimating the financial impact of a decision is called *prior analysis* in statistical language.

Option 2   The second option, for Mr Khanna is to not rely completely on his experience, but to conduct a market survey, and assume that the result of the survey may be treated as the exact reflection of the way the brand will perform in the market when launched (*perfect information*). In other words, the brand should be launched if the survey indicates that the total gain from launching it will be positive, and not be launched otherwise. The possible gain in this case would be

$$(0.3 \times 20) + (0.5 \times 5) + \{0\,(-10)\} = \text{Rs 8.5 lakh}$$

The probability of the third outcome, i.e., the company suffering a loss of Rs 10 lakh is 0 in this case, because if the survey indicates the chance of the market share being 1% and the loss, therefore, being Rs 10 lakh, the brand would not be launched. The survey would result in a net additional gain to the company of at least Rs 2 lakh (Rs 8.5 lakh – Rs 6.5 lakh = Rs 2 lakh), and that is, therefore, the maximum amount they should be willing to pay for the research.

Option 3   Mr Khanna is a realist and understands that the probability of the results of the market survey being replicated exactly in the national market is not one hundred per cent. He, therefore, conducts the survey, and uses the Bayes theorem to estimate the probability of achieving a certain market share, given that the same market share was indicated by the survey (*conditional probability*).

For convenience of estimation, he decides to divide the possible market shares indicated by the survey into three broad categories: market share of 10% or more (Z_1), market share between 3–10% (Z_2), and market share below 3% (Z_3), as shown in Table 2.3. Similarly, he decides to divide the possible post-launch expected market share into three categories: 15% or more (S_1), 5%–15% (S_2), and less than 5% (S_3) as shown in Table 2.4.

He will then calculate the total payoff for each market-share level, and choose the action (launching or not launching the brand) that will give him the highest payoff. As the first step, he puts down the following definitions:

- $P(S_i / Z_i)$ = the conditional probability that the brand achieves a market share of S_i, given that the market survey had indicated a market share of Z_i ($i = 1, 2, 3$)
- $P(Z_i / S_i)$ = the probability that the survey had indicated a market share of Z_i, given that the national market share has finally been observed to be S_i ($i = 1, 2, 3$)
- $P(S_i, Z_i) = P(Z_i, S_i) = P(S_i / Z_i) \times P(Z_i) = P(Z_i / S_i) \times P(S_i)$ = joint probability of S_i and Z_i occurring simultaneously

Table 2.3　Probable Outcomes of Market Survey Z_i

MS in the Survey	Probability 'P' of Survey MS
Z_1 (10%)	0.3
Z_2 (3 – 10%)	0.5
Z_3 (< 3%)	0.2

Table 2.4　Calculation of Final Market Shares S_i in the National Launch

National MS	Probability of National MS	$P(Z_1/S_i)$	$P(Z_2/S_i)$	$P(Z_3/S_i)$	Total Probability
S_1 (15%)	0.3	0.6	0.3	0.1	1.0
S_2 (5–15%)	0.5	0.3	0.5	0.2	1.0
S_3 (<5%)	0.2	0.1	0.2	0.7	1.0
Total Prob.		1.0	1.0	1.0	

On the assumption that the outcomes of the survey will reflect the true market share, Mr Khanna works out all permutations and combinations of market survey Z_i and the final market shares S_i in the national launch, as shown in Tables 2.3 and 2.4, respectively.

In statistical terms, the marginal probability of occurrence of any event S_i ($i = 1, 2, 3, \ldots$), which is dependent on the possible prior occurrence of another event Z_i ($i = 1, 2, 3, \ldots$), is the total probability of S_i, for all possible values that Z_i may take.

$$P(S_i) = P(S_i/Z_1) + P(S_i/Z_2) + P(S_i/Z_3) + \ldots$$

Accordingly, still continuing with the subjective probabilities for S_1, S_2, and S_3, he calculates the chances (*marginal probabilities*) of S_i ($i = 1, 2, 3$) being the most likely national market share (Table 2.5), and being reflected correctly by the market survey, i.e., the joint probability of S_i and Z_i ($i = 1, 2, 3$) as shown in Table 2.5.

Table 2.5　Marginal Probabilities

Survey Market Share Z_i

Final MS	Z_1	Z_2	Z_3	Marginal $P(S_i)$
S_1	0.3 × 0.6 = 0.18	0.3 × 0.3 = 0.09	0.3 × 0.1 = 0.03	0.30
S_2	0.5 × 0.3 = 0.15	0.5 × 0.5 = 0.25	0.5 × 0.2 = 0.10	0.50
S_3	0.2 × 0.1 = 0.02	0.2 × 0.2 = 0.04	0.2 × 0.7 = 0.14	0.20
Marginal $P(Z_i)$	0.35	0.38	0.27	1.00

Since the market-survey outcomes, Z_i, should reflect the final launch outcomes, S_i, Mr Khanna is now in a position to refine his possibilities $P(S_i)$ by using the Bayesian theorem.

$$P(S_i/Z_i) = \frac{P(Z_i/S_i)\,P(S_i)}{\text{Total}\,[P(Z_i/S_i)\,P(S_i)]}$$

The final (*posterior*) probabilities of S_i, therefore, are as shown in Table 2.6.

Table 2.6   Posterior Probabilities of Market Share

Final MS	Market-survey Results		
	Z_1	Z_2	Z_3
S_1	0.18/0.35	0.09/0.38	0.03/0.27
S_2	0.15/0.35	0.25/0.38	0.10/0.27
S_3	0.02/0.35	0.04/0.38	0.14/0.27
	1.00	1.00	1.00

Table 2.7   Calculation of $E(A_1)$ under Z_1

Conditional Probability $P(S_i/Z_1)$	× Profit Under S_1
.18/.35	× 20
+ .15/.35	× 5
+ .02/.35	× (−10)

Now that Mr Khanna has obtained the probabilities of each of the three relevant market shares, in the event of a national launch from the market survey, he can calculate the expected profit from each action, conditional upon each market-survey outcome. The two possible actions being to launch the brand (A_1) or to not launch the brand (A_2), he is aware that $E(A_1)$, the expected profit of A_1, and $E(A_2)$ will vary depending on the market-survey outcomes Z_1, Z_2, and Z_3.

For example, under the market survey outcome Z_1 with the marginal probability 0.35, conditional probabilities $P(S_1/Z_1)$, $P(S_2/Z_1)$ and $P(S_3/Z_1)$, and the corresponding payoffs as indicated in Table 2.7, the total expected payoff $E(A_1)/EPMA_1$, would be

$$(0.18/0.35) \times 20 + (0.15/0.35) \times 5 + (0.02/0.35) \times (−10) = 11.86$$
$$\text{and} \quad E(A_2) \quad = 0$$

Similarly, profits under Z_2 and Z_3 can be calculated for both actions A_1 and A_2.

The final profit of A, considering the likelihood of all three possible market-survey results Z_1, Z_2, and Z_3, is equal to

$$P(Z_1) \times E(A_1/Z_1) + P(Z_2) \times E(A_1/Z_2) + P(Z_3) \times E(A_1/Z_3)$$

Figure 2.3 has been adapted from Green and Tull's (1978) book, *Research for marketing decisions*, and presents a diagrammatical explanation of the method of calculating the final profit from launching the brand, using the Bayesian decision theory.

All research activities cost something. The net gain from market research is, therefore, calculated under the decision-making perspective as

Expected value of additional information − Cost of acquiring it

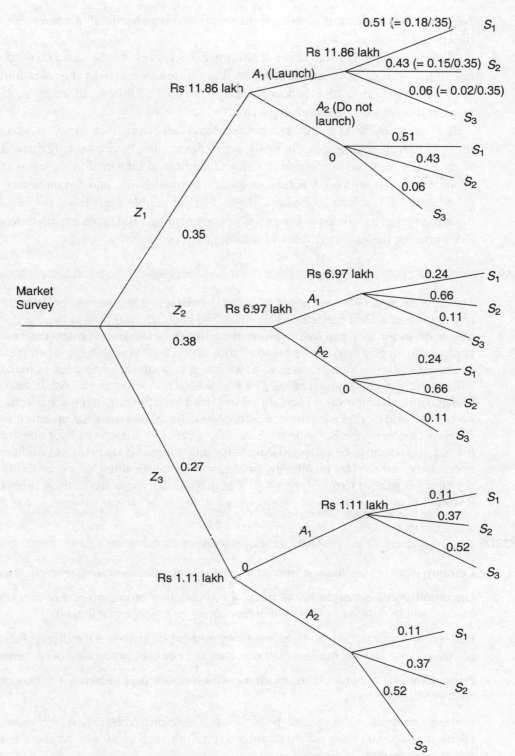

Fig. 2.3 Determination of Expected Payoff after Market Survey
Source: Adapted from Green and Tull 1978

No method of collecting additional information is worthwhile if it costs more than the net gain from it.

However, one major limitation of this method of assessing the value of marketing research has to do with the assumption that the total expected value of additional information and, thus, also the loss resulting from such additional information, can be measured completely in monetary terms.

If a company like ITC, for example, were to conduct a market survey to determine the feasibility of setting up 'e-choupals' across the country before actually doing it, the study would measure the 'expected value of additional information' in terms of the probability of the company achieving specific market shares, and the monetary gain from attaining each market-share level. The intangible gain from the resultant improvement in the company image will not be quantified and taken into consideration in computing the expected value of additional information.

SUMMARY

The decision about whether or not to undertake marketing research is not automatic for any organization, but depends on the time and cost involved. It also depends on the degree of uncertainty and risk involved in the decision. The kind of marketing research appropriate for any marketing situation varies depending on whether it is being carried out to establish the attractiveness of a marketing opportunity or to address marketing issues arising in current operations. Since all research involves some cost, it should be undertaken only if the value of information gained from the research is greater than the cost of carrying it out. Using the concepts of conditional and marginal probability from the Bayes theorem, the Bayesian decision theory provides a framework for determining the net gain that may be expected from a marketing research study under conditions of uncertainty and risk, by quantifying uncertainty in statistical terms of probability and defining net gain in terms of the profit that may be derived under various probability levels.

KEY WORDS

Certainty refers to a situation where the outcome of a decision is completely known.

Uncertainty in a situation arises when the probability of occurrence of any one of many possible out-comes of the different courses of action is not known.

Risk refers to a situation where each of many possible outcomes of the different courses of action has a known, but less than one hundred per cent probability of occurrence.

Prior analysis is the process by which a decision-maker uses judgement to choose the most profitable option.

Posterior analysis is the process by which the most profitable option is chosen after taking into account new information received from sources as well as the decision-maker's judgement.

Conditional probability refers to the probability, $P(S_i/Z_i)$, of the event S_i occurring, given that the event Z_i has already occurred.

Marginal probability refers to the total probability, $P(S_i/Z)$, of the event S_i occurring, given that the all possible values that event Z could take have been taken into account.

Perfect information is the complete and accurate information about the consequences of the various alternatives being considered, leading to zero risk.

Expected value of perfect information (EVPI) has been defined by Green and Tull (1978): 'If we had perfect information about which actual state of nature prevails, we would always be able to take the best action available to us...However, *before* the fact, we do not know which event will occur. Hence, we must multiply each of the best payoffs (profits) under various conditions by the prior probability that further enquiry will reveal the true state...The *difference* between EVPI and the best expected payoff (profit) under the *prior* probabilities case represents an upper bound on what we should pay for even perfect information.'

CONCEPT REVIEW QUESTIONS

1. Does Company A, introducing a new-to-the-world product so that it is the only player in the market, require marketing research before launching the product? Give reasons for your answer. What kind of marketing risk should it take into account while introducing the product?

2. How would the situation change if Company A was not the first entrant in this market, but had to face many competitors?

3. Jayesh Kumar, a popular Hindi film star, has been considering running for the Lok Sabha seat in the general elections. His major opponent in his chosen constituency is Krishna Kant, who has been representing that constituency for the past three elections. Jayesh Kumar does not want to take the final decision about entering the fray unless he can be reasonably certain of winning. What kind of research questions should he seek answers to in order to estimate his chances?

4. Company XYZ, a major player in the cigarettes and tobacco industry, is considering entering the casual wear market. What kind of internal risk factors should it take into account in arriving at the final decision?

5. Give two examples each of marketing decisions taken under situations of certainty, risk, and uncertainty. When, under each of these three situations, is marketing research required?

CRITICAL THINKING EXERCISES

1. Company X, a major manufacturer of small kitchen appliances, is considering entering the market for microwave ovens. On the strength of their reputation, they expect to achieve fairly good results in the market by the end of the first year.

Analysis of competitive data suggests that companies similar to them in size and image have usually been able to achieve about 5 per cent share of the market in the first year. If Company X were to get a market share of 5 per cent, it would translate into a net gain of Rs 20 lakh, after excluding all promotion costs. Most managers in Company X estimate that they have at least a 40 per cent chance of achieving a 5 per cent share. However, the all-India sales manager believes that, taking into account the growth in the demand for microwave ovens in the previous few years, he could put at 35 per cent, the chances of the company, to acquire a market share of 9 per cent in the first year, giving them a net gain of Rs 35 lakh. Mr Mohan, the marketing manager and one of the senior-most employees, believes that in taking the decision they should keep in mind an estimate of the minimum market share they might end up with, and the costs involved, since this estimate would give them the range within which the market's response is likely to lie. His worry is that if they were to draw a parallel with Company B, another kitchen appliances major that launched its brand of microwave ovens the previous year, they should estimate 25 per cent chances of ending up with as low a market share as 1 per cent resulting in a loss of Rs 10 lakh.

(a) Should the company decide to launch its brand of microwave ovens?

(b) Ramesh Chandra, the young product manager for small appliances in Company X above, suggests that they might undertake a market survey to get an estimate of their chances of success. What is the maximum amount they should be willing to spend on the market survey?

(c) Ramesh Chandra is authorized by the company to commission the market survey. The survey reveals that the probability of getting a market share of 9 per cent or more (Z_1) is 35 per cent; that of getting a market share between 5 per cent and 9 per cent (Z_2) is also 35 per cent, and the probability of getting a market share of less than 5 per cent (Z_3) is 30 per cent.

When asked by Ramesh Chandra to predict the chances of getting the expected market shares in the national market as mentioned in Question 1, if the market survey revealed these chances of getting various market shares, the agency suggests the conditional probabilities as shown in Table 2.8.

Calculate the final unconditional payoff after the market study.

Table 2.8 National Market Share (S_i)

Market-Survey Share	S_1 (5%)	S_2 (9%)	S_3 (1%)
9%	0. 3	0.5	0.2
5% – 9%	0. 5	0.4	0.1
<5%	0. 2	0.1	0.7
Total	1.0	1.0	1.0

2. Describe how one would structure the decision of which business school to choose, as a problem in Bayesian analysis.

PROJECT ASSIGNMENT

LG, the consumer appliances major, has recently entered the homecare products market under the name 'LG Care', and is targeting HLL and P&G products as major competitors. It has been marketing its premium detergent, Super Enz, at Rs 159 a kilogram. In order to improve its market share, it is now considering offering the 'LG Double Rich Shampoo', which is worth Rs 99, free with a one kilogram pack of Super Enz, thus bringing its prices down substantially compared to P&G's 'Ariel', which is being marketed at Rs 99 a kilogram. Discuss with company executives what kind of market shares they expect and with what probability, as a result of this promotion. If you were to offer to undertake a market survey to verify their estimates, what is the maximum cost the company is likely to agree to incur on the study?

CASE STUDY

Pomegranate Marketing

Mr Kolamkar heads Maharashtra Marketing Agency (MMA), an NGO working in Maharashtra which helps farmers market their produce. Fifty-nine-year-old Mr Kolamkar worked with a public sector pesticides company for about 35 years before retiring in 1999 as General Manager—Marketing. He started the MMA along with some friends the same year. His work with pesticides gave him ample opportunity to work with farmers and understand their problems. He had earlier been based in Nagpur, marketing his company's products to the orange growers there. In 1989, he moved to Mumbai following a promotion and his responsibilities increased to encompass the marketing of pesticides for a variety of crops, including fruits, vegetables, and food grains. Pomegranate is a popular fruit in the country, and Maharashtra is a major pomegranate-growing state. Mr Kolamkar often toured the pomegranate-growing areas in the state, specially the Satara and Sangli districts. During these visits, he observed the sales pattern of various crops, including those for which his company supplied pesticides. Mr Kolamkar's conversations with the farmers revealed that most of them did not have a proper knowledge of the method of grading fruits, though they all claimed to separate the diseased, defective, and overripe fruit from the better-quality pomegranates before selling them. Most farmers grade pomegranates by colour (78 per cent) or weight (68 per cent). The fruit is then packed in cardboard cartons of standard size for sale. Almost 70 per cent of the farmers growing pomegranates sell them to middlemen or merchants, instead of selling them directly in the market. One of the major reasons for this practice is that the markets are far away, and transporting their produce to these markets is an expensive and time-consuming event. In addition, the available transportation facilities are quite inadequate. About 18 per cent farmers sell pomegranates against contracts, and it is only the remaining 12 per cent who sell the fruit in the local market. Mr Kolamkar was intrigued by the distribution pattern of pomegranate sales, and collected some data which gave him greater insights into its markets. He found a rather interesting distribution pattern. The fruit is marketed mostly in Delhi (45.5 per cent), followed by Mumbai (37.5 per cent). The marketwise details that he was able to collect have been given in Table 2.9.

Table 2.9 Market Distribution of Pomegrenate Sales

Market	Percentage of Sale
Delhi	45.5
Mumbai	37.5
Kolkata	34.0
Nasik	28.5
Benaras	24.0
Ahmedabad	14.5
Local Markets	12.5
Surat	10.5

Mr Kolamkar was quite intrigued by this distribution pattern. Why is Maharashtra not the largest market for a fruit grown in the state? Why does the sale seem concentrated in larger cities and towns? What about the southern states? All these questions spurred him on to delve deeper into the issues relating to the marketing of pomegranates. He made a practice of having long conversations on the subject with farmers during his frequent field trips. Over a period of time, though he did not get the answers to all his questions, he was able to draw up a fairly exhaustive list of the problems that the farmers faced in marketing pomegranates. These have been listed here.

Constraints perceived by farmers in marketing of pomegranates:

- cost of packaging material
- availability of packaging material
- lack of knowledge regarding grading
- high transport costs
- distance to markets
- non-remunerative/fluctuating market rates
- high commission by middlemen
- delay in payment
- non-receipt of payment

What this suggested to Mr Kolamkar was that the farmers seemed to be in a bind. Neither did they have the money or the capacity to pay for the transport costs themselves, nor did they have a knowledge of the markets. They were not aware of the kind of packaging that would attract buyers, and had to borrow money from middlemen for buying packaging material. Since the farmers did not supply directly to the customers, they did not see the need to upgrade their packaging. In order to reduce their inventory costs and the risk of the fruit spoiling, they pledged the crop to middlemen before it was harvested. At that stage, the prices they were able to realize were much lower than the price at which pomegranates are sold in the cities. In addition, the cost of the packaging material was deducted from the prices they were paid by the middlemen. To Mr Kolamkar, all this seemed like large-scale exploitation. He decided to do something to help the farmers improve their marketing of pomegranates. It was for this purpose that he set up the MMA. Since then he has been trying to place the entire effort of the farmers on a more professional level, and has even conducted some surveys to understand buyer expectations.

The example of NOGA that he had come across during his Nagpur days made Mr Kolamkar consider the possibility of branding the pomegranate from the region, and also diversifying into items like bottled pomegranate juice. About a year ago, he came across another product called 'Litchica', the bottled juice and squash of Litchies, being marketed by a company called Litchica International, based in Muzzarffarpur, Bihar. He recollected that Bihar is a major producer of litchies. The example of Litchica further strengthened Mr Kolamkar's resolve to professionalize the marketing of pomegranates and make it more profitable.

Questions

1. How would you structure a plan, using Bayesian analysis, to help Mr Kolamkar decide whether he should conduct any marketing research study to be able to help the farmers improve their lot?

2. If you were called in by Mr Kolamkar as a consultant, what brief should he give you for designing such a study?

3. How would you design such a study? What environmental factors should be explored by the study? Define the objectives of the study. From whom will you collect data?

REFERENCES

Cooper, D.R. and P.S. Schindler (1999), *Business Research Methods*, Tata McGraw-Hill, pp. 15–18.

Green, Paul and Donald Tull 1978, *Research for Marketing Decisions*, Prentice Hall, pp. 16–18.

Sethi, A. and G. Chandrasekhar 1993 'Strategic Cube Analysis for Brand Equity Leverage', *Brand Equity and the Challenge of Branding,* book of papers submitted to the MRSI/ESOMAR Conference.

3 Practical Tips for Researchers

OBJECTIVES

After reading this chapter, the readers will be able to understand:

- the need for and the nature of the detailed dialogue between the researcher and the manager at different stages of a research project
- where the researcher's role stops and what he/she can do to provide an actionable research
- the difference between marketing intelligence and marketing research
- the need to go beyond the mere presentation of statistical data and provide actionable interpretations and recommendations based on the data

INTRODUCTION

Earlier, we discussed the role of research in marketing decision-making. Depending on the specific decisions to be taken, the requirements from research will vary. The expectations and framework of opportunity analysis research, for example, will normally be quite different from problem-solution research. The difference between good and bad research, i.e, between research which (a) is based on a detailed understanding of the issues involved, (b) answers the manager's concerns comprehensively, (c) provides conclusions based on rigorous and appropriate analysis, and (d) provides actionable recommendations, and bad research that is lacking in one or more of these, is the result not only of the quality of concepts applied and the research techniques used, but also of the understanding of its antecedents and implications. Therefore, prior to initiating a project, it is essential for researchers to understand the practical considerations involved in carrying out the research. The manager, too, must treat the researcher as a partner in decision-making and be willing to provide all the information needed, keeping in mind that any research will be only as good as the brief provided to the researcher. What must be kept in mind is whether the research is being outsourced or being carried out by an in-house marketing research department. The group/individual carrying out the research is rarely the same as the marketing manager/executive who will be using that research and commissioning the research. It is equally important to present the research findings from the research user's point of view. No research, no matter how sophisticated, will serve much purpose for the user organization unless it provides answers to the immediate concerns of the user, to the issue that is the reason for commissioning the research. Only such research will lead to more informed decision-making.

MANAGER–RESEARCHER DIALOGUE

Chapter 2 explained how research support is required at various stages in the marketing-decision process. It is important to understand the nuances of the requirement at each stage of the life cycle of the product and the business, and to determine what really is at issue. Listed below are some of the factors influencing the marketing decision and the planning and strategy process preceding that decision.

The research brief

There is a lot of data influencing marketing decisions. The key considerations of a brief are discussed here.

1. macro environment of the market:
   - government policies or changes in these policies that might influence industry in general, such as taxation vs savings policies, globalization trends, industry reservation policies, industry incentives, environment policies, five-year plans, budgetary outlays, politico-legal and regulatory trends, etc.
   - socio-economic trends, such as literacy levels, age trends, disposable income, inflation rates, percentage of women working, nuclear vs joint families, urbanization patterns, etc.
   - industry associations like FICCI and CII and their strengths
2. market and competition characteristics:
   - market size and growth, market clutter, location and distribution
   - market segmentation, i.e., definition of segments and dispersion of customers along these segments
   - market intermediaries, i.e., channel members, their strength and growth, media channels, their growth and dispersion, regulatory bodies, and trends in the growth of intermediaries

---

Coke it is! Or is it?

The story of the research study that formed the basis for the temporary withdrawal of Classic Coke and the launch of the new version of Coke has gone down in the annals of marketing as a celebrated example of how not to conduct research. It is a classic example of research based on inadequate identification of relevant research issues and poor insights into consumer perceptions. Commissioned to find reasons for the steady loss of market share to major competitor Pepsi, the research compared the standard and the modified Coke with Pepsi. It concluded on the basis of blind taste tests that the new version of Coke was considered equal to, if not better than Pepsi in taste and recommended that the classic Coke be withdrawn and the new Coke be launched. At no point were the two versions of Coke compared with each other, neither did the research try to determine what Coke really stood for in consumer perception. As is well known, the results were disastrous, and the Coca-Cola company had to reintroduce the classic version in order to protect their market share.

3. consumer characteristics:
   - market segments to which the brand/firm's customers belong
   - demographics and psychographics of the consumer, media habits
   - attitudes, brand knowledge, brand perceptions, perceptions of competing brands, influences on purchase, involvement levels, brand expectations
   - brand behaviour, i.e., purchase patterns, frequency and size of purchase, brand loyalty, channels of purchase, etc.

The researcher and the manager both need to identify the factors listed above before the focus of the marketing research can be defined adequately.

The Coke story indicates that research which compares product features with a competitor, for example, can fall far short of the mark when the real issue can be the identity of the brand. To conceptualize the experience of Coke, it is crucial that the actual issue underpinning a market situation be understood in its entirety before research is commissioned.

This could require exploring and understanding a much larger range of issues in the case of opportunity analysis research, which is typically less structured than problem-solving research. In either case, it is essential to discuss all these issues with the client often enough to ensure that (a) a common understanding of the rationale of the research is finally reached, and (b) all related issues that might impinge on the design of the study and the ultimate decisions have been explored. In other words, (a) the manager commissioning the study should give all pertinent information on the subject to the researcher and explain exactly what information is required from the study, (b) the researcher should be clear on what is the basic problem underpinning the need for research and should be certain that the requirements of the manager have been understood clearly, (c) any additional, related information that could influence the structure of the study, though it may not necessarily form a part of the survey, should be conveyed to the researcher, and (d) any information that could influence the final decision on the issue should be conveyed to the researcher.

Often, the manager commissioning the study would have been addressing the problem for so long that the person would tend to take for granted the responses to many of the unstated dimensions of the problem being studied. It is, therefore, important that the researcher ask questions to clarify the problem entirely.

After the first briefing, the researchers must take certain steps to ensure that the research is as successful as possible. These have been discussed below.

- The researcher must send minutes of the discussion to the client so that there is clarity in understanding the issues involved.
- It is good to prepare a questionnaire putting down all queries that the researcher may want to raise with the client before working out the detailed proposal. This is not the questionnaire that will be used in the field, but merely a list of items on which information is needed to be able to design the study. It will also help the

researcher understand if the interpretation of the client's requirements are exactly as they exist in the client's mind. It is important not to presume prior knowledge of all issues either on the part of the manager or the researcher.

- Researchers should obtain information from the manager regarding the decisions that will be based on the study. This not only helps determine the importance being attached to the study, whether the results will be implemented in the short or the long term, and whether the manager has really thought the problem through in its entirety, but also helps set up hypotheses and structure the design of the study. For example, a post-launch product study will be designed quite differently if its primary purpose is to determine consumer response to the new launch, than if the main objective is to determine whether the distribution channels employed for the same product are suitable and adequate.

- The researchers must collect all related information, in the case of problem-solution research, that has ostensibly contributed to the problem; action taken to date; and the different viewpoints bearing upon the problem that may prevail in the organization. This might necessitate meetings with other people in the organization apart from the manager commissioning the study. In such situations, the manager should be requested to set up these meetings.

- If the client agrees to it, then the researchers must go through the prior research on the subject that may be available in the client organization. This serves to give an idea of the angles from which the issue has already been studied. However, there are those who perceive that this can create a negative impact. Some researchers believe that prior research is likely to bias the new study, and should be avoided.

Research design

After the manager and the researcher have discussed and finalized the research brief, the research design and the methodology of the study need to be decided. This is the responsibility of the researcher and, though it is discussed with the client—its relevance and benefits explained—it should not be left to him/her to decide. Highly research-oriented clients sometimes insist on following a particular methodology. Unless the researcher has reason to believe that the client's suggestion is methodologically valid for the problem under study, the reasons behind the unsuitability of the method suggested must be explained, and so must the reasons why an alternative method would be more suitable. This same argument applies to sampling methodology and size as well.

Presentation

It is always a good idea to discuss the findings of the study with the manager commissioning the study, before a formal presentation is made. This provides an opportunity to incorporate in the results any specific analysis/information that the manager might want to emphasize. Semantics can sometimes make a significant difference to the acceptability of a study, regardless of the accuracy of the findings. In a recent image survey the author undertook for a large public sector bank, the results had to be discussed three times between the researchers and the project coordinator, before all the issues the client group wanted highlighted could be presented to their satisfaction.

Prior discussion with the manager also provides the researcher with an opportunity to understand the likely reactions of various members of the organization, and can help obtain the manager's support for the explanation of any controversial findings. A major dilemma for the researcher is whether and how to present findings that are contrary to the client's expectations and disprove the hypotheses. Apart from the unpleasantness involved, negative findings tend to get discredited, especially if they show up any particular department in a bad light. It is, therefore, important that such findings be totally factual and supported by adequate hard data, which can be submitted at the presentation.

DEFINING THE BOUNDARIES OF MARKETING RESEARCH

It is important to understand that the role of research is recommendatory, not decisive. An enthusiastic researcher may sometimes lose sight of this pertinent fact and start

---

Acting on Recommendations: The Manager's Prerogative

In October 2001 the marketing department of Company A, a large manufacturer of branded tea, faced a problem of steady decline in the sales of 'Tropica' over six months. Since Tropica was its largest brand, it decided to bring in the marketing research department to conduct a study on the possible reasons. The study was assigned to Ms X, who did a very competent job and confidently presented the findings to marketing. The main conclusion of her study was that retailers were substituting their brand's shelf space for a new brand from the major competitor. The reason for this was that the new brand was a major seller abroad and the competitor was committed to making it a big brand in India, one of the largest tea markets. Her recommendations were to run a sales promotion campaign for their brand and raise dealer margins immediately. The marketing manager thanked her effusively and commended her on a job well done.

Two months later, no action had been taken, brand sales continued to decline, and Ms X was fuming. 'These marketing guys! They don't know what is good for them. Why did they ask for a study if they did not want to act on the results? I could take care of the brand today if I was in their place,' she complained to her boss, the marketing research manager. The MR manager was intrigued and decided to check this out with the marketing manager. The latter's reply was revealing: 'Of course, she did a very good job, and for once we got definite actionable recommendations. But for one, she has to understand that while her job is to recommend action, it is our job to decide whether or not action is to be taken. We already knew about the new brand, and had guessed they (Competitor B, the marketer of the new brand) would be wanting to make a splash. But it is the end of November now. We cannot do much at this stage; our budgets for the brand are more or less exhausted. Since the new financial year begins from January, we are trying to work out a deal with the retailers that will tie them in for the entire year next year. Besides, it is not easy to raise margins for just one brand and that too in our kind of mass-distribution business. Moreover, we cannot keep doing it each time a competitor comes in with a big brand. Sorry, we should have talked to her about this.'

trying to tell the marketing department how to do their job. This is particularly likely with in-house marketing research departments, as they probably have access to most of the information about other departments, and are part of the same decision-making environment. It must be understood that even if the manager accepts the research findings, there may, at times, be reasons why they cannot be implemented.

Reasons for non-implementation of research findings can be divided into two groups: those to do with the research itself and those related to marketing or organizational factors extraneous to the research study:

- The first group of factors that can influence non-action on a research report has to do with the research quality. The factors could be the 'nothing-new' syndrome, where the manager interprets the findings as a mere confirmation of earlier studies or expectations; lack of clarity in defining the purpose of research; a temptation on the part of the researcher to be abstruse and talk down to the manager, or present conclusions based on very little analysis; or lack of clear recommendations in research, for example, the 'on-the-one-hand/on-the-other-hand' or the 'fiddler on the roof' syndromes. This is a frequent failing of research studies, especially from in-house research departments that are usually aware of organizational politics and may want to keep everyone happy. Since the research study is the product that the marketing researcher offers to the client, it is important for a long-term relationship that the quality of research be established early in this relationship, and that the manager be able to regard the research report as 'actionable'.

- Even with clear, acceptable findings, sometimes the research results do not get implemented for a host of reasons that are not reflections on the study. Some of these are inter-departmental politics; change in environment and marketing objectives since the research was commissioned; use of research as window-dressing or as a political tool; and cost of implementing research findings.

Though these causes for non-action are usually beyond the control of the researcher, it helps future relationships to ascertain these causes as far as possible from the manager commissioning the study. Often, a presentation given to an inter-departmental group can enhance the chances of acceptance, since all rational reservations can be discussed during the presentation and the study is not viewed as 'owned' by the manager who has commissioned it. This is possible provided the researcher has been adequately briefed on the orientations of the various members of the group.

Whatever the reasons for the response, the actions of the researcher must be limited to making recommendations. It is important for the researcher to understand this basic difference between marketing research and marketing decisions: good marketing research results provide actionable recommendations; good marketing decisions are concerned with action.

MARKETING INTELLIGENCE AND MARKETING RESEARCH

We have already provided a list of information requirements that are prerequisites for the structuring of a good research project in the section on research briefs. Many of these are items of marketing intelligence, or information that the marketing department must maintain on a regular basis.

These are a part of the ongoing process of acquisition of data about a firm's macro-environment in general, such as information relating to the government's economic and industrial policy, industrial and consumer protection laws, demographic and socio-economic trends in the country, trends in the industry in which the firm participates, as well as data relating to competitors—their market performance, sales, market shares, financial performance, expansion plans, collaborations, etc.

Marketing intelligence also includes internal data about the firm's own operations: overall sales; market shares; product-wise, region-wise, and territory-wise data on sales; information about channel members, their classification according to their current and potential turnover and contribution to the company's sales. In industrial markets, similar data has to be maintained about customers as well.

All this data is essential for marketing planning as well as operations in general and need not be restricted to a product category or a specific research study. It should be maintained by the marketing intelligence section of the client organization. A market researcher called in for a specific project should usually not need to collect this data as part of the project; the manager must have access to such information on a continuous basis, independent of marketing research.

Marketing research is the process of collecting information that is concerned with providing answers to a specific issue. As mentioned in Chapter 2, it could be concerned with analysing a specific marketing problem related to any aspect of the marketing mix, or it may involve assessing the size and suitability of an opportunity. It usually involves discrete, time-bound projects with a specified budget, which are often outsourced to marketing research agencies. Again, marketing research projects may often be planned and carried out within the framework of marketing intelligence data, which helps define the marketing research problem, frame the hypotheses and the research objectives, and define the sample.

Table 3.1 Marketing Intelligence and Marketing Research

Marketing Intelligence	Marketing Research
1. Ongoing process	1. Discrete data, relating to specific issues
2. Concerned with general, environmental, and industrial issues	2. Provides answers to specific issues pertaining to the marketing mix or to assessment of market opportunities
3. General in nature	3. Focused on a specific issue
4. Continuous	4. Time-bound
5. No specific budget assigned	5. Operates within a specific budget
6. Part of department's activity	6. May be outsourced to agencies

The distinctions between marketing intelligence and marketing research are summarized in Table 3.1. The two processes are complementary and together constitute the marketing information system of an organization.

ACTIONABLE RESEARCH

The need for actionable research recommendations can be illustrated with the example of company A's market research on the reasons for the decline of its 'Tropica' brand of tea. As discussed earlier in the chapter, the marketing manager explained that they could act on the researcher's (Ms X) recommendations to curtail this fall in sales only from the next financial year.

The following year, Company A announces a major sales promotion campaign spread over three months for the retailers of Tropica. The scheme involves an all-expense-paid trip for two to Darjeeling for the two winners of the scheme, which is linked to the achievement of the sales target of Tropica. Simultaneously, they announce attractive gift schemes for the consumers. The campaign succeeds in not only arresting the decline in Tropica's sales, but the brand also registers a 10 per cent increase during the quarter, compared to the same period the previous year. The marketing manager commissions a survey to determine the contribution of the two strands of the campaign: the retailer push and the consumer demand generation. Ms Y from the marketing research department is assigned the project and at the end of the month presents a detailed, voluminous report. The marketing manager goes through the report, and gets on the phone to the marketing research manager, 'Thank you for the report on Tropica. There is a lot of detailed data here. I have a bit of a problem, though. Data is all there seems to be in this report. What am I supposed to do with it? I had asked for answers, not just data. Could you please ask Ms Y to explain this data to me, and tell me what conclusions she is drawing from it? And do not mind my saying this, but I will be happier if she does not tie me up in a lot of statistical details. She should have offered to present the findings to me without my having to ask, anyway.'

The marketing research department is fortunate that the marketing manager does not just file the report but actually asks for an explanation and a presentation. The researcher must always keep in mind that while it is important to put the data in the report, mere data is not enough. Detailed interpretations of all tables, and the conclusions drawn from them, must form the major part of the report.

Just as it is important to ensure that the conclusions drawn are actually based on the data and relevant statistical analysis, and are not a result of the researcher's assumptions, likewise it is essential not to confuse the client with a great deal of involved statistical computation. The researcher has to guard against both extremes: reporting results that are not statistically valid on the one hand, and talking down to the manager using statistical jargon on the other. The difference between statistics and marketing research must also always be borne in mind. Therefore, it is important to provide an actionable interpretation of data. Mere tables and charts are likely to result in a summary treatment of the report. A good rule of thumb while reporting is to link the findings of the study to objectives: each objective or area of enquiry must be answered individually. Statistical analysis of the right kind will also ensure that definite and clear-cut findings are reported. Actionable recommendations are a must in every report.

SUMMARY

Requirements from research vary substantially over the life-cycle of the product or even of the business. It is, therefore, essential for the researcher to indulge in frequent dialogue with the manager for total clarity to be obtained on what is at issue in the research required, before designing the final research plan.

The dialogue will also help clarify the manager's thoughts on the subject. The pre-brief should be written down, and the decisions dependent on the findings of the survey should be known to the researcher, in order to design a study that exactly fits the client's requirements. Responsibilities of the two partners should be clearly defined from the very inception of the project.

Marketing intelligence is usually not the responsibility of the researcher, unless specifically asked for. The role of marketing research is to provide actionable recommendations on the issue at hand; the implementation of the action is the responsibility of the manager. There may be a variety of reasons preventing or delaying the implementation of the recommendations. The researcher must take care that a lack of trust in research quality is not one of them. Recommendations should be data based and properly analysed using statistical tests, but should go beyond the presentation of masses of data. Involving other departments from the client's organization in the presentation of the report usually enhances the chances of acceptance of the recommendations, since it creates an opportunity for various doubts, reservations, and concerns to be clarified. This should, however, be done only at the behest of the manager commissioning the survey.

KEY WORDS

Role of research refers to the contribution marketing research is expected to make to marketing decisions in the form of recommendations based on rigorous analysis of detailed, systematically obtained, and objective data collected for the specific purpose of the study on hand. The role of research is to make recommendations, and not to take the final marketing decisions.

Good research is research that (a) is based on a detailed understanding of the issues involved, (b) answers the manager's concerns comprehensively, (c) provides conclusions based on rigorous, appropriate analysis, and (d) provides actionable recommendations. Bad research would, therefore, be lacking in one or more of these.

Immediate concerns are marketing decisions that are dependent on the information which is provided by the marketing research study.

Focus is the key issue giving rise to the study, different from the many related issues that may have influenced different dimensions of the marketing decision which the study will impact. The 'immediate concerns' of marketing will govern the focus of the marketing research study.

The ultimate decision refers to the marketing decision arising from the marketing research study.

Unstated dimensions of the problem refer to a number of issues that may have directly or indirectly influenced the marketing decision under consideration. The manager commissioning the study is often aware of these at the subliminal level. While briefing the researcher, these should not be articulated as issues influencing the development of the marketing research problem.

Prior research relates to the product, service, or concept under study which may have been carried out by another agency earlier to investigate a marketing decision similar to the one currently being studied.

Relevance and benefits of methodology refer to any sampling or analytical methodology that has to be based on the framework within which the marketing decision has to be taken, and the various constraints and limitations governing the study. For example, the focus group method of data collection may not be relevant for a marketing decision that will be based on quantitative analysis of a large sample.

Presentation refers to the live reporting of the findings to a group as against a written report.

CONCEPT REVIEW QUESTIONS

1. What would you do as a researcher, if: the manager of a plastics products company, who commissioned a survey to assess the size of the market for a new product, is transferred halfway through the study? When you present your research findings to the new manager, she is extremely dissatisfied and claims that what you have found is already known. Instead, she needs to know the regional distribution strength of all major competitors and regionwise projections of the sales of the company's new product, which is something that the study has not reported in detail.

2. You had to present the findings of a study to the product manager concerned, including details of various statistical tests carried out, and explain why specific tests were used. After going through the report, when you call up to ask for his reaction, he replies angrily that you are trying to talk down to him, and that what he needs is specific recommendations and not a lesson in statistics. How would you handle such a situation?

3. After you present the findings of a study to the product manager concerned, he asks you where the analysis is. You expected him to take your word for all the recommendations, without checking why you had used some specific analytical methodology. What would you do now?

4. You are making a detailed presentation to an interdepartmental group on the consumer acceptance of a revised version of one of their major brands, and at the end of the presentation the finance manager asks why your presentation does not have any

data on the amount of money likely to be saved through the introduction of the new version. How would you provide an explanation to him?

5. Your survey for a psychotropic drug marketed by a major pharmaceutical company suggests that their drug is normally not prescribed in the early stages of the disease and the general manager—sales, disagrees strongly, saying he had had a conversation with a leading psychiatrist just a week earlier, and the doctor had assured him that he prescribes the company's drug from the very inception of the disease. What is your perception?

PROJECT ASSIGNMENTS

1. In the Coke study referred to earlier, what is the issue that should have been addressed? What data would be needed to provide appropriate information on it? Please list both marketing intelligence and marketing research data needed as well as the sources of these data.

2. Assume that you are the marketing research consultant for Company A that markets Tropica and have just completed the three-month sales-promotion campaign for retailers and consumers. How would you list the objectives of the study and structure the findings? You do not have to report just findings, just indicate the structure.

3. If a large toiletries company was planning to introduce a new brand of shampoo in the country, what kind of market research information would they require for determining the market potential of the shampoo? If you were the marketing researcher selected for the assignment, what kind of information would *you* need from the company for designing the study? Select a company operating in your city and discuss the project with the appropriate person to ensure that you have identified all the relevant requirements. What would be the designation of this person?

4. Select a large company in your area and find out what kind of marketing research it usually undertakes in a given year. For what marketing decisions does it usually utilize research? How often are its marketing decisions based on marketing research? What are the most frequent problems it has with the research?

REFERENCES

Aaker, David A., V. Kumar, and G.S. Day 1999, *Marketing Research*, 6th edition, John Wiley and Sons, New York.

Deshpande, R. and Gerald Zaltman 1982, 'Factors Affecting the Use of Marketing Research Information: A Path Analysis', *Journal of Marketing Research*, February, pp. 14–31.

Deshpande, R. and Gerald Zaltman 1984, 'A Comparison of Factors Affecting Researcher and Manager Perceptions of Market Research Use', *Journal of Marketing Research*, February, pp. 32–38.

Nargundkar, R. 2002, *Marketing Research: Text and Cases*, Tata McGraw-Hill, New Delhi, p. 5.

PART TWO

Planning for Marketing Research

- **Stages in Planning Marketing Research**

- **Types of Research**

- **Types and Sources of Data**

- **Experimentation**

- **Interview Techniques**

- **Sampling**

- **Designing Questionnaries and Interview Guides**

- **Building Attitude Exploration into Questionnaires**

Part Two

4

Stages in Planning Marketing Research

OBJECTIVES

After reading this chapter, the readers will be able to understand:

- the client's definition of the need for marketing research and the specifications of the problem: the marketing research brief
- how to derive the marketing research problem from the marketing problem
- the components of the marketing research problem
- the researcher's interpretation of the marketing research problem and planned approach to the solution: the marketing research proposal

INTRODUCTION

In the first part of this book, we examined the need for marketing research and defined its role in marketing decision-making. Once a decision has been taken to go in for research, the next step is to develop a framework, or plan, for research. As we saw in Chapter 3, this requires detailed discussions between the client and the researcher so that the research problem and its context are both understood clearly by the researcher. These discussions are needed to ensure that all the dimensions of the real problem, and not merely its symptoms, are addressed. As the ensuing sections indicate, satisfactory research can only be undertaken if all the dimensions or sub-problems related to the apparent marketing problem have been articulated and prioritized. Preliminary discussions and a written marketing research (MR) brief from the client form the basis for the marketing research proposal. This chapter discusses the definition of the marketing problem, the marketing research problem along with its sub-problems, the hypotheses relating to the various sub-problems, and the specific research objectives or the areas of enquiry. The proposal, which has also been looked at in this chapter, includes all these and the proposed sample, the data collection methodology, the outline of the analysis methodology, as well as the time and cost estimates for conducting the study.

THE MARKETING RESEARCH BRIEF

An inadequate understanding of the 'MR brief' on the part of the client is not uncommon. The client often does not distinguish between an MR brief and a two-line specification of the study the researcher is required to carry out. The framework for this specification is not always clearly defined. The client does not always indicate to the researcher, at least initially, why the research is required, what marketing realities within the organization have given rise to the need for this research, or what decisions are dependent on it.

As D. Aaker et al. (1999) say in their book, *Marketing Research*, 'Seldom will research problems come neatly packaged with obvious information requirements, clear-cut boundaries, and pure motives on the part of the decision makers. Research problems are more likely to be poorly defined, only partially understood, and missing possible decision alternatives that should be analysed.'

Seeking Information

Mr Suresh Mathur, a second-generation entrepreneur who manufactures and markets cigarettes, noticed that many smokers tend to buy cigarettes loose, in ones and twos. He was curious to know why, and whether this would spell an opportunity for him to market cigarettes in packets smaller than the 10-cigarette packs. He wrote to Market Researchers, a large marketing research agency based in Mumbai, suggesting that they conduct a study to determine the market potential for such a pack.

Market Researchers wrote back asking for an appointment to discuss the project. When the agency's representatives arrived, Mr Mathur was quite surprised to find that they had not brought along a research proposal. He indicated that he was in a bit of a hurry to have the study carried out. He had expected a proposal that could be discussed and finalized at the meeting so that the agency could begin work on it from the following week.

The agency's representatives were surprised in their own turn. Raka Mehta, the research director, pointed out that they had come prepared for the preliminary meeting with some industry data that they would present to Mr Mathur, and that they would need some discussion about the project he had in mind. She said they would need a brief from him before they could submit the proposal.

'But I sent you a brief!' was Mr Mathur's astounded reply. From the folder his secretary had placed before him, he produced a copy of the 'brief' he had sent to the agency. It was the same request that he had sent them, asking them to carry out the study to assess the market potential for a small pack. He could not understand what more the agency needed in order to start work. If any background information was required, it was their job to collect it—that was precisely what he wanted to engage them for.

Wal-Mart's India Strategy

At the National Retail Federation convention held in New York, Wal-Mart's CEO, Lee Scott, said that while China had the potential to replicate its success in the US, it is Russia, along with India, that is ripe for retail expansion. Wal-Mart's company officials in India will not confirm whether they have been conducting market research to develop an entry strategy, but they say, 'We are looking to expand our retail operations globally. Because of its population and demographics, we are interested in the Indian market. But India has laws forbidding foreign direct investment (FDI) in the retail sector and hence we cannot enter at this time. We would like to see this FDI regulation liberalized. However, at this time we are not lobbying actively for change'.

Given that 26 per cent FDI in retail is likely to be allowed by the government soon, is Wal-Mart going to enter India? In that case, Wal-Mart needs to identify a suitable entry partner in India.

Source: The Times of India, 28 May 2004.

The case discussed on Wal-Mart's strategy glosses over a number of questions that Wal-Mart will need to get answers to before it takes a decision about entering India. For example, what growth rate is the organized retail market likely to exhibit in the country over the next few years? In which regions will it grow the fastest? What will be the government's final policy about allowing FDI in this sector? How much will be allowed?

If Wal-Mart considers entering India, which part of the country will be the most promising? What route should it adopt: licensing, franchising, or a joint venture? Who are the potential partners it should consider? Research will be needed first to identify all the issues involved and then to find answers to them. If all the relevant questions are not answered, the final result may jeopardize Wal-Mart's entry into the country.

A research based on the kind of inadequate brief given by Mr Suresh Mathur to Market Researchers would probably result in findings that are not relevant, not usable, or even quite different from what the purpose of the research was in the client's mind. Such research is bound to lead to dissatisfaction; mutual finger pointing; waste of money, time, and effort for both the client and the researcher.

Any research is only as good as the brief given by the client, however competent an agency may be. A good research brief is a document that outlines the marketing problem the client wishes the researcher to address, the genesis of the problem, its impact on the organization's performance, and the organizational objectives that the marketing activity in question aims to achieve.

The absence of a good brief, however, does not absolve the researcher from the responsibility of determining the details of the problem at hand, the various dimensions of the problem, the internal and environmental trends that have given rise to the problem, the decisions that are likely to be taken on the basis of the research, and so on.

A marketing research brief given by the client must provide all this information and will usually emerge only after a series of discussions between the researcher and the client.

DEFINING THE MARKETING RESEARCH PROBLEM

A researcher must realize that from a client's point of view, the marketing decision is germane to the problem; the client tends to think in terms of marketing issues, not marketing research.

The responsibility, therefore, lies with the researcher to translate the marketing problem into a marketing research problem, with all its ramifications. A competent researcher will delve deep into the genesis of the marketing issue at hand to achieve this objective.

What is the difference between a marketing problem and a marketing research problem? Using the term 'problem' in the generic sense that includes both 'opportunities' and 'problems faced', a marketing problem is concerned with marketing decisions, while the domain of the marketing research problem is the information required to take the decision.

The Marketing Research Problem and Sub-problems

In the small cigarette pack case discussed earlier, the marketing problem that Suresh Mathur faces is whether or not to introduce a smaller pack, and the optimum size of this 'smaller' pack. His decision will be dependent on the incremental sales he can hope to garner from such a pack. He needs the agency to provide him with information that will help him take this decision. The agency, thus, needs to answer the questions: how much will be the annual demand for a smaller cigarette pack and what will be the optimal size of such a pack?

Implicit in the definition of the marketing research problem are issues related to its various dimensions, or sub-problems. These must be defined and addressed clearly so as to provide complete information that will help the client take an informed decision.

Once again, these sub-problems will have to be identified through discussions with the client. These discussions are crucial since the client may not even have considered some of the sub-problems explicitly. This is particularly likely if the marketing decision requiring research has not been discussed extensively within the client's organization.

Such a situation is more likely to occur in small, owner-manager-driven organizations in which there are not many people with whom the issues can be discussed or in cases where similar studies have in the past been carried out for other products in the organization.

The tendency, in the case of the adhesive bandages, is to look upon the new study as a replication of earlier product studies, and not to consider dimensions that had

---

Market Positioning of Small Adhesive Bandages

The manufacturing division of a multinational company noticed that in the process of manufacturing their well-known brand of pre-medicated small adhesive bandages, the wastage was very high. Although the supplier of the material produced the sheets in standard sizes, the cloth used for the backing had to be cut to a specific size. It was suggested that the material currently being wasted could be used to produce very small adhesive strips. Since these small strips would also be carried in the same packs in which the standard size strips were packed, packaging and marketing costs would be minimal. The entire project would result in huge savings in manufacturing, on the one hand, and would generate incremental sales, on the other. In a market where competition is getting more aggressive by the day and product-differentiation rests largely on the company's reputation, small adhesive bandages provide a major boost to the mother brand. The idea was met with enthusiasm within the company. The brand manager in charge of adhesive bandages called in the research agency and explained the concept to it. She asked the agency to prepare a proposal for a study to estimate the market potential for the small strips. During the discussion, the agency representatives wanted to know what market positioning was being considered for these strips. Were they, for example, to be targeted specifically at small children? Or very small cuts? How was the company intending to ensure that the small strips led to additional sales instead of cannibalizing the sales of the mother brand? Was the price of the pack going to be raised, or were the additional small strips to be put into the pack as 'free' promotion? The brand manager admitted that these questions had not been considered and promised to revert to the agency after discussions with her colleagues.

not been considered relevant to the decision then or had been inadvertently left out. The researcher, therefore, has the advantage, as an 'outsider', of bringing to the table such unarticulated issues and thus providing a richer backdrop for the study.

In the small cigarette pack case, the relevant sub-problems requiring investigation would be:

- the definition of a 'small' pack, as perceived by the smoker
- the target consumer section
- the likely price that smokers will be willing to pay for the small pack
- the likely frequency of purchase of the small pack
- the probability of the small pack cannibalizing the sales of the regular packs, and the probable extent of cannibalization
- the chances of the loose-cigarette buyer upgrading to the small pack and thus contributing to increased sales
- the chances of factors, such as brand loyalty, limiting the switch by the smokers of other brands to the small pack

In order to determine whether to manufacture the smaller cigarette pack, the client will need information on all these aspects of the problem. Obviously, the amount of time and effort required for obtaining such information cannot be standardized. Some problems move quickly from the client's initial questions to problem identification and the definition of sub-problems. Others are so complex, they almost defy diagnosis. Like a good doctor, a researcher must be willing to spend time moving from the general and the symptomatic (e.g., 'sales are declining') to the specific and the actionable.

HYPOTHESES GENERATION

Once the specific problems, i.e., the sub-problems have been articulated, the next step is to transform them into testable hypotheses (Fig. 4.1). These hypotheses are essentially assumptions that the people in the organization (and sometimes others such as the dealers and even the general public) will have formed about the possible causes of the issue at hand in the case of 'problem' research, and about the likely outcomes of what we have elsewhere termed 'opportunity' research. In other words, they are tentative explanations for specific events.

The testing of the hypotheses is the essence of most marketing research approaches (a major exception is the exploratory research, which will be discussed in later chapters). This methodology has a parallel in day-to-day life. When confronted with a given situation, we tend to make assumptions about its causes. In trying to make sense of the situation—mentally, behaviourally, or through information exchange with others—we check out this list of possible causes.

How do we arrive at the hypotheses to be tested?

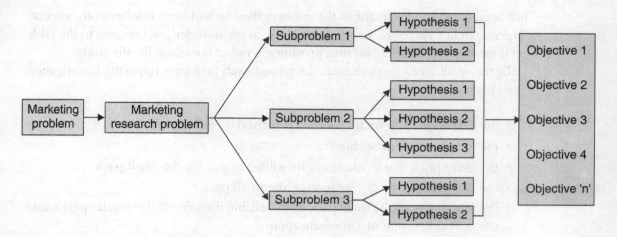

Fig. 4.1 Stages in Planning Marketing Research

- Hypotheses are best arrived at either by the client organization or by the researcher through discussions with the client and through an examination of external data.
- It is useful to involve a large number of sources (and people) in arriving at these hypotheses since the different explanations for the marketing issue are likely to provide a richer basis for identifying the realities on which the marketing decision must be based. At the same time, the explanations provide a focus for the process of investigation, thereby saving the researcher a lot of time that could otherwise have been spent chasing irrelevancies.
- Hypotheses should lend themselves to tests through quantifiable measures. A hypothesis such as 'This product makes the owner happy' is not testable unless the construct 'happy' has been defined in specific terms. Similarly, it is not possible to test the hypothesis 'This advertisement campaign has been effective' unless relevant connotations of 'effectiveness' have been defined. It is, therefore, essential to define all constructs and variables to be measured in the study in specific terms. The 'effectiveness' of an advertisement campaign, for example, means delivering on the objectives of the campaign: awareness building, increasing brand recall or consumer-information about the product, creating preference, etc. A campaign that is meant to enhance brand preference cannot be considered 'effective' if it has increased brand recall substantially but not gone beyond that.
- Another implicit requirement of good research is to limit the number of hypotheses that may be tested in one study to a manageable few.

This apparent contradiction is best understood when we note that, though it is crucial to begin with as exhaustive a list of likely explanations for a marketing event as possible,

Hypotheses

In the small cigarette packet study, Market Researchers, the agency, decides to talk to various executives in the organization to assess their beliefs about the likely 'fit' of the small pack with the existing product mix, and its likely contribution. It talks to the executives in the marketing area as well as in sales and production. Some interesting assumptions are articulated.

Market Researchers realizes that some of these hypotheses overlap. Moreover, the last hypothesis about the production cost vs sales revenue is beyond the ambit of their study since it relates to production costs and not to marketing issues to be checked out in the marketplace. They, thus, summarize the list of hypotheses to be tested out as follows:

- A pack of four to five cigarettes will be ideal since a light smoker smokes about three to four cigarettes a day.

- Light smokers who generally buy loose cigarettes, say, one or two at a time, will not want to buy a pack, since they will be worried that access to a pack will result in an increase in their daily consumption.

- Moderate to heavy smokers will not consider this pack of four to five cigarettes convenient or economical since they will have to buy more packs and will end up spending more money since the unit cost of two packs of five will be higher than the cost of one pack of ten cigarettes.

- People who want to reduce smoking will downgrade their purchase from packs of tens to small packs. Small packs will thus cannibalize the sales of packs of ten.

- People smoking other brands and wanting to reduce smoking will switch to this small pack and thus contribute to increased brand sales— at least till their regular brand introduces a similar small pack.

- The small pack will result in a net increase of 10 per cent in sales revenue of the brand.

- The incremental sales revenue generated by the small pack will not justify the manufacturing cost of the small pack, which will be only marginally lower than the pack of tens.

- The new pack will generate incremental sales revenue of 10 per cent for the brand in the first year.

- Most of the sales of the new pack will come from light smokers, i.e., those who smoke five or less cigarettes a day.

- The major reason for light smokers to buy the small pack will be the convenience of buying one small pack instead of buying loose cigarettes many times in the day.

- In the first three months, the new pack will derive sales more or less equally from buyers of large packs of competitor brands and the mother brand.

- Competitors will launch their own versions of small packs within three months.

all of them will not have equal bearing on the event in reality. It is, therefore, good practice to prioritize the list of hypotheses in consultation with the client and concentrate on the more relevant ones.

The list of hypotheses discussed for the small cigarette packet study thus concerns itself with the expected sales, the source of sales (brand switch vs additional sales), consumer perceptions of the small pack, and likely competitor reaction.

Production costs of the new pack will be available to the production and purchase departments of the organization and will involve decisions relating to packaging material, printing, and designing costs, etc. These are matters internal to the manufacturing decision, and need not concern the marketing research agency. The hypothesis relating to the net incremental profit from the small pack is, therefore, not included in the study.

THE MARKETING RESEARCH PROPOSAL

Once the client has finalized the marketing research brief, the researcher has to work out a detailed proposal. Fig. 4.2 outlines the components of a marketing research proposal. A research proposal has been defined in various ways by different authors. D. Aaker et al. (1999) describe a research proposal as 'a plan for conducting and controlling a research project'. According to D.R. Cooper and P.S. Schindler (1999), P.D. Leedy has defined the proposal as a 'work plan, prospectus, outline, statement of intent, or draft plan'. However, the paragraphs that follow attempt a somewhat more detailed explanation of what a research proposal is.

A proposal is essentially a detailed statement of the entire research plan from the researcher's point of view. Briefly stated, it includes the rationale of the study, i.e., the reasons why the client desires the study, and the research design, which includes:

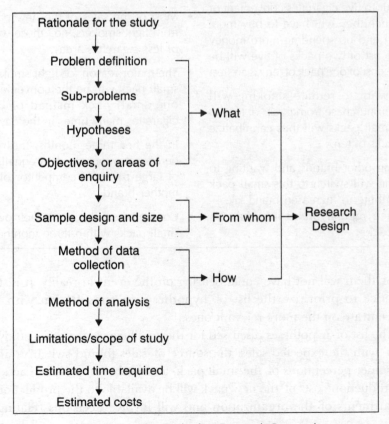

Fig. 4.2 The Marketing Research Proposal

- the 'what', i.e., the definition of the research problem, sub-problems, hypotheses, and research objectives,
- the 'from whom', i.e., the design and size of the sample from whom the information will be obtained, and
- the 'how', i.e., the method of data collection and analysis.

Defining Research Objectives

What are 'research objectives'? Once the hypotheses to be tested have been defined and prioritized for the study, the specific areas of enquiry relating to each hypothesis need to be spelt out. Often, each hypothesis will have multiple dimensions to be explored, and each of these dimensions is labelled as a research objective.

Many researchers like to differentiate between 'primary' and 'secondary' objectives, which may be defined in terms of the priority assigned to the hypotheses being tested. Primary or major objectives are those that relate to the more important hypotheses being tested; secondary or minor objectives relate to the less crucial hypotheses. For example, if Hindustan Lever were commissioning a study to determine consumer perceptions of their Lux brand of soap versus Lux International, the hypotheses may be defined as follows.

H_1: Consumers regard Lux International as more 'upmarket' than Lux, which is seen as a mass market brand.

H_2: Consumers who usually buy Lux would buy Lux International only for special occasions.

H_3: The users of other premium brands do not distinguish between Lux and Lux International and, therefore, do not buy either of the two brands.

H_4: People who have tried both Lux and Lux International do not consider the price difference between the two justified by the additional benefits offered by Lux International.

If the main purpose of the study is to determine why a buyer would opt for Lux over Lux International or vice versa, hypothesis H_3, which relates to the users of other premium brands, is less important than the other three hypotheses. The objectives of the study would then be as they have been listed here.

Primary objectives

1. The demographic profile of the current users of Lux and Lux International
2. The frequency of usage of Lux among current users of Lux International
3. The frequency of usage of Lux International among current users of Lux
4. The occasions of the use of Lux among current users of Lux International, and of the use of Lux International among current users of Lux
5. The major benefits desired in a toilet soap by the users of Lux and Lux International

6. The perception of major benefits delivered by Lux, Lux International, and other major brands among the users of Lux and Lux International

7. The perception of acceptability of the price of Lux and Lux International among the current and the past users of these brands

Secondary objectives

8. The demographic profile of the current users of the other premium brands of soap

9. The past usage of Lux and Lux International among the users of the other premium brands

10. The major benefits desired in a toilet soap by the users of other premium brands

11. The reasons for the non-usage of Lux/Lux International or the switch from these brands among the users of other premium brands

As is apparent from this list of objectives, it is not always necessary to draw up separate lists of primary and secondary objectives. The secondary objectives 8, 9, and 10 are merely extensions of primary objectives 1, 2, 3, and 5 to 'other premium brands of soap', and may be combined without any loss of information.

When the study is being planned, it is often tempting to examine all possible related issues at once. This attempt, although laudable in theory, is not practical since it will result in making the study too long, unwieldy, and difficult to manage. As in the case of hypotheses, so it is with objectives. In any study a good policy would be to limit the number to a few: a thumb rule is that the list of objectives pertaining to any study must not exceed eight to ten.

THE SAMPLE

The next essential step is to define the source of information for the study. Most studies limit the source of information to a subgroup, i.e., a sample of the relevant population, rather than undertaking a complete census. This keeps the time and costs of the study within manageable limits. Major decisions while deciding on a sample are concerned with the following issues:

• Who should form a part of the sample (i.e., the definition of the sampling unit and the sampling element)?

• How should these be selected from the population (i.e., the technique that is to be employed for sampling)? Usually the choice between probability and non-probability techniques depends on factors such as the accuracy desired, the heterogeneity in the population, and the details in the information to be obtained. These influencing factors on the choice of the sampling technique will be discussed in detail in later chapters on sampling.

- How many should be selected (i.e., the size of the sample)? This is the decision that has to take into consideration the accuracy required as well as the time and cost constraints.

Detailed discussions about the sample will follow in Chapter 9.

Method of Data Collection and Analysis

The research proposal must specify the method to be used for data collection. For example, will a qualitative or a quantitative approach be used? Will the emphasis be on desk (secondary) research or primary (field) research? In the latter case, will the data be collected through observation, experimentation, or a survey? What will be the kind of survey: personal, telephonic, mail, or online? Who will collect the data?

The methods of analysis should be specified depending on the expected response. Analysis takes many forms and shapes, ranging from simple cross-tabulations to complex statistical analytical designs. If statistical techniques are to be used, they should be mentioned. Similarly, qualitative analytical techniques, if required, should also be specified in some detail.

Limitations and Scope of the Study

A market research study is not a 'universal truth'. It is meaningful only within a specific framework. Time and cost constraints; the number of objectives that may be addressed without making the study unwieldy, and to that extent ineffective; the specific parameters being studied and the manner in which they are being defined; the assumptions under which the client's brief is being interpreted; the size and structure of the sample—all these factors influence the relevance and efficacy of the study. These limitations must be specified in the proposal, thus defining the scope, or 'outer boundaries', of its relevance.

Time and Cost Estimates

The decision to conduct research is dependent on a cost-benefit analysis. Similarly, the utility of the study is governed to a great extent by the amount of time taken to complete it and present the results. Since decisions that are going to be based on the study are time-bound, it is essential that the degree of sophistication and the details of a market research study be decided keeping these decision-requirements in mind. This information, therefore, constitutes a necessary element of the research proposal.

While preparing the budget for a marketing research study, a good rule is to list all the activities involved in the study and apply standard costs for each activity. Similarly, a realistic time budget must also be prepared, specifying the amount of time likely to be required for each activity. This method provides the researcher with a good estimate of the time and costs likely to be incurred at each stage of the study. Also, in case the client asks for any reduction in the allocation of either monetary or time resources, it provides a ready basis for examining where and how much modification is feasible.

SUMMARY

For marketing research to provide effective support to marketing decisions, it is essential to begin with a detailed marketing brief, which explains all the relevant dimensions of the marketing decision being considered. The initial step in planning a research study is to list the details of the information required for such a marketing decision. The defining of the marketing research problem, derived from the marketing problem, is an iterative process, i.e., the result of many discussions between the client and the researcher.

A detailed plan, or marketing research proposal, for the marketing research study to be undertaken is essential and must be submitted to the client before the study is actually initiated. This proposal should specify the actual marketing decision that is the genesis of the study and the marketing research problem or information needed to arrive at the decision. Other essential components of the proposal are, the sub-problems into which the marketing research problem may be broken up; the hypotheses being tested; the specific areas of inquiry or objectives of the study; the sample; the methodology to be employed in data collection and analysis; and the time and cost schedules of the proposed study.

KEY WORDS

Research brief refers to the client's view of the marketing issue for which a research study is being contemplated, including the background, the specific areas of enquiry, and the decisions that will be based on the study.

Research problem refers to the marketing issue to be studied through the marketing research study; it may be concerned with opportunity analysis or problem solution.

Sub-problems refer to those aspects of the research problem that deal with a specific dimension of the problem.

Hypothesis refers to an assumption about the cause of a sub-problem.

Objectives refer to the specific areas of enquiry into which a sub-problem is divided.

Qualitative research refers to the exploration of the reasons behind an individual's behaviour, attitudes, beliefs, thinking, and the interrelationships between these variables.

Quantitative research refers to measuring behaviour, attitudes, beliefs, thinking, and the interrelationships between these variables.

CONCEPT REVIEW QUESTIONS

1. Give two examples to illustrate the difference between an MR brief and an MR proposal. Is an MR proposal required if the research is being conducted internally, i.e., by the company's own marketing research department? Why?

2. A business school wants to explore the possibility of introducing a course in health-care management. Develop a research design to determine the health-care industry's expectations from such a course and its market potential. How would this study be different from one examining the market potential of a product?

3. Is it necessary to always break up a marketing research problem into sub-problems? One view is that this limits creativity in research and thus also its contribution to marketing. Comment.

CRITICAL THINKING EXERCISES

1. In the Wal-Mart case, what kind of information should the company's representatives ask a marketing research agency to collect if Wal-Mart wants to determine its market potential in India? Draw up a list, in addition to the questions raised in the text, and explain why you consider the listed items important so as to assess market potential for the company.

2. *The Times of India*, the English language daily, has changed its design, format, and content substantially over the years. While this has led to a tremendous increase in the circulation and readership of the newspaper, some executives worry that this growth might have been achieved at the cost of a decline in its editorial quality and image. If a study were to be conducted to check out this contention, how would you define the marketing problem that is to be addressed? Also, state the marketing research problem.

3. Both Coca-Cola and Pepsi have traditionally used celebrities extensively to advertise their products. One of the companies now wants to assess the extent and nature of the impact of celebrity advertising on their brand. Define the marketing research problem and list the objectives in detail.

4. Company X, a leading manufacturer of plastic-based household appliances, such as buckets, breadboxes, chairs, etc., is considering diversifying into pallets for industrial organizations. You have been engaged as a consultant to assess the market-potential for this product. What information would you require from the manufacturer in order to develop a research proposal?

5. Assuming that you have obtained all the information you needed from Company X, develop a marketing research proposal, justifying your time and cost estimates.

PROJECT ASSIGNMENTS

1. Your business school wants to improve its interface with the industry.

   (a) What dimensions of this interface need to be explored as a first step? Whom will you talk to in order to find out which dimensions would be the most relevant?

   (b) Design and conduct a study to determine how this interface may be improved.

REFERENCES

Aaker, D., V. Kumar, and G.S. Day 1999, *Marketing Research,* sixth edn, Wiley, p. 46.

Corporate Dossier, *The Times of India,* pp. 1–2; Friday, May 28, 2004.

Cooper, D.R. and P.S. Schindler 1999, *Business Research Methods*, sixth edition, Tata McGraw-Hill, New Delhi, p. 86.

Leedy, P.D. 1980, *Practical Research: Planning and Design,* second edition, Macmillan, New York, p. 79.

5

Types of Research

After reading this chapter, the readers will be able to understand:

- the exploratory, descriptive, and causal research approaches
- the kinds of research needed at different stages of the marketing decision process

INTRODUCTION

Understanding the marketing decision of a client and developing a plan for the kind of marketing research support needed are imperative to conducting market research. The next step is to determine the most suitable research approach. This approach will vary, depending on the nature of the problem being addressed as well as the extent to which it has acquired a structure. The most suitable approach must be determined because this will influence what information will be collected and how it will be done. Decisions relating to the implementation of the research design will follow once the research approach has been decided. This chapter discusses in detail the three basic research approaches: exploratory, descriptive, and causal or diagnostic.

The research approach that is adopted influences the time and cost required for the study. It also affects the degree to which the complexities in the interrelationships between the variables being studied are brought out. The need for exploring such complexities is not always the principal purpose of any research. Depending on the decision to be taken, the research need may be for an in-depth exploration or, alternatively, for painting a broad canvas with definite, firm strokes. One will not do where the other is required. In the very early stages of marketing decision-making, when the purpose is to acquire a clear understanding of the various contours of the problem more than to find out why the problem has arisen, the exploratory approach is essential. Once the problem has been clearly defined, further exploratory research with a larger sample or with different respondent groups will not serve much purpose. It then becomes essential, depending on the nature of the problem that is now clearly delineated, to undertake a descriptive study to identify and prioritize the variables involved as well as to comprehend their general relationship, or a causal research to establish the exact causality between dependent and independent variables.

Later sections are directed towards this end, i.e., a discussion on the appropriate research approaches at different stages of the marketing decision process.

Acme Pharma, a well-known multinational pharmaceutical company, was known for its nutritional supplements, especially Calmin, its multivitamin syrup. Although a large seller, Calmin had always been the No. 2 brand in the marketplace and a close competitor to the market leader. When its volume of sales began to rise beyond the ambitious target in 1995, everyone was pleased. Calmin was, after all, a major revenue earner for the company. However, Ajoy Bose, the marketing manager, was perplexed. The brand had always been supported well by the company, but no exceptional effort had been put in during the year. After two months, during which Calmin continued to exceed the sales target, he decided to call in the marketing research agency.

'But why?' asked the sales manager. ' What is wrong if the brand is doing so well? What are you worried about?'

'I need to know why it has suddenly taken off. I agree that it has always been a big brand, but what has opened the floodgates? It is not as if any of our major competitors is out of the market or doing badly. Nor is Calmin a new brand. If I don't know today why it is doing well, I would not know why, if it starts to slip tomorrow!'

The MR agency recommended some exploratory research to begin with.

RESEARCH APPROACHES

All research can be classified into the three categories: exploratory, descriptive, and causal or diagnostic.

Exploratory

This approach is often used when the research problem has not been clearly defined, 'or its real scope is as yet unclear. It allows the researcher to familiarize him/herself with the problem or concept to be studied, and perhaps generate hypotheses to be tested' (*www.ryerson.ca*). It is the initial research, often undertaken to get insights into the problem. As we saw in Chapter 2, the hypotheses in exploratory research are either not defined at all, or at best, vaguely defined.

The major objective of exploratory research is to identify and define the problem or sharpen its definition and scope, and thus help to arrive at the best research design, method of data collection, and sample. Exploratory research is typically characterized by highly flexible, unstructured, and, at times, informal research methods. Dependence on secondary sources of data or on discussions with the experts can be quite high.

'Another common reason for conducting exploratory research is to test concepts before they are put in the marketplace, always a very costly endeavour. In concept testing, consumers are provided with either a written concept or a prototype for a new, revised, or repositioned product, service, or strategy.' (*www.ryerson.ca*)

Since exploratory research depends on small samples and aims primarily at identifying or sharpening the definition of the problem, it should ideally be regarded as the initial stage of research, and its results treated as inputs for the next stage, rather than as supportive data for the final decisions.

Green and Tull (1978) have defined the three stages of exploratory research:

1. search for secondary data
2. discussion with experts
3. examination of analogous situations

The search for secondary data

In the Calmin case, the first step would be to examine retail audit reports. How is the market growing? How are the major competitors faring? Have there been any significant changes in the marketing mix of any of the competitors? Is Calmin's growth keeping pace with or outstripping the growth rate of the market? Such questions need to be explored in detail to establish whether there is a problem, to begin with. It is possible that there may be a spurt in the market growth for various reasons, and Calmin is merely growing at the rate of the market, maintaining a constant market share. In such a case, what needs to be determined is why the market is suddenly growing so rapidly rather than examining Calmin's growth patterns. If there does appear to be a problem, viz., Calmin's growth really is significantly higher than that of the market, the problem becomes more complex and it becomes essential to determine the reasons.

In general, data published regularly or studies conducted earlier on the same (or related) subject are available that will provide partial or, at times, complete answers to the problem. It may take the form of quantitative data regarding the environment or the industry. Reference to this secondary data in the early stages of the investigation is essential. The reasons behind the necessity for obtaining secondary data are many.

- Some marketing problems may lend themselves completely to solutions through secondary information.
- Saves time and cost: since part of the answer to the problem being addressed is obtained by referring to information already available, it becomes possible to narrow down the scope of the problem to which answers must be obtained through primary investigation.
- Direction and framework for the investigation: secondary data helps to identify the aspects of the problem that have already been resolved, the period over which the earlier data had been obtained, and the method used for data collection. Secondary information provides guidelines about the content, time frame, and sample required for the study to be undertaken.
- In addition, sometimes the review of (such) literature may provide pointers to some aspects of the issue under investigation that had not been considered earlier, adding to the utility of the study. Secondary sources, thus, serve to both limit and add to the scope of the study.

Table 5.1   Some Sources of In-company and External Information

In-company Information	External Information
• Sales and market-share data: by product, territory, dealer, month/year, contribution to total turnover, major territories	• Sales and market-share data of major competitors: by product, territory, dealer, month/year, contribution to total turnover, major territories
• Production data: product, month/year, plant	• Production data: by product, month/year, plant
• Dealer data: by location, product sales, A-B-C categorization by turnover	• Dealer data: by location, product sales, A-B-C categorization by turnover
• Major customers by sales (in case of industrial product companies)	• Major customers by sales (in case of industrial product companies)
• Sales-promotion strategies used; their impact in sales terms	• Sales-promotion strategies used; their impact in sales terms
• The size of the sales force by territory; sales performance of individual sales-force members—total and by product/brand	• The size of the sales force by territory; sales performance of individual sales-force members—total and by product/brand
• Reports of market studies conducted earlier	• Consumer perception and brand-usage data
	• Published industry data
	• Government/ministry/bank/agency reports
	• Annual reports of companies

• Secondary data on behavioural and sociological trends could provide extremely useful insights that may themselves act as the basis for modifications in the marketing mix, such as changes in the product or communication, or serve as hypotheses that may be tested.

The two major sources of secondary data are (a) in-company information and (b) external sources of information. Table 5.1 lists some examples of the more frequent sources of each kind.

Discussions with experts

Once secondary data has been obtained, the next step is to discuss the issue under study with 'experts', i.e., people who are likely to be knowledgeable about the subject. If the subject were related to detergents, for example, it would be beneficial to discuss it with housewives, who would be aware of the expectations from such a product, the problems with brands currently available in the market, the experience, and the usage patterns. Such discussions will, of necessity, have to be freewheeling in order to ensure that all aspects of the problem are addressed and so that the housewives may discuss the subject without any restraint or diffidence. At this stage, we are less interested in a representative cross-section of opinions than in getting special insights.

These discussions with the 'experts' may be carried out on a one-to-one basis, or it may take the form of a 'focus group', where the emphasis is on understanding influence patterns, product perceptions, and usage behaviour. The discussions usually continue till the incremental cost of information collection begins to exceed the additional information obtained.

Examination of analogous situations

Another approach to exploratory research is the examination of analogous situations. This may be done through an analysis of case studies or through simulation. Information on similar situations is usually available. These studies provide for a *post-facto* analysis and, thus, serve as guidelines to structure the study. They may help to define the nature of the problem and provide indications of relevant variables, as well as their interrelationships. This helps in defining hypotheses, which may later be checked out through larger-scale studies. Findings from the analysis of case studies should, however, be taken as suggestive rather than decisive since the environment is only broadly similar. It is not possible to manipulate the variables to determine the impact of a changed emphasis on each.

In the Calmin case, for example, the starting point in the study could be the analysis of some other brand of the company that had faced a similar situation of sudden growth, with no major apparent changes in the marketing environment. An examination of the case history of the company's own products would be particularly useful since similarities in the internal environment are likely to remain high. The details of the decision-making process, interrelationships of variables, and even some information on the process of manipulation of the variables involved may be available.

Another method of analysing analogous situations is through simulation. Simulation consists of developing and manipulating models that may be used for finding numerical solutions. These models are flexible in providing for the manipulation of variables and for understanding their nature and interrelationships. Computer-based simulation models that assist in marketing decision-making are now available. However, since the models employed are based on the examination of numerical relationships, they do not lend themselves well to the understanding of intangible variables such as changes in consumer perceptions and attitudes.

Descriptive

The largest type of research comprises descriptive studies. As the name suggests, these studies are concerned with defining the 'who', 'where', 'when', 'how', and 'what' of a decision problem, i.e., the descriptions of market characteristics. The simplest kind of descriptive research is concerned with a univariate issue. For example, in a descriptive study on Calmin, we may be interested in determining the sales or market share of the brand, the demographic profile of its users, its dealer-wise or territory-wise growth, and so on.

Descriptive studies may range from the very basic, concerned with identifying the values of one defined variable, to the extremely complex, defining a large number of variables and describing their interrelationships. In the Calmin case, a descriptive study might examine the variation in sales by age group, for example. Or it might be aimed at determining the effect of a patient's age and the duration of the use of Calmin on the patient's state of health, defined in terms of specific parameters.

Unlike causal studies that will be discussed in detail later, descriptive studies do not explain the relationship between variables, they merely describe the association. As such, descriptive studies are not always useful in predicting the impact of one or more independent variables on the dependent variable. Even so, there may be situations when it is not necessary to understand causality in order to predict change. For example, if a soap dish falls into a bucket filled with water up to the brim, water will overflow. It is not necessary to know the Archimedes principle of displacement in order to make that prediction; an average user will be able to make that prediction as well as a physicist. The point to note here is that there are many situations in which the description of the relationship between two variables, as in a descriptive study, is adequate for making a reasonably good prediction, without necessarily establishing causality.

Descriptive studies are also different from exploratory studies in that they are concerned with examining well-formulated hypotheses. The Calmin study for determining brand market share, for example, could aim at testing the hypothesis that the market share of Calmin is 60 per cent. These descriptive hypotheses might, at times, result from earlier exploratory research.

Descriptive studies are characterized by a fair degree of structure in research design.

Unlike an exploratory study, which is marked by a high degree of flexibility, a descriptive study requires identified hypotheses that are to be tested in the study, a clearly defined list of areas of enquiry, and a detailed plan of the sources of data as well as the method of data collection to be employed. It also needs substantially larger samples than those employed in exploratory research in order to control sampling errors within specified limits, since the information obtained is aimed at serving as a basis for decisions and not merely as a base for further research.

Causal or Diagnostic

These studies are concerned with finding answers to the 'why' aspect of a problem. For example, let us assume that the price of Calmin is reduced by 10 per cent during a month. If sales at the end of the ensuing quarter rise by a percentage significantly higher than in the corresponding quarter the previous year, could the change be attributed to a reduction in price? Although it is possible, as mentioned above, to make predictions about the future state of a variable without determining the cause of its occurrence, the determination of causes of an observed phenomenon helps to improve the quality of prediction, and also lets the decision-maker exercise better control over the implementation of a decision. Typically, such studies tend to be more complex than either exploratory or descriptive research, and require a very well-defined structure of research design, sources of data, and method of data collection. Although it is never possible to completely identify one or more variables as the cause of another variable, a well-structured causal study aims at optimizing the degree of accuracy with which the relationship between an observed (dependent) variable and its possible causes, i.e., independent variables, is identified.

P. Green and T. Tull (1978) have discussed two kinds of causation—deterministic and probabilistic.

Deterministic causation

This defines the necessary and sufficient condition(s) for any change in an observed variable. Let us consider the case of a change in the price of Calmin. Suppose that the only change in the marketing-mix of Calmin has been this change in price. If Calmin is the only brand in its category to have reduced prices, and there has been no other major change (e.g., no change in the marketing-mix of major competitors), the change in the price of Calmin can safely be identified as the variable causing the change in the sales of the brand. There is no other causal variable. The change in price may, therefore, be said to be the *deterministic cause* of the rise in the sales of Calmin. It is the necessary and sufficient condition for the change in its sales.

Probabilistic causation

Also referred to as a 'producer' of an event, a probabilistic cause is a necessary but not a sufficient cause of the event's occurrence. For example, let us once again consider the case of a change in the price of Calmin. Suppose that in addition to a reduction in the price of Calmin, the brand's major competitor is in short supply during the same period. Since the two are independent events, the influence of one on the other is nil. A change in the price of Calmin, although occurring at the same time as the shortage in the supply of the competing product, X, neither influences the shortage nor is influenced by it. It is, therefore, not possible to predict one from the other. At the same time, both influence the rise in sales (R_c) of Calmin. In other words, the rise in sales R_c is a function F of P_c and S_x. This may be expressed as

$$R_c = F(P_c, S_x),$$

where P_c is the change in the price of Calmin and S_x is the non-supply of competitor X. Both these independent variables influence the sales of Calmin separately. Each of them is thus only a partial cause of this change, i.e., a necessary but not sufficient condition for the change. In other words, such a change in the independent variables is the cause but neither of the two is an adequate explanation by itself, i.e., a sufficient cause for the change in the sales of Calmin. Such a relationship between R_c and each of the independent variables is called a *probabilistic causation*. Figure 5.1 depicts both these kinds of causation.

Causal relationship

How are causal relationships determined? Relationships between two variables may take any of the following forms

Symmetrical   Two variables may vary together, either in the same direction or in opposite directions. This is a 'concomitant variation' and may happen because the two variables are indeed associated; hence, a change in one results in a change in the

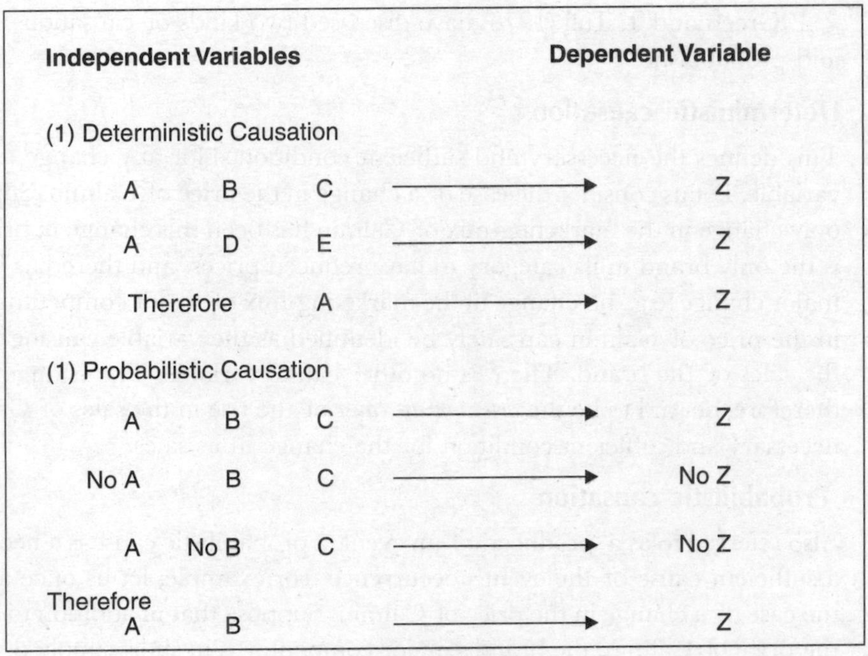

Independent Variables				Dependent Variable
(1) Deterministic Causation				
A	B	C	⟶	Z
A	D	E	⟶	Z
Therefore		A	⟶	Z
(1) Probabilistic Causation				
A	B	C	⟶	Z
No A	B	C	⟶	No Z
A	No B	C	⟶	No Z
Therefore				
A	B		⟶	Z

Fig. 5.1 Causation

other. However, this does necessarily suggest that one variable causes the other. For example, an increase in the sales of Calmin and a shortage of another brand in the same category may occur simultaneously, but this does not necessarily imply that the increase in the sales of Calmin has been caused by the shortage of the other brand. In order to establish such a link, it will have to first be determined that Calmin is perceived by doctors and users alike as the closest substitute of the other brand, and also that such substitution is considered acceptable, and not likely to carry any major risk.

Reciprocal Two variables may influence each other positively or negatively. For example, high levels of afforestation lead to increased rainfall as trees attract rain and, simultaneously, high levels of rainfall lead to growth in vegetation and afforestation. Correlation is the major measure of such a relationship.

Asymmetrical In such a relationship, the occurrence of one variable (independent) influences the occurrence of the other (dependent) variable. The converse is not necessarily true. The reasons for this are as follows:

(a) The occurrence of one (dependent variable) is the result of the occurrence of the other (independent variable), for example, an increase in the awareness of a brand, such as Calmin, may be the direct result of its TV advertisement campaign.

(b) The occurrence of both variables is influenced by the occurrence of a third variable, not being studied explicitly. For example, let us assume that the TV campaign for Calmin is offered on a long-running TV serial, whose viewership

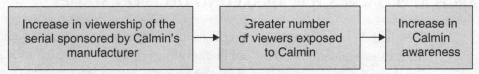

Fig. 5.2 Stages of Brand Awareness

has increased significantly over the year. Thus a significant increase in brand awareness follows the sequence given in Fig. 5.2.

In other words, the increase in brand awareness is not a direct result of any increase in the frequency of the TV commercial, which has been maintained at earlier levels, but a result of the fact that more people are now watching the sponsored programme and are, therefore, being exposed to the TV commercial.

Researchers are most often interested in such asymmetrical relationships in order to find answers to 'why'. D.R. Cooper and P.S. Schindler (2000), in their book *Business Research Methods,* have discussed four types of asymmetrical relationships, as listed below.

1. *Stimulus-response relationship* An event or occurrence that evokes some response from the dependent variable, such as an increase in brand preference, as a result of an advertisement campaign.

2. *Property-disposition relationship* An enduring characteristic (property) that cannot be manipulated artificially but influences the subject's response, such as a change in attitude towards saving (disposition) with a change in age (property).

3. *Disposition-behaviour relationship* Dispositions influence behaviour. For example, a variety-seeking disposition leads to the frequent trial of new products in the market.

4. *Property-behaviour relationship* In addition to disposition, enduring characteristics, such as social class, also influence behaviour. For example, the involvement of the family in investment decisions among the higher social classes.

The relationship between two variables is causal if and only if all the three conditions listed below are met.

*   *Concomitant variation* There is a concomitant variation between the two. For example, an increase in price and a decline in sales occurring together.

*   *Sequence of events* A change in the status of one variable follows a change in the status of the other variable, i.e., a price increase is followed by a decline in sales.

*   *Absence of other possible causes* There is no change in the status of any other relevant variable. For instance, in the price-sales relationship example above, there should be no increase in the competitive activity or decline in product quality availability of the product, or the communication frequency/quality.

RESEARCH APPROACHES FOR MARKETING DECISION STAGES

The suitability of research approaches for reducing risk in various marketing situations varies substantially. The use of an inappropriate research approach may not only not give the right information, but may also give the wrong information. It is, therefore, extremely important to be conversant with the compatibility of the research approaches with the information required for specific marketing decisions. The discussion that follows examines various marketing decisions required at different points in the life of an organization. It investigates, in some detail, the suitability of various research approaches for them. These decisions can be grouped under three broad heads.

- pre-introductory
- post-introduction
- strategy-related

Table 5.2 lists these applications in detail.

Pre-introductory Decisions

Pre-introductory decisions are most often concerned with the definition of a market opportunity and an evaluation of its attractiveness.

Opportunity definition and evaluation

In the early stages of an examination of a business or a product opportunity, the marketer is dealing with an area without possessing sufficient knowledge. The marketer's primary concern is with spelling out the various dimensions of the opportunity that appears to present itself and with drawing inferences that help in decision-making. The marketer has to perforce use a very flexible approach, capable of modification and an extension of the initial assumptions. Since information about the area being studied is very limited, no formal hypotheses may be formed on which to structure the examination of the opportunity. The most suitable and rewarding approach at this stage is, therefore, an exploratory one, following in the sequence mentioned earlier in this chapter.

1. secondary data analysis
2. surveys with experts
3. focus-group discussions
4. two-stage design

Secondary data analysis should begin with the company's internal data. Reports of prior research studies, if any, provide valuable information on the nature of the earlier approach, the conclusions arrived at, and, if so, the reason(s) why the project was not proceeded with. This should be followed up with retail audit reports and other published data.

Table 5.2 Suitable Research Approaches at Various Stages of Marketing Decision-making

Marketing Decision Stage	Research Approach		
	Exploratory	Descriptive	Causal

Pre-introduction	• Opportunity identification:
	  – Idea generation
	  – Idea evaluation
	  – Concept test
		• Concept test
		• Tests of various marketing elements: product, price, communication strategy; marketing channels
		• Test marketing
		• Market segmentation studies
		• Market potential
		• Sales forecasts
		• Positioning studies	

Post-introduction	• Consumer attitude to company and competitive market offering • Repositioning studies • Motivation research • Customer-satisfaction studies at brand/product level	• Studies related to specific marketing issues: consumer, product, price, communication, channels, competition, market segments • Purchase patterns, trial and repeat rates for new products/services; profile of major market segments • Usage patterns; heavy-, medium-, and low-use consumers • Brand-loyalty studies; brand-image and brand-identity studies; perceptual mapping of brands; brand positioning studies • Customer satisfaction studies at brand/product level	• Predictive studies to determine the degree and nature of influence exercised by marketing elements on sales, profits, etc. • Post-facto studies to determine the impact of changes in specific competitive variables on company's market-offering
Strategic	• Market and industry analysis • Perceptual mapping of company and competitors • Studies to choose growth strategies: market development, product development, diversification	• Assessment of market-performance • PLC analysis; studies for identification of appropriate market strategies • Corporate branding studies • Identification • Customer perception surveys • Opportunities for innovation	• Impact of specific environmental variables on company performance

Let us consider the case of an MNC, dealing in baby products, examining the possibility of introducing nappy pads marketed abroad successfully by its principals. A preliminary discussion within the marketing group reveals that a similar product, called a 'nappy liner', had been test-marketed by the company earlier and had been discontinued because of unfavourable results.

Checking up on the earlier test-market reports, the product manager in charge of the project finds that (i) the product nappy liner did not serve the clearly defined needs of keeping the baby or the nappy dry, (ii) it had not been positioned clearly in terms of the target group or the benefits offered and, as a result, had been perceived by mothers as not delivering on its promise, (iii) the market had been overestimated—the assumption had been that all households in the socio-economic classes A and B with a baby below six months would provide the potential market for the product, (iv) no marketing research had been conducted before the launch to determine the size of the potential market, and (v) the product had been perceived as too high-priced for the limited utility it was seen as providing.

The test-market reports provide extremely useful insights for the product manager, and a list of 'what-not-to-do' activities. As a first step, she sets about organizing a discussion with a few mothers of babies below six months in age, to understand the need for such a product more clearly. The line of questioning includes: In what situations would it be used? What do mothers currently do about the problem? How serious is the problem? Would mothers buy a product from the market to solve the problem? In other words, the 'survey with experts' is conducted.

In the case of the baby products company, the results of the discussion provide 'leads' for focus groups with women in different socio-economic and demographic segments. The objective is to determine the user-related and the product-related factors that might provide the predisposition to use nappy pads. How would mothers perceive such a product? What would be the psychographic profile of a mother likely to use it? How will it be different from that of a non-user? What would be the self-concept of such a mother? What would be the motivations behind using a nappy pad? The answers to all these questions emerging from the focus group discussions lead to the following hypotheses:

- The user is a young mother on her own, without the support of her mother's/mother-in-law's experience. The baby is her first child.
- She is likely to belong to the upper-middle income group, is educated, and is a working woman, most often in an executive position.
- She sees herself as modern, efficient, and well-organized. Proud of having become a mother and caring deeply for the baby, she wants baby care to fit into her everyday life, and not disrupt her daily routine. She sees the baby as fun, and does not want to start thinking of it as forcing her to give up having fun.

The product manager is now ready to test these hypotheses on a large sample. The focus group, as the first stage of the research study, has provided the preliminary definition of the target respondent and the specific areas of enquiry. The second stage is a descriptive study that would bring into sharper focus the target buyer, patterns of purchase, motivations that would provide the communication cue, the competition as perceived by the mother, the most acceptable channels of marketing, and the acceptable price.

Sharpening the definition of an opportunity Exploratory studies are thus most useful in the pre-introductory stages of defining and evaluating a market opportunity. These would include studies involving idea generation and evaluation. The studies may also be used in later stages, such as

- identifying the appropriate target population
- repositioning a brand
- sharpening communication strategies

By their very nature, the studies are not very useful for evaluating hypotheses that have already been formed, or in describing the contours of an opportunity that has already been well defined. The characteristically small sample used in such studies may, in fact, lead to unreliable results.

Another major area of use of marketing research is in defining the marketing-mix. In sharpening the definition of the opportunity, once the target segment has been identified, in the pre-introductory stages, it is necessary to identify (i) the appropriate positioning and identity of the market-offering, (ii) the product or service attributes and benefits, (iii) the prices that will be regarded as providing value, (iv) the packaging that will convey the desired identity, (v) the right communication strategy, i.e., suitable creative and media strategy, and (vi) the markets that will promise the greatest potential. The framework for the project would already have been defined and relevant hypotheses formed, and all these parameters have to be assessed with a large enough sample to minimize the risk involved in the decision. As such, descriptive research is the most appropriate at this stage.

Test marketing is often the next stage, especially in the case of consumer products, requiring the frequent use of marketing research. Here again, descriptive research is the most frequently required approach. The selection of test markets is based on computer-based analytical techniques, such as cluster analysis, which will be discussed in a later chapter.

Since the objective of the test market is to identify the most appropriate marketing-mix, research at this stage is concerned with determining the response of the consumers and the market intermediaries to various levels of the marketing-mix. A frequently used method is to set up consumer and dealer panels and conduct periodic descriptive studies with them, aimed at determining brand awareness, pre- and post-purchase opinion, experience with the product, trial and repeat rates, and response to the communication among the consumers, stocking and repeat order patterns, support to merchandizing strategies, and satisfaction levels with the incentives/sales promotion schemes among the retailers. Similar studies are also conducted to identify the competing brands from which the maximum attrition occurs. All these descriptive studies provide crucial inputs for determining the optimal marketing mix and for forecasting the sales turnover and market share the brand is likely to achieve.

Post-introductory Studies

Post-introductory studies account for the greatest percentage of all marketing research studies related to any organization's market-offering, and may be related to any issue concerned with the target user group, the marketing mix, or the competition.

Since these studies are almost invariably concerned with testing well-defined hypotheses, the descriptive approach is most often used for them. Again, the need for such studies may arise at any stage of the product's life cycle, ranging from the post-introductory, growth, maturity, to the decline.

Other post-introductory studies are concerned with determining the cause-effect relationship between marketing variables. A company may be interested in determining

- the impact of the specific elements of its marketing mix on its sales or profit, e.g., the change in sales as a result of a new sales-promotion campaign, or
- the impact of competitive activity on its sales or profit, e.g., the change in its sales as a result of an increase in the price of the major competitive product, or
- the impact of specific environmental variables on its sales or profits, e.g., change in its sales as a result of reduction in import duty on the price of some raw material.

Such studies are usually concerned with obtaining after-the-fact information on a marketing variable. This may be done through historical data on both the dependent and the independent variable(s), using models that study the exact nature of the relationship between the two. The objective is to determine the degree and direction of causality.

Strategy-related Studies

Another situation where causal studies are useful is when the objective is to identify the strength of the relationship between a dependent variable, such as sales, and more than one independent variable, such as sales promotion, advertising frequency, and change in price. In this case, research is required in order to assist in devising marketing activities, such as a promotion strategy or even the complete marketing strategy, and will often take the form of market experimentation. The methodology adopted is the manipulation of one or more independent variables to study their relative impact on the dependent variable, while controlling the change in all other independent variables. The findings of the study will then be used to decide on the exact quantum of variation required in the independent variable studied in order to achieve a specific change in the dependent variable. Market experiments are the most common form of causal studies, and will be discussed in detail in later chapters.

Another major area of use of marketing research is at the strategic level, which may be concerned with such decisions as defining the future direction of the organization. As depicted in Table 5.2, this area of marketing research relates to strategy issues and moves through the following stages:

- *Situation analysis* This involves the identification of market trends, existing gaps in consumer-need satisfaction, threats, and opportunities.
- *Strategy development* This involves the identification of major players, their strategies and competitive positions, competitive positions available, market segments to be targeted, consumer analysis, and performance objectives.
- *Marketing programme* This involves the marketing mix to be implemented.
- *Monitoring the implementation of the marketing programme* This involves the achievement of performance objectives and the corrective action desired in the case of non-achievement.

SUMMARY

All marketing research is based on one of three approaches: exploratory, descriptive, and causal. Exploratory studies are marked by a flexible approach and are most useful before definite research hypotheses have been formed. They are, in fact, to be used in developing hypotheses. They follow these stages: secondary data, 'expert' surveys, focus group discussions, and development of hypotheses. In terms of applications in marketing decision-making, the exploratory approach is to be used most often in the initial stages, such as in developing and evaluating a market opportunity.

The descriptive approach, which is adopted for the largest percentage of marketing research studies through the organization's life, is used for testing, rather than for developing hypotheses. It is concerned primarily with describing the relationships between various parameters being studied in a given situation. In terms of the stages in marketing decision-making; the descriptive approach is to be used once hypotheses have been formed and the framework of the study defined, all through the post-introductory stages of growth, maturity, and decline.

Causal studies, which aim at providing the 'if and only if' linkage between dependent and independent variables, are used for defining such causality at any stage after introduction. These studies usually adopt either the post-facto models and equations or experiments for explaining the causes of observed phenomena.

KEY WORDS

Exploratory studies refer to the initial, unstructured research aimed at developing hypotheses.

Descriptive research refers to the studies concerned with defining and describing the relevant variables and their interrelationships.

Causal research refers to the studies concerned with determining causality between two or more variables, i.e., establishing the degree to which one or more independent variables influence the occurrence and the level of the dependent variable.

Secondary data refers to the data that is already available either through studies conducted earlier, or through other reports and statistics, and not the data collected for the study in question.

Experts refer to any respondent group, especially in exploratory studies, who, because of their life-situation, experience, or knowledge, may be consulted in order to define hypotheses and variables.

Post-facto analyses/studies refer to the studies conducted after the occurrence of an event. It is not possible in such studies to manipulate the level of different variables to determine the ideal level of causality.

Simulation refers to developing and manipulating analytical or behavioural models that aim to create conditions in which the relevant variables and their interrelationships may be established, observed, and analysed.

Deterministic causation refers to the change in the value of the independent variable(s) that is necessary and sufficient for a change in the value of the dependent variable.

Probabilistic causation refers to the cause of any event or change in the value of the independent variable(s) that is necessary, but not sufficient, for a change in the value of the dependent variable.

Symmetrical causal relationship refers to a relationship in which two variables vary simultaneously, either in the same direction, or in the opposite directions. This is also called 'concomitant variation'.

Reciprocal causal relationship refers to a relationship when two variables influence the occurrence of each other.

Asymmetrical causal relationship refers to a relationship in which the occurrence of one variable (independent) influences the occurrence of the other (dependent) variable, but the converse is not necessarily true.

Test marketing refers to a marketing experiment aimed at testing the marketing mix of a new market-offering from a company. Test marketing is undertaken after all the relevant marketing elements have been tested out individually, and modified suitably. It differs from simulation and most other types of marketing experiments in that here the market-offering is actually introduced in the market, and its performance studied in a live situation.

CONCEPT REVIEW QUESTIONS

1. How do exploratory, descriptive, and causal studies differ from each other? How do these differences influence their utility at the different stages of marketing decision-making?

2. Company XYZ, a major player in the cigarettes and tobacco industry, is planning to enter the casual wear market. What market factors should it study before entering

the market? Should the company undertake an exploratory, descriptive, or causal study for this purpose?

3. Why is a small sample size adequate for an exploratory study but not for a descriptive one? What kind of information will not be reliable if a small sample is used in a descriptive study?

CRITICAL THINKING EXERCISES

1. You are the brand manager for Company X's nationally marketed brand of ballpens. The brand has been losing sales volume consistently for the last three months. You ask the marketing research department to do a study to determine the reasons for the decline.

   (a) Is this an exploratory, descriptive, or causal study?
   (b) What will be the objectives of the study?
   (c) How will the study need to be designed to meet these objectives?

2. Company A, manufacturers and marketers of precoated steel, is applying to the government for enhancement of its manufacturing capacity. Before applying, it wants to assess the market potential of the product and the opportunities for its brand.

   (a) What kind of study will be required for this purpose—exploratory, descriptive, or causal?
   (b) From where will the data for the study be obtained?
   (c) Are any sources of secondary data available for the study? List some such sources of secondary data.

3. Herbal Care Ltd, a well-known toiletries company, is considering an expansion of its product range to include herbal cosmetics, especially lipstick, mascara, and eye-shadow. Before launching the products, it would like to know who would be the most likely users, and what would be their perception of a herbal range in such a product category. What kind of a study should be employed to get such information? Why?

4. Herbal Care Ltd has increased its total advertising budget for its well-established brand of toothpaste 'Dentafresh' in order to counter the increased activity from its major competitor. Since the competitor brand is priced at about Rs 1.50 cheaper than Dentafresh, Herbal Care decides to offer a price discount of Rs 2 on each tube of Dentafresh for two months. The sales of Dentafresh increase significantly at the end of these two months. What kind of study should the company undertake if it wants to determine whether advertising or the price discount was responsible for this growth? To what extent did each of these contribute to the growth? Design the study.

PROJECT ASSIGNMENT

Choose a private hospital, a five-star hotel, or a BPO company from your area. Study its operations and identify a new opportunity area for it. Assess the potential the opportunity may have over the next three years and prepare your recommendations for the organization.

REFERENCES

Aaker, D., V. Kumar, and G.S. Day 1988, *Marketing Research*, John Wiley and Sons (Asia) Pvte Ltd, pp. 73–75.

Cooper, D.R. and P.S. Schindler 2000, *Business Research Methods*, Tata McGraw-Hill, p. 146.

Green, P. and D. Tull 1978, *Research for Marketing Decisions,* Prentice-Hall, pp. 66–74, *www.ryerson.ca*

6

Types and Sources of Data

After reading this chapter, the readers will be able to understand:

- the primary and secondary types of data used in research
- the various methods of data collection, their applicability, and limitations
- how to anticipate and safeguard against the kind of errors that infect data

INTRODUCTION

Fundamental to the process of scientific decision-making in marketing research is the understanding of the differences between data, information, and research. Data, collected scientifically and for a purpose, is pivotal to research-based decisions. This chapter explores in detail the nature of the data required for research in marketing.

The pre-eminent source of data in marketing research is the 'respondent', i.e. the individual or group from whom information is obtained, either by direct or indirect questioning or through the observation of behaviour in real-life, experimental, or simulated conditions. As discussed in the earlier chapters, such questioning or observation may not necessarily be restricted to the issue under study. It may take place in a general environmental context or even in the context of some other issue, directly or indirectly related to the current one. Again, what does such data measure? Marketing decisions require information on past and intended behaviour and behavioural change, as well as on attitudes, beliefs, perceptions, and influences that govern them. The first section discusses the sources of such data in detail. Methods available to obtain such data are discussed in the next section, along with the applicability and limitations of each method.

Research data is, by and large, obtained from a 'sample', i.e., a section of the population under study. However, even the best of efforts are subject to errors. A later section in the chapter discusses the various kinds of errors, their impact on the veracity of the data, and how to minimize or totally avoid them.

CLASSIFICATION OF DATA

Data is the quantification of tangible and intangible facts. It is, therefore, the only means of proving or disproving facts to arrive at marketing decisions. Data can be classified in two ways—by the purpose of collection and by the nature of the variables studied.

By the purpose of collection

Primary data is that which is collected specifically for the purpose of providing information on the decision under question. *Secondary data* is that which is not collected specifically for providing information on the decision under question; nevertheless, the data has significant bearing on the decision being examined. Such data may have been collected for some other purpose, or may be obtained from an earlier study on the same issue.

Secondary data may be classified under various heads.

- *Socio-economic trends* include data regarding demography, social trends, e.g., change in employment levels, increase in the ratio of working women to the total population, urbanization, immigration patterns, consumption patterns, and changes in the GNP and the GDP.
- *Industry trends* include the extent of industrialization, the growth of various industries, changes in ownership patterns, such as privatization, the entry of MNCs in various industry sectors, major players, and their performance and growth strategies.
- *Government policies* include data on especially those policies that have a direct or an indirect impact on industry growth and on economic, legal, fiscal, and international policies.
- *Internal company data* includes internal company policies; data on sales and production; budgets, distribution strengths, and channels; number of distributors, wholesalers, and retailers; sales by each channel member; markets covered; the performance of major brands; information on major competitors; major brands; and earlier market-research reports.

Secondary data is essential for all marketing research for the following reasons, even in situations where the primary data is ultimately not found to be necessary:

- Secondary data often helps to provide the direction in which the marketing research study should be structured. For example, secondary data relating to a study on the reasons for growth of new retailing formats might indicate that malls have been coming up with increasing frequency in upcountry towns. It would then become necessary for the primary research to extend the study beyond the metros to include smaller towns in the sample, and examine the retailing patterns in the two town categories for differences, if any.
- The analysis of secondary data, whether in company reports or from an external source, often indicates that some of the required information for the study is already available and, therefore, defines the content of the new study. In addition

to helping define the content of primary research, secondary data could thus help save on the costs and time of the primary data collection.

- The choice of the sample for the field-study is another area in which prior recourse to secondary data is essential.

Annexure 6.1 lists some commonly used sources of secondary data.

By the nature of the variables studied

Data can also be classified on the basis of the nature of the variables studied, in the following way:

Data related to past or future behaviour For example, information on purchase, brand usage, the mode of purchase, the quantity and frequency of purchase, the occasions of purchase, etc. usually require quantitative data.

Data related to attitudes, perceptions, beliefs, etc. Qualitative data is required for this purpose.

Primary and secondary data could relate to information regarding past or intended respondent behaviour or past or current respondent attitudes, perceptions, and beliefs. One major use of data regarding intended behaviour is in forecasting future sales. However, data on intentions can never predict future sales absolutely and accurately since future sales would be influenced by additional factors. These would include competitive activity, changes in purchasing power, introduction of new products, and many other variables beyond the control of the marketer.

Both types of data are needed by the marketer for understanding the current market trends, which would help in assessing the impact of past marketing decisions, as well as in planning future marketing strategy, and predicting future market trends, which is also needed for planning.

METHODS OF DATA COLLECTION

The actual data collection method for marketing research depends on the research approach — exploratory, descriptive, or causal — in addition to the nature of the data required.

As the example of the paint manufacturer suggests, extensive enquiries of this kind will require the use of various kinds of research approaches. In many cases, in practice, the requirement may be restricted to data needing one or the other research approach. At the same time, one method cannot substitute another. Secondary data, though essential for all research, cannot always provide the complete answer, for example, to consumer behaviour with respect to a product (Aaker *et al* 1998; Green and Tull 1978). Even if the internal-company data is available in the form of earlier research, it will be necessary to verify its validity over time and with different groups of users with the help of primary data collection. Many other limitations of secondary data have been listed in Table 6.1.

Gathering the right data

Company X, a major manufacturer of paints for the industrial segment, was considering expanding into the decorative paints market, primarily the household paints segment. It conducted a quick SWOT analysis of the organization and came up with these findings: it was the largest manufacturer of paint, even though it was not participating in the most attractive segment; it had the most advanced paint technology in the industry; it was not too well known in the household segment; it did not have the distribution channels required for the household segment since it had been operating all along in the industrial paints segment exclusively; the decorative paints market was crowded with at least six players in the organized sector and innumerable participants in the unorganized sector; the growth in the future, according to industry reports, was likely to come more from the household segment than from the industrial paints segment.

Company X realized that if it were to enter the decoratives segment, it would need a great deal of information about the market. It had no idea about the attractiveness of the decorative segment beyond the fact that it constituted the major and faster-growing segment of the paints market. The sources of data to which the company currently had access included the annual reports of major competitors in the organized sector, the current five-year plan of the government of India, and the report of the Ministry of Chemicals and Fertilizers. These reports gave the company information on the size and the projected growth of the market, the major competitors and their performance, and the fact that the housing construction industry was set to boom in the coming years, thus providing further growth opportunities for household paints.

The company decided to call in a marketing research agency, with a rather unusual brief. 'List all the kinds of information that will be required for taking this decision, and then list all the ways in which this data will be collected.'

Market Finders Ltd., the research agency, made a detailed list of all the data it considered relevant to Company X's request, and told the company to collect the following:

- Secondary data about the market in addition to the data already collected by the company: This includes the annual and monthly sales of paints in the decorative paints segment for the previous five years; the market shares and the growth rates of major players for these five years; the state-wise sales of the industry and the major players; the larger-selling pack sizes, colours, and prices; the major distribution channels for decorative paints; the promotion strategies employed by the major players.

- Information about consumer behaviour: This includes the companies preferred; the shades and types of paint preferred; the frequency of getting the house painted; the major occasions for it; the level of knowledge about the product category and the various brands; the decision-making process; the influencers; the usual quantity purchased; the variations in all these behavioural factors, if any, by region and by town.

- Information about consumer attitudes towards paints: This includes involvement levels, the relationship with paints and the painting process; the parameters influencing brand choice; the brand perceptions, the positioning, and the identity of major brands.

The agency suggested that since the company already had some secondary data about decorative paints, it should start with collecting the remaining secondary data. The next step would be exploratory studies to obtain information on consumer attitudes and, finally, information about consumer behaviour should be collected in order to devise a marketing strategy for entry into the decorative paints segment.

Table 6.1 Limitations of the Various Data-collection Methods

Types of data	Methods of data collection	Limitations
Secondary data		• Information may relate to a different period and may not be relevant any longer. • Sample or database may be different. • Rigour in collecting data cannot be vouched for.
Primary data	Observation	• Does not answer the question 'why'.
	Surveys	• Scope for rationalized responses. • Quality of data will vary with the skill of the interviewer. • Cannot tap into issues that are part of the subconscious mind.
	Experiments	• Can study only one dependent variable at a time. • Make assumptions that are not always sustainable in reality. • Difficult to replicate and, therefore, to generalize from. • Results may be vitiated by environmental variables and competitive activity.
	Qualitative	• Difficult to generalize. • The quality of data is highly dependent on the skill of the interviewer.

Collection of Primary Data

Primary data may be collected through any of the following four methods.

Observation of consumers

This method is useful in collecting information about current consumer behaviour and sometimes about past behaviour. It may be used to great effect in point-of-sale situations. The interaction between the consumer and the retailer may be observed by the researcher to understand the degree and the kind of influence exercised by the retailer on brand choice. Similarly, the observation of the process of brand and pack selection and the number of packs selected by the buyer in a self-service retail outlet provides more reliable information than later questioning. Another area in which observation may prove to be a useful method of research is in determining in-store responses to sales-promotion schemes of the 'one-free-on-"x"' kind.

Survey

This is the most popular method used in collecting primary data. Its versatility makes it suitable for collecting data of varying degrees of complexity. Surveys are almost a necessity for collecting a wide variety of data including those on behaviour, attitudes, knowledge, awareness, and behavioural intent. Considerable skill in planning and administration is required if surveys are to provide detailed, accurate, and relevant information.

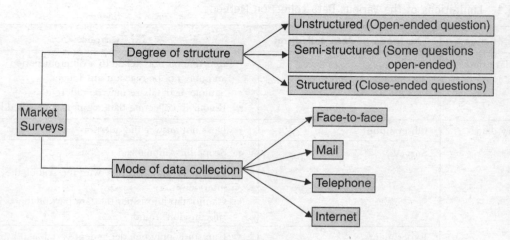

Fig. 6.1   Modes of Classification of Market Surveys

As we will see in later chapters, surveys may be classified in various ways depending on the degree of the structure and the mode of data collection. Fig. 6.1 explains this classification.

The modes of classifying surveys will be discussed in detail in Chapters 8.

Experiments

Controlled experiments are used frequently in marketing to draw causal inferences. So called because they require the marketer's (or the researcher's) planned intervention, i.e., control, experiments make it possible for the marketer to vary the levels of marketing variables and study their impact on specific dependent variables. As is the case with all the other methods of primary data collection, experiments—controlled and natural— also help obtain data from a sample of respondents that is later extrapolated. Controlled experiments are particularly useful in planning the marketing-mix and in determining the impact of a specific level of marketing-mix or even of a particular marketing element. One example of this is the impact of advertising on dependent variables, such as brand awareness, brand preference, or sales. These will be discussed in detail in the next chapter.

Natural experiments are those that do not involve any intervention by the researcher, but comprise the observation and recording of relevant variables, their interrelationships, and lateral or spatial changes in their levels.

Qualitative techniques

An accurate assessment of data related to psychological factors, such as attitudes, beliefs, and perceptions, requires methods of data collection that can delve into the individual's subconscious and obtain spontaneous, not rationalized, responses. Qualitative techniques of data collection, such as focus-group discussions, in-depth interviews, projective techniques and psychometric tests, neuro-linguistic programming and semiotics, aim at obtaining such data. These will be discussed in detail in a later part of this book.

Any method of data collection used in marketing research, as mentioned earlier, is based on the samples of respondents. Even the most rigorously selected sample, precisely because it is a sample and not a census, may fail to take into account some characteristics, displayed by only a very small part of the population. Samples on which marketing studies are based, even the most representative ones, are thus always subject to some errors. The effort in good research is to eliminate errors that are within the researcher's control and to minimize those that cannot be eliminated.

ERRORS IN DATA COLLECTION

Errors in data, whether primary or secondary, arise from a variety of sources.

Errors in Secondary Data

Some of the errors in secondary data may result from the limitations discussed in Table 6.1.

Outdated or irrelevant data Consumption trends sometimes depict a discontinuous change over time. Old data may not, therefore, present a comparable basis for drawing conclusions. The growth of mobile telephony in India is a typical example. Market penetration in the late 1990s was a mere 0.08 per cent of the population, and government policies, permitting only two service providers per 'circle' (group of states/metro cities), projected a growth rate of 100 per cent in the following decade. In reality, with the change in government policy and the introduction of CDMA technology by players such as Reliance, the market for mobile phones has grown much faster during this period. A prospective player examining this market for possible entry on the basis of secondary data alone towards the turn of the century would have missed a very attractive opportunity.

Inappropriate sample A recent report from the Census Commission of India about the population growth in various religious communities during the decade 1991–2001 in the country became the subject of a major political and social controversy when it averred that the population growth rate among the Hindus was much lower than that among Muslims. The reason for the inaccuracy was the fact that the data being compared was based on samples that were not strictly comparable: the 1991 census data did not include some Muslim-majority states, such as Kashmir, while the 2001 census data did.

The use of secondary data presumes that the basis for comparison and projections is valid, i.e., the database used for comparison has not undergone any significant changes during the period of comparison. Any comparison based on data that has undergone a significant definitional change, e.g., the definition of poverty line, the base year for calculation of consumer price index, etc., is erroneous.

Uncertainty about the data-collection methodology   Sometimes it is not possible to investigate and vouch for the accuracy of past data on which the projections or the conclusions are to be based.

Other errors   Other errors from the use of secondary data may arise for the following reasons.

Use of 'guesstimates' in the absence of a rigorous database   Every marketer uses certain data about the size of the target market to make projections about the market potential.

A marketer of up-market baby products would like to estimate the number of SEC 'A' urban households in the country with children below 12 months of age. Since such detailed data is not available at the national level, the researcher's best bet would be to arrive at this figure in three stages: (a) obtain data on all households with children below one year of age, (b) assess the proportion of all households in SEC 'A' across the country, and (c) multiply (a) by (b). A conscientious researcher might extend the exercise to each state and arrive at the sum total for the entire country.

Such extrapolations may lead to overestimation or underestimation of the variable being studied. Worse, it is usually not possible to assess the degree or the direction of the deviation.

Data 'twisting' to fit in with foregone conclusions   Ramchandra, the product manager for Company A's famous brand of cooking oil, is preparing for the annual marketing review. He will be required to present data about the performance of his brand. He is aware that the promotion budget sanctioned for the coming year will depend on how well the brand is perceived to have responded to the current year's budgetary allocation. As per the organizational norm, he settles down to calculate the brand's compound annual growth rate (CAGR) over a five-year period, from 1999 to the current year.

Ramchandra is disconcerted to find that since the brand had registered an unusually high growth rate in 1999 because of price reduction in a price-sensitive market, using 1999 as the base year will result in a relatively low CAGR compared to that for 1998–2003. He decides to use 1998, an 'average' year, as the base, thus hiding the fact that he is presenting a six-yearly CAGR, and not a five-yearly CAGR, as is the norm.

Sometimes organizational compulsions may thus motivate the researcher to use secondary data to 'prove' a result that the client or the researcher himself wants proved, regardless of the reality. Such planned errors may result from a variety of organizational reasons: the need to provide a 'window-dressing' for a decision that has already been taken, or interdepartmental or even interpersonal rivalries, in which data is sought to be used to prove or disprove claims.

Errors in Primary Data

Data collected specifically for answering the queries raised in a study may also be subject to various errors. These have been illustrated in Fig. 6.2.

Sampling error

This error has been discussed earlier in the chapter. Since a sample draws conclusions based on only a part of the population data, it does not ever present a totally accurate picture of population characteristics. This deviation of sample characteristics from population characteristics is a 'sampling error'. By its very nature, therefore, it is not possible to ever bring the sampling error down to zero. A researcher must, however, attempt to minimize the sampling error. Certain techniques of sampling based on the probability theory undertake to do this. As we will discuss in the chapter on sampling, this is achieved by predefining the degree of error acceptable in a study and calculating the sample-size accordingly.

Missing response error

This kind of error occurs when a response cannot be obtained from some of the units (individuals or groups) included in the sample. Such a situation may arise either because the respondent refuses to provide the information required (non-response) or because of the repeated non-availability of the respondent (not-at-home error).

Both these situations will lead to a reduction in the planned sample size and, therefore, to error. *Non-response error*, in particular, does not lend itself to any easy solutions. An option usually tried in both cases is to select a sample larger in size than is required for a predefined sampling error. Since the units included in the sample are usually matched with regard to the major characteristics under study, a larger-than-required sample will contain units that may be treated as substitutes for the ones that refuse to respond. It must, however, be ensured that respondents do indeed match

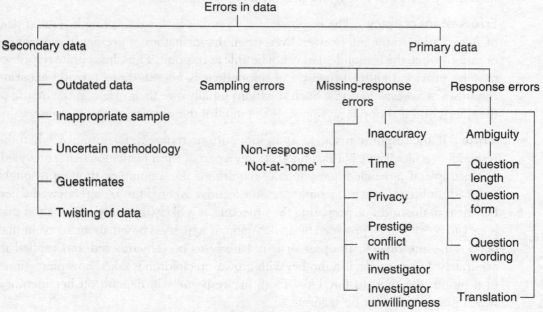

Fig. 6.2 Errors in Data

with respect to significant characteristics. In surveys with doctors, for example, it is difficult to get responses from doctors with a busy practice. But substituting them with another doctor in the same area may not yield the required data if the substitute does not have a practice (and, therefore, experience) of a similar size (Susan Kraft 1991).

The *not-at-home error* is usually sought to be minimized in practice by repeated calls, often varying the time of the day during which the call or the visit is made. It has, however, been found that units that cause the not-at-home error often display characteristics markedly different from those that are available for response. For example, in a sample of women, working women may not be available for interview during the day. But their opinions and world-view are likely to be markedly different from those of full-time housewives. Similarly, it is difficult to obtain responses from people who travel a great deal, but their experiences are likely to be more varied and to differ substantially from the stay-at-homes.

Response errors

Sampling errors and missing-response errors are largely beyond the researcher's control. Errors of the third kind, i.e., response errors, on the other hand, owe their presence almost totally to communication problems between the researcher and the respondent. Communication theory tells us that communication is not complete unless the message delivered is understood by the recipient as it was intended to by the sender, and the response given by the recipient understood by the original sender as it was intended to by the recipient. It is, therefore, the responsibility of the researcher to ensure that the process of data collection is kept free of gaps in communication that are likely to lead to such errors. These errors may be grouped under three major heads—errors of inaccuracy, errors of ambiguity, and errors of translation.

Errors of inaccuracy   The respondent is often not inclined to provide a great deal of information to the interviewer. Even when the inclination is present, there may be occasions when the respondent may not be able to respond. Thus, inaccurate responses may be provided either because the respondent is not *willing* to provide accurate responses or is *unable* to do so. Such situations usually owe their origin to the nature of the query, and it is not always possible to establish the veracity of the response.

Time   If the response is sought at an inopportune moment, for instance, when the respondent is busy, there is a likelihood of only a part of the information being provided. For example, if a detailed questionnaire requiring a fair amount of thought is sought to be administered at a retail outlet, or an executive is sought to be interviewed when he/she is in the midst of preparing for a meeting, it is likely that only information that is easy to recall will be provided, if at all. Again, if a query is posed about an event that occurred some time in the past, it is not likely to be remembered and replied to accurately. For example, if a mother with grown-up children is asked how many times in a month she used to buy baby food, her response will depend on her memory, which may or may not be accurate.

Privacy Questions relating to subjects that the respondent considers private will either not elicit any response or will elicit an inaccurate one. Questions relating to subjects such as personal habits ('How many times in a day do you brush your teeth?'), age, and income will usually not draw an accurate response. Cultural factors, of course, must be taken into account in judging what is 'personal'.

Prestige Questions to which an accurate response may involve some loss of prestige are often likely to draw inaccurate replies. For example, in response to a query about which place a person belongs to, it is usual for a person from a rural area to cite the nearest district, town, or even city. Similarly, in a survey on media habits, the more 'high-brow' publications are likely to be cited far more often than the truth warrants.

Conflict with the investigator The respondent may engage in a conscious or latent conflict with the interviewer for a variety of reasons, the most frequent one being the difficulty in identifying with the perceived socio-economic class, education, age, or gender of the interviewer. It is not uncommon for a woman interviewer collecting data on smoking habits of men in small towns of India to encounter difficulties in being taken seriously. Similarly, doctors are often not willing to give detailed interviews to 'non-medical' persons. This is one of the issues that must always be taken care of in planning fieldwork.

Investigator unwillingness This is a frequent source of error in primary data. The reasons may be the following:

- wrong selection of interviewers
- particularly difficult-to-interview sample of respondents because of the non-availability or geographical scatter of respondents or the 'confidentiality of the information', as perceived by respondents
- too long or too complex a questionnaire, which respondents are often unwilling to complete
- unrealistic targets for interviewers in terms of the number of interviews to be completed per day or the number of days over which the fieldwork is to be completed
- poor briefing or training to investigators, resulting in their inability to explain the questionnaire to the respondents or to answer their queries
- poor payment
- lax supervision of fieldwork
- a combination of these

While it is obviously not usually possible to eliminate this kind of error totally, proper care must be exercised to minimize the 'investigator error'. The solution to this problem is obvious. It lies in eliminating or reducing the causes through a rigorous process for the selection of investigators, efficient and well-supervised fieldwork, a questionnaire that has been pilot-tested in the field and has had its defects corrected, and reasonable fieldwork targets. Fixing a daily quota of interviews to be conducted and setting the number of days over which the fieldwork has to be completed, has its limitations. A reasonable amount of flexibility must be built into the fieldwork schedule.

The researcher must also resist the temptation to ask 'too many' questions in one study. The interviewers must be briefed in detail, preferably in the presence of the client, so that last-minute clarifications can be sought and credibility built. Most good researchers like to have the interviewers go through at least one 'practice interview' before the fieldwork actually commences.

Errors of ambiguity   These errors, labelled thus by Green and Tull (1978), arise if the respondent has not understood the query, i.e., the formulation of the query is ambiguous and the respondent answers according to a personal interpretation of the query. These errors may also occur because the response is ambiguous and it is classified and analysed as per the researcher's interpretation of it. The cause of such errors can almost inevitably be traced to the formulation of the query.

As indicated in Fig. 6.2, the reasons for the errors of ambiguity can be grouped under three major heads—those relating to the length of the question, those arising from its form, and those resulting from its wording.

Question length   Consider the question asked of consumers in a survey on polio vaccine: *'If you had to make a choice between the oral polio vaccine, which is painless, and the Salk polio vaccine, which has to be injected and thus goes directly into the bloodstream to act faster, which one would you prefer?'* When confronted with such a question, the respondent is likely to miss the import of one or the other part of the question. The response will, therefore, be based only on the part of the question that was grasped by the respondent, and will not follow from a complete understanding of the choices. The problem will be aggravated if the question forms part of a face-to-face interview with the interviewer, since the respondent may hesitate to ask for the question to be repeated.

The question is more likely to generate the correct response if it is divided into two parts, the first part providing the comparative information about the two vaccines, and the second part asking for the preference: *'The polio vaccine is available in two forms: the oral form, which is painless and reaches the body through the digestive process, and the injectible form, which acts faster as it goes directly into the bloodstream but is painful. Which one would you choose for your baby?'* Long questions must always be divided into sub-questions for an easier and a more complete understanding of the respondent.

Question form   Questions may be asked in any of the three alternative forms—dichotomous, in which the respondent has to choose from two possible responses; multiple-choice, in which a choice must be made from a list of possible responses; and open-ended (free answer), in which the answer is in the respondent's own words. According to P.E. Green and D. Tull (1978), the three forms differ significantly in the probability of ambiguity error (Table 6.2).

Table 6.2   Relative Probability of Ambiguity

Form of Question	Question	Answer
Free answer	Lowest	Highest
Dichotomous	Average	Lowest
Multiple-choice	Highest	Average

Source: Green and Tull 1978

Let us examine the question, *'The last time you visited a sale, did you notice if the products on sale were not available in all pack sizes?'* Such a question, besides being difficult to interpret, is also difficult to answer. It is not clear whether the question asks if the respondent noticed the fact, or if it asks whether all the pack sizes were indeed not available. Such 'double-barrelled' questions must always be avoided if an accurate response is desired.

Another question form that is quite likely to draw a wrong response is the 'leading' question, a question worded in such a manner that it leads the respondent to only one kind of answer. Consider, for example, *'Don't you think brand 'x' is the best in this product category?'* It would take a courageous respondent to say no!

A third kind of question form that leads to error in response is the multiple-choice question that does not provide an adequate number of options. For example, consider the following.

Q Are you satisfied with the quality of Brand 'A' of fruit juice?

A   Yes   No
       ☐   ☐

Such options do not provide for the very real possibility that the respondent may be less than fully satisfied, or less than totally dissatisfied.

The use of a dichotomous question when a multiple-choice question would provide a more accurate response should be avoided. Similarly, dichotomous and multiple-choice questions constrain the respondent to make a choice from a limited number of options. In situations where the researcher is not familiar with the subject being investigated, as in exploratory studies, the use of such a structured format of questions may force the respondent to provide the wrong answer. In such cases, it is best to use free answer questions to obtain complete and accurate responses, even though the tabulation and analysis of dichotomous and multiple-choice questions is far easier.

Question wording   The choice of words and correct grammar is a serious consideration in designing data collection formats that would produce accurate, unambiguous answers. Errors related to the wording could result from

- the use of long or unfamiliar words
- the use of jargon

- the combining of more than one question into one, such as *'Which of these would you say is a better and cheaper city to live in, Mumbai or Kolkata?'* The respondent's mention of one or the other city could relate to the 'better' part, or the 'economical' part.
- the use of terms that are not specific and are open to various interpretations. For example, in the previous question, the term 'better' is open to different interpretations, such as 'more sophisticated', 'more culture-conscious', 'cleaner', 'more friendly', 'providing more opportunities', and 'having a better quality of life'. Respondents would interpret the term differently and respond according to their interpretation.

Ways to minimize response errors   Response errors can be minimized by pre-testing the data, alternating the wording, pantry check, and reducing translation errors.

Pre-testing data   The pre-testing of the data collection format is essential for taking care of response errors. The pretest should be carried out with at least ten or fifteen target respondents. The parameters to be checked out in the pretest include the flow of the questions as well as the respondent's ease in understanding the language.

Alternate wording   Another method for reducing response error is to alternate wording wherever possible. For example, in a dichotomous question, it is useful to rotate the order in which the units being compared are presented to the respondent. For example, if the question is aimed at determining the respondent's preference between *Business Today* and *Business World*, it should be presented to half the respondents as, *'Between* Business Today *and* Business World, *which do you prefer?'* and to the other half as *'Between* Business World *and* Business Today, *which do you prefer?'* If the order of administration influences the response, this kind of randomization will take care of the problem. Similarly, alternative forms of questions could be tried.

Pantry check   Pantry check is another method of reducing response error. This method consists of the respondent being asked to actually show the item under discussion to the interviewer. This helps in verifying physical attributes, such as the brand name, quantity consumed, and pack size. However, this method is dependent on the respondent's willingness to physically demonstrate the item.

Minimizing errors of translation   This is a serious implementation problem in multilingual communities such as India. Market studies and data collection formats are usually planned in one language, most often in English. A study being conducted in different parts of the country needs to communicate in the local language, especially if the respondents are consumers—householders or housewives—and if it is to be understood well. The local idiom and lingual nuances must be preserved in the communication. Some words may lose their meaning completely or substantially in translation. Technical terms are particularly difficult to translate. Therefore, it becomes essential to have the questionnaire or other data collection formats translated into the local language in advance, and to have the responses translated back into English.

This helps avoid the risk of investigators translating questions on the spot during the interview, and then translating the responses back into English. This is quite a daunting task, especially in the case of a multi-centric study causing, inevitably, some loss of information in translation, leading to errors that cannot be eliminated completely.

SUMMARY

Data can be classified by the purpose of collection, such as secondary and primary data, or by the variables studied, such as behaviour, attitudes, beliefs, and perceptions. Secondary data is always required in marketing research, even though it may sometimes be possible to dispense with primary data. Primary data can be collected through observation, experiments, surveys, and qualitative techniques. All methods of data collection are prone to error. Primary data is subject to sampling errors, missing response errors, and response errors of various types. Sampling errors and missing response errors are largely beyond the researcher's control, but response errors can be avoided with care.

KEY WORDS

Respondent refers to an individual or a group from whom the data for a study is collected.

Sample refers to a carefully selected section of the population that is deemed to represent all the major characteristics of the population.

Primary data refers to data gathered from the respondents specifically for the purpose of the study.

Secondary data refers to data that has a significant bearing on the decision being examined, but is not collected specifically for answering questions related to it.

Survey refers to a method of collecting data by interviewing a large number of respondents in a planned, systematic manner.

Experiment refers to a method of collecting data from a sample of respondents through market intervention to vary one or a predetermined number of variables and observing and recording the impact on respondent behaviour.

Sampling error refers to the error that results when data is obtained from a sample, i.e., a part of the population, and not the whole population.

Non-response error refers to an error that results from the refusal of some members of the sample to provide information.

Not-at-home error refers to an error that results when some individuals or groups selected in the sample may not be available for interviewing.

Response error refers to an error that occurs in data because of inaccurate or inadequate responses from the sampling units (respondents).

Error of inaccuracy refers to an incorrect response obtained because the respondents are either unable to or unwilling to provide accurate information.

Error of ambiguity refers to an error obtained in the data because either the respondent is unable to understand/interpret the question accurately or because the interviewer is unable to understand/interpret the response accurately.

CONCEPT REVIEW QUESTIONS

1. Under what conditions would (a) past behaviour and (b) behavioural intent be a reliable indicator of future behaviour?

2. A well-known media group is considering launching a business weekly aimed at management students and young executives. What kind of primary and secondary data would it need in order to determine its market potential?

3. Make a list of the research data required to develop a business and another list to track the performance of that business. Are there any common features in the two lists? Why is this information common to both?

4. Give two examples each of errors of inability, unwillingness, and ambiguity. How can such errors be avoided?

5. *'Surveys are more useful for identifying current problems than for identifying opportunities. Extrapolations based on secondary data may be more useful for the latter.'* Do you agree or disagree with the statement? Give reasons for your opinion.

CRITICAL THINKING EXERCISES

1. ' Wegrow', an NGO working with urban women from low- to middle-income groups, has been offering a start-up training programme in small business. Over the years, although the organization's executives make extensive efforts to track the growth of businesses started by its alumni, they usually overestimate the percentage of businesses likely to survive for five years. What data should they examine to determine the possible causes of this error? What could be the possible causes of error?

2. Geeta Press, Gorakhpur, well-known publishers of religious books in Hindi, observed that over the years, the sales of the 'pocket edition' of *Ramcharitmanas*, the Avadhi dialect version of the *Ramayana* written by poet Tulsidas, has been declining. Secondary research shows that the market for religious books in regional dialects has been declining steadily at about 12 per cent per annum for about six years. This information, however, is not adequate to explain the decline in the sales of *Ramcharitmanas*. Draw up a list of issues to be evaluated through a study that may provide answers to the problem of decline.

3. Examine the following questions. If you were to include them in a questionnaire, would you leave them as they are or would you change them? If you think they should be changed, rewrite them as you believe they should be asked.

   (a) If you have ever used Brand X, how many packs did you last buy?

(b) Are you satisfied with the car you currently drive?
   Yes _____ No _____
(c) Do you think higher proportions of TFM improve the quality of the soap?
(d) Do you like apple juice?
(e) Between Barista and Café Coffee Day, which one would you say is better in terms of ambience and price?

If you think the questions should be changed, what kind of error does each suffer from?

4. In a study examining children's consumption pattern of snacks, a biscuit manufacturer discovered that all the respondents were mothers of children aged between five and twelve years. Upon enquiry, the product manager concerned was told that mothers of children below five years were not free to be interviewed when the investigator reached their house, usually between 9:00 am and 11:00 am. Do you think this pattern of response will affect the results of the study in any way? What steps could the interviewer have taken to gather responses from the 'below-five' group?

PROJECT ASSIGNMENTS

1. Choose an industry and, using secondary data sources, obtain its sales, sales of major players, and growth rates. What additional secondary information would you need in order to ascertain whether the industry currently offers a promising opportunity for a new entrant? Draw up a list of relevant sources of such secondary data from your library.

2. Work out the plan for a study to determine the market potential for the industry you chose for Question 1.

REFERENCES

Aaker, D., V. Kumar, and G.S. Day 1998, *Marketing Research,* John Wiley and Sons (Asia) Pte Ltd, pp.105–110.

Birn, R.J. 2004, *The Effective Use of Market Research,* Kogan Page and Sterling, London, p. 54.

Day, George S. 1975, 'The Threats to Marketing Research', *Journal of Marketing Research,* 12 November, pp. 462–467.

Green, Paul E. and D. Tull 1978, *Research for Marketing Decisions,* Prentice-Hall, pp. 76–79, 101–128.

Kraft, Susan 1991, 'Who Slams the Door on Research?' *American Demographics,* September, p.14.

ANNEXURE 6.1

Sources of Secondary Data

A. Government Publications and Reports

Publication	Published By
Annual Survey of Industries	Central Statistics Organisation, New Delhi
Basic Statistics Relating to Indian Economy	Planning Commission
Census Report	Registrar General of India
Currency and Finance Report	Reserve Bank of India
Estimates of National Product, Savings and Capital Formation	Central Statistics Organisation, New Delhi
National Sample Survey	Ministry of Planning
RBI Bulletin	Reserve Bank of India
Statistical Abstract of India	Central Statistical Organisation
Wholesale Price Index Number	Ministry of Commerce and Industry
Five Year Plans	Planning Commission, Government of India
Annual Economic Survey	Ministry of Commerce, Government of India
Reports on Various Industries	Ministry Reports
Journal of Trade and Industry	Ministry of Commerce
Sarvekshana	National Sample Survey Organisation
Reports on Demographic and Socio-Economic National Trends	National Council for Applied Economic Research (NCAER)
Report on Finances of Public Ltd Companies	Business Standards Research Bureau
Annual Budget	Ministry of Finance

B. Non-Governmental Publications and Reports

Publication	Published By
Commerce Yearbook of Public Sector	Commerce Publications Ltd, New Delhi
Directory of Foreign Collaborations in India	Indian Investment Centre, New Delhi
Handbook and Directory of Indian Industries	Bombay Market, 213, Yusuf Meherally Road, Mumbai 400 003
Kothari's Industrial and Economic Guide of India	Kothari Enterprises, Kothari Building, Nungambakkam Road Chennai 600 034
SIRI Directory of Industries in India	Small Industries Research Institute, New Delhi 110 007
Industrial Products Finder	IPFonline Limited
RK Swamy BBDO Guide to Urban Markets	RK Swamy BBDO Advertising Pvt. Ltd
Thapar's Indian Industrial Guide	Thapar International Information Service
Directory and Import-Export	1/E, Giriraj Building
Directory of the Entire World	11, Altamount Road, Cumballa Hill, Mumbai

(Table B Continued)

(*Table B Continued*)

Publication	Published By
The Hindu Survey of Indian Industries	The Hindu, Chennai 600 002
Business India	Wadia Building; 17/19, Dalal Street, Mumbai 400 023
Financial Express	Newspaper House, Colaba, Mumbai 400 001
Industry/Trade Reports	Industry/Trade Associations (CII, FICCI, ASSOCHAM, SIAM, IMC, WIAA, Plastics Manufacturers Association of India, etc.)
Indian Trade Journal	1 Council House Street, Kolkata 700 001
Industrial India	14, Sidhprasad, Ghatkopar Marol Road, Mumbai 400 089
ISI Bulletin	Manak Bhavan, Bahadur Shah Zafar Marg, New Delhi 110 002
National Readership Survey	National Readership Studies Council
Indian Readership Survey	Media Foundation
The Observer Statistical Handbook	The Observer
Productivity	Productivity Council, 5–6, Institutional Area, Lodi Marg, New Delhi 110 003
The Economic Times	Times of India Press, Mumbai 400 004
The Financial Express	The Indian Express Group of Newspapers, Mumbai 400 021
The Business Standard	Amrit Bazar Patrika Group, Kolkata
Statistical Outline of India	Department of Economics and Statistics, Tata Services Ltd.
Various publications relating to the economy and industry	Centre for Monitoring Indian Economy (CMIE)
Retail Audit Reports on Various Industries/Product Groups	AC Neilsen–ORG-Marg
World Development Report	World Bank
Human Development Report	United Nations Development Programme (UNDP)
TAM Peoplemeter	AC Neilsen

C. Some Websites

www.msn.com
www.google.com
www.rediff.com
www.indiainfoline.com
Capitaline*
Managementor*
CMIE*
Individual company websites

*Paid packages

7

Experimentation

OBJECTIVES

After reading this chapter, the readers will be able to understand:

- the concept of experimentation and its application in marketing research
- the need for internal and external validity in an experiment
- the types of experimental designs commonly used in marketing research
- the limitations of marketing experiments

INTRODUCTION

The purpose of experimentation in marketing remains essentially the same as it is in the physical sciences, from which it has been borrowed. This is to determine causality—its degree and nature. Effective marketing planning must be able to determine the cause(s) of observed marketing phenomena so that it may be manipulated to deliver optimal advantage. Most of the techniques discussed so far are able to provide snapshots of the status of the relationship between two or more variables but do not explain what causes the relationship. Experiments serve to explain this causality.

There are a number of marketing variables, some of which are likely to be influenced by others. Experiments in marketing aim at determining the impact of varying the levels of independent variables upon the dependent variable under controlled conditions. In other words, experiments aim at defining the causal relationship between the sets of variables. They identify (a) the variables whose occurrence is dependent on others, i.e., dependent variables, and independent variables that cause but are not caused by the other variables being examined, (b) the nature of the relationship between these dependent and independent variables, and (c) the independent variables that exercise the most influence on the occurrence of the dependent variable. Understanding these three dimensions of the cause-effect relationship contributes a great deal to the ability to control and improve marketing decisions. This chapter discusses these three objectives of experimentation in detail. First, we discuss the concept of causality in some detail, recapitulating some of the ideas discussed in Chapter 5. The nature of the relationship between dependent and independent variables as well as the various techniques (or designs of experiments) for determining this relationship, that have been discussed at length later in the chapter, point out the limitations of experiments and the experimentation method.

CAUSALITY

Aaker et al. (1998) in their book, *Marketing Research*, and Green and Tull (1978) in *Research for Marketing Decisions* discuss the concept of causality. Causality, according to them, could take any of two forms.

Deterministic causation

If the dependent variable Y (sales, in the above example) is completely explained by the occurrence of the independent variable X (say, advertising), the relationship is said to be that of deterministic causation. It is necessary and sufficient to know the level and the quality of advertising, and the form of its relationship with sales in complete detail in order to estimate sales.

Probabilistic causation

If the dependent variable Y is a function of two or more independent variables, say $X_1, X_2,\ldots, X_n$, none of them individually is sufficient to explain Y, although each of

---

Causality in Action

Arvind Verma is the brand manager of 'Sunshine', a brand of shampoo manufactured and marketed by Everest Home Products Ltd (EHPL). Although the brand has been facing increasing competition over the past few years, it has managed to retain its premier position in the market. Verma has to necessarily allocate his promotion budget optimally between above-the-line and below-the-line activities. With competition nipping at his heels, he has to decide between conventional wisdom, which allocates the pride of place to advertising, and a quick increase in sales, which suggests concentrating on sales promotion and PR.

Verma argues to himself that he cannot take the risk of knocking one off totally in order to boost the other and must arrive at an optimal combination of the two. He decides that he will allocate funds for the two activities in proportion to their ability to generate increased trials among new customers. In order to allow the impact of advertising to build up, he decides to run a campaign for three months in Vadodara, one of his

average-sized, steady markets. During the third month of this campaign, he launches a sales promotion scheme in Pune, a market pretty similar to Vadodara in terms of market size, growth pattern, competitive environment, and pre-campaign sales of Sunshine. He has ensured that the advertising campaign in Vadodara is restricted to the local media, and the sales promotion scheme being run in Pune is restricted to the city. At the end of the fourth, fifth, and sixth months, he will compare the effect of the two means of promotion on sales, to assess their relative impact in terms of the extent of growth and the rate of change in sales in the two cities.

Verma's questions can be answered by the concept of causality. What caused the change in sales? Which of the two media was more effective in causing this change? Was there any other event occurring simultaneously that might have caused or contributed to the change in sales in either city? Was this an event that Verma could have controlled?

them is necessary for the occurrence of Y. In other words, each of them individually can only predict the probability of the occurrence of Y. Since $X_1, X_2, ..., X_n$ are independent variables, they cannot explain each other either.

An experiment is thus, a method of explaining how an independent variable (or variables) causes change in the dependent variable, and in the case of multiple independent variables, the degree of influence each exercises on the dependent variable.

EXPERIMENTS IN MARKETING RESEARCH

Marketing is concerned with two types of experiments—natural experiments and controlled experiments.

Natural Experiments

The role of the researcher here is restricted to identifying the independent variables that could influence the dependent variable and observing a) the nature of the relationship and b) the change in the dependent variable as a result of a change in one or more independent variables over time. The time series, a kind of experimental design discussed later in the chapter, is an example.

Controlled Experiments

In these experiments, the researcher is concerned with actively manipulating (or 'controlling') the levels of the independent variables and tracking the impact of these changes on the dependent variable. The objective here is to identify the nature of the relationship, as in the case of natural experiments and determine the optimal levels of each independent variable required for a desired level of the dependent variable in order to plan the most suitable marketing-mix.

Conditions of Causality

Three conditions are essential for the occurrence of either of the two kinds of causation discussed earlier.

Associative variation

If the occurrence of one variable is always associated with the occurrence of another variable, and the degree of change in one is associated with the degree of change in the other, the two variables are said to vary in association. In the preceding example, if a change in the advertising levels and quality and a change in sales occur simultaneously, they are said to vary in association.

Sequence of events

This is the second condition of causality. In a causal relationship, the occurrence of the independent variable(s) is always followed by the occurrence of the dependent variable.

Absence of other possible causes

The third and conclusive condition of causality is that there is no other possible cause for the change in the dependent variable except the independent variable(s) being studied.

A natural experiment aims at determining these three conditions in studying the relationship between the dependent and the independent variables, while a controlled experiment actively attempts to create these three conditions in order to study causality among the variables being studied. In the remainder of the chapter, we will concern ourselves with controlled experiments alone.

VALIDITY IN EXPERIMENTS

According to D.R. Cooper and P.S. Schindler (1998) in *Business Research Methods*, the purpose of an experiment is to provide information about the causal relationship between the variable of interest (dependent variable) and other selected influence factors (independent variables). It is therefore, essential that the results of the experiment have *internal* and *external* validity.

Internal validity Internal validity implies that the relationship demonstrated by the experiment between the dependent and the independent variable could not be attributed to any other cause. William G. Zikmund (1996) in *Exploring Marketing Research* defines it as 'the ability of an experiment to answer the question whether the experimental treatment was the sole cause of changes in a dependent variable. Did the manipulation do what it was supposed to do?'

External validity To paraphrase Zikmund again, external validity implies that the results demonstrated by the experiment must be true across other time-periods, samples, and individuals.

In the example of the shampoo brand, the objective is to identify the promotion medium that is most likely to lead to higher sales on a sustained basis. Arvind Verma's experiment aims to do just that—using sales as the dependent variable, he will track the effect of advertising as the independent variable on a change in sales in one city, and the effect of sales promotion as the other independent variable in the second city. Why is it necessary for Verma to choose two different cities to study the impact of the two media he is considering? The answer is the need for external validity. Why does he need to take steps to restrict the media to the two cities where he is conducting the experiment? If he extends the advertising or sales promotion beyond the boundaries of the city, it will be difficult to measure the impact of the experiment. Why is it necessary to observe the results over an extended period of time? Once again, the demand for external validity makes it essential to determine if the results are valid over a period of time.

Factors Affecting the Results of an Experiment

In order to determine the internal validity of an experiment, it is necessary to examine some other factors that may influence the results of an experiment.

History or environment

A marketer conducts an experiment in an environment over which he has only limited control at best. Environmental factors, such as competitive activity, governmental regulations, change in consumer tastes, and economic conditions, could interfere with the results of the experiment and produce results that do not truly reflect the effect of the independent variables on the dependent variable. For example, the respondents in Vadodara may buy more of Sunshine, not necessarily because its advertisement has more impact than the sales promotion scheme but because summer sets in by the time Verma decides to extend the experiment to Vadodara, and people wash their hair more often in summer.

Maturation or learning

With the passage of time, respondents as well as those conducting the experiment change their behaviour as they acquire greater familiarity with the experiment. For instance, as time passes, users may discover that Sunshine is mild enough to be used more than once a week without harming the hair. They may, therefore, increase the quantity they purchase and use. This is not the result of effective advertising or sales promotion but a result of time-related brand experience.

Testing

The very awareness of the fact that their behaviour is being studied is likely to produce changes in the behaviour of the respondents. This change may, at times, be mistakenly attributed to the effect of the experiment. In the Sunshine case, if a group of consumers are queried on their awareness of the advertising campaign, the very fact that they are being questioned may heighten their awareness of the campaign to higher-than-usual levels and may, therefore, influence their purchase of the brand. This increase in sales can, therefore, not be strictly attributed to the effectiveness of the advertisement campaign.

Instrument

Yet another factor that may influence the results of the experiment is the method of data collection. The time when respondents are queried (e.g., immediately after seeing the advertisement), and the way the questions are asked ('Will you buy Sunshine the next time you need to buy a shampoo? Please answer "yes" or "no".') could result in an overestimate or underestimate of the likely purchase level.

Selection

How respondents are selected to participate in an experiment greatly influences its validity. If the selection procedure is randomized, the variation between the experimental group and the population being studied can be said to be due to random variation. However, selection that is purposive, non-random, or chosen by the investigator could lead to non-random errors that would vitiate the results of the experiment.

TYPES OF EXPERIMENTAL DESIGNS

Designs of marketing experiments and, for that matter, all business experiments can be divided into two categories—classical experimental designs and statistical designs of experiments. Fig. 7.1 describes the different types of experimental designs in detail.

We shall use the following notations and symbols in our discussion of these designs.

E: Experimental group

C: Control group

R: Random assignment of units to a group

M: Matching of the experimental group and the control group with respect to some relevant characteristics

O: Observation or measurement of the dependent variable

X: The exposure of experimental units to the experimental treatment

Classical Designs

These designs study only one treatment of an independent variable at a time. They are further divided into pre-experimental designs, true experimental designs, and quasi-experimental designs.

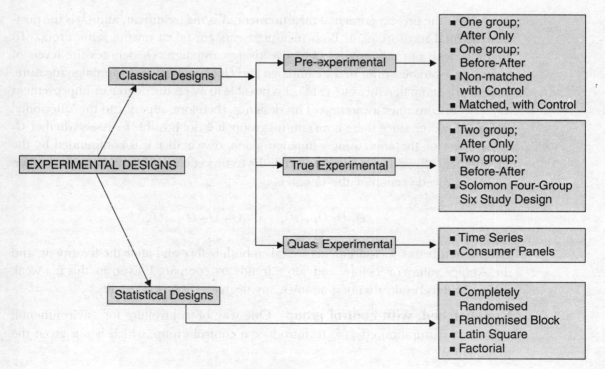

Fig. 7.1 Designs of Experiments

Pre-experimental designs

These are not experiments in the true sense since they do not control extraneous variables to any significant extent. They are, thus, weak at controlling the major threats to the internal validity discussed earlier. However, they do lead to hypotheses regarding causal relationships, which can then be confirmed through more rigorous research.

After only; one group   This kind of design can be denoted typically as

$$X \qquad O_1$$

In other words, an experimental treatment is given to a group, and post-experiment measurements on the dependent variable are taken. For example, an advertising campaign, X, for a brand may be run and its consumer awareness, O_1, measured after the campaign. It is obvious that such an 'experiment' does not control environment, maturity, or testing. Since there is no pre-measurement, it is not possible to determine whether there has been any improvement in consumer awareness. Such experiments do not provide any valid conclusions and should not be used as far as possible.

Before–after; one group   This experimental design is denoted as

$$O_1 \qquad X \qquad O_2,$$

where O_1 is the pre-experimental measurement, X is the treatment, and O_2 is the post-experimental measurement. Both measurements are taken on the same group. To continue with our example of the advertising campaign, O_1 denotes the levels of consumer awareness prior to the campaign and O_2 denotes its post-campaign measure. Since a pre-campaign measure exists, it is possible to assess the degree of improvement $(O_2 - O_1)$ in consumer awareness. This design is, therefore, superior to the 'after only' design. However, since there is no control group, it is not possible to assess whether O_2 is the effect of the advertising campaign alone, or whether it is confounded by the environment effect. The maturity effect or the testing effect cannot be controlled either.

An improved version of this design is

$$O_1 \, O_2 \, O_3 \ldots O_n \quad X \quad O'_1 \, O'_2 \, O'_3 \ldots O'_n$$

Here, a number of measurements are taken both before and after the treatment, and the average values or 'before' and 'after' trends are compared. Even so, this is a weak design, and its results do not guarantee any degree of internal validity.

Non-matched, with control group   One way of controlling for environmental effect and maturation effect is to introduce a control group, which is not given the treatment X.

$$E: \qquad X \qquad O_1$$
$$C: \qquad \qquad O_2$$

This design has many advantages over the ones discussed earlier. The comparison $(O_2 - O_1)$ of O_2 and O_1 measures the impact of the treatment X (the advertising campaign in our example), simultaneously controlling for the testing and the instrument effects. However, since there is no pre-measurement, and the experimental group E and the control group C are not matched, the design does not control environment. The selection bias could also affect the results since the design does not provide for any randomization or matching of the control and experimental groups.

Matched, with control group   This design is illustrated as follows.

$$E: \qquad M \qquad X \qquad O_1$$
$$C: \qquad M \qquad \qquad O_2$$

where M is the pre-treatment measure in the experimental group, matched with a similar measure in the control group. It reduces the problem of the selection bias left unsolved by the earlier design. However, if the two groups are self-selected by the respondents, some degree of selection bias could still remain. A comparison of the pre- and post-measurements in the two groups will control the environment effect as well as the maturation effect, though not the testing effect, except in the sense that it is present in both the groups.

In practice, the experimental and the control groups are sometimes selected post-facto, especially if the data is being collected from consumer panels. For example, after the advertisement is released, consumers who have seen it may be put into the 'experimental' group and those who have not seen it can become the 'control' group. A comparison of brand awareness in the two groups would then provide a measure of the effect. However, in such cases of self-selection, some bias has still been reported; research reveals that the users of the brand, or those who are at least aware of it, are more likely to notice the advertising campaign than those who are not aware. Also, acquiring a 'match' is much more difficult in practice than it may appear at first. If, for example, two cities are to be matched in terms of the current sales of the brand, they may still differ substantially in terms of past growth patterns, competitive activity, or total market size. In such cases, more reliable results may be obtained from consumer panels in which the allocation of respondents to the experimental and the control group has been randomized totally.

True experimental designs

Randomization means assigning any respondent, i.e., any member of the population, to either the control group or the experimental group in such a way that at any point any respondent has an equal probability of being assigned to either of the two groups. This process controls for selection bias.

Experimental designs that display the following two characteristics are called true experimental designs.

- the presence of a control group and random assignment of units to experimental and control groups
- active manipulation of at least one independent variable

True experimental designs are, therefore, not possible in natural experiments, in which the researcher's role is confined to the observation and recording of the treatment and the output. As will be obvious, true experiments take care of most of the problems of internal validity. We will examine some more commonly used true experimental designs in the sections that follow.

Two groups; after only   This is pretty similar to the 'matched control group' pre-experimental design, except that the units are assigned to the experimental and the control group in a randomized fashion.

$$E: \qquad R \qquad X \qquad O_1$$
$$C: \qquad R \qquad \qquad O_2$$

If the sample size is large enough, E and C will be similar. Any differences in O_1 and O_2 can then be attributed to the treatment X with some degree of validity. However, the design does not assess the maturity effect. The environment effect may be assumed to be similar for both the groups, except in cases in which a competitor may learn of the experiment and step up activity in the two groups at different levels in order to vitiate the results of the experiment. In their early days in the Indian market, Coke and Pepsi were known for such competitive activity at local levels.

The design would find application in any situation in which the test units may be assigned to the experimental group and the control group at random without any loss of information or objectivity as in, for example, a team of sales executives being studied for the impact of a new sales training programme. The team may be divided into two groups, with team members being assigned to the experimental group or the control group at random. Let us assume that the experimental group is put through a week-long training programme, while the control group is not. The sales achievement of the members of the two groups may then be compared at the end of the month. In such situations, matching is assured since both the experimental group and the control group are obtained essentially from one large sample that has been divided into two.

Two groups; before–after   If the above design is extended to include a 'before' effect in both the control group and the experimental group, we obtain a much more sophisticated experimental design.

$$E: \qquad R \qquad O_1 \qquad X \qquad O'_1$$
$$C: \qquad R \qquad O_2 \qquad \qquad O'_2$$

This design takes care of most factors that could affect the internal validity of an experiment, offering as it does three ways of evaluating the results.

- $(O'_1 - O_1)$ measures the treatment effect confounded with the testing effect and the maturation effect.
- $(O'_2 - O_2)$ measures the testing effect confounded with the maturation effect.
- $(O'_1 - O_1) - (O'_2 - O_2)$ measures the treatment effect exclusive of the testing and maturation effects.

Randomization controls for the selection bias and the environment effect may be ignored since it can be considered to be the same in both the groups, unless the kind of situation discussed earlier develops. The design does not usually control the instrument effect since the same instrument is usually used for measurement in both cases in a sequential manner.

A design of this kind may be used quite effectively in controlled situations such as the clinical trials of drugs. For example, in a clinical trial for a drug for hypertension, patients matched for the demographic profile (age, gender, smoking habits, occupation, obesity levels, etc.) may be assigned at random to the control or the experimental group. Each group is then measured for the duration and severity of disease (the duration and level of hypertension, for example). The experimental group could then be treated with the drug being studied, while the control group is given a placebo. The progress of the disease may be measured in both the groups after a specified period; the comparison would determine the treatment effect.

One limitation of this design is that it does not control for interaction effects. In practice, it makes sense to observe that in addition to the effect of the five factors discussed earlier, which influence the internal validity of an experiment, these factors also tend to interact with each other. In the sales training example, for instance, even if a 'before' measure is added to the design so that it is similar to the 'before-after' design, the maturity effect in both groups is measured by $(O'_1 - O_1)$ and $(O'_2 - O_2)$. However, the fact of measuring or 'testing' will also contribute to these differences. It is not possible in this design to segregate the contribution of each of these effects. The Solomon design, or the four group-six study design, attempts to measure the interaction effects.

Four group-six study design   This design, first introduced by R.L. Solomon (1949), is denoted as

$$
\begin{array}{ccccc}
E: & R & O_1 & X & O'_1 \\
C: & R & O_2 & & O'_2 \\
E: & R & & X & O'_3 \\
C: & R & & & O'_4 \\
\end{array}
$$

It is obvious from the design that it provides a large number of ways for evaluating the effect of the treatment — $(O'_1 - O_1), (O'_2 - O_2), (O'_1 - O'_2), (O'_3 - O'_4), (O'_1 - O_1), (O'_2 - O_2)$. Other effects can be established in the same manner as in the earlier designs. In addition, the four group-six study design also facilitates the measurement of the 'interaction' effects. To quote from P. Green and D. Tull (1978), 'The "after" treatments provide a useful basis for drawing inferences about the testing effect as well as that of treatment. They can be placed into a 2×2 table as follows:

Table 7.1 Showing the Effect of Treatment

Steps	No X	X
'Before' measurements taken	O'_2	O'_1
No 'before' measurements taken	O'_4	O'_3

The effect of the treatment can be estimated from the difference in the column means. The difference in the row means provides the basis for estimating the testing effect. The differences in the individual cell means can be used for testing the *interaction* of testing and treatment.'

Setting up such an experiment is prohibitively expensive and control is extremely difficult. However, this design provides the maximum amount of information about the treatment effects and interaction effects. Like most pre-experimental and true experimental designs, this design also has the inadequate promise of external validity, perhaps even more so than the others, since like most experimental designs discussed so far, this design too is very difficult to replicate completely in another place or time.

Quasi-experimental designs

According to Zikmund (1996), quasi-experimental designs were developed primarily to deal with external validity. The researcher lacks complete control over the scheduling of treatment or must assign treatment in a non-random manner. Even so, quasi-experimental designs provide more measurements and more information than a typical pre-experimental design. The two most popular quasi-experiments are time series and extended consumer panels.

Time series This experimental design is quite similar to the 'one group; before-after' design except that it involves obtaining data from the same sample over successive time points. Zikmund refers to 'interrupted time-series designs with or without control', in which the treatment interrupts repeated measurements. Although it is not easy to obtain a comparable control group in a time-series design, since the series is concerned with temporally varying measures, such a possibility should always be explored to obtain a design such as

$$O_1 \ O_2 \ O_3 \ O_4 \quad X \quad O'_1 \ O'_2 \ O'_3 \ O'_4$$
$$O_5 \ O_6 \ O_7 \ O_8 \qquad\qquad O'_5 \ O'_6 \ O'_7 \ O'_8$$

It is even more difficult to select the control group at random and yet ensure that the two groups are matched. However, even in the absence of randomization, the presence of a control group implies that it is possible to test for environment, maturation, and testing effects. A variation of time series is *trend studies*. It differs from time series in that measures over time are taken from separate samples of the same population. The data from trend studies can be analysed only in the aggregate form in which they are collected. The studies provide a great deal of the information on which marketing decisions are based. Often, they are essential for identifying significant changes in environmental, industrial, organizational, or brand patterns, and for identifying causal relationships. They take care of most of the effects that influence internal validity of the experiment, and usually control for external validity as well.

Panels   A 'panel' is a group of respondents that agree to be interviewed and/or provide data over a period of time. The respondents may be addressed on a one-time basis, when they are referred to as a 'consumer jury' or, as is more common, they may be contacted for information over a period of time. A panel is particularly useful in longitudinal studies in which changes in behaviour have to be tracked.

The most commonly used panels are as follows.

Consumer panels   Companies such as Hindustan Lever Ltd. use these panels extensively for tracking sales and brand switch into and out of their brands. They use a 'diary method', in which a selected group of housewives is given incentives for maintaining a record of brands in specific product categories bought by them during the month, the quantity bought, and the frequency of purchase during the period. The researcher visits them regularly and collects this data.

Consumer panels are also used extensively for testing new products, especially in test markets. The use of a panel helps determine the rate at which a trial builds up and stabilizes over a period of time, as well as the repurchase rate and the build-up of loyalty. Attrition rates, too, can be tracked as well as the reasons for dropouts. Some well-known models, such as John D.C. Little's model for forecasting new product sales, are based on data from continuous consumer panels.

Product improvement tests, such as taste tests and pack tests, often make use of a consumer jury, which is a matched sample of respondents who are presented with a variety of options on the product variable being tested to choose the one they like best.

Audience measurement panels   These are akin to product panels, and are used for testing the response of the audience to advertisements, especially on TV.

These panels are organized by independent agencies that collect data repeatedly from selected households at regular intervals. Electronic meters attached to the television are used to ensure the objectivity, accuracy, and ease of data collection. The Market Research Society of America was the first agency to introduce the concept of electronic measurement of an audience with its television audience measurement (TAM). An Indian equivalent of TAM is the Indian television audience measurement (INTAM), a service offered by AC Neilsen–ORG-MARG, a well-known marketing research agency in India. These services are used for providing audience viewership figures of various TV programmes, on which TV viewership ratings are based.

Dealer panels   These panels are used to provide information on manufacturer sales to dealers, or retailers, and in some cases, on retailer sales to final consumers. In India, ORG-MARG runs three major panels—retail audit of retail sales to consumers, pharmaceutical audit that provides information on manufacturer sales to chemists, and prescription audit that records company-wise, drug category-wise, and brand wise prescriptions by specific categories of doctors. The retail panels provide brand-wise, pack-wise sales volumes, sales values, market shares, and growth rates for urban and rural markets on a monthly and quarterly basis. They provide very useful data for tracking the progress of the product category, the company's own brand, and the competitor brands. They, thus, help in planning the marketing activity as well as in monitoring the impact of marketing decisions.

One of the limitations of panels is that the data is obtained through self-reporting. Although they are supposed to provide a record of the actual purchase data (or sales data, in the case of retail panels), in reality the respondents often do not make these entries at the time of the transaction, but rely on their memory to provide the data at a later date. Also, the testing effect is conspicuous since the respondents are aware that they will be interviewed repeatedly. If the same instrument is used for data collection, the instrument effect is also quite significant. There is no control group to evaluate the environment effect. If the panel is not chosen through the process of randomization, selection bias could creep in. Even if the panel is selected at random, the 'attrition effect' reduces the representativeness and reliability of the results, rendering the data progressively less representative. However, in spite of these limitations, the wealth of data that a panel is capable of generating makes this design a very effective source of information.

Statistical Designs

These designs of experiments differ from the classical and the quasi-experimental designs in that they permit the examination of the effects of more than one independent variable at a time as well as of different treatment levels of the experimental variable. In addition, some statistical designs provide for the examination of interaction effects as well.

Statistical designs are generally 'after-only' designs, and require the use of relatively complex analytical techniques, such as ANOVA, for obtaining the results of the effects of various independent variables and treatments. The most commonly used statistical designs of experiments are completely randomized designs, randomized block designs, Latin square designs, and factorial designs.

Completely randomized designs

Let us examine Arvind Verma's dilemma again. Let us assume that he decides to choose sales promotion as the major means of promotion. Now he has to choose one from among three different sales promotion schemes. In order to decide between the three schemes, he chooses three different stores in the city at random from a large group of general stores, and assigns the three sales promotion schemes to the three stores, one to each, completely at random. His objective is to identify the scheme that delivers the highest sales. He would design his experiment as

$$
\begin{array}{llll}
E_1: & R & X_1 & O_1 \\
E_2: & R & X_2 & O_2 \\
E_3: & R & X_3 & O_3
\end{array}
$$

where the Xs are the sales promotion schemes and the Os are the post-promotion sales. There is no control group since each of the three experiments serves as a control for the others. The randomized selection of stores and the randomized allocation of the schemes to each of them solves the problem of selection bias and the environment effect, which can safely be assumed to be the same for all three cases. There is no testing effect, since this is an 'after-only design'. However, the design does not test for the maturity effect or the instrument effect.

In practice, Mr Verma is quite likely to know the pre-promotion sales in the three experimental groups, and will be more interested in determining the relative increase in sales as a result of the three schemes, rather than just the post-promotion sales. The design then gets modified as

$$
\begin{array}{lllll}
E_1: & R & O_1 & X_1 & O'_1 \\
E_2: & R & O_2 & X_2 & O'_2 \\
E_3: & R & O_3 & X_3 & O'_3
\end{array}
$$

It is assumed that the randomization of the three stores to the three treatments, i.e., the three sales-promotion schemes, will make the three groups equivalent. Comparison of the $(O' - O)$ values in the three groups will be a good enough measure of the maturity effect.

These are two variants of the 'completely randomized design', the most basic statistical designs of experiment. If the assumption of equivalence resulting from randomization cannot be sustained, a more sophisticated design called the randomized block design is required.

Randomized block designs

If the sample is not large, as may happen in field experiments in, say, agriculture or the kind of clinical trials discussed earlier, mere randomization will not necessarily bring about equivalence. In the stores example above, for instance, the three stores could belong to three different income-group areas. In such cases, care has to be taken to ensure randomization as well as matching with respect to the relevant differentiating characteristic. Once this characteristic is identified through research, the randomized

Table 7.2 Block Design

	B$_1$ (High income)	B$_2$ (Low income)
X_1 R	O_1	O'_1
X_2 R	O_2	O'_2
X_3 R	O_3	O'_3

block design controls for it by introducing a block effect. The design would then appear as shown in Table 7.2.

Here Blocks 1 and 2 have been selected to differ with respect to one major extraneous variable, i.e., income. But each is assigned the same three treatments, i.e., three different sales-promotion schemes. In effect, the same experiment with three different sales-promotion schemes is repeated in two different blocks. It is, thus, possible to determine the impact of income groups on the response to the sales promotion schemes as well as to study the difference, if any, in the response to the three sales promotion schemes. It is, therefore, possible to measure both the main effects (difference in sales because of income and difference in sales because of the three schemes) and the interaction effects, i.e., the differential response to the three schemes in the two different income groups. The analysis of these interactive effects will be discussed in detail under 'factorial designs'.

Randomized block designs are effective in improving the accuracy of the measurement if they are able to minimize the variance within blocks and maximize the variance between blocks. In such cases, they could provide a good basis for a segmentation strategy.

Latin square designs

If the experiment is likely to get affected by two extraneous variables, and not one as in the case of randomized block designs, a Latin square design is appropriate. This design allows for the testing of all the main effects with a much smaller number of observations than required in the more detailed factorial design that will be discussed later. For example, in the case of Arvind Verma's sales promotion problem, let us assume that in addition to the influence of income, he also wants to control for the frequency of visits, or patronage, to the stores. The design suitable for this purpose is either a Latin square, or a factorial design. The Latin square is more parsimonious and, hence, popular in marketing research but it operates under the constraint that the extraneous variables as well as the number of treatments have to be examined at an equal number of levels. Treatments are randomized, as in the case of the designs discussed earlier. The design would then appear as shown in Table 7.3. Here, A, B, and C are the three sales promotion schemes.

Note that in this design, every cell is given one and only one treatment. This is what provides for parsimony in the design, with no loss of information. However, if we were to test for only two sales-promotion schemes, both the income group and the

Table 7.3 Latin Square Design

Frequency of Visits	Block 1 High Income	Block 2 Middle Income	Block 3 Low Income
High	A	B	C
Medium	C	A	B
Low	B	C	A

patronage levels will have to be combined into two levels each, resulting in some loss of detail in information. Moreover, the design can control for only two external variables at a time, and works on the assumption that the interaction effects are negligible.

Factorial designs

A factorial experimental design measures the effects of at least two independent variables for at least two levels. Unlike the statistical designs discussed so far, this design measures the main effects as well as the interaction effects, although it is necessarily more elaborate and more complex in use. Let us assume, for example, that in the sales-promotion experiment, in addition to the external variables, the income of the customer and the patronage level of the store, the dependent variable, and the sales-promotion scheme, an additional internal factor to be considered is variation in the price of the product. If we consider two price levels, P_1 and P_2, the design will appear as shown in Table 7.4.

Such a design ensures that every possible combination of variables is presented in one cell. In the preceding example, this would require at least $3 \times 3 \times 2 = 18$ observations. If the three patronage levels are added to the design, it will result in $3 \times 3 \times 3 \times 2 = 54$ observations. Thus, while the factorial design provides exhaustive information, it is rather cumbersome to set up, and is, therefore, more likely to lead to error.

One major advantage of the factorial design is that it measures both the main effects and the interaction effects. From the point of view of practical applications, therefore, it is a most useful design since it provides information not only on the most important variables, but also the most important *combination* of variables.

Table 7.4 Factorial Design Treatment

Store	X_1 (Sales Promotion 1)	X_2 (Sales Promotion 2)	X_3 (Sales Promotion 3)
1	P_1	P_1	P_1
	P_2	P_2	P_2
2	P_1	P_1	P_1
	P_2	P_2	P_2
3	P_1	P_1	P_1
	P_2	P_2	P_2

Table 7.5   Laboratory vs Field Experiments

Factor	Laboratory	Field
Environment	Artificial	Realistic
Control	High	Low
Reactive error	High	Low
Demand artefacts	High	Low
Internal validity	High	Low
External validity	Low	High
Time required	Short	Long
Number of units involved	Small	Large
Ease of implementation	High	Low
Cost	Low	High

Source: Adapted from N.K. Malhotra 2004.

THE LIMITATIONS OF EXPERIMENTS

Experiments that produce information based on observation and measurement suffer from some major constraints that limit their role in data collection.

The more the information an experiment is likely to produce, the more complex is its structure and, therefore, the higher the setting-up costs. Besides, issues such as 'matching' and randomization are much more difficult to ensure in practice than are apparent. If two markets have to be matched for observing the impact of a sales promotion scheme or a sales training programme given to the sales force, it is virtually impossible to find two markets that can be matched in terms of sales volume, sales growth, as well as competitive activity.

Table 7.5, adapted from Malhotra (2004), compares laboratory experiments with field experiments of the kind common in agricultural studies. One major limitation of laboratory experiments is that they are carried out in artificial conditions, which are difficult to replicate. This has an adverse influence on the *external validity* of the experiment, which, in turn, influences its cost effectiveness.

SUMMARY

The main function of an experiment is to identify the independent variables influencing the behaviour of the variable under study, called the dependent variable, and the nature and strength of the relationship between dependent and independent variables. Experiments aim at determining causality. Causation may be either deterministic or probabilistic, depending on whether each independent variable involved explains the dependent variable fully or in parts. Most experiments in marketing are of the controlled kind, concerned with actively manipulating the levels of the independent variable and tracking the impact on the dependent variable. Natural experiments, which are not very frequent in marketing, on the other hand, concern themselves only with observing and tracking changes in the dependent variable as a result of temporal or environmental changes in the independent variables.

It is important for the experiment to maintain internal validity as well as external validity. Internal validity could be vitiated by factors, such as the environment effect, maturation effect, testing effect, selection bias, or instrument effect. External validity would influence the experiment's capacity to be replicated over time and place. It is, therefore, important to design an experiment to minimize these effects.

The designs of experiments may be broadly classified into classical designs and statistical designs. Classical designs may again be categorized as pre-experimental, true experimental, or quasi-experimental designs. Each of these designs attempts to control the internal validity of the experiment in a larger or smaller measure. Statistical designs vary from the very basic completely randomized design to the factorial design. They are superior to the classical designs in their ability to provide measurable levels of accuracy, using statistical techniques of analysis and measurement such as the analysis of variance and covariance. In addition, they can provide for measurement of the effect of more than one independent variable at a time. Some of them can measure interaction effects in addition to the main effects of the independent variables.

Experimental designs suffer from some major limitations, for example, setting-up costs, control, and difficulty in replication. The utility of laboratory experiments is particularly limited by the artificiality of the conditions under which they are conducted.

KEY WORDS

Dependent variable refers to a variable whose variation in values is largely dependent on the variation in other variables.

Independent variable refers to a variable whose variation in values is caused by time or environment, but not by any of the other variables being studied.

Deterministic causation refers to a causal relationship in which the independent variable can explain the variation in the dependent variable completely.

Probabilistic causation refers to a causal relationship involving more than one independent variable, each one predicting the probability of occurrence of a dependent variable such that the probability is less than 100 per cent.

Natural experiments refer to experiments in which the researcher does not actively manipulate the independent variables but merely tracks the impact of change in their values on the dependent variable.

Controlled experiments refer to experiments in which the researcher acts to consciously vary or manipulate the value of the independent variable(s) to study its impact on the dependent variable.

Internal validity refers to the experimental result that ensures that the relationship demonstrated by the experiment between the dependent and the independent variable cannot be attributed to any other cause.

External validity refers to a validity that implies that the results of the experiment are valid across time, place, or individuals.

Environment effect refers to the environmental factors that may influence the results of an experiment.

Maturation effect refers to the change that could take place in the values of the dependent variable over a period of time, independent of the influence of the experiment.

Testing effect refers to the change that takes place in the value of the dependent variable because the respondents are aware they are being tested and, therefore, tend to give conditioned answers.

Selection effect refers to the bias that creeps into the results of the experiment because the subjects have been selected in a non-random manner.

Instrument effect refers to the conditioning in the responses that takes place because of the limitations of the data collection instrument.

CONCEPT REVIEW QUESTIONS

1. How do experiments differ from the survey method of data collection? Can they be used to determine change in attitudes as well as behaviour? Give reasons for your answer.

2. Can statistical designs be used as substitutes for classical designs? Explain your answer with examples.

3. What factors are likely to influence the internal validity of an experiment? Discuss some measures the researcher can take to improve the internal validity of an experiment.

4. What is a time series? Explain the difference between a standard time series and trend analysis. When would each be a more suitable method of data collection?

5. Compare the various statistical designs of experiments with each other for the advantages and disadvantages of each.

CRITICAL THINKING EXERCISES

1. ASTRA, a company marketing protein beverages, is interested in launching a 'sugar-free' version, 'Life-S', of its well-known brand of protein beverage for diabetics, 'Life'. The brand manager is trying to decide whether to make it available through chemists as usual, general stores and supermarkets, or provision stores. His worry is that the income and education levels of the patients might influence their choice of the outlet type, and as such, the sales of 'Life-S', which is more expensive than 'Life', might get affected. What kind of experiment would you advise to design to answer his problem?

2. Company XYZ is considering the idea of promoting its insurance policies through SMS on mobile phones. Design an experiment to do so. The experiment should check for (a) change in sales levels, (b) change in the company's ability to monitor and control the insurance agent's performance on a daily basis.

PROJECT ASSIGNMENT

Contact a manufacturing company in your city. Design an experiment to compare the change in productivity levels, defined as the number of pieces produced per day, among factory workers as a result of change from (a) a six-day, eight-hours-a-day week to a five-day, eight-hours-a-day week, (b) a six-day week with seven-and-a-half hours on Monday and six-and-a-half hours on the remaining five days, and (c) a five-day week with 25 per cent productivity-linked bonus for extra hours worked. Request the company to allow you to run the experiment and observe and report on the results. What design would you choose? Why?

REFERENCES

Aaker, D., V. Kumar, and G.S. Day 1998, *Marketing Research,* John Wiley and Sons (Asia) Pvte Ltd, pp.337–369.

Campbell, D.T. and J.C. Stanley 1963, *Experimental and Quasi-experimental Designs for Research,* Rand McNally, Chicago, p.5.

Cooper, D.R. and P.S. Schindler 1998, *Business Research Methods,* Tata McGraw-Hill, pp. 378–405.

Green, Paul E. and D. Tull, 1978, *Research for Marketing Decisions,* Prentice-Hall, pp. 80–92, 342–45

Malhotra, N.K. 2004, *Marketing Research: An Applied Orientation,* Pearson Education, p. 224.

Solomon, R.L. 1949, ' An Extension of Control Group Design', *Psychological Bulletin,* 46, pp.137–150.

Zikmund, William G. 1996, *Exploring Marketing Research* (PowerPoint of the chapter 'Primary Data: Experimentation'), Thomson Learning.

8

Interview Techniques

OBJECTIVES

After reading this chapter, the readers will be able to understand:

- how to select the appropriate respondents
- various survey techniques and how to choose the correct method of survey
- some popular qualitative methods of data collection
- how to select the most suitable mode and technique of interview

INTRODUCTION

The four major methods of collecting primary data are observation, experimentation, survey, and qualitative research. Both the observation and experimentation methods essentially use the *observation approach*. While the observation method is concerned with observing behaviour to determine consumer response to a given set of stimuli, experimentation collects data by manipulating the stimuli and observing consumer response to them. The other two methods, i.e., survey and qualitative research, use what D.R. Cooper and P.S. Schindler (1998) refer to as the *communication approach*. Both these methods go beyond studying behaviour to providing an understanding of the factors that influence and shape behaviour. This includes the cognitive and affective aspects of attitudes (such as consumer awareness and the knowledge of products and services), influences from the environment and experience, and consumer motivation and the resultant perceptions. Both qualitative research and surveys, thus, examine the consumer decision process in its entirety, making it possible to understand the current decision and to predict future decisions.

The survey method is the most popular method of primary data collection because of its versatility, efficiency, and economy. Moreover, it is easy to extrapolate the results of data from a survey. The method is not without limitations, as we noted in Chapter 6. It is, therefore, important to use surveys with an awareness of their limitations. Some of these limitations will be discussed again in the ensuing paragraphs.

This chapter mainly concerns itself with details of the survey method. It discusses the basic approach to the survey method—the choice of the appropriate respondent; the various survey techniques and their suitability for specific research problems;

and the time and cost considerations in choosing survey techniques, in other words, 'when to use which method'.

The other communication-based approach, i.e., qualitative research, has been discussed briefly in this chapter. Qualitative research techniques provide ways of understanding what is in the respondent's mind, sometimes beyond the stated obvious. These methods are, thus, most useful in collecting information about things that cannot be directly observed or measured. They are based on the assumption that 'an individual's organization of a relatively unstructured stimulus indicates the person's basic perception of the phenomenon and his or her reaction to it' (Kerlinger 1986). This chapter discusses these issues in detail and explains their relevance in finding solutions to marketing problems.

THE CHOICE OF RESPONDENTS

This 'direct' approach is the essence of reliable collection of primary data. In any such situation, it is essential to identify the appropriate respondent, usually the actual user. While selecting the respondent, it is useful to keep certain qualifications in mind.

- As far as possible, the respondent must be an individual, and not a group. Some exceptions are focus group discussions or, as in the case of children, 'party interviewing'. Similarly, in a study on the use of contraceptives, better data was obtained when couples were interviewed jointly. In general, the tendency of the entire household to gather and attempt to respond to an interview aimed exclusively at the housewife should be discouraged.

- The respondent's capacity to answer questions must be kept in mind. As mentioned earlier, it is difficult to obtain information through a questionnaire from children, who might perceive it as an examination, may not have the patience to sit through an entire interview, or may not wish to answer the questions of a stranger. In such cases, data must be obtained through projective techniques or games. At the same time, it is better to obtain data directly from the children rather than their parents, except where a parent is the one who makes the decision and the child does not, in any measure, influence it. In case a study involves infants, the parents will obviously have to be interviewed.

Market trends and segment profiles also influence the choice of appropriate respondents. For example, for many items of personal consumption, the housewife in urban middle-class households is no longer the decision-maker, with multiple brand-usage being a common phenomenon. In a survey on toothpastes, face creams, or garments, for example, interviewing the housewife in such households will not yield reliable data on motivations or reasons for choice.

Choose the Right Respondent

ABC Ltd, a large multinational company marketing lubricants in the country, had been running a high-decibel promotion campaign for three months and was eager now to determine its impact on consumer awareness and the extent of brand switch it had succeeded in generating from the public sector oil majors. The Research Co. (TRC) had been commissioned to collect this information. Mr Ramamurthy, the marketing manager for lubricants, 'Ramu' to his colleagues, gaped in amazement at the TRC proposal on his desk. 'But why do you want to interview dealers for this purpose?' he asked Narhari Menon, the young project executive from TRC.

Narhari, or 'Naru' as he was popularly known, was in turn surprised at the question. 'How else will we find out the consumer's buying pattern, the brand switch? It is the dealers who will be able to tell us which brand is moving faster, isn't it?' he responded.

'Why not speak to the consumers themselves?' Ramu asked patiently.

Naru's response took him by surprise. 'See, the way we look at it, the dealer will be able to track the switch—who was buying what and switched to what. I agree that the same information may be obtained directly from the consumer, but how will we vouch for its veracity? Besides, one dealer will be able to provide us with data for which we will otherwise have to contact many consumers. It is certainly more efficient, reliable, and quicker. And works with a smaller sample size, so we charge you less,' he smiled disarmingly at Ramu.

Ramu gave up the argument but was quite convinced that TRC's approach was wrong. To begin with, no dealer, at least not in India, kept a record of which customer bought what and why, except in cases where a customer actually complained about a product. A satisfied customer did not always praise the product to the dealer—he just bought it regularly. Brand switch was certainly not a phenomenon a dealer kept track of, except at the general, macro level, maintaining records of brands that were gaining sales and those that were losing sales. The dealer usually would not know the reasons for a brand switch, except as conjecture. So how would the dealer be able to provide any assessment of the impact of the promotion campaign?

Ramu made up his mind. He was going to insist that TRC interview the users, not the dealers, except perhaps to verify the trends that their data from the consumers threw up. Why interview the dealer to find out what the consumer thought when the consumer was available for a direct check?

SURVEY TECHNIQUES

Surveys are the most popular method of collecting primary data. There are quite a wide variety of survey methods available for research. The applicability of these methods varies with (a) the degree of structure needed in the data collection format, depending on the depth of data exploration required; (b) the need for revealing to the respondent the actual purpose of research; and (c) the most appropriate means of data collection to be used. Fig. 8.1 depicts these different methods.

Surveys almost always involve questioning the respondent. A few exceptions occur, as mentioned earlier, because of the characteristics of the respondent (for example, children); the respondent's unfamiliarity with the language of the survey; the unwillingness of conservative women to answer questions; etc.

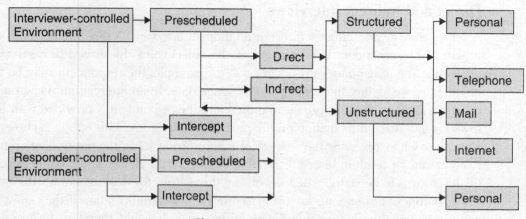

Fig. 8.1 Survey Methods

Survey Environment

Surveys may be conducted in an *interviewer-controlled environment*, such as the interviewer's office, shopping areas, entertainment areas, such as cinemas, or even hired accommodation as in the case of focus group discussions or simulated test markets. Alternatively, they may be conducted in *respondent-controlled environments* such as the respondent's residence, office, or college.

The choice of the environment depends on the convenience of location, the ease of availability of the respondent, the comfort level, and the detail and complexity of the data required. For example, a detailed study about the respondent's attitude to a product category, purchase motivations, and future purchase intent cannot easily be conducted in a supermarket or outside a cinema. Opinion polls that require the respondent to answer 'yes' or 'no' on the other hand, may be conducted anywhere—at the respondent's residence, on the road, or even in a bus. The choice of the appropriate environment—location, time, activity engaged in at the time of the survey, companions—has a major influence on the respondent's willingness to cooperate and the quality of data obtained.

A related question is the choice between conducting a prescheduled survey or an 'intercept'. Again, a detailed interview may only be conducted successfully with a prior appointment, when the respondent will be in a position to spend time on the interview and provide the required details. A brief, structured interview, requiring answers to a few elementary questions, may be conducted with a respondent 'intercepted' at a retail outlet or, as an experienced interviewer from Mumbai would tell you, inside the ladies compartment of the suburban local train. Both prescheduled and intercept interviews may be conducted in an environment controlled by either the respondent or the interviewer.

Direct and Indirect Interviews

A survey may involve either a direct or an indirect interview. A direct interview is one in which the respondent is fully aware of the objective of the survey. In a survey to determine the usage pattern of shampoos, for example, the respondent may be told of the purpose of the study and asked for usage data. In an indirect interview, on the other hand, the actual purpose is disguised and the respondent is provided with only broad, generalized information on the purpose of the study. This option is chosen in a situation where revealing the purpose of the study may invite the respondent's refusal to cooperate or result in biased or rationalized responses. If, for example, the purpose of the study is to determine the level of and the reasons for dissatisfaction with brand 'A' of shampoo, respondents are likely to provide biased information if they know the actual purpose, thus limiting the efficacy of the survey. It would, therefore, be necessary to couch the actual purpose in general terms, such as 'a survey on shampoos', to obtain a reliable response. The researcher must understand that this approach does not violate the code of ethics in research, involving as it does the collection of relevant data on the product category.

Structured and Unstructured Interviews

An interview may be structured, i.e., be based on a formal questionnaire consisting predominantly of close-ended questions, all questions being arranged in a predetermined order. Alternatively, it may be unstructured, i.e., based on open-ended questions, the order and wording of which may vary with the kind of responses obtained to earlier questions. In such cases, the interviewer is only provided with a general guideline on the kind of information required and often approaches the interview armed merely with an 'interview guide', i.e., a list of the items of information needed.

It is possible to combine these two bases of classification to yield four kinds of interviews that are commonly used in a variety of situations:

- structured direct interview
- unstructured direct interview
- structured indirect interview
- unstructured indirect interview

Structured direct interview

This is the simplest and the most common kind of interview, where the respondent is aware of the purpose of the queries. It takes the form of undisguised, structured questions. Structured direct interviews are most useful in descriptive studies, particularly in intercept interviews in a respondent-controlled environment. This is because the probability of response to short, close-ended questions and cooperation from the respondent increases substantially. Such interviews are also used extensively in

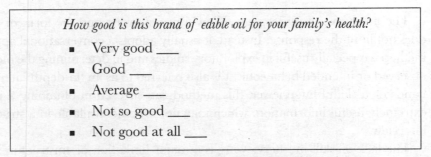

Fig. 8.2 A Multiple-choice Question

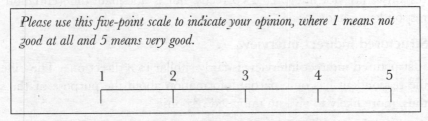

Fig. 8.3. Rating Scale

experiments. One of the attractive features of structured interviews is that they can be planned and tested in advance since the order of the questions remains the same for all respondents. As a corollary, the results of such interviews are not very dependent on the interviewer's skills. Relatively less-skilled interviewers can, therefore, conduct the interviews. Moreover, this kind of interview provides maximum control over the data collection process.

Questions in structured interviews can take one of two formats—*multiple-choice questions* or *rating scales*. In both formats, the respondent usually has to make one of many theoretically possible choices. For example, a question about the perception of a new brand of edible oil could be asked as shown in Fig. 8.2 and 8.3.

Simpler versions would take the form of answer options like 'yes', 'no', and 'don't know'.

A major shortcoming of structured direct interviews is the possibility of rationalized and inadequate answers since there is little scope for 'probing' behind each question. The responses get limited to a choice of one of the many alternatives provided.

Unstructured direct interview

An unstructured direct interview aims at taking care of these problems. Although the respondent is aware of the purpose of the study, the interviewer gives only general guidelines about the purpose of the study and the information required. The interviewer is thus free to modulate the question to the comfort level of the respondent. The language and vocabulary can be modified to suit the respondent's understanding, and questions may be asked to probe the response provided earlier. This process may continue as long as the interviewer considers it necessary to explore the reasons behind the earlier response.

The interview, thus, does not follow a preset order, and the form of the question does not limit the response. Instead, it usually adopts a conversational approach. This method is especially useful in exploratory studies and in determining the motives behind observed or intended behaviour. It is also referred to as an 'in-depth interview'. In the hands of a skilful interviewer, this method can succeed in obtaining a great deal of extremely useful information, which may not become available in a structured direct interview.

The lack of skill in interviewing is a major limitation of unstructured interviews. The interview then becomes a tedious process and loses a great deal of its utility. The responses are not interpreted correctly, nor is adequate differentiation between the respondents made.

Structured indirect interview

A structured indirect interview is fairly similar to a direct one. The difference is that the respondent has only partial information about the purpose of the study, and is, thus, more likely to give an unbiased response.

Unstructured indirect interview

This is the most complex method of primary data collection, although it is the most rewarding in terms of the richness of data obtained. This method has been adapted in marketing research from psychology. It is based on the premise that, in many situations, the respondent will be unable or unwilling to provide spontaneous, complete, and genuine answers to direct questions. Therefore, techniques that employ an indirect means of obtaining information must be used.

These techniques, usually referred to as *projective techniques*, require the respondent to interpret some seemingly non-personal, generalized situations. They provide the respondent with the freedom to interpret the situations presented in the light of personal experience. In the process, the respondent's personality characteristics, thought processes, and experiences are projected onto the situation. These techniques include simple, less personalized ones, such as word association, sentence completion, story completion, picture or cartoon interpretation, role-play, third person technique, and 'shopping list', to more complex, personalized techniques such as the thematic apperception test (TAT) and the Rorschach inkblot test.

Word association These are among the oldest projective techniques. The test presents the respondent with a set of stimulus words, which when heard, must be responded to quickly with the first word that comes to mind. It is expected that the instantaneous response will result in the strongest association being revealed. A variation is to present the respondent with two lists of words to be matched. Another variant used extensively in brand personality tests is to present the respondent with a brand name and ask, 'If this brand were an animal/film actor/vegetable/political leader (only one category is to be stated), which one would it be?' The purpose is to determine brand perceptions. The understanding of the response can be sharpened by either asking the respondent the reasons for such an association, or by determining, at another point in the interview, the characteristics the respondent associates with the stimulus.

Sentence completion tests   These are similar to word association tests in concept and objectives. The respondent is presented with a part of a sentence ('sentence stem') and asked to complete it with the first phrase that comes to mind.

Story completion tests   These are an extension of the sentence completion test. Here, the respondent is presented with the beginning of a situational narrative and asked to complete it.

Cartoon/picture tests   These tests similarly require the respondent to narrate the story that is depicted in the figure.

Role-play   Role play requires the respondent to adopt the role of another person. The method usually requires more than one 'player'. Through the 'enactment' of their interaction, the perceptions of the respondent about the given situation are verbalized.

Third person technique   It involves asking the respondent to describe the response of an imaginary 'average person' to the situation of interest. In doing so, the perceptions of the respondent are projected onto the 'third' person. This technique is quite effective in situations where the respondent may be expected to provide biased responses for reasons of prestige or privacy to a direct question.

Shopping list   This is a variant of the third person technique. Here, the respondents are given a typical shopping list and asked to describe the shopper. The technique may be used to compare the perceptions of the users of two brands in a product category.

An accurate interpretation of these projective techniques, especially the more complex ones, requires a great deal of skill and experience. But the relatively more commonly used ones, such as the word association test and sentence completion test, may be used effectively by a researcher with a reasonable degree of understanding. In marketing research, these tests have been used most often with consumer products. Some of the more popular uses of these tests are brand recall, perception studies, and motivation research. The author has also used them to good effect in the post-testing of advertisements.

The thematic apperception test   This test has been used extensively in entrepreneurship training programmes (Easwaran 1993–2004) to determine the entrepreneurial aptitude and achievement motivation levels among aspirants.

In practice, almost all interviews are a combination of structured and unstructured methods, and may be referred to as 'semi-structured', with some questions being close-ended (structured) and others open-ended. It is the degree of structure that may vary, depending on the kind of data required.

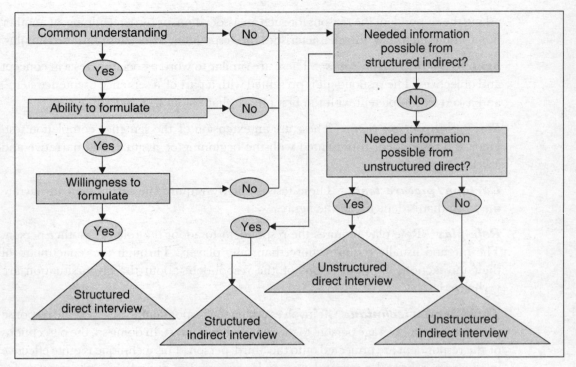

Fig. 8.4   The Process of Selection of an Appropriate Interview Method

The choice of the most appropriate method of interview has been given in the flowchart outlined in Fig. 8.4, adapted from D. Tull and D.I. Hawkins (1976).

THE APPROPRIATE INTERVIEW METHOD

The other factors that must be borne in mind while choosing the most suitable method of interview are the cost of the interviews and the time involved. We had discussed cost vs benefits of research in Chapter 2. The more complex the data collection technique, the higher the costs and the greater the amount of time involved. The utility of research in marketing decision-making must always be kept in mind while deciding on the survey technique. The costs and time required for the study must always be balanced against the quality of research aimed at.

The Mode of Interview

The argument between effectiveness and efficiency may be extended further to the mode of data collection—personal interview, telephone calls, mail surveys, or Internet-based interviews. Table 8.1 provides a comparison of these various methods with regard to a variety of parameters.

The table suggests that the personal interview remains the most effective means of collecting primary data even though it tends to be expensive and time-consuming.

Table 8.1 Comparative Strengths of Various Modes of Interview

Parameters	Personal Interview	Mail Survey	Telephonic Interview	Internet Interview
Complexity of issues covered	High	Low	High to low	High to low
Non-verbal communication	High	Low	Low	Low
Scope for open-ended questions	High	Low	High	Low
Time required for interview	High	Low	High	Low
Flexibility of interview-time	Low	High	High	High
Cost	High	Low	Low	Low
Response rate	High	Low	High to low	Low
Ambiguity of questions	Low	High	Low	High
Ambiguity of answers	Low	High	Low	High
Sample selection	High	Low	Low	Low
Flexibility	High	Low	High	Low
Privacy	Low	High	High	High
Anonymity	Low	High	Low	High
Familiarity required with technology	Low	Low	Low	High

However, in case the data being obtained is related to issues regarded by the respondent as private, the chances of a response are better in a telephonic interview, when the respondent is provided with a certain degree of privacy by the mere fact of not facing the interviewer. The probability of ambiguity of questions as well as answers is high in mail and Internet surveys since there is little scope for explaining the question and the answer. For this reason, mail and Internet surveys are best suited to structured interviews, with all questions being close-ended.

The response rates are usually low in these two types of interviews. Also, some degree of self-selection creeps into all non-personal methods; it is usual for a respondent to ignore the questionnaire, and those who respond often have a profile different from those who do not. Telephonic interviews in India, for example, suffer from the limitation that phone subscribers usually belong to a higher socio-economic class than non-subscribers. This is especially true in non-metro towns. Mail surveys, traditionally, elicit a very poor response in India. In addition, someone other than the targeted respondent may, at times, fill in the questionnaires. At the same time, non-personal methods of interview score in terms of the flexibility of time in responding since the respondent can fill the questionnaire or instrument at a convenient time.

Qualitative Techniques

Most of the survey methods discussed so far are best suited for eliciting information within a predefined framework, i.e., for testing hypotheses. They are, therefore, most useful in descriptive or causal studies. Whenever hypotheses have to be formed and the researcher wishes to explore the respondent's mind for the purpose, it is necessary to use another set of techniques called 'qualitative techniques'. These will be discussed in detail later in the book. However, a brief exposition of some of the major qualitative techniques is given here, and outlined in Fig. 8.5.

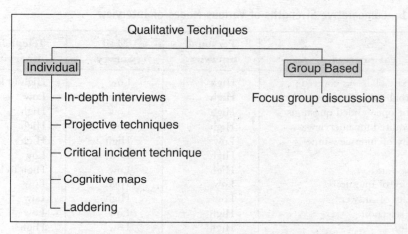

Fig. 8.5 Qualitative Techniques of Data Collection

In-depth interviews and projective techniques

In-depth interviews and *projective techniques* have already been discussed in the earlier sections of the chapter.

Critical incident technique (CIT)

This method was introduced by J.C. Flanagan (1954) 'for getting a subjective report while minimising interference from stereotypical reactions or received opinions'. Bob Hayes (1998) defined a critical incident as 'a specific example of the service or product that describes either *positive or negative* performance. A positive example is a characteristic of the service or product that the customer would like to see every time he or she receives the service or product. A negative example is a characteristic of the service or product that would make the customer question the quality of the company'. The objective of CIT is to link the respondent's perception of the reasons behind the outcome of an activity to a specific, important incident rather than to general opinions. The method usually employs an interview and aims at retrospectively determining the criticalness of the incident. It requires the respondent to

- describe an incident that had a strong positive influence on the final result of the activity,
- trace the history of the incident, i.e., describe what caused the incident, and
- describe how the incident influenced the success of the activity.

When at least one such critical incident has been recorded, the procedure is repeated with the respondent being asked to focus on incidents that had a strong negative influence on the result of the activity. There will be some variation in the number of positive and negative incidents that the respondents recall. It is usual to start with a positive incident in order to set a constructive tone with the respondent.

The data obtained may then be used to provide quantitative information on the frequency with which a certain feature may have been found helpful or unhelpful in some context. Alternatively, the effort is to collect enough contextual information to be able to 'place the critical incidents in scenarios or use cases' (Flanagan 1954). Johnson and Gustafsson (2000) have used the method as the basis for developing the questionnaire for a customer satisfaction survey that is the forerunner to the reputed American Consumer Satisfaction Survey (ACSS) conducted by the University of Michigan Business School every year.

Cognitive maps

Cognition is defined as 'the mental models, or belief systems, that people use to interpret, frame, simplify, and make sense of otherwise complex problems'. 'They are built from past experiences and comprise internally represented concepts and relationships among concepts that an individual can then use to interpret new events' and decide on the appropriate response. The importance of cognitive maps stems from the fact that adoption (or non-adoption) of an innovation or change is influenced significantly by the individual's cognitive map.

Many cognitive mapping techniques have been developed. They use different methods to 'elicit from an individual, key concepts and relationships among concepts and to construct a map for that individual'. 'All cognitive mapping techniques reveal concepts that people hold to be important but they vary in terms of the nature of the relationships among concepts that they identify.'

The major utility of congnitive mapping techniques lies in

- providing means for 'revealing peoples' significant subjective beliefs in a meaningful way so that they can be examined not only by the individual for whom the map is constructed, but also by other individuals and groups' (Eden 1992). The identification of these subjective beliefs contributes useful knowledge that leads to improved decision-making.
- providing the decision-maker with the means for understanding and appreciating alternative perspectives to a problem by examining maps constructed for other group members.
- explaining the hidden differences among individuals to help understand their personalities.
- identifying beliefs shared by a decision-making group by combining maps from different individuals into a composite map that represents the beliefs of the group (Eden 1992, Bougon et al 1977).

Laddering

This is a psychology-based technique that attempts to explain the consumer's relationship with products and services by examining 'how concrete aspects of the product fit into the consumer's life' (Reynolds 1988). It is based upon J. Gutman's (1982) 'means-end' theory, which operates on the premise that consumers learn to choose products containing attributes that are instrumental to achieving their desired consequences. The 'means-end theory simply specifies the rationale underlying why consequences are important, namely, personal values'. It thus seeks to explain product preference through the 'attribute-consequences-values (A-C-V) ladder' concept, originally developed by Reynolds and Gutman (1988).

Based on a one-to-one in-depth interview method, the laddering technique involves the use of a series of directed probes, typified by the 'Why is that important to you?' question. The objective is to determine the 'higher order knowledge structures' or perceptual orientations defined by associative linkages, or 'ladders', between product attributes (A), their consequences (C), and consumer values (V), that customers use to process information, identifying more personally relevant product attributes, leading to customer choice.

The analysis of the laddering data is a two-step process—first, content-analysing the data obtained from the interview, and then drawing up a specific type of cognitive map based on this data called the 'hierarchical value map (HVM)'. The technique of content analysis will be described in later chapters dealing with the analysis of data.

Focus group interviews

This method has its origin in sociology, but is now used extensively in marketing research, especially in exploratory studies and problem definition. It is important to note that focus group discussions (FGDs) should ideally be used for generating hypotheses and not for testing hypotheses. The technique will be discussed in greater detail in a later chapter.

Unlike the other interview methods discussed so far, FGDs obtain their data from respondents discussing the marketing problem in a group. The role of the interviewer, or 'moderator', is minimal and restricted to keeping the discussion on track, ensuring a smooth flow of discussion, with all group members getting an opportunity to participate, and obtaining all the data required. The group usually consists of eight to ten participants who share a common background or similar experience with respect to the problem being researched. It is best to use cohorts for this purpose. If it is necessary to obtain viewpoints of respondents with different backgrounds, it is best to conduct multiple FGDs, each consisting of a distinct cohort, differentiated from the other respondent groups.

The objectives of FGDs are similar to face-to-face in-depth interviews, but they usually result in richer data since the involvement and discussion with other group members provide an opportunity for greater spontaneity and candour. In the hands of a skilful moderator, respondents piggybacking on each other's ideas can produce very creative solutions to the problems being discussed. Since the size of each group is necessarily kept small in order to encourage interaction, the data obtained cannot be treated as the final solution but instead provide the basis for later quantitative studies in which the hypotheses generated can be tested.

SUMMARY

Interview techniques, comprising surveys and qualitative research, collect information on the cognitive and affective aspects of respondent attitudes in addition to behaviour. The survey method is the most popular method of primary data collection because of the versatility, efficiency, economy, and convenience of extrapolating data. Qualitative research techniques go beyond the stated obvious in exploring the consumer's mind. To optimize the efficacy of the communication approach of data collection, it is important to choose the respondent carefully. As far as possible, it is better to interview the actual user or the decision-maker(s).

The choice of the appropriate survey method depends on the degree of structure required, the need for disguise or directness, and the suitability of the mode of data collection to be employed as well as the cost and time involved. Survey methods include the structured direct, structured indirect, unstructured direct, and unstructured indirect interviews. The last category is also referred to as 'projective techniques' and includes a variety of methods such as word association, sentence completion, story completion, picture or cartoon interpretation, third person technique, role-play, 'shopping list', Thematic Apperception Test (TAT), and Rorschach Inkblot Test. These techniques are particularly useful in obtaining spontaneous responses from the interviewee because of the lack of structure and the freedom to interpret the situations presented in the light of personal experience.

Similarly, the choice of the environment depends on the convenience of location, ease of availability and comfort level of the respondent, and detail and complexity of the data required. The modes of interview available include the face-to-face interview, telephonic interview, mail survey, and Internet interview.

Whenever hypotheses have to be formed and the researcher wishes to explore the respondent's mind for this purpose, it is necessary to use another set of techniques called 'qualitative techniques'. This chapter outlines, in addition to in-depth interviews and projective techniques, some individual qualitative techniques, such as the critical incident techniques, cognitive maps, and laddering, as also the well-known group interview technique called focus group interviews.

KEY WORDS

Observation approach refers to a method of data collection based on the observation of the respondent's behaviour.

Communication approach refers to a method of data collection based on interaction with the respondent through interviews and qualitative research techniques.

Intercept interview refers to a method of data collection in which the respondent may be met without an appointment, usually outside the person's residence, office, or college, for an impromptu interview.

Prescheduled interview refers to a method of data collection in which the respondent may be met with an appointment, usually in a respondent-controlled environment.

Structured direct interview refers to a method of interview in which the respondent is aware of the purpose of the interview and which is characterized by close-ended questions.

Structured indirect interview refers to a method of interview in which the actual purpose of the interview is disguised from the respondent and which is characterized by close-ended questions.

Structured direct interview refers to a method of interview in which the respondent is aware of the purpose of the interview and which is characterized by open-ended and freewheeling questions.

Unstructured indirect interview refers to a method of interview in which the actual purpose of the interview is disguised from the respondent and which is characterized by open-ended and freewheeling questions.

Qualitative research techniques refer to data-collection techniques that aim at exploring the consumer's mind to determine qualitative parameters, such as respondent attitudes, perceptions, and motivations. These techniques usually do not use formal questionnaires but use methods derived from psychology and sociology.

CONCEPT REVIEW QUESTIONS

1. When is a structured direct interview a better option than an unstructured one? Give two examples to support your answer.

2. Why is the focus group discussion method not usually suitable for testing hypotheses? When is a focus group discussion to be preferred over an in-depth personal interview? Why?

3. What are the limitations in interpreting responses to projective techniques? How can they be overcome?

CRITICAL THINKING EXERCISES

1. (a) A manufacturer of a cough syrup for children wants to determine the perceived efficacy of the syrup among the consumers. From whom should he collect data?

   (b) The sales manager in the company suggests that a brief questionnaire could be designed and inserted into the carton of the syrup. This would help maximize the sample of respondents at the least possible cost. What is your view? Give reasons for your answer.

2. You are the product manager for your company's popular brand of biscuits. A new advertising campaign has been developed for the brand by an advertising agency, which also handles advertising research for the brand. It recommends conducting focus group discussions to test the effectiveness of the new campaign. What is your response? Why?

3. What method of data collection would you employ in the following situations? Why?

   (a) A study to determine consumption patterns for your company's brand of chocolate confectionery.
   (b) A study to identify satisfaction levels with postgraduate management education in India.
   (c) A study to determine market potential for a new brand of cell phones in the market.
   (d) A study to determine opinions regarding beauty contests in the country.

4. Develop a questionnaire to determine the most recognized brand of toothpaste in the country using word association and other appropriate projective techniques. Indicate a plan for interpreting the results.

PROJECT ASSIGNMENT

Your business school is considering launching a postgraduate programme in retail management. Plan and conduct a study to determine the market potential for such a programme and the most appropriate structure for it.

REFERENCES

Cooper, D.R. and P.S. Schindler 1998, *Business Research Methods,* Tata McGraw-Hill, pp. 378–405.

Kerlinger, F., *Foundations of Behavioural Research,* Third Edition, Holt, Rinehart and Winston, New York, as quoted in D. Aaker, V. Kumar, and G.S. Day 1998, *Marketing Research,* John Wiley and Sons (Asia) Pte Ltd, pp. 337–369.

Easwaran, S., Entrepreneurship Training Programmes conducted during 1993–2004 at NM Institute of Management Studies, India.

Tull, D. and D.I. Hawkins 1976, *Marketing Research: Meaning, Measurement and Methods,* Macmillan.

Hayes, B.E. 1998, *Measuring Customer Satisfaction: Survey Design, Use, and Statistical Analysis Methods,* ASQ Quality Press, Milwaukee, Wisconsin, p. 17.

Flanagan, J.C. 1954, 'The Critical Incident Technique', *Psychological Bulletin*, 51.4, pp. 327–359.

Johnson, M.D. and A. Gustafsson 2000, *Improving Customer Satisfaction, Loyalty, and Profit,* University of Michigan Business School Management Series, Jossey-Bass.

Tolman, E. 1948, 'Cognitive Maps in Rats and Men', *Psychological Review*, 55, pp. 189–208; quoted in 'Instructor's Guide Trainer Notes: Cognitive Mapping Techniques', omni.bus.ed.ac.uk/opsman/Oakland/inst18.htm.

Instructor's Guide Trainer Notes: Cognitive Mapping Techniques', omni.bus.ed.ac.uk/opsman/Oakland/inst18.htm.

Eden, C. 1992, 'On the Nature of Cognitive Maps', *Journal of Management Studies*, 29, pp. 261–265.

Bougon, M., K. Weick, and D. Binkhorst 1977, 'Cognition in Organizations: An Analysis of the Utrecht Jazz Orchestra', *Administrative Science Quarterly*, 22, pp. 606–639.

Reynolds, T.J. and J. Gutman 1988, 'Laddering Theory, Method, Analysis, and Interpretation', *Journal of Advertising Research*, February/March, pp. 11–29.

9

Sampling

OBJECTIVES

After reading this chapter, the readers will be able to understand:

- the purpose and the benefits of sampling
- the different stages and techniques of sampling
- the importance of sample size and methods for determining the sample size

INTRODUCTION

Having discussed the techniques of data collection in some detail, we now proceed to the next stage in planning the research design, i.e., deciding *whom* to collect data from—choosing the sample of respondents, the who, how many, and how.

Data is usually required to assess one or more characteristics of the population, i.e., of a group of individuals or objects, which share some characteristics relevant to the study. For example, in a study aimed at determining the market share of this textbook, the relevant population would be MBA students taking marketing research as a core or elective course. The characteristic shared in this case is the study of the course in marketing research. The sharing implies that these characteristics begin to repeat themselves after they have been ascertained from a certain proportion of the population members. Once one starts investigating the courses MBA students take during their two years at business school, a pattern indicating the frequency of choice of the marketing research course will emerge. The greater the sharing, the smaller the proportion of population that needs to be studied. This is the basic idea behind *sampling*—by studying a sub-group of a population, the characteristics of the population can be ascertained. This chapter discusses the idea of sampling in detail—the need for sampling, its advantages, and limitations. The different types of sampling techniques have been described in later sections.

While deciding to use sampling, the question of 'how many units to study' arises because the repetitive pattern in a population usually makes it unnecessary to check it out in its entirety. Once a sufficiently large sub-group, or *sample*, has been approached, the pattern will demonstrate itself, and another equally large sub-group will not throw up any significant differences. The question of 'how many' is, therefore, concerned with determining the size of the sample that will, by and large, adequately identify this critical characteristic. We will discuss the process of determining 'how many', i.e., the size of the sample.

SAMPLING

The basic logic behind sampling is that, in most cases, the underlying patterns in a population become clear after a certain section or sub-group has been examined, thus making a complete census unnecessary. Sampling will also mean a reduction in both the *costs* and the *time* required for a study, since a smaller number of units have to be investigated.

The other crucial issue is that of *accuracy*. In a population that is reasonably homogeneous with respect to the characteristic under study, the researcher need not expect substantial variations within, or even between sub-groups. One sub-group or sample can be expected to represent another sample and, therefore by implication, the entire population fairly accurately.

If, on the other hand, heterogeneity levels in the population are high, the sample cannot be expected to accurately account for all the variations in the population with respect to the characteristic being studied. The options in such a case are to either study a sample that is large enough to take into account most of the variation, or to dispense with sampling altogether and study the entire population, i.e., conduct a *census*. A balance has to be struck between the benefits of savings in cost and time and the question of accuracy. The two often seem at first to work at cross-purposes. A large sample, while more accurate as it is closer to the total population in size, will cost more and take longer, which can, at times, be a self-defeating exercise. It may not provide the required information in time to assist decision-making. Besides, as we have seen earlier, in a reasonably homogeneous population, such a large sample does not always provide a significant increase in accuracy.

If a study requires complex data, errors in data collection are likely to get compounded in a census. In such a case, a sample is more likely to provide higher levels of accuracy than a census.

Samples usually provide a greater degree of flexibility than do censuses. If a population is too large, it may not be practicable to take a complete census. In such a case, the choice is between taking a sample and not doing anything at all. For example, it is not possible to take a census of all the diabetics in the country, but a sample may be studied and the sample data extrapolated to estimate the total number in the population.

In studies requiring highly trained, expert investigators as well, a census is not a feasible proposition. Such a study has to be necessarily based on the extrapolation of data from a sample. Similarly, in cases involving destructive testing, as in many manufacturing processes, a census is not a practicable proposition at all; for example, destructive testing of the tensile strength of a load-bearing steel chain used in cranes, or of the life of a light bulb.

In sum, the major benefits derived from sampling are as follows:

- reduced costs
- reduced time
- greater accuracy
- greater flexibility of scope

How is a sample to be selected? We have seen earlier that a sample is actually a sub-group of a large group or population, sharing some characteristics, including the one under study. The process of sampling will need to go through the many stages that have been discussed in detail here.

Defining the Population

The most basic and the most crucial step in the implementation of a research study is the identification of the relevant population. If the population is defined incorrectly, we may end up talking to the wrong people, or not getting answers to the questions that are the means of collecting relevant data.

Why are MBA students the relevant population in the example of this book's market-share study cited earlier? The characteristics to be considered here are not age, income, number of years of education, or location. All these, or many of these characteristics may be shared, but they do not clearly define the appropriate population for this purpose. The defining characteristic is the *opportunity to use* any textbook on marketing research on a regular basis.

The largest groups of individuals, who are likely to have such an opportunity, are current MBA students, though business school libraries, undergraduate management students, and teachers of marketing research could also form a secondary target group. However, this secondary group is not an adequate definition of the population in this case, since the members of the group will not be major users of current books on this subject. While defining the population, we must, therefore, keep the following in mind:

The research purpose

The purpose of research, as we have seen earlier, defines the research question, the hypotheses to be investigated, and the scope of the study. It will, therefore, suggest the appropriate respondent group. As we will see later, it also influences the size of the sample.

The alternatives

All alternative populations should be evaluated in order to determine the most appropriate one. For example, we have discussed the possibility of defining these alternative populations—MBA students, undergraduate management students, libraries of business schools, and teachers of marketing research. MBA students were defined as the primary population after examining the size of the prospective group, the urgency of their need, and the frequency of their requirement.

The sampling unit

Who specifically will be the unit of study—households, retail outlets, or corporate organizations? In the above example, we have identified MBA students as the appropriate unit of study. In some cases, as in this one, it is relatively easy to define the appropriate sampling unit. In other cases, for example, in a study to determine parental attitudes towards male and female children, it may not be quite so easy to decide whether the sampling unit should be the household including the extended family, the couple, the father, or the mother. This choice again will influence the quality of the response.

The area

It is necessary to define the physical scope, i.e., the area that constitutes the population for the purpose of the study. The users of shampoos, for example, may be found all over the world, and in different age groups, but a study aimed at determining the market potential of a brand need not study the entire world market, since it will not have the capacity to cater to the entire shampoo market in the world. Such a study should, therefore, regard as the relevant population only the users and potential users in the market the brand aims to serve.

Time

This is another constraint that should limit the scope of the population. In talking of the users of shampoo, while the term should include past as well as present users, the definition of 'past users' has to be qualified by assigning a lower limit to the last usage—whether a past user is one who used the brand a month ago or one, two, or three years ago must be specified.

The convenience

Other things being equal, it makes eminent sense to choose a population that is easy to interview. Two alternative populations may differ in terms of locational distance, availability during the day, or comfort levels with the language of the interview. The convenience of sampling will influence the quality of data obtained because of the time and cost constraints, and also because if it is difficult to meet respondents or conduct the interview, the temptation for the interviewer to produce dishonest results increases.

The Process of Sample Selection

The process of sampling selection is illustration in Fig. 9.1. The following points must be taken into consideration when selecting a sample section from the population:

The sampling frame

A sampling frame is a detailed record or list of members of a population. Census lists, telephone directories, lists of subscribers to magazines, members of an association, and databases of customers maintained by various corporations are all examples of sampling

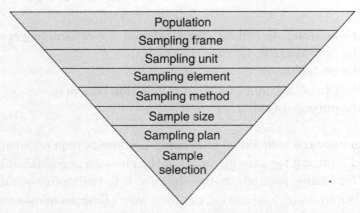

Fig. 9.1 The Process of Sample Selection

frames. With the advent of computerized databases, it has now become relatively easy to access detailed sampling frames. In theory, it is the enumeration of the population, but in practice it often differs from the actual population. Lists are not updated often enough. Thus, those who have ceased to be members of the group may not have had their details weeded out, and new members of the community may not have been included. Migratory populations often do not provide stable sampling frames.

The sampling unit

As we have seen, defining the sampling unit is not always an easy task. In a survey to assess brand preferences of refrigerators, should we interview households or dealers? The choice of the sampling frame that provides the source for identifying the sampling unit will depend on this decision and, again, it is not always available.

The sampling element

Identifying the actual respondent is another extremely important decision. Who the respondents should be and where they are to be located are not always easy questions to answer. In the preceding study on refrigerators, assuming that the household is identified as the sampling unit, who should be interviewed—the housewife, the head of the household, or the entire family? Again, where should they be met—in the store, at their work place, or at their residence? These are obviously crucial decisions in designing a study.

A well-known method of selecting the sampling element in household surveys is the 'Kish Grid', named after Leslie Kish (1965), the statistician who invented it. This is a table of numbers. The number of people in a household is determined, and a random number is chosen to select a particular person as a respondent. List (2005) has explained the method in detail, but has also pointed out that it may result in a high refusal rate.

The sampling method

The sampling theory discusses many methods of choosing a sample, explained in detail later in this chapter. The decision regarding the most appropriate technique for a given situation depends on

- the accuracy desired, i.e., the maximum size of sampling errors acceptable,
- the time available for data collection,
- the costs involved,
- the extent of control sought over selection bias, and
- the purpose of the research.

Exploratory research aimed at defining hypotheses requires small samples, but they should represent the extreme values of the phenomenon under study. This is valid for most qualitative research. If the objective is to determine quantitative estimates of population parameters or to forecast their values, large samples are necessarily required.

The basic choice is between the probabilistic procedure and the non-probabilistic method of sampling, i.e., whether the units in the sample are selected randomly, with each unit of the population being assigned a certain non-zero probability of inclusion in the sample, or whether they are chosen by the researcher on the basis of some other criterion such as familiarity with the units, or ease of availability. We will discuss all these procedures in a later section.

Probability sampling usually offers more reliable estimates for reasons that will be discussed in detail in the section dealing with sampling techniques. Even so, we will see later that a lot of the sampling undertaken in marketing research is non-random, or non-probabilistic, in nature. In particular, non-random sampling is widely used in qualitative research as a method of selecting respondents who may be more articulate or otherwise in a position to give greater or more reliable responses. Both methods have their own advantages and limitations, as indicated in Table 9.1. The final choice depends on the requirements mentioned earlier.

The next decision relates to whether sampling should be with replacement or without replacement, i.e., whether a respondent has the opportunity of being interviewed more than once. In practice, the 'without replacement' method is followed since it is not always possible to contact a respondent more than once to obtain information. Even if it were possible, the chances of obtaining new information from the same respondent are very slim.

The size of the sample

The major criterion governing the choice of the size of the sample is how well it represents the characteristics of the population. This includes the following criteria:

- The sample should be large enough to reproduce all the variations in the population, but not so large that the purpose of sampling, i.e., economy of time and money, is defeated. In other words, the sampling error should be minimized.
- All samples of the same size drawn from a population should provide more or less the same estimate of the parameter under study. In other words, the sample size should be such as to result in reliable estimates.

Table 9.1 Comparison of Characteristics of Probability and Non-probability Sampling

Probability Sampling	Non-Probability Sampling
1. Sampling error can be controlled.	1. Sampling error cannot be controlled.
2. The selection process depends on the specific technique and is, therefore, not influenced by the expertise of the researcher.	2. Selection bias can be very high.
3. Time and costs involved may be high.	3. Usually a low-cost, quicker alternative
4. It is possible to test the hypotheses through formal, rigorous tests of significance and, thus, obtain more reliable results.	4. Parametric tests of significance not applicable; the reliability of results is, therefore, not very high.
5. More reliable and representative if the population is heterogeneous.	5. May be more useful in a homogeneous population.
6. Preferable if complex, detailed estimates of are required.	6. Reasonably useful if parameters to parameters be estimated are at broad, aggregated levels, such as market shares or total sales.
7. Accuracy may be poor if the population is high.	7. Accuracy in such situations is quite scattered.
8. Formal sampling frames required.	8. Can be effective even in the absence of an elaborate sampling frame.
9. May be very inconvenient if the cheaper geographical spread of the population is high and likely to have lower	9. More convenient, less time-consuming, non-sampling errors.

In probability sampling, which assumes a knowledge of the underlying distribution of the population, it is possible to provide quantitative values for these constraints and thus determine the sample size, independent of the researcher's judgement. No such assumptions can be made in non-probability sampling, so that the size of the sample is based on the researcher's judgement.

The sampling plan

The operational details of the sampling process, i.e., the fieldwork, need to be specified. This includes details of the interview procedure, the sampling element, the time of the interview, the operational process of selecting the specific sampling unit and the sampling element, such as the 'right-hand rule', and the call-back procedure.

Some practical considerations regarding the population that influence the size of the sample need to be kept in mind while selecting the sample. These are as follows:

- Marketing populations tend to be geographically clustered. As such, non-probability sampling methods are likely to give a lower error than would be expected.
- They are finite and limited in size.
- They tend to display a high degree of mobility so that the address provided through the sampling frame may not actually deliver the sampling unit selected. It is, therefore, necessary to plan for a larger sample than the one suggested by the dictates of statistics.

- The members of the population usually demonstrate a low degree of cooperation. This also implies that non-response is likely to be high and, therefore, the actual size of the sample should be larger than suggested by theoretical considerations.
- Considerable prior knowledge is usually available about the population characteristics. This helps in operating with a relatively smaller sample size.

SAMPLING TECHNIQUES

When a decision has to be taken about the most appropriate technique of sampling, the basic choice is between the probability and the non-probability techniques of sampling. As defined earlier, probability sampling is

a method of sample selection in which each unit in the population has a definite, non-zero chance of selection in the sample, following some objective statistical rule.

The major advantages of probability sampling are that it is possible to determine the size of the sampling error, to estimate the population parameter, and to deliver a relatively small selection bias since the sample selected is not dependent on the expertise or preference of the researcher or various other considerations such as time constraints, spread of the population, costs involved, etc. This becomes even more important if the cost of errors resulting from selection bias is likely to be high.

In non-probability sampling,

the selection of the sample is based on such criteria as convenience, time, cost, and the researcher's perception of the respondent's knowledge of the subject under study.

The selected sample does not, therefore, follow any statistical guideline, but is instead based on the researcher's expertise.

Choice of the Sampling Technique

The choice between probability and non-probability methods of sampling is dependent on the following:

Kind of information needed   If the information is required at an aggregate level, such as the percentage of users of a product category or a brand, or total consumption, non-probability methods will provide adequately accurate information.

Error tolerance accepted   If the population parameter estimates are required to be highly accurate (e.g., sales forecast for a particular quarter), it is better to use probability sampling.

Likely size of non-sampling errors   Non-probability sampling is likely to provide a more representative sample if the non-sampling errors are expected to be high.

For example, in a survey of general practitioners, a probability sample is likely to include doctors with large as well as very small practice. If the objective is to ascertain the doctor's experience with a new medical formulation in the market, such a sample will not be as informative as a purposively selected sample of doctors with a large practice, who would have had more opportunity to prescribe the formulation and observe its efficacy.

Homogeneity of population If a population is reasonably homogeneous, the impact of the selection bias that is inherent in a non-probability sample is likely to be minimized. On the other hand, in a heterogeneous population, a probability sample is more likely to be representative, since it is likely to include respondent units representing all the variations in the population.

Cost of errors The high cost of errors suggests the need for minimizing selection bias and the ability to control sampling error. A probability sample is, therefore, most suitable in such a situation. For instance, if an organization is interested in estimating the usage rates of a new product, the proposed investments in manufacturing and marketing will be high. In such a case, it is safer to adopt probability sampling to obtain reliable estimates.

In sum, if non-sampling errors are expected to be high, non-probability sampling methods are more suitable. In case large sampling errors are expected, probability sampling should be used.

Both probability and non-probability methods of sampling include a large number of techniques, as shown in Fig. 9.2. They have been discussed in some detail later in this chapter.

PROBABILITY SAMPLING TECHNIQUES

Certain probability sampling techniques have been discussed here.

Random sampling

This method of sampling selects *n* units from a population in such a way that each of these units and, therefore, every one of the possible samples, has a predefined

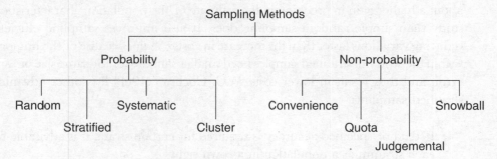

Fig. 9.2 Traditional Sampling Methods

probability of being selected. *Simple random sampling* is a special case where each unit and each possible sample has an *equal* probability of selection. This is the most commonly used method of random sampling when there is no extraneous reason to assign greater probability of selection to some units.

The implementation of the simple random sampling method is quite straightforward. The units in the population may be assigned an identification number each, and this number may be written on a piece of paper and put in a bowl. These slips of paper are then mixed thoroughly and the required number of slips drawn out one at a time. In practice, the 'without replacement' method is followed. It is most important to ensure that the slips are mixed thoroughly. An alternative method for ensuring complete randomization is to use random number tables. In spite of their limitations, 'random samples are always preferred as only random samples permit statistical inference'. Aaker et al. (1999) have explained the use of this method in detail.

Sometimes it is better to use the random sampling method with *unequal* probabilities of selection. For example, in the case of general practitioners discussed earlier, a solution would be to ascertain the doctor's experience in years, and assign a greater probability of selection to those with greater experience, following some selection rule. In practice, other methods of sampling are often preferable to random sampling, which may be non-representative, time-consuming, and/or expensive.

Stratified sampling

This is a special case of random sampling. In this case, the total population is divided into strata that are internally homogeneous with respect to the characteristic being studied, and as distinct as possible from the other strata. A random sample is selected from within each stratum such that these sub-samples together constitute the total sample. For example, the entire student population in a business school may be divided into different strata that consist of classes—first year students from different divisions, second year students majoring in marketing, finance, human resources, or IT, part-time students in various classes, and so on. A random sample may then be drawn from each stratum in proportion to the class size.

This method minimizes the within-stratum variation and maximizes the between-strata variation to reduce the overall variation in the sample data. It, thus, brings about a higher gain in precision in the estimate of the population characteristic under study than simple random sampling does. It also improves sampling efficiency by reducing variations faster than the increase in costs. Again, because of the homogeneity within the stratum, stratified samples need smaller samples for the same size of sampling error, and thus result in lower costs. W.G. Cochran (1960) lists other advantages of stratified sampling.

• If data of specified accuracy is required for certain strata, it is advisable to treat each stratum as a population in its own right.

- Administrative convenience may dictate the use of stratification; e.g., the agency conducting the study may have field offices in different parts of the country, each of which can then conveniently be treated as a distinct stratum.
- Sampling problems may differ markedly in different parts of the population. For example, a bank might like to treat its corporate clients and retail clients as two separate strata, since the issues faced by them and their reactions to the bank's initiatives will be quite different.

The sample size in each stratum is usually decided on the basis of the following:

(i) *Within stratum variation* The greater the variation, the larger the sample will need to be, to take into account all the heterogeneity.

(ii) *The cost of sampling within each stratum* The sample size usually tends to be inversely proportionate to the sampling cost.

Sometimes the sample size in each stratum is taken to be proportional to the ratio of the stratum population to the total population.

Cluster sampling

Sampling literature defines 'sampling efficiency' as A/C, the ratio of the accuracy (A) desired to the sampling costs (C). Efficiency may be improved either by reducing costs or by improving accuracy. In cluster sampling, unlike in stratified sampling, sampling efficiency is improved by decreasing costs faster than improving accuracy. The method involves, quite unlike the case of stratified sampling, dividing the population into sub-groups, such that each sub-group or cluster represents as much as possible of the variation in the population. A random sample of sub-groups or clusters is then selected and all the units in the cluster are studied. In the extreme case, the sample may consist of just one cluster, since it is expected to represent all the heterogeneity present in the population. It is, thus, a very cost-effective method. For example, let us assume that a study is to be conducted in the city of Mumbai to determine the perception of second-year marketing students about job opportunities in the field of marketing research. The samples could be drawn in any one of the following ways:

- Second-year marketing students may be approached in all the 25-odd business schools in the city and a random sample of the required size may be drawn, treating the entire group as the relevant population. This is obviously a time-consuming and expensive method, and the researcher may be tempted to leave out schools located in far-flung areas or those known to have small numbers of such students. Moreover, it does not provide any additional accuracy compared to the other methods that we will examine later.
- Each of the classes of the second-year marketing students in the various business schools may be treated as a stratum, and a simple random sample of a size

proportional to the class size may be drawn from it, adding up to the total sample of the required size. This method will provide better accuracy if there is reason to believe that perceptions on the subject vary from school to school. It will, however, not provide any saving in time or cost.

- The classes of the second-year marketing students in the various business schools may be treated as clusters if there is reason to believe that opinions on the subject among students of each school may be equally divergent. In such a case, depending on the required sample size, classes in a few schools may be selected and studied in their entirety. If the required sample size is equivalent to the size of the class in any one school, then only one class may be studied. This cluster-sampling method obviously provides for a substantial saving in time and cost, provided the assumption of divergence of opinion is valid.

However, in practice, it is not usually possible to ensure that each cluster will represent all the variations in the population. Therefore, the method could result in imprecise samples. It is, therefore, used only when clusters representing the entire population can be identified with some acceptable degree of accuracy.

David G. Garson refers to *multi-stage sampling* as a version of cluster sampling, where the researcher divides the population into strata, samples the strata, then stratifies the samples, and then resamples, repeating the process until the ultimate sampling units are selected at the last of the hierarchical levels. When the strata are geographic units, this method is called *area sampling*. This method has been used extensively in agricultural studies, and many well-known retail audits in India, such as those conducted by the agency ORG–MARG, make use of this method.

Systematic sampling

Sometimes one comes across populations or sampling frames where the units appear to follow a certain order. Consider, for example, a telephone directory, the rooms in a hostel, or the houses in a lane that are numbered successively. If a sample is to be selected from such a population to study some characteristic unrelated with this ordering pattern, the *systematic sampling* method would deliver an efficient sample. This approach involves systematically spreading the sample through the list of population members (Aaker et al. 1999). In other words, to select a sample of n units from a population of size N, we take a unit at random from the first k units, such that $kn = N$, and every kth subsequent unit. Cochran (1960) lists the following advantages of a systematic sample:

- It is easier to draw such a sample and often easier to execute without mistakes.
- Intuitively, systematic sampling seems likely to be more precise than simple random sampling. In effect, it stratifies the population into n strata, which consist of the first k units, the second k units, and so on. We might, therefore, expect the systematic sample to be about as precise as the corresponding stratified sample with one

Table 9.2 Possible Systematic Samples with $N = 24$ and $k = 5$

Systematic Sample Number				
I	**II**	**III**	**IV**	**V**
1	6	11	16	21
2	7	12	17	22
3	8	13	18	23
4	9	14	19	24
5	10	15	20	

unit per stratum. The difference is that in a systematic sample the units all occur at the same relative position in the stratum, whereas in a stratified random sample the position in the stratum is determined separately by randomization within each stratum. The systematic sample is spread more evenly over the population This fact has sometimes made systematic sampling considerably more precise than stratified random sampling.

In practice, the population size N will not always be an exact multiple of k. In such a case, different systematic samples of size n from the same finite population may vary by one unit in size. Thus with $N = 24$ and $k = 5$, the number of units in the five possible samples will be as shown in Table 9.2.

It is, therefore, obvious that the reliability of systematic sampling is the highest in the case of finite populations, which are exact multiples of 'k', the sampling interval. Again, if there is any implicit or explicit ordering inherent in the data, systematic sampling will result in greater accuracy.

For example, in selecting a sample of customers arranged in the order of purchase volume, a systematic sample will necessarily include customers with low purchase volume as well as high purchase volume and will, therefore, result in a representative sample. In fact, it will produce results comparable to a stratified sample, where the customer population is stratified by purchase volume. Both methods will be more representative than simple random sampling.

Systematic sampling, however, tends to result in poor representativeness if the items are ordered in such a way as to produce a cyclical pattern. For example, it is known that in the city of Mumbai, road traffic is heaviest on Fridays and Mondays since transporters attempt to avoid the weekend hiatus. Therefore, in a survey aimed at assessing average daily road-transport tonnage, a systematic sample based on data collected every Friday or every Monday will certainly overestimate the average tonnage. This will also give rise to problems in estimating the population variance from the sample variance. This is one of the reasons systematic sampling finds limited use in practice, in spite of its advantages.

NON-PROBABILITY SAMPLING

Non-probability techniques have been discussed here.

Convenience sampling

Also referred to as 'availability sampling', convenience sampling is a method by which the respondents are selected on the basis of the interviewer's convenience, or on the basis of availability. For example, a study of attitudes towards self-employment among management students may be conducted among students from one or two business schools where the students are known to the interviewers.

Similarly, a retail study about the market share of a brand of biscuits may be conducted among shoppers at a specific store using the 'intercept' method, as the shoppers emerge from the store. Since it is not possible to select the sampling units on the basis of predefined parameters, this method suffers from serious selection bias, and most authors and researchers warn against it. Aaker et al. (1999) have referred to it as 'indefensible'.

At the same time, it has been accepted that convenience sampling is a useful method for assessing quick reactions to any concept, or for pre-testing questionnaires. A useful variant is to select sampling units at the interviewer's convenience from a well-defined, well-structured sampling frame.

Quota sampling

This method is similar to convenience sampling in that units are selected at the interviewer's convenience, with the constraint that the population is divided into strata on the basis of some control variables, and the proportionality of the sample by strata is preserved. This method, thus, results in samples that are more representative of the population. Representativeness can be improved if care is taken to ensure the following:

- The controls are recent. For example, in a quota sample stratified by age groups, care may be taken to use the latest census figures as the basis.
- The controls are easy to use.
- The controls are closely related to variables under study. For example, in a study to determine the consumption of alcohol among different age groups, it is not meaningful to stratify the population by income groups.
- The controls result in a reasonable number of strata.

Judgement sampling

This is another variant of convenience sampling, where the units are selected on the basis of the interviewer's judgement to ensure a better quality of response. For example, the interviewees may be experts in a field. Depending on the interviewer's expertise and familiarity with the subject, this method may, at times, result in smaller sampling errors than simple random sampling, especially for small samples.

Snowball sampling

Also called 'chain referral sampling', snowball sampling is a method of sampling in which the first unit may be selected at random or on the basis of the interviewer's judgement. The next unit is referred by the first, the third unit may be referred by the first or the second, and so on. This method is appropriate and very efficient when it is necessary to reach small, specialized populations. For example, in a study to determine the initial response, it may be used to identify housewives who have tried a newly introduced brand of household detergent.

This information may not be available from either the manufacturer or the retailer, and the population of household detergent users is too vast to throw up a reasonable probability of identifying the users of a new brand. On the other hand, since housewives tend to exchange notes on such matters, a user is likely to be able to provide referrals. The method obviously suffers from serious selection bias since most of the respondents would be known to each other. This should be balanced against its cost and time efficiency.

DETERMINING THE SAMPLE SIZE

The purpose of sampling is to obtain data that is representative of the population, without having to incur the time and cost involved in studying the entire population. It is, therefore, essential to choose a sample that is large enough to approximate all the variation likely in the population and, yet, small enough to provide significant savings in cost and time.

The size of the sample depends on the following four factors:

- The number of groups and sub-groups within the sample that will be studied separately. The sample size for each of these sub-groups should be large enough to provide for an accurate analysis.

- The importance or the value of the information required from the study. If the information required is not very important, it may not be necessary to conduct the study at all. On the other hand, if the information required is extremely important and, therefore, needs to be accurate, it will need a sample size large enough to be representative.

- The cost involved. As mentioned on many occasions, the size of the sample is always the result of a trade-off between the cost of the study and the utility of the study. The lower the cost of the study, the larger the size of the sample that may be considered.

- The extent of variation in the population data. The greater the variation, the larger the sample needs to be in order to capture all the variation.

There are many ad hoc methods which provide reasonably good bases for arriving at the appropriate sample size. In addition, statistical theory provides two distinct methods for determining the size of the sample—the traditional or the *Neyman–Pearson approach*, and the *Bayesian approach*.

Ad hoc Methods

Ad hoc methods of arriving at a sample size have been discussed in the following paragraphs.

Rule of thumb   A common rule of thumb that provides the upper and lower boundaries for the size of the sample is to select a 1 per cent sample from a finite population, provided this results in a sample size of at least 25 to 30. This would improve the representativeness of the sample. In practice, a sample would usually include sub-groups that need to be compared with each other with regard to the characteristic being studied.

Each of these sub-groups should contribute a sample that is large enough to be meaningful in itself. For example, in a study of the usage patterns and frequency of usage of a beverage brand, it is usual to compare the frequency and usage patterns between heavy, medium, and light users. These three sub-groups should each consist of sub-samples of at least 25 to 30 each by the same logic, providing for meaningful comparisons.

If the population is large enough to asymptote to normality, the traditional Neyman–Pearson method for determining sample size discussed later may be used.

Budgetary constraints   One of the reasons behind sampling, as we have seen, is to reduce the costs that would be incurred in complete enumeration. This is of even greater significance if the budget for the study is limited, especially since the costs of the study cannot be reduced below a certain level. The option, then, is to settle for a sample size that can be accommodated within the given budget. If this results in too small a sample, it might be better not to undertake the study at all.

Time constraints   The influence of time constraints on the sample size is similar to budgetary constraints.

Comparable studies   Aaker et al. (1999) have listed this as another ad hoc method of determining the sample size. If it is possible to locate similar studies, their sample size may be taken as a guide in determining the sample size for the new study. This method is particularly useful in longitudinal studies, studies of the same product over two points in time, or studies of the same product with two comparable but distinct populations.

The Neyman–Pearson Approach

This approach involves two methods—the *confidence interval* method, which is used most commonly, and the *hypothesis testing* method. Let us first define some symbols before we discuss the two methods.

- population mean (or any other measure being considered) μ
- sample mean m
- population standard deviation σ
- sample standard deviation s
- standard error σ_m
- sample size n
- confidence interval [$m \pm$ *standard error*]

The confidence interval method   Basic statistics will tell us that any sample drawn from the population will have a sample average, m, close to but not exactly the same as the population average. As such, the means of various samples drawn from a population will also vary from each other. This variation in the sample average is measured by *standard error* σ_m. In other words, standard error may be referred to as the standard deviation of the frequency distribution of the sample means m.

Also, the larger the variation in the population, the larger will be the variation in the sample. As the sample size increases, this variation reduces, since more population units are included in the sample and the extreme values tend to average out. The standard error of m is thus a ratio of the population standard deviation, σ, to the sample size.

$$\sigma_m = \sigma_x / \sqrt{n} \tag{1}$$

A representative sample should provide an estimate m of the population characteristic μ such that μ may be expected with a specific degree of confidence to lie within a certain range of m. This range or interval would be defined as m plus or minus some multiple of the standard error, i.e., μ will be expected to lie in the interval $m \pm z$ (*standard error*), where z is the specified multiple.

How is this multiple z to be defined?

If μ is expected to be in the interval $m \pm z$ (*standard error*) with, say, 95 per cent confidence, i.e., if it is desired that in at least 95 out of 100 samples drawn, the value

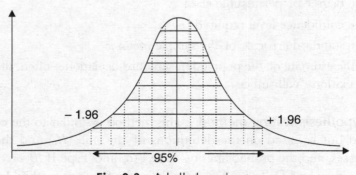

Fig. 9.3 A bell-shaped curve

of μ should be within this interval, and the population is assumed to be normally distributed, we may say that the probability of this event is 95 per cent.

$$P[m \pm z \ (standard \ error)] = 95\% \qquad (2)$$

In other words, this interval will cover 95 per cent of the area under the normal curve, i.e., the familiar bell-shaped curve shown in Fig. 9.3.

The values of the variable x (or z) that provide the boundaries of this interval are -1.96 and $+1.96$. We may then rewrite Eqn (2) as

$$P[m \pm 1.96 \ (standard \ error \ \sigma_m)] = 95\% \qquad (3)$$

This is the '95 per cent confidence interval' of m.

If the acceptable deviation of m from μ is specified as E, then we have another interval for μ :

$$m \pm E \qquad (4)$$

Putting Eqns (3) and (4) together, we get, at 95 per cent confidence level,

$$E = 1.96\sigma_m \qquad (5)$$

Substituting from Eqn (1), we have

$$E = 1.96\sigma_x/\sqrt{n}$$

So that the sample size is obtained as

$$n = (1.96\sigma_x /E)^2 \qquad (6)$$

In sum, this method provides for the determination of the sample size, given information on the following:

- the degree of permissible error E
- the confidence level required
- the standard error σ_m of the sample mean m
- some estimate of the population standard deviation—often, the sample standard deviation s will suffice

The hypothesis testing method   This method is similar to the confidence interval method but is based on the definitions of the null (H_0) and the alternative (H_1) hypotheses, and the probabilities of Type I (α) and Type II (β) errors associated with it. P.E. Green and D. Tull (1978) have defined a five-step method for determining the sample size on this basis.

A Question of Accuracy

Let us now study the requirements of a product manager who wants to estimate the trial rate for his newly launched brand of toilet soap in the market. The agency he approaches asks him how accurate he would expect the estimate to be, considering that a sample survey will not provide 100 per cent accuracy. The product manager indicates he would be satisfied if the sample response is 5 per cent less or more than the actual figure (degree of permissible error E).

The agency representative hums and haws a bit, and then says, 'Sorry, but we cannot guarantee that just any sample we draw from the population of users will give you that kind of accuracy. With the best of intentions and effort, samples are samples, and not all will be equally representative, you know.'

A little annoyed at this string of ifs and buts when all he expects is a reasonably reliable estimate of the trial rate, the product manager answers that he will be willing to take the chance if the agency can at least deliver this accuracy in 95 out of 100 cases (confidence level).

The agency representative looks sheepish, and mumbles, 'Yes, that 95 per cent level confidence in the sample accuracy would give us a standard error of 1.96σ.'

'What does that mean?' asks the befuddled product manager. He has never heard of 'standard' vs 'non-standard' errors.

The agency man quickly draws a bell-shaped curve on a piece of paper and explains the concept. In effect, he says, it means there is a 95 per cent probability that the sample measure of the trial rate will fall within ± 1.96 times the population standard deviation σ.

The product manager thinks he has understood, when the agency representative mumbles again, 'But...'

The product manager is aghast. 'Now what?' he splutters.

The agency man indicates that a difficulty has appeared that is common to all problems in the estimation of sample size—the sample size n depends some property of the population from which the sample is to be drawn. In this case, it is some estimate or 'guestimate' of the extent of variation, or the standard deviation σ_x. Is the product manager in a position to provide some such estimate?

The product manager is amused, 'So you are asking me to provide an estimate of the measure that I want you to estimate? Well, on the basis of our experience with similar products in the past, I would be very surprised if the trial rate varied by more than 30 per cent from sample to sample. Yes, you may take your standard error as 0.3.'

This information is enough to calculate the sample size, assuming that the population is normally distributed. From Eqn (6)

$$n = (1.96\sigma_x/E)^2$$

If the permissible error $E = 0.05$ and the product manager has given the value of σ_x as 0.3, we get a sample size of 138. If the z value is extended to 2, instead of 1.96, in the interest of greater rigour, the sample size increases to 144.

1. Specify the values of m under hypotheses H_0 and H_1.
2. Specify the acceptable probabilities of the two types of error α and β.
3. Determine the standard errors corresponding to these probabilities.
4. Provide some estimate of the population standard deviation σ.
5. Calculate the sample size that meets the α and β error requirements by defining the critical values (CV) as

$$(\mu_0 + Z_\alpha \sigma / \sqrt{n}) = \mathrm{CV} = (\mu_1 - Z_\beta \sigma / \sqrt{n}),$$

$$n = \frac{(Z_a + Z_\beta)^2 \sigma^2}{(\mu_1 - \mu_0)^2}$$

These methods can, similarly, be used to determine the sample size for other measures such as proportions just as for means. The confidence interval method is easier to use and, thus, more popular, although the hypothesis testing method takes care of both α and β errors and is, therefore, more rigorous. It suffers from the additional limitation of needing an exact, focused specification of the alternative hypothesis H_1.

The Bayesian Approach

In sample size determination, the Bayesian approach differs from all other methods discussed earlier in that it takes sampling costs explicitly into account in the process. Following the concept of the 'expected payoff' discussed in Chapter 2, the size of the sample under this approach is based on the principle that the ideal sample is one that results in maximum expected net gain from sampling. The process of determining the sample size then consists of:

- determining the expected value of information from samples of various sizes, as discussed in Chapter 2
- estimating the cost of obtaining each of these samples
- calculating the net gain from the information obtained from each sample
- choosing the sample that provides the largest gain

This method thus provides the optimal balance between sampling costs and the information obtained. Even so, its complexity restricts its use in the process of sample size determination. In stratified sampling, this complexity increases manifold since the size of each sub-sample has to be determined using this approach under the limitations of the total budget and the total sample size.

SUMMARY

The need for sampling arises in order to save on time and cost, and to minimize the repetition involved in obtaining the same underlying patterns in a population. Sampling also provides greater flexibility than does a complete census. If the data is complex, it may provide greater accuracy as well. The size of the sub-group appropriate for providing an accurate representation of the population varies with the degree of heterogeneity in the data. The process of sample selection has to go through various stages—defining the population, identifying the sampling frame, defining the sampling unit and the sample element, choosing the sampling method, estimating the sample size, and determining the sampling plan. The choice of the sampling method is one of the most crucial decisions in the sampling process. Sampling methods are divided into two broad categories—probability sampling and non-probability sampling. Under probability sampling, the units in the sample are selected randomly, with each unit of the population being assigned a certain non-zero probability of inclusion in the sample. In non-probability sampling, the units are chosen on the basis of criteria such as the researcher's familiarity with the units or the ease of availability. The choice between the two categories of sampling methods depends on the accuracy desired, the time and funds available, the extent of selection bias permissible, and the basic purpose of the study. The major methods of probability sampling are simple random sampling, stratified sampling, cluster sampling, and systematic sampling. Convenience sampling, quota sampling, judgemental sampling, and snowball sampling are the frequently used non-probability methods of sampling.

The choice of the sample size is another crucial decision in the sampling process. The factors on which this choice depends include the degree of heterogeneity in the population, the number of sub-groups explicitly required to be studied, the value or importance of the information to be obtained, the time available for the fieldwork, and the cost of the study. Sampling methods are divided into two broad categories. The ad hoc methods include the rule of thumb, choices based on budget considerations, time constraints, and sample size used in comparable studies, and the traditional methods include the Neyman–Pearson approach and the Bayesian approach. Both these methods assume that the population from which the sample is to be drawn is normally distributed. The Neyman–Pearson approach again includes two methods—the confidence interval approach and the hypothesis testing method. The Bayesian method is the only method that takes the cost of sampling explicitly into account. Under this method, the optimal sample size is the one that maximizes the net expected gain from sampling.

KEY WORDS

Sample refers to a part or sub-group of a population that displays the same characteristics as the population.

Census refers to the complete enumeration of a population with regard to the presence of the characteristic under study.

Sampling unit refers to the sub-group within a sample that includes the sampling element.

Sampling element refers to a particular member of the sampling unit from which data regarding the study is obtained.

Sampling frame refers to the detailed record or the list of members of a population that provides the basis for selecting the sample.

Sampling plan refers to the operational framework for selecting the sample and implementing the fieldwork.

Probability sampling refers to a sampling method in which each unit in the population has a definite, non-zero chance of selection in the sample, following some objective statistical rule.

Non-probability sampling refers to a sampling method in which the selection of the sample is based on such criteria as convenience, time, cost, and the researcher's perception of the respondent's knowledge of the subject under study.

Error tolerance refers to the extent of acceptable variation of the sample estimate from the actual population value.

Random sampling refers to the method of selecting *n* units from a population in a way that each of these units and, therefore, every one of the possible samples has a predefined probability of being selected.

Stratified sampling refers to a special version of random sampling in which a random sample is selected from within each of the internally homogeneous, distinct strata into which the total population is divided.

Cluster sampling refers to the method of dividing the population into sub-groups, such that each sub-group or cluster represents as much as possible of the variation in the population. One or a few of these clusters are selected in the sample and studied completely.

Systematic sampling refers to a probability sample selected from a population where the units appear in a certain pre-specified order.

Multi-stage sampling refers to a version of cluster sampling in which 'the researcher divides the population into strata, samples the strata, then stratifies the samples, and then resamples, repeating the process until the ultimate sampling units are selected at the last of the hierarchical levels'.

Sampling efficiency refers to the ratio of accuracy of sampling results to the cost of drawing the sample.

Convenience sampling refers to the method by which the respondents are selected on the basis of the interviewer's convenience or on the basis of availability.

Quota sampling refers to a variant of convenience sampling in which the sample is divided into strata, and sub-samples are selected from each stratum to be proportionate in size to the size of the stratum.

Judgement sampling refers to another variant of convenience sampling, where the units are selected on the basis of the interviewer's judgement to ensure a better quality response.

Snowball sampling refers to a method of sampling in which the first unit may be selected at random or on the basis of the interviewer's judgement; the next unit is referred by the first; the third unit may be referred by the first or the second; and so on.

Permissible error refers to the degree of variation of the sample estimate from the popula-tion parameter that is acceptable for the results of the study to be considered valid.

Confidence interval refers to the interval within which the sample estimate may be expected to deviate from the population parameter with a given degree of confidence.

Standard error of the mean refers to the average variation in the sample average obtained from a large number of samples from a population.

CONCEPT REVIEW QUESTIONS

1. Distinguish between
   - population and sampling frame
   - standard deviation and standard error
   - stratified sampling and quota sampling
   - the Bayesian approach and the ad hoc approach based on budgetary considerations for determining the sample size
   - systematic sampling and cluster sampling

2. Why is a snowball sample not treated as a probability sample, even if the first unit is selected at random?

3. How would you choose between probability sampling and non-probability sampling?

4. What advantages does the confidence interval approach offer over the hypothesis testing approach?

5. What are the limitations of convenience sampling?

CRITICAL THINKING EXERCISES

1. An NGO promoting entrepreneurship wants to interview final year management students in the city of Mumbai to determine their attitude to self-employment. Assuming there are 5,000 students in the final year, spread over 30 business schools across the city, how would you arrive at a suitable sample size for the study? What method of sampling would you use? Why?

2. In the above study, suppose you are required to complete data collection within a week and you decide there is no way to do so using probability sampling methods. You decide to use a non-probability method. You are able to obtain detailed lists of the students, with information about their age, gender, grades, family income, and prior work experience. How would you arrive at a reasonably reliable sample?

3. Company XYZ, a major manufacturer of soft drinks, is considering introducing its leading brand of soft drink in flavours other than orange. It has already developed a new, mixed fruit flavour that it would like to test for acceptance of taste. It has 4,000 employees in its plant where the drink is usually produced. It decides to conduct the taste test on them, providing each of them with a sample of the new flavour and a brief, structured questionnaire to determine their feedback. The employees will also be given a free 200 ml pack of the drink (worth approximately Rs 10) as payment for participating in the study. Give your comments on the appropriateness of the methodology and the reliability of the sample.

PROJECT ASSIGNMENT

In the previous chapter you were asked to plan a study to determine the market potential for a postgraduate programme in retail management. Whom would you interview for this purpose? Specify the most appropriate sampling technique for selecting a sample for the study, and give your reasons for this choice. Determine the appropriate sample size and indicate the assumptions under which you arrive at that size.

REFERENCES

Aaker, D., V. Kumar, and G.S. Day 1999, *Marketing Research,* Sixth edition, Wiley & Sons.

Cochran, W.G. 1960, *Sampling Techniques,* Asia Publishing House, Mumbai.

Garson, David G., http://www2.chass.ncsv.edu/garson/pa765/index.htm, Multivariate Analysis in Public Administration; North Carolina State University, Raleigh.

Green, Paul E. and D. Tull 1978, *Research for Marketing Decisions,* Prentice-Hall, pp. 204–236.

Kish, Leslie 1965, *Survey Sampling,* John Wiley, New York.

List, Dennis 2005, *Know Your Audience: A Practical Guide to Media Research,* Original Books, New Zealand.

10 Designing Questionnaires and Interview Guides

After reading this chapter, the readers will be able to understand:

- the importance of a well-designed questionnaire
- the funnel approach
- the categories of questions and how to choose between them
- how to avoid errors
- mail, telephone, and Internet surveys
- how to collect data from in-depth interviews
- what to look out for when reproducing a questionnaire

INTRODUCTION

It is said that a survey is only as good as the questionnaire that it uses to collect data. This postulate flows logically from the need for a survey, the primary purpose of which is to collect data to examine hypotheses. To this extent, a questionnaire that is used for collecting data, acts as a means of communication.

Communication theory tells us that for communication to actually take place, the message from the sender must be received by the recipient as it was intended, and the response by the recipient must also be understood by the sender exactly as it was meant. As Deborah Tannen, author of the best-selling books, *That's Not What I Meant* (1986) and *You Just Don't Understand* (1985), says, 'Questions, like everything we say, work on two levels at once: the message and the metamessage'. She also states that 'Information conveyed by the meaning of words is the social message', in other words, communication is embedded in the social context. Therefore, while the social context, influences the possibility of communication taking place, this possibility is certainly enhanced by the choice of the language used and the ease of its interpretation. If the questionnaire is to address survey needs adequately and appropriately, it must comprise questions that take into account the language as well as the social context. This would provide the right kind of information, thus improving the value of marketing research.

In addition to language and context, 'well-defined goals are the best way to assure a good questionnaire design. When the goals of a study can be expressed in a few clear and concise sentences, the design of the questionnaire becomes considerably easier. The questionnaire is developed to directly address the goals of the study'. A well-designed questionnaire also helps improve the internal consistency of data.

It goes without saying that the subject matter, as well as the structure of the questionnaire, must interest and involve the respondent, without putting the person on the defensive or creating a bias. This suggests the use of the 'funnel approach', discussed in this chapter. In addition, this chapter discusses the issue of the length of a questionnaire. A long questionnaire is less likely to be answered fully than a short questionnaire, i.e., a long questionnaire has greater chances of non-response. The relative merits of both long and short questionnaires have been discussed.

A later section in this chapter elaborates on the various categories of questions and the choice of the right question. This section is primarily concerned with the role of the appropriate question in minimizing errors in data collection. It discusses the ways and means of avoiding and minimizing errors, especially the flow chart approach to questionnaire formation.

The purpose behind the study, i.e., the way the information provided by the study is to be used, governs the format of the questionnaire and the degree of structure appropriate for it. A standardized or reasonably structured questionnaire, according to N.K. Malhotra (2004), 'will ensure comparability of the data, increase speed and accuracy of recording, and facilitate data processing'. When the study aims primarily at exploration—attempting to understand the consumer's persona or to climb into the consumer's mind—detailed information can only be obtained from an unstructured and conversational style of questioning, so that the thoughts of the respondent may be expressed without being constrained by the framework of the question. This chapter also discusses interview guides that are most appropriate for this purpose and also goes on to talk of the modifications required in the structure of a questionnaire if the data is to be collected telephonically, through mail, or through an Internet survey.

DESIGNING A QUESTIONNAIRE

A new researcher, when presented with a marketing research project, is very tempted to rush into preparing a questionnaire. No scientific theories or rules govern the development of the 'ideal' questionnaire; developing a questionnaire is an experience-based skill. Yet, a questionnaire can never be a stand-alone exercise; it can be developed only in the context of the management decision required, the definition of the marketing research problem, and the research design. In order to develop an understanding of the process of questionnaire formulation, we will revisit the following three stages in designing research:

(i) understanding the management dilemma, i.e., the marketing problem: What is it that the management needs an answer to?

(ii) definition of the marketing research problem: What is the specific information to be obtained in order to help solve the management dilemma? (The information may pertain to the extent of knowledge the respondent has relating

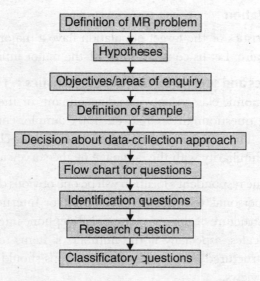

Fig. 10.1   Flowchart for Questionnaire Design

to the marketing issue being explored, or to respondent's attitudes and opinions on a specific subject, or a combination of the two).

(iii)   The research design: From whom is the information to be obtained? What will be the particular medium of data collection (face-to-face, telephonic, mail, or Internet interviews) and the specific interview approach—structured vs unstructured, disguised vs non-disguised, etc.? In a face-to-face or personal interview, the respondent has physical access to the interviewer and any clarifications required may be obtained easily. Mail surveys require short and close-ended questions.

The answers to these questions provide a framework for the development of the questionnaire. This process, as depicted in Fig. 10.1, has to take into account the type of information needed, as well as issues such as the target population, the type of questions to be asked, the order of questions, and the content of questions. This section examines the question of the target population and discusses in detail the choice of the type of questions in a questionnaire. The last two, i.e., the order and content of questions, have been discussed in a later part of this chapter.

The type of information needed

It is always useful to make a detailed list, in advance, of the exact information required from the survey. This helps define the kind of questions needed to be asked; the order of questions; the structure of questions—open-ended, dichotomous, or multiple-choice; whether a single question is enough to obtain information on an item or more than one question is required to get complete information on it; etc.

Target population

The characteristics of the target population have a major influence on the design of the questionnaire. Let us consider some of the major influencing characteristics.

Demographics and socio-economic characteristics   The respondent's age, gender, and socio-economic class are obvious determinants of the complexity, language, and length of the questionnaire. Children, for example, can rarely be subjected to a questionnaire. The education levels and socio-economic class will often determine the respondent's familiarity with the language of the survey and the choice of words.

Location   The respondent's location will be one obvious determinant of the interview method, i.e., personal, telephonic, mail, e-mail, or Internet survey. This, in turn, will influence the structure of the questionnaire. Telephone interviews, for example, cannot use ranking scales, especially if the number of items to be ranked exceeds three. Similarly, unstructured and open-ended questions should not be used much in non-personal interviews.

Occupational status   The absence of working women from home during the day may make it difficult to personally administer a questionnaire, especially in a time-bound survey. This will influence the choice of the survey method—self-administered questionnaires that may be left behind with the respondent, or telephonic, Internet, e-mail, or mail surveys.

Type of questions

In Chapter 6, we had discussed three types of questions—dichotomous, multiple-choice, and open-ended. Scales are one form of multiple-choice questions that are used extensively for quantifying qualitative data or for classification of data into categories. They are discussed in detail in the next chapter. An introduction to the concept of scales will be given later in this chapter. In designing a questionnaire, one major dilemma is to decide which form of question is most suitable in a given situation. The following are the influencing factors.

Relevance to the information sought   *Structured questions* of the dichotomous or the multiple-choice type are most suited to questions relating to behaviour. They provide satisfactory answers to the 'what', 'when', 'how', 'how much', and 'where' aspects of the information required, but usually not to the 'why' issues, which involve the exploration of perceptions and attitudes. These issues require the use of open-ended questions, and of 'probes'. *Probes* are questions that aim at delving deeper into a research issue; they follow the initial question. They may not be built into the questionnaire but will need to be framed on the spot by the investigator to take the respondent through the entire process of describing an experience, the reasons for a relationship with a brand, and so on. They have to be necessarily non-directive, but aimed at eliciting information from the respondent in an indirect and conversational manner.

For example, let us consider a survey on cigarettes, the purpose of which is to determine the smoker's reasons for preferring a particular brand. After identifying the respondent's preferred brand, the researcher needs to further explore the brand perceptions and reasons for brand preference. The questions in this case may be as follows.

- *Which brand of cigarette do you usually smoke?*
  The response may be
  (a) *(Brand A, B, C, ...)* or (b) <u>No fixed brand</u> (In case of non-regular smokers)
- *While selecting a brand, what do you look for?*
  This question may be designed as a structured multiple-choice question, with various desired benefits and attributes listed, such as:
  - *Taste*
  - *Strength*
  - *Price*
  - *Brand reputation*
  - *Company reputation*
  - *Kind of tobacco*
  - *Presence of filter*
  - *Price*
  - *Advertising*
  - *Popularity among my peers*
  - *Others (Please specify)*

This would appear to be quite an exhaustive list but it does not explore the image of the brand in the respondent's mind or the relationship of the brand with the smoker.

Alternatively, the question may be left open-ended and, depending on the answer provided by the respondent, the researcher may frame the next question to 'probe', i.e., explore deeper into the matter. This involves an attempt at getting more detailed answers from the respondent, and assessing what the brand stands for in the respondent's mind. Some examples of the image dimensions that may be explored are 'a macho image', 'sophistication', 'unconventional', 'cool', 'youthful and trendy', 'relieves tension', and so on. This information cannot be derived from a structured list but requires the researcher to lead the respondent into a description of brand usefulness.

Respondent profile   The demographic characteristics of the respondent, such as age, literacy, occupation, and familiarity with the language in which the interview is being conducted are all factors that should be taken into account while designing the questionnaire since they influence the respondent's ability to understand and answer the questions in detail.

Location The location of the interview should be kept in mind since it influences the length of the questionnaire, i.e., how many questions may be asked as well as the form of the questions. In an 'intercept' interview at a shopping centre or a movie hall, long questionnaires or questionnaires with many open-ended questions will not elicit detailed answers and many questions may go unanswered.

Similarly, interviews at the respondent's work place need to be designed keeping in mind the limited amount of time the respondent will be able to spare, even with a prior appointment, and the frequent interruptions that are likely to be the norm during the interview. It is, therefore, necessary to include short and clearly worded questions in the questionnaires for such interviews. If it is necessary to ask the respondent open-ended and probing questions, it helps to divide the questionnaire into various parts and ensure that the open-ended questions are administered first, through a face-to-face interview. The structured parts may then be left with the respondent for collection later, or may even be mailed or e-mailed to the respondent.

Focus groups aim at eliciting spontaneous responses from respondents in a group setting. They need to be conducted in informal surroundings where the respondents may be able to relax and share their experiences and ideas. Also, the questions from the moderator in a focus group discussion (FGD) need to be few, short, and non-directive.

ERRORS IN QUESTIONNAIRE DESIGN AND THE FLOW CHART

The issue of the 'type' of questions to be included in a questionnaire inevitably leads to a consideration of the order in which the questions should be asked and the content of the questions. All three must be dealt with in detail when designing a comprehensive and useful questionnaire that is convenient to administer and analyse.

The Order of Questions

In developing a questionnaire, the sequence of questions is important. Each question that is asked must relate to the others in the questionnaire, especially to the question that follows.

The funnel approach The questions should proceed from the general to the specific. The initial questions are aimed at building a rapport with the respondent and putting the person at ease. They should introduce the respondent to the broad area of enquiry, generate an interest in the study, and gradually lead to the queries relating to specific information. According to D.R. Cooper and P.S. Schindler (1998), in their book *Business Research Methods*, 'The objectives of this procedure are to learn the respondent's frame of reference and to extract the full range of desired information while limiting the distortion effect of earlier questions on later ones.'

Moreover, it is important not to confront the respondent early in the questionnaire with questions that require a great deal of complex information. The questioning process should begin with simple queries and then gradually move on to the more complex and specific ones. It is useful practice to start with dichotomous or multiple-choice questions, which are easier to understand and answer than open-ended questions.

Classificatory questions   The questions included in a questionnaire can be divided into three parts—*identification questions,* which obtain information on the name, address, telephone number, and e-mail address of the respondent for later reference; *research questions,* which relate to the specific purpose of the study and form the main body of the questionnaire; and *classificatory questions,* which qualify the respondent. Classificatory questions which provide information about the respondent's demographics, are the only kind that are invariably best asked at the end, for practical reasons. Such a sequence of questions in the questionnaire reduces the chances of a respondent's fatigue-linked non-response to questions specifically related to the research issue. In addition, some of the data required to be included in the classificatory list is usually already available to the researcher and the possibility of not having to obtain it again from the respondent does reduce respondent fatigue as well as investigator fatigue. This becomes even more relevant in a long questionnaire.

Flow chart   'Branched' questions, in which the response to a question determines the subsequent questions that will be asked, form an integral part of any questionnaire. Let us consider the following example:

Do you smoke (a) *cigarettes* (b) *cigars* (c) *bidis* (d) *others* (e) *nothing*

Q1. Investigator: *Go to Q2. if answer is (a), (b,) or (c), and to Q3. if the answer is (d). Terminate interview if the answer is (e).*

This is an example of a branched question that could lead to one of the three possible directions for the subsequent part of the interview. A typical questionnaire will include many such branched questions, which will divide responses and respondents into various categories, such as users vs non-users, users of one brand vs the other, and those intending to buy the brand in future vs those not intending to. In order to ensure a smooth flow while not repeating questions on the one hand and not leaving out important queries on the other hand, it is useful practice to prepare a rough flow chart of the questionnaire before developing the final version. For example, the preceding list of questions may be presented in a flow chart form as shown in Fig. 10.2.

It is good practice to prepare a similar flow chart of the entire questionnaire before writing it out in text form. Apart from ensuring proper coverage and a smooth flow of the order of questions, it also helps the fieldwork. It is annoying for the respondent to be faced with a question repeatedly if it has already been answered earlier, either directly, or in the process of elaborating on the response to another question.

Scales   In research, we are often interested in quantifying the characteristics of a variable that cannot be measured physically. For example, we may want to measure the public perception of a cricket team, the degree of preference for a brand, the

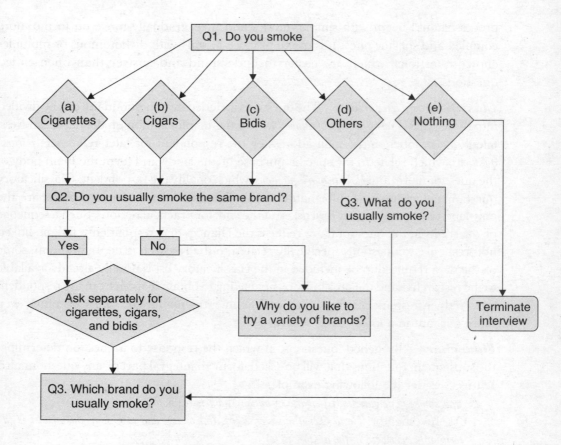

Fig. 10.2 A Part of a Questionnaire Depicted as a Flow Chart

relative market position of a brand in a product category, or even the growth of an economy. These characteristics are quantified by linking them to other, familiar concepts that are relatively easy to measure. For example, the growth of the economy may be measured by determining the change in the country's GDP over the years in question and the relative brand position may be determined by the market share of the brand. These measures, which attempt to assess the degree of presence of an intangible characteristic in the variable being studied, are called 'scales'.

The purpose of scaling is to measure a variable in such a way that it can be expressed on a continuum or a discrete category. In marketing research, scales are used most frequently to measure the direction (positive, negative, or neutral) and strength of attitudes. For example, in a consumer study of a brand of toilet soap, the extent of satisfaction, an intangible characteristic that cannot be measured physically, may be measured through a multiple-choice question that uses a scale along the 'satisfaction continuum'.

Q. How satisfied would you say you are with Brand 'X'? Please choose the option that best matches your opinion.

- *Highly satisfied* _____
- *Reasonably satisfied* _____
- *Not really satisfied*
  but not dissatisfied either _____
- *Rather dissatisfied* _____
- *Highly dissatisfied* _____

The choice of one of the options in this multiple-choice question will give the direction and the extent of satisfaction (or dissatisfaction) in the respondent's mind.

The Content of Questions

The actual text of the question must take into account the purpose of the question; the extent to which it needs to be disguised; the scope of the question (how much information it is expected to provide); and the wording of the question (the respondent's ability and willingness to answer it).

Purpose Every question included in a questionnaire must serve a specific purpose and provide definite information. In unstructured interviews, it is often necessary to ask questions that may not have a direct bearing on the subject of the interview but are aimed at creating a rapport with the respondent and leading the person in the general direction of the study. In a questionnaire, on the other hand, such 'conversational' questions should be avoided as far as possible. They should be reserved for explaining a preceding question to the respondent, if the need arises, i.e., for defining the meaning of a question in words the respondent may find easier to understand. If the original question has been framed properly and pre-tested, this necessity should not arise.

The need for disguise At times, disguise is necessary to reduce bias. The query to the respondent must be couched in general terms, without making the specific objective of the study too obvious. For example, in a study to determine the influence of price on the selection of brand X, a rather expensive brand, suppose the respondent is asked, '*How much does price influence your choice of brand X?*'

Such a direct question is likely to result in respondents understating the influence of price on their purchase. On the other hand, suppose the question is framed as, '*How would you rate these brands that you have used in terms of price?*'

	Exorbitant	*A bit expensive*	*Not worth the price*	*Reasonable*	*Good value for money*
Brand A	_____	_____	_____	_____	_____
Brand B	_____	_____	_____	_____	_____
Brand X	_____	_____	_____	_____	_____

A question that uses a scale is more likely to provide an unbiased answer since the respondent is now being cast in the role of an expert. In addition, being asked to compare three brands minimizes the respondent's need to be defensive about the price of Brand X.

In general, the decision about whether or not to disguise questions may be made depending on the following four situations.

- *When the respondent has the information at the conscious level and is willing to share it:* In such a case, the question need not be disguised.

- *When the respondent has the information and is aware of it, but is unwilling to share it:* For example, let us consider the case of a survey about live-in relationships. The respondent may have a definite though socially undesirable view on the issue but may not be willing to share it with the interviewer. In such a situation, a reliable response may be obtained by disguising the question or by using projective techniques to elicit a response.

- *When respondents have the information at the conscious level, but have not given it much thought:* At times, there are issues about which respondents may not have thought enough to take a definite stand. Environmental and political issues would form a frequent example of such cases. Asking a direct, undisguised question in such cases would motivate the respondent to express opinions that are not very strongly held and will, to that extent, lead to wrong estimates of the survey results. In such cases, it is best to use the in-depth interview approach, discussing the issue on a one-to-one basis with the respondent.

- *When respondents are not consciously aware of a subject, though they may have some opinion about it at a deeper level:* In such cases, it is best to use projective techniques for eliciting genuine respondent opinions.

Coverage/scope   The question should be worded in such a way that it will provide all the relevant information. For example,

(a) When trying to determine the reasons for behaviour or attitude, it is not enough to ask 'why'. Probing is required, and that may involve more than one question.

(b) Open-ended questions should be asked in a manner that they do not provide an opportunity for the respondent to restrict the answer to 'yes' or 'depends'.

(c) Questions need to be specific in order to elicit complete information. For example, if we are trying to establish the usage or brand preference for a household product, it is not enough to ask for the family's usage or preference because the various members of the family may use or prefer different brands. In answer to such a question, the respondent will, therefore, be likely to give incomplete information It is better to obtain such information by age groups and, if necessary, by gender of the household members.

(d) Multiple-choice questions in a questionnaire administered by the researcher pose a problem that the respondent may not always be able to remember all the options offered. The response will, therefore, be based on what the respondent remembers. The use of show-cards aids memory and facilitates easier and complete responses. The use of graphics is also a useful tool, particularly if the question is complex, or requires responses indicating difficult-to-verbalize reactions to an experience. They are also useful when interviewing children or people not very fluent in the language in which the interview is being conducted.

(e) It is always better not to assume that the respondent will definitely know or will take a definite stand on the subject of the interview. Filter questions that determine the awareness of the subject must be asked first, before the researcher plunges into a discussion of the topic with the respondent.

Willingness/ability of the respondent   Errors in primary data arise from the wording of a question that does not take into account the respondent's ability or willingness to answer the question. These include errors resulting from

- use of words that are unfamiliar to the respondent,
- imprecise or open-ended terms that may be interpreted differently by different respondents,
- leading questions,
- questions that use an unfamiliar framework, or ask for very old data,
- questions that ask for information regarded as private or personal by the respondent,
- inadequate alternatives in the case of multiple-choice questions,
- very long questions, or
- double-barrelled questions.

All these errors must be kept in mind while framing the questionnaire. In addition, a questionnaire must always be pre-tested before finally being administered in the field.

Pre-test   The pre-test is the administration of the questionnaire to a small sample of respondents, before it is finalized and used on the final sample. The purpose of the pre-test is not primarily to collect data but to check for suitability of the type of questions, the order in which they have been asked, their content, and the length of the questionnaire. We have seen earlier that the meaning of a question needs to be clear to the respondent if meaningful answers have to be obtained. For example, in a study to determine consumer perceptions of a software company, consider the question, *'How safe do the customers feel in dealing with the employees of the company?'* What does *safe* mean in the context of a software company? If the meaning of a question is not clear, the respondent will tend to modify it in a way that makes it easier to understand and respond to it accordingly. In this case, the respondent may interpret 'safety' as 'no hacking', or 'no inadvertent revelation of private information'.

It is equally important to determine whether the questionnaire will hold the respondent's interest till the end. Other things being equal, too long a questionnaire will lead to higher non-response rates. It is, therefore, essential to conduct the pre-test with a sample similar to the final sample. Management students often give in to the temptation to pre-test the questionnaire with their classmates or members of the family. This is acceptable only as long as these classmates or members of the family are similar to the members of the final sample—the very purpose of the pre-test is to determine how the members of the actual sample will respond to the questionnaire's language, structure, content, and length.

Another important point to remember is the size of the pre-test sample. Pre-testing with too small a sample is worse than no pre-test, since it might set the researcher off on a totally wrong track. Although there are no specified techniques for determining the correct size of a pre-test sample, according to Aaker, Kumar, and Day (1998) in their book, *Marketing Research*, a good rule of thumb is to use a sample of at least 15 if the questionnaire is short and direct, and at least 25 for a long or complex questionnaire.

The actual administration of the questionnaire and the care needed in the process is in the domain of fieldwork. This will be discussed in Chapter 12.

QUESTIONNAIRES FOR TELEPHONE AND INTERNET SURVEYS

One of the major limitations of the non-personal interviewing techniques, for example, by mail and Internet surveys, is the scope of misinterpretation of the questions. Therefore, while preparing questionnaires for mail/Internet surveys, it is important to

- use structured questions as far as possible.
- use graphics frequently, especially when attitudinal/perceptual response is being elicited. Not only does it break the monotony of the questionnaire, it also makes the choice of options being offered clear.
- use multiple-choice or dichotomous questions extensively even when graphics are not being used.
- use short questions in the interest of clarity.
- use 'why' questions with care and, preferably, as rarely as possible. Such questions are open to a variety of interpretations, as the following example will show.

Q. Why do you use brand 'X' of toilet soap?
A. I have always seen it being used in my family.
Or
A. It is good for my skin.
Or
A. My friend recommended it.
Or
A. It is good value for money.

The term 'why' can thus be interpreted as enquiring about loyalty levels, the source of influence, the benefits relevant to the respondent, or even the important product attributes. Since the interviewer is not present in a non-personal interview to explain the exact intent of the question to the respondent, all these possibilities must be anticipated while designing the questionnaire. It will be useful to ask four focused questions separately, rather than a single 'why' question, in order to ensure that the respondent does not get confused.

It is also important to keep the questionnaire brief. Response rates are known to be usually very low in non-personal interviews. In the absence of an interviewer to motivate and persuade the respondent, the chances of a questionnaire being left incomplete and not being returned go up in proportion to the length of the questionnaire.

There are two factors that should help improve the response rate to non-personal methods of interviewing.

Anonymity   In a mail/telephone/Internet survey, it is not essential for the respondents to reveal their identity any more than they wishes to. This cover of anonymity could help provide information regarding their perceptions, attitudes, and opinions about sensitive issues relatively more readily.

Ability to answer at leisure   A mail questionnaire or one on the Internet, unlike one administered by an interviewer, need not be answered all at once. The respondent may answer it in stages, as and when they desire. This should encourage more respondents to complete and return the questionnaire.

As a result, the coverage of the sample can be much higher in a mail/Internet survey at a proportionately lower unit cost. However, people who do not find the subject of the survey interesting have the freedom not to respond. Thus, the information obtained will not be from an unbiased sample—the sample responding and providing data is more likely to be one biased in favour of the subject. Multiple mailings to the same respondents might improve response rates somewhat, but it has been found that incremental improvement in response tapers off beyond three reminders.

Telephonic surveys suffer from the additional limitation that the respondent may disconnect at will. Therefore, in such an interview, it is essential to seek the respondent's permission before starting the interview. Keep the questionnaire brief and clear, and stay away from controversial topics.

PROJECTIVE TECHNIQUES AND INTERVIEW GUIDES

We had earlier discussed situations in which respondents may not have consciously thought about a subject despite being aware of it at a deeper level, or where respondents may be aware of the subject but unwilling to share their views with the interviewer. In such cases, projective techniques are the best means of eliciting information without putting the respondent on the defensive or being limited to socially desirable responses. These techniques were discussed in Chapter 8.

We have also noted that projective techniques require asking questions that will provide the respondent with the freedom to interpret the question as referring to a third person or a generalized situation, that 'takes the respondent outside of him/herself', so to speak. In such situations, the respondent's experience and attitudes are projected onto another, a 'third person', and the information is provided without going on the defensive. It is important while using this technique to present the questions in a truly neutral manner.

The structure of an interview guide differs from a formal questionnaire in many ways. For one, an interview guide does not include formal, structured, complete questions, but only a list of the areas of enquiry. Also, the interview guide used in projective techniques and in-depth interviews aims at obtaining information on all relevant issues but does not necessarily follow a predetermined order or structure of questions. The attempt is to follow the respondent's line of thought and even encourage the person to put in words thoughts, feelings, and motivations that may not have been consciously considered earlier. This might, at times, require the interviewer to follow the respondent into a labyrinth of thought processes and may necessitate asking for the same piece of information more than once, using different terms, to ensure that all 'links' to the conscious opinions and behaviour are explored fully. The order of enquiry in an interview guide, therefore, unlike in the case of a formal questionnaire, does not follow a predetermined flow but may require going back and forth on one issue. This might, on occasion, also necessitate completing an enquiry into one area and then reverting to an issue that has been discussed earlier.

Data collection when interviewing children

We have seen earlier that the format of the means of data collection is influenced significantly by the characteristics of the respondent population. The use of projective techniques is of special relevance when interviewing children. Children, typically, have a very short attention span. The use of projective techniques, based on interview guides, helps maintain their interest levels for an adequate length of time and increases the probability of spontaneous answers without their having to resort to help from parents, other adults, and peers. A projective method structured like a game, a riddle, or a story is more likely to get the children involved and produce genuine answers than a questionnaire, which might give an impression of an 'examination' and put children on the defensive. The methods of data collection when interviewing children, involve keeping the following points in mind.

(i) A significant amount of observation. A child's reaction to a situation, brand, or product category, as well as the interaction between the group of children being interviewed, requires a great deal of observation, i.e., a passive mode of data collection on the part of the interviewer.

(ii) Short and focused questions relating to the child's response to a specific situation that is part of an experience. Questions should not be asked about abstract situations.

(iii) Very limited questioning, supported by the creation of situations that give the children the opportunity to piggyback on each other's ideas and present innovative solutions to the marketing problem, which must be tacitly defined.

REPRODUCTION OF THE QUESTIONNAIRE

A secondary but influential characteristic of the interviewing instrument is its physical quality and visual appeal. This is particularly important in personal, specially self-administered interviews as well as in e-mail/Internet or mail surveys. Care needs to be taken to ensure that the questionnaire does not look like an advertisement. At the same time, all the care that is needed with the layout of an advertisement should be taken with a questionnaire as well to ensure that it draws the respondent into reading it. It should be well produced, and if it is printed, the quality of paper used should be good. Nothing puts off a respondent more than a smudged copy of a badly printed questionnaire, which is full of typographical errors. E-mail/Internet questionnaires need to be even more carefully designed since the entire initial impact of an Internet questionnaire is derived from its visual appearance, without the support of other factors, such as good quality paper.

In multi-lingual countries like India, it is often necessary to translate the questionnaire into languages other than the one in which it was originally designed. This issue is not treated with the seriousness it deserves, frequently being left as the interviewer's responsibility. This works on the oft mistaken assumption that the interviewer will necessarily be adequately fluent in both languages (the original language of the questionnaire and the one spoken by the respondent) to be able to correctly translate the questionnaire on the spur of the moment and also translate the response back into the original language. It is extremely important to ensure that the questionnaire is correctly translated, without any errors of a culturally sensitive nature. Although the interviewer will often be faced with the need to explain some points in vernacular to the respondent, as far as possible the onus should not be on the interviewer.

SUMMARY

Questionnaires are a record of questions that comprise messages as well as meta-messages. A well-designed questionnaire addresses the goals of the study. Appropriate questions play a major role in minimizing data collection errors. In particular, the flow chart approach to questionnaire formation helps minimize such errors by defining the flow and the structure required in the questionnaire. The funnel approach to designing the questionnaire ensures that the series of questions moves from the general to the focused, and helps improve the internal consistency of data. The purpose behind the study. i.e., the way the information provided by the study is to be used, also governs the format of the questionnaire and the degree of structure appropriate for it. Structured questionnaires are most useful in descriptive studies and they also help facilitate speedy data tabulation and analysis. Exploratory studies, on the other hand, require the flexibility of an unstructured interview and interview guides.

To develop a meaningful questionnaire, it is necessary to understand the management decision required, and define the marketing research problem and research design. The latter will involve decisions on the sample, data-collection medium (face-to-face, telephonic, mail, or Internet interviews), and specific interview approach—structured vs unstructured, disguised vs non-disguised. Once these issues have been settled, the process of questionnaire development deals with defining the target population, the type of questions to be asked, the order of questions, and the content of questions. The socio-economic characteristics of the target population, the location of the interview, and the time when the respondent is likely to be available influence the language of the questions, the appropriate length of the questionnaire, and the degree of structure required.

Questions are of three types—open-ended, dichotomous, and multiple-choice. The choice between them depends on the type of information sought—behavioural or attitudinal; the respondent's profile; and the location of the interview. Scales are multiple-choice questions that attempt to quantify essentially qualitative data.

In terms of content, questions may again be divided into three categories—identification questions, which provide the reference point for the respondent; research questions, which deal with specific research problems; and classificatory questions that qualify the respondent. In a questionnaire, the identification questions must be asked first, the research questions should form the main body of the questionnaire, and the classificatory questions should be asked at the end. Branched questions are questions the answers to which determine the choice of the succeeding question. The actual text of the question should be governed by its purpose, scope, wording, and extent of need for disguising the question. The greater the need for disguise, the greater the utility of projective techniques in data collection.

It is essential to pre-test a questionnaire to determine the suitability of the type of questions asked, their order, content, and length.

Non-personal modes of interviewing, such as telephonic, mail, e-mail, and Internet surveys usually need to be as short and structured as possible to improve response rates and reduce the chances of misinterpretation of questions. The twin benefits of anonymity and the ability to answer at leisure, except in case of telephonic interviews, usually operate in favour of improving response rates, which are generally quite low in non-personal interviews.

Interview guides are a specialized means of interview, which do not include questions but only list the areas of enquiry, and need not be administered in a pre-specified order. Rather, the order depends on the respondent's statements. Similarly, the instruments for collecting data from children need to have the minimal amount of structure, and should ideally be a combination of games and observation. Projective techniques are quite well suited to interviewing children.

KEY WORDS

Metamessage literally means 'beyond message' and refers to the messages implied and 'embedded' in the communication, beyond what is said at the superficial or the obvious level.

Questionnaire structure refers to the details regarding the type of questions that will be included (dichotomous, multiple-choice, or open-ended), the order of questions, and the length of the questionnaire.

Funnel approach refers to a questionnaire design that proceeds from the general to the focused questions.

Flow chart approach refers to the method of designing a questionnaire that is based on drawing up a flow chart of all the information required, before the formal format of the questionnaire is finalized.

Unstructured style of questioning refers to a conversational style of asking questions where the respondent is not constrained by the structured framework of the questionnaire, and provides spontaneous and detailed responses to questions.

Scales refer to the multiple-choice questions used for quantifying qualitative data or for classifying data into categories.

Probe questions refer to questions that aim at exploring deep into the experience of the respondent and determining the reasons for a stated behaviour or attitude. These are usually not included in the questionnaire in advance but are framed by the interviewer depending on the respondent's answer to a question.

Identification questions refer to the initial questions in a questionnaire, usually asked in order to determine the respondent's identity, such as details of name, address, and telephone number.

Research questions refer to those questions that are concerned with the main body of research in a study.

Classificatory questions refer to those questions relating to age, occupation, ownership of certain products or brands, and family structure. These questions are asked at the end of the study and aim at categorizing the respondent.

Branched questions refer to multiple-choice questions that are followed by one or the option of response/action, that depend on the choice made in the previous question.

Conversational questions refer to the open-ended questions that aim at building rapport with the respondent in unstructured questionnaires.

Disguised questions refer to questions that are framed in such a manner that their real purpose and focus are not obvious to the respondent.

Filter questions refer to those questions that aim at determining the respondent's familiarity with and interest in the subject.

Show cards refer to the cards or slips that are aimed at assisting the respondent's memory by repeating some categorical options included in the questionnaire.

Pre-test refers to the administering of the draft questionnaire to a small sample of the target population before final use in the field. The objective of pre-testing is to determine the suitability of the type of questions, their content, order, and length of the questionnaire.

Interview guide refers to the list of areas of enquiry that is used to collect data and ask questions on all relevant topics in an unstructured, indepth interview or focus group discussion.

Research design refers to the framework of the research study being undertaken, that provides answers to the 'what' (research problem), 'from whom' (sample), 'how' (methodology of data collection and analysis), 'when' (time frame), and 'at what cost' questions specifying the study.

CONCEPT REVIEW QUESTIONS

1. What are the steps that should be considered before designing a questionnaire?

2. How will you decide what form of questions will be used for collecting data for a given marketing research problem? What problems do open-ended questions pose?

3. What problems in the designing of a questionnaire will the use of a flow chart solve?

4. What role does pre-testing play in developing a questionnaire? What errors should one take care to avoid?

CRITICAL THINKING EXERCISES

1. In view of the Government of India's directive that any foreign company interested in entering the Indian retail market must do so with a minimum 10,000 sq. ft. of space and a population-to-outlet ratio of a million-to-one, Wal-Mart wants to estimate its market potential in India. Define the marketing research problem for a market research study that Wal-Mart may commission for this purpose. What method of data collection will you use for this problem? Why?

2. Company XYZ is a major player in the FMCG market, with a huge consumer demand for its products. But it does not get much support from the retailers, who do nothing to actively push the company's brands to the consumers. XYZ offers similar terms as its major competitors do to its retailers. XYZ would like to conduct a study to determine the reasons for the attitudes of the retailers. What data-collection instrument would you suggest? Why? Develop the instrument. You may make whatever assumptions you consider relevant.

3. Godrej Foods have recently launched a soymilk-based beverage called 'Sofit' in ready-to-consume cartons. The brand is positioned on the health platform but emphasizes that unlike most soy-based drinks, Sofit has a great taste. The company would like to commission a research to determine the initial consumer trial and user opinion of the product. Design a flow chart to help develop a questionnaire for the study.

4. The following questionnaire was developed by the marketing research agency that was asked by Company ABC to determine the market potential for a four-cigarette pack, which is smaller than the regular pack of ten. ABC has briefed the agency that

the target consumer of the pack will be the light smoker who usually buys cigarettes loose in order to keep his consumption down.

Examine the questionnaire and indicate whether you would like to retain the questionnaire as it is presented here or if you would like to make any changes. In case you would like to make changes, please write down the changes you suggest and give your reasons for suggesting the change.

Consumer Questionnaire

1. First name (optional) ....

2. How old are you? .... yrs .... months

3. Are you a smoker? Yes .... No ....

4. How many cigarettes do you usually smoke in a day?

   1–5 .... 6–10 .... 10–20 .... More than 20 ....

5. Which brand do you smoke? ....

6. Do you buy a whole pack of cigarettes or do you buy them loose? ....

7. If loose, then how many cigarettes do you buy at a time?

   1 .... 2–3 .... 3–5 .... >5 ....

8. Have you tried brand 'X'? Yes .... No ....

9. If yes, how often have you tried it'

   Once .... Twice .... More than twice ....

10. What is your opinion of brand 'X'? ....

11. Are you satisfied with this new brand? Yes .... No ....

12. Would you recommend it to others? Yes .... No ....

13. What do you like most about this brand? ....

Classificatory Data

Address ....Tel. No. ....

Income Category: Below Rs 5,000 pm ☐
Rs 5,000–Rs 10,000 pm ☐
Rs 10,000–Rs 20,000 pm ☐
Above Rs 20,000 pm ☐

Occupation: Student ☐   Self-employed professional ☐
Service ☐   Industrialist ☐
Trader ☐   Other ☐

PROJECT ASSIGNMENT

1. You represent the Marketing Research Company, which company XYZ, a well-known company manufacturing 'Waterguard', a new brand of water purifiers, has approached. Assume that Waterguard is the first brand in its category of solar-powered water purifiers, and the concept has been supported by scientists across the country. The brand is marginally more expensive than the conventional water purifier. Three months after an extensive launch, a survey reveals that the purchase rates for Waterguard have been substantially below expectations in the target population, defined as the urban, middle class to upper class households. The study also provides some attitudinal and other data regarding water purification.

   • Unclean water is seen as a major health hazard.
   • Health is a high-concern area for most households, especially for the target households.
   • Treating drinking water through some means, such as boiling, adding chlorine or alum, etc., is common practice in target households.
   • One in every five target households owns an electrically operated water purifier.
   • Non-buyers of Waterguard were found to belong to the same socio-economic class as buyers.

   What areas would you explore to determine the reasons for the low trial of Waterguard? Define the marketing research problem, list the objectives of the study, and develop a questionnaire. You may make whatever assumptions you deem necessary about the brand.

REFERENCES

Aaker, D., V. Kumar, and G.S. Day 1998, *Marketing Research,* Sixth edition, Wiley, Singapore, p. 324.

Cooper, D.R. and P.S. Schindler 1998, *Business Research Methods,* Tata McGraw-Hill, p. 346.

Malhotra, N.K. 2004, *Marketing Research: An Applied Orientation,* Fourth edition, Pearson Education, p. 280.

Statpac Survey Software

Tannen, Deborah 1985, *You Just Don't Understand,* Ballantine Books, New York.

Tannen, Deborah 1986, *That's Not What I Meant!,* Ballantine Books, New York, pp.15, 45.

11 Building Attitude Exploration into Questionnaires

OBJECTIVES

After reading this chapter, the readers will be able to understand:

- the different categories of data—nominal, ordinal, interval, and ratio—and how each of these is measured
- the concept of attitude scales
- the various ways of classifying scales and the information they provide
- some well-known scales
- the reliability and validity of attitude scales
- how to develop scales

INTRODUCTION

Sumit Khanna was planning to get formally engaged to his girlfriend of two years and was considering gifting her a diamond ring on the occasion. He confided to his friend, Ramesh, that he had no idea how to select a diamond. 'I do not have a clue about these things, and you know my mother passed away three years ago. Dad is as bad as I am. How do I tell a good diamond from a not-so-good one? Suppose Supriya is not happy with the one I select?'

Ramesh scouted around for information to help his friend and located some literature on diamonds. According to the literature, diamonds are usually evaluated on the basis of four Cs—carat, colour, cut, and clarity.

'Let us look at the diamonds at Bhimji Bhai Zaveri, the well-known jewellers, on this basis. Those people will give us accurate information; they are very reputed jewellers and can be relied upon to be honest. The other three things can even be checked out visually. Besides, there are definite measures and specifications for each of these factors, on the basis of which we can choose diamonds. Sounds easier than buying good quality gold,' Ramesh told Sumit.

Sumit brightened for a moment, 'Wow, Ramesh, you are a genius. Where did you get this information? Let us go.' And then he stopped.

'Now what?' asked Ramesh.

Sumit hung his head. 'How will I be able to figure out exactly how happy she is with it?'

This is the kind of measurement situation that calls for the use of scales. Measurement involves assigning numbers to specific events in accordance with some rules. Establishing such a correspondence between tangible events or objects and numbers is easy, but more sophisticated methods, such as scaling, are required for measuring intangibles such as preferences, perceptions, and motivations.

In the previous chapter, we defined scales as 'measures that attempt to assess the degree of the presence of an intangible characteristic in the variable being studied'. In other words, a scale is a continuum on which an object may be plotted according to the degree to which it possesses the characteristic being studied. In marketing research, scales are usually required for the measurement of attitudes.

Scales can be classified in a variety of ways—by the nature of the data being classified, by the focus of the variation being studied, by the number of attributes studied, or by the method of data collection. This chapter discusses the measurement of data and the various kinds of information that scales provide. The different types of scales—their characteristics, limitations, and application—have been discussed in later sections. This chapter also discusses some specific scales that are used frequently in marketing research, some guidelines for developing a good scale, and the desirable qualities of a good scale, such as validity and reliability.

MEASUREMENT OF DATA

The measurement of data or sets of data uses real numbers. Measurement involves assigning symbols and values to the properties of objects so that these symbols have the same relationship to each other as the objects they represent. Numbers are the most frequently used symbols.

The properties being measured may be classified into elemental/basic properties or composite concepts.

Either of these two categories of properties may be tangible or intangible.

Methods of Measuring Data

Measurement methods can vary depending on what is measured and how sophisticated the measure is required to be, i.e., the amount of information it is expected to produce.

Numerical measurement methods classify data into four categories, depending on these two requirements. A detailed description of these categories in the order of increasing sophistication follows. Each category provides more information than the preceding one. Table 11.1 summarizes the information about various scales based on data categories.

Nominal data

This classification aims at a one-to-one correspondence, and groups data into internally homogeneous, exhaustive categories, such as men–women; black–white–green; or wooden vs plastic. No values relating to order, distance, size, or origin are ascribed to the data in any category by this method, except that all the variables grouped together, and only those, should be similar with respect to the characteristic being studied.

Table 11.1 Classification of Scales Based on the Types of Data

Type of Data	Type of Scale	Rule for Classification	Statistical Processes
Nominal	Dichotomous	Objects identical or different	Totals, Percentages, Mode, Chi-square
Ordinal	Rank order, Comparative	Objects greater or smaller	Percentile, Median Rank correlation, Friedman ANOVA
Interval	Likert, Thurstone, Stapel, Semantic differential	Differences between adjacent ratings are equal	Mean, Standard deviation, Correlation coefficients, t-Test, F-Test, Factor analysis
Ratio	Special scales	Fixed point of origin or zero	All statistical operations

As such, scales using nominal data are the least restrictive and, therefore, the least informative of all. Scales classifying age, income, or sex belong to this category. The only statistical operations that may be performed on nominally measured data are totals and percentages. Even so, nominal data is useful in classifying respondents into specific categories for further analysis. Such data is especially useful in exploratory studies, where the emphasis is more on uncovering underlying relationships rather than numerical analysis.

Ordinal data

As the name suggests, data in this category are ordered, or ranked, with respect to the characteristic being studied. The order or rank is preserved with respect to only one attribute at a time. The category thus provides information on the *direction* of the attribute under study, in addition to the category information given by the nominal grouping. In other words, ordinal data provides information about the direction of the difference between two successive elements in a category, not information about the actual difference. For example, let us consider the marks obtained by three students in a marketing research class.

Student	Marks (Out Of 100)	Rank
A	87	I
B	73	II
C	71	III

Expressed in ordinal terms, that is, in terms of rank order, the three students are ranged as A>B>C. Thus A is ahead of B, who is ahead of C. However, this ordering only provides the *direction* in which the difference in the marks of the three students occurs. It does not reveal the *degree* of difference, i.e., the fact that the difference between the marks of A and B is much larger than the difference between the marks of B and

C. Any transformation of this kind of data preserving the order is valid—the ranks of the three students will remain the same even if their marks were changed as follows:

Student	Marks
A	94
B	82
C	53

As such, any statistical measure of ranked data that is influenced by such transformation is not meaningful—the concept of 'average rank' does not have any meaning.

If some items are ranked with respect to a variety of attributes in turn, the researcher is often tempted to attach weights to the rankings and develop 'indices' of 'average rankings' so that it may be possible to make meaningful statements about the 'overall' relative ranking of the items. This can lead to incorrect conclusions, as depicted in the following example.

Let us consider the case of a housewife ranking three brands of microwave ovens with respect to her perception of their utility and aesthetic appeal (Table 11.2 and 11.3).

Table 11.2 A Housewife's Ranking of Three Brands of Microwave Ovens

Brand	Ranking with respect to		Weights assigned to		Weighted
	Utility	Aesthetics	Utility	Aesthetics	Index Rank
A	1	3	0.6	0.4	1.8
B	2	1	0.6	0.4	1.6
C	3	2	0.6	0.4	2.6

Table 11.3 Rank-preserving Transformation

Brand	Ranking with respect to		Weights assigned to		Weighted
	Utility	Aesthetics	Utility	Aesthetics	Index Rank
A	12	25	0.6	0.4	17.2
B	22	15	0.6	0.4	19.2
C	34	18	0.6	0.4	27.6

We notice that even with the rank-order preserved and the same set of weights assigned to the two attributes, we do not get the same ordering in the final index ranks (Table 11.3). This is so because the transformation of ranked data does not necessarily preserve the *degree* of separation, only the *direction* of separation, whereas measures such as 'average' assume equidistant variation between the variables being studied. However, ordinal data can be analysed using order-preserving measures such as median, quartile, and percentile.

Interval data

Interval data possesses all the qualities of nominal and ordinal data. In addition, these provide information about the degree, and not merely the direction of the distance between successive values of the variable being studied. All interval data assumes the *equality of distance:* the interval between 1 and 2 is the same as the interval between 2 and 3. Similarly, the interval between Monday and Tuesday is the same as the interval between Tuesday and Wednesday. However, we cannot meaningfully state that any value on an interval scale is the multiple of any other. For example, let us consider the measurement of Sumit's fiancée, Supriya's, happiness over the diamond engagement ring in the example discussed earlier through numerical measures 5, 4, 3, 2, 1, in which 5 stands for 'extremely happy', 4 stands for 'quite happy', 3 stands for 'neither happy nor unhappy', 2 stands for 'rather unhappy', and 1 stands for 'very unhappy'.

This does not suggest that 'extremely happy' is twice that of 'quite happy'. It merely suggests that it denotes a greater degree of happiness than 'quite happy'. However, it is possible to measure the distance between the values—the difference between 'extremely happy (5)' and 'quite happy (4)' is equivalent to the difference between 'quite happy (4)' and 'neither happy nor unhappy (3)'. These comparisons remain valid under any transformation. In other words, if we were to define the numerical measures of the various states of happiness as: +2 stands for 'extremely happy', +1 stands for 'quite happy', 0 stands for 'neither happy nor unhappy', –1 stands for 'rather unhappy', and –2 stands for 'very unhappy', the information provided by the new measures about Supriya's happiness would remain the same as provided earlier. In this scale, '+2' provides exactly the same information as '5' in the earlier scale; '+1' here provides the same information as '4' in the earlier scale; therefore, the difference between '5' and '4' in the earlier scale is the same as the difference between '+2' and '+1' in the new scale. The scales are, therefore, unique up to a transformation of the kind $y = a + bx$, for any positive value of b. Green and Tull (1978) have pointed out that '*differences* between interval-scale values can be expressed in terms of multiples of one another because, by taking differences, the constant in the above linear equation drops out in the computations'.

It must also be noted that the origin, or zero point, of the scale is arbitrary—the value of '0' in the scale (+2, +1,…,–2) provides exactly the same information as '3' in the (5, 4,…,1) scale. Since the numerical measures are merely denoting the quantification of the 'extent of happiness', the starting point, or zero, may take any numerical value, as long as the distance between successive values remains constant. A third scale, with numerical values 50, 40, 30, 20, and 10, given to successive categories denoting the different degrees of happiness, for example, will again provide the same information as the other two scales, although the starting point here is '50', corresponding to 'extremely happy'. To put it differently, whether the scale ranges from +2 to –2, 5 to 1, or 50 to 10 will make no difference to the information provided, as long as the interval between 5 and 4 in Scale 1 is taken to be the same as the interval between +2 and +1 in Scale 2 and between 50 and 40 in Scale 3.

Most statistical measures such as the arithmetic mean, standard deviation, and correlation coefficient, and most common parametric statistical tests such as the t-test and F-test can be used for analysing interval data. However, measures such as the geometric mean and the harmonic mean may not be applicable to interval data.

Ratio data

The data in ratio scales possess all the characteristics of interval data and, in addition, they have a fixed origin or zero point. Scales based on ratio data are the most sophisticated of scales. They measure the actual physical characteristics of objects, such as weight, height, distance, and area. In marketing, they may be used to measure entities such as sales, market share, the population size of a market, and any such physically verifiable characteristics. They retain their interrelationships under any transformation, and all statistical measures may be used to analyse them. However, they are not used much in attitude measurement as the concept of a 'fixed zero' is not usually relevant in this field.

Attitude Measurement

Attitudes are defined along three dimensions—cognitive (relating to knowledge, or cognition), affective (relating to feelings, perceptions, and motivations), and conative, also known as behavioural (relating to intent to act). Various types of scales are available for measuring each dimension. The information a scale can provide would belong to one of the following three categories:

- The presence or absence of a characteristic, e.g., aware vs not aware; user vs non-user.
- The importance of a characteristic, e.g., the influence of price vs fragrance when choosing a toilet soap.
- The desirability of a characteristic: A characteristic may be desirable, but not important. A patient may like his medicine to have a pleasant taste but taste may not be an important factor in the choice of a brand of medicine.

Attitudes cannot be measured directly. Hence, various attitude scales have been developed that measure the response to stimuli aimed at one or the other dimension of the attitude. For example, we may use a scale to determine the extent of awareness of a brand as follows.

1a. If I mention the words 'soft drinks' (*stimulus)*, which brand(s) comes to your mind first? (Top-of-mind recall)

1b. Which other brands of soft drinks have you heard of? (Unaided recall)

1c. Which of these brands have you heard of? (Aided recall)
- Coke
- Pepsi

Q. '*How likely are you to buy this brand the next time you are buying into the product category?*'

- *Will definitely buy*   ____
- *Very likely to buy*   ____
- *Might buy*   ____
- *Not likely to buy*   ____
- *Will definitely not buy*   ____

Fig. 11.1 A Conative Scale

- Thums Up
- Sprite
- Mirinda

In this scale measuring awareness, i.e., the cognitive dimension of attitude, brand awareness is checked at three levels—top-of-mind (spontaneous recall), which is considered to be the highest level of recall; unaided recall, which suggests high recall but the brand is not recalled spontaneously as soon as the product category is mentioned; and aided recall, which is a weak recall level, where the brand is recalled only when memory is aided through the direct mention of the brand name. These three levels of the scale may be given numerical weights of 3, 2, and 1 to indicate the relative degrees of recall.

An example of a scale to measure the affective component of attitude was given earlier when we examined the measurement of Sumit's fiancée's happiness on receiving the diamond ring. Similarly, a conative scale may attempt to measure the respondent's intention to purchase a new brand, as shown in Fig. 11.1.

TYPES OF ATTITUDE SCALES

Scales vary depending on whether the underlying data is nominal, ordinal, interval, or ratio. An additional basis of difference between scales is the item being measured. A scale may measure the variation across respondents with regard to their attitude to an object, such as the proportion of Indians strongly in favour of the Congress party compared with those only mildly in favour, or those against.

Alternatively, the scale may measure the variation between objects or stimuli, such as the brands of soft drink preferred by a group of respondents. Here, the respondents are the judges of the stimuli. Whatever the item being measured, there is a variety of attitude scales available for different kinds of measurements. The more popularly used ones are depicted in Fig. 11.2.

Single-item Scales

These scales use only one item, or attribute, to measure the respondent's attitude to the stimulus. They assume that the underlying data are nominal or ordinal scaled.

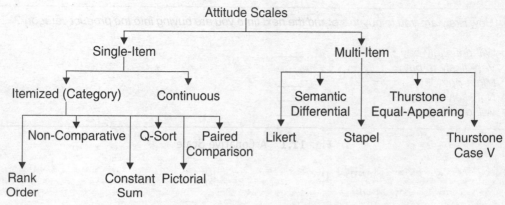

Fig. 11.2   Types of Attitude Scales

The scale may be balanced, i.e., there may be as many positive categories for measuring the attribute as there are negative categories; or it may be unbalanced, with more positive or more negative categories. Single-item scales may be *itemized,* where the data is divided into categories, or *continuous.* The itemized scales result in a one-to-one correspondence between the position of the object as perceived by the respondent and the number assigned to that category. The responses are thus sorted into predetermined categories. An example of an itemized category scale was given earlier, in measuring Supriya's happiness with the engagement ring, as shown in Fig. 11.3:

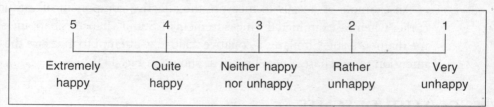

Figure 11.3 An Itemized Scale

Itemized scales are the most commonly used single-item scales.

A *continuous scale*, on the other hand, is expressed as a line that runs between the two extremes of the scale, and only these two extremes are labelled, such as '5' ('Extremely happy') and '1'('Very unhappy'), in the preceding scale. The categories in between are not specified. This has the advantage of getting more accurate and detailed information from the respondent, who may put a mark anywhere on the scale to indicate an exact perception, as in Fig. 11.4. Once these markings have been obtained, the researcher divides the line into as many categories as desired, and assigns scores to the respondent's ratings depending on the categories into which the ratings fall. The scores are treated as interval data. The advantage of the ease of construction of the scale is offset by the limitation that the comparison of the responses from two respondents and the interpretation of such responses become very difficult and subjective.

Again, single-item scales may be *comparative*, also known as *dyadic*, or *non-comparative*, also known as *monadic.* Comparative scales attempt to compare different stimuli to

---

Q. How would you rate the taste of this new brand of soft drink?[Please indicate your opinion with an 'x'.]

Extremely Good |____X_____| Extremely Bad

Fig. 11.4 A Continuous Scale

determine ordering or ranking. *The reference point in such cases is always the other stimulus.* Objects may, therefore, be ranked in order of the presence of an attribute, or attributes may be ranked in terms of the relative importance or relative desirability.

Rank-order scales

Among ranking scales, the rank-order scales are the most commonly used comparative scales. There are a variety of ranking, or ordering, methods. Some of these are listed here.

- A full rank-order, in which all n objects may be ranked in increasing or decreasing order with respect to some property of the object.
- Selecting any k out of n objects and ranking them. For example, from a list of eight attributes of men's shirts, the respondent may be asked five most important attributes. The next step may be to ask the respondent to rank these five in the order of their relative importance.
- The paired comparison method, which asks the respondent to compare or rank two objects at a time out of n, each object being ranked against every other object in turn. There are, therefore, $n(n-1)/2$ such rankings in all. Such scales will be discussed again later in this section.

Rating scales

Rating scales, or monadic scales, on the other hand, are used if the objective is to sort the responses into pre-determined, ordered categories as in the earlier ring example. Here, the information being sought is the respondent's perception of the object in the absolute sense, without reference to any other object. In their simplest form, rating scales may have only two categories, such as *yes/no, heavy/light, important/unimportant.* These two-category scales are useful when a dichotomous response is adequate. Most rating scales, especially those measuring attitudes, need to have multiple categories in order to properly assess all the variations in attitudes. They may take many forms— verbal, numerical, or a combination of numerical and verbal—as shown in Fig. 11.5. Some of these forms assume that the items are being measured along categories that are at equal intervals from each other and may, therefore, be regarded as based on interval data. This treatment of category data as interval data is not always valid, as some of the forms in Fig. 11.5 will show.

It will be noted that Forms (2) and (4) in Fig. 11.5 have to be necessarily based on category data. The levels of satisfaction and quality perception cannot be measured

Form 1		Form 2	
Totally agree	_____	5. Very satisfied	_____
Agree somewhat	_____	4. Reasonably satisfied	_____
Neither agree		3. Neither satisfied	
nor disagree	_____	nor dissatisfied	_____
Disagree more		2. Rather	
than agree	_____	dissatisfied	_____
Disagree totally	_____	1. Very dissatisfied	_____

Form 3		Form 4	
1. ☐ Will definitely try		Excellent	☐
2. ☐		Very Good	☐
3. ☐		Above average	☐
4. ☐ Might try		Average	☐
5. ☐		Below Average	☐
6. ☐		Poor	☐
7. ☐ Will definitely not try		Very Poor	☐
		Extremely poor	☐

Fig. 11.5 Forms of Rating Scales

meaningfully by the respondent over a continuum, even though theoretically it may be possible to think of them as moving along a continuum. Similarly, we may consider examples, such as age, income, or family size distribution, all of which are necessarily category-scaled variables.

Scale representations, such as in Form (3), are often mistaken for a continuous scale, since the labelling is restricted to the two extremes and the middle category. It must, however, be noted that ratings need to be provided across pre-specified categories. Purchase intention, like age distribution, cannot be rated along a continuous scale, since the degree of purchase-intent is necessarily a discrete variable.

Constant sum scales

Constant sum scales are essentially comparative scales that provide information not only about the direction of difference between two successive categories (e.g., ascending or descending, greater to lower, or vice versa) but also the degree of difference. Such a scale operates by asking the respondent to divide a fixed number of points, usually 100 or 10, between the number of items to be rated, in a manner that the points assigned to each item should be indicative of the importance of each item relative to the other items. The ratings given to all items should, of course, add up to 100 (or 10). The following example will illustrate the method.

Let us assume that three brands of painkillers, A, B, and C, have to be compared in terms of the consumer's perception of their relative efficacy. For this purpose,

Consumer X is asked to divide 100 points between the three brands to indicate his relative preference for each. He responds with the following division:

A	50
B	40
C	10
Total	100

This suggests that in the opinion of X, A is the best brand, followed by B, and C is the most inferior. Moreover, the perceived difference between A and B is significant, but not extraordinarily so. On the other hand, C gets a relative rating of just 10, compared to 40 for B, the brand rated second. In other words, in X's perception, A and B are relatively similar, compared to C, which is perceived to be substantially inferior.

This is a very popular scale because of its simplicity coupled with the significant amount of information it provides. Its limitation, however, is that it cannot be meaningfully applied to a comparison of more than a maximum of five items. With a large number of items, the response becomes mechanical, and the respondent's concentration is more on ensuring that the totals add up to 100 than on providing item ratings that are a true reflection of the perception of the item being rated.

A modified version of the scale allows points to be allocated to various alternatives to indicate the respondent's perception with the proviso that if the total exceeds 100, the base is revised to 100 and the points allocated to all the alternatives are reduced proportionately to add up to 100.

Q-sort scale

Certain comparative scales operate by permitting a tie between the items being rated. The scale operates on the assumption of equal intervals between categories, which are typically lower in number than the stimuli. The stimuli, or items, may be assigned to the same or different categories as per the respondent's perception. There are two variants of this kind of scale.

- In one variant, the number of items to be assigned to a category are fixed in advance.
- In the second variant, the respondent's perception may help assign the stimulus to any category. The assumption in this case is that the distribution of stimuli in each category follows the normal distribution.

An example will make the application of this method clear.

Let us consider the case of 20 business schools being rated by prospective students on the competitiveness of admission. The scale divides the schools into three categories:

- extremely competitive
- moderately competitive
- not very competitive

The two variants of the scale may operate as:

- Assign each of the 20 business schools to any one category. You may assign the five schools you consider most competitive to the category 'extremely competitive', the next eight to the second category, and the remaining seven to the last category.
- Assign each of the 20 business schools to any one category, depending on your perception of the degree of competitiveness of their admission process.

The Q-sort scale is a special version of this kind of comparative scale, and was first proposed by psychologist William Stephenson. It is used when the number of items to be rated is very large (more than 75), so that any attempt at ranking them will make the task tedious and mechanical, and is likely to result in biased responses. The classical Q-sort scale rates attitude statements. These statements are required to be divided into 11 piles, ranging from 'agree most with' to 'agree least with'. The primary objective is to assess the extent to which each respondent's responses are similar to every other respondent's. This is achieved by correlating each respondent's numerically coded responses with every other respondent's responses, using methods such as factor analysis and cluster analysis.

Pictorial scales

The difference between pictorial scales and other usual rating scales is that in the former, the category labels are not verbal, but pictorial or graphic. This makes it easy to administer the scales to individuals who cannot read, such as children or illiterate people. To be effective and meaningful, therefore, pictorial scales must define the categories quite sharply and accurately. Some of the most popular pictorial scales are the smiley scales and thermometer scales. These have been depicted in Fig. 11.6.

Paired comparison

This is a modified version of the ranking scale, in which each of the *n* stimuli is compared pair-wise with every other stimulus. The preferred stimulus of the two with

---

Q. How satisfied are you with this brand? Please tick on the appropriate 'degree' to indicate your satisfaction level, if 1 = totally satisfied and 5 = totally dissatisfied.

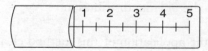

(a) Thermometer scale

(b) Smiley scale

Fig. 11.6 Pictorial Scales

respect to a specific attribute or an overall perception is determined in the form of ranking or ordinal scale, although the original data are assumed to be interval or ratio scaled. This is one of the most popular comparative scales. The scale will thus result in $n(n-1)/2$ comparisons. The example below will make the process clear.

Let us assume that a group of 50 management students is asked to indicate their perception of five business schools A, B, C, D, and E. A student has to indicate his preference for each school compared to every other school, with the preferred school being rated 1 and the other school being rated 0. Suppose the responses of any one student are as shown in Fig. 11.7, with preferences being indicated along rows.

The data show that School B is regarded by the student as superior to the other four schools, followed by C, D, A, and E. Similar pair-wise comparisons between the other business schools suggest C>D>A>E. Such comparisons made by all the 50 students may be aggregated and the aggregate matrix may be analysed to obtain pair-wise and overall ranking of the business schools. Other analyses of this data may be made to obtain the percentage of students who prefer any one business school. This method can thus be used to classify information by respondents as well as by stimuli.

An essential assumption on which the validity of the paired comparison scale is based is that of *transitivity of preference*—if A>B and B>C, then the transitivity rule assumes that A>C. Under this assumption and the additional assumption that no two schools (stimuli) are considered equal by any respondent (i.e., A = B is not possible), it is possible to derive aggregate rank-orders for all the schools, starting with pair-wise comparisons. What happens if these assumptions are not true? For instance, a student may prefer Business school A to Business school B, and Business school B to Business school C, but may find A and C similar. This is possible if the stimuli are compared on a large number of dimensions in the respondent's perception, and the differences between the ratings of stimuli are not significant in the respondent's mind. Green and Tull (1978) have quoted M.G. Kendall's (1962) summary measures and statistical tests for determining the incidence of tolerable levels of intransitivity. Malhotra (2004) has also referred to literature relating to this issue of transitivity.

Another limitation of the paired comparison scale is that it is useful only when the number of brands or stimuli being compared is limited. If the number of brands is

		Business Schools				
		A	**B**	**C**	**D**	**E**	**Total Preference**
Business Schools	**A***	x	0	0	0	1	1
	B	1	x	1	1	1	4
	C	1	0	x	1	1	3
	D	1	0	0	x	1	2
	E	0	0	0	0	x	0

* A cell value of '1' implies that the row school is preferred to the column school.

Fig. 11.7 Paired Comparison Scale

large, as may happen in real-life situations, the pair-wise comparison becomes unwieldy and mechanical. Moreover, in the market-place, consumers have a clear preference for one or a few out of a large number of brands; they do not usually make a pair-wise comparison. Again, what happens if the respondent does not like any one stimulus in absolute terms, although in comparative terms one of the stimuli may be liked more than the others? In these situations, the scale actually provides information only on 'the least disliked'.

Considerations in developing single-item scales

Single-item attitude scales are very widely used in marketing for assessing perceptions, opinions, and preferences. Even so, unlike some multi-item scales that will be discussed later, they do not have a defined structure, so that decisions about what makes a good scale often taken on an ad hoc basis and are open to question. A discussion of some decision areas relating to the construction of a good scale follows.

Number of scale categories How many categories should there be in a scale? Theoretically, the number can range from two, as in a dichotomous 'yes-no' scale, to infinity, as in a continuous scale. Too few categories, such as two or three, do not discriminate adequately between different degrees of opinions or perceptions. Too many categories, on the other hand, end up confusing the respondent, by offering more than the actual number of options that may be taken into consideration. The choice of categories should ideally depend on the purpose of the interview, the capability of the respondent, and the mode (telephone, face-to-face, or mail) of interview. When interviewing a relatively less educated person or conducting a telephonic interview where the respondent does not have access to all options simultaneously, it is best not to offer too many options. A good rule of thumb is to not use less than four categories and usually not more than seven categories.

Odd or even number of categories It is often thought that odd-numbered categories (3, 5, 7, etc.) are a more realistic option, since they provide the respondent with the opportunity to take a neutral stand (the mid-point) in case of lack of a definite opinion on the subject. At the same time, odd-numbered categories run the risk of what is referred to as 'the medium tendency', or 'the escape-route'. It is easier to choose the mid-point when the respondent does not want to make the effort of choosing, or does not want to express a view that may be controversial. The choice between odd and even number of categories should again depend on the purpose of the interview. For example, it makes sense to use an odd-numbered category scale with a neutral point in the middle when asking about the purchase-intent of a new product that the respondent may not have tried, only heard of. In a scale assessing the respondent's awareness of various environmental dimensions, on the other hand, a neutral mid-point is not a relevant option.

Balanced or unbalanced scale Another decision concerns whether the scale should be balanced, i.e., should there be equal number of positive and negative categories, or should the scale be unbalanced, i.e., should it have more positive or more negative categories? The decision again depends on the purpose of the question, as shown in Fig.11.8.

In the figure, in Q.1, the researcher is interested in finding out how well the respondent liked the taste of the new soft drink brand, and if it was not liked, the degree of dislike is not relevant. Therefore, the scale lays emphasis on determining the degree of liking, and all negative responses are clubbed together under the head 'didn't like it'. In the second question, on the other hand, the researcher's interest is in determining the possibility of the purchase of the new brand in future. Therefore, the difference in the levels of purchase-likelihood, including the difference between 'not likely to buy' and 'will definitely not buy' categories is relevant and must be recorded.

As this example illustrates, the decision about balanced or unbalanced scale depends on the purpose of the question. There is no strict rule in favour of or against a uniform decision to always prefer a balanced scale.

Unipolar or bipolar scale Scales need to have verbal descriptors at the extreme ends, indicating the degree of the strength of the adjectives defining the categories. Most scales have at least the two extreme category poles labelled, thus providing the boundaries for the adjective being considered. An exception is the Stapel scale, which will be discussed later. This is a unipolar scale, where only one pole is labelled. It has the advantage of being easy to construct, but suffers from the major limitation that respondents may differ in their interpretation of the strength of the other, unlabelled pole. Comparisons between respondents will then be based on a non-uniform understanding and interpretation of the scale.

Labelling of categories Another decision relates to whether or not to provide verbal descriptors for all categories. Continuous scales can obviously not have all points between two extremes labelled. In the case of category scales, labelling all categories reduces ambiguity but restricts the respondent's freedom to accurately indicate an exact perception.

These decisions are needed for constructing a good single-item scale, but will vary depending on the requirements of the study.

(a) Unbalanced Scale	**(b) Balanced Scale**
Q. 1 How did you like the taste of this new soft drink?	Q. 2 How likely are you to buy this new brand of soap?
• Liked it very much (+3) ☐	• Will definitely buy (+2) ☐
• Liked it a fair bit (+2) ☐	• Quite likely to buy (+1) ☐
• Liked it, but not much (+1) ☐	• Not sure; might or might not buy (0) ☐
• Neither liked it (0) nor disliked it ☐	• Not likely to buy (−1) ☐
• Didn't like it (1) ☐	• Will definitely not buy (−2) ☐

Fig. 11.8 Balanced vs Unbalanced Scale

Multi-item Scales

Attitudes to an object are usually the result of its cognitive, affective, and conative evaluation along a large number of dimensions. The more complex the object and the greater the respondent's involvement with it, the greater the number of dimensions on which it is evaluated to form the overall attitude. To measure the attitude towards complex, high-involvement objects, scales that comprise a large number of dimensions must necessarily be used. Respondents rate the object on these dimensions. The scores on the various dimensions are added up to develop some kind of an average 'attitude score'. The underlying assumption, of course, is that all these dimensions together constitute the overall, or the major part of, attitude to the object in question. Some well-known multi-item scales have been discussed in the paragraphs that follow.

Likert scale

The psychologist Renesis Likert (1932) first proposed this scale. This is an ordinal scale, also called the summated scale, since the individual scores of the respondents on a large number of items (statements) are added to form the overall attitude score of the respondent. Respondents are then grouped into various categories, indicating the degree of strength of their opinion about an object. The final scale is thus unidimensional, assuming that each statement reflects some part, or dimension, of the overall attitude.

The original Likert scale is a five-point scale, consisting of a number of statements about the object being studied, which the respondent scores on any of the five categories ranging from 'totally disagree (−2)' to 'totally agree (+2)'. This popular scale has been expanded by many researchers to a much larger number of categories. The popularity of the scale is evident from the fact that any five-point 'agree-disagree' scale, including a single-item scale at times, is often referred to as a Likert scale. It is more appropriate to refer to such scales as 'Likert-type scales' unless they are developed using the following procedure. The development of a Likert scale is a multiple-step process.

1. The researcher develops or gathers a large number (often 75 or more) of statements about the object under study.

2. These statements are classified by the researcher as generally 'favourable' or 'unfavourable'.

3. These items are evaluated by a small number of experts (usually not more than 15) who indicate their approval or disapproval of the items on a five-point scale, ranging from 'strongly approve' to 'strongly disapprove'. Each response is given a numerical score, ranging from +2 (strongly approve) to −2 (strongly disapprove).

4. These scores are assigned such that the 'unfavourable' items get a positive numerical score (+2, +1) for a negative response and a negative score (−1, −2) for a positive response. For example, let us consider the statement, 'Advertising on billboards merely distracts motorists.' This statement is classified as 'unfavourable' by the researcher in a study on the impact of outdoor advertising

on sales. A score of '+2' or '+1' assigned to this statement would indicate an approval of the statement, i.e., an agreement that billboard advertising indeed has a negative impact on sales.

5. Each expert's responses on all statements are added up to get a total score.

6. The scores are divided into four quartiles and the two middle quartiles are eliminated as not discriminating adequately between the positive and the negative items.

7. The mean differences between the two extreme groups are compared for each item. The 20 or so items with the most significant difference are retained in the list as those that are most discriminating between the favourable and the unfavourable opinions.

8. Steps 3 to 5 are repeated with the larger sample, using these 20 to 25 items. The respondents are then divided into four quartiles:

   • Quartile 1: Most favourable opinion
   • Quartile 2: Somewhat favourable opinion
   • Quartile 3: Somewhat unfavourable opinion
   • Quartile 4: Most unfavourable opinion

It must be noted that at the first stage, the quartiles separate the items into four categories, but at the second stage, it is the respondents who are separated into four categories expressing the strength of favourable opinion. A part of a Likert scale has been depicted in Fig. 11.9.

Another use to which the Likert scale can be put is in developing a 'profile analysis'. This involves comparing responses at the level of individual items rather than in the

	Totally agree (+2)	Agree somewhat (+1)	Neither agree nor disagree (0)	Disagree somewhat (−1)	Disagree totally (−2)
1. Advertising through billboards improves product recall.	☐	☐	☐	☐	☐
2. The most economical method of generating awareness is billboard advertising.	☐	☐	☐	☐	☐
3. There is very little one can communicate through billboard advertising.	☐	☐	☐	☐	☐
4. Colourful billboards brighten up the landscape.	☐	☐	☐	☐	☐
5. Billboard advertising exposes children to undesirable visuals.	☐	☐	☐	☐	☐
6. All that billboard advertising does is to clutter up the roadsides.	☐	☐	☐	☐	☐

Fig. 11.9 A Part of a Likert Scale Measuring Attitudes to Billboard Advertising

aggregate. Such a comparison provides information about the dimensions on which opinions differ substantially as well as dimensions on which opinions are largely positive or negative. Such analyses, in conjunction with the aggregate analysis or independently, provide guidelines about the perceived strengths and weaknesses of the object being studied, so that corrective managerial action may be taken.

Researchers often find the method of developing the Likert scale cumbersome and tend to avoid the first stage for this reason. It must, however, be kept in mind that the items selected in the final scale must be truly capable of discriminating between the different shades of opinion. Despite its popularity, the Likert scale suffers from certain limitations.

- This is a multi-dimensional scale, but the conclusions drawn from it about the overall opinion of the respondents are based on the aggregate scores (sum of responses on each item) alone. The process of aggregation ignores the direction and the degree of ratings on specific items. As a result, respondents with very divergent opinions on specific dimensions could ultimately be grouped together as having a 'very favourable' or 'very unfavourable' opinion. The profile analysis, described above, takes care of this problem to a great extent.

- If the number of dimensions considered for administering the scale is not large enough or if the dimensions considered do not discriminate adequately, the scale does not assess the variation in respondent opinions satisfactorily.

- The Likert scale also suffers from the potential for inaccuracy in results that might arise because of the manner in which respondents react to various degrees or the intensity levels of opinion that each category expresses. Some respondents may rarely go beyond '+1' to indicate a favourable opinion or '−1' to indicate an unfavourable opinion while others are more willing to rate the extreme '+2' or '−2' to express the same strength of opinion.

Semantic differential scale

This is a set of scales that rates the object under study on a number of itemized rating scales bounded by a set of bipolar adjectives. This scale is often used for a profile analysis of companies, products, institutions, and brands. It is also used as the basis for further, more sophisticated analysis such as Fishbein's attitude model (1967), discussed later, or multi-dimensional scaling (MDS).

The classical semantic differential scale is a seven-point scale, with a neutral middle position. Osgood, Suci, and Tannenbaum (1957) were the first to propose it. The scale assumes that the raw data are interval-scaled. It measures the direction and the intensity of attitudes to the object in question on three sets of dimensions:

- evaluative (good vs bad)
- activity (active vs passive)
- potency (strong vs weak)

The total number of adjectives used in a semantic differential scale should never be less than seven or eight, covering all these three dimensions. They may be expressed as words, or preferably as phrases, but care should be taken to ensure that the labels at the two extreme poles of the scale are truly bipolar. One way of doing this, if adjectives are being used to label the category, is to refer to a dictionary of antonyms. Alternatively, a group of respondents/experts may be asked to suggest the most appropriate antonym pairs, and the most popular ones get chosen.

The categories in between are not labelled verbally but are assigned integer values ranging from (+3) to (–3) or from 1 to 7. The respondents rate the object under study on each item on this seven-point scale.

The analysis of a semantic differential scale involves averaging the response to each item (adjective/phrase) across all respondents and plotting this average on the graph. The average values of all items are joined in what is usually referred to as a 'ladder' or a 'snake-chart' (see Fig.11.10). If the responses indicate a large variation, it is better to use the median value rather than the arithmetic mean. This graphic representation of the semantic differential scale makes it possible to compare two or more objects (brands, companies, institutions) visually.

The rating of the two stores, A and B, using a semantic differential scale has been depicted in Fig.11.10. It presents a part of the scale, taking into account four adjectives relating to the price, freshness of stock, variety of stock, and friendliness of the staff. The scales indicate that Store A rates better than Store B on all counts. Store A is seen as having lower priced items and as having fresher stock, more variety, and more friendly staff. In absolute terms, it is considered quite satisfactory on price and variety, but just above average on freshness of stock, and average on friendliness of staff. Therefore, these are the areas the management should concentrate on. Store B is rated as average or below average on all four counts. It is perceived as particularly inferior to Store A in terms of economy. Its items are rated as high-priced, and that is the parameter on which Store A has been rated at least three points higher (+2 compared to –1). The major corrective strategy that Store B needs to employ is to change the consumer's perception of it as being high-priced.

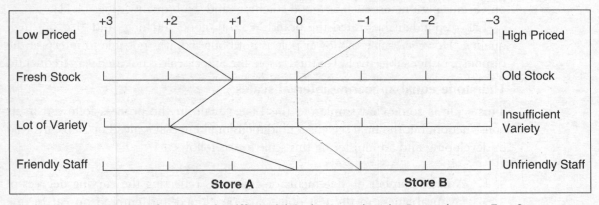

Fig. 11.10 Part of a Semantic Differential Scale Measuring the Perceptions on Two Stores

Martin Fishbein proposed an attitude model defined as

$$A_0 = \sum_{i=1}^{n} B_i a_i$$

where A_0 is the overall attitude towards the object, B_i is the respondent's strength of belief that the object has some attribute x_i, and a_i is the evaluation of the importance or the desirability of the attribute x_i. Here B_i and a_i are usually measured with the help of the semantic differential scale. For example, in a survey for the attitude to a newspaper, B_1 and a_1 may be defined as

B_1 = The newspaper provides detailed coverage of international events.

and a_1 = It is very important for a newspaper to provide detailed coverage of international events.

Given its convenience of construction and reasonable reliability, the semantic differential is one of the most popular attitude scales used in marketing research.

Stapel scale

This scale, developed by Jan Stapel (1969), is a modified, simpler version of the semantic differential scale. The assumptions under which the scale is applicable remain the same as in the case of the semantic differential scale, so that it produces interval data. However, this is a unipolar scale with ten categories numbered from +5 to –5, without a neutral point. It is, therefore, easier to construct, although more difficult to interpret accurately. It is possible to use it even when the questionnaire is being administered through non-personal modes of interview such as the telephonic interview.

The scale is usually presented vertically, and respondents are asked to indicate how accurately the adjective or term describes the object being studied. The more accurate the description is supposed to be, the higher the number that should be assigned to it. For example, let us consider the case of a brand of readymade shirts being evaluated on various parameters such as 'good stitching' and 'high quality' (Fig. 11.11).

The respondent has rated the brand '+3' on 'good stitching' and '+2' on 'high quality'. However, since the lower pole is not bounded, it is possible to interpret the responses rather subjectively. For this reason, the Stapel scale is not used very frequently.

Thurstone equal-appearing interval scales

This scale is somewhat similar to the Likert scale in the process followed in its construction, but the final scale is a unidimensional interval scale. The steps involved in developing and administering this scale are as follows.

1. A large number of statements or adjectives reflecting the varying degrees of favourableness to the test object are developed and entered on cards, one statement per card.

Q. *How would you rate Brand 'A' of shirts on 'good stitching' and 'high quality' using the 10-point scale given below? The more accurately you think a term describes the brand, the higher the number you should allocate to it. Please allocate negative numbers to a term if you think it describes the brand inaccurately.*

Good Stitching		High Quality	
+5		+5	
+4		+4	
+3	x	+3	
+2		+2	x
+1		+1	
−1		−1	
−2		−2	
−3		−3	
−4		−4	
−5		−5	

Fig. 11.11 A Stapel Scale

2. The statement cards are given to a large number (50 or more) of judges, who evaluate them in terms of '(1) relevance to the topic, (2) potential for ambiguity, and (3) the level of attitude the represent' (Cooper and Schindler 1998).

3. The judges are asked to classify the statements into 11 piles or categories, ranging from 'very favourable' to 'very unfavourable', and a 'neutral' position in between. All 11 categories are assumed to range at intervals equidistant from each other. The judges are not asked to express their opinion about the statement, merely to indicate the extent to which they consider the statement favourable to the object.

4. The median position of each item is calculated as its scale value.

5. Items that are placed in many categories are discarded as ambiguous.

6. The remaining 10 to 20 items are included in the study and presented to the final set of respondents. The respondents have to select those items that best reflect their opinion about the object.

7. The average score of all the items selected by the respondent is the respondent's attitude score.

The method is time consuming, cumbersome, and expensive to construct although easy to administer. Moreover, it does not provide an explicit response to each item in the scale. The scale values of an item could be influenced by the opinion of the judges. It is, therefore, not used frequently nowadays.

Thurstone Case V scaling

This procedure develops a unidimensional interval scale from ordinal data, specifically, from paired comparison data. The assumption is that people react to a stimulus through their *discriminal* process, i.e., they are likely to respond differently each time they are presented with a particular stimulus. As such, the response to a stimulus is not constant over time, but follows a frequency distribution. Green and Tull (1978) mention Thurstone's concept of the *modal discriminal response*, i.e., the most frequent response when presented with a stimulus. The difference between the modal discriminal responses to two stimuli is called the *discriminal difference*. Under the assumption that the frequency distribution of the response is normal, as assumed by Thurstone, the modal response will be equal to the mean, and the discriminal difference will also follow the normal distribution.

In other words, if R_i and R_j are the responses to stimuli i and j, the difference X_{ij}, between them is a standard normal variate.

$$R_i - R_j = X_{ij}$$

The average value of X_i, over all js may then be calculated and then such averages may be calculated for all X_i. Treating the smallest value of X_i as the origin, the revised values of all average responses may be plotted on an interval scale. The example below will make this scaling method clear.

Let us consider the case of 100 car owners being asked to indicate their preferences between four brands of small cars—Maruti 800, Santro, Palio, and Swift. They are asked to compare the cars pair-wise, and indicate the one they prefer. Their preferences are indicated in Table 11.4.

Table 11.4 Preferred Brand

Brand	Maruti 800	Santro	Palio	Swift
Maruti 800	0.50	0.75	0.80	0.70
Santro	0.25	0.50	0.45	0.55
Palio	0.20	0.55	0.50	0.60
Swift	0.30	0.45	0.40	0.50

Under the assumptions of normality made for the Thurstone scale, these proportions of preferences may be treated as areas under the normal curve for each discriminal difference, and the corresponding standard normal variates, X_{ij}, may be obtained from the normal tables, as shown in Table 11.5.

Table 11.5 Corresponding Normal Variates X_{ij}

Brand	Maruti 800	Santro	Palio	Swift
Maruti 800	0	0.67	0.84	0.53
Santro	−0.67	0	−0.13	0.13
Palio	−0.84	0.13	0	0.26
Swift	−0.53	−0.13	−0.26	0
Total	−2.04	0.67	0.45	0.92
Average $\overline{X}$	−0.51	0.17	0.11	0.23
Interval value for brand	0	0.68	0.62	0.74

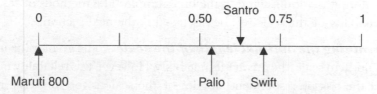

Fig. 11.12   Graphical Representation of the Scale

These values suggest that if we treat Maruti 800 as the origin, Palio is the closest to it, followed by Santro, and then Swift. Also, the perceived difference between Swift, Santro, and Palio is much less than that of Maruti 800 from all these cars. Graphically, this scale may be represented as shown in Fig. 11.12.

Considerations in developing multi-item scales

Multi-item scales are often used in marketing research to measure abstract concepts such as perception. The development of these scales requires a fair amount of skill. The considerations that must be taken into account while developing multi-item scales have been discussed earlier and are summarized as follows.

Definition of the construct to be measured   It is important to clearly define the construct to be measured, since the definition would govern the dimensions to be studied, and accordingly, the items to be included in the scale.

Number of items to be included   Abstract constructs are defined by a large number of dimensions. Each dimension is usually measured by at least one item. In order to capture the meaning behind the construct in as much detail as possible, it is important to generate a large number of items so as to define it completely.

Evaluation of items   Multi-item scales have to ultimately work with a limited number of items in order to be manageable, and also so that all items included in the scale may be relevant, meaningful, and capable of discriminating between different shades of opinion. It is, therefore, essential to have them evaluated by experts.

The choice of an appropriate scale   Depending on the construct to be measured, and the level at which information about it is required, a suitable scale must be chosen. For example, if attitudes or opinions are to be measured and rated in the aggregate, the Likert scale is a better option. Again, it is the appropriate scale to be used if the variability between respondent opinions is to be measured. If, on the other hand, the purpose is to determine the variability between objects, such as products or brands, about which respondents are required to express their opinions, then scales such as the semantic differential or the Stapel scale should be used.

Pre-testing the scale   The scale, once developed through the third and the fourth steps, must be administered to a small initial sample. The primary objective of this pre-test is to test the validity of the scale, and also to check if it is understood by the respondents. Any modifications suggested by this pre-test must be incorporated in the scale before it is administered to the final sample. The methods of testing the validity and reliability of the scale will be discussed in the next section.

Determining the optimal length of the scale The greater the number of items in a multi-item scale, the greater its reliability. However, this reliability must be balanced against the risk of respondent fatigue—if the scale is too long, the respondents are likely to lose interest in completing the scale and the responses will become mechanical.

RELIABILITY AND VALIDITY OF SCALES

Attitude scales, like any other measure, are useful only if they are accurate. Accuracy requires that the observed score on a scale should be the same as the true score. In other words, the scales should be *valid*, that is, they should measure what they are supposed to measure. They should be *reliable*, that is, they should provide consistent measures; in other words, they should deliver the same value of the measure in question over time. In practice, however, there is always a risk of the observed score (S_o) being a composite of the true score (S_t), the systematic error (E_s), and the random error (E_r):

$$S_o = S_t + E_s + E_r$$

A valid measure must be free of both the systematic error and the random error, such that,

$$S_o = S_t$$

In order to be valid, a measure should be reliable, but that is not an adequate precondition of validity. Reliability is a necessary though not a sufficient condition for validity. An example will make this clear. Consider the case of a room thermometer. If it gives the correct measure of temperature inside the room, it is valid. If it does so every time the temperature is checked, it is both reliable and valid. If, however, it consistently reports the temperature as 2 °C higher than the actual temperature, it is reliable, though not valid. In order to be valid, it is, therefore, essential for the thermometer to be a reliable measure of the temperature in the room. However, merely being reliable is not adequate. If it is consistently overestimating the actual temperature, it is consistently inaccurate and, therefore, not a valid indicator of the actual temperature.

Reliability of Scales

Reliable scales are thus free from random error up to a measurable degree. Reliability can be measured in terms of stability, equivalence, or internal consistency.

Stability A stable scale provides consistent results when measurements are taken on the same sample at different points in time. One way of checking stability is the *test–retest method*, which operates by administering a scale to a sample of respondents and then repeating it with them after a specific time interval. Usually, this is done with a gap of two weeks. If the scale yields similar results, it is considered reliable.

This method of determining reliability has certain limitations.

- If the time interval is too short, say a week or less, the respondent may remember the answers that were provided on the first occasion and repeat them. This leads to a loss in the reliability of the scale.
- If the respondent becomes aware of the purpose of the study, the answers will be biased and result in a loss of reliability.
- If the time interval between the two tests is, on the other hand, too long, it may result in a change in the environmental factors that could influence the response, regardless of the reliability of the scale.
- Often, the first test sensitizes the respondent to the scale, resulting in 'learning', which influences the response.

For all these reasons, the test–retest method is not used often for determining the reliability of a scale.

Equivalence   Unlike stability, equivalence is concerned with comparisons at the same point in time. The concern is with assessing differences between different respondents and different scales. Two scales may be considered equivalent if they classify a rater's responses across different items similarly. The method used here is *interrater reliability*, which consists of determining correlations between the scale-ratings given by different judges.

If the objective is to compare different scales instead of different respondents, the method of *parallel* or *alternative forms* is used, in which the same respondent may be given two different forms, X and Y, of the same scale (test) simultaneously, and the responses to the two are correlated. The limitation here is that too long a form may lead to incorrect answers because of respondent fatigue. This may lead to an erroneous conclusion of low reliability. In order to solve the problem, sometimes a *delayed parallel forms method* is used wherein the two forms X and Y are administered with a time lag. Half the respondents may be administered Form X, followed by Form Y, and the process may be reversed in case of the other half. The responses to the two forms are then correlated. It is, however, not easy to develop parallel forms that are exactly equivalent. Moreover, the limitations of the test–retest method are present in this method as well.

Internal consistency   This approach is concerned with determining consistency among the various items used in a multi-item scale. It is most useful when the scale consists of a large number of similar items for the respondent to rate.

One method used for determining internal consistency is the *split-half technique*. Here the scale is administered to the respondents and then split either into half—all odd-numbered items may form one half and all the even numbered items may form the other half—or randomly. Responses to the two halves are then correlated.

The method has the following limitations:

- The level of internal consistency is influenced by the manner in which the original scale is split.
- The longer the scale, the greater the reliability. At the same time, a long scale will lead to respondent fatigue, increasing the chances of random responses.

One other popularly used method of assessing the internal consistency of a scale, one that is free from the limitations of the split-half method, is called *Cronbach's coefficient alpha*. It is the average of all possible split-half correlation coefficients. Usually, a Cronbach's alpha value of less than 0.6 denotes poor internal consistency for the scale.

Validity of Scales

It was mentioned earlier that a valid scale measures what it is supposed to measure, consistently, each time it is administered. A valid measure is, therefore, invariably reliable as well. Any differences in the scores obtained by a totally valid scale may be considered to reflect the true differences in the actual scores among the respondents on the characteristics being studied.

The validity of a scale may be measured in a variety of ways, as depicted in Fig. 11.13.

Content validity The content validity of a scale, also known as *face validity*, is concerned with the extent to which the scale items are able to adequately measure the characteristics being studied. For example, in a study of the public image of a company, a scale that only measures the public image of the company's product quality will not have content validity. This is because, in the respondent's perception, an 'image' will consist of perception on a variety of items, such as the marketing-mix, quality of service, company profitability, perceived honesty, concern for the consumer, and concern for employees.

Criterion validity This aspect of validity measures the accuracy and suitability of the items used for measuring the characteristics being evaluated. It is, therefore,

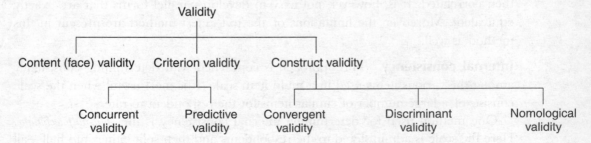

Fig. 11.13 Validity of scales

concerned with whether or not the scale accurately estimates the current presence of a characteristic (*concurrent validity*), and whether it accurately predicts the future occurrence of a characteristic (*predictive validity*). For example, a scale that aims at determining brand awareness should be able to establish brand recall at the top-of-mind, unaided, and aided levels to have *concurrent validity*. An aptitude test (scale) administered to MBA aspirants will be said to have *predictive validity* if the candidates rated high on the scale also do well in placement, that is, job interviews at the end of the MBA programme. Similarly, a future purchase-intent scale will have predictive validity if the respondents indicating high purchase probability towards a brand on the scale actually buy the brand quite frequently. Of course, terms such as 'high purchase probability' and 'frequent purchase' must be quantified. The validity in both these cases will be measured by the degree of correlation between the two measures, 'purchase probability' and 'purchase frequency'.

Construct validity This is the most complex aspect of validity, and is concerned not only with demonstrating whether a construct works but also with developing a theoretical basis explaining why it works. For example, in determining the validity of a scale to measure the 'effectiveness' of an advertising campaign, we would first need to define the term 'effectiveness', that is, the theoretical base underpinning the construct. Should it be taken to mean the generation of or an increase in awareness, brand knowledge, brand preference, purchase intent, or a combination of all or some of these responses? A scale measuring awareness generation is not valid if the objective of the study is to measure the post-campaign brand preference.

Construct validity includes convergent, discriminant, and nomological validity. *Convergent validity* refers to the extent to which two or more different methods of measuring a construct provide the same result. The degree of correlation between the outcomes of the two methods (both methods need not be scaling techniques) is then a measure of the validity of the scale. *Discriminant validity*, on the other hand, is a measure of the extent to which the scale measures the differences between two constructs. In the advertisement campaign example, the scale that differentiates between respondents who interpret 'effectiveness' as 'increased awareness' and those who interpret it as 'increased preference', will have discriminant validity. *Nomological validity* is concerned with relating measurement to a theoretical model that leads to further deductions, tests, and interpretations. For example, according to one consumer behaviour theory, first generation immigrants tend to prefer brands that are symbolic of the culture of their home country. A scale that measures the relationship between brand preference and brand symbolism would have nomological validity.

Generalizability

One major objective of the use of scales is to be able to generalize the findings of a sample to other samples, situations, and times. The determination of the validity of scales, especially of construct validity, is essential for this reason, although establishing construct validity may not always be easy.

Chandon et al. (2005), in a recent article, have warned against generalizations based on what they term 'internal accuracy' (measuring the purchase intent towards a brand/product in a sample of respondents and then comparing it with the actual purchase of the brand/product made by the same sample) of purchase-intent measures because of 'self-generated validity'. They postulate that purchase-intent studies that are used to forecast purchase behaviour have an inbuilt bias, since the very act of being questioned on purchase intentions would influence the respondent's purchase behaviour to the brand or product. According to them, 'Commonplace procedures and models that measure the intentions and behaviour of the same sample of consumers overestimate the strength of their association'; these should not be generalized to 'non-surveyed' consumers.

CONSIDERATIONS IN SCALE CONSTRUCTION

We have seen that scales are a versatile set of measuring tools for measuring intangibles, for example, attitudes. Most of them are not very difficult to construct either, provided some basic rules are followed and the assumptions under which they are valid are observed. Scales such as the Likert and the semantic differential scale owe their popularity to these reasons. At the same time, it is neither possible nor necessary to restrict the measurement of intangibles to these standard scales. A good researcher may develop scales to satisfy specific requirements that are not adequately met by these standard scales. However, certain criteria for scale development must be borne in mind while doing so. Some considerations in developing and evaluating scales have been discussed earlier. We will now examine this issue in greater detail.

Objective of scaling A scale may be designed to measure the characteristics of the respondents and group them according to the intensity of this characteristic, as in the Likert scale, or the characteristics of the stimuli, using the respondents as judges, as in the semantic differential scale. In the first case, the emphasis is on understanding the attitudinal differences in the sample of respondents, and in the second case, on the differences in respondent perceptions of the stimuli.

Comparative or non-comparative response The structure of the scale will vary depending on whether the objective is to understand respondent perceptions of the stimuli in absolute or comparative terms. Rating scales are suitable in the first case; ranking scales should be used in the comparative case. Scales providing similarity or preference judgements are another kind of comparative scales.

Dimensions Another major consideration is whether to construct a unidimensional scale or a multi-dimensional one. This is usually not an either-or decision, since the two types of scales differ in their areas of application. According to Green and Tull (1978), 'More progress has been made in the construction of scales for measuring attitudes along a single dimension than in dealing with the more complex cases of multidimensional attitudes.' At the same time, perception, consideration, and the choice of brands is usually a response to a large number of stimuli and will, therefore, be measured more accurately on a multi-dimensional scale. The choice of scale dimensions is thus a difficult question to resolve and needs very careful consideration.

Scale properties The underlying nature of the data used, whether nominal, ordinal, interval, or ratio, will also influence the kind of statistical analysis the scale may be subjected to and, therefore, the sophistication of the final output.

Reliability and validity We have discussed earlier that these scale characteristics may each be measured in more than one way, and some ways are simpler to obtain and assess, but less useful in measuring the dependability and the consistency of the final measures obtained. The choice of reliability and validity measures that can be obtained for a scale reflect the quality of the scale since they directly influence the confidence with which the conclusions drawn from the scale may be generalized.

On the basis of these considerations, scales can be developed in any of the following ways.

Arbitrary scales Scales developed on an ad hoc basis may or may not measure the concepts they are designed to measure, but they are popularly used because they are easy and inexpensive to construct. The usual method is to collect a large number of items that are expected to reflect the dimensions of the characteristic under study, and measure all of them along the same categories. The quality of the scale may be improved through the measurement of the reliability and validity of the scale and through methods such as factor analysis, that provide information about the interrelationships between the items.

Consensus scaling This method involves the selection of items by a panel of judges on the basis of their relevance, the potential for ambiguity, and the level of the attitude they represent. A classical example of this approach is the Thurstone equal-appearing intervals scale. As discussed, such scales are difficult to construct, and do not provide the benefits that would justify the complexity of their approach. They are, therefore, not used much in marketing research.

Item analysis The steps this method involves are as follows.

1. collecting a large number of items related to the object indicating a definite favourable or unfavourable position about the item
2. obtaining scores on them from a group of respondents
3. calculating the total scores on all the items for each respondent, dividing them into quartiles on the basis of their scores, and later excluding the scores of the two middle quartiles from further consideration
4. calculating the average score for each item separately for the high and the low scorers
5. comparing the average for each item across the two groups using the t-test, to retain the items with the most significant t-value, which provide the final scale

One popular example of scales based on item analysis is the Likert scale. It is relatively easy to construct, and each item in the final scale has been tested for its discriminating ability.

Factor scales These are multi-dimensional scales developed using a variety of techniques that aim specifically at studying multi-dimensional content, identifying latent dimensions that have not been identified, and detecting the intercorrelations between various dimensions. The net result is a reduced set of factors, each representing some intercorrelated dimensions.

One of the most popular factor scales is the semantic differential scale—the bipolar, seven-point scale that has been discussed earlier. The category labels in this scale range from +3 to –3. Three factors contribute most to the inter-dimensional variation in this scale—evaluation, potency, and activity. The evaluation dimension or factor explains 50 per cent to 75 per cent of the inter-dimensional variation, and the remaining two factors explain another 25 per cent or so. The versatility of this scale makes it one of the most popular scales for studying corporate and brand image, comparing objects on various dimensions as well as on an overall basis.

In later chapters, we will study some other, more complex scales such as multi-dimensional scaling and conjoint analysis. The choice of scales ultimately depends on the objectives of the study and the level of detail at which analysis is needed.

SUMMARY

Scales are tools for the measurement of intangible characteristics that cannot be measured directly in the objects being studied. They can be classified in a variety of ways—by the nature of the data being classified, that is, whether nominal, ordinal, interval, or ratio data is being examined; by the focus of variation being studied, that is, whether the purpose of study is the variation between respondents or that between objects that the respondents are judging; by the number of attributes studied, that is, whether unidimensional or multi-dimensional; or by the method of data collection, that is, whether the data being collected is of interest at the aggregate level or at the level of individual dimensions. Nominal scales do not provide any information about the objects being studied beyond merely classifying them into mutually exclusive categories. Ordinal scales rank them in increasing or decreasing order, thus providing information about the direction of variation between them. Interval scales, among the most popular ones for measuring attitudes, give information about the degree as well as the direction of variation between the objects. The most sophisticated of the scale categories is that of ratio scales, which explain the degree and the direction of inter-object variation from a fixed origin.

Attitude scales can be divided broadly into single-item and multi-item scales. Single-item scales base judgement about attitudes on the measurement of one item. Popular itemized (discrete) scales include the rank-order scale, the group of non-comparative, or rating scales, the constant-sum scales, paired comparison, q-sort, and pictorial scales. While devising single-item scales, the major factors that have to be taken into consideration are the appropriate number of categories, whether to opt for odd or even number of categories, whether all categories or only the extreme poles should be labelled, whether the scale should be balanced or unbalanced, and whether it should be unipolar or bipolar. The major multi-item scales are the Likert, semantic differential, Stapel, Thurstone case V, and Thurstone equal-appearing interval scales. Multi-item scales, unlike single-item scales, are based on the assumption that attitudes are complex constructs and it is necessary to use scales that comprise a large number of dimensions. The Likert scale is a summated ratings scale that categorizes respondents on the basis of the intensity of their attitude towards the object being examined. The semantic differential is a multi-dimensional, bipolar factor scale that measures attitudes towards stimuli on the basis of adjectives and their antonyms. Attitudes are measured by three factors—evaluation, activity, and potency. Both Likert and semantic differential scales assume that the raw data is ordinal scaled. The Thurstone Case V scale is based on the concept of a 'discriminal process' that the respondent employs in evaluating stimuli and converts ordinal data into an interval scale. The Thurstone equal-appearing scale is similar in the process of construction and operation to the Likert scale, but more cumbersome. It is not used much in research because of its complexity.

The construction of multi-item scales must take into account the exact definition of the construct being evaluated, since these scales measure complex constructs. In addition, factors such as the optimal number of items and the suitability of the items included in the scale must be considered. The scale most appropriate to the objectives of the exercise must be selected; the length of the scale must be balanced against the improvement in reliability because of the coverage of a larger number of items in a long scale. All such scales must be pre-tested with a group of experts to ascertain their suitability, reliability, and validity.

Validity and reliability are two characteristics essential to any good measure, and so also to attitude scales. Validity refers to the ability of a scale to measure what it is supposed to measure, that is, to be free from systematic error. Reliability implies consistency, that is, freedom from random error. Validity includes measures of content validity, criterion validity, and construct validity. Reliability can be measured through tests of equivalence or internal consistency. Cronbach's coefficient alpha is a popular and robust measure of scale reliability.

KEY WORDS

Nominal scale refers to a scale that categorizes objects to establish a one-to-one correspondence, and groups data into internally homogeneous, exhaustive categories such as men-women, black-white, etc.

Ordinal scale refers to a scale that assigns ranks to objects to indicate the direction of variation.

Interval scale refers to a scale that measures the degree as well as the direction of difference between objects, measured from a subjectively defined origin.

Ratio scale refers to a scale that measures the degree and direction of variation between objects from a fixed zero, or point of origin.

Itemized scale refers to a scale that is divided into discrete, labelled categories.

Continuous scale refers to a scale that has only the two extreme poles labelled, and no structured division into categories.

Single-item scale refers to a scale that uses only one item to measure the respondent's perception or opinion about an object.

Multiple-item scale refers to a complex scale that uses multiple items to assess the respondent's opinion about the various dimensions of a construct relating to an object.

Ranking scale, also called an ordinal or a dyadic scale, refers to a scale that measures objects in comparative terms with respect to any construct.

Rating scale, also called a monadic scale refers to a scale that measures respondent perception of an object in absolute rather than relative terms.

Constant sum scale refers to an ordinal scale that operates by dividing a fixed number, such as 10 or 100, between various objects to indicate the respondent perception of the relative presence of the characteristic under study.

Q-sort refers to a scaling technique that, like the constant sum scale, divides the objects into 11 graded piles to determine the extent to which objects are seen as similar and the extent to which each respondent's pattern of scores is correlated with each of the other respondents' score.

Pictorial scale refers to a scale that uses pictures, such as smiley faces and thermometers, instead of verbal labels to define interval categories.

Paired comparison refers to a method that requires the respondent to compare a large number of stimuli on a pair-wise basis with respect to an item, so that each stimulus is compared with every other stimulus as a pair.

Likert scale refers to an ordinal, multi-item scale that ultimately results in a single scale dividing respondents, and not stimuli, into categories to indicate the variation in their attitudes towards a stimulus.

Semantic differential refers to a bipolar, seven-point multi-item scale that measures respondent perception of one or more stimuli, using adjectives with opposing meanings to define the two endpoints.

Stapel scale refers to a unipolar, 10-point scale, similar to the semantic differential scale, which uses adjectives at one end of the scale to measure the stimulus on various dimensions.

Thurstone's equal-appearing interval scale refers to a multi-item scale similar to the Likert scale, which develops median scores for each item and obtains aggregate scores for each respondent by totalling the scores for the selected items.

Thurstone Case V scale refers to a multi-item scale that operates on the assumption of the 'discriminal process', and derives an interval scale using paired comparison data.

Balanced scale refers to a scale that has equal number of positive and negative categories.

Factor scale refers to a multi-item scale that determines the inter-correlation between item variables through methods such as factor analysis, and works with a reduced number of uncorrelated factors.

Validity of scales refers to the property of a scale to be free of systematic errors, so that it consistently measures what it is supposed to measure.

Reliability of scales refers to the property of a scale to be consistent, i.e., free from random errors.

Content validity refers to the property of a scale to measure what it is supposed to measure.

Criterion validity refers to the aspect of validity that measures the accuracy and suitability of the items used for measuring the characteristics being evaluated.

Concurrent validity refers to an aspect of criterion validity concerned with determining whether the items used for measuring the characteristics being evaluated estimate it correctly in the short term.

Predictive validity refers to an aspect of criterion validity concerned with determining whether the items used for measuring the characteristics being evaluated predict it correctly in the long term.

Construct validity is concerned with demonstrating whether a construct works, and also with developing a theoretical basis explaining why it works.

Convergent validity refers to an aspect of construct validity that refers to the extent to which two or more different methods of measuring a construct provide the same result.

Discriminant validity refers to the extent to which a scale measures the differences between two constructs.

Nomological validity refers to relating measurement to a theoretical model that leads to further deductions, tests, and interpretations.

Consensus scaling refers to the selection of items by a panel of judges on the basis of their relevance, potential for ambiguity, and the level of the attitude they represent.

Item analysis refers to a method for evaluating a scale on the basis of how well it discriminates between respondents with high and low scores.

CONCEPT REVIEW QUESTIONS

1. What are the relative advantages and disadvantages of ranking scales and paired comparison scales? What role does the concept of transitivity play in ensuring that the results of a paired comparison test are meaningful?

2. What is the difference between the Likert scale and the semantic differential scale? Which of the two would you use if two brands of toilet soaps have to be compared by a group of housewives? Why?

3. Why is validity an important requirement of a good scale? Give an example of convergent validity in developing a scale to measure the belief that MBAs make better managers.

4. Researchers sometimes try to use rating scales as substitutes for ranking scales. What are the limitations of this approach?

CRITICAL THINKING EXERCISES

1. Develop a semantic differential scale to compare the corporate image of the two companies, Infosys and Wipro.

2. You have administered the paired comparison test for four brands of automobiles to a group of 100 young people. Their responses are given in the following table.

Preferred brand

	Wagon R	Santro	Palio	Alto
Wagon R	–	60	75	50
Santro	40	–	45	35
Palio	25	55	–	25
Alto	50	65	75	–

i. How do these brands rank in terms of overall preference?

ii. Develop an interval scale for these brands using the Thurstone Case V scaling method.

3. The Government of India recently announced some guidelines for permitting foreign direct investment (FDI) in the country. These include limitations on the location and on the outlet size. Only in cities where the population-to-outlet ratio will be one million-to-one, and are not less than 10,000 sq. ft, is FDI permitted. Develop a suitable scale to test the reaction of some major retailers from the USA, UK, and Sweden to this directive.

4. Develop a suitable scale to evaluate the perception of the public of Mumbai of the way the local government handled the extremely heavy rains in the city on 26 July, 2005. How would this scale appear if it were (a) a Likert scale, (b) a semantic differential scale, (c) a Stapel scale, and (d) a Thurstone Case V scale?

PROJECT ASSIGNMENTS

1. From a marketing journal in your college library, select an article that uses the scaling method for data collection. Examine the scale for its appropriateness to the purpose of the study. Which other scale could you have used?

2. Develop a different scale for the same purpose and test it for construct validity.

3. Develop a Likert scale to determine the attitude of working women in your city to television. List the ambiguous items. Collect data using the scale. What is the

distribution of the women in your sample according to their overall attitude towards television?

CASE STUDIES

1. Post-launch Survey for *The Daily Reporter*

It had been among the biggest stories in the specialized world of Mumbai's print media early this year. A breakaway group of senior journalists from some well-known newspapers had come together to launch *The Daily Reporter,* the first English newspaper in the new format to be launched in this city, traditionally known as the 'Times of India city'. The launch had been preceded by high-profile promotion, with large billboards depicting catchy visuals and witty one-liners dotting the city for a month before the launch. As some cynics said, you had to be blind and deaf not to realize that *The Daily Reporter* was about to be born, considering the amount of noise that was being made about it. The promotion itself followed an extensive pre-launch survey, designed to determine what the average Mumbai reader of English dailies really wanted in the newspaper with a morning cup of tea.

The Daily Reporter was now three months old, and the print order was going up steadily. Though pleased with its success, the marketing department of the newspaper decided it was time to find out how it was being received by its readers, that the print order was not adequate indication. Sudhanshu Mehra, GM, Marketing, decided he needed to know the profile of the reader, the extent of subscription versus off-the-stands purchase, and 'everything else about it', as he put to his colleague and senior editor, Shyam Naik. 'Why do people it? What do people read in it? What do they read first? What paper have they switched from? Or is TDR (*The Daily Reporter)* a second paper in the household? Why have the switchers switched? How regularly do they read it? What do they think of it? Do they see it as different from the other papers? Would they stay with it, or is it just curiosity...' 'Hey, hold it, hold it. You are taking my breath away,' Shyam Naik interjected, laughing. 'One thing I am reasonably certain of is it cannot be just curiosity for three months. I am sure we have regular readers now.' 'How do you know it is the same people reading it, or new readers getting added on, while the older ones drop out?' was Sudhanshu's worried rejoinder. Shyam pondered over the answer for a few moments. 'You have a point there. And I do understand that if that is happening, we are not building up a regular reader base. For myself, I would like to know what they think of the content, the language, the layout, the pictures... The total editorial angle, in other words. Is there anything they are not happy with, or anything they would like included? Would they like it to be more, or less, serious? More analytical, or less?'

Sudhanshu grinned, 'Now who is asking a lot of questions?' and then in his characteristic quick manner, he decided, 'I am going to ask those two summer trainees to take this up as a project. I will brief them on the entire history of the newspaper, and the concerns we have. Let them develop a questionnaire and bring it to me tomorrow.' 'Why not ask each of them to develop one independently? We could merge them later, if necessary,' suggested Shyam. Sudhanshu agreed, but suggested they list down the main issues they wanted explored in the survey. The outcome of their combined labour was as follows.

- The profile of the TDR reader.

- Which other paper had the reader switched from, or added TDR to? What was the frequency of switching, compared with adding TDR as a second paper?

- How long had the average reader been subscribing to TDR?

- The reasons for switching to or adding TDR.

- The reading pattern: where read; the items most frequently read; the items read first; the frequency of reading TDR.

- The perception of TDR in terms of editorial matter, coverage, language, and features, compared to other newspapers.

Ruchira and Ranjan, the two summer trainees, brought in their questionnaires the next day, and asked for an appointment with Sudhanshu Mehra. He called Shyam Naik in, and the two of them went through the two questionnaires together. They could not reach a decision on whether either of the two questionnaires was adequate, whether they required improvement or additions, and whether merging the two questionnaires would serve the purpose. They decided to administrator the two questionnaires independently to a few friends outside the office.

Ruchira's Questionnaire

Introduce yourself.
Name of Respondent: ....
Telephone.: ....
Address: ....
....

1. Which newspaper do you read regularly?
   ....

2. How long have you been reading it?
   ....

   [If TDR mentioned in answer to Q. 1, go to Q. 5. Otherwise ask Q. 3a]

3a. Have you heard of *The Daily Reporter?*
   Yes ....   No ....
        ↓   ↓
   [Go to Q. 3b]   [Terminate Interview]

3b. Have you ever read it? If yes, do you remember when? ....

4. Why do you not read it now? ....

5. What do you read first in the newspaper?

   Headlines   ☐
   Sports Page   ☐
   Business News   ☐
   Page 3   ☐

Others_____ ☐
    (Pl. specify)
No specific preference ☐

6. How would you rank the following aspects of a newspaper in terms of their importance to you?

News coverage ☐
News analysis ☐
Variety in coverage ☐
Freshness of news ☐
No. of pages ☐
Language ☐
Size ☐
Style ☐

7. How would you rate (a) your current newspaper and (b) *The Daily Reporter* on the given five-point scale for each of the listed parameters? [Scale: 1: v. good, 2: good, 3: average, 4: poor, 5: v. poor]

	TDR	Your Current Newspaper
News coverage	☐	☐
News analysis	☐	☐
Variety in coverage	☐	☐
Freshness of news	☐	☐
No. of pages	☐	☐
Language	☐	☐
Size	☐	☐
Style	☐	☐

Thank you

Sex: Male/Female
Date of Birth: ....
Education:..
Occupation: ....

Ranjan's Questionnaire

Good morning/evening. We are conducting a survey on the newspaper-reading habits of Mumbai. Could you spare some time and answer some of my queries?

Name (Optional) ....

Telephone No. ....

Address ....

....

1a. Which newspaper do you read currently?
    [Please tick]
  b. Which paper did you read before this?
    [Please tick]

Newspaper	(A)Current	(B)Previous
The Times of India *Indian Express* *Asian Age* *Hindustan Times* *The Daily Reporter* *DNA* Any other _____ (Pl. specify)		

2. How long have you been reading your current newspaper?

    0–3 months ....   12 months–2 years ....
    3–6 months ....   2–5 years ....
    6–12 months ....   More than 5 years ....
    [If TDR not mentioned so far, ask Q. 3, otherwise go to Q. 5]

3. Have you heard of *The Daily Reporter*?
    Yes ....   No ....
    (Go to Q. 4a)   (Terminate interview)

4a. Have you ever read *The Daily Reporter*?
    Yes ....   No ....

4b. If yes, why did you stop reading it? ....

4c. If no, what is your reason for not having read it so far? ....

5. Where do you usually read your daily newspaper?
    At home ....
    At work/In College ....
    On the way to work ....
    College ....

6. What do you read first when you pick up the newspaper?
    Headlines ....   Front Page ....
    Business News ....   Society News/Page 3 ....
    Sports News ....   Editorial ....
    No fixed pattern ....

7. Please list below the five features that you consider most important in a newspaper.
    (i)   ....
    (ii)   ....
    (iii)   ....
    (iv)   ....
    (v)   ....

8. How satisfied are you with (a) your current paper, and (b) TDR on these five parameters? Please use the scale below to indicate your satisfaction.

1: Totally satisfied ...   5: Totally dissatisfied

Parameters	(a) Current Paper	(b) TDR
(i)	....	....
(ii)	....	....
(iii)	....	....
(iv)	....	....
(v)	....	....

9. How likely are you to subscribe to *The Daily Reporter* in future?
Very likely ....
Somewhat likely ....
May or may not ....
Somewhat unlikely ....
Very unlikely ....

Thank You

Classificatory Data

Age:

Up to 15 years	....	30–40 years	....
1–20 years	....	40–50 years	....
20–25 years	....	50 years or more	....
25–30 years	....		

Sex: Male/Female

Marital Status: Married/Single

Occupation:

		Monthly Household Income:	
Service	....	Up to Rs 10, 000	....
Business/Industrialist	....	Rs 10, 000–20, 000	....
Self-employed professional	....	Rs 20, 000–30,000	....
Student/Housewife	....	Rs 30, 000–40,000	....
Retired	....	Rs 40, 000–50, 000	....
Other (Pl. specify)	....	Rs 50, 000–75, 000	....
		Rs 75, 000 or more	....

Questions

1. If you were asked for advice, which of the two questionnaires would you recommend to Sudhanshu Mehra? Why?

2. Do you think either of the two questionnaires will serve Mehra's purpose as they stand, or should they be modified? What modification, if any, would you suggest? Why?

2. Anjali Mukerjee's Health Total

Anjali Mukerjee's Health Total (AMHT) is an eight-year old, Rs 3 crore company in the market for health/fitness programmes. The company has established itself fairly well in the major cities of the country. The brainchild of a nutritionist, it is a proprietary company, owned jointly by Dr Anjali Mukerjee and her husband Saurabh Mukerjee, who is the Chairman and Managing Director of the company. The company offers two related product lines: three health programmes and nine health foods in the form of snacks. The brand aims at delivering two major promises: health through nutrition and beauty through health. It has thus positioned itself on a 'health and beauty through nutrition' platform, distinguishing itself from other fitness programmes such as Talwalkars, VLCC, etc. As a brand, AMHT had been growing well till recently, and now employs 109 people in Mumbai and New Delhi. Catering to SEC A1, A, and B customers through four centres in Mumbai and two in New Delhi, it registered a compound annual growth rate of over 30% in the first five years of its existence, but growth has been erratic since then. It has now mounted a serious examination of ways and means to recover its position. In addition to the new products it is planning for delivering beauty through the health route, the company sees opportunities in preventive health care and is aiming at growth through collaboration in this area, expanding its presence into at least the top ten Indian cities. It also plans to expand the shores of India into at least four countries, aiming primarily at the NRI market. The market for health/fitness and beauty programmes cannot be defined as an industry in the strictest sense of the word. It straddles the health care and the beauty industries, and is highly fragmented in structure. A report published in *The Economic Times* in 2001 had pegged the total 'health and fitness industry' at Rs 2000 crore. This gives AMHT a miniscule market-share of 0.15%, with both its strategic business units (SBUs), health programmes and health foods, grouped in the 'question mark' category in the BCG matrix. In other words, though both the SBUs are participating in high-growth markets, their own growth is open to question. The health-and-fitness market may be segmented as below in terms of consumer perceptions:

- health programmes such as AMHT
- national level fitness programmes such as Rama Bans, VLCC, Talwalkar's
- smaller local players in different parts of the country, of which there are scores

Though there is a fair amount of overlap between 'health programmes' and 'beauty programmes', some programmes such as Shahnaz Hussain's and Jamuna Pai's have been able to acquire a distinct consumer perception as 'exclusively beauty oriented programmes'. The health/fitness and beauty programmes attract a lot of indirect competition from yoga and meditation programmes like Siddh Samadhi Yoga and from Ayurvedic centres, gyms, and the like. This unstructured and fragmented nature of the market makes it difficult to guess its size and growth, except in purely qualitative terms. Most well known programmes were traditionally concentrated primarily in metros, mini metros, and Class I cities, but of late, they have seen a spurt in growth in smaller towns as well. In the Mumbai market, Talwalkar's and VLCC are the largest players. VLCC is the most heavily advertised, and Talwalkar's is the oldest. Most programmes other than VLCC, including AMHT, use event marketing and articles in the print media as their major means of promotion. Tie-ups with beauty pageants are a very popular means of promotion. AMHT, a small but well known and influential player in this market, has now reached the stage where the focus on strategy for further growth has became vital to its continued well-being and to a successful move from entrepreneurial to managerial decision making and operational style. The company would like to identify an appropriate growth strategy and put in place business process systems which will increase managerial accountability and install performance-based managerial reward process for its young team of professional managers. As the CMD, Mr Mukherjee looks after the marketing and finance functions in the company. Strategy decisions are taken jointly with his wife, whose main responsibility areas are research and product development, in addition to the day-to-day supervision of the fitness centers. Mr Mukerjee had retained some consultants for help with planning out the long-term strategy of the organization. The consultants believed that before expanding into new products and new markets, it was important for the company to assess how the consumers, most of whom the company believes to be women, perceive AMHT as a brand. To this end, they had initiated a small study in Mumbai two months ago. The report that had just come in is attached to the letter from the consultant:

Dear Saurabh,

The results of the consumer-perception study that we had carried out are given in the pages that follow. You will remember that we had decided to cover both men and women above 15 years of age, and had planned on a sample of 50, equally between the two groups. We ended up interviewing 31 men and 35 women, 66 in all. I am afraid the study does confirm your fears that AMHT is not very clearly positioned, falling between the two stools of health and beauty instead. Of course, awareness about AMHT is quite high. Anjali's articles in The Bombay Times have a particularly strong recall. But unlike with other health programmes, the conversion from awareness to trial does not seem too high in case of AMHT. Being a 'diet only' programme, on the one hand it does not have as strong a link with health and fitness as other 'exercise and diet' programmes, and on the other hand, since its communication does not directly emphasize beauty but only health, it is not seen as a beauty programme, either. Availability is another negative—four centres in a city the size of Mumbai are far too few. The customers do not seem very keen on travelling long distances three to four times a week to AMHT centres, when they do not know WHAT it is about AMHT for which they should take the trouble; and there are so many alternatives available! Well, the news is not all bad: Anjali is perceived by the women as quite the expert, and they would like greater interaction with her. Maybe we could do something with that while working out the strategy. After you have gone through the findings in the attached sheets, do give me a call. I am available for a presentation whenever you are.

Regards.

The Consumer Perception Study

1. Objectives: To determine

1. the importance attached to health and beauty by men and women

2. the methods used for maintaining health and beauty
3. awareness of specific programmes including AMHT
4. use of various AMHT programmes
5. perceptions and positioning of AMHT and other competitive programmes
6. future usage-intent

2. **Sample:** The sample for the study is shown in Table 11.6.

Table 11.6 Sample for the Study

	Proposed	Actual	Age-wise Distribution		
			15–25	26–35	36+
Men	25	31	14	6	10
Women	25	35	16	6	13
Total	50	66	30	12	23

Note: All respondents were from SEC A, A and B.

3. **Findings:** The findings of the study are listed below:

   i. *Importance of health and beauty:* Of the list of six drivers of individual satisfaction in life that the respondents were presented with, health was rated most important by both men and women (men: 4.65 out 5 and women: 4.71 out 5). The next most important parameters for both men and women are education (rated 4.63 and 4.68 respectively), followed closely by financial security (rated 4.61 and 4.63 respectively). Men rated occupational status as extremely important (4.25), ahead of women (3.97); the ratings were reversed for 'appearance' (men: 3.68; women: 4.03). A good address was rated the least important of these six, at 4.25 and 3.97 respectively.

   Most respondents claim to take some active steps for maintaining good health and staying fit. The responses may be grouped under four heads: exercise, diet related action, medical consultation and/or health supplements like vitamins, and other action like yoga meditation, massage, etc. The most popular steps are exercise and diet. Here too, gender-wise preferences are distinctly different: men go more for exercise related options, while women prefer dietary control. Convenience is the most frequently cited reason for this choice, suggesting that for greater penetration it is extremely important for any health programmed to be convenient in terms of time-schedule and location.

   ii. *Awareness of health/fitness programmes:* More than 83% of the respondents claimed to have heard of some fitness/health programmes. At 94%, the proportion was significantly higher among women. Unaided awareness was highest for Talwalkars (65.5%), followed by VLCC (60.0%). AMHT was mentioned by only about 11% at this stage, including weaker linkage with health. Total awareness for AMHT was, however, a gratifying 93%, and among women it was 100%. Even so, the fact the respondent had to be prodded thus suggests that the link between AMHT and health needs to be strengthened.

iii. *Source of information:* Most respondents mentioned newspaper, specially *The Bombay Times* (52.9%) and magazines (15.7%) as the source of information. Predictably, the proportions were much higher among women. Friends and relatives were mentioned by only about 20%. This is an encouraging sign in that it suggests that health being a high involvement area, even the relatively low-profile media campaign has been noted and recalled by respondents. At the same time, the relatively low 'word-of-mouth' promotion is a matter for concern: usually in India this is the most frequent source of reference for any product or service. About 14% respondents spontaneously mentioned having seen (and in some cases tried) Anjali Mukerjee's products in the shops at this stage.

iv. *Trial of AMHT:* The sample reported extremely low rates of trial of AMHT: only about 7% of those who knew of some health/fitness programme, and about 8% of those who were aware of AMHT, had tried the brand. It must, of course, be borne in mind that only about 55% of those who are aware of health programmes actually try out some programme.

This amounts to about 45% of the targeted market. A rough estimate of the market-share of AMHT would thus appear as in the table below:

- Sample size N 66   (=100%)
- Awareness of health programmes   55   (=83.3% of N)
- Awareness of AMHT   51   (=77.39% of N)
         (=92.7% of aware)
- Trial of health programmes   30   (=45.4% of N)
         (=55% of aware)
- Trial of AMHT   4   (=6.1% of N)
         (~ 7.3% of those aware of programmes)
         (~ 7.8% of those aware of AMHT)
         (~13.3% of those trying some programmes)

v. *Basis for selection of a health programme:* From the responses to this question it is apparent that the image of health programmes is closely linked to exercise and gyms in the respondent's mind. In response to an open-ended question about the basis for selection of a health programme, the largest percentage (18.2%) mentioned proximity to residence as the major determining factor, followed by low price, technical superiority of the place, referrals, and personal attention. These choices were further confirmed by the answers to a structured question, which indicated that 'long-lasting results' are what the largest number of respondents look for (84%), followed by proximity and absence of side effects (67% each). It is thus logical to assume that in a competitive market, a large network of outlets would improve market-share.

vi. *Experience with AMHT and brand perceptions:* In the small group who had tried out the AMHT weight loss programme, the overall experience appears to have been reasonably satisfactory. Individual in-depth discussions with respondents however indicated that being a 'diet only' programme, AMHT is seen as relatively weaker than other exercise based programmes. The average educated, aware consumer believes that diet is something she can manage on her own without expert advice. As such, the brand communication that is not customized to individual requirement and does not give information about maintenance after attending the weight-loss programme is seen as providing no significant benefit.

Also, the brand is identified very strongly with Dr Anjali Mukherjee, and user expectations of value for money are defined in terms of interaction with her. The rapport with the trainer is an important fact influencing the choice of the programme and AMHT is not seen as providing this link to the extent other programmes do. At the product level, the diet items given out are seen as 'tasteless' and 'boring'.

At the same time, detailed discussion with the respondent revealed that AMHT is not seen as a 'beauty' programme, unlike programmes offered by Shahnaz Hussain and Jamuna Pai, and, to an extent, VLCC. This inspite of the fact that AMHT is perceived as a 'diet only' programme, and diet is seen as a significant contributor to appearance, specially as a part of skin care. As Table 11.7 indicates, 'eating sensibly in general' is the most popular method of maintaining and enhancing appearance, followed by exercise and workouts. Visits to a beauty parlour follows in the third place.

Table 11.7   Methods of Maintaining/Enhancing Appearance

Methods	M	F	%	Total
• Visit a beauty parlour	7	27	34	51.5
• Exercise/workout at home	23	15	38	57.6
• Seek a doctor's/beauty therapists's advice	3	6	9	13.6
• Follow a formal diet	12	9	21	31.8
• Eat sensibly in general	23	25	48	72.7
• Use good quality beauty aids	5	26	31	47.0
Total	31	35	65	100.0

Gender-wise analysis reveals, though, that among women, visits to beauty parlours and use of beauty aids are marginally higher than dependence on nutrition. It is the men who seem to depend more on exercise and nutritional care for taking care of their appearance. This suggests some opportunities for AMHT: (1) highlight the link between appearance and eating habits and (2) target their messages to men as much as to women. They may not opt much for use of external enhancers like beauty aids, but do claim to rely a great deal on internal aids like nutrition for taking care of their looks, primarily because, as discussions revealed, they are seen to be easy and natural. As with health programmes, ease of use appears to be a major basis of choice of any beauty programme, with both men and women.

vii. *Future use intent:* The probability of trial of AMHT in future is extremely low at 10.9% among all those who are aware of the programme, and only slightly higher than the current 'aware-to-trial' conversion rate of 7.8%. Enquiry into major reasons for this response reveals perceptions about AHMT that need to be corrected:

- No need/satisfaction with : 29.1%
   current programme
   (No differentiation perceived in AMHT)
- Economy consideration : 21.8%
   (AMHT seen as not giving value for money)
- Location & Timings : 9.1%
   (lacking convenience of proximity)
- Not enough information : 7.3%
   (poor/inadequate communication)

Questions

1. Discuss the role of marketing research in helping AMHT increase its market-share.

2. What should be the positioning of AMHT?

3. Develop the outline of a marketing strategy plan based on this research for improving AMHT's consumer-perception and acceptability. What additional information should marketing research provide?

REFERENCES

Chandon, Pierre, V.G. Morwitz, and W.J. Reinartz 2005, 'Do Intentions Really Predict Behaviour? Self-Generated Validity Effects in Survey Research', *Journal of Marketing*, vol. 69, no. 2, pp. 1–14.

Cooper, D.R. and P.S. Schindler 1998, *Business Research Methods*, Tata McGraw-Hill, p.195.

Fishbein, Martin 1967, 'A Behaviour Theory Approach to the Relations between Beliefs about an Object and the Attitude towards the Object', *Readings in Attitude Theory and Measurement*, John Wiley, New York, pp. 389–400.

Green P.E. and D.S. Tull 1978, *Research for Marketing Decisions,* Prentice Hall, Englewood Cliffs, New Jersey, pp. 167, 172, 180–87.

Kendall, M.G. 1962, *Rank Correlation Methods*, Hafner Publishing Company, New York.

Likert, Renesis 1932, 'A Technique for the Measurement of Attitudes', *Archives of Psychology*, 140, p. 55.

Malhotra, N.K. 2004, *Marketing Research: An Applied Orientation*, Fourth edition, Pearson Education, p. 243.

Osgood, C.E., G.J. Suci, and P.H. Tannenbaum 1957, *The Measurement of Meaning*, University of Illinois Press, Urbana, Illinois.

Stapel, J. 1969, 'About 35 Years of Marketing Research in the Netherlands', as quoted in Malhotra, N.K. 2004.

PART THREE

Implementing Research:
Quantitative Surveys

- Fieldwork, Data Editing, Tabulation, and the Basic Concepts of Analysis

- Specific Techniques for Analysis of Data

- Computer Based Techniques of Data Analysis

12 Fieldwork, Data Editing, Tabulation, and the Basic Concepts of Analysis

OBJECTIVES

After reading this chapter, the readers will be able to understand:

- what to watch out for in fieldwork; how to build checks and controls
- the editing and the tabulation of data—marginal tabulation and cross-tabulation
- the basic concepts of analysis
- how to test associative relationships—association, correlation, and regression
- how to test for differences— ANOVA

INTRODUCTION

In the earlier chapters, we examined the 'what' and 'why' of issues involved in a marketing decision, and tried to explore the 'how' through discussions on the methods of data collection. This chapter will take us further in the examination of the 'how' aspect of decision-making, through an understanding of the ground processes of data collection, the nitty-gritty of data editing and tabulation, and the basics of data analysis. The implementation of the details of the data-collection process in the field is the primary driver of the quality of data obtained. It influences the quality of conclusions that may be drawn on the basis of that data and also, therefore, the accuracy and the quality of the marketing decisions taken on the basis of that data. Understanding the nature of the fieldwork and the steps involved is, thus, extremely important to ensure quality. This chapter begins with a description of these steps and discusses the controls required to ensure quality in fieldwork, including in the training of fieldworkers.

Once the data has been collected from the field, it must be 'cleaned'; no matter how much care is taken in fieldwork, some data editing is invariably needed before the further stages of data tabulation and analysis are considered. The concepts of data editing and tabulation have been discussed in this chapter, followed by a discussion on some basic concepts of analysis.

FIELDWORK

The data for a survey may be collected, broadly, through two methods—the interactive method, such as personal interviews at the respondent's residence or place of work, intercept interviews in the shop, or telephonic interviews, and the non-interactive method, such as interviews by mail, email, or the Internet. Interactive methods obviously require an interviewer to administer the survey instrument.

Fieldwork may be undertaken by the marketing personnel of the organization itself or, as is often the case, may be outsourced to a marketing research agency. In either case, interviewers trained for the purpose carry out the fieldwork. These interviewers may be a part of the agency's regular roster of interviewers, or may be recruited ad hoc for a particular study. There are agencies that specialize exclusively in conducting fieldwork. They usually maintain a database of interviewers, who are not necessarily regular employees of the agency but are available on call. Even so, fieldworkers suitable for a study have to be selected keeping in mind the particular requirements of the study.

Process of Fieldwork

The steps involved in the process of fieldwork are given in Fig. 12.1.

Specification of job requirements   Once the research brief has been given to the agency and a proposal has been prepared by it, the requirements of the job need to be specified in detail. These specifications should provide information on the profile of the respondents, where and how many times they are to be interviewed, and the most suitable method of data collection. The specifications will influence the choice of fieldworkers.

Specification of fieldworker characteristics   Once the job requirements have been identified, the criteria for the choice of the fieldworker flow directly. Some general requirements of a good fieldworker are physical stamina, persistence, reasonably acceptable education levels and communication skills, comfort levels with people (especially strangers), pleasant appearance, initiative, and integrity. Gender, age, and experience are other criteria that must be taken into account while determining the suitability of a potential fieldworker for a particular study. It is important to choose fieldworkers with whom the respondents may be able to identify. For example, a female fieldworker may not be suitable for a survey on alcohol consumption habits among lower income group males, although she is likely to be more suitable than a male for eliciting information from small children. Similarly, doctors usually do not find non-medical interviewers acceptable. Some level of domain knowledge is a major advantage. Experienced fieldworkers have the advantage of being familiar with the potential problems and are, therefore, easy to brief. They are more likely to have developed the skills of obtaining respondent cooperation. However, the disadvantages may be that they tend to be rigid in their views and, therefore, difficult to train. Also, since they are more familiar with the opportunities for cheating, they could prove to be less reliable.

Briefing the fieldworkers   The interviewers, or fieldworkers, regardless of their intelligence level, domain knowledge, and experience, need to be briefed in detail about the survey for which they have been hired to collect data.

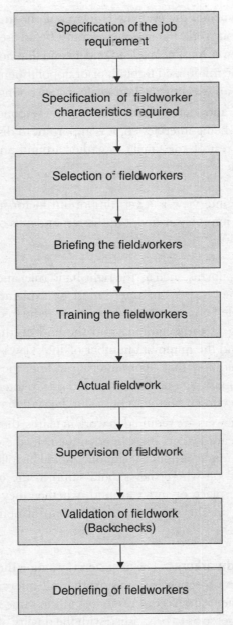

Fig. 12.1 The Process of Fieldwork

- To begin with, the fieldworker must be given a background of the survey—the rationale and the client's requirements from the study.
- The profile of the respondent must be clearly explained to the fieldworker.
- The most suitable time and place for the initial contact in the case of a personal interview must be specified. It is usually preferable to interview a working woman

at her residence in the evening. However, if she indicates a preference for being interviewed at work, the interviewer must be advised to fix a prior appointment. The interviewer must be made to understand that non-response and 'not-at-home' errors can be minimized through prior appointments, irrespective of the respondents being an executive, a housewife, or a working couple.

- All the 'dos' and 'don'ts' with respect to the respondent must be explained—if a housewife is being interviewed, it is important to discourage the tendency on the part of the rest of the family to gather around and start providing answers or modifying her responses.

The time of the interview is a very important factor in telephonic interviews. It is essential that the interviewer finds out the respondent's convenience before launching into the interview.

- Interviewing norms, such as 'the right-hand rule' and 'the number of households' to be interviewed per apartment must be explained to the fieldworkers. They must be briefed on reporting requirements—the frequency of reporting, the time of reporting at the beginning and the end of the day's work, the period of fieldwork, and the minimum number of interviews expected per day. The right-hand rule requires that upon entering a lane, the interviewer must choose at random an apartment on the right-hand side to interview; the next sampling unit must also be chosen on the right, using the systematic sampling technique.

- If the interviewers are required to work in teams, they must be assigned to specific teams and team leaders must be identified. In the case of intercept interviews, too, the systematic sampling technique should be followed. The interviewers need to be briefed on where they should stand in the outlet—whether they should stand in one place or move around, whether they should try to interview the respondent on the spot or take an appointment suiting the respondent's convenience.

Training the fieldworkers   The next step is training the fieldworkers in the specifics of the study. The objective is to ensure that all interviewers administer the data-collection instrument and record responses in the same manner. The client must be present at this stage, so as to be satisfied with the quality of the supervision, and also to provide any product- or company-related information that has a bearing on the study. This training should extend to fieldworkers, team leaders, supervisors as well as the research executive in charge of the project.

- The first step is for all investigators to read through the data-collection instrument fully and note down any points of doubt or lack of clarity. They should then be given an opportunity to ask questions and clear their doubts.

- Next, the instrument must be discussed in detail, preferably question by question. The relevance of each question should be explained and all possible answers pointed out. The relevance of each answer to the question that follows must be explained. This is particularly important in the case of an open-ended question.
- The third step is the 'mock interview'. Its objective is to prepare the interviewer for the variations in the responses that come up and for the researcher to get an understanding of how each interviewer is likely to handle difficult responses and unusual situations in the field. At this stage, each interviewer is required to run through the complete instrument, interviewing the research executive or the supervisor. This helps caution the fieldworkers in advance that the executive or the supervisor intends to play the role of a difficult respondent. This may involve non-response, an uncooperative attitude, or inadequate or generalized and non-actionable answers such as 'maybe', 'depends', etc. The purpose is to expose the fieldworker to difficult situations, understand how to handle them, and provide the necessary guidance. The mock interview should run through all the stages from the introduction to the wrap-up. Each interviewer should be put through this exercise in detail. Sometimes this exercise may even point out the need for modifying or introducing some questions that may not have come up when the data-collection instrument was pilot-tested. Some guidelines for interviewing and recording responses must be provided to the interviewers at this stage.

  - Do not get into an argument with the respondent.
  - Do not talk down to the respondent or start providing answers.
  - Record the responses verbatim. Sometimes, the respondent starts giving detailed answers, which may include situations, experiences, and anecdotes that may not appear totally question-specific. Record all these as far as possible. This provides two benefits—an apparently 'rambling' response may provide insight into the respondent's motivations, experience, and overall approach to the subject of study. Moreover, such rambling responses may provide advance answers to the questions that are to follow. These questions may then be avoided. The interviewer may, in the course of the interview, convey concern about not wasting the respondent's time. This helps enhance the respondent's goodwill and makes the rest of the interview easier.
  - Use the respondent's own words instead of modifying or paraphrasing them. This will pose difficulties if the respondent is not very fluent in the language in which the data-collection instrument is worded. The interviewer may need to translate the questions and the responses. To the extent possible, this problem may be minimized by using questionnaires that have been pre-translated into the respondent's language and by recording the responses in the same language. Subsequently, these responses may be translated into the original language of the study.

- Terminate the interview only after all data have been obtained and recorded. However, questions to which the respondent has already provided answers in the course of answering other questions need not be repeated. Similarly, the respondent's time may not be wasted for obtaining personal data such as qualifications, phone number, and address, which may be obtained from other sources.

- Whenever possible, the respondent's visiting card or signature must be attached to the response sheet. In focus groups or long in-depth interviews, it is customary to present the respondent with a small gift to express appreciation.

Supervision of fieldwork   This step is essential in controlling the quality of data gathered from the field. The purpose is to ensure that the interviewers are following all the procedures, there is no dishonesty, and any unanticipated problems are taken care of immediately. The quality of fieldwork may vary for the following reasons.

1. *Inappropriate sample*   The interviewer may not always follow the sampling specifications but may select sampling units on the basis of convenience or accessibility.

2. *Inadequate sample*   The non-response levels may be high because of a wrong database, inappropriate interview timings, or the interviewer's inability to strike a rapport with the respondent. This may, at times, be restricted to some questions because the respondent may have refused to answer the question and the interviewer did not or could not persuade the respondent to do otherwise.

3. *Falsification of data*   The interviewer may fill in inaccurate or false information in part or in the entire questionnaire. This may happen either because of the interviewer's inherent dishonesty, very long questionnaires, and/or very impractical deadlines.

4. *Inadvertent errors*   Information may be filled in incorrectly in the wrong slot, or erroneous information may be filled in. This is likely to happen when, for example, the interviewer has to translate the questions on the spot from one language to another and back, or in the case of numerical responses.

5. *Inflated costs*   When the compensation rules are not clearly explained in advance clearly to the interviewers or when a part of the compensation is for actual expenses incurred, there is a possibility of transportation costs being inflated.

Validation of fieldwork   Most of the problems cited above need to be taken care of through stringent field supervision. Issues such as unwieldy questionnaires and impracticable deadlines must be identified and sorted out before the survey is taken up in the field. In order to validate the responses, the supervisor or the team leader must follow strictly the norm of 'backchecking' a certain percentage, usually 10 per cent to 15 per cent, of the interviews conducted by each interviewer. Backchecking means, literally, checking back to verify whether the interviews were actually carried out.

Further, the team leader must ascertain whether all the questions were actually administered by questioning the interviewer. If the responses vary substantially from the ones indicated in the response sheets submitted by the interviewer, it is a pointer to likely cheating, especially if there appears to be a pattern to the responses in all questionnaires completed by an interviewer and they differ from those obtained by other interviewers. The interviewer must be queried on these discrepancies. This practice must be followed on a daily basis so that errors and cheating are minimized.

Debriefing of the interviewers The debriefing of the interviewers is undertaken along with the editing of field data. It has two objectives—the verification of the responses obtained by the interviewer, as explained above, and a feedback for the interviewers as well as an evaluation of their work. All fieldwork-related criteria should be considered for this purpose—to check for the quality of interviews and data obtained, response rates, time taken for data collection, and costs incurred.

CODING AND EDITING OF DATA

We shall now discuss the process of coding and editing data in detail.

Coding of Data

Coding means assigning unique numerical or symbolic values to the various responses to each question obtained through a data-collection instrument. It is the first step in the process of the collation of data. Coding involves assigning a column position (field) to some specific information about a respondent. Usually respondents are assigned 'respondent IDs' and their opinions about one of the set of items being studied are assigned a 'record'. For example, let us assume that data from 50 respondents, indicating their awareness and usage pattern of three brands of toilet soaps and three brands of shampoo, collected by one interviewer, is to be coded. Data relating to toilet soaps is labelled Record 1 and data relating to shampoos is labelled Record 2. Since there are only two distinct product categories, the column relating to records will occupy only one space. This would be true up to 99 product categories. The part of the code book that gives coding instructions relating to toilet soaps is indicated in Table 12.1. Coding is most easily and effectively done on a spreadsheet, such as MS EXCEL.

Data results may be *precoded* or *postcoded*. All responses to structured questions can be precoded since it is possible to define before the fieldwork the various categories into which responses to a question may fall, as in the example discussed earlier. In the case of unstructured questions, it is not possible to anticipate all the answers, so it is necessary to list all the responses after the fieldwork, and postcode them.

It is good to have fixed-field codes, i.e., to try to have the same number of records and the same data appearing in a particular column for each respondent. If possible, missing values should be assigned the same standard values. To minimize variations in coding, written instructions should be given to those editing and coding data.

Table 12.1 Codebook Excerpts Showing Information for the First Record: Toilet Soaps

Column No.	Variable No.	Variable Name	Q. No.	Coding Instruction
1–2	1	Respondent ID		(01–50)
3	2	Record No.		1–2
4	3	Interviewer code		1 (Same for all respondents)
5–10	4	Date code		As coded on the qr.
11–15	5	Time code		As coded on the qr.
16–17		Blank		Leave these two columns blank
18	6	Who buys	1	Housewife = 1
				Male head = 2
				Others = 3
				Input the number circled
19	7	Awareness of Brand 1	2a	T-o-M =1
				Unaided = 2
				Aided = 3
				Missing values = 9
				For Q. 2a–2c Input the response number obtained
20	8	Awareness of Brand 2	2b	
22	10	Awareness of other brands	2d	T-o-M =1
				Unaided = 2
				Aided = 3
				Missing Values = 9
				For Q. 2a–2d Input the response number obtained
23	10	Usage of Brand 1	3a	Ever Used =1
				Currently Used = 2
				Missing Values = 9
				For Q. 3a–3c Input the response number obtained
24	11	Usage of Brand 2	3b	
25	12	Usage of Brand 3	3c	
26	13	Blank		Leave this column blank

Note: T-o-M = Top of the mind recall

Coding of open questions and content analysis   Post-coding is necessary for open-ended questions. The semantic content of a response is measured with the help of *content analysis*. This is a relevant method for coding and analysing communication data rather than objects or behaviour. Berelson (1952) described it as 'a research technique for the objective, systematic and quantitative description of the manifest content of a communication'. Today the definition has been expanded to include latent content, symbolic meaning, and qualitative analysis as well. According to Stemler (2001), this can be a useful technique for determining the focus of an individual, a group, or an institution as well as for allowing inferences that may later be corroborated by other methods of data collection.

The first step in content analysis is to select the coding scheme. Coding units may be of various kinds.

- *Syntactical*, such as words, sentences, or paragraphs. The assumption in the word-frequency count is that words (or phrases/sentences) that are repeated most often reflect the areas of greatest concern. However, this may not always yield the desired results. For example, synonyms may at times be used for the purpose of improving the writing style. Certain words may not be used often for cultural reasons. Alternatively, a word may be used in different contexts and, therefore, may not convey the same meaning.

- *Referential* coding unit is concerned with the way persons, objects, or events are referred to. This is particularly relevant when making inferences about attitudes, opinions, preferences, or values. For example, a brand of car may be referred to as 'old-fashioned', 'fuel-guzzler', or 'aspirational'.

- *Propositional* units use complex frameworks and require breaking down the text into subframes in order to examine the assumptions involved and the relationships between the entities. Stemler (2001) quotes an example from Krippendorf (1980) to say that the statement, 'investors took another hit as the stock market continued its descent' has to be broken down into two propositions: 'The stock market has been performing poorly recently/Investors have been losing money.'

- *Thematic* According to Cooper and Schindler (1999), 'These units are higher level abstractions inferred from their connection to a unique structure or pattern in the content.' The theme may be temporal (e.g., 'consumer incomes have improved in recent years'; 'people could not afford these products earlier'), geographical (e.g., 'incomes in urban areas have been growing faster than in rural areas'; 'consumer lifestyles in semi-urban and rural areas are following the pattern of metros'), and so on.

- *Time and space measure* Coding units are concerned with the length or duration of the communication. For example, 'whether a sentence or two paragraphs have been devoted to a message' could help assess the importance attached to the topic of discussion.

The use of more than one coding unit in the repeated analysis of data or combining different coding units usually provides richer information.

Editing Data

Editing the data is essential to maintain consistency and uniformity in the data and exclude ambiguous or incomplete data before tabulation begins. Editing includes the following steps.

1. *Checks for veracity* This is best done at the stage of debriefing of the interviewer. The objective is to determine whether the response has been genuinely obtained from the respondent or the interviewer made it up, partially or completely. This has been discussed already.

2. *Consistency checks* Responses that appear contradictory, illogical, ambiguous ('maybe', 'depends', 'now that you are talking about it, I might consider using it', etc.), or are questions in response to a question ('What do *you* think it should be?') provide no insight into the respondent's thinking and cannot be included in any response category. They are, therefore, best omitted from tabulation.

3. *Missing responses* This situation arises either because the response may not have been provided by the respondent, may not have been recorded by the interviewer, or may have been edited out because of inconsistency. Editing is required then to

   - substitute an average response instead of the missing value.
   - substitute a likely response, if possible. Sometimes, especially in the case of qualitative answers, the response to a question may be imputed from the overall trend of the responses, i.e., derived from the consistent pattern of the rest of the responses.
   - work with a reduced sample, excluding the missing responses to a question, or totally excluding the questionnaires with missing responses. This is a feasible option only if the number of missing responses is not so large as to introduce bias in the analysis and reduce the reliability of the sample.

Statistical adjustment of data

A major part of editing is concerned with the statistical adjustment of data to make it more meaningful and to reduce the inherent anomalies that may be present in it because of individual styles of the respondents. Major procedures for data adjustment include the following.

Weighting   This is a process by which individual responses are assigned a certain number, i.e., weight, according to some pre-specified rule, so that the data become more representative on certain characteristics. For example, in ranked data, responses ranked higher may be assigned greater weight compared to lower-ranked responses. This helps to be truly more representative of the respondents' assessment of the relative importance of the characteristics being ranked. Weights may be assigned to data to adjust the sample to attach greater importance to respondents with some characteristics. For example, in a study on the public opinion of electoral processes, responses from people with higher education levels may be assigned higher weights; in a study of skin moisturizing lotions, responses from older women may be assigned a higher weight, as they are likely to be the heavier users of the product.

Variable re-specification   Sometimes the data may be re-specified to make it more consistent with the objectives of the study or to make the measurement of a variable more meaningful. For example, a large number of response categories may be grouped together, often through processes, such as factor analysis, in order to make better sense out of data and to make it easier to work with while not losing any significant information. Another process of re-specification involves the introduction of *dummy* variables. For example, let us consider a question on the current usage of a brand of butter, as 'Are you using (Brand A) now?' The usage could then be expressed as a dummy variable, with the current usage being assigned a value of 1, and the current non-usage a value of 0.

Scale transformation This is another common procedure for adjusting data statistically. It involves manipulating scale values to make them comparable with other scales. This may be needed in a study, because different scales may be used to measure different variables, making a meaningful comparison difficult. Also, even when the same scale is being used, some respondents may tend to consistently use lower ratings, while some others may consistently use higher ratings. For example, consider the case of two divisions of second-year MBA students being given a test in marketing research. A strict instructor may mark the students in a narrow range of 60 to 75 marks, while another, more lenient instructor may mark them in the range of 65 to 90. In order to make the two sets of evaluation comparable, the data must be transformed using letter grades, ranging from A (the highest) to E (the lowest). This kind of transformation will even out the variations in evaluation resulting from the instructor's predilections. One of the most common forms of scale transformation is *standardization*. This takes care of the variation in responses because of the difference in scales. The process is to calculate the mean $\bar{X}$ and the standard deviation S_X of each variable X and redefine the variable as

$$Z_i = (X_i - \bar{X})/S_{\bar{X}}$$

TABULATION OF DATA

Tabulation is the final step in preparing data for analysis. Simple tabulation involves merely counting the number of responses in a category and presenting them as *frequency tables*, i.e., the number of times different responses to a question are obtained. For this purpose, the kind of responses that are required and the categories into which the responses to a question must be grouped must be decided in advance. The coding of data helps in this exercise, since it serves to list all the possible responses to a question. The totals of frequencies in each category are called 'marginal totals' and this process is called 'marginal tabulation'. In the example of coding related to soap and shampoo brands mentioned earlier, the frequency distribution of the awareness of the three brands of soap is tabulated as in Table 12.2.

In addition, information on the frequency of responses that occur simultaneously in two categories of variables is usually required. Such tabulation is termed *cross-tabulation* or *contingency tables*. Cross-tabulation is needed to define the relationships between variables and to provide greater insights into data. The numbers within the brackets in the awareness level column of Table 12.2 indicate the code. This kind of simple tabulation is called marginal tabulation.

Table12.2 Frequency Distribution of Brand Awareness of Three Brands of Toilet Soap

Brand	Awareness Level	Usage	
		Frequency	% of N
1	Top-of-the-mind (1)	15	30.0
	Unaided (2)	10	20.0
	Aided (3)	7	14.0
	Total	32	64.0
2	Top-of-the-mind (1)	8	16.0
	Unaided (2)	8	16.0
	Aided (3)	14	28.0
	Total	30	60.0
3	Top-of-the-mind (1)	2	4.0
	Unaided (2)	7	14.0
	Aided (3)	11	22.0
	Total	20	40.0
4 (Others)	Top-of-the-mind (1)	25	50.0
	Unaided (2)	25	50.0
Total samples N		50	100.0

In practice, percentages may be computed row-wise, as shown in Table 12.2, or column-wise. An illustration of such computation for Brand 1 is given in Tables 12.3 and 12.4.

Table 12.3 Usage by Brand Awareness

Brand Awareness	Usage %		Row total
	User	Non-user	
T-o-M	100.0%	0.0%	15
Unaided	80.0%	20.0%	10
Aided	0.0%	100.0%	7

Table 12.4 Brand Awareness by Usage

Brand Awareness	Usage %	
	User	Non-user
T-o-M	65.2%	0.0%
Unaided	34.8%	22.2%
Aided	0.0%	77.8%
Column total	23	9

While Table 12.3 displays the computation of usage levels of Brand 1 among respondents with different levels of brand awareness, Table 12.4 shows the relative levels of awareness of the brand among users and non-users. The usual practice is to compute percentages along the independent variable, across the dependent variable. Although the percentages in Table 12.3 have been computed treating usage as the dependent variable so that the data is interpreted as a 'per cent of users among respondents with different levels of brand awareness', the usual practice would be to look for 'brand awareness levels among users and non-users', as shown in Table 12.4. In general, this computation depends on the objectives or areas of enquiry of the survey.

An example of the cross-tabulation of brand awareness and usage from the preceding data is shown in Table 12.5. The table depicts the levels of usage of the brand among respondents demonstrating the different levels of awareness—those with top-of-the-mind (T-o-M) recall of a brand are all users of the brand. Among those who registered unaided, but not with top-of-the-mind recall of that brand, are some non-users. It stands to reason that the brand currently in use would have top-of-the-mind recall, as shown in the table. Other brands which are either high profile as a result of the longevity or high levels of advertising would be familiar to all those who have either used the brand some time or have been exposed to the advertising for the brand. Among those registering unaided recall of Brand 1, 80 per cent were users and 20 per cent were non-users. Others who have not used the brand may not always recall the brand at this stage, i.e., without any assistance in the form of an oral or written list. Such a list, providing an 'aid' to recall, is most likely to bring about the recall of brands that have been heard of even if these do not form part of the respondent's immediate consciousness.

Table 12.5 displays cross-tabulation between two variables, i.e., bivariate cross-tabulation. The table shows the percentage of users among respondents with different levels of awareness. Similar cross-tabulation could be and, at times, is required to be undertaken between three or more variables. For instance, in the soap-and-shampoo example discussed earlier, information may be required about the use of soap and shampoo brands among those demonstrating different levels of awareness of the brands of two categories, as well as the use of different brands of shampoo among those using each brand of soap. A multi-brand FMCG organization may want to know the 'basket' of its products used by an average user household—the number of products

Table 12.5 Usage of Three Brands of Toilet Soap Among Respondents Demonstrating Different Levels of Awareness

| Brand | Awareness | | Usage | | | |
	Level	Frequency (N)	Users	% of N	Non-users	% of N
1	T-o-M	15	15	100.0	0	0.0
	Unaided	10	8	80.0	2	20.0
	Aided	7	0	0.0	7	100.0
	Total	32	23	71.9	9	28.1
2	T-o-M	8	8	100.0	0	0.0
	Unaided	8	6	75.0	2	25.0
	Aided	14	1	7.1	13	92.9
	Total	30	15	50.0	15	50.0
3	T-o-M	2	2	100.0	0	0.0
	Unaided	7	4	57.1	3	42.9
	Aided	11	1	9.1	10	90.9
	Total	20	7	35.0	13	65.0

normally used as well as the particular categories generally used together. The introduction of the third variable often serves to explain or refine the original relationship. It may indicate that the relationship is actually spurious, the two variables initially considered are actually related not to each other, but each to the third variable, or if the third variable is taken into consideration, it may be found that a relationship between the original variables actually exists where none had been indicated. However, cross-tabulation of more than three variables at a time is usually quite tedious, and does not often provide particularly useful insights.

Some guidelines must always be kept in mind while preparing tables.

- Tables must be prepared with the survey objectives or the areas of enquiry in mind. Each table must provide information on a survey objective or at least some of the variables being studied in relation to that objective, so that two or three tables together fully provide data that answer the queries raised through that objective. Once all tables have been prepared, all the data needed to answer the queries should become available through them.
- Table titles must be self-explanatory.
- The response categories listed must be exhaustive and mutually exclusive.
- Percentages should be calculated in the direction of the independent variable.
- The final row and column totals must always tally with the size of the sample or the variable totals. Differences between these two sets of totals can arise only if there are missing responses. These must be indicated under the heading 'not answered', so that the totals add up and a clearer picture of the response pattern emerges.
- To the extent possible, tables should present the frequencies as well as percentages.
- In a marketing research report, graphs and charts are not substitutes for numerical tables—both should be presented.

The identification of a meaningful relationship between variables leads to the next step, viz., investigating the reasons underlying the relationship. Control variables, as discussed in Chapter 7, are useful in answering these questions. They indicate the conditions under which the relationships exist and the reasons for the relationship. The use of statistical packages, such as SPSS, Systat, Minitab, and SAS, help in developing n-way tables in which multiple control variables may be used. .

Data mining

For handling large amounts of dynamic data requiring complex analysis, data mining is often needed. Cooper and Schindler (1999) have described this as the process of obtaining information from formal databases. The two major functions that data mining serves are as follows:

- determining patterns in the data, including the relationships underpinning data structures
- predicting trends and behaviours, including predictive models

Since data mining is used for both retrospective and prospective dynamic data delivery at multiple points, it is necessarily dependent on computer-based statistical techniques. Some of the popular techniques are clustering, neural networks, tree models, classification, and association-based techniques such as market-basket analysis.

PRELIMINARY ANALYSIS OF DATA

Once the data have been tabulated, analysis can be taken up. Data analysis is not an end in itself but aims at answering all the queries raised in the survey and at assisting in decision-making. It should, therefore, provide clear responses to each area of enquiry on which the decision will be based. The choice of a data analysis strategy should thus be based on the following:

- the objectives of the survey
- the degree of detail required in the analysis
- the characteristics of the statistical techniques being considered
- the comfort level of the researcher with the various techniques

Now we will discuss some basic techniques of analysis, such as the tests of hypotheses relating to the average values in the sample and the population, and those related to association, dependence, and interdependence between variables. A student must be familiar with the basic concepts of statistics such as measures of location and dispersion.

The formulation of hypotheses in a testable form is an essential step in planning marketing research. Almost all analyses in marketing research are concerned with testing and verification of hypotheses. Quantitative research, in particular, is concerned with testing hypotheses that are stated in a quantifiable, measurable form, such as the average value of a frequency distribution, the dispersion of values in a distribution, and the degree of association between two variables. A hypothesis stated in totally qualitative terms, such as the following one, cannot be tested statistically and, therefore, has to be modified and expressed in more specific terms before it may be verified numerically.

$$H_0 : \text{women like shopping}$$

This statement is an assumption, expressed in extremely general terms. In order to verify it, we will have to limit its interpretation in terms of one of the following options at a time.

1. women's shopping orientation compared to that of men

OR

2. women's preference for shopping as compared with other activities they spend time on

OR

3. women's preference for shopping as compared with their preference for getting someone else to do it

This generalized statement may be open to many other interpretations. Expressions such as 'like' also need to be defined in measurable terms—how would we measure 'liking' to be able to decide whether or not shopping is 'liked'? What degree of positive inclination may be termed as 'liked'?

The testing of hypotheses is dependent exclusively on the information obtained from the sample. Since even the most accurate sampling data are bound to differ somewhat from population data, the testing of hypotheses is concerned with determining whether or not these differences are statistically significant, i.e., whether the differences could be due merely to chance random error or there is reason to believe that the sampling data are not adequately representative of population characteristics. We may, therefore, define the steps in the testing of hypotheses as follows.

- The first step in the analysis is the definition of a hypothesis, H_0 (or all hypotheses being tested), called the null hypothesis, in specific, measurable terms.
- The statistic to be measured for testing the hypothesis is then defined.
- The alternative hypothesis, H_1, is specified.
- The test appropriate for testing the null hypothesis and the appropriate probability distribution is identified.
- The acceptable significance level is specified.
- The sample is specified and data collected.
- The test statistic is calculated.
- The critical value of the test statistic corresponding to the significance level is specified.
- The probability of the test statistic at this level is specified.
- The calculated and critical values of the test statistic are compared.
- The hypothesis is rejected if the probability of the test statistic is greater than the significance level, in other words, if the calculated value of the test statistic is greater than the tabulated value, indicating that the deviations in the sample are too large to be due merely to chance. If the calculated value is smaller than the tabulated value, the variations could be attributed to chance, so the hypothesis cannot be rejected at this level of significance. Note that it is not 'accepted', but merely 'not rejected', since more stringent tests at different significance levels may indicate different results.

Univariate, Bivariate, and Multivariate Analysis

The tests of statistical hypotheses may relate to a single measurement of each of the n sample objects $(x_1, x_2, ..., x_n)$ or several measurements of each object but on each variable $x, y,$ or z in isolation $[(x_1, x_2, ..., x_n); (y_1, y_2, ..., y_n) ..., (z_1, z_2, ..., z_n)]$. This is referred to as *univariate analysis*. Alternatively, statistical hypotheses may be concerned with the study of relationships between two variables (*bivariate analysis*) $[(x_1, y_1)\ (x_2, y_2)\ldots(x_n, y_n)]$ or many variables (*multivariate analysis*) $[(x_1, y_1, z_1),\ (x_2, y_2, z_2)\ldots(x_n, y_n, z_n)]$ simultaneously and there may be two or more measurements of each variable.

Tests relating to univariate techniques vary, depending on whether the underlying data are measured on nominal, ordinal, interval, or ratio scale. Metric data, i.e., data based on interval or ratio scales are tested using *parametric tests* and are based on the assumption that the underlying frequency distribution is normal or asymptotically normal. Data based on nominal or ordinal scales, on the other hand, are tested through *non-parametric tests*, which do not require any such assumptions about the data distribution. Again, tests may vary depending on whether a single sample or multiple samples are involved, and whether the multiple samples are dependent or independent. Figure 12.2 describes the various kinds of univariate tests.

For metric data, the t-test and the z-test (normal test) are most commonly used to test for differences, especially for one or two samples. To determine if more than two

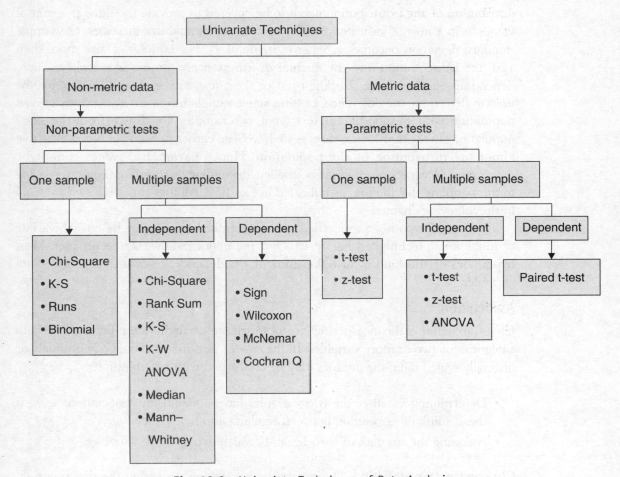

Fig. 12.2 Univariate Techniques of Data Analysis

given samples have all been drawn from the same population, the analysis of variance (ANOVA) must be used.

One-sample tests are needed when we have a single sample and wish to test the hypothesis that the sample is derived from a specified population. For example, we may wish to test the success potential of a new brand of shampoo on the basis of the hypothesis that at least 40 per cent of the users find the shampoo acceptable. In other words, the sample has been derived from a user population 40 per cent of whose members find the shampoo acceptable.

The t-test is based on student's t-distribution, and the z-test is based on the normal distribution. The two distributions are similar in appearance, being bell-shaped and symmetric. However, the t-distribution has a narrower 'bell', i.e., there is less area in the centre and more in both tails compared to the normal curve. This is because the t-test is applicable when the population variance σ^2 is unknown and has to be estimated by the sample variance s^2. Since the sample standard deviation s lacks the precision of σ, this imprecision makes the spread necessary, as a greater area in the frequency distribution of the t-distribution needs to be covered to provide the same per cent of values as in a normal distribution. However, as the sample size increases, the sample standard deviation becomes a better estimate of σ. For samples of size more than 120, the t-distribution and the normal distribution are almost identical. As such, depending on the sample size, the t-test or the z-test, as mentioned earlier, may be used to determine the difference, i.e., if a single sample has been drawn from a given population with specific parameters, or if two samples are drawn from the same population. In the non-metric case, as we have seen earlier, no information is available about the distribution of the population. Hence parametric values cannot be determined. A variety of tests may be applied, depending on specific conditions relating to the sampling distribution, as indicated in Fig. 12.2. All these are discussed in detail in the following chapter.

The tests of hypotheses concerned with two or more variables are based on bivariate or multivariate techniques. Figure 12.3 lists the major multivariate techniques. Most hypotheses of this kind involve the study of the dependence or interdependence of variables.

Association

Cross-tabulation is the measurement of observations occurring simultaneously in data categories of two or more variables. In the case of non-metric data, i.e., nominally or ordinally scaled data, the analysis may be concerned with two questions:

- Determining whether the two variables have a significant association—e.g., is there a link or association between smoking and lung cancer?
- Assessing the strength of association between two or more variables

Chi-square (χ^2) Statistic   The χ^2 statistic is used for answering the first question, i.e., measuring the significance of association between two variables when the data

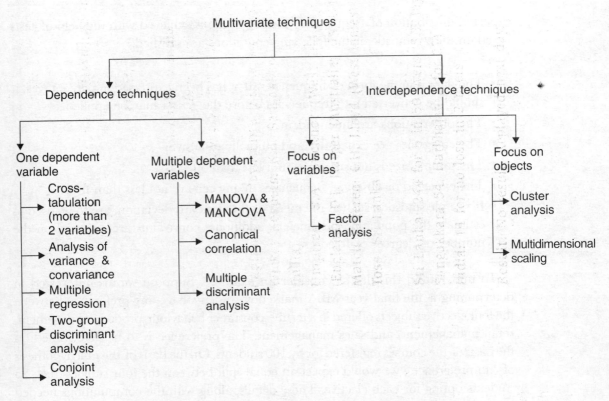

Fig. 12.3 Multivariate Techniques of Data Analysis
Source: Adapted from Malhotra 2004.

are expressed as frequencies. The χ^2 variable is the sum of the squares of normal variables. It has a skewed frequency distribution, the shape of which becomes more symmetrical as the number of degrees of freedom increases. For example, the χ^2 table[1], which lists the upper-tail areas of the χ^2 distribution, shows that for one degree of freedom, the upper-tail area of 0.05 has a value of 3.841. In other words, when the distribution has one degree of freedom, the probability of exceeding a χ^2 value of 3.841 is greater than 0.05, or when the significance level is .05, the critical value of χ^2 with one degree of freedom is 3.841. The second question is relevant only if the association between the variables is significant. The strength of association, i.e., the answer to the second question, is determined by various measures based on the χ^2 statistic.

In marketing research studies, the χ^2 distribution is typically used for testing two kinds of hypotheses.

Goodness of fit   In data analysis, we are often concerned with determining whether the observed distribution of frequencies is compatible with any theoretical or expected distribution based on the null hypothesis, i.e., how well the observed data 'fits' the

---

[1] Readers are advised to refer to the standard Chi-square tables available in the market.

expected distribution of frequencies. This objective is achieved with the help of tests based on the χ^2 statistic, if the following conditions are satisfied:

- The data is in the form of frequencies. If it has been expressed in percentages, it should be converted into frequencies before the χ^2 test may be applied.
- The observations are independent.
- The categories are exhaustive and mutually exclusive.
- The sample size is not small, i.e., not less than 50.
- The expected or observed frequencies in any cell are not less than five.
- If sample statistics, such as the mean or the standard deviation, are to be used to estimate the population parameters, additional constraints are imposed on the number of degrees of freedom.

To understand this, let us consider an example. Suppose we are interested in determining if the final year MBA marketing students have any preference between the four elective subjects offered in a term—consumer behaviour, product management, retail management, and sales management. The preference is to be determined on the basis of the courses registered for by 100 students. On the basis of the null hypothesis of 'no preference', we would expect an equal split between the four subjects, i.e., 25 students opting for each elective. These details, along with the computations needed to test if the observed frequencies of preference are compatible with this distribution, are given in Table 12.6.

Since there are four options, the χ^2 statistic for testing preferences is computed with three degrees of freedom as

$$\chi^2 = \sum (O_i - E_i)^2 / E_i = 24$$

Under the null hypothesis, the value of the χ^2 statistic with the three degrees of freedom at a 95 per cent level of confidence is given in the χ^2 table. Since the computed value at 24 is much larger than this tabulated value, the differences in preference for the four electives obtained in the sample could not have been due to chance, and the null hypothesis is, therefore, not accepted. It must be noted that the test merely

Table 12.6   Observed versus Expected Frequencies in the Goodness-of-Fit Test

Subject	Observed Frequency of Preference (O_i)	Expected Frequency of Preference (E_i)	$O_i - E_i$	$(O_i - E_i)^2 / E_i$
Consumer Beh.	15	25	−10	100/25 = 4.00
Product Mgmt.	45	25	20	400/25 = 16.00
Retail Mgmt.	25	25	0	0.00
Sales Mgmt.	15	25	−10	100/25 = 4.00
Total	100	100		24.00

determines whether or not the difference in preferences is significant; it cannot indicate the strength of association between the four options.

Tests of independence   Two variables are said to be independent if the variation in the values of one has no bearing on (i.e., is not contingent upon) the values of the other. The χ^2 statistic is used for determining this independence. For example, let us consider the association between the undergraduate degrees of 100 MBA students and their choice of specialization at the MBA level, as indicated in Table 12.7, called a 'contingency table'.

In order to test the association between the choice of specialization and the undergraduate degree, we state the null hypothesis as 'no association between undergraduate degree discipline and the specialization chosen at the MBA level'. Under this hypothesis, the cell frequencies f_{ij} (given within brackets) would be expected to equal the ratio

$$f_{ij} = R_i \times C_j / N \qquad\qquad (i = 1, ..., s, j = 1, ..., t)$$

where R_i is the ith row, C_j is the jth column, and N is the total of all rows and columns, equal to the total sample size. If F_{ij} is the observed frequency of the ith row and jth column, and f_{ij} is its expected cell frequency, we calculate the χ^2 statistic as

$$\chi^2 = \sum_{j}^{t} \sum_{i}^{s} (F_{ij} - f_{ij})^2 / N$$

with $(s-1)(t-1)$ degrees of freedom, and compare it with the tabulated value of χ^2 at the α level of significance and $(s-1)(t-1)$ degrees of freedom. In the preceding example, the value of χ^2 is calculated to be 0.907. The tabulated value with six degrees of freedom and $\alpha = 0.05$ is 12.59. Since the calculated value is significantly lower than the tabulated value, we may safely accept the null hypothesis and conclude that the apparent association is only due to chance, and this sample does not indicate any significant association between a student's undergraduate discipline and the choice of the specialization area at the MBA level.

One major limitation of the chi-square test is that the statistic is proportional to the

Table 12.7   Observed versus Expected Frequencies in the Test of Independence

MBA Major	Undergraduate Degree				
	Engineering	Science	Commerce	Others	Total
Finance	18 (17.1)	7 (7.6)	8 (7.6)	5 (5.7)	38
Marketing	17 (15.75)	8 (7.0)	5 (7.0)	5 (5.25)	35
Others	10 (12.15)	5 (5.4)	7 (5.4)	5 (4.05)	27
Total	45	20	20	15	100

sample size. Chi-square analysis can be extended to deal with more than two variables. However, the procedure becomes too complex to justify the benefits of the test, since when the number of variables is large, cross-tabulation does not adequately examine inter-relationships between all of them. Even with two variables, the chi-square test measures only association, not causation. Also, it does not measure the strength of association. Some tests to determine the strength of association are discussed as follows.

Phi coefficient In the case of a 2×2 contingency table, the strength of association between the two variables is measured with the help of the 'Phi (Φ) coefficient', which is the square root of the ratio of χ^2 to the sample size n:

$$\Phi = \sqrt{(\chi^2 / n)}$$

The value of Φ ranges from 0 (no association) to ± 1 for perfect positive or negative association. A good feature of Φ is that it is not affected by variations in the sample size and its value can quickly indicate the strength of association between the two variables.

Cramer's V This is an extension of the Φ coefficient to tables larger than the 2×2 case. It is defined as

$$V = \sqrt{\chi^2 / n(k-1)}$$

where n is the sample size and k is the lesser of the number of rows or columns.

Contingency coefficient This statistic, proposed by Karl Pearson, is the extension of the Φ coefficient to the '$s \times t$' contingency table, where either s or t or both are greater than 2. It is defined as

$$C = \sqrt{\left[\chi^2 / (\chi^2 + n)\right]}$$

and is called Pearson's coefficient of contingency, or merely the contingency coefficient. It takes values between 0 and 1. It may be noted that $\Phi^2 = (C^2 / 1 - C^2)$, and both Φ and C are symmetric measures. Unlike Φ, C can never take the value 1, and contingency coefficients computed from tables with different values of s and t are not strictly comparable. The upper limit of C is $\sqrt{(k-1)/k}$. C is similar to the coefficient T proposed by Tschuprow.

$$T = \sqrt{\chi^2 / n(s-1)(t-1)}$$

Lambda coefficient This coefficient was proposed by Goodman and Kruskal. It assumes that both the variables being studied are nominal. The *asymmetric Lambda coefficient* treats one of the variables in the contingency table as independent and the other as dependent. It is based on the extent to which the frequencies of one variable offer predictive evidence about the frequencies of the other variable. The asymmetrical λ indicates the direction of prediction. It is calculated as

$$\lambda = \sum (f_{kR}^* - F_c^*)/(n - F_c^*)$$

where $f*_{kR}$ is the maximum frequency in each subclass of the row variable, F_c^* is the maximum frequency among the marginal totals of the column variable, and n is the sample size. The following example will make this clear.

Let us consider the case of MBA students discussed earlier. Suppose we want to determine whether there is any association between work experience and class performance as indicated by the student's CGPA, measured on a 9-point scale. The data gathered from the 100 students interviewed earlier is presented in Table 12.8.

Table12.8 Work Experience versus CGPA of MBA Students

	CGPA > 6	CGPA ≤ 6	Total
Work experience	32	8	40
No work experience	24	36	60
Total	56	44	100

Let us assume that the value of CGPA will be dependent on the student's work experience. The CGPA may then be treated as the dependent variable, and the work experience becomes the independent variable. Suppose we want to predict which category a randomly selected student would fall into with respect to CGPA. If we had no knowledge of the student's work-experience status, we would have only the column marginal frequencies to rely on. We could include the student in the CGPA > 6 category, the higher of the column marginal totals, and we would be wrong 44 times.

If, on the other hand, we had knowledge that the student has work experience, and put the student in the CGPA ≤ 6 category, we would be wrong only 8 out of 40 times, i.e., 20 per cent of the times. Including the student in the CGPA > 6 category with no work experience would make us wrong 24 out of 60 times. With information about the student's work experience, we would, therefore, have reduced the frequency of error from 44 to 8 + 24 = 32, i.e., a decrease of 12 errors. Using the formula given earlier, the value of λ will be

$$\lambda = [(32 - 36) - 56]/(100-56)$$
$$= 0.273$$

This suggests that 27 per cent of the errors in predicting the column variable (CGPA value) would be eliminated if we know the row variable (work experience).

The value of λ-asymmetric ranges between 0, indicating no ability to eliminate errors in predicting one variable on the basis of additional information about the other, and 1, indicating the complete elimination of such error.

In the preceding example, we worked out the λ–asymmetric that calculates the reduction in the error in the predicted value of the column variable on the basis of information about the row variable. Similarly, we may compute a λ–asymmetric that calculates the reduction in the error in the predicted value of the row variable (e.g., work experience) on the basis of information about the column variable (e.g., CGPA).

A λ-*symmetric index* may be calculated as the weighted average of the two λ-asymmetric indices. This index does not treat either of the two variables as the dependent variable, and measures the overall improvement as a result of prediction in both directions. In practice, however, the λ-asymmetric index provides more useful information since we usually treat one variable as independent and want to predict the values of the other, dependent variable, subject to the values of the independent variable.

OTHER MEASURES OF ASSOCIATION

In case both the variables being studied are ordinal, other measures of association may be used. Some of these are Kendall's tau b and tau c, Somer's d and Spearman's rho (better known as the rank-correlation coefficient ρ). They do not operate under the assumption of a bivariate normal distribution, but do have values ranging from –1 to +1. Within this range, the greater the magnitude of the coefficient, the stronger the association between the variables is taken to be. All these coefficients are based on the consideration of 'concordant' and 'discordant' ordering of variables. All pairs of cases corresponding to the two variables need to be examined to determine if the relative ordering of each pair is the same with respect to one variable as with respect to the other variable (concordant). Is the order reversed (discordant) or are the pairs tied? Most of these coefficients treat the tied values in different ways.

Correlation

When two variables are metric, i.e., measured on an interval or ratio scale, and have similar distributions, the association between them is measured through a coefficient called the *product moment correlation coefficient*. If the values taken by the two variables are displayed graphically, the coordinates of each point on the graph correspond to these values. Such a graph, depicting the scatter of the joint values of the variables x and y, is called a *scatter diagram* (Fig. 12.4). If the variables are associated, most points on the scatter diagram will be close together in the form of a line. The stronger the association or correlation between the two variables, the greater the number of points (x_i, y_j) that lie along the line. This visual presentation, therefore, gives an intuitive idea of the concept of correlation measured by the correlation coefficient.

Since the idea of a correlation coefficient was introduced by Karl Pearson, it is also referred to as Pearson's correlation coefficient. It measures the magnitude and direction

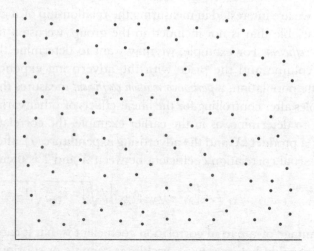

Fig. 12.4 A Scatter Diagram

of linear relationships, without dividing the data into dependent and independent variables. The symbol r is used to denote the correlation coefficient calculated from sampling data. When it is based on population data, it is denoted by rho (ρ). r is an estimate of ρ. It is a symmetrical measure and takes values between -1 and $+1$. The negative sign merely indicates the direction of the correlation—correlation coefficients with values -0.35 and $+0.35$ indicate the same magnitude of relationship, only the directions differ.

The variance of a variable X is defined as $\Sigma(x_i - \bar{x})^2$. Similarly, the covariance measure

$$\sum(x_i - \bar{x})(y_i - \bar{y})$$

should provide a measure for the simultaneous variation in variables x and y. The product moment correlation coefficient r is then defined as

$$r = \sum(x_i - \bar{x})(y_i - \bar{y}) / \sqrt{\sum(x_i - \bar{x})^2 \sum(y_i - \bar{y})^2}$$

Dividing both the numerator and the denominator by $(n-1)$, we obtain

$$r = (Cov_{xy} / S_x S_y)$$

where $\bar{x}$ and $\bar{y}$ are sample means, and S_x and S_y are sample standard deviations. The correlation is an absolute number and is independent of the unit of measurement. The proportion of variation in one variable that is explained by the other, i.e., the strength of association between the two variables, is measured by r^2, called the *coefficient of determination*. Its value varies between 0 and 1.

In case we are interested in measuring the relationship of a group of variables with another variable that is not included in the group, we use a measure called *multiple correlation coefficient*. For example, we may want to determine the joint association of the sales volume and the price with the advertising expenditure. Similarly, in a multivariate population, a *partial correlation coefficient* measures the correlation between two variables after controlling for the linear effects of other variables. For example, we may want to determine, as in the earlier example, the correlation between the sales volume of a product (X) and the advertising expenditure (Y), after controlling for price (Z). The partial correlation coefficient between X and Y is then defined as

$$r_{XY.Z} = \left[r_{XY} - (r_{XZ})(r_{YZ}) \right] / \sqrt{(1 - r_{XZ}^2)} \sqrt{(1 - r_{YZ}^2)}$$

The advantage of a partial correlation coefficient is that it can be used to determine if the relationship between two variables is genuine or spurious. For example, it was discovered that the increased production of cotton was correlated to delayed rainfall. Since cotton is traditionally not grown in low-rainfall areas, this conclusion was confusing. Further investigation revealed that food crops, such as rice, requiring heavy rainfall could not be grown in the usual quantities in these areas, which were, therefore, given over to cash crops such as cotton. Therefore, there did not exist a correlation between delayed rains and cotton, but a negative correlation existed between the cultivation of rice and the delayed rains, and the substitution of cotton for rice in such areas. A partial correlation analysis served to bring out these relationships.

The partial correlation coefficient described earlier, i.e., $r_{xy.z}$, is a first-order partial correlation coefficient. A second-order partial correlation coefficient, $r_{wx.yz}$, would control for the effect of two variables; a third-order coefficient would control for the effect of three variables; and so on.

In situations where the dependent variable Y presents itself as an array of values y_{ij} occurring with frequency f_{ij} corresponding to any given value x_i of the independent variable X, the definition of the correlation coefficient may be extended to give the *correlation ratio*. We define

$$\sum \sum f_{ij} y_{ij} = N\overline{Y}$$

where

$$N = \sum \sum f_{ij} = \sum n_i; n_j = \sum_j f_{ij} \text{ and } y = a + bx \text{ is the equation of the line of}$$
regression.

Using the principle of the least squares and minimizing $S = \sum \sum f_{ij}(y_{ij} - a - bx_i)^2$, we further obtain the correlation ratio

$$\eta_{yx}^2 = 1 - (S_{y'}^2 / \sigma_y^2)$$

where $\sigma_y^2 = \left[\sum n_i (y_i - \bar{y})^2\right] / N$ and S_y^2 is the mean square of deviations from the means of arrays.

Bivariate Regression

Correlation coefficient measures the strength of association between two variables. If we want to predict the values of one variable on the basis of the values the other variable takes, it is not possible to do so with the help of a correlation coefficient, since it does not divide the data matrix into dependent and independent variables. This function is served by the regression coefficient. Depicted graphically, the line along which the values of observations of two correlated variables are concentrated is called the *line of regression*. In general, when these value points are concentrated along a curve, the regression is said to be *curvilinear*. The algebraic expression of this line (Fig. 12.5) is given in the form of the equation

$$Y = a + bX$$

where Y is the dependent variable, X is the independent variable, and a and b are the constants of the equation, also called *regression coefficients*. It must be noted that here, Y is dependent on X, but it is not caused by X. Expressed in the form of the preceding equation, the values of the variable Y can be predicted or estimated from the values of X once the values of the regression coefficients have been determined. The most popular method used for this purpose is the *least squares method*.

Regression is one of the most widely used concepts in marketing research, since we are very often interested in being able to predict the values of one variable, given the values of the other. For example, we may want to determine

- the sales value of a brand, given the advertising expenditure on it.
- the attendance of students in a class, given the number of holidays in the preceding week, or the student-feedback rating of the teacher.
- the production of a crop in a year, given the amount of rainfall.

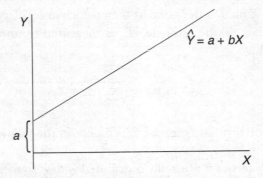

Fig. 12.5 Unstandardized Regression Equation

As mentioned earlier, the least squares method is a popular approach for determining the regression coefficients and thereby predicting the value of the dependent variable Y. Elementary statistics tells us that using the least squares method, we can estimate the value $\hat{Y}$ of the dependent variable Y as

$$\hat{Y} = a + bX$$

where a is the intercept and b is the slope of the line denoted by the above equation, i.e., the change in the value of Y for every unit change in the value of X. This line minimizes the sum of the squared deviations of the estimate $\hat{Y}$ from the observed values Y_i. The parameters a and b are estimated as

$$b_{est} = (\Sigma XY - n\overline{X}\overline{Y})/(\Sigma X^2 - n\overline{X}^2)$$

where n is the sample size and

$$a_{est} = \overline{Y} - b\overline{X}$$

The minimization of error does not necessarily mean zero error. There will often be some points that are at a distance from the least squares line that minimizes the distance between the estimates $\hat{Y}$ of Y_i and the observed values of Y_i. If this distance is denoted by the error term e_i, the model can be defined as

$$Y_i = a + bX_i + e_i$$

where e_i is the error term associated with the ith observation.

Sometimes it is necessary to standardize the data if X and Y are measured in units that are not compatible. Standardization, which we have defined earlier, implies that the line relating to the regression equation passes through the origin so that the intercept a is equal to zero (Fig. 12.6). In this case, the value of the regression coefficient b is the same as the correlation coefficient r between X and Y. Also, the coefficient b_{xy} of regression of X on Y is the same as the coefficient b_{yx} of regression of Y on X.

The accuracy of the estimate, $\hat{Y}$, is measured by the *standard error of the estimate* (SEE) defined as

$$SEE = \sqrt{\Sigma(Y_i - \hat{Y})^2/(n-2)}$$

The concept of bivariate regression is based on the following assumptions.

- The error term e is normally distributed with zero mean and constant variance; it is independent of X.

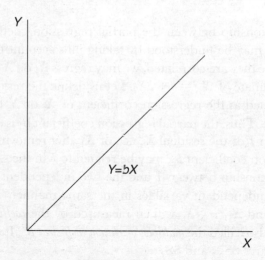

Fig. 12.6 Standardized Regression Equation

- Y is normally distributed for each value of X.
- The means of all normal distributions of Y, given the values of X, lie on a straight line that has a slope b.
- The error terms e are uncorrelated, i.e., the observations are drawn independently.

Multiple Regression

When we want to determine the strength of the relationship between a single dependent variable and two or more independent variables, we consider *multiple regression*. For example, we may be interested in determining the relationship between the sales value as the dependent variable and the advertising expenditure and the price as independent variables:

$$Y = a + bX_1 + cX_2 + e$$

where Y = sales value of brand P, X_1 = advertising expenditure on brand P, X_2 = price of brand P, and e = the error term.

The parameter Y is estimated as

$$Y = a - b_1X_1 + b_2X_2$$

The regression coefficients b_1 and b_2 are called *partial regression coefficients* because X_1 and X_2 are usually correlated, and b_1 represents the expected change in Y as a result of one unit of change in X_1 after controlling for X_2, while b_2 is the expected change in Y as a result of one unit of change in X_2 after controlling for X_1. In this sense, the partial regression coefficients b_1 and b_2 are different from the bivariate regression coefficient b. In the bivariate case, X_2 is ignored, and all the variation in Y that is shared by X_1 and X_2 is attributed to X_1.

The relationship between the partial regression coefficient b_1 and the bivariate coefficient b may be understood by taking into account the relationship between X_1 and X_2. Since they are correlated, we may regress X_1 on X_2, and estimate the equation X_{1est} (i.e., estimate of X_1) $= a + bX_2$. Let us define the residual $X_r = X_1 - X_{1est}$. Then b_r may be defined as the regression coefficient of X_r on Y, obtained from the equation $\hat{Y} = a + b_r X_r$. Thus, the partial regression coefficient b_1 is equal to b_r, the coefficient of regression on Y of the residual X_r, i.e., of X_1 after removing the effect of X_2. The partial correlation coefficient b_2, may be related to b in the same way.

This relationship between Y and the two independent variables may be extended to k $(k > 2)$ independent variables in the same manner. The strength of association between Y and $X_1, \ldots, X_n$ is then measured by the *coefficient of multiple determination*, $R^2_{Y \cdot X_1 \cdots X_n}$, also called the *multiple correlation coefficient R^2*. It is defined as the ratio of two sums of squares SS_{reg} and SS_Y.

$$R^2 = SS_{reg}/SS_Y$$

where $SS_{reg} = \Sigma(\hat{Y}_i - \overline{Y})^2$ and $SS_Y = \Sigma(Y_i - \overline{Y})^2$

Stepwise Regression

This method is used to select, from a large number of predictor variables, a small subset of variables that accounts for most of the variation in the criterion variable (Aaker et al 1999). The predictor variables are included in or are removed from the regression equation one at a time. There are various approaches to stepwise regression.

- *Forward addition* To begin with, there are no predictor variables in the regression equation. They are entered in the regression equation one at a time, if they meet certain criteria defined in terms of the *F*-ratio, to be discussed later. The order in which they enter the model depends on their contribution to the explained variation.
- *Backward elimination* This method is the converse of the forward addition method. Initially, all predictor variables are included in the model. They are removed one at a time depending on their contribution to the explained variance.
- *Stepwise method* In this method, the forward addition of predictor variables is combined with the removal of those that no longer meet the specified criterion at each step.

Stepwise regression does not produce optimal solutions in the sense of producing the largest R^2 for a given set of predictors. To identify the optimal solution, it may be necessary to obtain combinatorial solutions that examine all possible combinations. Even so, stepwise regression provides useful solutions when the sample is large relative to the number of predictors.

Multicollinearity

The problem of multicollinearity is said to exist when some or all of the predictor variables exhibit very high correlation among themselves. This poses a serious problem in the estimation of regression coefficients, since predictor variables are more often than not correlated at least to some degree. The following are the major problems that arise as a result of multicollinearity.

- The partial correlation coefficients may not be estimated correctly, as the standard errors are likely to be high.
- The size of the partial correlation coefficients may depend on the sample size, and may even change their signs in some cases.
- Predictor variables may be dropped incorrectly or get included erroneously in stepwise regression because of high standard errors.
- Explaining the relative importance of predictor variables in explaining the variation in the criterion variable may become difficult.

Since predictor variables almost invariably tend to be correlated, it is difficult to specify the degree of correlation that constitutes serious multicollinearity. The issues that engage analysts are the detection and solution of multicollinearity.

Though many rules of thumb have been developed for dealing with it, serious multicollinearity remains an ambiguous concept. One popular method is to examine the correlation between all the pairs of independent variables, and discard the pairs for which the correlation exceeds 0.9. Another method is to transform the set of predictor variables into a new, smaller set of uncorrelated variables using methods such as factor analysis or principal components analysis. These methods will be discussed in Chapter 14.

Regression models (as well as some other multivariate methods) tend to capitalize on chance variation in sample data. In order to minimize the problems resulting from this tendency as well as genuine multicollinearity, one popular method that is used is *cross-validation*. This method involves the following steps.

1. Separate the data into two parts—the estimation part and the validation part.
2. Estimate the regression equation from the estimation part of the data.
3. Fit the data kept aside for the validation part to this equation.
4. Obtain estimates Y_i of the various values taken by the dependent variable.
5. Calculate the coefficient of determination R_1^2 between these estimates. $\hat{Y}_i$ and the original values Y_i in the validation part of the sample.
6. Compare this value of R_1^2 with the original R^2 to determine the degree of difference, or 'shrinkage'.

This method is sometimes extended to *double cross-validation*, where the data is divided into two equal parts and each part is treated as the estimation part (and the other as the validation part) and vice versa alternately. Cross-validation is then performed on one estimation part and then repeated on the other part.

Analysis of Variance

We have mentioned earlier that for testing the difference between the means of more than two populations, the methods used are analysis of variance (ANOVA) and analysis of covariance (ANCOVA), introduced by Fisher (Green and Tull 1978). The data matrix is divided into dependent and independent variables, in which the dependent variable is metric and the independent variables are all non-metric and usually nominal. For example, we may want to test whether MBA students from engineering, science, and commerce backgrounds at the undergraduate level differ in their performance at the MBA level. The null hypothesis that we test is that all means (in this example, the average CGPA of students from all three streams) are equal. The independent variables are also called *factors*. The purpose is to test for the difference between the mean values of the dependent variable associated with the effect of the controlled independent variables *after taking into account* the effect of the uncontrolled variables. In the preceding example, the uncontrolled independent variables may be the performance of the students at the undergraduate level. A particular combination of factor levels is called a *treatment*. When we are examining the effect of only one factor, we are dealing with a *one-way analysis of variance*. In the above example, if we are merely comparing the average performance of students from three different undergraduate streams of study as described earlier, the analysis will be termed *one-way analysis of variance*.

To study of the process of one-way analysis of various, let us consider sales data for a shampoo brand from three stores. The process goes through well-defined stages.

- *Identify the dependent variable Y and the independent variable X* as depicted in Table 12.9, the sales are the dependent variable Y, with a sample size 8, indicating the sales of brand A of shampoo over eight periods. The three stores depict the independent variable X. Thus the total sample size in this example is $8 \times 3 = 24$.

- *Decompose the total variation in Y*, denoted by SS_Y, the sum of squares of the deviation of Y_i from Y, the average value of Y across all stores and all periods. This variation may be decomposed into two parts—the variation between/among groups, which measures the intergroup differences as a result of the influence of the independent variable X, and the variation within groups, which is independent of the influence of X. In the shampoo example, the intergroup, or the 'between' variation will be indicated by the difference in the sales value of the shampoo brand A among the three stores, and is denoted by SS_X, the sum of squares due to X. The intragroup, or 'within' variation, denoted by SS_{error}, is the variation in the sales value of the shampoo brand A over eight periods, and is not the result of the influence of X. This variation could, in fact, result from a variety of factors, such as consumer preference for other brands, price changes in the brand over the eight periods considered, promotion campaigns for brand A or other brands, and so on. Since these causes of variation are not being identified independently, and are instead all clubbed together as one entity influencing variation in the values of Y, these are termed 'errors' in the one-way analysis of variance.

- *Measurement of the effects SS_X and SS_{error} relative to SS_Y* we must remember that in one-way ANOVA,

$$SS_Y = SS_X + SS_{error}$$

The relative magnitude of SS_X increases as the variation in the average sales value $\bar{Y}_i$ among the three stores increases, or as the average variation within a store decreases over the eight periods being studied. We then define the ratio

$$\eta^2 = (SS_Y - SS_{error})SS_Y$$

as a measure of the relative significance of the effect of X on the variation in Y. For the purpose of measurement, we calculate the mean square (MS) corresponding to each sum of squares by dividing the SS by the appropriate degrees of freedom. In the preceding shampoo example, the number of degrees of freedom associated with MS_X is $3 - 1 = 2$, and that with MS_{error} is $(8 \times 3) - 3 = 21$.

- *Test the effects for significance* The hypothesis being tested here is that the samples have been drawn from the same population, i.e.,

$$H_0 = \mu_1 = \mu_2 = \mu_3 = \cdots = \mu_n$$

In the example being discussed, we will test

$$H_0 = \mu_1 = \mu_2 = \mu_3$$

for the three stores. In order to test the given hypothesis, we have seen that we need to determine the relative impact of SS_X and SS_{error}. Since the relative impact of SS_X increases with an increase in variation in the value of Y_i with $\bar{X}$, the ratios MS, taking the number of degrees of freedom into account, give a better estimate of the relative impact of the 'between group' variation to the 'within group' variation. We, therefore, test the relative significance of the two sources of variation through the F-ratio:

$$F = MS_X / MS_{error}$$
$$= [SS_X / c] / [SS_Y - SS_X)/(N - c)]$$

where c is the number of categories of X and N is the total sample size.

- *Interpreting the results* If the F-ratio is found insignificant in comparison with the tabulated F value with the same degrees of freedom, the independent variable does not exercise much influence on the dependent variable. If, on the other hand, the hypothesis is rejected, it becomes necessary to identify the nature of the effect the independent variable exercises on the dependent variable, and the samples that have been drawn from the same population. These examinations are based on certain tests that will be discussed in the later chapters.

If we are interested in studying the influence of two factors at a time—say, in examining the impact of three different streams of study (F_1) as well as the relationship of undergraduate-level scores with the MBA-level performance—we will be dealing with a *two-way analysis of variance*. For example, let us again consider the data of Table 12.8. Suppose in addition to studying the impact of differences in stores on the sales of brand A, we are interested in determining whether the variation in the monthwise sales is also a significant factor contributing to the overall variation in sales. We are then dealing with three questions.

- Are the differences in sales attributable to the performance of different stores?
- Do sales differ significantly from month to month?
- Do the store performances and monthwise sales interact to result in sales variation?

The answer to the first question may be obtained through the one-way analysis of variance, by averaging out the data across months; similarly, if we treat the time period as another independent variable, the answer to the second question may be obtained through a one-way analysis of variance, by averaging out the effect of stores. The answer to the last question involving interaction between the store data and the month-wise sales data requires additional analysis that can be performed only through the two-way analysis of variance. The analysis works by calculating an SS for the store

Table 12.9 Sales Data (in Units) for Shampoo Brand A from Three Stores

Sales (During)	Store 1	Store 2	Store 3	Total
January	200	131	386	717
February	245	174	313	732
March	314	274	224	812
April	223	263	367	853
May	331	222	174	727
June	451	391	448	1290
July	305	332	345	982
August	257	263	350	870
Total	2326	2050	2607	6983

variable, another for the months variable, and the error term, which includes the interaction between the stores and the months.

The analysis may be extended to an *n-way analysis of variance*. The analysis of variance is used most often in analysing experimental designs, discussed earlier. ANOVA is valid under certain assumptions:

- The set of data on which the analysis is performed consists of an exhaustive and mutually exclusive set of frequencies, i.e., the observations are drawn independently.
- The error term is normally distributed with zero mean and constant variance. It is independent of the predictor variable X.
- The error terms are uncorrelated.
- The categories of the independent or predictor variable are fixed.

Analysis of Covariance

If the independent variables being studied include nominal as well as metric variables, the technique of analysis is called the *analysis of covariance* ANCOVA as mentioned earlier. We are often interested in examining the differences in mean values of the dependent variable related to the effect of controlled independent variables, after taking into account the impact of uncontrolled independent variables, as in the following examples.

- In examining the variation in the purchase intent of consumers towards a brand of soap with different levels of advertising expenditure, it may be important to take prior brand knowledge into consideration.
- In determining differences in average crop yield expected in response to different levels of a fertilizer, we may also need to take into account the differences in soil quality.
- In determining the influence of advertisement recall on brand-purchase decisions, it may be necessary to also study the respondent's level of involvement with the product category.

Why is this method referred to as 'analysis of variance' when the hypothesis is comparing means? The logic becomes clear when we examine the fact that the total variance in the data may be divided into two parts—one reflecting the variance between different groups, such as the variation in the performance of students from the science stream compared with that of students from the commerce and the engineering streams, and the other relating to the variance in the performance of individual students within each group. If the null hypothesis is correct, not only are the means similar but also the variation *between* each of these groups is similar to the variation within each of the other groups (since they belong to the same population under the null hypothesis).

Combining the three groups should, therefore, not result in higher variation. If the combined variation of the three groups is larger than that within each group, it can only indicate that the groups belong to populations with different levels of variation, i.e., to different populations. In other words, the hypothesis can hold only if the variances between the three groups are equal.

The other techniques of analysis and tests of hypotheses, listed in Figs 12.2 and 12.3, have been described in later chapters.

SPSS COMMANDS

The detailed commands that may be used for computer-based frequency tables, cross-tabulation, the chi-square test, correlation, regression, and ANOVA are given in this section.

Frequency Tables

After the input data has been keyed in along with variable labels and value labels in an SPSS data file, go through the following steps to get the frequency table output for the kind of problem discussed earlier in the chapter.

1. Click on **Analyse** in the SPSS menu bar (in older versions of SPSS, click on **Statistics** instead of **Analyse**).
2. Click on **Descriptive Statistics**, followed by **Frequencies**.
3. A dialog box will appear in the window (Fig. 12.7). Select the variables for which **Frequency Tables** are required by clicking on the right arrow to transfer them from the variable list on the left to the **Variables** box on the right.

Fig. 12.7 Dialog Box Displaying Frequency Table Variables

4. Click on **OK** to get tables with counts and percentages for each of the selected variables.
   Note: If charts are *desired*, click on **Charts** in the main dialog box to get the dialog box shown in Fig. 12.8, select the required type of charts, and click on

Continue before the last step. Similarly, if the variables are interval scaled, you can click on **Statistics** in the dialog box to get the dialog box shown in Fig. 12.9 and request **Means**, **Standard Deviations**, and so on for each variable (Fig. 12.9). If you click on **Formats** in the main dialog box, you will get the dialog box shown in Fig. 12.10.

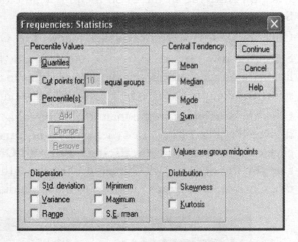

Fig. 12.8 Dialog Box of Statistical Frequencies

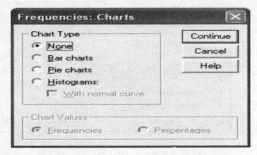

Fig. 12.9 Dialog Box for Frequencies of Charts

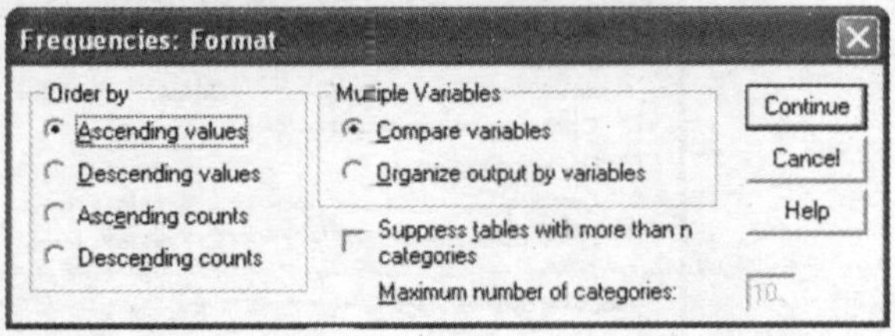

Fig. 12.10 Dialog Box for Counts of Selected Variables

Cross-tabulations and Chi-square Test

After the input data has been keyed in along with variable labels and value labels in an SPSS data file, go through the following steps to get the cross-tabulations and chi-squared test output for a problem.

1. Click on **Analyse** in the SPSS menu bar (in older versions of SPSS, click on **Statistics** instead of **Analyse**).
2. Click on **Descriptive Statistics**, followed by **Cross-tabs** (Fig. 12.11).
3. Select the row variable for a cross-tabulation by highlighting it in the variable list on the left side and clicking the arrow leading to the row variable box. Similarly, select the column variable in the cross-tabulation.
4. Click on **Statistics** in the main dialog box (Fig. 12.11) to get the dialog box displayed in Fig. 12.12. Then click on **Chi-square**. In the box titled **Nominal**, click on **Contingency coefficient**, **Phi and Cramer's V**, and **Lambda** to give you the statistics, which measure the strength of the association in a cross-tab. Click on **Continue** to return to the main dialog box.

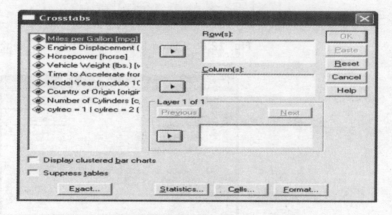

Fig. 12.11   Dialog Box of Cross Tabs

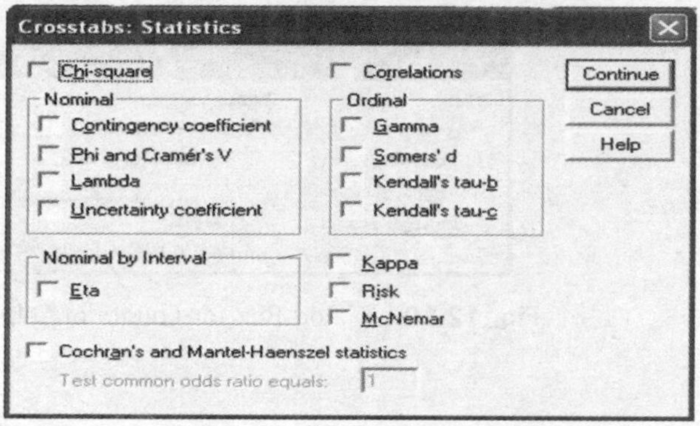

Fig. 12.12   Dialog Box Displaying Statistical Variables

5. Click on **Cells** in the main dialog box to get the dialog box in Fig. 12.13. Under **Percentages**, select either **Row** or **Column** depending on which is desired, as per the discussion and rule given in the text. Click on **Continue** to return to the main dialog box. Similarly, you can click on **Format** in the main dialog box to get the dialog box in Fig. 12.14 and select the row order.

6. Click on **OK** to get the output containing the required cross-tab, along with the chi-square test (Figs 12.15 to 12.17) and the measures of association such as lambda and contingency coefficients.

Note: The chi-square test requires frequencies in the cross-tables, and not percentages. The original data should use frequencies when applying this test.

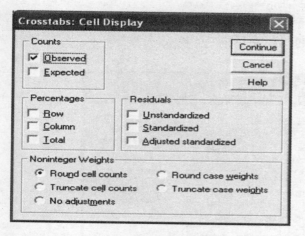

Fig. 12.13   Cross Tabs: Cell Display

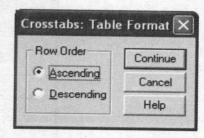

Fig. 12.14   Crosstabs: Cell Format

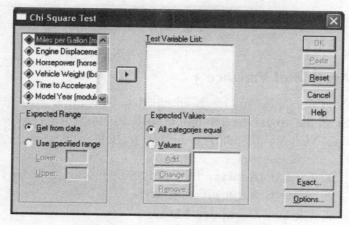

Fig. 12.15   Chi Square Test

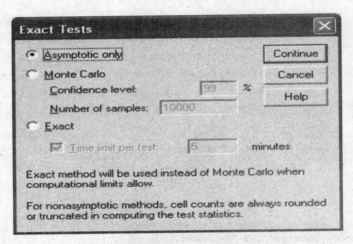

Fig. 12.16   Exact Tests

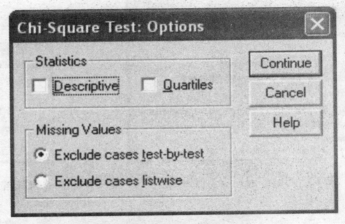

Fig. 12.17   Chi Square Test: Options

Analysis of Variance

After the input data has been typed along with variable labels and value labels in an SPSS file, to get the first output for a *one-way ANOVA problem* described in the chapter on ANOVA in the text, go through the following steps.

1. Click on **Analyse** in the SPSS menu bar (in older versions of SPSS, click on **Statistics** instead of **Analyse**).
2. Click on **Compare Means**.
3. Click on **One-way Anova**.
4. In the dialog box that appears (Fig. 12.18), select one appropriate variable as the **Dependent** by highlighting it in the left-hand side box and clicking on the

arrow towards the **Dependent** box. Then select another appropriate variable as a **Factor** (independent variable) from the list of variable labels that appears on the left side of the box and click on the arrow directing it to the **Factor** box. The variables should get transferred to the right-hand side boxes after the selection.

5. For the **Factor** variable, the minimum value and the maximum value have to be specified. To do this, click on **Range** just below the **Factor** variable, and type in the minimum and maximum values for the **Factor** (independent variable). For example, 1 and 3 could be the minimum and maximum values.

6. Click on **Continue** after specifying **Range**, and then on **Ok** to get the output for the one-way **ANOVA**.

   Note: Fig. 12.19 to 12.21 show the dialog boxes that will appear on clicking on **Contrasts**, **Post Hoc,** and **Options**, respectively, on the main dialog box (Fig. 12.18).

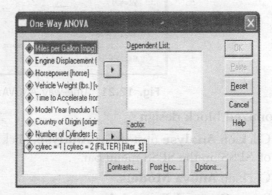

Fig. 12.18 Dialog Box Displaying One-way ANOVA Commands

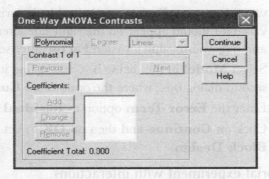

Fig. 12.19 One-way ANOVA: Contrasts

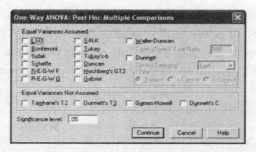

Fig. 12.20 One-way ANOVA: Post Hoc Multiple Comparisons

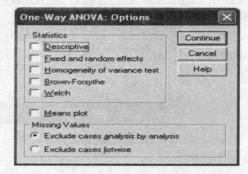

Fig. 12.21 One-way ANOVA: Options

Randomized block design

1. Click on **Analyse** (instead of **Analyse**, click on **Statistics** for older versions of SPSS) in the SPSS menu bar.
2. Click on **Anova Models**.
3. Select **General Factorial**.
4. In the dialog box that appears, select the dependent variable, the independent variable as one **Factor**, and the block variable as the second **Factor**. The variables should appear on the right side after this. Specify the minimum value and maximum value for each **Factor** after selecting the range of each in turn.
5. Select **Model** in the dialog box and define it as **Custom** by selecting it in the second dialog box, where the options are **Custom** and **Full Factorial**.
6. Enter the **Error Term** option as **Residual**.
7. Click on **Continue** and then on **OK** to get the output of the **Randomized Block Design**.

Factorial experiment with interactions

To get the output for a factorial experiment as described in the text with two or more factors including the main effects and the interactions, repeat steps 1 to 3 of the Randomized Block Design. Then go through the following steps.

1. Specify the dependent variable and all the **Factors**. Specify the range of each **Factor** as before.
2. Select **Model** and click to select **Full Factorial** (instead of **Custom**, which you had selected earlier).
3. Click on **OK** to get the output, which should have the main effects and the interactions.
   Note: There may be small variations in the commands depending on which version of SPSS is used. The user may experiment and find the correct set of menu choices from the dialog boxes in such cases.

Correlation and Regression

Let us now look at the SPSS Commands for Correlation and regression.

Correlation

After the input data has been typed along with variable labels and value labels in an SPSS file, to get the output for a *correlation* problem similar to that described in the text, go through the following steps.

1. Click on **Analyse** in the SPSS menu bar (in older versions of SPSS, click on **Stastics** instead of **Analyse**).
2. Click on **Correlate**, followed by **Bivariate**.
3. In the dialog box that appears (Fig. 12.22), select all the variables for which correlation is required by clicking on the right arrow to transfer them from the variable list on the left. Then select **Pearson** under the heading **Correlation Coefficients**, and select **Two-tailed** under the heading **Tests of Significance**.
4. Click on **Ok** to get the matrix of pairwise **Pearson** correlations among all the variables selected, along with the two-tailed significance of each **Pairwise** correlation.
   Note: On clicking on **Options** in the main dialog box (Fig. 12.22), the dialog box shown in Fig. 12.23 appears.)

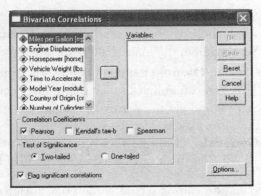

Fig. 12.22 Dialog Box Displaying Bivariate Correlation Commands

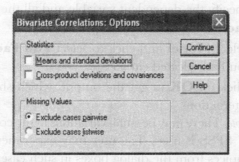

Fig.12.23   Bivariate Correlations: Options

Regression

After the input data has been typed along with variable labels and value labels in an SPSS file, to get the output for a *regression* problem similar to that described in the text, go through the following steps.

1. Click on **Analyse** in the SPSS menu bar (in older versions of SPSS, click on **Statistics** instead of **Analyse**).

2. Click on **Regression**, followed by **Linear**.

3. In the dialog box that appears (Fig 12.24), select a dependent variable by clicking on the arrow leading to the dependent box after highlighting the appropriate variable from the list of variables on the left side.

4. Select the independent variables to be included in the regression model in the same way, transferring them from the left side to the right side box by clicking on the arrow leading to the box called **Independent Variables** or **Independents**.

5. In the same dialog box, select the **Method**. Choose **Enter** as the method if you want all independent variables to be included in the model; **Stepwise** if you want to use forward stepwise regression; and **Backward** if you want to use backward stepwise regression.

6. Select **Options** (12.25) if you want additional output options, select those you want, and click on **Continue**.

7. Select **Plots** (Fig. 12.26) if you want to generate plots such as **Residual Plots**, select those you want, and click on **Continue**. Similarly, you can click on **Statistics** in the main dialog box to get the dialog box in Fig. 12.27.

8. Click on **Ok** from the main dialog box to get the **Regression** output.
   Note: You can go back to your data file by clicking on it, change the method at Step 5, and get the regression output using another method of your choice in the same way as described above.
   General: All output files can be saved using the **File Save** command (Fig. 12.28). They can be printed using the **File Print** command.

Input data also can be separately saved, or printed, using the same commands (**File Save, File Print**) while the cursor is on the input data file.

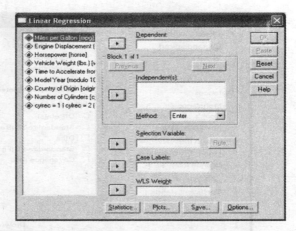

Fig. 12.24 Dialog Box Showing Linear Regression Commands

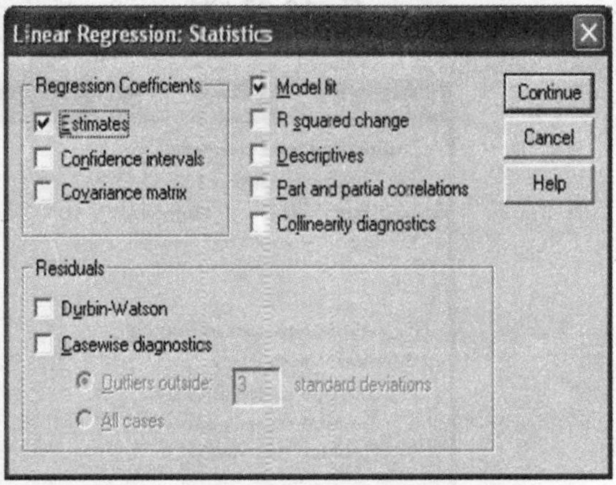

Fig.12.25 Linear Regression: Statistics

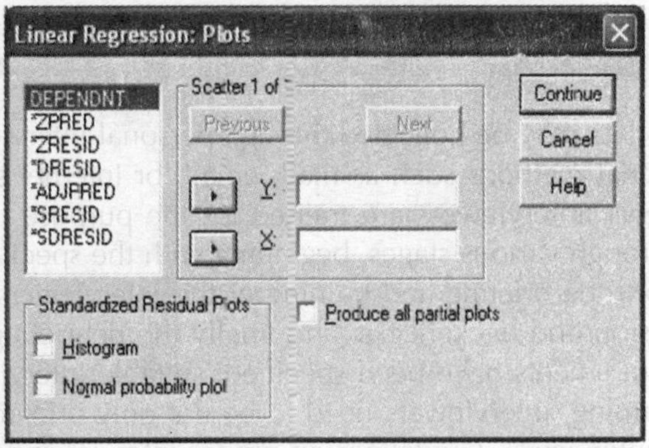

Fig.12.26 Linear Regression: Plots

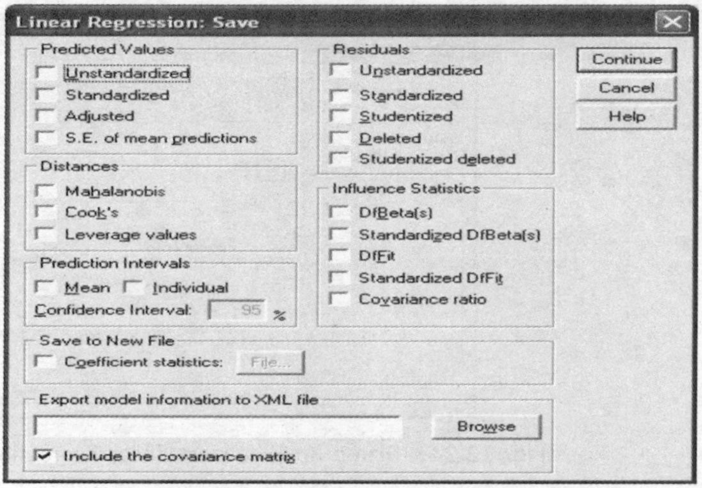

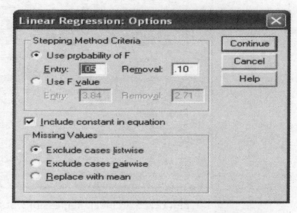

Fig.12.27 Linear Regression: Save

Fig.12.28 Linear Regression: Options

SUMMARY

Survey data may be collected through personal interviews of various kinds or through impersonal methods such as mail, email, or Internet surveys. In the case of personal interviews, interviewers are trained for the purpose of collecting data. This process goes through various stages, beginning with the specifications of the job requirement, selection, the briefing and training of the interviewers, actual fieldwork including its supervision and backchecks, and finally the debriefing of the interviewers. Once the job requirements have been specified, suitable interviewers are identified. As part of their training, interviewers need to be not only briefed in detail but also put through 'mock interviews'. Guidelines on proper interviewing procedures must be given. The supervision of fieldwork is essential to ensure the validity and reliability of data, and also to sort out any on-the-spot problems that the interviewer may be facing.

The coding of collected field data is an essential first step in the process of collation. While data can be precoded in the case of structured interviews, unstructured interviews require post coding and content analysis. Content analysis is needed for coding and analysing communication rather than objects or behaviour. Depending on the objective of the analysis, syntactical, referential, prepositional, thematic, or time/space measure-related content analysis schemes may be used.

The editing of data to check for veracity and consistency is the next important stage in preparing data for analysis. Depending on the objectives of the study, data may sometimes need some degree of transformation through weighting, data reduction, the use of dummy variables, or scale transformation.

Once the data have been put through all these stages of coding and editing, it is ready for tabulation. Tabulation is basically concerned with dividing the data into relevant categories, counting the responses in each category, and presenting them in the form of a frequency table. The process of obtaining totals by summing up each category is called marginal tabulation. The tabulation of the frequency of responses that occur simultaneously in the two categories of variables is called *cross-tabulation*. Data mining is required while handling large amounts of complex data for determining the relationship patterns between variables and for predicting trends and behaviours.

Once the data have been tabulated, they may be analysed in order to test the hypotheses that form the basic purpose of almost al marketing research. Analysis may relate to univariate, bivariate, or multivariate measurement. The choice of appropriate tests depends on whether the data are metric or non-metric, whether a single sample or multiple samples are involved, whether these samples are dependent or independent, and in the case of bivariate or multivariate analysis, whether we are interested in dependence or interdependence relationships between variables. In univariate analysis, the tests of metric data, called parametric tests, include the *t*-test and the *z*-test. The *t*-test and *z*-test are also used for testing for differences between two samples of metric data. Analysis of variance (ANOVA) is used for testing the differences between three or more samples. It is most frequently used for analysing experimental data. Hypotheses based on non-metric data are tested through non-parametric tests, such as the χ^2 test, the K-S test for one sample or two samples, the Mann–Whitney test, and many others. More complex techniques of analysis with a single dependent variable are discriminant analysis and conjoint analysis.

The analysis of bivariate or multivariate data is concerned with dependence or interdependence techniques. Dependence techniques may test for association between two variables through the χ^2 test or the correlation coefficient, or examine the data divided into dependent (criterion) and independent (predictor) variables for a relationship through bivariate or multiple regression. A two-group discriminant analysis is required for determining the relationship between a single dependent variable measured on a nominal scale and multiple independent variables measured on an interval scale. Multivariate dependence analysis includes, apart from multiple regression, canonical correlation, multiple discriminant analysis, and multivariate analysis of variance (MANOVA) and covariance (MANCOVA) Interdependence techniques include factor analysis, cluster analysis, and multidimensional scaling.

KEY WORDS

Fieldwork refers to the collection of primary data through personal interviews or impersonal methods.

Mock interview refers to the rehearsal of a personal interview between the fieldworker and the research executive, in which the fieldworker is required to administer the entire data collection instrument to the research executive.

Coding of data refers to the assigning of unique numerical or symbolic values to the various responses to each question in the instrument.

Precoding refers to developing in advance the various codes to be assigned to the alternative responses possible to a structured question.

Postcoding refers to the system of listing all the responses of an open-ended question, grouping them through methods such as content analysis, and then assigning unique symbolic or numerical values to each categorized response.

Content analysis is a research technique for the objective, systematic, and quantitative description of the manifest or latent content of a communication.

Marginal tabulation refers to the process of totalling the frequencies in each category of a frequency table, called *marginal totals*.

Cross-tabulation is the process of totalling the frequency of responses that occur simultaneously in two categories of variables.

Data mining is the process of obtaining information from formal databases that comprise large amounts of dynamic data requiring complex analysis.

Univariate analysis refers to the methods of testing hypotheses that relate to a single measurement of each of the n sample objects ($x_1, x_2, ..., x_n$) or several measurements of each object, but on each variable x, y, or z in isolation [($x_1, x_2, ..., x_n$); ($y_1, y_2, ..., y_n$)...; ($z_1, z_2, ..., z_n$)].

Bivariate analysis refers to the tests of hypotheses that are concerned with the study of relationships between two variables [(x_1, y_1) (x_2, y_2), ..., (x_n, y_n)].

Multivariate analysis refers to the tests of hypotheses that are concerned with the study of relationships between many variables [(x_1, y_1, z_1), (x_2, y_2, z_2), ... (x_n, y_n, z_n)] simultaneously; there may be two or more measurements of each variable.

Parametric tests are tests of hypotheses based on metric data, i.e., interval- or ratio-scaled data. They, therefore, assume a definite underlying distribution of the population.

Non-parametric tests are tests of hypotheses based on nominal or ordinal data. These tests do not make any assumptions about the population distribution.

Goodness of fit refers to the compatibility of observed frequencies with a theoretical distribution in the case of category data. Goodness of fit is measured with the help of the χ^2 test.

Contingency refers to the condition that the occurrence of one category variable will be associated with, or be contingent upon, the occurrence of another category variable.

Correlation refers to the association between two interval- or ratio-scaled variables with similar continuous distributions. This is measured by the product moment correlation coefficient r.

Scatter diagram is a graph that depicts the scatter of the joint values of the variables x and y, i.e., the scatter or distribution of the points (x_i, y_i) on a two-dimensional graph.

Coefficient of determination is the measure r^2, the square of the correlation coefficient, which measures the proportion of variation in one variable that is explained by the other.

Correlation ratio is the measure of correlation between two interval-scaled continuous variables x and y, where y takes an array of values y_{ij} for every value x_j of x.

Regression is the process of determining the values of the dependent variable Y from the relationship it has with the independent variable X.

Stepwise regression is the method of determining the optimal subset from a large number of independent variables X_i that explain the maximum variation in the dependent variable Y by adding or removing one variable at a time and studying its impact on the level of variation.

Multicollinearity refers to the condition where some or all of the independent variables involved in a regression equation exhibit a high degree of correlation among themselves.

Cross-validation refers to the technique of validating a regression model by dividing the data into two parts, determining the model using the data of one part, and then fitting the data kept aside for validation to this model.

Analysis of variance refers to the method of testing the hypothesis that the means of three or more populations are equal, i.e., the corresponding samples have been drawn from the same population.

Sum of squares of error refers to the measure of variation of the values of the dependent variable from the total variation in the sample, excluding the variation explained by the independent variable.

Analysis of covariance refers to the method of analysis of the differences in the mean values of the dependent variable related to the effect of the controlled independent variable after taking into account uncontrolled independent variables.

CONCEPT REVIEW QUESTIONS

1. What are the limitations of correlation analysis? How does regression overcome them?

2. What factors should be taken care of to minimize the scope of a fieldworker cheating or an error?

3. What are the different types of coding units under the various coding schemes in content analysis? Give two examples of each.

4. Define the null hypothesis for a one-way ANOVA involving four samples. What is the basic statistic used for testing this null hypothesis? How is it computed?

5. 'Why waste time doing basic data analysis? Why not just conduct sophisticated multivariate data analysis?' Discuss.

PROJECT ASSIGNMENTS

1. In the project relating to the manufacturer of Waterguard in Chapter 10, how would the fieldwork be conducted? Develop a detailed plan for administering the questionnaire you developed in Chapter 10. Define suitable interviewers for conducting the fieldwork. Prepare all the instructions for the interviewers and the field supervisors and specify the kind of checks that will be necessary for ensuring the validity of the data.

2. For the following pairs of variables, indicate which is dependent and which is independent.
   a. Crop yield and the consumption of fertilizers
   b. Point-of-purchase display and brand awareness
   c. Age and income
   d. Family size and pack size purchased
   e. Advertising expenditure and sales revenue

3. Refer to Question 4 in the list of concept review exercises in Chapter 10 and develop a coding scheme for Questions 4 to 8 in it.

4. Assume that Dabur India, the makers of the Real brand of fruit juices, want to determine whether the preference for fruit juices is linked to gender. In order to test this hypothesis, they conducted a survey to determine the preferences of men and women in the age group 30–45 years for two popular flavours of fruit juices, A and B, and two well-known brands of aerated drinks, C and D. The following preferences were indicated by the sample.

	A	B	C	D	Total
Men	15	25	40	20	100
Women	20	30	25	25	100

(a) Is this an appropriate test of the hypothesis being studied?

(b) Are gender and preference for fruit juices associated on the basis of this test?

5. A manufacturer of household detergents is interested in determining consumer preferences among three pack sizes before launching a new 'giant' pack of their popular brand of detergent. A survey with 200 housewives revealed that 35 per cent preferred the 500-g

pack, 30 per cent preferred the 100-g pack, and the remaining 35 per cent preferred the 2-kg giant or family pack. Does the survey data indicate any distinct preference? What test would you use to test preference? Why?

6. Your college is interested in verifying the theory being put forward by some faculty members that older students score better marks in exams. The data on total marks obtained by 20 final year students in their terminal examinations were compared along with their ages in order to test this hypothesis.

Table 12.11 Students Data

Student Serial No.	Age in Years	Total Final Marks (out of 500)
1	22	285
2	24	315
3	21	431
4	26	334
5	23	269
6	22	397
7	27	345
8	25	423
9	23	300
10	26	240
11	27	450
12	24	316
13	21	308
14	23	403
15	26	322
16	27	419
17	21	254
18	22	373
19	24	478
20	25	359

(a) Plot the age data (X-axis) against marks (Y-axis) and interpret the diagram
(b) Conduct an appropriate analysis of the data. Do the data support the hypothesis?

REFERENCES

Aaker, D., V. Kumar, and G.S. Day 1999, *Marketing Research*, 6th edn, Wiley, p. 46.

Berelson, B. 1952, *Content Analysis in Communication Research,* Free Press, New York, p.18.

Cooper, D.R. and P.S. Schindler 1999, *Business Research Methods*, Tata McGraw-Hill, New Delhi, pp. 417–419.

Green, P.E. and D.S. Tull 1978, *Research for Marketing Decisions,* Prentice Hall, New Jersey.

Krippendorf 1980, *Content Analysis: An Introduction to Its Methodology*, Sage, Newbury Park, California.

Malhotra, N. 2004, *Marketing Research: An Applied Orientation*, Fourth edition, Pearson Education.

Stemler, Steve 2001, 'An Overview of Content Analysis', *Practical Assessment, Research & Evaluation*, 7(17), Yale University, http:// PARE online.net/getvn.asp

13

Specific Techniques for Analysis of Data

OBJECTIVES

After reading this chapter, the readers will be able to understand:

- how to choose between parametric and non-parametric tests
- application of some popular parametric tests
- some popular non-parametric tests and their applications

INTRODUCTION

So far, we have discussed the role of statistical hypotheses in marketing research and the importance of tests of significance in the context of these hypotheses. Chapter 12 talked about the need for defining hypotheses in measurable terms, so that it may be possible to assess their acceptability. We have also established that this need for testing hypotheses arises because in research we almost invariably work with sample data, which, if truly representative of the population from which it has been drawn, should be more or less indicative of the true properties of the population. Tests of hypotheses are aimed at confirming, on the basis of the examination of one or more parameters, that the sample is indeed representative of the population. Since what we usually have available is sample data, it becomes necessary to determine whether the empirical findings follow a pattern or are merely random. This is done by checking the assumption that the sample estimate of a population parameter is more or less the same as the actual population parameter, and would be exactly the same if the sample were larger.

Since most populations follow a defined frequency distribution, the nature of the population parameter gets defined by the nature of the distribution. No single test for examining the hypothesis that the sample estimate of the population parameter is identical to the actual parameter is valid for all kinds of frequency distributions. For this reason, it is important to know the frequency distribution of the population in question. If this distribution is known, as in the case of interval-scaled or ratio-scaled data, specific tests of hypotheses called *parametric tests* may be applied for testing the hypothesis. However, with discrete data based on category (nominal) variables or rank-ordered (ordinal) variables, it is not always possible to define the frequency distribution. In such cases, we need to apply tests that are not dependent on the knowledge of the frequency distribution of the population. Such tests are referred to as non-parametric tests. This chapter discusses the differences between these two types of tests, and provides some guidelines for choosing between them. Tests for specific hypotheses concerning metric data (continuous variables with a known frequency distribution) and those relating to non-metric data, i.e., non-parametric tests, have also been discussed in detail.

PARAMETRIC AND NON-PARAMETRIC TESTS

We have seen that hypotheses relating to interval- and ratio-scaled data require parametric tests, since the basic assumption with such data is that the underlying distribution of the population is completely known and, therefore, the parameters are defined. Often, the population is assumed to be normal, or transformations may be found that will reduce it to the normal form. In practice, however, we often do not have adequate knowledge of the parent population to be able to find such a transformation. According to Kapur and Saxena (1960) in their book *Mathematical Statistics*, 'In such cases we need tests that do not depend on any assumption about the form of the population'. These tests are called non-parametric or distribution-free tests. The advantages of these tests are that they (a) are simple, (b) have wider applicability, and (c) are not dependent on complex sampling theory.

Parametric tests most commonly use the mean and the standard deviation as the measures of location and dispersion. These measures do not make any assumptions about order in the sample. Distribution-free methods, on the other hand, most often use the median, quartiles, the inter-quartile range, and similar measures which are based on *ordered statistics* or *ordered samples*. In other words, in these tests we assume that the sample $(X_1, X_2, ..., X_n)$ is ordered, so that the sampling units $X_1, X_2, ..., X_n$ appear in ascending or descending order of magnitude. Non-parametric tests are similar to parametric tests in that they test hypotheses using probabilities. Although presently there are fewer non-parametric tests compared to parametric tests, according to Statistical Testing Services (2005), there exist non-parametric analogues for many of the most common parametric tests. However, both types of tests require randomization of data.

In statistical testing of hypotheses, we have only two options: (a) either we reject the null hypothesis, in which case we accept the alternative hypothesis or (b) we fail to reject the null hypothesis—this option is commonly and somewhat erroneously taken as 'accept the null hypothesis'. If we reject a true null hypothesis on the evidence of sample data, we are committing a type I (α) error. α is called the *level of significance* and is the *probability of rejecting a true null hypothesis*. If, on the other hand, we fail to reject a false null hypothesis, we are committing a type II (β) error, and β is the probability of the type II error. *The power of a test is $1 - \beta$, i.e., the probability of rejecting a null hypothesis* *when it is false.* Parametric tests are more powerful in the sense that the probability of rejecting a false null hypothesis is higher in a parametric test. A parametric test based on a sample of size 30 will have the same probability of rejecting a hypothesis H_0 when it is false as that of a non-parametric test on a sample of size 50. Gibbons (1993) has discussed the related concept of asymptotic relative efficiency of two tests in his book *Nonparametric Statistics: An Introduction:* 'The asymptotic relative efficiency of test A relative to test B is the ratio of the sample size required by test B relative to the sample size required by test A in order for both tests to achieve the same power at the same significance level under the same distribution assumptions with large sample sizes'.

Parametric tests can accommodate more complex designs and interactions than non-parametric tests. As discussed earlier, both parametric and non-parametric tests are available for one sample, two independent samples, and for two related samples. We will now discuss various types of parametric tests.

PARAMETRIC TESTS

In marketing research an often faced problem is that of drawing some inferences about the population mean. This may be done through tests of the hypothesized value of the population mean. The choice of the appropriate test depends on (a) the definition of the hypothesis (for example, whether the sample mean is equal to, greater than, or less than the population mean), (b) whether the population standard deviation σ is known, and (c) the size of the sample. When we are dealing with metric data and the standard deviation σ of the population is known, the population distribution may be assumed to be normal, and we use the z-test for testing the hypothesis about the mean. If σ is not known, the choice of the probability distribution depends on the size of the sample, and the t-test is often used for this purpose. The definition of the hypothesis will govern the choice between a one-tailed and a two-tailed test.

One-sample Tests

In marketing research, we are often interested in determining whether a variable from a population conforms to a given hypothesis. For example, we may want to determine if the monthly sales of a brand average Rs 75 lakhs, or if the recall of an advertising campaign is 40 per cent within the target group, and so on. These hypotheses may be tested through the z-test or the t-test, depending on the sample size and whether or not σ is known. The steps to be followed in testing these hypotheses have been specified in an earlier chapter.

Case I: Known population standard deviation
Let us consider the case of testing for a population mean, given the population standard deviation σ. The z-test would be applicable, since σ is known. A numerical example will make the procedure clear:

Defining the hypothesis   The null hypothesis is always the hypothesis that is tested. Let us test the hypothesis that the average monthly sales of a brand are Rs 75 lakh, i.e.,

$$H_0: \mu = 75$$

against the alternative

$$H_1: \mu \neq 75$$

This leads to a two-tailed test, since we are interested in testing the null hypothesis against the alternative that the average brand sales are not Rs 75 lakhs. We could instead have tested the null hypothesis against the alternative that average sales are more than Rs 75 lakh ($\mu > 75$) or that average sales are less than Rs 75 lakh ($\mu < 75$).

Test statistic   Since the parameter to be tested is the population mean, the appropriate test statistic corresponding to it is the sample mean $\bar{X}$.

Test   If the population standard deviation σ is known to be 1.5, the z-test is appropriate.

Acceptance significance level   Let us assume that the hypothesis is being tested at the acceptable value of $\alpha = 0.05$, known as the significance level; i.e., the hypothesis will be accepted if the value of the calculated test statistic exceeds the tabulated value in 5 or less out of 100 samples.

Sample   Let us suppose that the brand sales figures have been collected for 24 months at random, and average sales during this period is found to be Rs 70 lakh, i.e., the value of the sample mean $\bar{X}$ is found to be 70.

Test statistic   The test statistic z for the two-tailed test is then calculated as

$$z = (\bar{X} - \mu)/(\sigma/\sqrt{n}) = (70 - 75)/(1.5/\sqrt{24})$$
$$= 5/0.306186 = 16.3299$$

Critical value of test statistic   The critical value of z given in the table 1 is 1.96 for $\alpha = 0.05$.

Comparison of the calculated and critical values   Since the calculated value 16.33 is greater than the tabulated value 1.96 of z, the null hypothesis is not accepted. In other words, the average monthly sales cannot be said to be Rs 75 lakhs.

If the hypothesis to be tested was $H_0 \geq 75$, the alternative would be $H_1 < 75$. In this case, a one-tailed test would be applicable. The calculated value of the test-statistic z remains the same as in the two-tailed test, but for a one-tailed test with a significance level $\alpha = 0.05$, the area under the normal curve to be studied is under the left or right

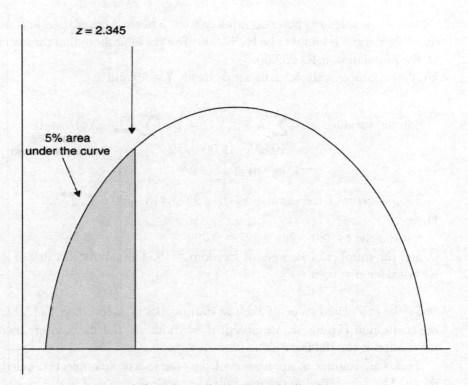

Fig. 13.1 The Normal Distribution

tail of the normal curve, as shown in Fig. 13.1. The value of z for this area at $\alpha = 0.05$ is 2.345. The calculated value of z in this case is

$$z = (\overline{X} - \mu)/\sigma/\sqrt{n}) = (70 - 75)/(1.5/\sqrt{24})$$
$$= -5/0.306186 = -16.3299$$

The rejection rule for a left-tailed test is to reject the null hypothesis if the calculated value of z is less than $-z_\alpha$. Since $-16.3299 < -2.345$, we reject the null hypothesis.

Case II: Population standard deviation not known If the population standard deviation σ is not known and the sample size is not large, the test to be applied is the t-test. In this case, the sample standard deviation s is used to estimate the population standard deviation σ, and the standard error of the mean is defined as $s/\sqrt{n}$. The test-statistic t is then defined as

$$t = (\overline{X} - \mu)/(s/\sqrt{n})$$

This t-statistic follows the t-distribution with $n - 1$ degrees of freedom. The following numerical example will illustrate the application of this test.

Twenty people are chosen at random from a normal population and their average monthly income is found to be Rs 30,000. Test the hypothesis that the average income of the population is Rs 28,000.

Here, the sample statistics are sample mean $\bar{X} = 30$ and

$$\text{Sample variance } s^2 = \sum (\bar{X}_i - X)^2 / (n-1) = (\sum \bar{X}_i^2 - nX^2)/(n-1)$$
$$= (19{,}885 - 18{,}000)/19$$
$$= 99.21053$$

Sample error of the mean $= s / \sqrt{n} = 9.960448 / \sqrt{20} = 2.227$

Hence,

test statistic $t = (30 - 28)/2.227 = 0.898$

and the number of degrees of freedom $= 19$. The tabulated value of $t_{19} = 2.09$ if we consider $\alpha = 0.05$.

Since the calculated value of the test statistic (0.898) is less than t_{19} (2.09), we do not reject the null hypothesis; we accept the hypothesis that the average income of the population is Rs 28,000.

This is an example of application of the *t*-test to a one-sample, two-tailed test for the mean. The adaptation to the one-tailed test is similar to that in the case of the *z*-test.

Case III: Test for proportions In real-life situations, we are often interested in estimating proportions rather than averages. Suppose we want to test the hypothesis that the percentage of the target audience that could be expected to recall an advertising campaign run for brand A by its marketer is 40 per cent.

This hypothesis is described as

$$H_0: P_0 = 0.40$$

where P_0 is the proportion in the population of the target audience who recall the advertising campaign for brand A. This also means $Q_0 = 0.60$, where Q_0 is the percentage of population who do not recall the advertising campaign. For a two-tailed test, this sample data provides

$$H_1: P_0 \neq 0.40$$

We study a sample of 225 individuals in the target group and find that only 35 per cent of the respondents recall the campaign.

$$p = 0.35$$

Therefore,
$$q = 0.65$$

In order to test the hypothesis for proportions, we need to calculate the standard error of the proportion as

$$\sigma_p = \sqrt{(PQ/n)} = \sqrt{0.4 \times 0.6/225} = 0.0337$$

at a level of significance $\alpha = 0.05$, the test statistic can be computed as

$$z = (p - P_0)/\sigma_p = 0.05/0.0337 = 1.48$$

Since the tabulated value of z at $\alpha = 0.05$ is 1.96, which is greater than the calculated value 1.48 of z on the basis of this sample, we accept the null hypothesis, i.e., the proportion of target audience recalling the advertising campaign may be accepted at 40 per cent.

We must note that this test for proportions is applicable only to large samples.

Two Independent Samples

Researchers are often interested in comparing parameters from two different populations: viewership of a television programme among men and women, usage levels of a brand among different income groups, ownership of CDs of a certain music genre among different age groups, and so on. Such comparisons are often useful for marketing decisions such as determining the market potential a brand among different segments or brand health in different user groups. Samples drawn at random from such populations are *independent samples* and are used for testing hypotheses regarding these populations. Here again, the most commonly tested hypotheses relate to population means or proportions.

Testing the significance of the difference between two sample means

Let us first discuss the testing of hypothesis relating to two sample means.

Case I: Two populations with the same variance   Given two independent random samples $(x_{11}, x_{12}, \ldots, x_{1n})$ and $(x_{21}, x_{22}, \ldots, x_{2n})$ drawn from normal populations with the same variance, sample means $\bar{X}_1$ and $\bar{X}_2$, and sample standard deviations S_1 and S_2, we test the hypothesis that the two populations have the same population mean. To carry out the test, we calculate the statistic

$$t = (\bar{X}_1 - \bar{X}_2)/S\sqrt{(1/n_1) + (1/n_2)}$$

where $\bar{X}_1$ and $\bar{X}_2$ are the sample means from the two independent samples with sample sizes n_1 and n_2. S^2 is the pooled estimate of the population variance, and is defined as

$$S^2 = [(n_1 - 1)S_1^2 + (n_2 - 1)S_2^2]/(n_1 + n_2 - 2)$$

where S_1^2 and S_2^2 are the sample variances of samples 1 and 2, respectively.

The t-statistic defined above follows the t-distribution with $n_1 + n_2 - 2$ degrees of freedom.

Case II: Two populations with unequal variance   Malhotra (2004) has quoted various authors on the situation in which the two populations cannot be assumed to have equal variances. In such a situation, it is not possible to have a common estimate S^2 of the population variance, and only an approximation to the t statistic can be computed.

Testing the significance of the difference between proportions from two independent samples

Suppose two large random samples of size $n_1 = 60$ and $n_2 = 50$ are taken from two populations of first year students from two business schools. The proportions of students from the two samples intending to opt for the marketing discipline in the second year are compared and found to be 45 per cent and 38 per cent, respectively. We want to test the hypothesis that there is no difference in the proportion of students from the two populations opting for marketing. This kind of hypotheses involving proportions are tested with the aid of the test-statistic defined as

$$z = (p_1 - p_2)/\sqrt{pq(1/n_1 + 1/n_2)}$$

where

$$p = (n_1 p_1 + n_2 p_2)/(n_1 + n_2)$$
$$q = 1 - p$$

A z-test is applied to the statistic z at a pre-selected level of significance α. In the example described above, we have $p_1 = 0.45, p_2 = 0.38, n_1 = 60$, and $n_2 = 50$. Therefore,

$$p = (27 + 19)/110 = 0.4182, \; q = 0.5818$$
$$z = (0.45 - 0.38)/\sqrt{0.4182 \times 0.5818(1/60 + 1/50)} = 0.7407$$

At $\alpha = 0.05$ ($\alpha = 0.01$), the tabulated value of $z = 1.96$ (2.58) for a two-tailed test. Since the calculated value of $z = 0.7407$ is much smaller than 1.96 (2.58), the null hypothesis can be accepted and we conclude that on the basis of the samples studied, there appears to be no significant difference between the groups of students opting for marketing in the two schools.

It must be noted that the sample size influences the value of z in this test.

Matched Samples

If the size of the two samples is the same, say n, and the data are paired or the data have been obtained twice from the same sample, then the definition of the t-statistic given for two populations with the same variance, which assumes independent samples, is not appropriate. It is, therefore, modified to

$$t = (d - 0)/(S/\sqrt{n})$$

where $d = \Sigma d_i/n$ is the average of d_i, d_i being the difference between the ith pair of values of the variables from the two samples (i.e., say, $x_i - y_i$). This statistic follows the t-distribution with $n-1$ degrees of freedom.

Hypothesis Testing and Confidence Intervals

In the preceding discussion, we have assumed that the population being studied has a known mean, though the population variance may or may not be known. If, on the other hand, the population standard deviation σ is known but the population mean μ is unknown, we have to estimate μ. The sample mean $\bar{X}$ will provide an estimate of μ only within some limits, i.e., within a specified interval. The relative deviation of $\bar{X}$ from μ which defines this interval is the ratio z of $(\bar{X} - \mu)$ to the standard error $S_x = \sigma/\sqrt{n}$ of the sample mean, i.e.,

$$z = (\bar{X} - \mu)/(\sigma/\sqrt{n})$$

If z is not significant at a specified level of probability, say 5 per cent, then this relative deviation must lie inside the area (in a normal distribution) whose outer boundary is defined by the tabulated value of z; for example, the 5 per cent shaded area in Fig. 13.1, whose boundary value x is 1.96. In other words, $z < 1.96$, or taking the chances of $\bar{X}$ being greater than or less than μ,

$$\left| (\bar{X} - \mu)/(\sigma/\sqrt{n}) \right| < 1.96$$

This equation translates to

$$\bar{X} - 1.96\sigma/\sqrt{n} < \mu < \bar{X} + 1.96\sigma/\sqrt{n}$$

This is the 95 per cent confidence interval of μ. It gives the limits for μ beyond which the probability of the observed sample mean $\bar{X}$ being equal to μ is less than 5 per cent. Alternatively, we may say that the critical or cutoff limits for μ can be calculated by using the formula

$$\mu \pm 1.96 S_x$$

If $\bar{X}$ lies beyond this range, we reject the null hypothesis that X is equal to μ.

NON-PARAMETRIC TESTS

The concept of non-parametric tests was discussed in detail in Chapter 12 and then again at the beginning of this chapter. In this section, we will discuss some common non-parametric tests.

All non-parametric tests are based on three assumptions:

1. The sample size is less than 20.
2. The variables involved are ordinal or nominal.
3. No prior assumption is made about the underlying distribution of the population from which the sample is drawn.

In addition, assumptions specific to a particular test may be made. Like parametric tests, non-parametric tests are also available for one sample, two or more independent samples, and related samples.

One-sample Tests

One of the most popular non-parametric one-sample tests is the chi-square test, which has been discussed in detail in the previous chapter. We will discuss other one-sample tests in this section.

Kolmogorov–Smirnov test Sometimes it is necessary to compare the observed sample distribution of a random variable X with a theoretical distribution. The Kolmogorov–Smirnov (K-S) test is one of the goodness-of-fit tests used for this purpose. It is more powerful than the chi-square test and, hence, more suited to small samples. It compares the cumulative frequency distribution of the observed sample with the theoretical cumulative frequency distribution on a base of 100. The hypothesis for this test is defined as

$$H_0: O_i = F_i$$

where

$$O_i = \left(\sum_{1}^{i} o_i\right)\% \text{ and } F_i = \left(\sum_{1}^{i} f_i\right)\%$$

O_i and F_i being the observed and theoretical frequencies, respectively.

The test is based on the maximum absolute difference between O_i and F_i:

$$D = \text{Max}|O_i - F_i|$$

The larger the value of D, the greater the probability of H_0 being false. The theoretical distribution of D for various levels of significance and sample sizes is given in the table

'Kolmogorov–Smirnov statistic for one-sample test'[1]. The decision rule is to reject H_0 if D exceeds the $(1 - \alpha)$ quantile $(V_{1-\alpha})$. For sample sizes greater than 40, the statistic approximates to the normal distribution and the critical values of D^* for various probability-value levels are the following:

One-sided test	$p =$	0.90	0.95	0.975	0.99	0.995
Two-sided test	$p =$	0.80	0.90	0.95	0.98	0.99
	D^*	$1.07/\sqrt{n}$	$1.22/\sqrt{n}$	$1.36/\sqrt{n}$	$1.52/\sqrt{n}$	$1.63/\sqrt{n}$

Consider an example of preference for five business schools, administered to 20 candidates. The hypothesis to be tested is that the preference pattern for the five schools is uniform across the sample. Using the K-S test, the calculations have been shown in Table 13.1.

$$\text{Max } D = 0.10$$

Now, for $n = 20$ and $p = 0.95$, the quantile W_p of the Kolmogorov–Smirnov test, as given in the table, is 0.294, which is greater than 0.10. Hence, the hypothesis H_0 is not rejected and we may conclude on the basis of this sample that there is no difference in the candidates' preference for the five business schools.

Runs test This test is applicable to dichotomous variables. It tests for randomness by assessing whether or not the order in which the observations occur is truly random. It was introduced by Bradley in 1968.

According to the *Engineering Statistics Handbook* (2005), 'a "run" is defined as a series of increasing values or a series of decreasing values. The number of increasing or decreasing values is the length of a run. In a random data set, the probability that the $(i + 1)$th value is larger or smaller than the ith value follows a binomial distribution, which forms the basis for the runs test.'

Table 13.1 Calculations Using the K-S test

Schools	Observed Frequency O_i (1)	Cumulative Frequency O_i (2)	% Cumulative Frequency O_i (3)	Expected Frequency F_i (4)	Cumulative Frequency F_i (5)	% Cumulative Frequency F_i (6)	$D = (O_i - F_i)$ (6)−(3): (7)
A	5	5	0.25	4	4	0.20	0.05
B	3	8	0.40	4	8	0.40	0
C	2	10	0.50	4	12	0.60	0.10
D	6	16	0.80	4	16	0.80	0
E	4	20	1.00	4	20	1.00	0
Total	20						

[1] Readers are advised to consult the table for Kolmogorov–Smirnov Statistic for one-sample test available in books on research methodology.

Let $x_1, x_2, ..., x_n$ denote the observations in the order obtained. The first step in the test is to compute $(x_i - x_{i-1})$. $x_i > x_{i-1}$, it indicates an increasing order, and $x_i < x_{i-1}$ indicates a decreasing order. Let each observation be indicated by a if it is higher than the sample median and by b if it is lower than the sample median. We then obtain a sequence such as, say,

$$aa, bbb, ab, aa, bb, ...$$

This sequence provides runs of two a's, three b's, one a followed by one b, two a's, two b's, and so on. It is obvious that if the sample is truly random, then the a's and b's will be well-mixed and the number of runs would be large. The test, therefore, consists of counting the number of runs in the combined ordered sample and rejecting the null hypothesis if the total number of runs is less than the number determined from the distribution of runs and the level of significance. This number is, however, independent of the distribution of the parent population. Under the null hypothesis of a random sample, with an even sample size n and continuous population data, the number of runs above and below the sample median is a random variable with

$$\text{Mean} = (n+2)/2$$

and

$$\text{Variance} = (n/4)[1 - (1/n - 1)]$$

Another alternative is to treat the values above the median as positive and those below the median as negative.

Binomial test   This is another goodness-of-fit test for dichotomous variables. It tests the goodness-of-fit of a sample of observations to a theoretical binomial distribution. The sample consists of the outcomes of n independent trials, with two possible distinct outcomes. Let us assume that n_1 is the number of outcomes of type 1 and n_2 is the number of outcomes of type 2. Each trial has the probability p of outcomes of type 1, constant across all trials. The null hypothesis is the following.

For a two-tailed test,

$$H_0: p = p*$$

against

$$H_1: p \neq p*$$

For a one-tailed test,

$$H_0: p \leq p*$$

against

$$H_1: p > p*$$

or

$$H_0: p \geq p*$$

against

$$H_1: p < p*$$

We test the statistic $T = n_1$

The decision rule is, for the two-tailed test, given $P(y \leq t_1) = \alpha_1$ and $P(y > t_2) = \alpha_2$, where α_1 and α_2 are the sizes of the upper and lower tails and $\alpha_1 + \alpha_2 = \alpha$, reject H_0 if $T \leq t_1$ or $T > t_2$. The values of t_1 and t_2 may be obtained from the binomial tables with parameters n and $p*$.

For the one-tailed test, reject H_0 if, for $P(y > t) = \alpha$, $T > t$, where y follows the binomial distribution with parameters n and $p*$ for $H_0: p \leq p*$. Similarly, reject H_0 if, for $P(y \leq t) = \alpha$, $T \leq t$ for $H_0: p \geq p*$.

Multiple-sample Tests

Let us now discuss various multiple-sample tests.

Independent samples

The chi-square test for independent samples has been discussed in detail in Chapter 12. In this section we will discuss other popular non-parametric tests for independent samples.

Kolmogorov–Smirnov two-sample test The K-S two-sample test is used when two independent samples of ordinal data are to be compared to determine whether both the samples have been drawn from the same population. This is among the most useful, general, and, therefore, popular non-parametric tests.

As in the one-sample case, here also we use the cumulative distribution functions of the two samples to compare the two distributions, on the basis that if the two samples indeed belong to the same population, their cumulative distributions should be fairly similar, except for random deviations from the population distribution. The test statistic is again D_{max}, where D_{max} is the maximum D_i and D_i is the difference between the ith cumulative frequencies, converted into percentages, of the two samples. The number of frequency intervals used in this test should be large, so that D_{max} is not obscured. Critical values of the theoretical distribution of D are given in the table 'Kolmogorov–Smirnov two-sample test'[1] available in textbooks on research methodology.

Mann–Whitney U-test Also called the 'rank sum test', this is the most powerful non-parametric test. It is the non-parametric equivalent of the t-test for independence of two means in the parametric case. It is applicable for two samples when the larger of the samples is of size 20 or less. The objective of the test is to determine whether or not the two samples have been drawn from the same population. The null hypothesis is defined as

---

[1] Readers are advised to refer to the table 'Kolmogorov Smirnov two-sample test' available in the market.

$$H_0: F(X) = G(Y) \text{ for all } X \text{ and } Y$$

against

$$H_1: F(X) \neq G(Y) \text{ for at least some } X \text{ and } Y$$

where $F(X)$ and $G(Y)$ are the distribution functions of the populations $\{X_i\}$ and $\{Y_j\}$ from which the two samples of sizes n_1 and n_2 have been drawn.

The test consists of the following steps.

1. Combine the two samples and list the $n_1 + n_2$ observations sequentially.
2. Rank the observations from 1 to $n_1 + n_2$ in order of magnitude in the combined series. If there are ties, give the successive observations, say x_i and y_j, the average rank.
3. Sum up the ranks obtained by the observations in the two samples for each

    sample, i.e., $R_1 = \sum_1^{n_1} X_i$ and $R_2 = \sum_1^{n_2} X_j$.

4. Compute the test statistic U as

    $$U = n_1 n_2 + [n_1(n_1 + 1)/2] - R_1$$

    or

    $$U' = n_1 n_2 + [n_2(n_2 - 1)/2] - R_2$$

    Under the null hypothesis, $U = U'$.

5. Decision rule: Reject H_0 if $U < W_{\alpha/2}$ or $U > W_{1-\alpha/2}$ at level of significance α. W_α is the αth quantile of the Mann–Whitney statistic, as given in the Mann–Whitney U-test table.[1]

    When $n > 20$ in any one of the samples, the sampling distribution of U approaches normality with

    $$\text{Mean} = \mu_U = n_1 n_2 / 2$$
    $$\text{Standard deviation} = \sigma_U = \sqrt{n_1 n_2 (n_1 + n_2 + 1)/12}$$
    $$\text{Test–statistic } z = (U - \mu_U)/\sigma_U$$

Kruskal–Wallis test   This is the generalized version of the Mann–Whitney test, similar to the parametric case of analysis of variance, which is a generalized version of the *t*-test. It tests the hypothesis that the three (or more) samples being studied have been drawn from the same population. The test procedure is similar to the Mann–Whitney test. Majumdar (1991) has listed the steps in conducting the test as follows.

---

[1] Readers are advised to consult the Mann Whitney U test table available in the market.

1. Pool all scores from the various samples.
2. Assign ranks to all the pooled scores from the smallest to the largest.
3. Calculate the rank sum of each sample, with tied observations being assigned average ranks.
4. Compute the test statistic U as

$$U = 12[(\sum_{i=1}^{G} T_j^2 / n_j) - 3(N+1)] / N(N-1)$$

where T_j = sum of ranks in column j,
n_j = number of cases in the jth sample,
N = total number of cases, and
k = number of samples

In the case of multiple ties, a correction factor (C) should be computed and used for correcting T as

$$C = 1 - \{\sum (ti^3 - ti) / (N^2 - N)\}$$

where G = total number of tied observations, ti = number tied in any set N_i, *and* $U' = U/C$.

The test statistic U' follows the chi-square distribution with $k-1$ degrees of freedom.

Median test Cooper and Schindler (1999), in their book *Business Research Methods*, have defined the median test as a test which is 'used to test whether two samples are drawn from populations with the same median. The median of the combined data set is calculated and each original observation is classified according to its original sample (A or B) and whether it is less than or greater than the overall median. The chi-square test for homogeneity of proportions in the resulting 2×2 table tests whether the population medians are equal.'

The test works as follows. Suppose two samples of size n_1 and n_2 are drawn from two populations $f(x)$ and $f(y)$. The data from the two samples will be pooled to determine the combined median M. Now suppose that in sample 1, O_{11} is the number of observations greater than M and O_{12} is the number of observations less than M. We define O_{21} and O_{22} similarly. This data may be arranged in a 2×2 contingency table (Table 13.2).

Table 13.2 2 × 2 Contingency Table

Sample Values	Sample 1	Sample 2	Total
> M	O_{11}	O_{21}	a
≤ M	O_{12}	O_{22}	b
Total	n_1	n_2	$N(=n_1 + n_2)$

$$H_0: M_1 = M_2$$
$$H_1: M_1 \neq M_2$$

M_1 and M_2 are the medians of the two populations, respectively.

We calculate the test-statistic T as

$$T = (N^2 / ab)\left(\sum_1^2 (O_{1i} - n_i a / N)^2 / n_i \right) = (N^2 / ab)\left(\sum_1^2 O_{1i}^2 / n_i \right) - Na / b$$

Reject H_0 if $T > \chi^2(1-\alpha)$ with 1 degree of freedom.

This test can be extended to more than two samples as well.

Related Samples

The samples drawn from a population may not always be independent. At times the same sample may be studied at different points in time, such as before and after treatments, or the samples may be matched. In such cases the tests of hypotheses required are different from those discussed so far. Some common tests for related samples have been discussed in this section.

Sign test   When data is collected in pairs, this test is concerned with a measure of central tendency specified as the median M_d of the population of differences M between the pairs. It tests the null hypothesis that for pairs (X_i, Y_i), X_i and Y_i have the same measure of central tendency. Some authors prefer to use the mean rather than the median as the measure of central tendency. This test is particularly useful when we are trying to assess the impact of a treatment. For example, if we want to determine the impact of a sales promotion scheme on the sales of a brand, we may want to compare the sales of the brand before (X) and after (Y) the campaign from, say, 15 stores to check if there is a significant difference between the average sales before and after the campaign. The null hypothesis in this example is that there is no difference between the before and after sales.

The median of a continuous population divides the area under the distribution curve into two equal parts, so that the probability of a difference being positive or negative is half. We can, therefore, test the null hypothesis by treating the number of positive signs as a binomial variable with mean $= N/2$ and variance $= N/4$.

The working of the test is given below.

1. Within each pair (X_i, Y_i), calculate the difference $X_i - Y_i$.
2. Define the difference as '+' if $X_i > Y_i$, as '−' if $X_i < Y_i$, and as '0' if $X_i = Y_i$. In the last case, i.e., if there is a tie, the observations are usually ignored and the sample size N is adjusted for the reduction.

3. Define the null hypothesis as follows:

- For a two-tailed test, H_0: $M_1 = M_2$, where M_1 is the median of the population $f(X)$ and M_2 is the median of the population $f(Y)$, against H_1: $M_1 \neq M_2$.
- For a one-tailed test, H_0: $M_1 \geq M_2$ against H_1: $M_1 < M_2$ or H_0: $M_1 \leq M_2$ against H_1: $M_1 > M_2$.

4. Define the test statistic T as the total number of '+'s, i.e., pairs where $X_i > Y_i$. t follows the binomial distribution.
5. The decision rule for level of significance α is sample size ≤ 20 and $P = 1/2$.

- For the two-tailed test, reject H_0 if $T \leq t$ or $T \geq n - t$, where t is obtained from the binomial distribution table[1], using P $(B \leq t) = \alpha/2$, where B follows the binomial distribution with $(N, 1/2)$.
- For the one-tailed test, reject H_0 if $T \leq t$, where P $(B \leq t) = \alpha$. For $N > 20$, t approximates the normal distribution.

Wilcoxon signed-rank test This is another important test used for testing the differences between the locations of two populations on the basis of paired data (X_i, Y_i) obtained from them. This test takes into account not merely the sign but also the magnitude of the differences. It is more powerful than the sign test. In fact, under certain conditions it can even be more powerful than the t-test. The procedure for the test is as follows.

1. Find the difference score d_i between each pair of values (X_i, Y_i).
2. Rank the differences in order of their magnitude, without taking the signs into account. For example, if two pairs of values exhibit numerical differences 4 and −5, they are given ranks on the basis of the numerical values 4 and 5.
3. In case the d_i value for any pair is zero, i.e., if $X_i = Y_i$, it is dropped from further calculation. If two or more pairs have the same d_i value, their rank positions are averaged.
4. Add the signs relevant to the differences to the ranks corresponding to the values of the differences.
5. Calculate the test statistic T as the sum of the ranks with the less frequent sign.
6. For sample size $N < 25$, the test-statistic follows the Wilcoxon signed-rank test distribution.[2]
7. For sample size $N > 25$, T approximates to normality with

$$\text{Mean} = \mu = N(N + 1)/4$$

---

[1] Readers are advised to consult the binomial distribution table available in the market.
[2] Readers are advised to consult the Wilcoxon signed ranks test distribution available in the market.

$$\text{Standard deviation} = \sigma = \sqrt{[N(N+1)(2N+1)/24}$$
$$\text{Test statistic } z = (T - \mu)/\sigma$$

McNemar's test   This test is a variation of the sign test. It may be used with nominal or ordinal data and is useful before and after the measurement of the same sample, when the sample is administered some treatment and its effect has to be studied. It compares the proportion of the sample that registers change (positive or negative) with the proportion that does not change, in order to determine if the treatment has resulted in any significant change. The working of the test is as follows.

1.   the sample before the experiment is divided into two groups N_1 and N_2, where the subgroup N_1 depicts the characteristic C and N_2 does not. $N_1 + N_2 = N$, where N is the total sample.

2.   The sub-samples N_1 and N_2 are further divided into two groups each, depending on the proportion in each sample that depicts the characteristic C after the treatment.

3.   The data is thus represented in the form of a contingency table:

		After Treatment		
		X_{21}	X_{22}	Total
Before	X_{11}	a	c	N_1
Treatment	X_{12}	b	d	N_2
	Total	N_1'	N_2'	N

Here, a = proportion of the sample that exhibited the characteristic C before and after the treatment $(X_{11}X_{21})$, b = proportion of the sample that did not exhibit the characteristic C before the treatment but did so after the treatment $(X_{12}X_{21})$, c = proportion of the sample that exhibited the characteristic C before but not after the treatment $(X_{11}X_{22})$, and d = proportion of the sample that did not exhibit the characteristic C either before or after the treatment $(X_{12}X_{22})$.

4.   Cell frequencies b and c depict the extent of change. Cell b exhibits the positive change from the absence of C before treatment to its presence after treatment. Cell c exhibits the negative change from the presence of C before treatment to its absence after treatment. The other two cells depict no change: a depicts positive (present) to positive (present) and d depicts negative (absent) to negative (absent). Under the null hypothesis, the proportions b and c should be equal, depicting only random change, independent of the effect of the treatment.

5.   The null hypothesis is, therefore, defined as

$$H_0: \text{P}(b) = \text{P}(c)$$

against

$$H_1: \text{P}(b) \neq \text{P}(c)$$

6. The test statistic is $D = (|b - c - 1)^2/(b + c)$, which follows the chi-square distribution with one degree of freedom and level of significance α.

Cochran's Q-test   This is an extension of the McNemar test for ordinal data to k related samples. It is computed for binary variables for multi-way tables. 'Cochran's Q statistic is used to test the homogeneity of the one-dimensional margins', according Dallal (2000). If m denotes the number of variables and N denotes the total number of subjects, the test statistic is computed as

$$Q_C = (m - 1)\left[m\sum_{j=1}^{m} T_j^2 - T^2 \right] / \left(mT - \sum_{k=1}^{N} S_k^2 \right)$$

where T_j is the number of positive responses for variable j, T is the total number of positive responses over all variables, and S_k is the number of positive responses for subject k. Under the null hypothesis, Cochran's Q statistic is an approximate chi-square statistic with $(m - 1)$ degrees of freedom. This simplifies to McNemar's test for m = 2, i.e., for two binary variables.

Friedman's test   This is also a test for k matched samples with at least ordinal data, similar to the two-way analysis of variance. According to Gibbons (1993), this refers to 'a situation in which we want to compare T treatments using a design where $N = BT$ subjects are matched into B groups, each of size $N/B = T$. The T subjects within each group are assigned randomly to T treatments, the treatment effects are measured on at least an ordinal scale, and the comparisons of the treatments are made only within each group.' The response to each treatment by the subjects within each group is ranked from 1 to T. No comparisons are made between groups. These ranks are used to compute the test statistic S:

$$S = \sum_{t=1}^{T} [R_t - B(T + 1)/2]^2$$

S follows the Friedman distribution tables.[1] Tests based on multivariate techniques have been discussed in the chapters that follow.

SUMMARY

This chapter discusses tests of hypotheses, which aim at determining whether or not a sample is representative of the population from which it is drawn.

If the parameters of the population are known, the tests involved are called *parametric tests*. These are most often used with interval- or ratio-scaled data, for large samples.

---

[1] Readers are advised to consult Friedman distribution tables available in the market.

If the population parameters are not known, so that the distribution of the population cannot be defined, the tests involved are called *non-parametric* tests. These are based on small samples, usually of size less than 20, and use ordinal or nominal data. For larger samples, these tests approximate to the normal test. The level of significance, or type I error, is the probability of rejecting a null hypothesis when it is true. The power of a test or (1 – type II error) is the probability of rejecting a null hypothesis when it is false.

If the standard deviation of a normal population is known, and the sample is large and based on metric data, the test of hypothesis to be used is a *z*-test. If the standard deviation is not known, the *t*-test is applicable. These tests are applicable to testing the population mean in single samples, two independent samples, and related samples. For more than two independent samples, the analysis of variance technique is applied. It uses the *F*-test. As is the case with parametric tests, non-parametric tests are also available for one sample, two or more independent samples, and for related samples.

The most frequently used one-sample tests are the chi-square test of goodness-of-fit for nominal variables, the Kolmogorov–Smirnov (K-S) one-sample test for goodness-of-fit for ordinal variables, the runs test for randomness of data, and the binomial test for goodness-of-fit. Unlike the K-S test, the binomial test is applicable to dichotomous variables. The two-sample tests discussed are the chi-square test for independence, the K-S two-sample test, the Mann–Whitney test for difference of means (an analogue of the *t*-test), the Kruskal–Wallis analysis of variance, and the median test. The tests for related samples that have been discussed are the sign test, the Wilcoxon signed-rank test, the McNemar test, Cochran's *Q*-test, and the Friedman test, which is similar to ANOVA, except that it tests only the differences within the group.

KEY WORDS

Hypothesis refers to a measurable and testable assumption relating to specific distribution parameters that may be tested through empirical data and statistical tests.

Null hypothesis is a hypothesis that is being tested.

Parametric tests are statistical tests of hypotheses that are valid and applicable only under the assumption of a known and defined distribution of the population.

Non-parametric tests refer to statistical tests of hypotheses that do not require any assumption about the population distribution in order to be valid.

Distribution-free methods are the same as non-parametric methods of testing hypothesis.

Ordered samples are samples that have data arranged in ascending or descending order of the values of the variables.

Type I error is also called the level of significance, and is the probability of rejecting a null hypothesis that is true.

Type II error refers to the probability of accepting an erroneous hypothesis.

Power of a test refers to the probability of rejecting a hypothesis when it is false.

Asymptotic relative efficiency of a test can be defined as follows: the asymptotic relative efficiency of test A relative to test B is the ratio of the sample size required by test B relative to the sample size required by test A in order for both tests to achieve the same power at the same significance level under the same distribution assumptions with large sample sizes.

Independent samples are samples which are drawn from populations in a manner that the selection of sampling units from one does not in any way depend on the selection from the other.

Related samples refer to samples which are drawn from populations in a manner that the selection of sampling units from one depends on or is effected by the selection from the other.

Test statistic is the constant calculated from sample data that is used for testing the veracity of the null hypothesis.

Confidence interval is the range within which, given the sample value, the population value may be expected to have a predetermined probability of lying.

Goodness-of-fit refers to the probability that the observed frequency values are close to or the same as the frequencies of a theoretical distribution.

Decision rule is the rule, involving the test statistic, that is used for deciding whether or not the null hypothesis should be rejected.

CONCEPT REVIEW QUESTIONS

1. What is the power of a test? What is its influence on sample size?

2. Discuss the relative advantages and disadvantages of parametric and non-parametric tests.

3. What factors will you take into account in choosing a test for a particular application? Give examples of suitable applications of each:

   (i) *t*-test and Mann–Whitney *U*-test
   (ii) K-S one-sample test and binomial test
   (iii) McNemar test and sign test

4. A publisher of a women's magazine wants to test the claim that 40 per cent of its readers are males. A sample of 100 adults was selected at random, consisting of 60 men and 40 women. An in-depth interview with them revealed that 30 men and 24 women were regular readers of the magazine. Does the data support the claim?

5. In an attitude survey of two brands of ready-to-eat pizza, consumer ratings on a five-point scale of preference showed the following pattern in two samples of 300 consumers each:

Preference rating

1 = Like it very much, ..., 5 = Do not like it at all

	1	2	3	4	5
Brand A	50	43	67	80	60
Brand B	47	62	60	70	61

Test the hypothesis that both brands of pizza are perceived to be similar.

6. Company A wants to test whether the frequency of purchase of their brand B of a malted beverage in various households varies with the number of children below 15 in the families. A survey with 500 households undertaken for the purpose gives these results:

| Frequency | No. of Children < 15 in the Household | | |
of Purchase	Upto 1	2	3 or more
Twice a month	35	50	45
Once a month	40	60	20
Once a quarter	55	40	18
Less often	50	75	12

Test the hypothesis that there is no relation between the number of children and the frequency of purchase of brand B in a household.

7. Sales representatives from an organization were given a test on product knowledge. Then they were put through a training programme for a fortnight on the same content and a second test of equal difficulty was held at the end of this period. The marks obtained by a random sample of ten sales representatives in the tests before and after the training programme are given below. Do the marks in the two tests suggest that the training programme led to improved product knowledge?

Rep. no.	1	2	3	4	5	6	7	8	9	10
Marks in test I	24	21	23	19	22	15	20	17	11	18
Marks in test II	25	20	22	22	24	17	18	20	12	16

8. The sales representatives from the organization mentioned above were divided into two groups. One group was put through training programme I and the other group received training programme II. Two samples of 10 representatives each were drawn from the two groups, respectively, and the marks received by them in the post-training tests were compared. The marks obtained by the two groups are given below:

Rep. no.	1	2	3	4	5	6	7	8	9	10
Marks in test II	25	20	22	22	24	17	18	20	12	16
Rep. no.	11	12	13	14	15	16	17	18	19	20
Marks in test II	20	18	25	26	21	24	16	22	22	12

Test the hypothesis that the two training programmes produced the same kind of results.

PROJECT ASSIGNMENT

Obtain a copy of the most recent *National Readership Survey* (NRS). Develop the profile of the average reader of an English daily vis-à-vis that of a Hindi daily. What parameters will you need to take into account in defining the profile? Compare the two profiles using appropriate tests. Further, compare (a) the profiles of the readers of the *Times of India* in different states and (b) the all-India profile of the *Times of India* with the all-India profile of the *Indian Express*. Obtain a copy of an earlier *NRS*, and develop a profile of the average reader of the *Indian Express*. Compare the two profiles to determine whether the profile of the average *Indian Express* reader appears to have changed and in which way?

REFERENCES

Aaker, D., V. Kumar and G.S.Day 1999, *Marketing Research, 6th edn.*, Wiley, India.

Cooper, D.R. and P.S. Schindler 1999, *Business Research Methods*, Tata McGraw-Hill, New Delhi, pp. 417–419.

Dallal, Gerard E. 2000, *Non Parametric Statistics*, www.tufts.edu/-gdallal/npara.htm

Engineering Statistics Handbook 2005, NIST/SEMATECH e-Handbook of Statistical Methods http://www.itl.nist.gov/div898/handbook, accessed on 28 December 2005.

Gibbons, Jean D. 1993, *Non Parametric Statistics: An Introduction*, Sage, California, p. 3.

Kapur, J.N. and H.C. Saxena 1960, *Mathematical Statistics,* 2nd edn, S. Chand and Co., Delhi, pp. 335, 424.

Majumdar, R. 1991, *Marketing Research: Text, Applications and Case Studies,* New Age International, New Delhi, pp. 179–130, 183–184.

Malhotra, N.K. 2004, *Marketing Research: An Applied Orientation*, Pearson Education, Indian Branch, Delhi.

Statistical Testing Services 2005, http://www.statsconsult.com, Tutorial 11, Non-Parametric Tests, accessed on 22 December 2005.

The SAS/STAT User's Guide, The FREQ Procedure, http://www.id.unizh.ch/software/unix/statmath/sas/sasdoc/stat/chap.28/sec.26.htm

14 Computer Based Techniques of Data Analysis

OBJECTIVES

After reading this chapter, the readers will be able to understand:

- how to reduce and group data: canonical correlations and discriminant analysis; factor analysis; and cluster analysis
- how to identify underlying links in data: multidimensional scaling and conjoint analysis
- the influence of data analysis on research design

INTRODUCTION

In this chapter, we shall discuss some methods that assist in drawing conclusions about dependent and interdependent relationships between multiple variables. Some popular methods for data reduction and data grouping, such as canonical correlations, two-group and multiple discriminant analysis, factor analysis, and cluster analysis, have been discussed in detail. All these methods are based on the assumption of a two-dimensional variable space. For three-dimensional or higher order spaces, multidimensional scaling has also been discussed. In marketing research, multidimensional scaling is mostly concerned with the measurement of psychological judgements such as consumer preferences and perceptions. Conjoint analysis, which is an extension of multidimensional scaling, has also been discussed. It helps in developing the link between psychological measurements and their influence on physical measurements, such as amounts purchased.

REDUCTION AND GROUPING OF DATA

Complex data and detailed analysis require more sophisticated methods of analysis than the ones discussed in earlier chapters. In the given example, the problem discussed by Mr Mathur, which is discussed in this section, raises some issues often faced in marketing research: data collected from the field often provides such a large number of variables that analysis becomes difficult to manage. Moreover, the variables thrown up by field data are often fully or partially correlated with each other, so that no significant new information is provided by including them in the analysis. While discussing multiple regression in Chapter 12, we learnt that independent variables in a regression equation are more often than not highly correlated. In such cases, it makes sense to use a technique that can group all correlated variables together, so that they may be reduced to one common factor without much loss of information, but with the enhanced ease of handling.

Different Software for Different Requirements

Mr Mathur was staring at the data provided by his sales department. They had submitted the latest classification of dealers to him, grouped by sales turnover. He decided to call Atul Malhotra, the all India sales manager. 'Atul,' he began, almost before Malhotra could sit down, 'can we not get a more detailed classification of dealers than this data your department has submitted? If we really want to zero in on the best dealers, we can not only look at the sales turnover. I am sure it is possible to figure out why this turnover varies. There are so many factors that influence sales—the size of the shop, the location of the store, the period for which it has been around in the area, the competitors, the range of product categories and brands stocked ... . If we can get that information and classify dealers on that basis, we will be able to get a clearer picture and use it for future reference as well.' Atul Malhotra thought for a moment. There was substance in what Mr Mathur was saying, but how would his team go about collecting all this information? As it was, selling was a time consuming job, and this data collection was not quite what they considered their cup of tea. Besides, it was one thing for Mr Mathur to rattle off factors in this manner, but quite another for his team to develop a detailed list of parameters. And once it had been collected, what were they going to do with that data? How would it be analysed? Who would handle such massive amounts of information? He decided to play safe. 'Yes, sir, I agree totally. Maybe marketing research could be asked to collect this information. It is extremely important to have all this information, so we may be able to get a better understanding of our dealers. My team can help them (MR) out wherever needed. Till a few years ago, they could have done the entire job themselves, but now we have grown so much, that it is difficult for them to collect all this quickly, and also analyse it.' Mr Mathur hid his smile. Malhotra was not totally wrong. He called Gangadharan, the head of Marketing Research and put the proposition to him. Gangadharan's response was cryptic. 'Who decides on what parameters the dealers should be classified? And what analysis do you want?' 'Ganga, the parameters can be specified by marketing, so why do you not ask them? My worry is that all the brand managers will say the same thing in different words, or they will end up with a list of parameters, most of which will give you more or less the same information,' said Mr Mathur. The young marketing research manager tended to speak a language that others in the organization sometimes found difficult to understand. 'That is not a problem. We do have the required software for most of it. For what you are worrying about, we could run the data through factor analysis. But you have to specify your requirement. If you are only looking for the link between dealer characteristics and sales, we could run a multiple regression on sales with these characteristics. Alternatively, if you want the dealers divided into groups, we could do a cluster analysis. Once the data has been entered into the computer, a discriminant analysis could be run to give you the factors that distinguish between high and low sellers, as also the dealers who are included in each group. You simply tell me what information you need... .' Mr Mathur looked at Atul Malhotra out of the corner of his eye. Malhotra's jaw had dropped open a bit. He smiled, and said, 'Okay, Ganga, hold your horses and your jargon. Let us call a meeting of the Marketing and Sales people and work out what information we need and how to go about obtaining it.'

Canonical Correlations

Let us consider the case of the relationship between sales (Y) of Mango, a new upmarket international brand of apparel introduced in India, with its advertising expenditure (A), stores location (B), and average monthly expenditure on apparel in a SEC A class household (C). The relationship is defined through the multiple regression equation:

$$Y = aA + bB + cC + e$$

where a, b, and c are the regression coefficients and e is the error term. Y, the criterion variable and A, B, and C, the predictor variables are all interval-scaled.

Now suppose we want to study *two* criterion variables simultaneously: sales (Y_1) and brand image (Y_2). We are then concerned with determining the relationship between the battery (Y_1, Y_2) of criterion variables and the battery (A, B, C) of predictor variables. This is the problem of *canonical correlation*. Canonical correlation, which is an extension of multiple regression to the case of more than one dependent variable, can also be defined as the correlation between the linear combination of the criterion variables and the linear combination of the predictor variables. Some important facts about canonical analysis must be kept in mind. These are listed below.

- It is the maximal correlation between the two linear combinations.
- As in regression analysis, so also in canonical correlation a set of canonical coefficients or weights is obtained for each of the two sets, and their relative magnitude and signs are used for interpreting the combinations.
- The maximum number of canonical functions that can be obtained is equal to minimum (p, q), where p is the number of independent variables and q is the number of dependent variables.
- The degree of variance in one set of variables that is explained by the other set, measured by the square of the canonical correlation, the magnitude of the canonical correlation, and the level of significance of each canonical factor, is used to interpret each canonical factor.
- The correlation between the original variables and the canonical factor is called the 'canonical loading'. This may be used to interpret the canonical function.
- The significance of the canonical function is measured through Wilk's λ and the variables are evaluated through the F-statistic.

DISCRIMINANT ANALYSIS

The technique of multiple regression operates on a data matrix divided into dependent and independent variables, where both sets of variables are interval-scaled. However, in practice we often face situations where the independent variables are interval scaled, but the dependent variable is category scaled. For example, we may be interested in classifying a group of shoppers as 'users' or 'non-users' of a brand of protein beverage, on the basis of some characteristics, such as age, income, family size, number of children below twelve in the family, and so on. Similarly, banks often want to classify customers into 'good' and 'bad' risk categories. The classification may not be restricted to two groups, but might be extended to 'high', medium', or 'low' users of a brand, the demographic profile of people who indicate their preference for one of the six makes of cars, or students who opt for one of the various business schools in the country. In each of these problems, we are concerned with classifying a group of objects into one of a pre-specified number of categories, on the basis of the data we may have about them on a set of interval-scaled independent variables. This is the issue that 'discriminant analysis' addresses. It is, thus, concerned with the following.

- Determining linear combinations of independent variables or characteristics, using which it may be possible to separate groups of objects by maximizing between-group variance relative to within-group variance.
- Developing a rule for assigning new entrants, whose characteristics are known, to one or the other group.
- Testing, on the basis of values of group-means, whether significant differences exist between the groups.
- Identifying the independent variables that contribute most to the inter-group difference in mean-profiles.

Some terms used specifically in discriminant analysis are as follows:

Canonical correlation   This term has been described in detail earlier. In the context of discriminant analysis, it refers to the measure of association between the discriminant scores and the groups.

Centroid   This is the mean value of the discriminant scores of a group.

Classification matrix   It is also referred to as the 'confusion matrix'. It gives the number of objects correctly classified and misclassified by discriminant analysis.

Discriminant coefficients   These coefficients are the weights assigned to the original predictor variables in the discriminant function. Discriminant coefficients obtained when the variables have been standardized to mean 0 and variance 1 are called 'standardized discriminant coefficients'.

Discriminant function   This is the linear equation that divides the objects into internally homogeneous groups that are distinct from the other groups with respect to the predictor variables being considered.

Discriminant scores   The values of the predictor variables for each object, multiplied by the values of the discriminant coefficients obtained in the discriminant function and summed together, provide the discriminant score for the object.

Eigenvalue The ratio of the between-groups to within-groups sum of squares for any discriminant function is its eigenvalue. It is also referred to as the 'discriminant criterion' of the discriminant function.

Pooled within-group correlation matrix The pooled within-group correlation matrix is obtained by averaging the covariance matrices of all the groups.

Structured correlations Also known as 'discriminant loadings', they are the measures of correlation between the original predictor variables and the discriminant function.

Wilk's lambda This is the ratio of the within-group sum of squares to the total sum of squares for each predictor variable. Large values of λ suggest small difference between group means.

Discriminant analysis assumes that the data is drawn from a multivariate normal population and the sample for each group is drawn from a population with the same covariance matrix.

Two-group Discriminant Analysis

Let us consider the case of a group of participants in a training programme for women on New Venture Creation. It was found that at the end of the four-month long training programme, on the average 40% of the participants started their own venture; the remaining 60% did not. The organizers of the programme were interested in determining what characteristics distinguished those who started a business from those who did not. They also wanted to acquire a decision rule using this information that would help them predict which of the future applicants would be likely to start their own business.

Two-group discriminant analysis was used for this purpose. The two-group analysis is quite similar to multiple regression analysis, with the dependent variable, defined as D (Training Outcome) coded as a dummy variable with only two values—0 (not starting the venture) and 1 (starting the venture). The independent variables considered in this case were as follows:

$$X_1 = \text{Age of the participant}$$
$$X_2 = \text{Monthly family income}$$
$$X_3 = \text{Presence of children below school-going age in the family}$$
$$X_4 = \text{Presence of elderly dependents in the family}$$
$$X_5 = \text{Previous work experience}$$

The discriminant analysis model involves linear combinations of the following form:

$$D = a_0 + a_1X_1 + a_2X_2 + a_3X_3 + a_4X_4 + a_5X_5$$

where

D = discriminant score

X_i = the ith independent variable

a_i = the unstandardized discriminant coefficient related to the ith variable

The objective of the analysis, as in the case of multiple regression, is to estimate coefficient a_i so that the difference (or distance, shown geometrically in Fig. 14.1) between the two groups A and B is maximized, while the intra-group distance between points included in each of the two groups is minimized. For this purpose the ratio of between-groups sum of square to the within-groups sum of square for the discriminant scores D_0 and D_1 is maximized. However, it must always be remembered that the objective of multiple regression is to define relationships between the dependent and the independent variables for the purpose of prediction, while the objective of discriminant analysis is to determine similar relationships for the sake of classification.

Figure 14.1 plots the two groups in only two of the five dimensions denoted by the predictor variables X_i. The discriminant function is denoted by D. Annexure 14.1 provides another example of discriminant analysis, using the Statistical Package for Social Sciences (SPSS).

The stages in conducting two-group discriminant analysis are as follows:

1. formulating the problem
2. estimating the discriminant coefficients

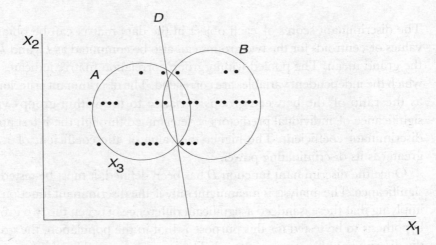

Fig. 14.1 Graphical Illustration of Two-group Discriminant Analysis

3. determining the significance of the discriminant function
4. interpreting the results
5. determining the validity of the analysis

In the example in Annexure 14.1, the problem has been formulated as described. The key problem in discriminant analysis is to find a new axis, so that the projections of the points on that axis maximize the separation between group means relative to the linear combination *D*. In general, as mentioned earlier, the dependent variable is a category variable. If it is interval-scaled or ratio-scaled, it must be converted into a category variable, as described earlier.

The next step is to estimate the discriminant coefficients. For this purpose, the data may be divided into two parts: (a) the estimation sample, used for estimating the discriminant function and (b) the validation sample, reserved for validating this function. Two methods are available for this purpose: the direct method and the stepwise method, as in multiple regression analysis. The process of estimating the weights is quite similar to the least square method adopted for multiple regression analysis. However, in addition we need to find a set of sums of squares and cross-products that relate to within-group variation. The data is first divided into the two groups being studied (in the example above, the two groups are *A*, i.e., those starting their ventures, and *B*, i.e., those not starting their ventures). The groups may be of equal or unequal sizes. The data is standardized for estimating the discriminant coefficients and the coefficients are then obtained using a method analogous to the least square method. Once the standardized discriminant weights a_i' are obtained, we may define the discriminant function as

$$D = a_1'X_1 + a_2'X_2 + a_3'X_3 + a_4'X_4 + a_5'X_5$$

The discriminant scores of each object in the data matrix can be obtained, and the values of centroids for the two groups can also be computed as $\bar{D}_0$ and $\bar{D}_1$, where $\bar{D}$ is the grand mean. The pooled within-group correlation matrix indicates the extent to which the independent variables are correlated. The discriminant criterion is calculated as the ratio of the between-groups variance to the within-groups variance. The significance of individual predictors is determined through the F-test applied to each discriminant coefficient. The higher the value of the coefficient of a variable, the greater is its discriminating power.

Once the discriminant function *D* has been defined, it must be tested for statistical significance. The analysis is meaningful only if the discriminant function is significant, implying that there is indeed a significant difference between the two groups. The null hypothesis to be tested for this purpose is that in the population, the group means of the discriminant functions are equal. The test statistic used for this purpose is Wilk's λ, the ratio of the within-group sum of squares to the total sum of squares, and the corresponding F-values. The significance level is estimated on the basis of a chi-square transformation of Wilk's λ. Larger values of λ, ranging between 0 and 1, indicate that group means are not significantly different.

After the discriminant scores D_0 and D_1 have been obtained, and their distance from the discriminant function D has been estimated, it is then possible to interpret the data. Some of this interpretation may take place on an intuitive basis by examining the distance between group means and their distance from D.

The value of the coefficient of an independent variable is dependent on the values of the other variables. Since the independent variables often tend to be correlated, it is not always possible to clearly identify which variable has the maximum importance in discriminating between the two groups. However, the *discriminant loadings*, i.e., the correlations between the individual predictors and the discriminant function, provide a measure of the importance of the predictor variable: the greater the discriminant loading, the greater the importance of the predictor. Even so, like the standardized coefficients, these correlations must be viewed with caution, keeping in mind that unless the sample size is large relative to the number of predictor variables, the standardized coefficients as well as their loadings tend to be unstable. A good thumb rule for this purpose is to work with a ratio of at least 20:1 between cases (objects) and independent variables.

Classification and validation

One of the objectives of discriminant analysis is to develop a rule for classifying a new entrant in the data matrix to the correct category. The discriminant equation provides this rule: once the values of the predictor variables X_i for the new entrant have been fitted into the equation, its value may be compared with $\bar{D}$ the grand mean. Values less than $\bar{D}$ may be assigned to one group, and greater values may be assigned to the other group. However, in order to do that, we need to first assess the ability of the discriminant equation to correctly classify a new unit. For this purpose, we construct a *classification matrix* (or confusion matrix, as it is sometimes called) using the validation sample (see Fig. 14.2). Discriminant scores are calculated for all objects in the validation sample, and the matrix compares the actual grouping of each object with the grouping predicted by the discriminant score. The numbers n_1 and n_4 on the diagonal of the

		Predicted Groups		
		D_0	D_1	
Actual	D_0	n_1	n_2	$n_1 + N_2$
Groups	D_1	n_3	n_4	$n_3 + n_4$
		$n_1 + n_3$	$r_2 + n_4$	$N(=n_1 + N_2 + n_3 - n_4)$

Fig. 14.2 Classification Matrix

matrix represent the number of correct classifications, while the off-diagonal figures n_2 and n_3 indicate the number of incorrect classifications:

The ratio $(n_1 + n_4/n)$, i.e., the percentage of correct classifications is a measure of the reliability of the decision rule. In general, when the two groups are of the same size, classification accuracy should be at least 75% for discriminant analysis to be considered reliable.

Application of the classification rule may be stated in these terms:

- Substitute the centroid of each group in the discriminant function and obtain the respective groups scores.
- For any new object compute the discriminant score and assign the object to the group whose group score is closer to it.

This rule assumes that the *prior* probabilities of a new case being part of any one group are equal for all groups, and the same assumption applies to the cost of misclassification of the object. It is, however, not essential for the probabilities to be equal. They could, for example, be weighted by the size of the group.

Finally, we need to test whether the group centroids differ significantly. This is similar to testing the correlation ratio R^2 for significance in multiple regression analysis. This test is conducted using the *Mahalanobis Squared Distance*, a measure based on the F-statistic.

Multiple Discriminant Analysis

When the dependent variable can be classified into more than two categories, we are dealing with the case of multiple discriminant analysis. For example, we may be interested in classifying users of a product category into users of one of the six major brands. The preceding discussion about two-group discriminant analysis may be directly extended to multiple discriminant analysis. The major difference is that in the latter case we compute more than one discriminant function, the number of such discriminant functions being Min $(N - 1, p)$, where N is the number of categories and p is the number of predictor variables. All these functions may not be statistically significant. The first function usually accounts for the highest proportion of between-groups to within-groups variability, the next function, for the next highest, and so on. It may, therefore, often be enough to compute only the first few functions.

The SPSS commands for conducting discriminant analysis are as follows.

1. Open the data editor screen in 'SPSS 13.0 for Windows' and enter data.
2. Click on **Analyse** in the menu bar; click on **Classify** in the drop-down window, and click on **Discriminant**.
3. The list of variables will appear in the window to the left (Fig. 14.3).
4. Select the dependent variable and click on the top arrow on the right to transfer it to the window titled **Grouping Variable**.

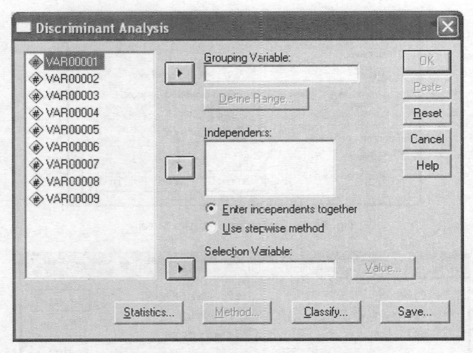

Fig. 14.3 Window Displaying Variables

5. Click on the **Define Range** bar and enter in the appropriate windows the maximum and minimum values that your dependent variable will take.

6. Select all relevant independent variables from the left window and click on the second arrow on the right to transfer them to the window on the right under **Independents**.

7. Click on **Statistics** at the bottom of the screen and open the **Statistics** screen (see Fig. 14.4).

8. Click on **Means** under **Descriptives**, **Understandardized** under **Function Coefficients** and **Within-groups correlation** and **Separate-groups covariance** under **Matrices**. Click **Continue** to revert to the main screen.

9. Click on **Classify** to open the classification screen (see Fig. 14.5).

10. Click on **All groups equal** under **Prior Probabilities**, **Case-wise results** and **Summary table** under **Display**, **Within-groups** under **Use covariance matrix** and **Combined-groups** under **Plots**. If needed, click on **Replace missing values with mean**. Click **Continue** to revert to the main screen.

11. Click on **Save** to open the relevant screen (Fig. 14.6). Click on **Predicted group-membership** and **Discriminant scores** and then click on **Continue** to revert to the main screen.

12. Click on **OK** on the main screen. The analysis will appear on the screen.

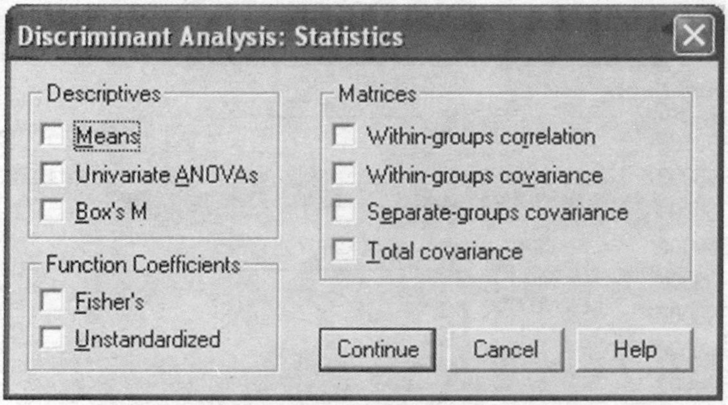

Fig. 14.4 Window on Statistics Screen

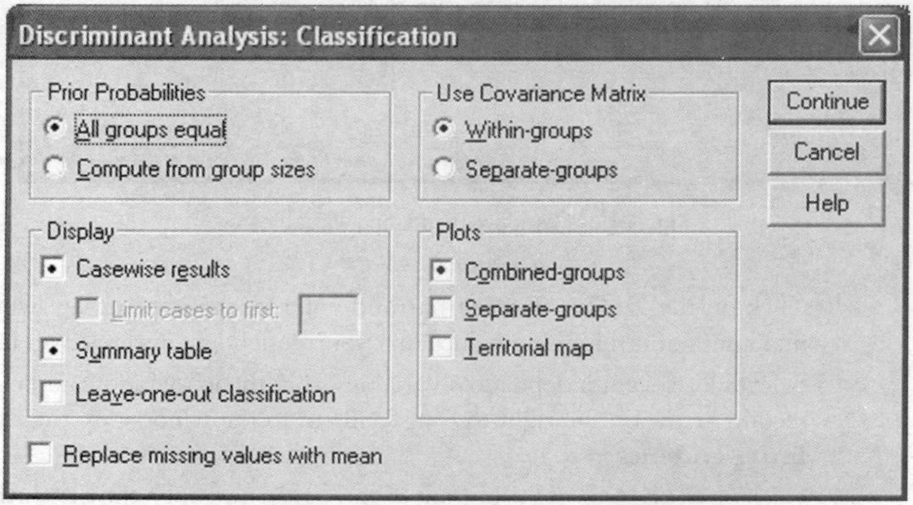

Fig. 14.5 Classification Options shown on Screen

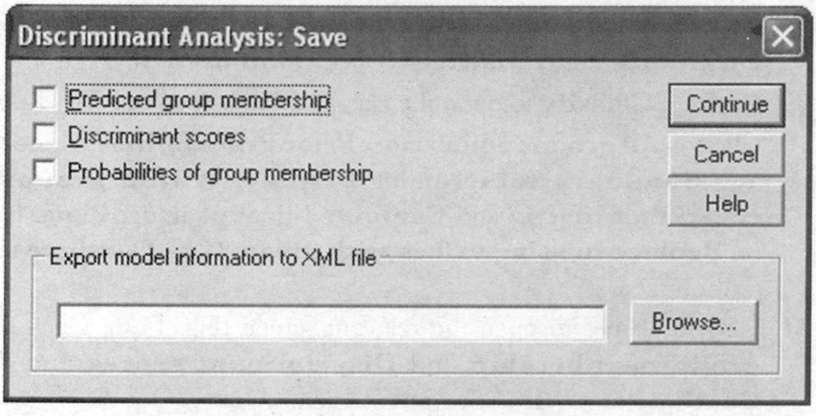

Fig. 14.6 Save Function

FACTOR ANALYSIS

Factor analysis is a popular technique used for the purpose of grouping together correlated variables. In Chapter 12, we had discussed the division of multivariate techniques into *dependence* and *interdependence* methods. As depicted in Fig. 12.3, factor analysis is an *interdependence* technique, i.e., it determines the relationship between variables without dividing the data matrix into 'dependent' and 'independent' variables. It, therefore, does not attempt identification of causal relationships. In research, it is instead used mainly for two purposes.

1. Reduction of data to manageable levels without loss of information, by combining into one factor the variables that are highly correlated with one another. The final data set then gets reduced to factors, smaller in number than the original variables, that are totally or largely uncorrelated with each other.
2. Determination of the underlying dimensions surrounding the variables that constitute a factor.
    A *factor* is, thus, a linear combination of the variables that are correlated with one another, with a_{ij} as the weights or factor score coefficients.

$$F_i = a_{i1}X_1 + a_{i2}X_2 + a_{i3}X_3 + \ldots + a_{in}X_n \tag{14.1}$$

Every variable X_i that is correlated with other variables to form factor F_1 shares some of the variance with these other variables, called communality. Communality is, thus, the percentage of variable X_i's variance that is common to other variables it is correlated with. In addition, it has a small unique element not shared with the others.

Again, the variable X_i may also be correlated with another group of variables, which are not very significantly correlated with the first group of variables, to form another factor F_2. This concept may be expressed diagrammatically as Fig. 14.7. As this figure shows, the variable X_1 is highly correlated with variables X_3, X_4, and X_5 and forms factor F_1 with them. It is also correlated with variables X_2 and X_6, with which it forms factor F_2. Variables X_2 and X_6, however, are not correlated with X_3, X_4 and X_5. Any such variable X_i can, therefore, be expressed as

$$X_i = A_{i1}F_1 + A_{i2}F_2 + A_{i2}F_3 + \ldots + A_{im}F_m + V_iU_i \tag{14.2}$$

where X_i is the ith standardized variable, $F_1, F_2, F_3, \ldots, F_m$ are the factors that X_i forms part of, A_{ij} is the standardized multiple regression coefficient of variable X_i on factor j, U_i is the unique element in X_i, and V_i is the regression coefficient of X_i on U_i.

The Process of Factor Analysis

The objective of factor analysis is to group the original variables into factors in such a way that all factors are ultimately uncorrelated with each other. For this purpose, it

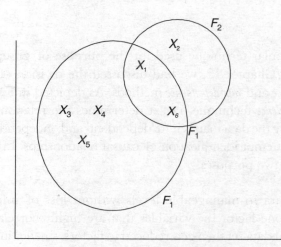

Fig. 14.7 Factors and Factorization

identifies variables that exhibit high intraset correlations and low interset correlations, determines how many such sets might exist, and explores whether the sets are uncorrelated themselves. Keep in mind the fact that factors must be inferred; unlike variables, they are not observed. The two techniques that are used most often for the purpose of extracting factors are (a) principal components analysis, used most frequently when the purpose is to summarize the information available, and (b) common factor analysis, used most often for uncovering dimensions underlying the original variables.

Factor analysis is usually applied only to interval- or ratio-scaled data, though there have been examples of its application to dichotomous or a mixed set of variables, as in Malhotra's (2004) book *Marketing Research: An Applied Orientation*. It is important to use an appropriate sample size: the ratio of variables to sampling units (cases) should be at least 1:5. In order to understand the technique, we will first discuss the definitions of some of the major statistics associated with it:

- *Correlation matrix* The matrix that displays the correlation of each variable with every other variable.
- *Factor* A group of variables that form a highly intercorrelated set, expressing a common dimension.
- *Factor loading* The correlation of a variable with a factor. These loadings are used to interpret factors. In the unrotated form, a variable usually loads on more than one factor, so that it is not possible to define independent factors that are uncorrelated with each other.
- *Factor matrix* The matrix that exhibits the factor loadings of all the standardized variables on all the factors extracted.
- *Residuals* The difference between the original correlations exhibited in the correlation matrix and the factor loadings as depicted by the factor matrix.

- *Communality* The percentage of variance explained by all the factors extracted, i.e., the percentage of variance of a variable that is shared with all other variables.
- *Eigenvalue* The amount of variance explained by an extracted factor.
- *Factor scores* Values for each respondent on each extracted factor.
- *Bartlett's test of sphericity* The statistic that tests the hypothesis that the variables are uncorrelated in the population. This is an important starting point for factor analysis, since the technique is useful only if the variables are correlated.
- *Kaiser–Meyer–Olkin measure of sampling adequacy* A measure of the appropriateness of factor analysis. Values above 0.5 indicate that factor analysis is appropriate.
- *Scree plot* A graph of the eigenvalues plotted against the number of factors in order of extraction.

The principal components method operates by arranging the factors in order of decreasing variance: the first factor extracted accounts for the maximum amount of explained variance, the next factor explains the maximum amount of variance left unexplained after the first factor has been extracted, and so on. It operates with standardized variables, with zero mean and unit variance. This is a two-stage process.

Stage 1 This is concerned with deciding how many factors will be extracted. Since each successive factor explains progressively lesser amount of variance, we can expect to ultimately reach a point where the last factor extracted explains just about the same amount of variance as the correlation matrix, so that the factoring process does not provide any additional information. Factor extraction beyond this point is not meaningful. Factors so extracted are called *principal components*.

At stage 1 we are therefore concerned with deciding how many factors to extract. Theoretically speaking, we can keep extracting factors till there are as many factors as there are original variables. This is obviously a self-defeating exercise. We, therefore, have to find other rules of thumb.

The drop in variance One such rule of thumb is to examine the 'drop in variance', i.e., to look for the point at which there is a sudden and substantial drop in the variance explained between two points. If the first factor explains, say 35 per cent of the variance, the second explains another 30 per cent, and the third explains another 3 per cent, then the third factor is not contributing much to the unravelling of the variance. It may, therefore, be adequate to extract only two factors.

Eigenvalue criterion The eigenvalue is the total variance explained by a factor. In the principal components method, each successive factor explains relatively lower amounts of variance; we have seen that below a certain level we do not get any incremental information from an additional factor. Since we are dealing with standardized variables with unit variance, this is the least amount of variance value which can provide useful information through factorization. Using the eigenvalue criterion, therefore, we extract factors up to the point where the eigenvalue of a factor becomes one. Factors with eigenvalue below one are not retained.

Percentage variance criterion This method takes into account the cumulative variance explained by the factors at various levels. Once enough factors have been extracted, the cumulative variance reaches a satisfactory level and no further factors need be extracted. The definition of a 'satisfactory' level is, however, subjective, and varies from case to case.

Significance test criterion It is possible to test the statistical significance of each eigenvalue, and retain only those factors with a significant eigenvalue.

Scree plot criterion We have seen that a scree plot is the graph of eigenvalues against the number of factors extracted. The point at which there is a steep drop in the graph is indicative of the number of factors that should be extracted. Figure 14.8 depicts this pattern. Six factors have been extracted, but after the first three, the slope curves steeply downwards, followed by a gradual tailing off later. We should, therefore, stop factoring after three factors.

Stage 2 This stage is concerned with rotating the factors so that each factor is totally uncorrelated with the other factor. This requires each original variable to load almost exclusively on only one factor, or at the most on a few factors. In geometric terms, this would imply that each factor in the reduced *m*-dimensional space is orthogonal, or perpendicular to every other factor. Rotation does not influence the communalities of the variables; nor does it affect the percentage of total variance explained. It is merely a way of expressing the factors in a way that is easier to interpret.

The most commonly used method of rotating factors is 'varimax rotation'. This method results in orthogonal factors that make the factors easy to interpret. Another method of rotation is 'oblique rotation', which does not result in factors orthogonal or at right angles to each other. Once factors have been extracted through either of the rotation methods, the next task is to interpret and label them.

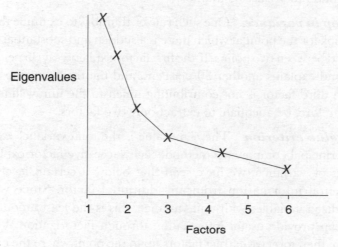

Fig. 14.8 Scree Plot

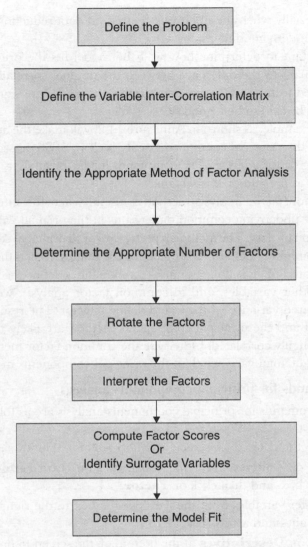

Fig. 14.9 Process of Factor Analysis
Source: Adapted from Malhotra (2004)

The interpretation and labelling of factors is facilitated by determining the variables that have large loadings on a factor, and determining the common dimensions of all such variables. The factor is then labelled in terms of this common dimension.

The process of factor analysis is described in Fig. 14.9. Once the factor has been interpreted, it is useful to determine factor scores for all the respondents. This may be done by applying the values of X_i for each respondent to Eqn (14.1), where the coefficients a_{ij} have been obtained from the factor matrix.

Sometimes it may be worthwhile to use surrogate variables instead of calculating factor scores. If any one variable loads significantly higher than the other variables on a factor, the researcher may decide to define the factor in terms of this variable as its surrogate, specially when the interest is centred on data reduction rather than interpretation of underlying dimensions.

It is important to determine how well the model fits the original data. We had defined 'residuals' as the difference between the original correlations and the factor scores obtained from the factor matrix. If these residuals are significantly large, the model cannot be said to be a good fit.

A worked example, as shown in Annexure 14.2, will make the application of factor analysis using the principal components analysis clear. SPSS provides the programme for conducting factor analysis. The commands for factor analysis used in SPSS have been outlined at the end of this section.

The common factor analysis method is useful when the interest is centred on identifying the underlying common dimensions in the original variables, rather than on the reduction of data. The method is pretty similar to principal components analysis, except that communalities are substituted for the unities ('1's) in the original variables correlation matrix. This is done because communalities define the variance a variable shares with other variables, and in common factor analysis, we are interested in identifying shared variance which would define a factor. The results of the common factor method and the principal components method are likely to be similar if the variables are highly correlated. Otherwise the common factor method may explain a lower amount of total variance than the principal components method.

SPSS Commands for principal components analysis

The SPSS commands for principal components analysis are as follows:

1. Open the data editor screen in 'SPSS 13.0 for Windows', and enter data.
2. Click on **Analyse** in the menu bar, click on **Data reduction** in the drop-down box, and then click on **Factor**.
3. Transfer variables from the left dialogue box to the right by clicking on the top right hand arrow (Fig. 14.10).
4. Click on **Descriptives** at the bottom of the screen to open the descriptives screen (Fig. 14.11).
5. Click on **Initial solution** under **Statistics**, and on **Coefficients**, **Significance levels**, **Determinant** and **KMO and Bartlett's Test of Sphericity** under **Correlation Matrix**. Click on **Continue** to revert to the main screen.
6. Click on the **Extraction** bar at the bottom of the main screen (Fig. 14.10) to open the 'extraction' screen (Fig. 14.12).
7. Click on **Principal components** under **Method**, and on **Correlation matrix** under **Analyse**.
8. Specify '1' in the dialogue box **Eigenvalue over** under **Extract**, and **Unrotated factor solution** and **Scree plot** under **Display**. Click on **Continue** to revert to the main screen.

9. Click on the **Rotation** bar at the bottom of the main screen to open the 'rotation' screen (Fig. 14.13). Click on **Varimax** under **Method**. Click on **Continue** to revert to the main screen.

10. Click on the **Scores** bar on the main screen to open the screen factor scores (Fig. 14.14). Click on **Save as variables** and **Display factor score coefficient matrix**. Click on **Continue** to revert to the main screen.

11. Click on the **Options** bar on the main screen to open the 'options' screen (Fig. 14.15).

12. Click on **Exclude cases listwise** or **Replace with mean** under **Missing values**. Click on **Continue** to revert to the main screen.

13. Click on **OK** on the main screen. The analysis will appear on the screen.

CLUSTER ANALYSIS

Suppose we have to determine how children in the age group 8–12 yrs choose the television programmes they would like to watch. We could ask them in unstructured interviews, why they prefer one programme over the other or what they find similar about two programmes. The responses could be in terms of timings, the level of entertainment ('fun' or 'excitement'), the kind of entertainment (technology, stories, humour, etc.), the kind of rewards, the extent of competitiveness, etc. We will find that different segments of children vary in the importance they attach to the programmes they prefer and the reasons for their preference. A technique like cluster analysis is useful in grouping respondents into different segments on the basis of characteristics such as perceptions, beliefs, and orientations.

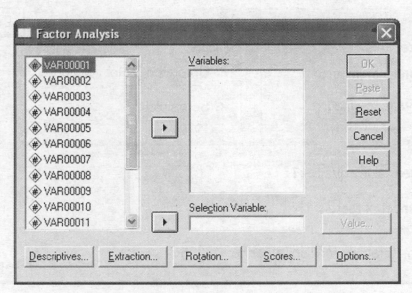

Fig. 14.10 Dialog Box with Factor Analysis Variables

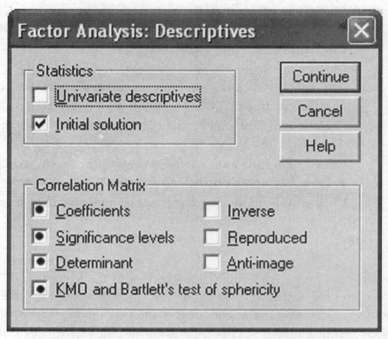

Fig. 14.11   Dialog Box with Descriptives Function

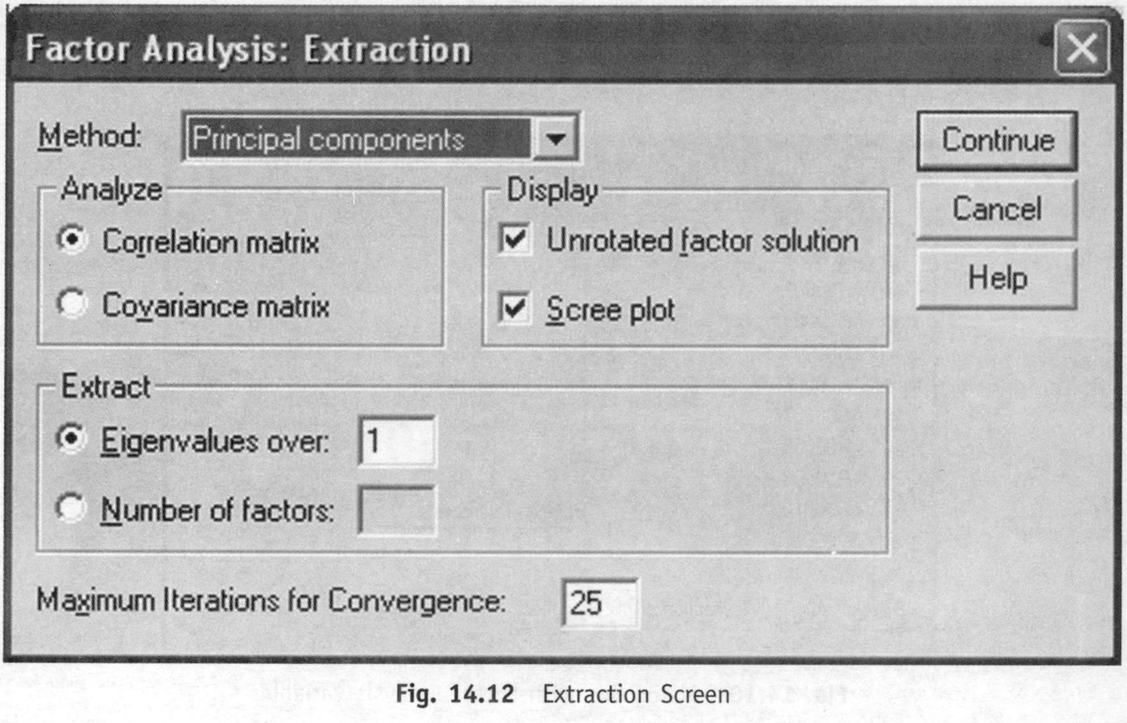

Fig. 14.12   Extraction Screen

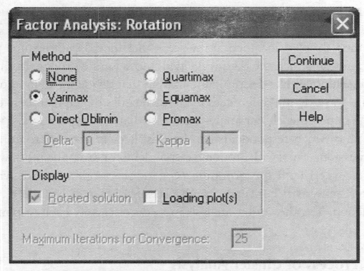

Fig. 14.13 Rotation Screen

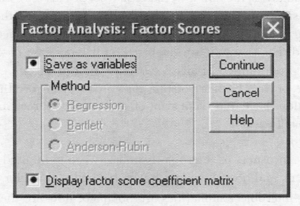

Fig. 14.14 Factor Scores

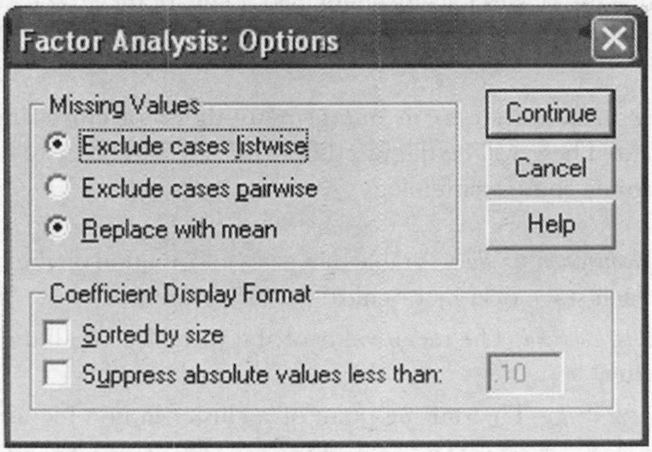

Fig. 14.15 Options

Cluster analysis, like factor analysis, is an *interdependence* technique used for grouping data, without dividing it into dependent and independent variables. Both the methods are, thus, pre-classificatory, in the sense that they do not assume prior knowledge of the bases on which the data is divided into separate groups. In this sense, they differ from techniques like discriminant analysis that divide the data into mutually exclusive groups to study the differences in characteristics of the members of different groups. At the same time, cluster analysis assumes that such separation is possible, i.e., clusters exist into which respondents can be classified. It also differs from factor analysis in that it is concerned with grouping respondents, or sampling units, while factor analysis is concerned with the grouping of variables. Again, unlike with factor analysis, cluster analysis is concerned with classification and grouping, and not with data reduction. Yet, the cluster analysis procedures classify each respondent into one, and only one, class.

The Process of Cluster Analysis

In cluster analysis, the aim is to establish a set of clusters so that cases within a cluster are more similar to each other than they are to cases in other clusters. This method finds numerous applications in marketing, and may be applied wherever segmentation is required. For example, we discussed earlier the case of children's preference for television programmes. Similarly, we may want to classify customers by their brand preference, or cities by their potential for a product category. In the process of clustering, four questions have to be kept sight of, according to Green and Tull (1978) in *Research for Marketing Decisions*:

- What measures of interobject similarity are to be used for developing exclusive clusters, and how should each variable be weighted for this purpose?
- After interobject similarities are obtained, how are the classes of objects to be formed?
- Once the classes have been formed, how are they to be defined?
- What inferences may be drawn about the statistical reliability of clusters?

Keeping these questions in mind, many different clustering methods have been developed. These will be discussed in detail later. In order to understand them, let us first examine some terminology:

- *Agglomeration schedule* A table that gives information on the objects being combined at each stage of a hierarchical clustering process.
- *Cluster centroid* The mean value of the variables for all the objects in a particular cluster.
- *Cluster centre* The starting point of a cluster in non-hierarchical methods.
- *Cluster membership* Defines the cluster to which an object belongs.

- *Dendogram* A graph displaying the clustering pattern. Vertical lines in a dendogram represent the clusters that are linked. The position of the line on the scale indicates the stage at which clusters were joined. It is read from left to right.
- *Inter-centre distances* The distances between clusters indicate how distinct they are. The further apart they are, the better the clustering.
- *Icicle diagram* This diagram, resembling a row of icicles, depicts the result of a clustering process. The columns correspond to the objects being clustered and the rows correspond to the number of clusters.
- *Similarity/Distance coefficient matrix* This matrix describes the pair-wise distance between objects.

Measures of interobject similarity

This is the first question that needs to be answered in conducting cluster analysis. The objective is to find a measure that will assess the proximity of any two points (objects) in the n-dimensional space on which they are defined, each dimension representing one variable. There are two types of measures: (i) distance measures, which measure the distance between two objects using the Euclidean distance measure, and (ii) matching-type measures, which describe the variables with regard to which the two objects are similar. The Euclidean distance method is stronger and is used most often. This defines the distance measure d_{ij} as

$$d_{ij} = \sqrt{\sum_{k=1}^{n} (x_{ik} - x_{jk})^2}$$

where x_{ik} and x_{jk} are the values of points i and j on the kth dimension.

Matching measures are usually applied to ordinal data. If two objects i and j are measured on a number of attributes using a binary scale (0, 1), then the simplest matching measure would be defined as:

$S_{ij} =$ (number of attributes on which both i and j have the same measure 0 or 1)/
  (total number of attributes on which i or j are measured)

Green and Tull (1978) extend this to the case in which the variables consist of mixed scales—nominal, ordinal, and interval. According to them 'Interval-scaled variables may be handled in terms of similarity coefficients by the simple device of computing the range of the variable R_k and finding

$$S_{ijk}^* = 1 - \left(\left| x_{ik} - x_{jk} \right| \right) / R_k$$

The measure S_{ijk}^* will then appropriately vary between 0 and 1, just like a similarity measure. This measure has been suggested by Gower as a device to handle both nominal- and interval-scaled data in a single similarity coefficient.' Other popular distance measures are as follows.

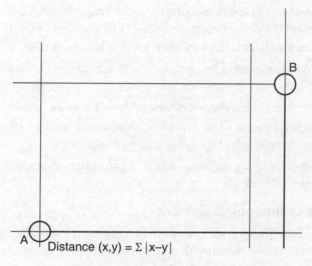

Fig. 14.16 City Block Distance

(i) Chebycheff measure: This measure is based on the absolute maximum difference between variable scores as: Distance $(x, y) = \text{Max} |x - y|$

(ii) City block or Manhattan distance: This measure follows the pattern of the route of the regular grid of roads in America, taking into account the fact that in most American cities, it is not possible to go directly between two points (see Fig. 14.16).

In cluster analysis, if the variables are measured in different units, it is usual to standardize them to zero mean and unit variance. This, however, may have the effect of reducing the distance between groups with regard to variables that best discriminate between clusters.

A non-Euclidean distance measure for interval data can also be defined as the cosine of the vectors of variables. This measures the similarity between two objects, and, as is always true of cosines, is equivalent to the correlation coefficient between two vectors:

$$\text{Similarity } (x, y) = \Sigma(xy)/\Sigma x^2 \Sigma y^2$$

There are other methods of measuring distances, especially measures of qualitative distance. For example, in terms of Euclidean distance, Bangalore is closer to Chennai than to Mumbai. However, if one were to measure the distance in terms of the city's characteristics, it is closer to Mumbai than to Chennai. The results of cluster analysis are sensitive to the kind of distance measure used. It, therefore, helps to use different distance measures and compare the results before finalizing the method of measuring distances.

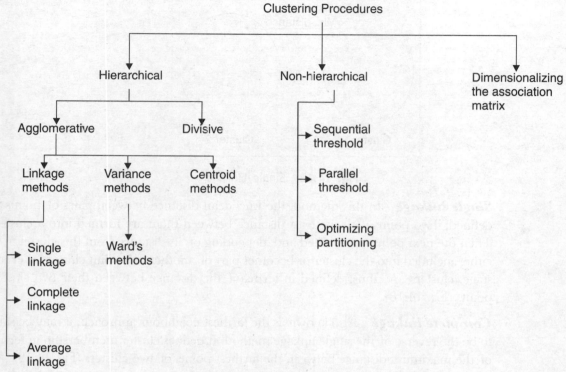

Fig. 14.17 Clustering Procedures

Selecting a clustering procedure

Once the appropriate measure of similarity/distance has been selected, the next step is to choose a procedure or algorithm for clustering, i.e., the rules which govern between which points distances are to be measured for determining cluster membership. We had discussed earlier that a variety of clustering procedures exists, broadly divided into hierarchical and non-hierarchical. Figure 14.17 lists the various methods of clustering. They may be broadly divided into three categories: (a) *hierarchical* or *linkage methods*, where the classification begins with a single-point cluster and has an increasing number of nested classes, forming a tree-like structure, (b) *non-hierarchical* or *nodal methods*, where a number of clusters may be formed in parallel, each around a 'node', such as in *k*-means clustering, and (c) methods based on *dimensionalizing the association matrix*, using techniques such as factor analysis.

Hierarchical methods Hierarchical methods may be *agglomerative*, or *divisive*. In agglomerative techniques, we usually begin with a single point cluster. These clusters are gradually merged together till one large cluster is formed. On the other hand, divisive techniques start with one large cluster of all points (objects), that are gradually broken down into smaller and smaller clusters.

Agglomerative techniques comprise three major methods of clustering: linkage methods, variance methods, and centroid methods.

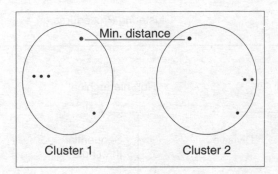

Fig. 14.18 Single Linkage

Single linkage In this method, the Euclidean distance between pairs of points is defined. Two points with the least distance between them are formed into a cluster. Then the next point is examined and, depending on its distance from this cluster, it is either included into the cluster or becomes part of another two-point cluster. At every stage, clusters are, thus, defined in terms of the distance between their two closest points (Fig. 14.18).

Complete linkage Also known as the farthest neighbour approach, it may be said to be the reverse of the single linkage method. It defines cluster membership in terms of the maximum distance between the farthest points of two clusters (Fig. 14.19).

Average linkage This method defines cluster membership in terms of the average of the distances between all pairs of points from two clusters. This method has the advantage of being based on the distance between all points, not only those minimally or maximally distant from each other.

Variance methods These methods aim at forming clusters that attempt to minimize within-cluster variance. The most popular of these is Ward's method. In this method, the cluster's membership is assessed by measuring the total sum of squared deviations from the mean of a cluster. As more clusters are formed, the total sum of squared deviations, i.e., the error sum of squares, increases. The rule for fusion is that the inclusion of the new member should cause the smallest possible increase in the error sum of squares.

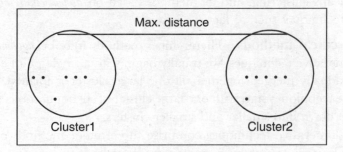

Fig. 14.19 Complete Linkage

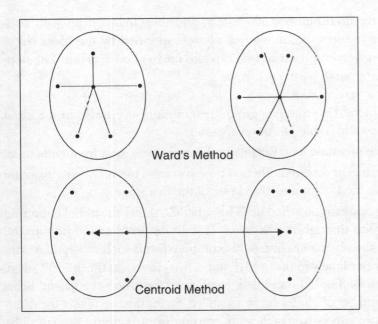

Fig. 14.20 Ward's Method and Centroid Method

Centroid method A 'centroid' in a cluster is the point whose coordinates are the means of all points in the cluster. In the centroid method (Fig. 14.20), the cluster membership is based on the distance between the centroids of clusters. Clusters are combined according to the distance between their centroids (the centroid of a single point cluster is the point itself); the clusters with the least distance between them are combined first.

Non-hierarchical methods Also known as *k*-means clustering these include three approaches.

Sequential threshold In this method, a cluster centre is chosen, and all the points within a prespecified threshold of that cluster centre are grouped together. Then a new cluster centre is chosen and the process is repeated. Once a point is included in a cluster, it is no longer included in any other cluster.

Parallel threshold In this method, as in the sequential threshold method, points are included in a cluster depending on their distance from the cluster centre. However, here a few cluster centres are selected simultaneously, and points are grouped into the cluster from which they are at the least distance.

Optimizing partitioning method In this method, points once assigned to a cluster may at times be reassigned to another cluster in order to optimize some overall criterion such as the average within-cluster distance.

Non-hierarchical methods require pre-specification of the desired number of clusters. The selection of cluster centres is also arbitrary. At the same time, non-hierarchical methods are quicker and of special utility when the number of objects to be clustered is large. The usual approach to good clustering is to first use a hierarchical approach to get the required number of clusters, and then follow it up with non-hierarchical clustering to form the number of clusters specified by the hierarchical method. The example given in Annexure 14.3 explains the method in detail. The steps involved in such a cluster analysis are as follows.

1. Define the problem. For example, group the customers as shown in the input data matrix shown in Table D, Annexure 14.3.

2. Select a distance measure. The Euclidean distance is the most frequently used.

3. Select a clustering procedure. The average distance hierarchical clustering procedure is the most commonly used one in the first stage.

4. Develop the agglomeration schedule. This schedule shows the initial clustering of pairs of objects through $(n-1)$ stages. It indicates from top to bottom the order in which the objects or clusters get combined with each other, till we are left with one cluster finally in the $(n-1)^{th}$ stage, two clusters in the $(n-2)^{th}$ stage, and so on upwards. The column titled 'coefficient' (or fusion coefficient) helps determine the number of clusters to be identified. So for this, we obtain the difference between two successive coefficients, starting from bottom upwards. The objective is to zero in on the smallest number of clearly segregated clusters. For this purpose, we do not stop at the difference between the $(n-1)^{th}$ and the $(n-2)^{th}$ stage, since that will return us to the stage of all points combined into one cluster.

5. Beyond that, we examine the stage at which the first significant difference between coefficients is compared with the difference between coefficients at the next stage. The first large difference in coefficient values between two successive stages determines the number of clusters to be extracted. If the same difference is obtained between coefficients at two different stages, it is left to the judgement of the researcher to decide whether to settle for the smaller or the larger group of clusters. The same information may also be obtained from the 'dendogram' or the 'icicle plot'. The next two columns in the agglomeration schedule indicate the first stage at which the two clusters being examined appear. The last column determines the stage at which these combined clusters get examined again for proximity to another cluster.

6. Select the appropriate clustering procedure for the next stage. Usually, at this stage the k-means non-hierarchical approach is used, based on the number of clusters ('k' means) determined in the hierarchical approach. It must be remembered that though the hierarchical approach used at the first stage does give clearly defined clusters and the second stage is not strictly essential, but the non-hierarchical approach usually gives more stable clusters and is therefore to be preferred. This method gives the initial cluster centres, the list of cases belonging to the various clusters, the final cluster centres giving the mean value of each variable for each of the clusters, and an analysis of variance table. The ANOVA table identifies the variables that contribute to significant inter-cluster difference.

Defining and interpreting the clusters

The clusters can then be defined in terms of values of these variables and the areas in which they differ from the other clusters. This profiling of clusters is the most crucial management decision in this analysis. We need to examine the cluster centroids for this purpose. The centroids, or mean value of the objects included in a cluster, provide information about each cluster by assigning it a name or a label. A comparison of the values of the variables in each cluster then helps us define the differences between the clusters. The clusters may then be profiled in terms of variables such as demographic or psychographic variables that may not have been used to derive the clusters, but may be treated as exogenous variables anchoring the clusters in measurable terms.

Assessing reliability and validity

As we may note, among all multivariate analysis procedures, cluster analysis procedures are among the most subjective and dependent on the researcher's judgement. It is, therefore, essential to get an estimate of the reliability and validity of the clustering solutions obtained. Malhotra (2004) suggests the following methods for assessing the quality of clustering solutions obtained:

- Cluster analysis may be performed on the data using different distance measures and the results may be compared across measures to determine the stability of the solutions.
- Different clustering methods may be used and the results compared.
- The split-half method: the data may be split randomly into two halves, cluster analysis performed separately on each half, and then the cluster centroids may be compared across the two halves or subsamples.
- Delete variables randomly, perform cluster analysis on the data with reduced set of variables, and then compare the results with the complete set of variables.
- In non-hierarchical clustering, make multiple runs, changing the order of objects in the data set till the solution stabilizes. This is done because in non-hierarchical clustering, the solution is sensitive to the order in which the objects appear.

Sometimes cluster analysis may be used to cluster variables rather than objects. The objective is to obtain homogeneous groups and to reduce the number of variables. Though this method does not usually explain as much variance as principal components analysis and is, therefore, not quite as reliable, such 'cluster components' are easier to interpret than principal components.

SPSS commands for cluster analysis

SPSS commands for cluster analysis is a two-stage process. The first stage helps define the number of clusters that should be formed, and the second stage defines the clusters.

Stage 1   The following steps are required in Stage 1.

1.   Open the data editor screen in 'SPSS 13.0 for Windows' and enter data.

2. Click on **Analyse** in the menu bar, click on **Classify** in the drop-down window, and click on **Hierarchical cluster** to go to the main screen displayed in Fig. 14.21.

3. Transfer variables from the left window to the right by clicking on the top right hand arrow.

4. Under **Cluster**, click on **Cases**; under **Display**, click on **Statistics** and **Plot**.

5. Click on **Continue** to revert to the main screen.

6. Click on **Statistics** in the menu bar; in the dialogue box that opens (Fig. 14.22), click on **Agglomeration schedule**; click on **None** under **Cluster Membership**.

7. Click on **Continue** to revert to the main screen.

8. Click on the **Plots** bar in the main screen to open the **plots** screen (Fig. 14.23). Click on **Dendogram**; under **Icicles**, click on **All clusters**; under **Orientation**, click on **Vertical** or **Horizontal** depending on the required orientation for the icicle plot.

9. Click on **Continue** to revert to the main screen.

10. Click on the **Method** bar in the main screen to open the relevant screen (Fig. 14.24). Under **Cluster Method**, click on **Between-group linkage**; under **Measure**, click on **Interval** and **Squared Euclidean distance**.

11. Click on **Continue** to revert to the main screen.

12. Click on **OK**. The analysis will appear on the screen.
    Note: On clicking on **Save** on the main screen, the dialog box in Fig. 14.25 appears.

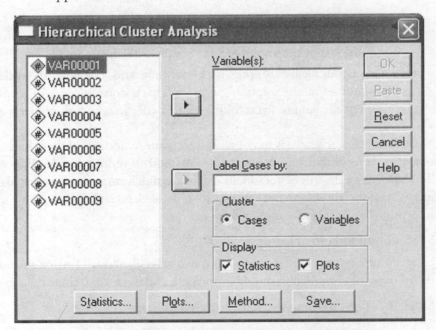

Fig. 14.21   Window for Hierarchical Cluster Analysis

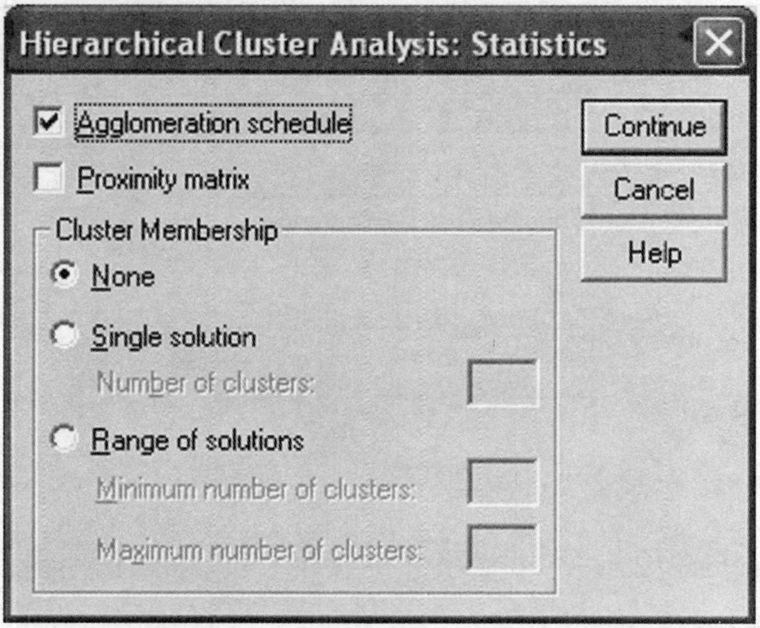

Fig. 14.22 Window for 'Statistics'

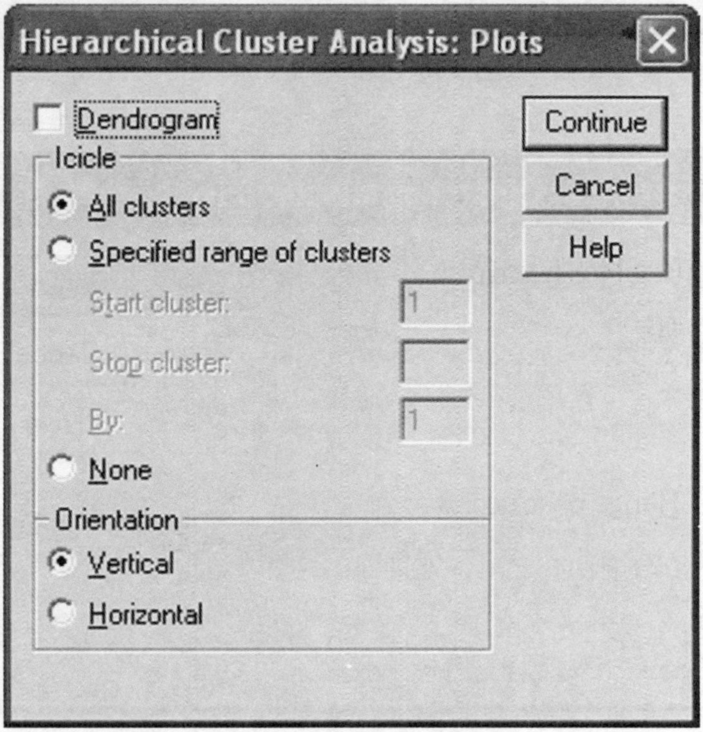

Fig. 14.23 'Plots' Window

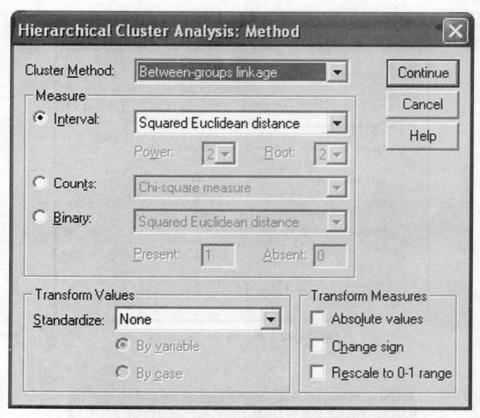

Fig. 14.24 Method Window

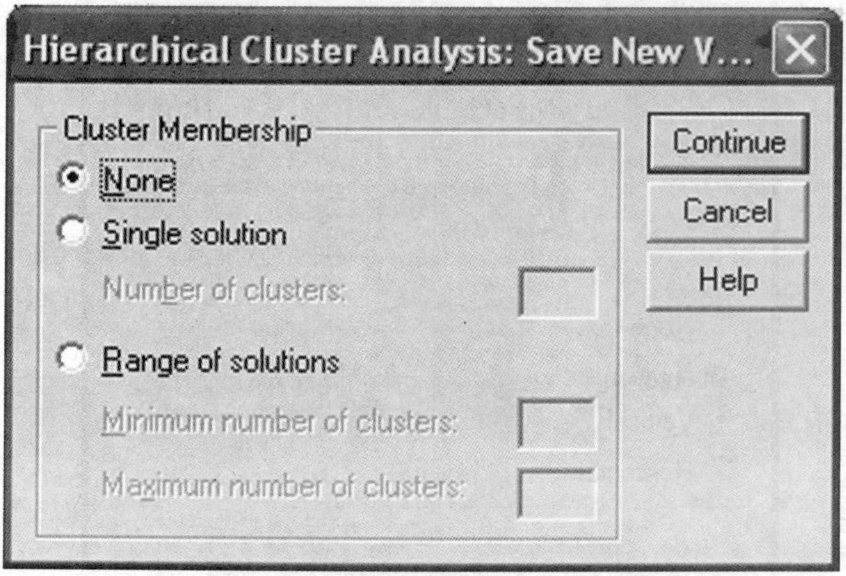

Fig. 14.25 'Save' Function

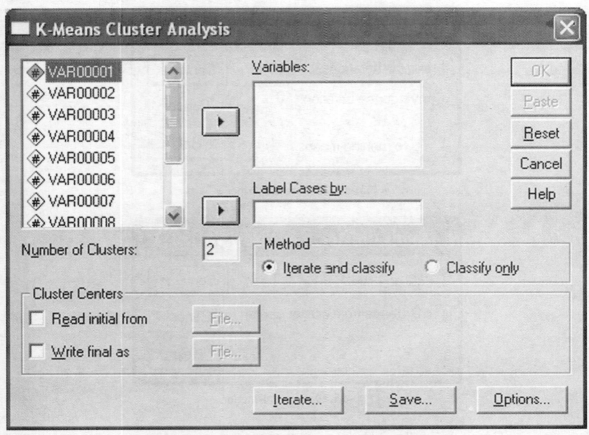

Fig. 14.26 'K-Means Cluster Analysis' Window

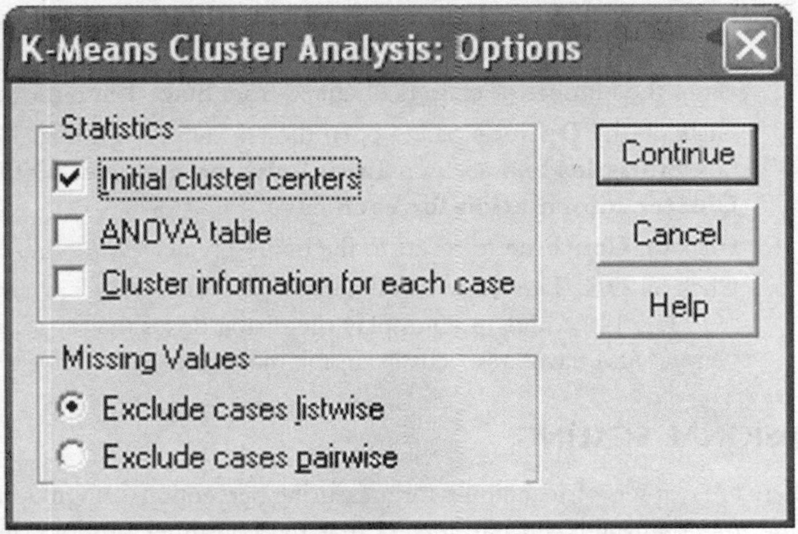

Fig. 14.27 Options Window

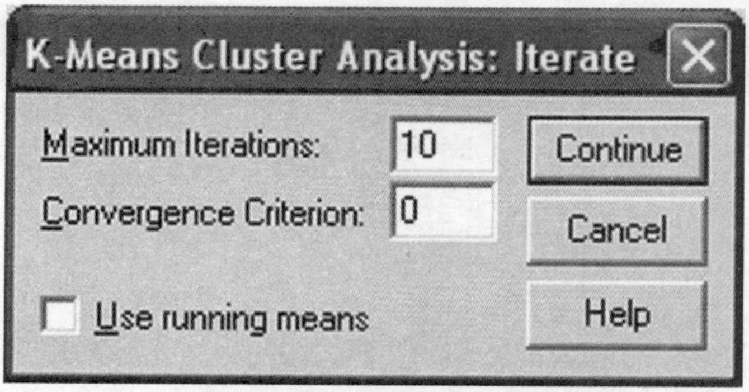

Fig. 14.28   'Iterate' Window

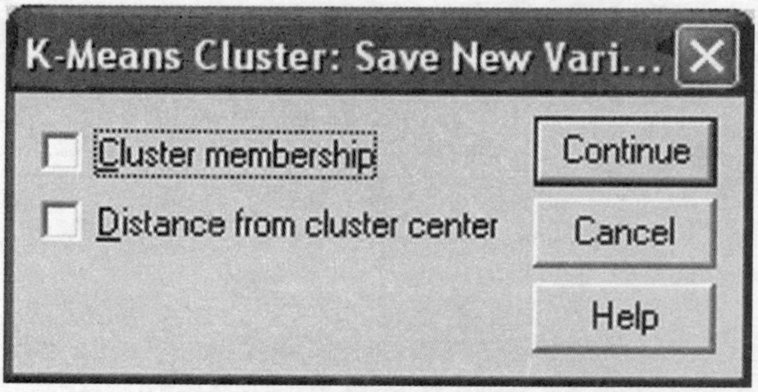

Fig. 14.29   'Save' Function

This analysis will provide the number of clusters required.

Stage 2   The following steps are involved in Stage 2:

1. Click on **Analyse** in the menu bar, click on **Classify** in the drop-down window, and click on **k-means clustering** (Fig. 14.26).
2. Enter the number of clusters obtained from Stage 1 into the appropriate box.
3. Click on the **Options** bar to open the relevant screen (Fig. 14.27). Open the box **Statistics** and click on **Initial cluster centres**, **ANOVA table**, and **Cluster information for each case**.
4. Click on **Continue** to revert to the main screen.
5. Click on **OK**. The analysis will appear on the screen.
   Note: Fig. 14.28 and 14.29 display the dialog boxes that appear on clicking on 'iterate' and 'save', respectively, in the main screen.

MULTIDIMENSIONAL SCALING

There are two sets of techniques for measuring perceptions and preferences, based on some underlying links in parameters that the consumer observes in objects under study—multidimensional scales and multi-attribute tradeoffs.

Let us consider the case of a group of students who are just graduating from a reputed MBA programme. A large number of them were interested in finding placement in the FMCG industry. In order to understand how they perceive and evaluate the companies they would like to work for, the placement coordinator of the business school asked them to indicate how similar they perceived the seven FMCG companies to be to each other. They did not have to specify the basis on which they judged them to be similar, but merely rank them on a 'similarity–dissimilarity scale' shown in Table 14.1, comparing each pair of companies for similarity. The pair of companies perceived by a student to be most similar was to be given the rank 1, the pair next most similar 2, and so on, till the least similar pair was ranked 21. The average rankings given by the students are depicted in Table 14.1.

It would be easier to understand the perceived similarities between the companies if these figures could be depicted pictorially. However, it is not easy to preserve the relationships between the pairs and depict them accurately if one tries to present them on a graph, as is apparent from Fig. 14.30.

Multidimensional scaling (MDS) refers to a set of techniques used for representing perceived similarities spatially through a visual display, called a *perceptual map*, where perceived links or relationships are represented geometrically as inter-point Euclidean distances in a multidimensional space. It is an extension of the procedure discussed earlier in scaling. The brands or objects that are perceived to be most similar will be represented by points that are closest together, and the ones which are most dissimilar or least similar will be farthest apart. This geometric configuration of points reflects the 'hidden structure' in the data and makes the relationships between objects much easier to understand. According to S.P. Borgatti (1997), 'in order to discover rather than impose the dimensions, the attributes on which the stimuli are to be judged are usually not specified'. If interval data is used instead of ordinal data for comparing objects, the similarities (dissimilarities) may be measured using Euclidean distances d_{ij}, where

$$d_{ij} = \sqrt{\sum (X_{ia} - X_{ja})^2}$$

Table 14.1 Perceived Similarities Between Companies

Co.	Company						
	A	**B**	**C**	**D**	**E**	**F**	**G**
A	–	1	8	10	14	18	2
B		–	19	3	17	20	21
C			–	9	13	5	15
D				–	4	16	6
E					–	11	12
F						–	7
G							–

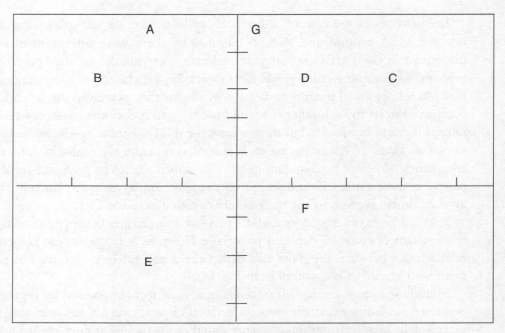

Fig. 14.30 MDS Solution Based on Data of Table 14.1

and X_i and X_j are the coordinates of points i and j on dimension a.

MDS has its origins in psychometrics, but the method has been used extensively in marketing to answer questions like:

- With whom do we compete?
- How are we perceived in relation to our competitors?
- On what dimensions does the consumer evaluate the brands in the product category we participate in? How is the consumer's ideal brand positioned on these dimensions?
- On what dimensions are we compared to our major competitors?
- What positioning strategy should be followed?
- Where are the gaps in this product category where a new entrant may profitably position itself?

There are several approaches to MDS. They vary in terms of the assumptions they are based on, the perspectives they take and the input data they use. Aaker et al. (1999) have described these various approaches as shown in Fig. 14.31.

The Process of Multidimensional Scaling

Factor analysis and discriminant analysis are two attribute-based methods of determining intra-group homogeneity of objects that have been discussed in earlier chapters. In this section we will concentrate on MDS. The emphasis in MDS, both attribute-based as well as non-attribute based as we have discussed, is different from

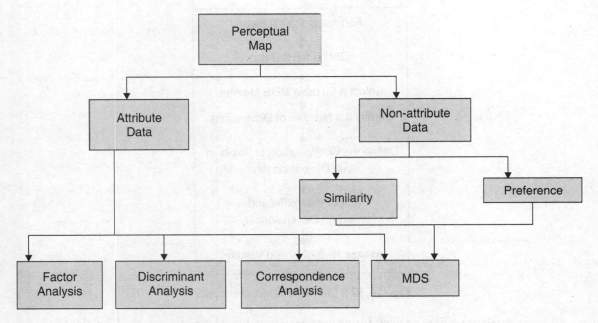

Fig. 14.31 Approaches to Perceptual Maps

these two techniques, in that it neither aims at reduction of data nor at classification, but rather at describing inter-object relationships.

According to Young (1985), one of the early proponents of the technique, 'MDS pictures the structure of a set of objects from data that approximate the distances between pairs of objects. The data, which are called similarities, dissimilarities, distances, or proximities, must reflect the amount of dissimilarity between pairs of objects.' Because of the variety of approaches available for carrying out MDS, it is important to formulate the MDS problem carefully, specify the form in which the input data should be obtained and select the appropriate MDS procedure. The stages in conducting MDS have been described in Fig. 14.32.

Formulating the problem   Problem formulation in MDS is concerned with, first, specification of the objective of the exercise, i.e., the purpose for which the results are to be used. The next step in problem formulation is the specification of the number of objects to be used and which specific objects are to be used. MDS should normally not be attempted with less than eight or more than twenty-five objects.

Obtaining input data   The choice of objects will usually govern the dimension specifications and the configurations, the two key objectives of MDS. Though traditional methods of MDS do not ask respondents to define in advance the dimensions on which they perceive the objects as similar or dissimilar, it is desirable to select objects for MDS so that the total set of objects selected may contain variations (dissimilarities) along many possible parameters or dimensions.

Traditional MDS was originally applied only to cases where the similarities could be measured in quantitative terms (Metric MDS). It has since then been extended to

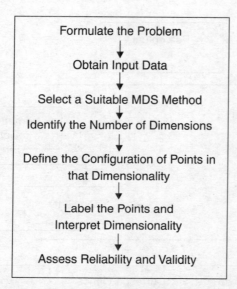

Fig. 14.32 Stages in Conducting MDS

qualitative data as well. Input data may now be obtained in the form of (a) derived or attribute-based approaches, where objects are compared through Likert-type scales in terms of attribute based perception of similarities, or (b) direct or non-attribute approaches, where the respondents are asked to compare pairs of objects in terms of overall similarities or preferences. Preference data orders the objects being compared in terms of the respondent's preference between pairs or groups of objects. Various methods for defining preferences may be used, such as rank-order scaling or paired comparison. The two methods, similarities and preferences, often yield significantly different results.

Direct approaches are easier for the respondents to handle and are more representative of actual behaviour. However, they are more difficult for the researcher to interpret, and the dimensions derived from the analysis may get influenced by the characteristics of the objects being compared. If, for example, only paracetamol based analgesic brands are being compared, then 'ingredients' may not emerge as a significant dimension for comparison, and the researcher may derive the erroneous conclusion that composition is not a significant basis for differentiation between analgesic brands.

On the other hand derived, or attribute-based, approaches are easier for the researcher to handle and easier to label in terms of differentiating dimensions. They, however, suffer from the disadvantage that comparisons are restricted to the dimensions or attributes specified, and objects that differ on some dimensions not taken into account may be wrongly labelled as similar. In order to minimize the chance of such errors, it is necessary to make comparisons on a large number of attributes.

Selecting the MDS method MDS techniques can be classified into different types, such as classical, replicated, and weighted. The *classical MDS* (CMDS) technique yields a single matrix with an unweighted model. *Replicated MDS* (RMDS) has several matrices with an unweighted model, whereas *weighted MDS* (WMDS) has several matrices using the weighted model. CMDS typically uses non-attribute based data.

According to Kruskal and Wish (1997), 'stimulus confusability is a measure of proximity arising in certain kinds of psychological experiments'. We usually begin the process of analysis by obtaining similarities or proximities between objects as shown in Table 14.1 earlier. The derived Euclidean distances are obtained so as to correspond to these proximities. If the derived distances are multiple or linear functions of the proximities, the method of analysis is referred to as *metric MDS*. It operates on the assumption that the input data is metric. This technique, the oldest of the CMDS set of techniques, was first proposed by Torgerson (1984), and requires the data to be dissimilar, complete (no missing values), and symmetric. The distance model is required to be Euclidean. The distances D are defined to be as akin to the similarities S as possible, and are defined using the least-square model as

$$L(S) = D + E$$

where $L(S)$ is a linear transformation of the similarities S; D is the distance matrix; and E is the error matrix. If ratio-scaled similarities data is used, the linear transformation has zero intercept. With interval data it can have non-zero intercept. The slope of the transformation is negative with similarities data, but positive with dissimilarities data.

On the other hand, if these proximities are expressed in terms of some ordinal measure of distances, such as ranks, so that the rank order of derived distances between the objects corresponds to the rank order of proximities data, then we are dealing with non-metric CMDS. Often respondents find it difficult to provide numerical comparisons about the degree of relative similarity or dissimilarity between objects, but do not have a problem making ranking-type judgments. This is a more flexible set of techniques, wherein the data is ordinal-scaled, may be complete or incomplete, and may be expressed as similarities or dissimilarities. In most cases, the two methods yield similar results.

Another decision required at this stage is whether the comparison between objects is to be made for an individual respondent or if responses are to be aggregated. Both methods have their limitations: individual level analysis, yielding spatial maps for each individual respondent, analysis and comparisons become unwieldy, and conclusions and decisions are difficult to arrive at. Aggregate level analysis, though it runs the risk of eclipsing some differences, is usually more meaningful from the decision point-of-view. A practical solution to the problem is to aggregate the comparisons at the segment level, and compare segment-wise perceptions. This is the approach used in RMDS and WMDS. These methods, in turn, may be metric or non-metric. The WMDS method generalizes the distance model so that the various similarity matrices S_k may be weighted to differ from each other systematically.

Identifying the number of dimensions The objective of MDS is to be able to present the proximities data in the form of a visual display, as mentioned earlier.

Borgatti (1997), in his book *Multidimensional Scaling*, defines dimensions as item attributes that seem to order the items in the map along a continuum. Since it is possible to visually examine only objects in two or at the most three dimensions, it is desirable to present this data in the minimum number of dimensions possible. At the same time, the fit between these derived distances and proximities data improves as the number of dimensions increases. It is, therefore, necessary to arrive at a compromise solution. Kruskal and Wish (1997) give a thumb-rule that there should be at least twice as many stimulus pairs as the number of dimensions.

A more rigorous decision in this regard is achieved through computation of a statistic called *stress*, which is a measure of the poorness of fit between the original data and the derived distances: the greater the value of stress, the poorer the fit. As with the scree plot in factor analysis and the error sum of squares plot in cluster analysis, the 'stress plot' indicates the optimal number of dimensions in MDS. We plot the stress values against the number of dimensions, and use the point at which the stress value jumps as the cut-off point for the adequate number of dimensions.

The analysis of MDS is sufficiently complex to be dependent on computer programmes. Most algorithms include the calculation of a *stress-index* (S-stress or Kruskal's stress) that ranges between 0 and 1. A stress-index of 0 indicates a perfect fit, and a stress-index value of 1 denotes the poorest fit. The following guidelines for determining the number of dimensions are based on Malhotra's (2004) book *Marketing Research*:

(a) *A priori knowledge* Based on theory or past research

(b) *Interpretability of the spatial map* We discussed earlier that the number of dimensions is often restricted by the consideration that it is difficult to interpret a spatial map in more than three dimensions

(c) *Elbow criterion* We discussed above the 'stress-plot' or elbow criterion. Plotting the stress index values against the number of dimensions indicates the point at which the stress value shows a steep change

(d) *Ease of use* It is usually easier to work with two-dimensional maps

(e) *Statistical approaches* Specific approaches available for determining dimensionality

According to Borgatti (1997), with reference to the dimensions used by respondents to distinguish between objects, 'it is important to realize that these substantive dimensions or attributes need not correspond in number or direction to the mathematical dimensions (axes) that define the vector space (MDS map). For example, the number of dimensions used by respondents to generate similarities may be much larger than the number of mathematical dimensions needed to reproduce the observed pattern. This is because the mathematical dimensions are necessarily orthogonal (perpendicular), and therefore maximally efficient. In contrast, the human dimensions, while cognitively distinct, may be highly intercorrelated and therefore contain some redundant information.'

Labelling the dimensions and interpreting the dimensionality The simplest method of defining the dimensions is through visual examination of the configuration and linking it to information that is available about the objects. If attribute data is being used, the object's ratings on attributes may be correlated with the dimensions to identify the attributes that correlate with specific dimensions. Kruskal and Wish (1997) recommend linear regression as the easiest method to understand. Here, dimensional coordinates may be used as the criterion variables and attribute ratings as predictor variables. The axes may then be labelled for the attributes with which they are most closely aligned. In case of non-attribute data too, the usual method is to identify some variables that are expected to have a relationship with the dimensions, and follow the same procedure.

Figure 14.33 depicts the perceptual map of seven brands of dishwashing detergents based on interviews with 75 housewives. The horizontal axis may be labelled as 'grease-removal strength' versus 'easy cleaning' ability. Brands *A, C, D,* and *F* have high positive values on this dimension, while brands *E* and *G* have high negative values (cleans easily). The vertical axis may be labelled as harshness versus softness on hands. Brand *D* has a high value on softness on hands. An opportunity gap seems to exist in the 'soft-on hands'/'cuts grease' area.

Often, the dimensions represent more than one attribute. The configuration may be interpreted by examining the coordinates and relative positions of the objects. If, for example, the MDS process is being applied to brands, the brands that are closer together may be perceived as closer competitors, while a brand located at a distance by itself along the axes may be expected to have a unique image. It may be possible to identify opportunities as gaps in the spatial map where no brands are located, while most current brands are grouped into one or more clusters.

The usual process in MDS is to start with one or two dimensions and if this is not found satisfactory, i.e., if the stress-index is high, then continue to add dimensions till the stress-index stops registering a noticeable change in value.

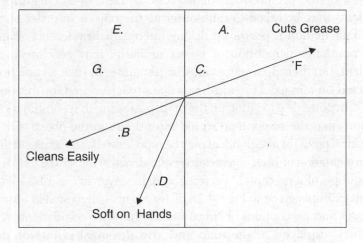

Fig. 14.33 Using Attribute Vectors to Label Dimensions

Assessing reliability and validity   In order to test the reliability and validity of an analysis, we must examine the value of R^2, the squared correlation index that measures the proportion of variance of the optimally scaled data accounted for by the MDS procedure. In other words, R^2 is the measure of goodness-of-fit. Values of R^2 above 0.6 are considered satisfactory for this purpose.

The stress-index, the measure of poorness-of-fit, is another indicator of the appropriateness of the analysis. Stress values below 5% are considered good for Kruskal's stress formula.

If the analysis has been done at the aggregate level, the data may be split into two parts, then the MDS can be performed separately on each part and the results compared. Alternatively, data may be collected at two different points in time (not very distant from each other) and the results may be compared for test/re-test reliability. Malhotra (2004) also suggests selectively eliminating objects from the input data, and performing MDS on the remaining data. Different objects may be eliminated at successive stages, and the results compared. An SPSS-based example of MDS is given in Annexure 14.4.

Models of Multidimensional Scaling

The various kinds of MDS models have been discussed here.

Perceptual maps   In applications of metric or non-metric MDS, we are by and large interested in scaling either only similarities or similarities and preference data. Most often, we plot only the objects, i.e., one set of points providing *simple-space configurations*. If based on similarities data, such configurations are called *perceptual maps*, as we mentioned earlier, and display distinct groups of objects that are perceived to be internally similar (or homogeneous) and dissimilar to objects in other groups.

Maps based on preference data   Sometimes, in addition to determining their perceptions of similarity (dissimilarity) of objects, we may be interested in studying the respondents' preferences for objects. In case of such joint-space solutions, respondents may be asked to rank order all the objects in order of preference. This kind of information is portrayed through perceptual-preference maps.

A respondent's perception of object similarity may be close to that of another respondent, but their preferences may be disparate. In such a case, how will such data be depicted on a map? The 'ideal-point' approach is used for this purpose. An 'ideal point' is a hypothetical location on the map, possessing that combination of the relevant dimensions that the respondent would most desire in the object. On the spatial map then the ideal point for a respondent may be represented by the respondent herself/himself. This representation of both objects and respondents on the spatial map is called unfolding.

An example of a perceptual-preference map is given in Fig. 14.34. In the dishwashing detergent example given in Fig. 14.33, if we are also interested in obtaining the brand-preferences and perceptions of 'ideal brand' from two respondents R_1 and R_2, we get the vectors displayed in the map and also the ideal points of the respondents.

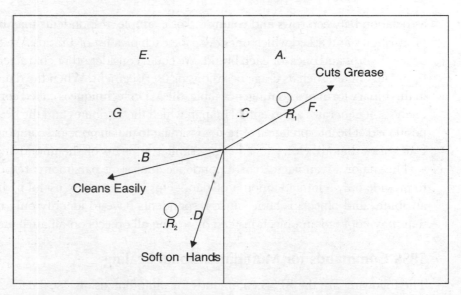

Fig. 14.34 Perceptual-preference Map based on Data given in Fig. 14.33

Respondent R_1's ideal point is high on 'cuts grease' and close to his/her preferred brand A, while respondent R_2's ideal point has a high value for softness on hands and is closer to his/her preferred brand D.

Vector models The location of the ideal point in preference analysis may be 'internal' or 'external'. In internal analysis, the ideal point may be located within the perceptual map, i.e., may be indicated as a point related to the preference data. On the other hand, in external analysis, the preference point may be at an extreme end, or even lie outside the range of the objects, indicating the direction of preference rather than a point located within the space. For example, in Fig. 14.33, the ideal point for a respondent may be in the direction of 'soft on hands' (as much as possible) and 'easy cleaning ability' (as much as possible), without specifying a point in the perceptual space. In this case, the 'ideal point' would be represented by the ideal vector rather than a point in the perceptual space.

Usually external analysis, involving ideal vectors, is preferred to internal analysis, for the reason that in internal analysis, perceptions may get confounded with preference data. In case, as discussed earlier, some objects are perceived to be similar and yet one is preferred to another, it is difficult to account for such variation in internal analysis. External analysis makes it easy to locate 'ideal points' of respondents having different preferences on the spatial map in a meaningful manner.

Correspondence Analysis This is an MDS technique for scaling attribute-based qualitative data. Instead of the conventional 5-point or 7-point scales used in factor analysis or discriminant analysis, correspondence analysis is based on binary scaling. The input data are presented in the form of a contingency table indicating a qualitative association between rows and columns. For example, respondents may be given a list of attributes and asked which ones describe each of a list of brands. We then obtain a series of zeros and ones for each brand. We could consider other characteristics besides brand attributes, such as usage occasions or user-segment. When the data is presented in this binary form in a contingency table, the MDS technique is called correspondence analysis. It generates a perceptual map in which the attributes and the brands are both positioned. The interpretation of results is similar to that in principal components analysis. Categories that are closer together are similar in terms of the underlying structure.

The major advantage of correspondence analysis is parsimony: respondents need to provide only a limited amount of data. This is particularly useful if the number of attributes and objects is large, since respondents have to identify only the attributes that may apply to an object, instead of scaling all objects on all attributes.

SPSS Commands for Multidimensional Scaling

The following are the SPSS commands for multidimensional scaling:

1. Open the Data Editor screen in 'SPSS 13.0 for Windows', and enter data as shown in Table 14.2.

2. Click on **Analyse** in the menu bar; click on **Scale** in the drop-down window, and click on **Multidimensional Scaling** (you may choose between PROXSCAL and ALSCAL, depending on whether you are using proximities or distance data).

3. If PROXSCAL has been selected, the **Multidimensional Scaling: Data Format** screen will appear (Fig. 14.35). Click on 'The data are proximities' under **Data Format**. Transfer variables from the left window to the right by clicking on the top righthand arrow (Fig 14.36). Click on the **Model** bar at the bottom of the screen.

4. The **Multidimensional Scaling: Model** screen will appear (Fig. 14.37). Key in the minimum and maximum dimensions desired, click on **Ratio, Interval, or Ordinal** under **Proximity Transformations,** depending on the level of measurement desired. Click on **Continue** to revert to the screen in Fig. 14.36. Click on the **Restrictions** bar at the bottom.

Table 14.2 Data For Multidimensional Scaling

Rin	Nirma	Ariel	Surf	Henko	Wheel	Tide	Vimal
0.00	2.00	3.00	5.00	4.00	2.00	1.00	8.00
2.00	0.00	5.00	7.00	6.00	4.00	1.00	3.00
3.00	5.00	0.00	2.00	5.00	1.00	8.00	7.00
5.00	7.00	2.00	0.00	3.00	4.00	7.00	8.00
4.00	6.00	5.00	3.00	0.00	7.00	3.00	2.00
2.00	4.00	1.00	4.00	7.00	0.00	5.00	6.00
1.00	1.00	8.00	7.00	3.00	5.00	0.00	2.00
8.00	3.00	7.00	8.00	2.00	6.00	2.00	0.00

5. The **Restrictions** screen will open as in Fig. 14.38. Click on **No restrictions** under **Restrictions on Common Space.**

6. Click on **Continue** to revert to the screen in Fig 14.36. Click on the **Options** bar at the bottom. The screen shown in Fig. 14.39 will appear.

7. Click on **Simplex** under **Initial Configuration**. Key in the required **stress convergence**, the **minimum stress**, and the **maximum iterations** desired under **Iteration Criteria.**

8. Click on **Continue** to revert to the screen in Fig 14.36. Click on **Plots**. The dialog box in Fig. 14.40 will appear. Click on **Common Space** under **Plots.**

9. Click on **Continue** to revert to the screen in Fig. 14.36. Click on the **Outputs** bar at the bottom. The screen on Fig. 14.41 will appear.

10. Click on **Common space coordinates** and **Multiple stress measures** under **Display.**

11. Click on **Continue** to revert to the screen in Fig. 14.36. Click on **OK**. The analysis will appear on the screen.

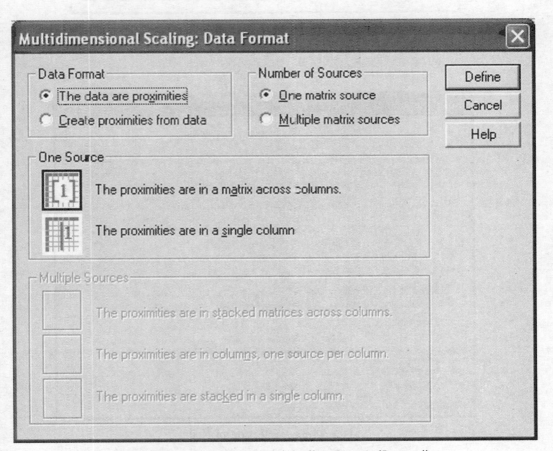

Fig. 14.35 Multidimensional Scaling Format (Proxscal)

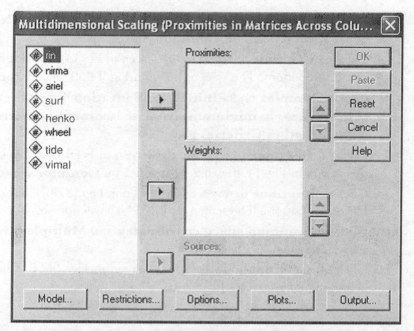

Fig. 14.36 Transference of Variables

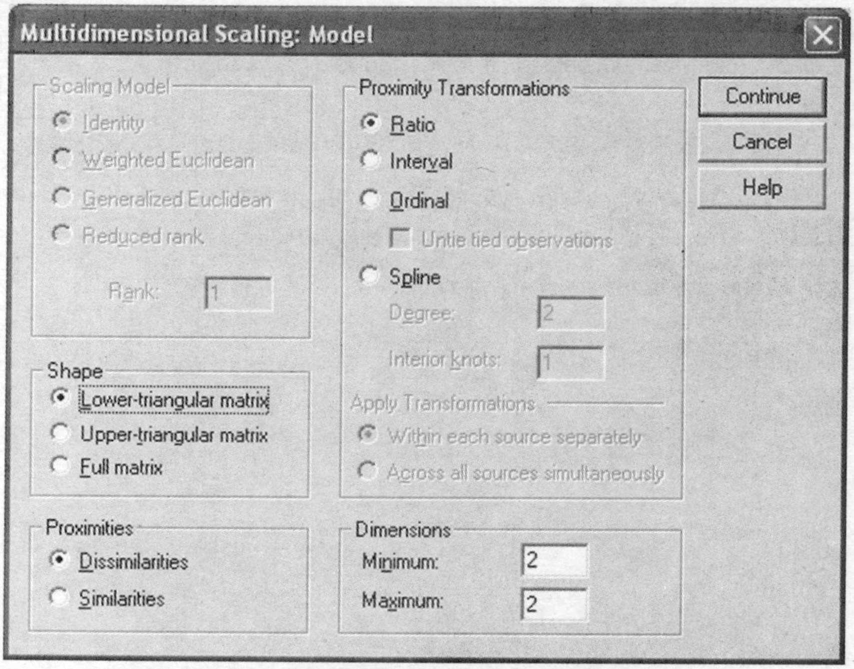

Fig. 14.37 Selection of Model

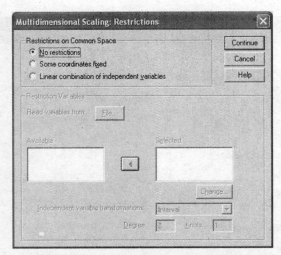

Fig. 14.38 Identification of Restrictions

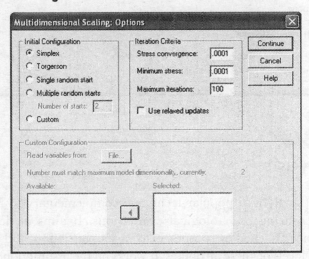

Fig. 14.39 Selection of Options

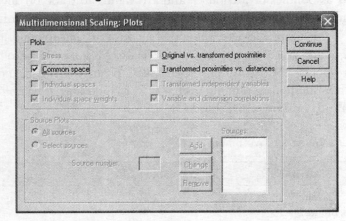

Fig. 14.40 Plots

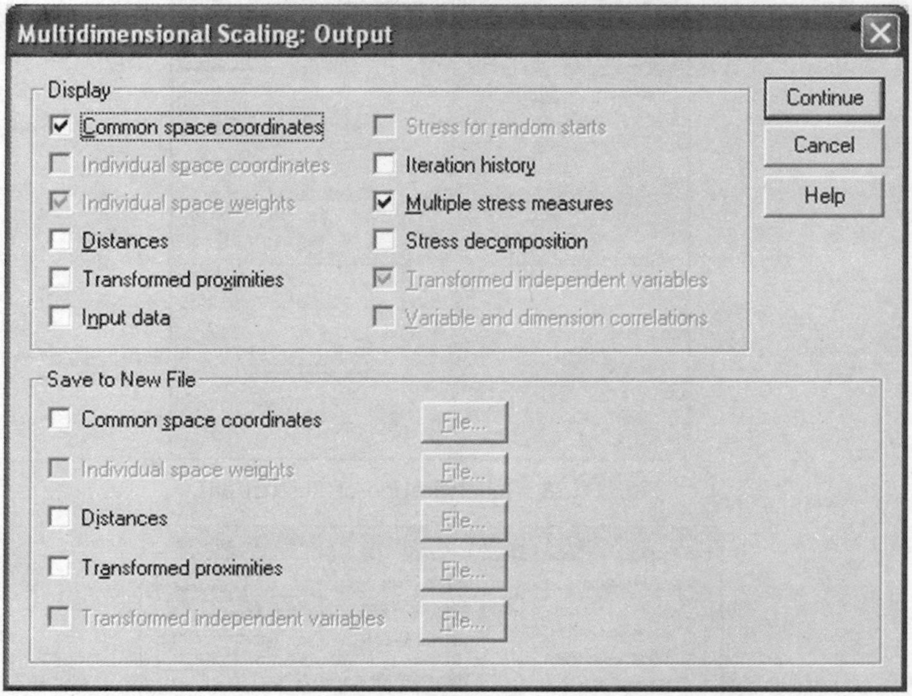

Fig. 14.41 Output

CONJOINT ANALYSIS

Conjoint analysis, a popular technique complementary to MDS, is also concerned with measuring psychological evaluations. It aims at determining the relative importance attached by consumers to various attributes, and to the values attached to different levels of these attributes. It works on the assumption that consumers evaluate objects as bundles of attributes, and are willing to trade off levels of attributes with less 'utility' or value for gaining higher levels of attributes that have higher utility for them. For example, let us assume that a consumer has to choose between two brands of tea, *A* and *B*. For choosing tea, he/she assigns importance to flavour, brand image, and freshness—in that order. When asked to rate the two brands on these attributes using a 5-point scale (ranging from 5 = 'very high' to 1 = 'very low'), she/he rates the two brands as shown in Table 14.3.

Table 14.3 Consumer's Rating for Two Brands

	Attribute	Brand A	Brand B
I	Flavour	4	3
II	Brand Image	4	4
III	Freshness	3	4

The consumer would be willing to trade off Brand B's superiority or higher score on freshness for Brand A's superiority or higher score on flavour, because greater value, or 'utility' is attached to flavour.

Conjoint analysis works on the principle that once we know the utility levels for each attribute of a product at each level, we can develop combinations of attributes that provide the highest utility to the consumer. The technique aims to develop these *utility* (or *part-worth*) functions, describing the utility or value consumers attach to various levels of each attribute. The objective, therefore, according to Green and Tull (1978) is to break down the 'overall responses to factorially designed stimuli so that the utility of each stimulus component can be inferred from the respondent's overall evaluations of the stimuli'. In other words, conjoint analysis aims to convert ordinal-scaled, or ranked-preference data into interval-scaled 'utility' data. The method obviously has significant applications in marketing in areas like new product development.

The stimuli in conjoint analysis are thus combinations of attribute levels determined by the researcher. As against this, in MDS the stimuli are the objects and the attributes are the dimensions to be identified. Both techniques aim at assessing the respondent's subjective judgment. Classical conjoint analysis deals with preference data, though its later versions have extended the technique to similarity data. The attributes to be evaluated are usually arrived at through past research, secondary data, or qualitative research, such as focus groups.

Some examples of the use of conjoint analysis in marketing are as follows:

- determining the relative importance of various brand-attributes in consumer choice
- estimating market-share of brands that possess different attribute-levels
- determining the consumer concept of the ideal brand (This is particularly useful in developing new brand-concepts.)
- identifying market segments that attach similar utility to group of brand attributes, distinct from attributes considered important by other segments
- identifying levels of marketing-mix variables considered useful by different consumer segments

The example of choice between two brands of tea is a simple one. In reality, we often face problems that (a) the attribute levels preferred may be in conflict or unrealistic (e.g., lowest possible price and best possible quality), (b) the range of levels opted for by different respondents may be too large, or (c) where the list of attributes is elicited from a focus group, the actual attribute and level of preferences of the respondents may extend beyond the range finally presented by the researcher. The concept of 'utilities' on which conjoint analysis is based takes care of these issues to a great extent.

Stages in Conducting Conjoint Analysis

The stages in conducting conjoint analysis are described in Figure 14.42.

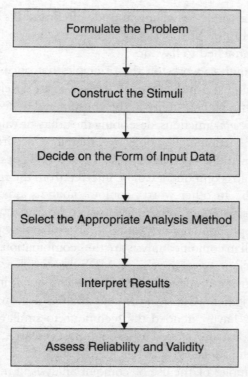

Fig. 14.42 Stages in Conjoint Analysis

Formulating the problem

As discussed earlier, the purpose of conjoint analysis is to decompose the consumer's overall preference for brands or other objects into the utility derived from specific attribute levels. The attributes must be salient in influencing brand choice, and must be actionable. The first step in problem formulation is, therefore, the identification of these attributes through previous research, secondary data, or qualitative research. At least six or seven attributes must be identified.

The next step in problem-formulation is identifying the relevant levels along which the attributes may vary between respondents. This specification of attribute levels is crucial in conducting meaningful conjoint analysis. The greater the range of differences in utility assigned by consumers to an attribute, the more important the attribute in the attitude towards the brand. On the other hand, if the utility assigned to an attribute by most consumers is more or less the same, the attribute is not very important from the point of view of conjoint analysis, since its level does not influence the choice of the object (brand). For this reason, the range of levels of an attribute offered to the respondents is very important: the greater the difference between the extreme levels of an attribute, the greater the variation in utility is likely to be. Consider, for example, the number of initial free calls offered by a cellphone company: if the range varies from 50 calls to 150 calls, the variation in utility is likely to be much greater than if it were to vary from 50 calls to 75 calls.

Constructing the stimuli

Two alternative approaches are available for constructing the stimuli for obtaining trade-off information in conjoint analysis: the *two-factor* (pairwise) approach and the *full-profile* approach. These are best explained through the example of tea that we discussed earlier. Suppose brands of tea are being compared on six attributes, each at three levels:

- Flavour
- Strength
- Colour
- Packaging
- Price
- Company reputation

In the two-factor approach, the respondent is asked to rank the nine combinations of, say price and flavour, in order of preference, or price and packaging, as shown in Fig. 14.43.

Pairwise data may be similarly collected for all pairs at all levels. In this example, there would be 15 such pairs being compared through this kind of 3×3 tables. The problem then is to find a set of utilities or part-worths; in this example, we need to get three numbers each for the six factors to indicate the utility the consumer derives from each level of each attribute.

Once these utilities have been obtained, we may estimate the overall utility of each two-way table, by adding the separate utilities for any two-factor table. The utilities for all the 15 pairs may then be ranked. These derived rankings should correspond as closely as possible to the respondent's original ranking.

In the full-profile or multiple-factor approach, complete profiles of brands are constructed for all the attributes. Hence, there would be 18 such profiles, each depicted on a separate index card. One such profile is shown in Fig. 14.44.

	Flavour					Packing		
	Strong	**Medium**	**Mild**			**Tetrapack**	**Plastic**	**Sachet**
Price (Rs/Kg) 500	9	4	2		**Price (Rs/Kg)** 500	4	1	7
250	8	3	1		250	5	2	8
100	7	6	5		100	6	3	9

Fig. 14.43 Two-factor Approach to Collecting Conjoint Data

Flavour	Mild
Strength	Medium
Colour	Gold
Packaging	Tetrapack
Price	Rs. 400/-
Company reputation	High

Fig. 14.44   Full Profile Approach to Collecting Conjoint Data

In practice it is neither always necessary nor always feasible to have all possible combinations evaluated. The pairwise approach is easier for the respondent, but may often end up being tedious and time consuming. In addition, after a while the responses may become mechanical. The greater the number of attributes and levels, the greater the chances of such mechanical responses. Besides, in real terms, a pairwise approach is not meaningful—respondents do not evaluate attributes in pairs. Rather, they tend to consider different levels of all attributes taken together, and choices are made holistically between entire sets of attributes, different options presenting different combinations of levels of attributes. The respondent may then be asked to rank the 18 cards in order of preference or perceived value, or they may be asked to divide them into three piles divided as follows:

- Definitely like
- Neither like nor dislike
- Definitely dislike

Within each pile, the cards may be arranged in order of preference.

This approach, as is obvious, requires more effort on the part of the respondent, since each card has a complete set of attributes to be evaluated and differentiated from the others. Even so, it provides a more realistic picture and is more commonly used.

Deciding on the form of input data

Input data may be in metric or non-metric form. If it is non-metric, the respondents provide evaluation in the form of rank order of preference. In the two-factor approach, ranked preferences are provided for all $n(n - 1)/2$ matrices, where n is the number of attributes. In case of the multiple-factor approach, ^nC_m profiles are ranked, where n attributes are evaluated, each at m levels.

If metric data is used, respondents are required to provide ratings rather than rankings. These ratings are independent judgments. Data is most often analysed in terms of preferences or intentions to buy, but other bases for analysis like actual purchase may be used at times.

Selecting the method of analysis

The analysis usually involves a kind of ANOVA, with the respondent's overall preferences as dependent variables and attribute levels as independent levels. Both the two-factor approach and the multiple-factor approach use similar computational methods, where the underlying conjoint model is

$$U(X) = \sum_{i=1}^{m} \sum_{j=1}^{k_i} a_{ij} x_{ij} \qquad (14.3)$$

where

$U(X)$ = the total utility of an alternative
a_{ij} = the utility of level j of attribute i
x_{ij} = 1, if the jth level of attribute i exists
= 0 otherwise
k_i = the number of levels of attribute i
m = the number of attributes

The importance of attribute i, following our earlier discussion, depends on the range of differences in utility perceived by the respondents. Let us define this range as D_i, where

$$D_i = (\max a_{ij} - \min a_{ij}) \text{ for attribute } i$$

This may be normalized as D_i', the ratio of the importance D_i of the attribute i to the total importance of all attributes:

$$D_i' = D_i / \sum_i D_i$$

The following points summarize the conjoint analysis approach.

- The respondent is presented with a set of object profiles constructed following the factorial design pattern.
- The respondent is asked to rank the objects according to some criterion, usually preference.
- The objective is to find the set of utilities for the factor levels such that the sum of each specific combination of utilities adds up to the total utility of that factor profile.
- The derived ranking of the object profiles is obtained to be as close to the original ranking, using the goodness-of-fit approach.

Somewhat like MDS, conjoint analysis may also be conducted at the level of the individual respondent, at the segment level, or across segments. Aggregate level analysis may be done in either of two ways: (a) consumers can be grouped into segments and average values can be obtained for all attributes for all consumers in a segment, to be compared across segments, or (b) analysis can be carried out at the individual level first and then respondents can be grouped together through cluster analysis on the basis of the similarities of their utility functions.

Individual level analysis is useful if the difference between the expectations of individual consumers is expected to be significant and they are each likely to contribute adequate volumes to make such customized exercise profitable, as in industrial markets. In the FMCG market, differences in requirements will usually be significant *between* segments, or sometimes not even then. In this case, the objective of conjoint analysis will be not so much to be able to identify *different* utility combinations for different consumers, so that segment-specific product requirements may be met, but to determine possible alternatives that provide the same utility levels.

Dummy regression variable approach   There are many approaches available for analysing conjoint data. Among the most popular of these is the dummy regression variable approach. Dummy variables, also called binary, dichotomous, or qualitative variables, are defined as variables that take the value '1' or '0' across their entire range. They enable the expression of non-quantitative data in the form of numbers.

The dummy variable method defines the predictor variables as dummy variables for the attribute levels, and preference rankings as the dependent variables. If the ith attribute has k_i levels, it is coded as $k_i - 1$ dummy variables. For example, let us once again consider the example of the tea brands discussed earlier. For the sake of convenience of discussion, let us suppose we are considering only three attributes— flavour, price, and packaging—each at three levels.

Table 14.4   Dummy Variable Approach for Analysing Conjoint Data

Flavour:	Strong (1)	Medium (2)	Mild (3)
Price:	(1) Rs 500	(2) Rs 250	(3) Rs 100
Packaging:	(1) Tetrapack	(2) Plastic jar	(3) Sachet

According to Table 14.4, we thus get $3 \times 3 \times 3 = 27$ combinations of attributes. Let us consider nine of these combinations, and depict them through numerical labels. Each of these attribute variables may be coded as (1, 2, 3), since each is considered at three levels. We may then present the nine profiles or combinations for one consumer and her/his preference ranking for them as depicted in Table 14.4.

These profiles may be interpreted as, say, (1, 1, 1) for the first profile, providing the combination (strong flavour, priced at Rs 500, in a tetrapack). Each of the attribute variables may now be expressed in terms of two dummy variables. For example, we define $X_1 = 1$ for strong flavour, and 0 for other flavours. Similarly, $X_2 = 1$ for medium flavour and 0 for all others. Once the dummy variables are defined in this manner, the third option mild flavour automatically gets defined. We treat it as the base level. Dummy variables may be similarly defined for the other two attributes. Data of Table 14.5 is then expressed in terms of dummy variables as shown in Table 14.6.

If we are dealing with metric data, ratings on interval-scales form the dependent variable. For non-metric data, the above manner of defining independent variables would mean comparing the brands in pairs for each attribute and assigning them values 0 or 1 depending on the absence or presence of the attribute, so that the predictor variables represent the differences in the attribute levels of the brands being compared. The regression model for estimating utilities based on Table 14.5 may then be expressed as

$$U = b_0 + b_1X_1 + b_2X_2 + b_3X_3 + b_4X_4 + b_5X_5 + b_6X_6$$

where the b_is are the coefficients estimating the difference between the utility for that level and the base level. For example,

$$b_1 = a_{11} - a_{13} \tag{14.4}$$

Table 14.5 Selected Profiles of Attribute Data

Selected Profiles				
Profile No.	Flavour	Price	Packaging	Preference Rating
1	1	1	1	9
2	1	1	2	8
3	1	2	2	7
4	2	1	1	6
5	2	2	1	5
6	2	1	2	4
7	3	1	1	3
8	3	2	1	2
9	3	2	2	1

Table 14.6 Data of Table 14.5 Expressed as Dummy Variables for Regression Analysis

Preference Rankings	Flavour		Price		Packaging	
	X_1	X_2	X_3	X_4	X_5	X_6
9	1	0	1	0	1	0
8	1	0	1	0	0	1
7	1	0	0	1	0	1
6	0	1	1	0	1	0
5	0	1	0	1	1	0
4	0	1	1	0	0	1
3	0	0	1	0	1	0
2	0	0	0	1	1	0
1	0	0	0	1	0	1

where b_1 is the coefficient of X_1 and a_{11} and a_{13} are the utilities as described in Eqn (14.3). With this dummy variable coding, where level 3 is the base level as described above, the coefficients b_i are, thus, related to the utilities or part-worths. We may define all the coefficients b_i in this manner and solve these equations to obtain the utility values.

The next step is to estimate the range of utilities, and the relative importance D_i' of each attribute as defined earlier. The SPSS computer package may be utilized to obtain the utilities directly. If the SPSS package available does not contain the conjoint programme, we may obtain utilities by converting the data to the multiple regression model as described earlier.

Interpreting results

In order to interpret the results of the analysis, it is useful to plot the graphs depicting the utility functions. The graphs make for easier interpretation of the analysis. The interpretation of the analysis aims at obtaining

(a) the most important attributes, i.e., the attributes with the highest utility in the respondent's perception;

(b) the most preferred level of each attribute, i.e., the level of each attribute with the highest utility; and

(c) the most preferred combination of attributes, i.e., combination of attributes that optimizes the total utility U.

As we have discussed earlier, if analysis is required at the aggregate level, this data may be averaged at each of these three levels. For segment-wise analysis, the data at each of the three levels may be aggregated into groups using cluster analysis.

Assessing reliability and validity

The use of conjoint analysis in marketing and marketing research has increased significantly in the past three decades or so. This in itself is a major evidence of the validity of the technique. It has been found to be effective in prediction studies, and results of conjoint analysis are usually found to correspond well with observed consumer behaviour. As is usual with predictive techniques, the internal validity of conjoint studies can be determined through what Aaker et al. (1999) have referred to as the 'hold-out sample': the total sample is divided into two parts. One part is used for prediction and the other part is used for validating the model developed through the predictive part. Other methods of assessing reliability and validity may also be considered. Some have been listed here.

(a) In case of the dummy variables regression model discussed earlier, R^2 may be calculated to assess the goodness-of-fit of the model.

(b) If aggregate level analysis is being conducted, the total sample can be split in a number of ways, and conjoint analysis can be performed on each sub-sample.

If the results are comparable across sub-samples, they indicate stable and reliable results of conjoint analysis.

(c) The test/re-test method of assessing reliability may be applied to conjoint results.

All applications of conjoint analysis are based on the assumption that all attributes that contribute to the utility of a product can be identified and are independent. It also assumes that trade-offs between parameters are a conscious action on the part of the consumer and that they consider trade-offs at the two-factor level. These may not always be totally valid assumptions and, to that extent, the results of conjoint analysis must be treated with caution. It might be possible to try and use metric data in cases where non-quantifiable attributes are involved or if multicollinearity is expected between independent variables and run a factor analysis on them. Utilities may then be computed for these factors.

THE INFLUENCE OF DATA ANALYSIS ON RESEARCH DESIGN

This chapter, more than any other in this book, brings to the fore the influence that the kind of data analysis planned exercises on the design of the research study: the form of data to be used, the detail required, the form of questions to be asked, etc. Primarily, the kind of assumptions made and analysis required and their influence on the structure of the study have been summarized in Table 14.7.

Table 14.7 Research Design Most Suited to Various Data Analysis Requirements

Requirements	Research Design
1. Interrelationships between independent variables or respondents are to be studied	Data matrix is not partitioned, as in factor analysis or cluster analysis
2. Influence of pre-identified independent variables on the dependent variable is to be studied	Multiple regression methods are to be used if the dependent variable is interval-scaled; discriminant analysis is required, if the dependent variable is nominal or ordinal
3. More than one dependent variable is to be studied	Canonical correlation methods are to be used
4. Reduction in the number of correlated variables	Principal components analysis, if the emphasis is on data reduction; common factor analysis if the emphasis is on identifying the commonality
5. Grouping of respondents on the basis of parameters that would provide internally homogenous groups and have to be identified	Cluster analysis

Table 14.7 continued

Table 14.7 continued

Requirements	Research Design
6. Grouping of objects on the basis of identified parameters for prediction purposes	Discriminant analysis
7. Spatial representation of brand/object perceptions in terms of perceived similarities measured in quantitative terms, when the dimensions on which objects are compared are not pre-specified	Metric multidimensional scaling (MDS) using similarities data
8. Spatial representation of brand/object perceptions in terms of perceived similarities measured in qualitative terms	Metric (MDS) using Likert-type scaled data
9. Spatial representation of brand/object perceptions in terms of perceived preferences	Rank-ordered data or paired comparisons
10. Spatial representation of an individual respondent's brand/object perceptions in terms of perceived similarities measured in quantitative terms	Classical MDS
11. Spatial representation of brand/object perceptions of a group of respondents in terms of perceived similarities	Replicated or weighted MDS, metric or non-metric
12. Defining and interpreting dimensionality in MDS when attribute–based data is used	Linear regression with dimensions as criterion variables and attributes as predictor variables
13. MDS when input data is available in a binary form in a contingency table	Correspondence analysis
14. Identification of perceived relative importance of attributes of objects and the levels of these attributes	Conjoint analysis

SUMMARY

Analysis of inter-relationships between multiple variables takes on many complex forms. Most of them are extensive and complex enough to require the use of computer-based techniques.In case correlation between independent variables and more than one dependent variable is to be simultaneously determined, the method of canonical correlations is employed. It is, thus, an extension of multiple regression to the case of multiple dependent variables.

Another technique similar to multiple regression is discriminant analysis, used when the dependent variables are nominal or ordinal rather than interval scaled. Discriminant analysis is used to determine linear combinations of independent variables, or characteristics, whose coefficients are called discriminant loadings, then we separate groups of objects by maximizing between-group variance relative to within-group variance. Once the groups are separated, they are tested for significance of inter-group differences. The variables that contribute most to this difference are identified, and a rule is developed for assigning new entrants to various groups.

When independent variables in a regression equation are correlated and one wants to reduce this data to smaller number of uncorrelated factors without much loss of information, two variants of factor analysis are popularly used. The principal components analysis method aims at reducing data to a smaller number of factors so that the major factors responsible for variation in data are extracted, in a manner that the first component explains the maximum amount of variation, the second component explains the next largest amount of variation, and so on. The common factor analysis method lays emphasis on grouping correlated variables with the objective of identifying underlying links between variables.

Cluster analysis is another inter-dependence technique. It differs from factor analysis in that it aims at grouping respondents, not variables, into different segments on the basis of characteristics such as perceptions, beliefs, and orientations. The objective of cluster analysis is, thus, classification and not data-reduction. The technique operates by identifying most suitable measures of interobject similarity for developing exclusive clusters. The important step is to define and interpret the clusters. Two other sets of techniques that have been discussed in this chapter, i.e., multidimensional scaling and conjoint analysis, measure perceptions and preferences based on some underlying links in parameters that the consumer observes in objects under study. MDS refers to a set of techniques used for representing perceived similarities between brands or other objects spatially through a visual display, called a perceptual map, where perceived links or relationships are represented geometrically as interpoint Euclidean distances in a multidimensional space. MDS techniques can be classified into different types, such as classical, replicated, and weighted. Classical MDS (CMDS) usually uses data based on the consumer's overall perception of similarities (proximities) or dissimilarities between objects, though it may also use derived or attribute-based approaches, using Likert-type scales. MDS technique yields a single matrix with an unweighted model. Replicated MDS (RMDS) has several matrices with an unweighted model, and weighted MDS (WMDS) has several matrices using the weighted model. All these may in turn be metric or nonmetric. The goodness/poorness-of-fit of the model is measured through computation of a statistic called *stress*. This is measured with the help of a statistic called the 'stress-index', which ranges from 0 to 1. The greater the value of the stress-index, the poorer the fit. Another MDS technique used for scaling attribute-based qualitative data is correspondence analysis. It is based on binary scaling with the objects being evaluated rated 0 or 1 depending on whether or not they are perceived to possess the attribute being considered. It, therefore, presents input data in the form of a contingency table. Conjoint analysis is a multivariate technique that aims at determining the relative importance attached by consumers to various attributes. It works on the assumption that consumers evaluate objects as bundles of attributes, and are willing to trade-off levels of attributes with less 'utility' or value for gaining higher levels of attributes that have higher utility for them. Its purpose is to decompose the consumer's overall preference for brands or other objects into the utility derived from specific attribute levels. Two alternative approaches are available for constructing the stimuli for obtaining trade-off information in conjoint analysis: the *two-factor* (pairwise) approach and the *full-profile* approach. The full-profile approach is considered closer to the consumer psychological processes and used most often. In either of the two approaches, the input data may be metric or nonmetric and may be obtained in the form of preference ratings or rankings.

Given the set of attributes being evaluated and the various levels at which they may be available in the form of a factorial design, the objective is to find the set of utilities for the factor levels such that the sum of each specific combination of utilities adds up to the total utility of that factor profile. The derived ranking of the object profiles is obtained to be as close to the original ranking, using the goodness-of-fit approach. The analysis is most often undertaken using the dummy regression variable approach. The major step here is to estimate the range of utilities. This may be done directly using the SPSS computer package, or through the regression model. The results may then be interpreted with the help of graphs.

KEY WORDS

Agglomeration schedule is a table that gives information on the objects being combined at each stage of a hierarchical clustering process.

Bartlett's test of sphericity tests the hypothesis that the variables are uncorrelated in the population, before factor analysis is undertaken.

Canonical correlation in the context of discriminant analysis, refers to the measure of association between the discriminant scores and the groups.

Centroid refers to the mean value of the discriminant scores of a group.

Classical MDS is a method of multidimensional scaling which displays only one similarity matrix.

Classification matrix (confusion matrix) refers to the matrix that gives the number of objects correctly classified and misclassified by discriminant analysis.

Cluster centroid is the mean value of the variables for all the objects in a particular cluster.

Cluster centre refers to the starting point of a cluster in non-hierarchical methods.

Cluster membership defines the cluster to which an object belongs.

Communality is the percentage of variance explained by all the factors extracted, i.e., the percentage of variance of a variable that is shared with all other variables.

Common factor analysis is the factor analysis that is primarily concerned with defining the underlying commonality between variables that are highly correlated with each other.

Configurations refers to the relative position of points (objects) on a perceptual map using a given number of dimensions.

Correlation matrix is the matrix that displays the correlation of each variable with every other variable.

Dendogram is a graph displaying the clustering pattern. Vertical lines in a dendogram represent the clusters that are linked.

Discriminant coefficients are weights assigned to the original predictor variables in the discriminant function.

Discriminant function is the linear equation that divides the objects into internally homogeneous groups that are distinct from the other groups with respect to the predictor variables being considered.

Discriminant scores refer to the values of the predictor variables for each object, multiplied by the values of the discriminant coefficients obtained in the discriminant function and summed together.

Eigenvalue refers to the ratio of the between-groups to within-groups sum of squares for any discriminant function, also referred to as the discriminant criterion of the discriminant function.

Factor refers to a group of variables that form a highly intercorrelated set, expressing a common dimension.

Factor loading is the correlation of a variable with a factor. These loadings are used to interpret factors. In the unrotated form, a variable usually loads on more than one factor, so that it is not possible to define independent factors that are uncorrelated with each other.

Factor matrix is the matrix that exhibits the factor loadings of all the standardized variables on all the factors extracted.

Factor scores are values for each respondent on each extracted factor

Icicle diagram is a diagram, resembling a row of icicles that depicts the result of a clustering process. The columns correspond to the objects being clustered and the rows correspond to the number of clusters.

Ideal point is the perceived location of the respondent's ideal brand on the perceptual map.

Kaiser–Meyer–Olkin measure of sampling adequacy is a measure of the appropriateness of factor analysis, where in values above 0.5 indicate that the factor the analysis is appropriate.

Multidimensional scaling (MDS) refers to a set of techniques for representing such perceived similarities spatially through a visual display.

Metric MDS method of MDS uses metric, i.e., interval-or ratio-scaled data.

Perceptual map (Spatial map) is a visual display of objects that presents the perceived similarities between them in terms of Euclidean distances. It, thus, depicts the perceived relationships between objects as geometric relationships among points in the multidimensional space.

Perceptual-preference maps are perceptual maps in the joint-space that depict respondent perceptions of similarity (dissimilarity) of objects, in addition to their preferences for objects.

Preference rankings refer to respondent perceptions of objects in terms of their preferences, where the objects being studied are ranked from the most preferred to the least preferred.

Principal components analysis is the method of factor analysis that groups correlated variables into factors such that the first factor explains the largest component of variation in the data, the next factor describes the next largest component, and so on.

Pooled within-group correlation matrix is obtained by averaging the covariance matrices of all the groups.

R-square is the squared correlation index that is a measure of the goodness-of-fit of the MDS model. It indicates the proportion of variance of the optimally scaled data explained by the MDS procedure.

Residuals refer to the difference between the original correlations exhibited in the correlation matrix and the factor loadings as depicted by the factor matrix.

Replicated MDS is the method of MDS which defines the distance –matrix so that it is simultaneously like all similarity matrices being generated.

Scree plot is a graph of the eigenvalues plotted against the number of factors in order of extraction.

Similarity/distance coefficient matrix describes the pairwise distance between objects.

Standardized discriminant coefficients are obtained when the variables have been standardized to mean 0 and variance 1.

Stress-index is the measure of poorness-of-fit defined as a function of the difference between the original similarities data and derived distances.

Structured correlations, or discriminant loadings, are the measures of correlation between the original predictor variables and the discriminant function.

Unfolding refers to the simultaneous representation of objects and respondents as points in the same space.

Weighted MDS also called individual differences scaling, is the method that generates more than one unique distance matrix, one for each data matrix.

Wilk's lambda is the ratio of the within-group sum of squares to the total sum of squares for each predictor variable.

CONCEPT REVIEW QUESTIONS

1. Discuss the similarities and differences between cluster analysis, discriminant analysis, canonical correlation and factor analysis in terms of (a) assumption structures and (b) objectives of the techniques.

2. Describe two problems in MR that you think might be amenable to factor analysis, and discuss how you would use factor analysis in each situation.

3. What are the key distinctions between dependence and inter-dependence techniques? Give two examples of each.

4. How would you decide on the most appropriate method of MDS in a situation where you think MDS may be the appropriate technique of analysis? Give an example of each method.

5. When are hierarchical methods of cluster analysis to be preferred to non-hierarchical methods? Why?

6. In using conjoint analysis, under what conditions and situations would the trade-off approach be preferred? When would you prefer to use the full-profile approach? Why? Are there situations when the two approaches would yield the same kind of results?

PROJECT ASSIGNMENTS

1. Consider these brands of toilet soaps: Pears, Liril, Cinthol, Lifebuoy, Chandrika, and Lux.

   (a) Collect data on their perceived similarities from a set of consumers and develop a perceptual map in three dimensions for these brands. Label the dimensions and identify the gaps, if any.

   (b) Develop a product concept to fit in this gap, defining three alternative levels at which the three major attributes may be available; using conjoint analysis, define the optimal combination of attribute levels at which the utility of this new brand may be maximized.

2. What kind of multivariate method would you recommend in each of the following cases? Why?

   (a) A client wants to develop an estimating equation that will be used to predict which applicants will come to its business school as students.

   (b) You have been studying a group of successful salespeople. You have given them a number of psychological tests and now you want to bring meaning out of these results.

3. A marketer of branded milk has developed three new package designs for the product that will enable the milk to last for upto one month without refrigeration. The marketer wants to know if any or all of these designs are likely to result in significantly higher sales than the current package design, which requires refrigeration and lasts for a maximum of one week under refrigeration. Suggest a suitable approach for evaluating the alternative package designs. What techniques would you employ to analyse the research data needed to satisfy the marketer's information requirements? Why would you use this technique?

4. A recruitment firm is trying to relate activity/interest scores to 'success' measures of applicants for the position of counter sales personnel in a large department store. Activity/interest scores and success scores are available for a group of retailing employees who have already been employed by the store. The activity/interest variables are—X_1: gregariousness, X_2: liking for outdoor sports, X_3: liking for music, and X_4: desire for travel. Y denotes the success measure. Higher values of the X_i denote higher interest or success respectively.

(a) Conduct a principal-components analysis on the 14 × 4 matrix of activity/interest scores.

(b) How would you interpret the first component?

Employee	X_1	X_2	X_3	X_4	Y
1	21	26	7	8	6.2
2	22	16	11	7	7.6
3	16	28	11	7	5.7
4	17	30	9	13	6.1
5	12	26	12	7	1.8
6	25	10	18	14	2.9
7	18	21	14	16	4.7
8	15	17	5	11	4.8
9	14	23	13	8	4.7
10	18	20	10	5	5.7
11	14	29	14	11	7.2
12	15	23	16	7	6.7
13	25	21	14	12	3.6
14	15	20	3	10	7.0

CASE STUDIES

Market Potential for Tatamida: Data Analysis in Marketing Research

Week 1

Raghavender Mateti and his colleague Supriya Chawla were waiting in the Rallis House reception area for their meeting with Aditya Chandrashekhar, the Marketing Manager of the Pesticides Division. Mateti's company, Innovative Strategy Consultants, had been providing consultancy services to Rallis for the past one year, and had now been called in for discussions on the new project that Rallis were evidently excited about. While waiting, Raghu (as friends and family called Mateti) took the time out to, once again, go over with Supriya the request put forward by Chandrashekhar. Rallis were planning to launch a new pesticide for the cotton crop, one of the largest cash crops in the country. The molecule, named Imida, was already in the market, introduced by archrival Bayer under the brand name Confidor. Rallis had now developed the molecule in their lab and were in a position to launch it in the market at a much lower rate. The phone at the reception desk rang before Raghu could get much further than the opening lines of the letter with Supriya. The receptionist spoke into the mouthpiece, looked at Raghu while cradling the phone against her chin and writing out the visitors slip, and smiled at him, ' You may go in now, sir'. Raghu and Supriya walked into Chandrashekhar's office, where Raghu made the introductions, 'Aditya Chandrashekhar; Supriya Chawla. Supriya is the one handling the research side of the project, Adi. I brought her along so that she may get the entire story straight from the horse's mouth. It will save time organizing the study'. Chandrashekhar inclined his head in acknowledgement, 'Hi, Supriya. Good that you came along. I assume Raghu has already briefed you about our new venture. So why not get down to brass tacks straightaway?'

'He has. But even so, it will be good to run us through the background. I will be able to clarify any doubts I may have,' Supriya replied. 'Very well, let us start at the beginning,' Chandrashekhar rejoined, 'How much do you know about the pests that affect cotton?' 'I know that cotton is affected by three kinds of pests at different stages in its life—sucking pests like aphids and jassids in the early-to-mid season; thrips and white fly in mid-to-late season; and there are the chewing pests and the boring pests. Of the lot, the white fly is the major sucking pest and heliothis is the main boring pest,' Supriya said.

'Very good, Supriya, go to the top of the class,' Chandrashekhar grinned, 'now let me tell you about the treatment and the market. That is where we come in, after all. Here is a small booklet that will serve as reference about the cotton pesticides and their market.'

The problem   Supriya and Raghu took turns flipping through the booklet while tea was being ordered. Over a cup of tea, Chandrashekhar resumed, 'You know that the pesticides market is very competitive, with both Indian and multinational companies operating actively. One of the major crops requiring pesticides is cotton. As you said, it is a crop plagued by a variety of pests all through its life. Pesticides are used for treatment, not much for prevention—it is difficult to determine what will cause a certain species of pests to infest the crop. Besides, many of these pests often infest the crop simultaneously, such as white fly and heliothis. Both these pests are very common, almost an annual occurrence, and the damage they cause can be very extensive. As a result, many pesticides are also used concurrently, such as Triazophos and Deltamethrin for controlling white fly and heliothis. This certainly pushes the costs up, but given the seriousness of the problem, the farmers have no choice. There are about eight to nine brands of Triazophos in the market currently. Besides, farmers work out their own combinations of pesticides as well as doses. Treatment of these various pests has evolved over the years from the early organochlorines such as DDT to the new ones like Acetamaprid (Pride), Thiomethoxam (Actara), and the latest kid on the block, i.e., Imidacloprid. All this is covered in the booklet. Bayer has introduced Imidacloprid as Confidor in India, and they are co-marketing it with Aventis and Pesticides (India) Ltd under two different brand names. The total market for Imidacloprid is currently estimated at approximately 3,00,000 litres. Confidor is currently the leading brand of Imidacloprid. At the moment, Bayer imports the total requirement of Imidacloprid and that makes it pretty expensive'.

'Imida is generally rated as the best product for controlling routine sucking pests such as aphids, jassids, and thrips. It also gives good control over white flies, but the dosage required for the purpose is about double as compared to the dosage required for controlling other pests. Bayer has not promoted Confidor for white fly, leaving the decision to the farmer'.

'We have now developed the same molecule in our laboratory, and would like to market it for white fly. There are three reasons for this decision. First, we avoid direct confrontation with Bayer this way. Second, the market for white fly is much larger than that for the other sucking pests. Third, other companies are sure to move into the white-fly-pesticide market with their brands of Imida, and we would like the first-mover advantage in repositioning it for white fly. But if the dosage has to be higher, we may have to reduce the price. Of course, our brand should be cheaper than Confidor, since it will be made within the country. The promotion will also have to be quite extensive, which brings in the question of profitability. Price-competition, I believe, is imminent, and it will be important for us to know what price the farmers will be willing to pay. Plus, how important is price to them in the final analysis?'

Supriya was noting down all these points assiduously, when Raghu broke in to ask, 'What about the dosage? If you recommend a relatively low dosage, would the farmer not compare the total expenditure with the overall gain from saving the crop, and yet find it worthwhile?' Chandrashekhar nodded, 'He might. But that will depend on the price at which we are able to market it, and on the dose the farmer uses. Actually, we have reason to believe that farmers tend to use pesticides in doses much higher than those recommended by the companies. This works to the company's advantage in case of conventional products that usually prescribe low doses, but if they try to follow the same practice with Imida at Bayer's price, it will put the product out of their reach, and eventually kill the product. So we really have three options before us: (a) not promote Imida for white fly, though it is a huge market; (b) price it much lower than Confidor; or (c) strictly enforce the dose, which is a tough proposition. Not promoting it for white fly means losing out on this fantastic opportunity staring us in the face.'

Raghu and Supriya gathered up their papers as Supriya finished taking notes, and left after promising to study the issue in greater detail. They would revert to Chandrashekhar at the earliest with their queries and the research proposal.

Week 2

A week later, Aditya Chandrashekhar opened his mail in the morning, and found this note from Supriya Chawla:

Dear Mr. Chandrashekhar,

Sub: *Survey to determine the market-potential for Tatamida*

Thank you for having spent time with Mr Raghavender Mateti and myself last Friday, discussing the background to the captioned survey. We have been discussing it at our end, and think that we have acquired some understanding of the issue. We believe we are now in a position to send you a formal proposal, but before doing that, I would like to summarize our understanding of the marketing problem, and a broad framework of how we would like to go about the study. The summary is appended, and I will appreciate it if you could go through it and let me have your comments. I am not putting in details about the market composition here. For that, in any case, we will be relying on the booklet you gave us.

Brand constraints as perceived by client (Rallis):

- Bayer is already well-accepted in the market.

- The price/cost of Imida in white fly control is high.

  As such, the issues you would like us to investigate are:
- Are farmers conceptually willing to use Imida as a tool for white fly control?
- Are the farmers' criteria for satisfactory control: (a) clean-up level (i.e., the % of pests removed) and (b) days of control required before the next spray?
- Other pests occurring along with white fly.
- Whether separate or combined treatment is preferred for pests infesting at the same time.
- Present delivery levels and satisfaction levels in terms of efficacy and costs.
- Awareness of new products and prices.
- What would motivate the farmer to try a new product or an old product at a higher dose: guarantee of efficacy alone or low price/gift/recognition in addition?
- Importance of price as a selection criterion.
- Major sources of information and influence.
- Communication strategies adopted by the marketers and frequency of visits by the field-force.
- Current usage patterns: products/brands used, quantity used each time, pattern of purchase, loyalty to companies/ brands, etc.
- Can the company capture the white fly pesticide market by reducing price?

I hope we have got it right so far. On the basis of this understanding, we are defining the objectives of the study as determining

1. the farmer's needs: pattern, frequency, and intensity of pest-infestation,
2. the treatment given, and an awareness of various pesticides and the frequency of their use,
3. the parameters on which various pesticides are evaluated,
4. the perceptions of various brands on major parameters, especially on price,
5. actual patterns of use of pesticides; reasons for variation from prescribed patterns; actual costs of use,
6. the response to the new product concept (Tatamida), and
7. future purchase intent towards Tatamida.

We intend to conduct the study in the four major cotton-producing states of Punjab, Haryana, Gujarat, and Rajasthan. As indicated by your office, Andhra Pradesh will not be covered. We will interview 720 farmers and 144 dealers in 16 districts in these states. The districts will be selected by your field-force. The farmers will be interviewed in the local language by our investigators who are based in those states. A semi-structured questionnaire will be used for the purpose, after it is approved by your office. The dealers will be interviewed either in English or in the local language by our staff, using a discussion guide approved by your office. The discussion guide for interviewing the dealers will also be sent to you for approval. Do let me have your response to these points at your earliest convenience, so that we may send you the formal proposal.

Regards,
Yours truly
Supriya Chawla,
Director, Marketing Services,
Innovative Strategy Consultants.

Chandrashekhar wrote back his approval immediately, asking them to add 'estimation of sales of Tatamida' as one of the objectives, and send their formal proposal including the total cost of the project as well as the time likely to be taken.

Week 8

A week after receiving the formal approval of the final proposal, the field staff of Innovative Strategy Consultants, Marketing Research Division, had spread out in the field. Data collection took two weeks. It was now eight weeks since the initial meeting that Raghu and Supriya had had with Chandrashekhar, and the field data that came in had been edited and tabulated. The research executive in charge of the project had just had the tables prepared when Supriya Chawla phoned, 'Aman, how is the progress on that Rallis project?' On being told that the data tables were ready, she asked him to bring them in to her office. Aman did as he was asked, and now they sat together, poring over the tables (Tables 14.8–17), as well as discussing the data and the information they revealed.

TABLE 14.8   Methods of Handling Pests

Methods	Punjab		Haryana*		Rajasthan		Gujarat		Total	
	No.	%	No.	%	No.	%	No.	%	No.	%
Use Pesticides	179	85.24%	181	86.19%	90	100.00%	195	93.00%	645	89.58%
Wait and See	18	8.57%	27	12.86%	0	0.00%	11	5.20%	56	7.78%
Use Kerosene etc.	7	3.33%	12	5.71%	0	0.00%	0	0.00%	19	2.64%
Don't do Anything	6	2.86%	0	0.00%	0	0.00%	4	1.90%	10	1.39%
Total no. of respondents	210	100.00%	210	100.00%	90	100.00%	210	100.00%	720	100.00%

* Multiple responses indicate simultaneous use of more than one method.

Table14.9   Trial of Pesticides

Pesticides	Punjab		Haryana		Rajasthan		Gujarat		Total	
	No.	%	No.	%	No.	%	No.	%	No.	%
Fenvalerate	160	76.19%	171	81.43%	90	100.00%	156	74.29%	577	80.14%
Acephate	174	82.86%	145	69.05%	87	96.67%	138	65.71%	544	75.56%
Ethion	184	87.62%	161	76.67%	90	100.00%	71	33.81%	506	70.28%
Cyper	144	68.57%	137	65.24%	90	100.00%	46	21.90%	417	57.92%
Confidor	174	82.86%	84	40.00%	38	42.22%	90	42.86%	386	53.61%
Alpha	147	70.00%	99	47.14%	80	88.89%	42	20.00%	368	51.11%
Hostathion	121	57.62%	114	54.29%	61	67.78%	72	34.29%	368	51.11%
Quinalphos	110	52.38%	105	50.00%	49	54.44%	102	48.57%	366	50.83%
Pride	110	52.38%	12	5.71%	6	6.67%	46	21.90%	174	24.17%
Actatra	83	39.52%	36	17.14%	6	6.67%	49	23.33%	174	24.17%

Table continued

Table 14.9 continued

Pesticides	Punjab		Haryana		Rajasthan		Gujarat		Total	
	No.	%	No.	%	No.	%	No.	%	No.	%
Delta	75	35.71%	48	22.86%	7	7.78%	15	7.14%	145	20.14%
Nagata	55	26.19%	28	13.33%	4	4.44%	37	17.62%	124	17.22%
Monchorto	0	0.00%	0	0.00%	0	0.00%	34	16.19%	34	4.72%
Avant	0	0.00%	0	0.00%	0	0.00%	17	8.10%	17	2.36%
Total no. of respondents	210	100.00%	210	100.00%	90	100.00%	210	100.00%	720	100.00%

Table14.10 Pesticides Commonly Used For Wf

Pesticides	Punjab		Haryana		Rajasthan		Gujarat		Total	
	No.	%	No.	%	No.	%	No.	%	No.	%
Confidor	127	60.48%	40	19.05%	22	24.44%	13	6.19%	202	28.06%
Ethion	82	39.05%	53	25.24%	19	21.11%	12	5.71%	166	23.06%
Monochrotophos	0	0.00%	71	33.81%	57	63.33%	23	10.95%	151	20.97%
Fenvalerate + mono	49	23.33%	77	36.67%	16	17.78%	5	2.38%	147	20.42%
Actara	33	15.71%	0	0.00%	1	1.11%	86	40.95%	120	16.67%
Acephate	36	17.14%	20	9.52%	0	0.00%	44	20.95%	100	13.89%
Endosulphan	64	30.48%	0	0.00%	3	3.33%	27	12.86%	94	13.06%
Cypermethrin	0	0.00%	0	0.00%	13	14.44%	44	20.95%	57	7.92%
Ecalux	0	0.00%	13	6.19%	0	0.00%	27	12.86%	40	5.56%
Others	60	28.57%	88	41.90%	6	6.67%	75	35.71%	228	31.67%
n.a.	39	18.57%	0	0.00%	0	0.00%	0	0.00%	39	5.42%
Total no. of respondents	210	100.00%	210	100.00%	90	100.00%	210	100.00%	720	100.00%

Table 14.11 Most Important Factors in Selecting a Pesticide

Factors	Punjab		Haryana		Rajasthan		Gujarat		Total	
	No.	%	No.	%	No.	%	No.	%	No.	%
Company's reputation	184	87.62%	107	50.95%	19	21.11%	141	67.14%	451	62.64%
No. of days of control	183	87.14%	47	22.38%	48	53.33%	149	70.95%	427	59.31%
% clean-up	171	81.43%	93	44.29%	47	52.22%	99	47.14%	410	56.94%
Price	144	68.57%	50	23.81%	16	17.78%	129	61.43%	339	47.08%
Prev. exp. with co.	85	40.48%	49	23.33%	32	35.56%	134	63.81%	300	41.67%
Dose pre acre	119	56.67%	39	18.57%	0	0.00%	78	37.14%	236	32.78%
Side-effects	27	12.86%	58	27.62%	5	5.56%	31	14.76%	121	16.81%
Relationship with rep.	18	8.57%	40	19.05%	0	0.00%	63	30.00%	121	16.81%
Whether Effective Alone	50	23.81%	9	4.29%	0	0.00%	20	9.52%	79	10.97%
Schemes/Gifts	4	1.90%	13	6.19%	0	0.00%	20	9.52%	37	5.14%
Others	8	3.81%	33	15.71%	0	0.00%	63	30.00%	104	14.44%
n.a.	0	0.00%	9	4.29%	12	13.33%	42	20.00%	63	8.75%
Total	210	100.00%	210	100.00%	90	100.00%	210	100.00%	720	100.00%

Table 14.12 Satisfaction Levels with Pesticides Used Most Often

Pesticides Used	Totally Satisfied		Mostly Satisfied		Dissatisfied		V. Dissatisfied		Total N		Average Satis. Index
	No.	% of N	No.	% of N	No.	% of N	No.	% of N	No.	% of N	
Fenvalerate	49	29.34%	71	42.51%	41	24.55%	6	3.59%	167	100.00%	3.0
Acephate	41	29.93%	69	50.36%	27	19.71%	0	0.00%	137	100.00%	3.1
Monocrtophos/Monosyl	47	36.15%	46	35.38%	37	28.46%	0	0.00%	130	100.00%	3.1
Confidor	37	30.08%	58	47.15%	26	21.14%	2	1.63%	123	100.00%	3.1
Cyper	24	23.30%	56	54.37%	23	22.33%	0	0.00%	103	100.00%	3.0
Ethion	8	7.84%	71	69.61%	21	20.59%	2	1.96%	102	100.00%	2.8
Hostathion	13	22.41%	35	60.34%	6	10.34%	4	6.90%	58	100.00%	3.0
Quinalphos	9	17.65%	25	49.02%	12	23.53%	5	9.80%	51	100.00%	2.7
Pride	2	8.33%	19	79.17%	3	12.50%	0	0.00%	24	100.00%	3.0
Alpha	0	0.00%	16	76.19%	5	23.81%	0	0.00%	21	100.00%	2.8
Endosulfan	0	0.00%	17	85.00%	3	15.00%	0	0.00%	20	100.00%	2.9
Actatra	2	15.38%	11	84.62%	0	0.00%	0	0.00%	13	100.00%	3.2
Delta	0	0.00%	3	100.00%	0	0.00%	0	0.00%	3	100.00%	3.0
Stallion	0	0.00%	3	100.00%	0	0.00%	0	0.00%	3	100.00%	3.0
Spark	0	0.00%	5	83.33%	1	16.67%	0	0.00%	6	100.00%	2.8
Tresar	0	0.00%	1	100.00%	0	0.00%	0	0.00%	1	100.00%	3.0
Thiovit	0	0.00%	1	20.00%	4	80.00%	0	0.00%	5	100.00%	2.2
Achook	0	0.00%	0	0.00%	1	100.00%	0	0.00%	1	100.00%	2.0
Others	2	9.52%	11	52.38%	10	47.62%	0	0.00%	21	100.00%	2.0

Table 14.13 Trial of Imida

Whether Tried	Brand/Molecule	Punjab		Haryana		Rajasthan		Gujarat		Total	
		No.	%	No.	%	No.	%	No.	%	No.	%
Yes	Imida (generic)	83	39.52%	108	51.43%	75	83.33%	71	33.81%	337	46.81%
		0	0.00%	2	0.95%	0	0.00%	16	7.26%	18	2.50%
	Confidor	83	39.52%	104	49.52%	75	83.33%	38	18.10%	300	41.67%
	Stallion	0	0.00%	2	0.95%	0	0.00%	5	2.38%	7	0.97%
	Jumbo	0	0.00%	0	0.00%	0	0.00%	12	5.71%	12	1.67%
No		115	54.76%	68	32.38%	0	0.00%	135	64.29%	318	44.17%
Don't Remember		6	2.86%	5	2.38%	15	16.67%	0	0.00%	26	3.61%
n.a.		6	2.86%	29	13.81%	0	0.00%	4	1.90%	39	5.42%
Total		210	100.00%	210	100.00%	90	100.00%	210	100.00%	720	100.00%

Table 14.14 Intent to Try New Formulation of Imida

Intent	Punjab		Haryana		Rajasthan		Gujarat		Total	
	No.	%	No.	%	No.	%	No.	%	No.	%
Will definitely try	149	70.95%	139	66.19%	54	60.00%	15	7.14%	357	49.58%
Likely to try	43	20.48%	50	23.81%	31	34.44%	0	0.00%	124	17.22%
Can't say at this point	11	5.24%	21	10.00%	3	3.33%	3	1.43%	38	5.28%
Not likely to try	1	0.48%	0	0.00%	2	2.22%	3	1.43%	6	0.83%
n.a.	6	2.86%	0	0.00%	0	0.00%	189	90.00%	195	27.08%
Total	210	100.00%	210	100.00%	90	100.00%	210	100.00%	720	100.00%

Table 14.15 Anticipated Effective Dosage Per Acre Against Wf

Anticipated Dosage	Punjab		Haryana		Rajasthan		Gujarat		Total	
	No.	%	No.	%	No.	%	No.	%	No.	%
40–60ml	30	14.29%	27	12.86%	16	7.62%	15	7.14%	88	12.22%
60–80ml	32	15.24%	15	7.14%	23	1095%	47	22.38%	117	16.25%
80–100ml	15	7.11%	4	1.90%	23	10.95%	56	26.67%	90	13.61%
100–150ml	8	3.81%	1	0.48%	15	7.14%	18	8.57%	42	5.83%
>150ml	9	4.29%	3	1.43%	9	4.29%	12	5.71%	33	4.58%
Can't say	80	38.10%	160	76.19%	4	1.90%	0	0.00%	244	33.89%
As company recommends	30	14.29%	0	0.00%	0	0.00%	0	0.00%	30	4.17%
n.a.	6	2.86%	0	0.00%	0	0.00%	62	29.52%	68	9.44%
Total	210	100.00%	210	100.00%	90	42.86%	210	100.00%	720	100.00%
Ave. Dosage (ml)	84.0		69.7		94.8		92.8		88.0	

Table 14.16 Anticipated Effective Dosage Per Acre Against Wf

Intent to Buy (Probability)	Punjab		Haryana		Rajasthan		Gujarat		Total	
	No.	%	No.	%	No.	%	No.	%	No.	%
At Rs. 450/- per acre										
V. likely	71	33.81%	93	44.29%	20	22.22%	32	15.24%	216	30.00%
Might try	45	21.43%	45	21.43%	37	41.11%	85	40.48%	212	29.44%
Can't say	46	21.90%	31	14.76%	9	10.00%	28	13.33%	114	15.83%
Not likely	35	16.67%	34	16.19%	12	13.33%	39	18.57%	120	16.67%

Table continued

Table 14.16 continued

Intent to Buy (Probability)	Punjab		Haryana		Rajasthan		Gujarat		Total	
	No.	%	No.	%	No.	%	No.	%	No.	%
Will certainly not try	7	3.33%	7	3.33%	12	13.33%	13	6.19%	39	5.42%
N.A.	6	2.86%	0	0.00%	0	0.00%	13	6.19%	19	2.64%
Total	210	100.00%	210	100.00%	90	100.00%	210	100.00%	720	100.00%
Ave. Purchase IndexIndex	3.68		3.87		3.46		3.21		3.54	
Probability of purchase	38.92%		45.48%		35.22%		31.68%		38.37%	
At Rs. 300/- per acre*										
V. likely	27	28.72%	50	69.44%	15	45.45%	17	18.28%	109	37.33%
Might try	29	30.85%	12	16.67%	7	21.21%	8	8.60%	56	19.18%
Can't say	13	13.83%	8	11.11%	5	15.15%	6	6.45%	32	10.96%
Not likely	17	18.09%	0	0.00%	6	18.18%	7	7.53%	30	10.27%
Will certainly not try	2	2.13%	0	0.00%	0	0.00%	42	45.16%	44	15.07%
n.a.	6	6.38%	2	2.78%	0	0.00%	13	13.98%	21	7.19%
Total	94	100.00%	72	100.00%	33	100.00%	93	100.00%	292	100.00%
Ave. Purchase Index	3.70		4.60		3.94		2.39		3.58	
Probability of purchase	39.20%		63.33%		46.36%		21.75%		41.62%	

* Asked of those respondents who were unlikely to or netural about buying Tatamida at Rs 450/- per acre.

Table 14.17 Intended Frequency of Use of Tatamida

Frequency	Punjab		Haryana		Rajasthan		Gujarat		Total	
	No.	%	No.	%	No.	%	No.	%	No.	%
Routinely	66	31.43%	139	66.19%	20	22.22%	21	10.00%	246	34.17%
Along with other pesticides	76	36.19%	41	19.52%	42	46.67%	78	37.14%	237	32.92%
Only in severe infestation	15	7.14%	23	10.95%	9	10.00%	21	10.00%	68	9.44%
If other pesticides don't work	21	10.00%	13	6.19%	8	8.89%	28	13.33%	70	9.72%
Can't say	9	4.29%	13	6.19%	0	0.00%	0	0.00%	22	3.06%
n.a.	23	10.95%	1	0.48%	11	12.22%	62	29.52%	97	13.47%
Total	210	100.00%	210	100.00%	90	100.00%	210	100.00%	720	100.00%

Supriya was particularly interested in the tables relating to the awareness of Imida and the future-purchase-intent of Tatamida. What conclusions would Aman draw from the tables? What techniques of analysis would he use? Why? Under what assumptions were those techniques being applied?

Questions

1. If you were the research executive instead of Aman, how would you analyse the data? How would the information pertaining to each of the objectives be obtained from these tables?

2. Give reasons for your choice of data analysis techniques.

3. What conclusions would you draw about the future-purchase-intent towards Tatamida? What price and dosage would you recommend?

REFERENCES

1. Aaker, D., V. Kumar, and G.S.Day 1999, *Marketing Research*, 6th edn, Wiley, India.

2. Borgatti, S.P. 1997, *Multidimensional Scaling*, www.analytictech.com.borgatti/mds.htm, accessed on 23 Feb 2006.

3. Cluster Analysis; *149.170.199. 144/multivar/hc.htm, accessed on 15 Feb 2006.*

4. Green, P.E. and D.S. Tull 1978, *Research for Marketing Decisions,* Prentice Hall.

5. Kruskal, J.B. and M. Wish 1977, *Multidimensional Scaling*, Sage Publications, California.

6. Malhotra, N.K. 2004, *Marketing Research: An Applied Orientation*, Pearson Education, Delhi.

7. Young, F.W.; *Multidimensional scaling* http://forrest.psych.,unc.edu/teaching/ p208a/mds/mds.html, Dec., 2005. Original *y* published in Kotz and Johnson (eds) 1985, *Encyclopedia of Statistical Sciences,* vol. 5, John Wiley and Sons Inc.

RELATED READING

1. Cooper, D.R. and P.S. Schindler 1999, *Business Research Methods*, Tata McGraw – Hill, New Delhi, pp 417 –419.

2. Kerlinger, F. 1973, *Foundations of Behavioural Research*, 2nd edition, Surjeet Publications, Delhi.

3. Sengupta, S. 1990, *Brand Positioning: Strategies for Competitive Advantage*, Tata McGraw-Hill, New Delhi.

ANNEXURE 14.1

An Example of Discriminant Analysis Using SPSS

Let us consider the case of 30 final-year MBA students from a business school. Midway through the placement season, the school authorities found that 15 out of these 30 students had already been placed, while the remaining 15 were still to find jobs. Various possible reasons were put forward by the faculty members for this apparent discrepancy. One view advanced was that students who received high scores in the school's entrance test had greater managerial aptitude and, therefore, were more likely to find jobs early. Some other faculty members suggested that the 'smarter' students, i.e., those obtaining better CGPAs (cumulative grade point averages) were the ones who got placed early. A third group was convinced that the student's performance in the placement interview conducted by the company is the most reliable indicator of whether she/he will finally get selected, though the company may take other factors like written tests into account. It was decided to run the scores of the 30 students on these various criteria through a discriminant analysis to determine which, if any, of these three variables most influence a student's chances of early placement. The data relating to this exercise is given below.

Table A   Discriminant Analysis Data for Student Selection

S. No	Score on MBA Entrance Test (out of 400)	Final CGPA (out of 9)	Score on Co. Interview (out of 50)	Selected (=1) Not Selected (=0)
1	250	5.5	20	0
2	270	6.2	25	0
3	300	8.3	35	1
4	325	8.0	30	1
5	200	5.4	25	0
6	360	7.5	40	1
7	210	6.0	45	1
8	290	6.4	30	1
9	250	6.9	30	0
10	320	6.6	35	0
11	240	6.5	20	0
12	300	7.0	40	1
13	280	7.8	25	1
14	290	7.5	25	0
15	250	7.5	30	1
16	320	8.1	40	1
17	275	5.2	25	0
18	260	5.0	30	0
19	300	6.6	35	1
20	250	7.8	20	0
21	300	8.2	40	1
22	275	7.9	35	0
23	360	8.5	35	1
24	205	5.5	20	0
25	270	7.4	30	0
26	250	5.0	25	0
27	250	7.2	35	1
28	325	6.4	25	0
29	330	7.5	35	0
30	260	6.2	30	0

Analysis Case Processing Summary

Unweighted Cases		N	Percent
Valid		30	100.0
Excluded	Missing or out-of-range group codes	0	0.0
	At least one missing discriminating variable	0	0.0
	Both missing or out-of-range group codes and at least one missing discriminating variable	0	0.0
	Total	0	0.0
Total		30	100.0

Group Statistics

VAR00005		Mean	Std. Deviation	Valid N (listwise) Unweighted	Weighted
0.00	VAR00002	265.8824	36.32472	17	17.000
	VAR00003	6.3824	.99952	17	17.000
	VAR00004	26.7647	5.28594	17	17.000
1.00	VAR00002	295.7692	42.41885	13	13.000
	VAR00003	7.4692	.78675	13	13.000
	VAR00004	35.3846	5.57582	13	13.000
Total	VAR00002	278.8333	41.22443	30	30.000
	VAR00003	6.8533	1.05233	30	30.000
	VAR00004	30.5000	6.36696	30	30.000

Pooled Within-Groups Matrices[1]

		VAR00002	VAR00003	VAR00004
Covariance	VAR00002	1525.145	17.342	58.739
	VAR00003	17.342	.836	.667
	VAR00004	58.739	.667	29.291

[1] The covariance matrix has 28 degrees of freedom.

Covariance Matrices[1]

VAR00005		VAR00002	VAR00003	VAR00004
0.00	VAR00002	1319.485	15.485	109.283
	VAR00003	15.485	0.999	1.846
	VAR00004	109.283	1.846	27.941
1.00	VAR00002	1799.359	19.817	−8.654
	VAR00003	19.817	0.619	−0.904
	VAR00004	−8.654	−.904	31.090
Total	VAR00002	1699.454	24.995	122.155
	VAR00003	24.995	1.107	3.024
	VAR00004	122.155	3.024	47.155

Analysis 1: Summary of Canonical Discriminant Functions
Eigenvalues

Function	Eigenvalue	% of Variance	Cumulative %	Canonical Correlation
1	0.927[1]	100.0	100.0	0.694

[1] First 1 canonical discriminant functions were used in the analysis

Wilks' Lambda

Test of Function(s)	Wilks' Lambda	Chi-square	df	Sig.
1	0.519	17.383	3	0.001

Standardized Canonical Discriminant Function Coefficients

	Function
	1
VAR00002	−0.090
VAR00003	0.570
VAR00004	0.797

Structure Matrix

	Function
	1
VAR00004	0.849
VAR00003	0.633
VAR00002	0.408

Pooled within groups correlations between discriminating variables and standardized canonical discriminant functions. Variables ordered by absolute size of correlation within function.

Canonical Discriminant Function Coefficients

	Function
	1
VAR00002	−0.002
VAR00003	0.623
VAR00004	0.147
(Constant)	−8.115

Unstandardized coefficients

Functions at Group Centroids

	Function
VAR00005	1
0.00	−0.813
1.00	1.064

Unstandardized canonical discriminant funtions evaluated at group means

Classification Statistics
Classification Processing Summary

Processed		30
Excluded	Missing or out-of-range group codes	0
	At least one missing discriminating variable	0
Used in Output		30

Prior Probabilities for Groups

VAR00005	Prior	Cases Used in Analysis	
		Unweighted	Weighted
0.00	0.500	17	17.000
1.00	0.500	13	13.000
Total	1.000	30	30.000

Table B Casewise Statistics

Case No.	Actual Group	Predicted Gp.	Highest Gp. P(D>d | G=g) p	df	Highest Gp. P(G=g | D=d)	Highest Gp. Squared Mahala. dist. to Centroid	2nd Highest Gp. Group	2nd Highest Gp. P(G=g | D=d)	2nd Highest Gp. Squared Mahala. dist. to Centroid	Discri Scores Function 1
Original										
1	0	0	0.131319322	1	0.990	2.276838457	1	0.010010738	11.46490998	-2.322315621
2	0	0	0.701752537	1	0.923	0.146655145	1	0.077234745	5.107706065	-1.196351788
3	1	1	0.651880553	1	0.931	0.203537437	0	0.068591272	5.420603249	1.514822912
4	1	1	0.596273254	1	0.683	0.280653431	0	0.317067277	1.815218177	0.533904341
5	0	0	0.471932895	1	0.957	0.517446674	1	0.042617543	6.741320634	-1.532733652
6	1	1	0.582299167	1	0.942	0.302532407	0	0.057641986	5.89080046	1.613701138
7	1	1	0.484636147	1	0.956	0.488412859	0	0.044213298	6.635431201	1.762537085
8	1	0**	0.666099722	1	0.721	0.186198341	1	0.278538331	2.08964547	-0.38188893
9	0	0	0.403385193	1	0.548	0.698211845	1	0.451841953	1.084674237	0.022194727
10	0	1**	0.512954992	1	0.630	0.428034453	0	0.369670101	1.495299135	0.409428257
11	1	0	0.38826283	1	0.967	0.744375545	1	0.032889066	7.506721462	-1.676168001
12	1	1	0.705874501	1	0.922	0.142432655	0	0.077980933	5.082635776	1.441074188
13	1	1	0.554720343	1	0.658	0.340920437	0	0.342335303	1.654737531	-0.22269434
14	0	0	0.703458973	1	0.740	0.144898528	1	0.259767835	2.239249691	-0.432740596
15	1	1	0.504340573	1	0.624	0.445790948	0	0.375564247	1.462628732	0.395995897
16	1	1	0.309432609	1	0.975	1.033096023	0	0.02485401	8.372232175	2.08008499
17	0	0	0.30890109	1	0.975	1.03536849	1	0.024803233	8.378699029	-1.830926573
18	0	0	0.710444887	1	0.921	0.137832991	1	0.078814159	5.054971259	-1.184654647
19	1	1	0.543219257	1	0.650	0.36960573	0	0.349662212	1.610654373	0.455719598
20	0	0	0.939407046	1	0.870	0.005778303	1	0.129613876	3.814532482	-0.889411138
21	1	1	0.260586979	1	0.980	1.265635911	0	0.020364213	9.012439387	2.188676527
22	0	1**	0.795006764	1	0.905	0.067503643	0	0.095402858	4.566265955	1.323486309
23	1	1	0.662200118	1	0.930	0.190862037	0	0.070322867	5.354342692	1.500549277
24	0	0	0.160091434	1	0.988	1.973362215	1	0.012146075	10.77041983	-2.218160102
25	0	1**	0.437591166	1	0.576	0.602590947	0	0.42443697	1.211761408	0.28740436
26	0	0	0.278246522	1	0.978	1.175634487	1	0.021946995	8.769501801	-1.897662786
27	1	1	0.905732855	1	0.823	0.014023902	0	0.17662188	3.092832624	0.945249122
28	0	0	0.69975101	1	0.923	0.148731013	0	0.076874211	5.119921099	-1.199052588
29	0	1**	0.907107825	1	0.824	0.013615935	0	0.176148706	3.098938902	-0.94698434
30	0	0	0.70666141	1	0.742	0.141634566	1	0.258214601	2.252172479	-0.437052308

** Misclassified case

Classification Results[1]

		VAR00005	Predicted Group Membership		Total
			.00	1.00	
Original	Count	0.00	13	4	17
		1.00	2	11	13
	%	0.00	76.5	23.5	100.0
		1.00	15.4	84.6	100.0

[1] 80.0% of original grouped cases correctly classified.

ANNEXURE 14.2

An Example of Factor Analysis Using SPSS

A study with entrepreneurs aimed at determining the reasons for success or failure of small businesses, a sample of 150 entrepreneurs was asked to indicate the perceived areas of strength of their organizations. Their responses identified 11 variables rated on a five point scale, where '1' indicated 'very weak area' and '5' indicated 'very strong area'. In the opinion of the research analyst, some of these 11 variables appeared to be correlated, and were therefore not providing a great deal of additional information. He felt that it would make sense to group the correlated variables together, so that it may be possible to work with a reduced set of data without losing out on much information. He opted for factor analysis for this purpose. The details of factor analysis performed by him on the data in Table C are shown in this section.

Table C Perceived Organizational Strengths

Sl. No	Location of firm/ business	Type of plant, equipment, and other physical facilities	Product/ service quality	Pricing of products/ services	Customer services	Innovations in product/ services offered	Cost control	Employee productivity	Marketing (personal selling, promotion, adv, etc)	Cash and finan- cial mgmt	Overall quality of mgmt
	1	2	3	4	5	6	7	8	9	10	11
1	3	3	5	3	5	4	2	2	4	3	3
2	4	1	4	4	3	3	3	—	4	—	4
3	5	5	5	5	5	5	5	5	—	—	5
4	4	—	5	5	5	5	5	4		5	5
5	4	4	5	5	3	5	4	4	5	4	5
6	4	5	5	5	5	5	4	4		—	5
7	4	5	5	5	5	2	4	4	2	4	5
8	5	5	5	5	5	5	5	—	—	—	5
9	5	5	5	4	5	5	4	4	5	5	5
10	5	—	5	5	5	5	—	1	3		5
11	4	3	5	4	5	5	3	4	2	4	5
12	4	3	4	5	5	5	4	5	3	5	5
13	3	4	4	5	5	4	4	4	—	4	4
14	—	—	4	4	5	—	4	4		2	3
15	1	—	5	5	5	1	5	2	5	5	5
16	2	3	4	2	4	4	3	—	2	4	4
17	4	3	5	4	5	5	4	3	2	5	5
18	4	5	5	3	5	4	3	4	1	4	5

(Table C continued)

(Table C continued)

Sl. No	Location of firm/business	Type of plant, equipment, and other physical facilities	Product/service quality	Pricing of products/services	Customer services	Innovations in product/services offered	Cost control	Employee productivity	Marketing (personal selling, promotion, adv, etc)	Cash and financial mgmt	Over all quality of mgmt
	1	2	3	4	5	6	7	8	9	10	11
19	5	1	5	1	5	1	3	3	1	5	5
20	3	3	5	4	4	5	4	4	4	4	4
21	5	4	5	-	5	5	5	5	3	5	5
22	5	5	4	3	4	2	2	2	-	1	3
23	-	5	5	5	3	5	5	-	5	5	3
24	5	-	4	5	5	-	4	4	3	4	4
25	4	4	4	3	5	4	3	3	4	4	5
26	5	-	5	5	5	-	5	4	5	5	4
27	5	3	5	3	5	4	3	4	1	4	5
28	4	3	5	3	5	2	2	5	2	3	5
29	3	5	5	3	5	4	3	5	2	3	4
30	5	4	5	5	5	4	3	3	3	5	5
31	5	3	5	5	5	4	4	3	1	4	5
32	5	2	5	5	5	4	3	3	1	4	5
33	5	4	5	4	5	5	4	4	2	3	5
34	5	5	5	5	5	3	3	2	2	5	5
35	5	-	5	4	5	5	-	-	-	-	5
36	5	4	5	5	5	5	-	5	-	5	5
37	5	-	5	5	5	3	-	3	3	3	5
38	3	-	5	4	5	5	4	3	3	3	3
39	2	4	5	4	5	5	4	4	3	3	4
40	4	3	5	4	4	5	5	3	5	4	5
41	-	4	5	3	5	5	2	5	2	3	3
42	5	5	5	3	5	4	5	3	5	5	5
43	5	5	5	5	5	5	4	5	5	5	5
44	3	4	5	5	4	4	3	4	3	3	4
45	3	5	5	5	5	5	4	3	4	5	5
46	5	-	5	5	5	4	-	3	1	3	5
47	5	3	5	3	5	5	3	3	4	4	5

48	5	4	4	4	4	5	5	3	5	2	5
49	4	3	2	3	3	3	5	5	5	5	5
50	5	4	4	3	5	4	5	5	5	5	5
51	5	4	3	4	3	5	5	3	5	3	5
52	5	5	3	3	5	4	4	5	5	3	1
53	5	4	3	3	3	3	5	5	5	4	3
54	5	5	1	5	—	5	5	5	5	5	5
55	5	4	2	4	4	5	5	3	5	3	5
56	5	5	—	3	4	—	5	5	5	—	3
57	5	4	3	4	4	3	5	5	5	5	3
58	5	4	1	4	4	3	5	5	5	5	3
59	5	4	2	4	4	5	3	3	5	2	4
60	5	4	2	3	3	4	4	4	4	4	4
61	5	—	4	4	4	5	5	5	5	—	5
62	5	5	5	2	—	4	5	5	5	3	5
63	5	5	4	5	5	—	5	5	5	—	5
64	5	—	—	4	—	5	5	3	5	5	5
65	5	5	1	—	—	2	5	3	5	4	5
66	5	5	2	4	—	4	5	5	5	2	5
67	5	3	1	5	4	3	5	5	5	4	4
68	5	—	1	3	4	5	5	4	5	1	4
69	5	4	5	4	3	5	5	3	5	—	5
70	5	—	1	—	4	5	5	5	5	4	5
71	—	—	5	—	—	5	5	5	5	—	5
72	3	—	1	3	—	3	5	5	4	—	3
73	5	4	5	4	4	5	5	5	5	—	5
74	4	—	—	—	—	5	5	4	5	—	3
75	—	—	1	—	4	5	4	4	4	3	—
76	—	—	3	3	—	5	5	4	5	—	4
77	—	—	—	4	—	5	4	4	4	3	3
78	—	—	—	—	4	—	5	4	4	—	3
79	4	4	5	4	4	4	4	—	5	4	—
80	4	4	—	4	5	4	4	4	5	5	4
81	4	3	1	3	—	4	5	4	5	—	4
82	4	4	4	4	2	5	4	5	5	2	4
83	5	4	4	4	3	3	4	3	5	4	5
84	5	4	4	3	3	5	5	4	5	—	5

(Table C continued)

(Table C continued)

Sl. No	Location of firm/business	Type of plant, equipment, and other physical facilities	Product/service quality	Pricing of products/services	Customer services	Innovations in product/services offered	Cost control	Employee productivity	Marketing (personal selling, promotion, adv, etc)	Cash and financial mgmt	Overall quality of mgmt
	1	2	3	4	5	6	7	8	9	10	11
85	5	3	4	1	3	4	2	2	4	2	4
86	—	4	5	5	5	5	—	3	—	—	5
87	4	—	5	5	5	5	3	4	—	5	5
88	5	—	4	4	5	3	3	3	5	5	5
89	5	3	5	5	5	4	3	3	4	4	5
90	4	4	5	5	5	5	4	4	5	5	5
91	5	—	5	5	5	5	—	2	5	4	5
92	5	3	5	5	5	3	4	4	1	4	5
93	4	3	5	4	5	3	3	3	1	3	5
94	5	5	5	3	4	4	3	5	3	4	5
95	5	3	5	5	5	4	3	3	3	4	3
96	5	1	5	5	5	1	4	3	5	5	3
97	2	2	4	4	5	3	2	4	1	2	3
98	1	5	4	4	3	5	4	4	2	3	5
99	5	4	5	3	4	5	3	4	5	4	5
100	5	—	5	5	5	5	—	—	5	—	5
101	—	—	5	—	5	—	—	—	—	—	5
102	5	4	5	5	5	5	—	3	2	5	5
103	5	4	5	5	5	5	—	—	—	—	5
104	5	—	5	5	5	5	5	5	—	5	5
105	5	5	5	5	5	5	4	5	5	4	5
106	5	5	5	5	5	5	—	4	5	—	5
107	5	2	3	4	5	5	5	—	—	—	—
108	—	—	—	—	—	—	—	—	—	—	4
109	—	4	3	5	5	5	4	—	5	5	5
110	1	—	3	—	5	5	5	5	—	5	5
111	2	—	5	5	5	4	5	3	4	4	5

	112	113	114	115	116	117	118	119	120	121	122	123	124	125	126	127	128	129	130	131	132	133	134	135	136	137	138	139	140	141	142	143	144	145	146	147	148	149	150
	4	4	5	3	5	4	4	3	4	5	4	–	5	5	5	3	5	4	5	5	5	4	4	5	5	5	–	5	–	–	5	4	5	5	–	–	5	–	5
	4	2	3	–	4	3	5	1	4	4	3	–	5	5	5	2	5	3	5	5	5	5	3	4	–	5	4	–	5	–	–	2	–	–	–	–	–	–	–
	4	4	2	–	4	5	3	–	4	–	3	1	5	–	5	2	1	3	2	2	3	3	1	–	2	1	–	–	–	–	–	1	–	–	5	–	–	–	–
	4	3	5	5	4	3	3	3	4	4	4	–	3	5	5	4	3	4	4	3	3	4	3	–	3	3	–	5	–	–	3	4	4	5	–	–			
	4	–	4	2	4	3	4	1	4	4	3	2	5	4	5	4	5	5	4	3	–	4	3	5	5	–	–	–	–	3	–	4	5	4	–				
	5	5	4	5	5	5	5	5	5	4	5	5	5	5	4	5	2	3	4	5	5	5	4	5	–	3	5	–	–	–	–	3	–	4	4	–	5		
	4	5	5	5	5	4	4	5	5	3	5	4	5	5	5	4	5	4	5	5	5	5	5	5	5	5	–	5	–	4	4	5	4	–	4	5			
	5	4	4	5	4	4	5	2	4	4	3	5	5	5	5	4	5	5	5	5	4	4	5	3	1	5	–	–	–	3	4	4	4	–	4	–			
	5	4	5	5	5	5	5	4	5	5	4	5	5	5	2	5	5	5	5	5	5	5	2	5	–	5	–	5	5	5	4	–	4	4					
	3	3	4	–	3	3	5	–	5	5	5	–	5	5	4	–	5	–	4	4	4	3	4	5	3	5	–	–	–	3	–	4	–	–	–				
	3	3	4	5	4	5	5	1	4	4	3	4	3	4	–	5	2	5	5	5	5	5	5	1	–	–	–	–	–	5	4	4	4	4	–				

Factor Analysis

Correlation Matrix

		VAR00001	VAR00002	VAR00003	VAR00004	VAR00005	VAR00006	VAR00007	VAR00008	VAR00009	VAR00010	VAR00011
Correlation	VAR00001	1.000	-.114	.317	-.008	.142	.022	-.185	.035	.127	.107	.217
	VAR00002	-.114	1.000	.120	.245	-.087	.170	.240	.168	.101	.212	.272
	VAR00003	.317	.120	1.000	.372	.214	.017	-.056	.070	-.026	.033	.019
	VAR00004	-.008	.245	.372	1.000	.193	.135	.304	-.023	.073	.307	.012
	VAR00005	.142	-.087	.214	.193	1.000	-.186	.147	.088	-.157	.255	.152
	VAR00006	.022	.170	.017	.135	-.186	1.000	.167	.097	.376	.032	.024
	VAR00007	-.185	.240	-.056	.304	.147	.167	1.000	.243	.312	.547	.294
	VAR00008	.035	.168	.070	-.023	.088	.097	.243	1.000	.083	.000	.178
	VAR00009	.127	.101	-.026	.073	-.157	.376	.312	.083	1.000	.238	-.077
	VAR00010	.107	.212	.033	.307	.255	.032	.547	.000	.238	1.000	.439
	VAR00011	.217	.272	.019	.012	.152	.024	.294	.178	-.077	.439	1.000

Communalities

	Initial	Extraction
VAR00001	1.000	.853
VAR00002	1.000	.625
VAR00003	1.000	.792
VAR00004	1.000	.788
VAR00005	1.000	.566
VAR00006	1.000	.607
VAR00007	1.000	.742
VAR00008	1.000	.571
VAR00009	1.000	.757
VAR00010	1.000	.792
VAR00011	1.000	.704

Extraction method: principal component analysis.

Total Variance Explained

Component	Intial Eigenvalues			Extraction Sums of Squared Loadings			Rotation Sums of Squared Loadings		
	Total	% of Variance	Cumulative %	Total	% of Variance	Cumulative %	Total	% of Variance	Cumulative %
1	2.481	22.556	22.556	2.481	22.556	22.556	2.003	18.210	18.210
2	1.657	15.068	37.624	1.657	15.068	37.624	1.587	14.431	32.640
3	1.365	12.408	50.032	1.365	12.408	50.032	1.507	13.696	46.336
4	1.200	10.910	60.942	1.200	10.910	60.942	1.366	12.414	58.750
5	1.093	9.936	70.878	1.093	9.936	70.878	1.334	12.128	70.878
6	.951	8.648	79.526						
7	.658	5.980	85.506						
8	.536	4.873	90.379						
9	.436	3.964	94.343						
10	.322	2.924	97.267						
11	.301	2.733	100.00						

Extraction method: principal component analysis.

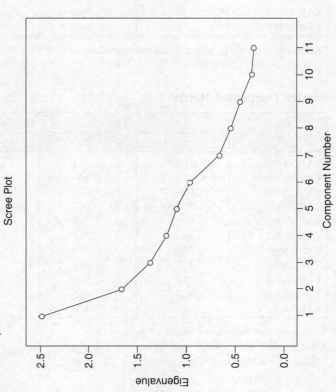

Scree Plot

Component Matrix[1]

	Component				
	1	**2**	**3**	**4**	**5**
VAR00001	.125	.467	.465	.611	−.171
VAR00002	.509	−.206	−.003	−.156	.547
VAR00003	.253	.534	.598	−.163	.242
VAR00004	.541	.182	.305	−.607	−.012
VAR00005	.289	.648	−.174	−.088	−.156
VAR00006	.304	−.524	.475	.116	.037
VAR00007	.750	−.249	−.289	−.119	−.141
VAR00008	.311	−.067	−.056	.351	.586
VAR00009	.383	−.513	.400	.210	−.378
VAR00010	.756	.096	−.246	.023	−.388
VAR00011	.544	.213	−.367	.452	.155

Extraction method: principal component analysis.
[1] 5 components extracted.

Rotated Component Matrix[1]

	Component				
	1	**2**	**3**	**4**	**5**
VAR00001	.012	.084	.079	.916	.020
VAR00002	.146	.161	.310	−.300	.626
VAR00003	−.140	−.057	.771	.395	.134
VAR00004	.297	.081	.815	−.162	−.052
VAR00005	.403	−.491	.291	.268	−.074
VAR00006	−.006	.751	.115	.004	.173
VAR00007	.760	.219	.086	−.266	.195
VAR00008	.015	.054	−.046	.087	.747
VAR00009	.273	.809	−.022	.130	−.103
VAR00010	.877	.056	.113	.088	.077
VAR00011	.538	−.178	−.156	.280	.529

Extraction method: principal component analysis.
Rotation method: varimax with Kaiser normalization.
[1] Rotation converged in 6 iterations.

Component Transformation Matrix

Component	**1**	**2**	**3**	**4**	**5**
1	.786	.259	.389	.060	.399
2	.053	−.740	.381	.546	−.078
3	−.429	.572	.548	.417	−.123
4	.022	.166	−.610	.697	.339
5	−.441	−.175	.177	−.198	.839

Extraction method: principal component analysis.
Rotation method: varimax with Kaiser normalization.

ANNEXURE 14.3

An Example of Cluster Analysis Using SPSS

In the study discussed in Annexure 14.2, the research analyst noted that some of the entrepreneurs appeared to adopt similar competitive methods, defined by 20 variables. Data on the extent of adoption of these competitive methods was obtained in the form of ratings on a five-point scale, with '1' indicating 'rarely or never used', and '5' indicating 'used very frequently'. All the 150 respondents were asked to provide such ratings, but one respondent did not provide the information. The research analyst decided to use cluster analysis to group the entrepreneurs according to their competitive methods. The data and the analysis are given below.

Table D Competitive Methods

v01	v02	v03	v04	v05	v06	v07	v08	v09	v010	v011	v012	v013	v014	v015	v016	v017	v018	v019	v020
2	4	2	5	3	2	4	4	3	4	5	.	.	.	.	.	.	.	.	.
4	4	4	4	3	.	.	.	.	.	.	.	.	.	.	.	.	4	4	4
5	5	5	4	.	5	.	.	.	5	4	.	.	4	1	5	5	.	.	1
4	5	5	5	3	5	5	1	1	5	5	1	4	1	2	5	5	1	5	4
4	5	5	5	4	5	5	.	.	5	.	5	5	1	5	5	5	5	1	5
.	.	.	5	.	5	5	.	.	.	.	.	.	1	.	.	5	.	.	-4
4	.	4	4	3	4	4	2	1	4	4	3	1	1	1	1	4	1	1	1
2	2	5	4	4	.	5	.	5	5	.	.	.	.	1	.	5	3	3	.
3	5	5	5	3	3	4	1	1	1	5	5	5	.	1	5	4	1	1	1
3	5	5	5	.	3	5	1	1	5	5	.	.	3	1	5	5	5	5	5
2	5	5	5	3	.	4	.	5	5	5	2	5	.	3	5	5	5	1	1
5	5	5	5	3	2	5	2	1	3	5	2	.	1	1	3	5	1	1	2
3	5	5	4	5	5	4	3	3	3	5	3	2	3	1	5	4	.	.	.
2	5	5	.	1	4	5	5	3	4	.	3	1	.	1	.	5	5	.	4
4	.	.	4	5	3	.	.	.	5	.	5	4	5	.	.	5	.	.	5
2	4	4	4	4	5	3	2	4	5	.	5	5	2	3	2	3	4	1	2
3	5	4	5	4	4	3	.	.	4	3	3	1	1	2	.	5	1	1	.
1	4	.	5	.	4	5	.	.	5	.	.	1	1	1	.	4	.	.	1
1	1	4	5	3	4	3	1	1	4	1	1	1	1	1	5	5	1	1	1
4	5	5	3	5	5	4	4	.	5	5	4	4	5	4	5	5	1	.	.
5	3	3	5	5	3	5	4	5	5	5	5	5	2	2	5	5	2	5	5
4	5	5	4	3	3	5	1	1	5	5	5	4	1	2	4	5	4	1	4
1	.	.	5	3	5	5	3	1	5	.	3	3	5	.	5	5	1	5	5
1	5	.	5	4	.	4	.	.	5	.	5	.	1	5	.	5	.	.	3
3	5	5	5	3	3	5	4	1	5	5	4	4	1	4	4	5	4	4	4

(Table D continued)

(Table D continued)

v01	v02	v03	v04	v05	v06	v07	v08	v09	v010	v011	v012	v013	v014	v015	v016	v017	v018	v019	v020
5	4	5	5	1	5	5	4	5	5	4	5	1	1	1	1	5	1	1	5
2	2	4	4	4	2	4	1	1	4	4	·	1	1	1	1	4	1	1	1
2	3	3	5	5	2	5	4	1	5	4	·	2	1	1	1	4	1	1	1
3	5	4	5	5	1	4	1	1	4	4	·	1	1	1	2	4	1	1	2
1	5	2	5	5	2	5	·	1	1	1	1	1	1	1	1	1	1	·	1
3	5	5	5	1	2	5	1	2	3	1	1	1	1	1	1	4	1	·	1
2	3	3	5	3	2	4	2	2	4	4	1	1	1	1	1	4	1	2	1
3	5	4	5	3	2	4	2	·	4	4	·	3	1	1	3	4	3	3	1
1	5	5	5	5	·	·	·	·	5	·	·	·	·	·	·	5	3	3	·
1	·	5	5	·	·	·	·	·	5	5	·	3	·	1	5	5	3	3	·
1	5	5	5	1	5	5	2	·	5	·	1	·	5	1	·	5	5	5	·
4	1	5	5	·	·	5	5	1	5	4	1	3	1	1	2	4	·	·	2
5	5	3	5	3	2	3	2	1	4	5	4	·	2	1	4	5	2	1	2
5	5	5	4	2	1	5	2	1	4	4	1	4	2	2	3	5	2	4	5
2	5	5	5	4	5	5	3	1	5	3	2	2	1	1	1	5	1	1	1
5	5	5	4	4	2	5	2	1	2	3	·	1	1	1	5	2	1	1	5
4	5	4	5	5	1	4	3	5	2	·	·	1	5	3	5	5	2	4	·
3	5	5	5	3	·	4	2	·	5	3	3	5	1	2	4	5	5	1	4
1	1	5	4	4	2	5	·	2	2	2	·	·	·	1	5	2	3	·	-3
3	4	5	5	·	·	5	5	1	5	4	1	1	1	·	1	5	3	2	1
5	5	4	5	3	·	·	2	1	4	5	·	1	1	2	1	4	1	5	1
5	2	5	5	2	3	4	3	1	4	1	3	1	1	2	1	3	1	3	1
2	4	5	5	3	2	3	2	1	3	4	·	2	1	5	2	4	1	1	1
5	5	5	4	3	4	4	4	1	5	4	3	1	3	1	4	5	1	4	1
5	5	4	5	3	3	4	1	1	4	5	·	5	·	1	5	3	4	1	5
1	4	5	5	2	3	4	4	5	1	1	1	1	1	2	5	5	1	3	2
2	5	4	5	5	3	5	2	1	5	5	·	5	1	5	5	4	3	1	1
1	5	5	5	2	·	3	·	1	4	1	3	1	·	1	4	4	1	·	·
5	·	4	4	3	3	5	2	1	5	5	·	·	·	·	·	5	·	·	1
5	3	2	5	4	3	3	3	3	5	·	·	4	3	1	3	5	3	5	1
4	4	4	4	4	4	4	3	1	5	5	1	1	1	1	1	4	1	1	·
2	2	3	4	2	3	3	·	·	4	4	·	·	1	1	1	4	·	1	1

·	5	5	·	·	·	1	1	·	·	5	·	·	1	·	·	4	4	·	4	·	2	1	·	5	·	·	·	1	3	5	1	1	1	·	1	4
2	5	1	·	3	·	·	1	·	·	5	5	5	1	·	·	4	·	4	·	2	1	1	3	·	5	·	·	1	1	1	1	1	·	1	5	
5	5	1	·	3	·	1	5	·	·	5	5	5	1	·	5	·	4	·	4	·	4	1	·	5	·	5	·	1	1	1	1	1	·	1	4	
5	5	5	5	5	5	4	5	5	5	·	·	3	·	5	5	3	·	4	·	4	5	5	5	·	·	·	5	4	4	3	5	5	4	5	
5	2	·	·	·	·	1	1	·	·	1	·	·	2	·	·	·	·	4	5	·	5	·	·	3	1	1	·	1	3	3	3	5	
1	·	·	·	1	1	·	1	1	1	1	·	1	·	·	1	·	3	1	2	·	2	·	1	2	1	1	1	1	1	
1	5	·	·	·	1	5	1	5	5	5	3	1	·	4	·	·	2	5	1	1	·	5	4	4	1	1	1	1	1	1	1	
·	2	·	·	·	2	5	·	·	·	1	·	·	4	·	1	3	·	1	1	1	3	5	
·	·	·	·	4	·	·	3	·	·	5	·	3	5	·	4	4	1	1	·	5	
5	5	·	5	·	4	1	·	5	·	·	4	·	·	·	5	·	5	5	4	·	4	5	1	3	2	4	5	3	5	
5	5	5	5	5	5	4	5	5	·	5	·	·	3	·	·	4	5	5	5	·	2	·	5	4	2	4	5	5	4	5	
4	4	·	·	2	1	·	1	·	1	1	·	3	·	1	·	3	2	1	1	1	1	1	3	
·	1	·	·	3	5	4	·	·	1	·	2	·	1	5	·	5	·	2	2	1	1	1	3	1	1	
5	5	·	5	·	4	4	5	5	·	·	4	5	4	·	·	4	3	5	5	4	5	5	·	5	4	5	4	4	5	2	1	
·	5	·	·	·	3	2	·	·	2	·	·	2	1	3	5	·	·	5	3	2	2	3	3	5	1	
·	4	5	·	3	5	4	5	5	5	·	2	·	2	·	·	·	43	3	4	3	4	·	4	5	3	2	3	3	5	2	5	
5	5	5	5	5	5	5	5	5	5	5	5	5	·	·	4	·	4	5	5	5	·	5	4	5	5	5	4	5	4	5	
5	4	·	5	·	3	1	5	5	5	5	5	4	·	4	4	·	1	5	·	5	3	4	5	5	1	5	5	5	3	
5	5	·	5	·	3	1	·	5	5	5	5	4	5	5	·	4	·	5	3	5	·	5	·	2	4	5	5	1	5	5	4	5	
·	1	·	1	3	5	3	1	·	4	·	1	4	3	3	3	3	·	3	·	4	2	2	1	·	1	4	3	3	5	2	5	5	

(Table D continued)

(Table D continued)

v020	1 5 5 . 4 . . . 5 3 3 5 1 3 1 . 3 1 . 4 5 4 1 5 5 1 1 3 1 1 . 1
v019	4 5 1 5 . . 1 . 1 2 . 5 4 5 . 2 4 5 . . 4 3 1 1 . . 1 4 . 3 5 2 1 3 3
v018	1 1 5 5 . . 5 . 1 5 . 5 5 1 2 5 2 . . . 3 3 5 1 . . 1 5 . 3 1 5 1 3 3
v017	3 5 4 5 . 5 5 5 1 5 3 5 5 1 5 5 5 5 5 5 5 5 5 5 3 5 5 5 5 5 5 5 5 5
v016	1 5 4 . 4 . 5 5 1 5 5 1 5 5 2 5 4 . . . 5 5 5 4 . . 4 5 . 1 . 5 5 5 5
v015	1 1 . 1 . 2 5 1 1 3 . 3 5 1 2 1 3 . 5 . 3 4 3 . 2 . 1 1 . 1 . 1 1 4 1
v014	4 5 2 . . 1 1 3 5 1 5 5 1 2 1 2 . 1 2 3 3 1 . 5 . 1 1 1 1 2 1
v013	2 5 1 . . 5 5 3 4 . 1 5 4 3 2 4 5 . 4 4 . 1 5 1 3 5 . 3 3 2 2
v012	1 1 . . 5 5 . 2 3 . . 3 4 . 5 . 1 3 5 5 . 4 . . .
v011	1 4 2 5 5 5 5 1 1 5 5 5 5 5 . 5 5 5 5 5 3 5 3 5 5 4 4 4 . .
v010	1 1 . 5 5 5 5 5 1 5 5 5 5 5 5 5 5 3 5 5 5 5 4 5 5 5 5 4 5
v09	1 2 . 1 5 3 4 1 2 1 . 1 3 2 4 2 1 5 5 . . .
v08	3 3 4 3 . 3 4 1 3 5 3 1 5 5 . 5 3 4 . 1 3 3 3 .
v07	3 5 4 4 5 5 5 5 5 5 5 5 5 5 5 4 5 4 4 5 4 4 5 5 5 5 5 5 5
v06	1 4 3 . . 1 5 1 4 4 3 4 2 4 3 5 5 3 5 4 3 5 5 4 4 3 4 4
v05	2 5 5 2 . 4 4 5 5 . 5 5 3 3 5 5 4 4 4 1 . 5 3 3 5 3 4 5 3 2 2
v04	3 4 5 5 . 5 5 5 5 5 5 5 5 5 4 5 5 3 4 5 4 5 4 . 5 4 5 5 5 5
v03	4 4 5 5 . 5 5 5 5 5 5 5 4 5 5 5 5 . 5 5 5 . 4 5 . . 5 5 5
v02	4 4 5 5 4 5 5 5 5 3 1 5 5 5 5 5 5 4 5 5 . 4 5 . 4 . 5 5
v01	5 3 2 . 4 . 1 1 1 4 1 2 1 5 5 4 3 5 4 5 4 3 4 4 5 4 3 4 5 3 2 1

·	1	·	·	2	1	5	4	·	5	4	1	·	5	5	5	·	·
3	1	3	·	·	1	·	·	·	·	·	1	·	·	·	·	·	·
3	4	3	·	·	1	·	·	·	·	1	·	·	·	·	·	·	·
5	2	5	5	5	4	5	5	·	4	5	5	5	5	5	·	4	5
5	4	·	·	·	4	·	·	·	5	·	·	·	·	·	·	·	·
1	1	1	1	2	1	·	·	·	·	·	1	·	·	·	·	·	·
1	3	·	·	1	1	·	·	·	·	·	·	·	·	·	·	·	4
·	2	·	·	5	·	·	·	·	4	·	·	·	·	4	4	·	·
·	2	·	·	5	·	·	·	·	·	·	·	·	·	·	·	·	·
·	4	·	·	4	5	·	5	·	5	5	·	·	4	5	5	·	·
5	2	5	5	5	5	·	·	4	·	·	5	5	·	·	·	·	·
·	2	·	·	·	·	·	·	·	·	·	·	·	·	·	·	·	·
2	5	·	·	4	1	·	·	·	·	·	·	·	·	·	·	·	·
5	3	5	5	2	4	4	4	·	4	·	·	·	4	4	5	·	·
·	3	·	·	3	2	·	·	4	·	·	·	·	·	·	·	·	·
1	4	4	·	3	3	·	·	·	·	·	5	5	5	·	·	·	·
5	4	5	5	5	5	·	4	5	5	4	5	4	4	5	·	4	4
5	4	4	·	3	5	5	5	·	5	5	·	·	5	5	5	·	·
5	4	5	·	3	5	5	5	·	5	5	·	·	5	4	5	·	·
2	3	1	1	2	3	4	3	·	4	4	3	3	4	5	4	3	·

Cluster Analysis for Competitive Methods
Case Processing Summary[1,2]

Cases					
Valid		**Missing**		**Total**	
N	**Percent**	**N**	**Percent**	**N**	**Percent**
149	98.7	2	1.3	151	100.0

[1] Squared Euclidean distance used
[2] Average Linkage (Between Groups)

Table E Average Linkage (Between Groups)

	Agglomeration Schedule					
	Cluster Combined			**Stage Cluster First Appears**		**Next Stage**
Stage	**Cluster 1**	**Cluster 2**	**Coefficients**	**Cluster 1**	**Cluster 2**	
1	66	137	0	0	0	58
2	81	83	0	0	0	63
3	10	136	2	0	0	47
4	132	133	3	0	0	43
5	68	146	5	0	0	17
6	53	95	5	0	0	13
7	13	86	5	0	0	18
8	34	69	6	0	0	12
9	141	148	7	0	0	49
10	52	76	7	0	0	22
11	40	50	8	0	0	21
12	34	49	8	8	0	16
13	53	139	8.5	6	0	15
14	74	75	9	0	0	105
15	53	57	9.333333	13	0	18
16	29	34	9.666667	0	12	20
17	68	145	11.5	5	0	36
18	13	53	12	7	15	26
19	21	62	13	0	0	46
20	29	30	13.25	16	0	32
21	40	60	14	11	0	24
22	9	52	15.5	0	10	30
23	27	120	16	0	0	31
24	31	40	16.33333	0	21	28
25	51	94	17	0	0	46
26	13	96	17.16667	18	0	35
27	67	102	18	0	0	84
28	31	35	18.25	24	0	32
29	33	55	19	0	0	40
30	9	125	19.66667	22	0	44
31	27	119	20	23	0	50
32	29	31	20.16	20	28	35
33	44	46	22	0	0	70
34	32	43	22	0	0	61

	Agglomeration Schedule					
	Cluster Combined			**Stage Cluster First Appears**		**Next Stage**
Stage	**Cluster 1**	**Cluster 2**	**Coefficients**	**Cluster 1**	**Cluster 2**	
35	13	29	23.4	26	32	44
36	58	68	23.66667	0	17	62
37	28	128	24	0	0	102
38	15	91	25	0	0	76
39	6	42	25	0	0	55
40	33	93	25.5	29	0	42
41	150	151	26	0	0	78
42	33	92	26.33333	40	0	64
43	132	134	26.5	4	0	80
44	9	13	26.72059	30	35	54
45	4	80	27	0	0	66
46	21	51	27	19	25	72
47	10	36	27	3	0	84
48	11	14	28	0	0	53
49	141	147	28.5	9	0	67
50	24	27	30.66667	0	31	55
51	114	115	31	0	0	74
52	18	135	32	0	0	69
53	11	41	33	48	0	60
54	9	97	34.19048	44	0	57
55	6	24	34.75	39	50	74
56	45	105	37	0	0	99
57	9	131	37.63636	54	0	60
58	20	66	38	0	1	90
59	25	100	39	0	0	95
60	9	11	39.30435	57	53	64
61	32	107	40	34	0	91
62	58	65	40.75	36	0	94
63	81	142	41	2	0	78
64	9	33	41.94231	60	42	75
65	77	88	42	0	0	115
66	4	82	42.5	45	0	105
67	141	144	42.66667	49	0	92
68	23	98	44	0	0	103
69	18	84	44	52	0	87
70	44	101	45	33	0	100
71	39	71	45	0	0	131
72	21	59	45	46	0	81
73	47	56	47	0	0	99
74	6	114	47.16667	55	51	85
75	9	113	48.36667	64	0	77
76	15	118	48.5	38	0	88
77	9	122	49.12903	75	0	87
78	81	150	49.33333	63	41	113

(Table E continued)

(Table E continued)

	Agglomeration Schedule					
	Cluster Combined			**Stage Cluster First Appears**		
Stage	**Cluster 1**	**Cluster 2**	**Coefficients**	**Cluster 1**	**Cluster 2**	**Next Stage**
79	48	110	50	0	0	112
80	38	132	50.33333	0	43	107
81	21	129	50.8	72	0	98
82	7	108	52	0	0	123
83	12	63	52	0	0	126
84	10	67	52.33333	47	27	97
85	6	112	52.5	74	0	95
86	121	130	53	0	0	138
87	9	18	53.76042	77	69	88
88	9	15	54.82857	87	76	96
89	22	138	55	0	0	119
90	20	85	55.33333	58	0	98
91	3	32	56	0	61	96
92	140	141	56.5	0	67	101
93	116	124	58	0	0	124
94	19	58	58.4	0	62	104
95	6	25	60.83333	85	59	103
96	3	9	61.86842	91	88	100
97	10	37	62	84	0	114
98	20	21	62	90	81	104
99	45	47	62.5	56	73	107
100	3	44	64.3254	96	70	108
101	140	143	65.2	92	0	110
102	28	123	66	37	0	120
103	6	23	66.90909	95	68	109
104	19	20	67.53333	94	98	117
105	4	74	68.5	66	14	121
106	54	111	69	0	0	109
107	38	45	69.625	80	99	128
108	3	99	71	100	0	116
109	6	54	73.96154	103	106	111
110	140	149	74.33333	101	0	143
111	6	87	75.13333	109	0	118
112	48	89	76	79	0	135
113	81	90	77.4	78	0	137
114	10	104	78.33333	97	0	136
115	77	103	83	65	0	133
116	3	72	84.02174	108	0	119
117	19	26	84.875	104	0	122
118	6	126	85.3125	111	0	123
119	3	22	86.47872	116	89	120
120	3	28	87.73469	119	102	124
121	4	61	89.4	105	0	132
122	19	117	89.88235	117	0	127

Agglomeration Schedule						
	Cluster Combined			Stage Cluster First Appears		Next Stage
Stage	Cluster 1	Cluster 2	Coefficients	Cluster 1	Cluster 2	
123	6	7	9C.23529	118	82	130
124	3	116	9C.51923	120	93	128
125	17	127	91	0	0	147
126	12	64	91	83	0	140
127	16	19	92.44444	0	122	134
128	3	38	93.79167	124	107	129
129	3	106	94.22581	128	0	130
130	3	6	98.48705	129	123	139
131	39	109	98.5	71	0	135
132	4	73	99.83333	121	0	144
133	77	78	100.3333	115	0	137
134	8	16	100.8421	0	127	136
135	39	48	103.3333	131	112	145
136	8	10	105.3714	134	114	142
137	77	81	107.6667	133	113	142
138	70	121	111.5	0	86	141
139	3	5	113.3537	130	0	140
140	3	12	114.261	139	126	141
141	3	70	124.0426	140	138	143
142	8	77	128.6222	136	137	144
143	3	140	136.0257	141	110	146
144	4	8	140.1583	132	142	145
145	4	39	146.6364	144	135	146
146	3	4	150.2429	143	145	147
147	3	17	163.9384	146	125	148
148	3	79	179.5676	147	0	0

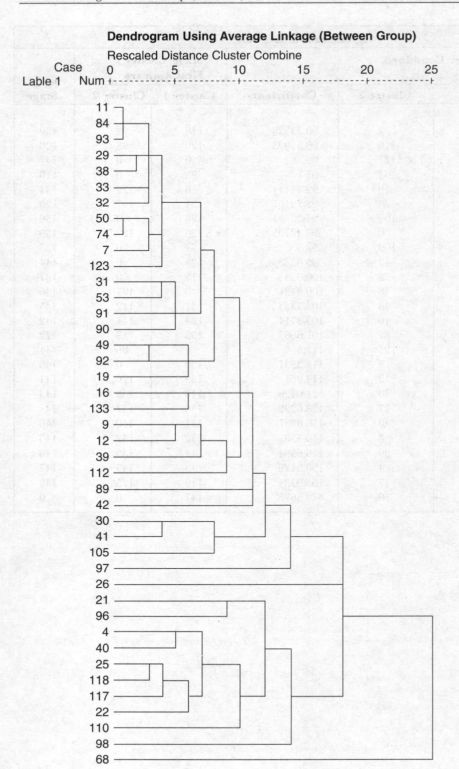

Dendrogram Using Average Linkage (Between Group)

Quick Cluster
Initial Cluster Centres

	Cluster	
	1	**2**
VAR00002	1.00	4.00
VAR00003	0.00	5.00
VAR00004	5.00	5.00
VAR00005	5.00	4.00
VAR00006	0.00	5.00
VAR00007	0.00	5.00
VAR00008	5.00	4.00
VAR00009	5.00	0.00
VAR00010	0.00	5.00
VAR00011	2.00	5.00
VAR00012	0.00	5.00
VAR00013	0.00	0.00
VAR00014	0.00	5.00
VAR00015	5.00	0.00
VAR00016	2.00	0.00
VAR00017	5.00	0.00
VAR00018	0.00	5.00
VAR00019	5.00	0.00
VAR00020	5.00	0.00
VAR00021	0.00	5.00

Iteration History[1]

	Change in Cluster Centres	
Iteration	**1**	**2**
1	8.912	7.431
2	2.152	1.119
3	0.606	0.348
4	0.500	0.270
5	0.428	0.265
6	0.166	0.109
7	0.140	0.093
8	0.149	0.101
9	0.079	0.055
10	0.000	0.000

[1] Converge achieved due to no or small change in cluster centres. The maximum absolute coordinate change for any centre is 0.000. The current iteration is 10. The minimum distance between initial centres is 18.000.

Final Cluster Centres

	Cluster	
	1	**2**
VAR00002	2.18	3.11
VAR00003	2.70	4.31
VAR00004	2.74	4.27
VAR00005	3.98	4.69
VAR00006	1.80	3.39
VAR00007	0.74	3.06
VAR00008	2.59	4.30
VAR00009	0.64	2.02
VAR00010	0.23	1.50
VAR00011	2.67	4.28
VAR00012	1.23	3.74
VAR00013	0.20	1.78
VAR00014	0.36	2.41
VAR00015	1.21	1.60
VAR00016	0.69	1.52
VAR00017	0.46	3.23
VAR00018	3.57	4.41
VAR00019	1.44	2.05
VAR00020	1.43	1.81
VAR00021	1.39	2.24

Number of Cases in Each Cluster

Cluster	1	61.000
	2	88.000
Valid		149.000
Missing		2.000

ANNEXURE 14.4

An Example of Multidimensional Scaling Using SPSS (Proxscal)

A company planning to enter the household detergents market would like to understand how the major detergent brands are viewed by housewives; i.e., how similar or how different from each other the eight selected brands are perceived to be. The objective is to identify the relative perception of these brands, and gaps, if any, in the perceptual space. The company entrusts this task to an MR agency, which decides to carry out a multidimensional scaling exercise for this purpose. A sample of housewives are requested to indicate their perception of how similar or how far apart the eight brands are, without having to define the parameters on which the brands are being compared by them. They are asked to use a ranking scale, where 1 indicates 'most similar' and 8 indicates 'least similar'. The Proxscal method of multidimensional scaling suited to measurement of proximities is used. The perceived similarity ranking by one housewife is given in Table F, followed by the SPSS based analysis.

Table F Perceived Similarities between Detergents

Detergents	Rin	Nirma	Ariel	Surf	Henko	Wheel	Tide	Vimal
Rin	0	2	3	5	4	2	1	8
Nirma	2	0	5	7	6	4	1	3
Ariel	3	5	0	2	5	1	8	7
Surf	5	7	2	0	3	4	7	8
Henko	4	6	5	3	0	7	3	2
Wheel	2	4	1	4	7	0	5	6
Tide	1	1	8	7	3	5	0	2
Vimal	8	3	7	8	2	6	2	0

Proxscal

Case Processing Summary

Cases		8
Sources		1
Objects		8
Proximities	Total Proximities[1]	56[2]
	Missing Proximities	0
	Active Proximities[2]	28

[1] Sum of all strictly lower-triangular and strictly upper-triangular proximities.
[2] Active proximities include all non-missing proximities.

Goodness of Fit

Stress and Fit Measures

Normalized Raw Stress	0.04257
Stress-I	0.20632[1]
Stress-II	0.58554[1]
S-Stress	0.11264[1]
Dispersion Accounted For (D.A.F.)	0.95743
Tucker's Coefficient of Congruence	0.97849

Proxscal minimizes normalized raw stress
[1] Optimal scaling factor = 1.044.

Common Space

Final Coordinates

	Dimension	
	1	**2**
rin	−0.085	−0.373
nirma	0.376	−0.419
ariel	−0.692	−0.027
surf	−0.649	0.496
henko	0.235	0.554
wheel	−0.500	−0.335
tide	0.526	−0.185
vimal	0.788	0.290

Object Points

Common Space

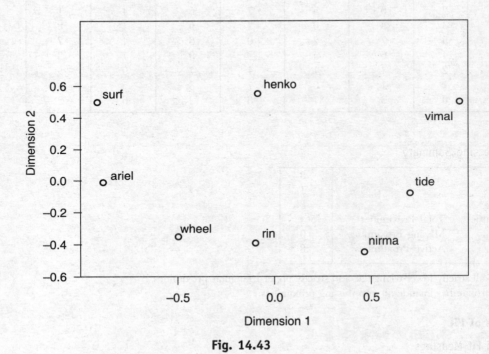

Fig. 14.43

PART FOUR

Qualitative Research and its Implementation

- Qualitative Research

- Qualitative Research Methodology

- Analysis and Interpretation of Qualitative Research Data

15

Qualitative Research

OBJECTIVES

After reading this chapter, the readers will be able to understand:

- what qualitative research delivers in terms of value in the context of a marketing research exercise

- where it can be efficaciously and effectively applied

- what a qualitative researcher needs to do in order to achieve value in research effort

- the relationship between qualitative and quantitative research approaches

- the strengths and limitations of qualitative research

- the steps in the process of conducting a qualitative research

INTRODUCTION

Qualitative research attempts to delve into the mindset of the consumers and bring forth a more holistic understanding of their needs in connection with products, services, and brands so that the marketer may be able to provide a product/service as close as possible to the consumers' verbalized as well as non-articulated expectations, i.e., an offering closer to their needs in comparison to that which the competition offers. This chapter discusses in detail the utility of qualitative research in aiding marketing decision making.

Both qualitative and quantitative research have clear-cut domains of consumer research to which they can do justice and these are not substitutable. Each has its own strengths and limitations. In fact, they complement each other in giving a robust understanding of consumer behaviour in the market. Traditionally, and most often, the approach is to begin a research study with a qualitative research module and then to conclude with quantitative research. The former generates insights which are then validated through measurement by the latter. However, sometimes, qualitative research can also come after quantitative research.

To elaborate on the point being made here, the marketer may begin with qualitative research to determine consumer perceptions *before* undertaking quantitative research in order to develop market potential estimates of the brand. This would be a safer route to marketing decision-making. However, if this is not done, qualitative marketing research may still be undertaken after the launch of the brand, to diagnose reasons behind the difference in consumer acceptance and sales of the two versions of the brand. This has been discussed in detail in a later part of this chapter on diagnostic studies.

It is important to note that qualitative research is not always used 'post-facto', merely to diagnose reasons for manifest problems.

This chapter discusses the various uses of the research approach and goes on to detail its applications in specific marketing situations, such as basic exploratory studies to generate hypotheses about consumer behaviour and provide foresight to the marketer for new product development; explore consumer beliefs, motivations, personality characteristics, and attitudes that are likely to impact behaviour and lead to consumer acceptance of or resistance to marketing decisions; and diagnose attitudinal issues that could be leading to market-related problems. Further, this chapter discusses in detail the use of qualitative research in developing marketing communication, which is a key and growing arena wherein qualitative research is gaining strength.

Limitations of qualitative research, characteristics of good qualitative research, and skills required of a good qualitative researcher have been discussed in the latter part of the chapter.

In the final section of this chapter, there is a brief introduction to the start of the research process, i.e., taking of the research 'instructions' (which is termed as a 'research brief') from the client and converting the same into a comprehensive research proposal which details the approach and understanding of the researcher vis-à-vis the client's information needs and objectives.

QUALITATIVE RESEARCH

We have looked at the 'what' and the 'how' of consumers' needs, and have arrived at quantifiable measures of the nature, intensity, and direction of these needs. If marketing research is to provide a complete understanding of consumer needs, it is equally important to understand the 'why' of these needs, i.e., why do these needs arise; why are decisions made in favour of one brand over the others; why does a consumer behave in a particular manner in a market situation; what factors in the environment and the individual's personal make-up influence her/his needs and behaviour; etc. The understanding of this 'why' will enable the marketer to fashion a market-offering truly aimed at satisfying the consumer better than the competition. The understanding of the reasons behind consumer thinking and behaviour enables the marketer to identify key and vulnerable touch points in the consumer upon which to peg her/his brand, and thus weave out a relevant and impacting marketing strategy.

Qualitative research is that strand of marketing research where the consumer is the focus—her/his multi-dimensional understanding is the core essence of qualitative research. For example, a cigarette manufacturing company might observe through a study of the market that well-known Western brands have the image of being superior to Indian brands, and are well-accepted by the target consumer at much higher prices than upper-end Indian brands. However, if the same Western brand is manufactured under license in India, consumers neither perceive it as having the same quality as its Western counterpart, nor are they willing to pay similar high prices despite the same brand name. This could result in wrong estimates of market-share prior to launching the brand, and a resultant loss in sales revenue. The explanation for this apparently irrational behaviour on the part of the consumer, i.e., the apparent disconnect between consumer perception of the Indian and foreign versions of the same brand, can be provided by qualitative marketing research. In the context of the cigarette example, the brand images of the respective Indian vs. foreign brands play a key role. Thus, qualitative research brings out the finer nuances in the perception of brands by the consumer.

Qualitative research, thus, is concerned more with understanding the reasons (with depths and dimensions) behind the manifested consumer behaviour than with measuring the degree and direction of the difference in which the consumer behaves and the marketer's response to it.

Qualitative research explores and understands—it unearths the 'whys'. To do this, the basic tenets of its approach are: open-endedness, dynamism, flexiblity, penetration of rationalized/superficial responses, depth of understanding, tapping consumer creativity, and providing richer inputs for marketing and creative teams (Fig. 15.1).

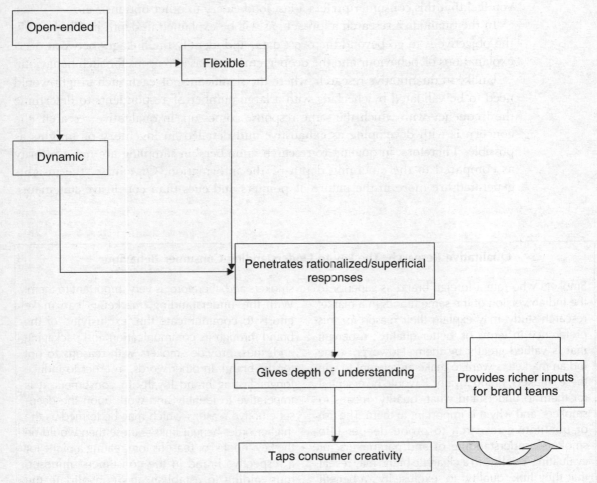

Fig. 15.1 Value-chain of Qualitative Research

Understanding the rational and overt reasons for a particular aspect of human behaviour is important. Quantitative research plays the important role of providing measurement of seemingly rational and overt reasons for human behaviour. Typically in quantitative research, the consumers respond to the options given to them in the questionnaire, while in qualitative research, the consumer is asked open-ended questions wherein he has the freedom to choose his options and respond in the way he sees his world, in the language that he wishes to respond in.

In other words, while a quantitative approach is based on a response framework created by the researcher, the qualitative approach is grounded in the language and symbols of the consumers who are the experts about their world.

A typical question in a quantitative questionnaire would be something like—'Who in your opinion is the main consumer of a fast food eatery—a) Children b) Young Adults c) Teenagers'. However, a qualitative questionnaire would be more on lines, such as—'Who do you feel is the main consumer of a fast food eatery?'; 'What makes you feel that this consumer prefers a fast food eatery to other options?; etc.

In the qualitative research approach, as will be explained in depth in Chapter 17, the objective is to go beyond the overt data, and identify the linkages between overt explanations of behaviour and the deeper, emotion-based reasons for such behaviour.

Unlike in quantitative research, where the significance of each such insight would need to be validated by checking with a large number of respondents to determine the frequency with which the same response comes up, in qualitative research, the concern is with developing as exhaustive and detailed an inventory of insights as possible. Therefore, in qualitative research, 'numbers' in sampling are not a priority as compared to the emerging depth of the information. Of course, the insights generated are more in the nature of pointers and cues than conclusive statements.

Qualitative Research: The key to Understanding Consumer Behaviour

Smokers who rate a foreign brand as superior to the Indian version of the same brand, in a market research study, may explain their reason for this preference in terms of 'better quality', a benefit that is valued greatly by them. However, if the Indian marketers were to make an attempt to win these smokers, brand loyalty, it would be essential for them to understand what 'quality' means to smokers' and why it is important to them. The use of qualitative research to probe deeper into smokers' understanding of and parameters for evaluating 'quality' in a cigarette brand may reveal that they link 'quality' to 'exclusivity', a benefit that relates to their self-concept as discerning smokers and, therefore, is very important to them. With this understanding, marketers can make efforts to communicate the 'exclusivity' of the brand through its communication and packaging and, thus, provide smokers with reasons to opt for the brand. In other words, in order to induce longer lasting brand loyalty in consumers, it is imperative to identify and work upon the deep-set emotive reasons which may be termed as the 'higher order benefit links'—these then would be the key 'hooks' or reasons for creating a niche for a respective brand in the consumers' mindset, thus, aiding to establish and consolidate the brand–consumer relationship.

Product–Benefit Relationship

If consumers are asked why they prefer to shop at Shoppers' Stop over other stores, they would perhaps talk of the quality of the Indian garments available there. Probed further on what they mean by 'quality', they might answer in terms of product attributes like unique cuts, eye-catching latest designs, soft fabrics, and an interesting section of mix and match Indian outfits. In this context, using the 'benefit laddering' approach, if the researcher were to probe deeper into why all the stated factors are important to them, they would perhaps respond by talking about what difference such clothes make to their lifestyles. Still further probing would reveal that that the benefits-perception is linked to their self-confidence amongst peers as well as their images as stylish or discreet shoppers:

Why Shoppers' Stop?

↓

'Quality of Indian garments—fabric, design, cuts, mix n match' (Level 1 product attribute)

↓

'Such clothes make me stand out in society' (Level 2 product benefit)

↓

'I am a stylish and/or careful shopper' (Level 3 product benefit)

Nevertheless, these insight have a fair amount of validity given the depth of the probing done—it is not the first layer of consumer reaction which gets mapped. Significantly, it is the deeper layers answering to the *why* in the probing that are the target for the qualitative researcher.

However, to re-emphasize this point, once the researcher is reasonably certain that all possible 'benefit links in the ladder', as described above, have been explored fully, the next step may be to check out these insights through quantitative research to determine the key reasons for patronizing Shoppers' Stop. One again, the above cited example also serves to show that the two approaches of quantitative and qualitative researches are not substitutes for each other; instead each has its own deliverable and value which is complementary to the other.

Qualitative Research in Application

Having understood what qualitative research entails and delivers, it is now imperative to understand its application context and arenas. Qualitative research can be utilized in five primary areas:

Generating hypotheses

It is used to generate hypotheses on attributes and dimensions of consumer behaviour, in order to evaluate in retrospect and/or develop foresight.

In qualitative research, most studies go into the realm of exploration and/or evaluation—and this attempt yields a lot of perceptions—be it vis-à-vis a product category or a brand. From these perceptions emerge hypotheses in the context of how the product/brand is connecting/not connecting with the consumers, the needs it fulfills for them, its relative assessment vis-à-vis competition, etc.

More often than not, these emerging hypotheses are then validated through the route of quantitative research.

Identifying a range of behaviour

Qualitative research is used for identifying a range of behaviour, therefore giving rise to the need to explore unseen, unknown areas. One of the key tasks of qualitative research is to answer questions such as: 'What is happening', 'What are the habits and practices?', etc. Therefore, in this endeavour, an attempt is made to map behaviour and work out a listing of different types of needs, motivators, barriers, habits, decisions, influencers, preferences, etc.

Exploring and explaining consumer behaviour

Qualitative research can both explore and explain the reasons underlying consumer motivations, attitudes, and behaviour, therefore satisfying the need to understand and/or get a feel of the consumer behaviour dynamics and unearth reasons that would explain certain observed phenomena and the 'how's of behaviour.

By definition, the core of qualitative research is to understand how to bring out the *reasons* behind a respective thought, feeling, decision, or behaviour. In this attempt, the probing of the consumers' mindset is done with the main objective of seeking an explanation. In other words, diagnosis is the goal of probing.

Providing creative inputs

Qualitative research can provide creative inputs to a future stage of research and/or development, therefore, emphasising the need for creative generation of ideas.

By nature, qualitative research is open-ended and penetrates the superficial to reach the emotive layers in the consumers' mind. Therefore, each consumer, along with the researcher, explores her/his own mind and brings out new thoughts and feelings which even she/he may have been be unaware of till the time of the research—these then become creative inputs for the researcher.

Thus, in a nutshell, the essence of qualitative probing is to reach to the depths of human thinking; this attempt helps to generate deeper and creative dimensions of consumer thinking and behaviour.

Importantly, as a process, qualitative research often uses the technique of brainstorming, wherein there is a free-wheeling of ideas. Brainstorming refers to creative sessions held to generate inputs for new product development as well as for developing brand communication and innovative marketing strategies for the client.

Providing preliminary inputs

Qualitative research may be used to provide preliminary inputs for quantitative validation as well as for the formation of the quantitative questionnaire. It is therefore used when there is a need to map consumer perceptions and language of expression.

Traditionally, in a research study, the qualitative research module precedes the quantitative research module—and, in such a case, qualitative findings are given as inputs to be validated and measured through the quantitative research approach.

Also, importantly, the language of the quantitative research questionnaire has to make sense to the consumer, it has to talk his language—only then will the respective questions be relevant and make sense to the consumer. For this the inputs from the qualitative research exercise are crucial.

Qualitative Research—Correct Usage

Having explained the basic scope of qualitative research, we will now discuss specific and frequently researched upon areas of information where qualitative research is most effective and valuable. These areas may be categorized as:

- basic exploratory studies
- diagnostic studies
- new product development studies
- communication development studies

Before we move to understanding each of these types of studies in more detail, it needs to be emphasized here that these studies are not necessarily mutually exclusive—in the sense that for new product development, as the starting point, one would require a basic exploratory phase, as also for diagnostic studies.

In other words, many a times the line of differentiation between one type of study may not be very distinct as compared to another type of study—the areas of enquiry are largely interrelated.

Basic exploratory studies

Qualitative research is frequently conducted to examine consumer attitudes and behaviour in relation to product categories or services, with the specific aim of understanding consumer relationships with brands. Here the objective of research would be exploration of the consumers' lives, perceptions, attitudes, and mindsets from the grassroot level—basically aiming to understand the emotive and sub-conscious processes, apart from the conscious ones, that underlie human attitude and behaviour.

Nature of the Study

In a study on one of the food items of an eatery, the client wanted to understand why their food product was not preferred as much as other products, especially considering it was a new product. The research was, of course, a diagnostic study; however, in the process of understanding the reasons behind the lack of preference for the product, a probing was first done to understand the palate preferences of the consumers followed by evaluation of the test product in the context of these preferences in order to understand the problem with the respective test product. Therefore, the research exercise was exploratory as well as diagnostic in nature.

Exploratory Studies

In a study conducted for a client manufacturing condoms, the objective was to attain an under-standing of the mindset, lifestyle, and needs of contemporary youth. They wanted to know 'what youth are like today and how they are likely to evolve tomorrow'. In this research, an attempt was made to understand the contemporary youths' basic beliefs, aspirations, weak-nesses, attitudes, etc.; in sum, their frames of reference in life. From this data the client wanted to derive cues for the communication strategy which would help the brand develop a better connect (at an emotive level) with this consumer segment that was their core target group.

In another study related to an eatery, the objective was to understand a certain city in terms of 'the psychographics and lifestyle of the city, what the people were like, their recreation preferences', etc. in general; the next-level objective was to understand their food consumption lifestyle, habits, and preferences along with their needs and expectations vis-à-vis eating out. Thus, from this data the client wanted to derive pointers on how to enhance the presence of their brand within the food consumption lifestyle of the consumers of the respective city—mainly to establish a stronger brand–consumer relationship and get the desired edge over competition.

Diagnostic studies

Diagnostic studies are related to exploratory studies, however, the objective of the former type of studies is more focused as compared to that of the latter. For example, in one kind of a diagnostic study the marketer gives the research agency a brief that their brand/advertising is not meeting the sales target—the agency must find out what and where the problem is (i.e., aiming to understand the 'wear-out' of brand, and/or its advertising) and also how to resolve the problem.

In another diagnostic study, the marketer could be faced with a question such as: 'Am I targeting the right consumer?'

Alternatively, the marketer can tell the researcher to understand and find out why the competition brand is selling better as compared to her/his brand—here the requirement would be to do some sort of a competition 'snooping'.

Diagnostic Studies

One marketer's problem was that the advertising of his brand (related to an eatery) did not seem to be making any impact on the target consumers as evident in the dropping sales transactions in his outlet. Also, he felt that the advertising of one major competing brands seemed to be doing very well in comparison. Thus, a qualitative diagnostic study was initiated wherein the first attempt was to understand the perceptions of the niche occupied by the client's brand and its advertising communication, the areas of satisfaction and dissatisfaction vis-à-vis the brand and its communication, and the needs gaps emerging

from the equation of expectations versus experience. Further, such similar objectives were fulfilled for the competition brand as well, leading to a comparative assessment of the two brands and their respective advertising, on the basis of consumer reactions. This assessment revealed clear-cut insights regarding where and why the competition brand and its communication was scoring over the client's brand. Continuing with this line of probing then came the generation of solutions, from the consumer point of view, as to how to leverage the client's brand and its communication over the competition brand.

Thus, in a diagnostic study, the key tasks of qualitative research for all the problems would be to explore, understand, and identify the reasons behind the stated problem as well as generate solutions.

New product development studies

An existing brand, in order to grow better in the market, from time to time may need to be infused with 'new life' so that new consumers get attracted to the brand, existing consumers become more loyal to it, etc. Therefore, a brand extension may be required—whether vertical or horizontal. In both cases, research is required to generate 'ideas'—this is then a study for new product development (NPD).

In such studies, qualitative research aims to find out where 'gaps' may lie for a new product, given the context of the consumer's evolving lifestyle and needs. Essentially, here the research would yield perspectives and pointers for the development of an NPD proposition, which need not be for a product alone, but could be in the realm of packaging, positioning, and promotion/advertising as well. In this endeavour, the task of qualitative research would be two-fold:

(i) Creatively explore the consumer's current need gaps and futuristic needs with respect to any aspect of the concerned brand/product.

(ii) Based on the NPD pointers that emerge, then develop these needs into baseline concepts and understand further the strengths and weaknesses of the 'new products' in order to guide the product architecture more comprehensively. One important question to answer at this stage is—why is an NPD study undertaken?

So, what is the need for an NPD study? The answer to this root question is as follows:

Over a period of time, boredom and fatigue affect the mind of the consumer with respect to a product/brand. Therefore, the marketer feels the need to bring in modifications in order to enhance into the brand–consumer relationship, either through new product variants such as a fast food joint coming up with a teen café or through a re-positioning of the brand, for example, a fruit juice brand positioned as a 'brand for fun' for the young adult could get repositioned as a 'good-for-health' brand for all consumers.

Brand Extension

If Mahindra Tractors bring out a new tractor that is specially designed for the transportation of people and goods, apart from farming application, then it will become a horizontal extension of the brand—wherein the brand is still within the same product category. However, if the brand starts to manufacture cranes for rural construction work under the same brand name, then this becomes a vertical extension of the brand—wherein the same brand name is now being used for another product category altogether.

Creativity and Brainstorming for New Product Development

In one study, the research task was to understand existing perceptions and needs vis-à-vis selling, related to the insurance sector. From this, through a process of creative brainstorming the client, through research, inputs on how to change the selling for this product—this process was a NPD effort—generating inputs for product as well as communication changes. Thus, the consumers were taken through a methodology which comprised of brainstorming and a creative session.

The marketer can also expand her/his market by bringing in new consumers with the introduction of new product variants under the same umbrella brand name. Thus, to attract new consumers and increase sales, the qualitative research approach would be two-fold:

(i) to generate a spectrum of unfulfilled, underlying needs of the consumer
(ii) to understand how the consumer wants these needs to be fulfilled – thus eliciting creative insights from brand/product development and positioning

Communication development studies

A client communicates her/his brand as per a strategy which has various components, such as—who to target for the communication, what should be the essence of the communication, which media avenue to choose, etc. From all these components, the task of developing the content (i.e., what to say, in what genre, in what language, etc.) of the communication is where qualitative research is being increasingly used. Such a study is defined as a communication development study.

To further explain the point made above, consider a client who, in tandem with the advertising and research agencies, develops a communication strategy for her/his brand—both in terms of selecting the media (i.e., from where and how to communicate) and communication target and content (i.e., whom to communicate to and what to say). Marketing research plays its role in both these contexts. Qualitative research has a special value to deliver in the second context, i.e., 'whom to communicate to' and 'what to communicate', by first understanding what the consumers need and what their touch-points are, and then by providing inputs as to what will connect with these touch-points such that the consumer–brand relationship is established and further strengthened.

Thus, in this context, qualitative research may be commissioned at three different stages in the advertising/communication development process:

(i) *Strategy definition* 'What' should the advertising communicate to the consumers? At this stage the qualitative research process will focus upon a more creative process to churn out communication cues and perspectives vis-à-vis the brand, and the product category.

(ii) *Executional guidance* Once the strategy is decided, then comes another question—'how' should the strategy be conveyed to consumers, in what format,

Communication Pretesting

In a market research study on a dishwashing liquid, the client first gave the research agency the product concept to be evaluated for appeal and credibility. Once the product concept got assessed qualitatively, baseline print communication concepts were worked out to find out which message and what words would connect well with the consumers. Based on this feedback, as the next step, pictorial storyboards were developed incorporating the brand message that was to be delivered to the consumers. When evaluating these storyboards against a pre-defined set of parameters, further executional cues were generated to refine the communication.

and what should be the specifics (in terms of communication genre, type of characters and their role, etc.) in an advertisement?

In other words, in order to achieve this objective, the qualitative approach will focus more upon how to translate the creative cues and perspectives into specific elements required in execution, for example, the requirement of the nature of characters to symbolize and convey the message and ambience of the advertising situation selected, etc.

(iii) *Pre-testing* Third in the sequence is the need to evaluate the chosen execution(s) to check the communication against the advertising objectives. To achieve this objective, qualitative research pre-sets evaluative parameters, such as clarity of comprehension, intended communication vs the nature of decoded communication, credibility, appeal, etc., and seeks to get reactions on these parameters in order to assess the communication concepts and arrive at the winner concept/execution.

Most often stages (i) and (ii) are combined in one research paradigm, given the time and cost constraints of the client. Stage (iii) would definitely have to be a separate research exercise altogether.

Qualitative Research—Some Words of Caution

As true of life, every perspective and approach has its advantages and lacunae. The main advantage of qualitative research is that the approach is open-ended; hence it is dynamic and flexible. These attributes of the approach enable the marketer to achieve depth of understanding, tap consumer creativity, penetrate rationalized/superficial responses, and, thus, be a richer source of ideas for marketing and creative teams. Also, during the fieldwork, learnings from one phase of the study can be carried over to another, thereby making the data collection process and its output richer due to this flexibility.

All these only highlight the point that nothing goes waste in the process of conducting qualitative research. Every step is a prelude to the next and is connected, thus contributing constructively to the next.

However, one limitation of this research approach is that, in terms of sampling (as will be discussed in the subsequent chapters), the numbers are small and, therefore, it becomes inappropriate to state *conclusions* based on qualitative data interpretation. What the qualitative researcher can say with confidence from the data and analysis is that the findings are 'significant pointers' and cues, although not conclusions and, therefore, these insights would need to be taken through quantitative measurement and validation in order to state them as conclusions.

It is also important to note the manner in which the data is to be reported to the client (this again will be dealt with in detail in Chapter 17). The researcher needs to ensure that what is reproduced is what was said by the consumer, and not the researcher's feelings and thoughts. It is not the researcher's point of view that the client wants to know; it is the consumer speak which has the highest salience for the client and her/his decision-making.

So, in a nutshell, qualitative researchers and qualitative data cannot

- state conclusions—it can only state trends, patterns, or perspectives;
- make categorical and strong statements;
- quantify the output in numerical terms; however, the reactions can be graded as per degree, e.g., weaker vs stronger; greater vs lesser; minority vs significance, and statements can be made in probable terms;
- state a researcher's personal point of view; or
- state data in the language of the researcher. There needs to be 'reporting' of consumer language. Importantly, verbatim responses (i.e., direct quotes of the consumer) cannot be reported in the language of the researcher or in the form of her/his interpretations—they need to be stated as they had been said and meant. There should be no tampering with the language or the meaning.

SKILLS REQUIRED IN A QUALITATIVE RESEARCHER

The skills that enable a qualitative researcher to deliver value are to be understood at two levels—(a) the output of the research, and (b) the specific traits in the researcher.

Output of the research

The consumer insights generated need to have marketing relevance; if the research data says that 'consumers belonging to a certain ethnic community dislike the colour black', the researcher needs to ask—'So what?' The moment she/he can connect the answer with the research task she/he had set out to achieve, the respective consumer insight becomes meaningful and relevant. Otherwise there will be a huge set of data which will be good-to-know information yet irrelevant. Every consumer insight generated must have the power in it to contribute to the research task meaningfully.

Specific traits in the researcher

The core personality traits required to do well as a qualitative researcher are sensitivity, empathy, and a keen sense of logic. Why? The importance of these traits has been explained here.

Sensitivity   This gives researchers the capacity of absorbing both the verbal and non-verbal communication of consumers with alertness. Also, this enables them to be receptive to anything that the consumers may unconsciously reveal about themselves, which could become an eye-opening insight vis-à-vis the task at hand.

Empathy   This may be explained by the statement 'what I do not feel I will not be able to understand'. Thus, the qualitative researcher must be able to *feel* what the consumer is saying in order to get a proper and indepth understanding of the consumer's viewpoint.

More importantly, the researcher needs to shed off personal points of view and biases, and understand how a consumer views a certain brand, given the latter's frame of reference. For each human individual, the frame of reference gets built up from one's experiences and learnings in life; in other words, the conditioning of a person's life over time and experience gives her/him 'windows' for perceiving and assessing life and people. The researcher too, by virtue of being human, would have her/his own frames of reference from which she/he would perceive and understand the consumer. It is these very personal frames of reference that the researcher must keep in check while attempting to understand a fellow human consumer.

A keen sense of logic   This is imperative for qualitative researchers because this will enable them to sift out the 'claimed' responses from the 'real' ones.

This issue of 'claimed vs real' is one of the hazards that come into play when consumers are spoken to (this will be dealt with in detail in the subsequent chapters). More often than not, researchers are faced with certain exaggerated consumer reactions vis-à-vis brands, their positives and negatives; these then are the 'claimed' reactions because there is an innate need of any human to appear 'good' and 'right' in front of others and, therefore, the consumer would try to state the 'right' and 'good' answers in front of the researcher as well.

Hence, at such times, the researcher needs to go beyond the data and logically seek connections between either the suspected claimed reaction and the earlier reactions of that consumer in related contexts, and/or verify such reactions against the market reality of the respective brand/product. If this is done then the researcher will be able to sift out the more 'real' reactions by using a keen sense of logic.

Finally, apart from the discussed skills, the other important requirement is good articulation (both verbal and written) because, at the end of the day, the researcher has to reproduce her/his understanding of the consumer in a language that is meaningful and makes sense to the client, keeping its essence intact.

Think logically

In one research study, during a warm up session, homemakers said that one of their most hated chores was that of washing utensils. Then they discussed what parameters were important for them in selecting a dishwashing product. At this point in time, packaging aesthetics (i.e., the 'look' of the pack, its colours, mnemonics on it, etc.) did not figure in their list of parameters. When the consumers were exposed to the new packaging of a dishwashing bar, one person said, 'now I will feel enthusiastic to wash the utensils because of the new packaging'. In such a case, the researcher should not take this reaction at face value because this could be just a claimed reaction, not really reflecting the truth. In order to decide whether to accept this reaction as a true evaluation of the new packaging, the researcher needed to logically understand and analyse the answers to two questions. One, was packaging a key factor in the dislike for the chore of washing utensils? Two, was packaging a key barrier or a key influencer in the decision-making process of the homemakers when it came to the purchase of a dishwashing bar? Analysis of the responses to these two questions would give the researcher the answer to the dilemma of sifting out the claimed vs. real reaction in the current example quoted. Only the logical thinking ability of a researcher would make it possible for her/him to think that there could be something inappropriate with the consumer reaction of 'now I will feel enthusiastic to wash the utensils', thereby encouraging her/him to look for other supporting comments and verifications in the rest of the data.

CLIENT–RESEARCHER RELATIONSHIP

In the context of today's evolving business scenario and its needs, research is not a product or an output, instead, it is a service, a relationship. This relationship needs to be understood as an interactive and ongoing process.

First, the client–researcher interaction has to go beyond the presentation of the data analysis. The researcher needs to understand the needs and problems of the client's business. Second, the researcher should work upon data interpretation to the extent that she/he delivers actionable pointers.

The researchers should, also, play the role of a consultant, and in this way ensure an on-going relationship with the client's brand. From time to time, value additional inputs should come from the researcher, whereby she/he must be able to correlate consumer dynamics with brand and market dynamics and, thus, extrapolate upon the data wherever possible.

Limiting one's role to that of being an academic researcher will only stunt the growth of a researcher's skills as well as business. Thus, the contemporary times of the business world demand such 'extended' services from researchers, be it a qualitative researcher or a quantitative one.

Innovation and relationship-orientation are the keys to establishing a meaningful and mutually beneficial relationship between the client and the researcher.

FORTE OF QUALITATIVE RESEARCH

'We want to conduct some focus group discussions'—these words have been heard many a time whenever a company faces some marketing issues as well as when the brand team wants to do a 'quick and dirty research (QDR)'.

However, the implications here are i) many managers assume that 'qualitative research' means 'focus groups'; (ii) decision-makers presume that qualitative research is a short-cut to solutions and are unclear about the deliverables of qualitative research.

Two of the most basic questions, asked at the start of any research, should be: 'What kind of answers do you need from a marketing research exercise?', 'Therefore, does this issue require qualitative or quantitative research, or both?' Failing to think these through will often lead to research that is not appropriate for the stated research objective and, hence, will be a wastage of resources.

As Harper W. Boyd (1966) says in his book *Marketing Research: Texts and Cases*, motivation research attempts to determine the 'why' of human behaviour. It is not limited to any specific type of behaviour, but includes the entire gamut of human behaviour that may be related to marketing.

It is based on the premise that, if approached correctly, people can give you rich information about how and why they behave or consume in the way that they do. In marketing, one of the uses to which it is put most extensively is to determine the reasons why consumers buy one brand or type of product instead of others, how they perceive and relate to brands, and what the areas of bonding are with the brand or the product category. The understanding and establishing of this bonding becomes imperative because this is the Achilles' heel of the brand loyalty of the consumer for a brand/product.

According to Boyd (1966), this information helps in designing the product, packaging, pricing, and advertising; especially the latter since all advertising communication aims at 'hooking the consumer by targeting her/his relevant needs and aspirations'. Moreover, this information also helps in repositioning a brand, or even modifying the entire existing marketing mix.

QUALITATIVE RESEARCH VS QUANTITATIVE RESEARCH

Qualitative research plays a major role in the initial stages of product planning, such as product opportunity identification and product idea generation. Research at this stage serves to answer questions such as: 'Where does the product category fit into the respondent's life?', 'What role does it play?', etc. Such questions cannot be answered within the structured framework of quantitative research.

It is important to emphasize here that qualitative research will provide a deeper understanding of how the consumer thinks, but it does not give measurement (i.e, a numerical validation) to the findings. This task is then left to quantitative research, which typically seeks to quantify the data and, more often than not, uses some form of statistical analysis to validate the insights derived from qualitative research.

But, one question that should come to mind is: Why is a validation required from quantitative research?' It is pertinent to ask this question because qualitative findings, although based on relatively smaller sample sizes, have depth as a proof of their validity. Why, then, do we use quantitative research to substantiate the validity and reliability of the qualitative findings?

Quantitative sampling, by virtue of its large sampling, comes closer to representing the universe. In addition, its statistical mode of data analysis leads to a quantification which then gives a finding of its correct significance and salience, whereas the stated language of qualitative research findings is more in probability terms. For example, a qualitative finding, most often, is stated as: 'The young adult consumer does not want to patronize a respective fast food outlet probably because he feels that the place is more for kids and not for him and his own needs'. However, to ensure that this statement is the voice of a majority of the young adults, a large sample and approach of quantitative research is required.

Marketers often get misled into using qualitative research to gather numerical data; and therefore ask questions such as how many people in the group liked the advertisement or what proportion of the respondents said that they would use this new product if it came to the market. A word of caution to marketers: qualitative insights cannot be regarded as conclusive and representative of the entire population as the sample is very small in size. Importantly, the promise of qualitative research is to deliver depth and not measurement and numbers!

Thus, while qualitative research provides insights into the *why* of the human mind, the question of *how many* is best handled by quantitative research.

To investigate a crucial issue fully it is ideal to conduct both types of research. A sound practice is to view the two kinds of research as complementary rather than as substitutes for each other.

For instance, take the example of a situation where a company has to decide on whether to change the name of one of its brands or not. Qualitative research can be used to explore how the current name is perceived, as also to assess the response to some potential new names in terms of the imagery that each name evokes and lends to the product, what each name connotes and symbolizes, and what the positives and negatives are of each name. At the end of this exercise one will have a clear picture of what each potential name 'means and communicates' to the consumer. What is missing is information such as, what proportion/percentage of the target market will have a positive response to each name, what will be the majority consumers' imagery and connotations for each name etc. For this purpose, quantitative research is required.

Thus, at the end of this two-stage exercise, the company will know whether to go in for a change in name or not, and, if yes, then which name is most suitable and preferred. In addition, they will know exactly what image the 'winner name' will bring to consumers' minds, also, they can use this information in developing or modifying their brand identity and brand communication.

Unfortunately, due to constraints of time and finance, this elaborate two-step approach cannot always be adopted. Sometimes you have to choose between the two. When making this choice, it is important to know what kind of information is more critical for the decision at hand. If one is looking for motives and behaviour for understanding a phenomenon and/or for exploring for new information, then, qualitative research can be used; but if the need is to quantify data and generalize it to a large group or to work out market estimations then it is a task for quantitative research.

In the above cited example of brand name selection, if the key information required is that of knowing the imagery evoked by and the connotations of the respective brand names, then a qualitative research study is advocated. However, if the key requirement is information on how many consumers prefer each brand name, quantitative research would be a more suitable approach.

RELATIONSHIP BETWEEN QUALITATIVE AND QUANTITATIVE RESEARCH

There has probably been more energy expended on debating the differences between, and the relative advantages of, qualitative and quantitative methods than almost any other topic in marketing research. In view of this, to say that one or the other approach is 'better' is simply trivializing what is far more complex than just an 'either–or' choice. An understanding of this *relationship* holds dual benefits for marketers.

First, they will able to decide what kind of research will be most suitable to their information needs and objectives and, therefore, they will be able to formulate an appropriate research brief for the research agency.

Second, they will know what to expect as 'research deliverables' at the end of a respective research exercise, and therefore, be better able to understand how to absorb and assimilate the data-inputs into their marketing plans and strategies. In other words, over-expectations will dissipate once they achieve an understanding of the relationship between qualitative and quantitative research approaches.

In any discussion involving this debate, it will be useful to distinguish between the general premises involved in qualitative and quantitative research. To understand qualitative research better, it is important to compare its assumptions and focus with those of quantitative research.

In their book, *Education research: Competencies for analysis and application*, Gay and Airasian (1999) compare the two research approaches. Their views have been summarized in the paragraphs that follow. They state that quantitative research uses a deductive approach to ascertain findings, forecasting, and testing of hypotheses. A large part of the data analysis of quantitative research is statistical, striving to show that the world can be looked at in terms of measurable reality. This is known as the positivist perspective. Contrary to quantitative research, qualitative research has a non-positivist perspective and uses an inductive approach. This theory postulates that the world is made up of different people with different perspectives and, therefore, has many different meanings and contexts.

The approach   Deductive research begins with a known theory and tests it, usually by providing evidence for or against a pre-specified hypothesis. Inductive research, on the other hand, begins by making observations, usually in order to develop a new hypothesis or to contribute to new theory.

Qualitative research usually begins with open-ended observation and analysis, most often looking for patterns and processes that explain 'how and why' questions. Quantitative research on the other hand starts with pre-specified objectives focused on testing preconceived outcomes. The difference is mainly in the perspective of quantitative research, which is based on the positivist approach (the belief that the world can be measured, understood, and generalized), and the non-positivist view (the belief that the world cannot be generalized) of qualitative research.

The data   Quantitative researchers work mostly with numerical and statistical data, while qualitative researchers use mainly non-numerical data, such as observations, interviews, interactions, etc., as sources of information.

The objective   Another difference between the two types of research is that whereas quantitative research seeks to find evidence, which supports or does not support an existing hypothesis, qualitative research allows hypotheses to emerge from patterns of recurring events. G.K. Huysamen (1997) discussed this issue in his book *Parallels between qualitative research and sequentially performed quantitative research*. Table 15.1 summarizes the relationship.

As suggested by Green and Tull (1978) in *Research for marketing decisions*, an appropriate method of inquiry for research problems depends, in a large part, upon the nature of a problem itself and the extent or level of existing knowledge regarding it.

Table 15.1   Comparison of Qualitative Research and Quantitative Research

	Qualitative Research	**Quantitative Research**
Type of reasoning	Inductive (Subjective)	Deductive (Objective)
Purpose	*Meaning*—describes multiple realities and develops deep meaning, capturing everyday life	*Causation*—deals with theory testing, prediction, establishing facts, hypothesis testing
Research Focus	*Process-oriented*—examines full context, interacts with participants, and collects data face-to-face from participants	*Outcome-oriented*—isolates variables, uses large samples, is often anonymous to participants, and uses tests and formal instruments
Research Plan	*Open-ended*—flexible and tentative; start with an initial plan that evolve as researchers learn more about participants	*Pre-specified*—structured and formal; developed before study is initiated
Data Analysis	*Interpretive* and *descriptive*	*Statistical* and *numerical*

The focus and purpose of qualitative and quantitative researches are different, hence each one can be used only for a specific research design. In fact, in almost every applied social research project, there is value in consciously combining both qualitative and quantitative methods—what is referred to as a 'mixed methods' approach. Increasingly, we find researchers who are interested in blending the two traditions, attempting to get the advantages of each.

Casebeer and Verhoef have mentioned in their article, 'Combining qualitative and quantitative research methods: considering the possibilities for enhancing the study of chronic diseases', that there is a slow but important movement towards a more collaborative use of both types of research methods. Positive suggestions for combining quantitative and qualitative approaches are emerging from some health-oriented disciplines. Sociology and nursing are fields that struggle with the divide often separating researchers who prefer one or the other research approach; however, some researchers in both fields are promoting greater harmony.

Table 15.2 provides an illustration of the respective roles of qualitative and quantitative researches, through the example of a paint company that wants to understand the dynamics between shop owners and painters, and to profile a typical painter undertaking shop painting jobs.

Table 15.2 Issues Addressed by Qualitative and Quantitative Research

Qualitative method investigates	Quantitative method investigates
the profile of the painter who does shop painting	*the profile of the painter who does shop painting*
<ul><li>a typical day in the life of a painter</li><li>his/her aspirations, wishes, desires, and fears</li><li>preferences between different kinds of painting jobs and the reasons</li></ul>	<ul><li>different painting jobs that a painter undertakes</li><li>characteristic of painters—skilled or unskilled, etc.</li><li>periods when painting as an activity is most prevalent</li><li>types of products regularly used</li></ul>
the role of the painter in the painting process and the dynamics with the shop owner	*the role of the painter in the painting process and the dynamics with the shop owner*
Painter:<ul><li>description of the actual painting process—days and time involved, role in the process, methodology, number of actual people at work, etc.</li><li>how a painter gets the leads in the business</li><li>problems faced in day-to-day working environment</li></ul>	Painter:<ul><li>extent to which a painter influences the choice of paint/colour/brand used</li><li>where the materials are bought and who purchases</li><li>the types of paints purchased most often</li><li>the quantities of the various paints purchased</li></ul>
Shop owner:<ul><li>how and from where the shop owner gets the painter</li><li>interactions with the painter and any need gaps</li><li>nature and extent to which the shopkeeper is price sensitive</li><li>perceptions of promotions</li><li>problems faced during the whole painting process and the interaction with the painter</li></ul>	

STRENGTHS AND LIMITATIONS OF QUALITATIVE RESEARCH

For the right application of qualitative research and for a good understanding of the respective situations in which qualitative and quantitative researches are specifically suitable, it is essential to understand the strengths and limitations of qualitative research.

Strengths of qualitative research

Qualitative research helps in understanding those aspects of the world which cannot be understood in terms of numbers and objectivity. These techniques are used to define a problem, generate hypotheses, identify determinants, and develop quantitative research designs. Qualitative research tries to understand the human mind with a mirror and not with a yardstick. It is more reflective than calculative, and better than quantitative research at probing below the surface for affective drives and sub-conscious motivations.

Qualitative research provides the opportunity to develop a rich understanding of and insight into individual attitudes, beliefs, concerns, motivations, aspirations, lifestyles, culture, behaviours, and preferences. This makes this approach valuable for exploring an issue in-depth.

In sum, qualitative research

- is flexible,
- allows exploring the meaning of concepts and events with target audience,
- produces valid/relevant data as issues are explored in sufficient depth to provide a clear understanding,
- helps discover motivations and patterns of association between factors that underlie behaviour,
- provides insights into how and why individuals behave, think, and feel in a particular way, and
- allows observation of the process by which people adopt new behaviour within the context of their daily lives.

Limitations of using qualitative research

In theory, therefore, it seems that qualitative research would be the best route to take in every research situation. After all, it takes into account the fact that each person is an individual with a different perspective on the world, different reactions to occurrences, and different opinions—variations that quantitative research hardly takes into account. So why do researchers continue to use quantitative methods, instead of qualitative methods that give a more in-depth understanding of a topic?

One answer could be that, by their very nature, these exploratory research methods are based on very small samples that cannot be used to generalize to the whole population. At times, therefore, numerical data based on a large sample is necessary in order to test a hypothesis.

Some lacunae of the qualitative research approach are discussed in this section.

A time-consuming exercise Qualitative analysis, for reasons explained in this section, is often rejected as a research choice when there is a time constraint. It is the very nature of qualitative research (in-depth process of data collection as well as analysis) that makes it a long process.

Data collection process The semi-structured style of inquiry takes up a lot of time as the framework of the inquiry keeps developing and modifying depending upon the respondents. Information from each individual consumer, if it has to adequately explore the issues involved, needs to be developed through a gradual and unstructured process of questioning.

Analysis It is also a continuous process where themes keep changing and the framework is continuously evolving and adapting accordingly. Besides, acceptance of the fact that each consumer is an individual with her/his own approach to products, issues, and life in general suggests that, in order to derive maximum benefit from qualitative research, the analysis should be detailed enough to bring out these very differences, so that richer and more subtle meanings and interpretations may be made possible. At the same time, this also means that there are many instances when, though qualitative research is necessary, there is not enough time or money resources in order to conduct an adequately detailed research.

Subjectivity of the researcher and the process Qualitative research brings out the 'inner view' of consumers. However, for that to happen, we need unbiased and skilled researchers.

Interpretation One disadvantage of qualitative research is the dependence of accuracy on the interpretations of researchers. Because the researcher is a thinking and feeling person like the participants, it is possible that the researcher may have personal biases which might affect the reasoning processes. Hence, this could cause results to be unreliable as a researcher's biases may colour the research findings.

Presentation The skill and experience of the researcher also influence how well and how objectively the data is analysed and interpreted to derive insights that are useful for subsequent planning.

Accuracy Some consumers could express views that are consistent with those of others in the group. They try not to articulate views generally not considered acceptable. This need for social acceptability may lead respondents to censor their actual views, especially when they are in a group setting. This affects the integrity of data that is obtained.

Findings The important implication of this limitation is that researchers should refrain from drawing any conclusions about the actual frequency of concerns, attitudes, or beliefs among the target audience.

This discussion of the limitations of qualitative research should act as a significant source of caution to the researcher or the buyer of research who tends to favour qualitative research indiscriminately.

The Right Application of Qualitative Research

Qualitative research is distinguished by its emphasis on describing, understanding, and explaining complex phenomena, such as the relationships, patterns, and arrangement among various factors or the context in which behaviour takes place. The focus is on understanding the full multidimensional and dynamic picture of the issue under study. Qualitative methods are useful not only for providing rich descriptions of complex phenomena, but also for constructing or developing theories and for generating hypotheses to explain those phenomena.

Critically, it is important to understand that the qualitative research findings are not the end in themselves. In fact, they open up perspectives and thinking avenues wherein ideas get generated, paving the way for further thinking on the marketing strategy for the brand, and developing new products and avenues for reaching out to the consumer. Therefore, qualitative research findings are strong pointers and directional cues which need to be optimally and realistically interpreted and utilized by the client's marketing team.

More often than not, the core demands of the clients' marketing team are the following:

- an explanation and description of what is happening, and what can and should happen
- information about what they do not know and understanding the consumer multi-dimensionally—penetrating the rational, superficial thoughts to reach to the latent/deeper/emotional responses and reasons underlying consumer behaviour
- an attempt to yield deep, richer insights—all answering two core questions:

   1) Why do consumers think and behave in a particular manner?
   2) How to increase/enhance this thought and behaviour in the direction that benefits the client's brand?

Therefore, to put it succinctly, it can be said that the success of a qualitative research study depends upon the extent of depth and dimensions that get discovered vis-à-vis the objectives under study. Such depth and dimension are achieved when researchers keenly seek answers to the following:

- What did the respondent say?
- Why did she/he say it?
- What could be the possible immediate triggers in her/his mind vs long-standing reasons?
- What did she/he actually *mean* by it?
- Is there a deeper meaning behind what he is telling me?

Fresh Food Foil Wraps

We may consider the case of a manufacturer of foil wraps, who wants to know how mothers pack food for school-going children, the possible role of foil wraps, in keeping food fresh, motives for using foil wraps and reasons for using competing brands of foil wraps. This requirement necessitated the use of qualitative research. No quantitative research technique would have been able to unearth the answers to the numerous questions of 'why' underpinning this seemingly simple query. This is so because a detailed discussion on the subject might explore the mother's concern with providing safe and hygienic food to her child, her worries about the child's health, and her own self-concept as a caring mother, apart from a lot of other information about her caring for her child's needs and health.

Caution to be Exercised

Care should be taken to ensure that qualitative research is not reduced to just carrying out focus group discussions or depth interviews and using just only projective techniques just for the sake of application. Often, due to lack of proper direction, any indiscriminate application of clinical psychology techniques (e.g., the TAT, the Rorschach test) to marketing studies is regarded as qualitative research. It must be noted that each study is unique in itself and might need to be dealt with differently, depending on its requirements and constraints of resources.

For example, all qualitative studies need not produce best results through one-on-one and in-depth interviews. In certain situations involving personal, private issues, a joint interview with two close friends would work better, as respondents find security with a known person, which helps them open up better; compared to a one-on-one interview, where one is all alone with the researcher, who is a stranger, and so feels inhibited and unwilling to share experiences and views. In certain other cases, it would be necessary to meet people in their own natural environment instead of in a formal group discussion set-up. The methodology adopted in a qualitative research study, thus, is depended upon the objective of optimizing the consumer's comfort level, so that inhibitors to response are minimized.

A variety of research methods can be used to study human behavior and its causes. Depending upon the type of consumer segment to be covered/objectives of the study, qualitative research methodologies have to be selected. Qualitative methods will be discussed in detail in Chapter 17. The focus in choosing a method should be on its relevance in giving the correct understanding of the human behaviour under study and not on using fancy methods and probing techniques.

COMMENCEMENT OF THE QUALITATIVE RESEARCH STUDY

Every research study requires a different handling as each study is commissioned for a specific purpose. However, certain steps are essential in every study. The basic requirements of a research study are listed below.

   (i)   taking a research brief from the client
  (ii)   working out a research proposal on the basis of the research brief
 (iii)   preparation of the recruitment questionnaire
 (iv)   detailing the probing process in the format of a discussion guide
  (v)   converting all findings and analysis into a presentation format which is then presented to the client

Qualitative Research Brief

Every research study begins with a research brief and, as they say, a research study is as good as its brief—this means that the research brief given by the client and taken by the researcher needs to have accuracy and clarity. Therefore, when recording the client's information needs and objectives, which comprise a research brief, the researcher must take note of the following points:

Language   In the research brief we should look for words that can help indicate the main thrust of the project. For example, 'Is a market to be *explored*, a phenomenon in the market to be *explained*, advertising to be *evaluated*, new product ideas to be *developed* or hypotheses to be *generated*?'

Words like these give an indication of whether to adopt a qualitative research approach, a quantitative research approach, or an amalgamated one. Also, the researcher will get to know the key 'problem' and 'information need, of the client'.

Prioritization   Next, clarity is required vis-à-vis the core and peripheral objectives. This will help prioritize the researcher's time when it comes to asking relevant questions during the qualitative interview sessions in order to do complete justice to the desired research objective.

Rationale   In the research brief, the researcher must attempt to understand the reasons behind client's suggestion of the respective research centres, the profile of the consumers to be met, etc.

In the context of the specified consumer segments to be understood, again it is imperative to ask the client what would be the core information required from each respective consumer segment. This will enable the researcher to have the appropriate focus in her/his probing.

Analysis   It is extremely important that the researcher seeks to understand, at the time of recording a research brief, how the client wants the data to be analysed, i.e., does he want to understand perceptions and differences as per the different regions covered, or as per gender of the consumers, or as per any other variable basis on which the consumer segments have been designed. The information on the analysis variables is important for the researcher as it would help bring out maximum relevance in the insights derived from the analysed data.

Clients' context   Other relevant information in the research brief that the researcher must find out is about regards the brand's position in the current market scenario—

information about market shares, competition positioning vs. positioning of the client's brand, etc. This 'context' information will help the researcher to understand the marketing relevance of the research study better.

Expected research value   Last, but not the least, a key question which the researcher must ask the client is: What are the end-deliverables of the study? That is to say, to what 'use' would the research findings be put? This information will enable the researcher to weave out relevant and actionable recommendations on the basis of the research findings.

The research findings must have application value, i.e., they need to have marketing relevance for the client's brand. Therefore, an understanding of the scope of application and relevance of the findings for the client is imperative for delivering appropriate value from the research study.

Qualitative Research Proposal

Based on the research brief given by the client, a research proposal, which is the blueprint of the approach of the researcher, needs to be worked out for two reasons:

(i) It gives an assurance to the client that the researcher has understood with complete clarity the client's needs and brand scenario.

(ii) It gives the client clarity as to how the researcher will approach the study, what will be the data collection process, and how will she/he bring value to the client's brand under study.

Thus, in the working out of the research proposal, the guidelines given below should be adhered to in order to give the research approach depth and relevance.

- the need to flesh out the client's core problem by suggesting alternative perspectives of looking at the given problem, that is, by adding dimensions to the research approach
- hypotheses should be worked out, then follows the attempt to verify these in the course of the study—every research needs to start with one or a set of hypotheses; this will give a framework within which the research processes will get fine-tuned
- the need to give a reasoning/rationale behind every suggestion (be it a centre, sample segments, analysis variables, etc.)—e.g., why is something being suggested, what is the relevance of a respective suggestion vis-à-vis the research objectives, etc. This will give the client a clear understanding of the 'why' behind the suggestions of the researcher
- the need to give a very clear blueprint of the researcher's thought process vis-à-vis the research objectives and how she/he would proceed in terms of fieldwork—detailing every aspect, step-wise (see Annexure 15.1)

Research Instruments

The next stage after an approval of the research proposal, is to translate all the thought processes into action. For this, two key research instruments are critical.

(i) Recruitment questionnaires, based on which, the consumer sample is selected and recruited for the fieldwork.

(ii) Discussion guides, which are the are blue-prints of the manner in which the researcher will conduct the interview or group session; the kind of questions that will be asked, the sequence of the questions, the manner in which the questions will be put forth to the consumer, etc.—all these aspects get detailed in a discussion guide.

Recruitment questionnaire Based on the mutually (i.e., between the client and the researcher) decided-upon 'sample profile' to be covered for the respective study, a recruitment questionnaire is prepared. These are used in the field to select consumers and recruiting them for the interviews/group sessions. This questionnaire contains profile parameters such as demographic details, attitudinal profile variables, etc., based on which consumers are sifted and appropriately selected (See Annexure 15.2).

Discussion guide This is a process blue-print of what the researcher will ask the consumer and how it will be asked. A discussion guide consists of various isues, such as the ones listed below.

- How will the qualitative probing session begin, proceed, and end?
- How will consumer be led from one question to the next?
- What kind of questions will be asked to achieve the objectives of the study?
- What 'projective techniques' will be used in questioning?
- What will be the language (e.g., English vs. Hindi, simple versus technical, whether examples are to be used to explain the meaning of a respective question, etc.) of the questions asked?
- What instructions will the researcher need to follow while moderating the session vis-à-vis how to probe, what to focus upon, what to write and note down, what to emphasize upon and where, etc.

Therefore, in working out a discussion guide, certain guidelines have to be adhered to. These have been discussed in the following paragraphs.

At the very beginning, complete instructions should be given to the moderator in terms of

- how to warm up the session at the start;
- how to put the consumers in the right perspective, i.e., tell them what they are supposed to do and why they should not feel inhibited to talk; and
- how to begin and conclude the session.

It is essential to give time approximation for each section so that the researcher is clear, during the session, as to how much time to devote in probing a certain information arena.

The questions should be phrased as colloquial as possible. Technical jargon will not be comprehended well by the consumer and, therefore, simple language should be used, a language with which the consumer is familiar.

The researcher must keep in mind the sequence in questioning. For example, either one goes with the funnel approach or the inverted funnel approach. Ofen, when a concept testing is carried out, the inverted funnel approach is adopted, that is, the session begins with the concept discussion. (Any other 'exploratory' discussion prior to the discussion on the concept will bias reactions to the concept.) Once this is over, the discussion moves to other information areas.

In most exploratory, diagnostic, and new product development studies, the funned approach in questioning is adopted, that is, moving from broad information areas to specific core areas.

It is important to keep in mind the sequencing and linking of questions, use of loaded vs neutral/biased words, etc.

An attempt must be made to make the discussion guide more interesting and 'conversation-like'—thereby making it less mechanical and boring! (See Annexure 15.3)

The discussion guide must deliver comprehensively to the objectives of the study. Therefore, there is a need to check

- whether all the relevant objectives are being covered in terms of time and types of questions asked,
- whether pertinent questions are being asked,
- whether funneling, i.e., moving from fundamental/general questions to the core information arenas is used, and
- whether the language is simple/colloquial or wordy, complex, ambiguous, or full of jargon.

Presentation of Findings

Once the analysis is in place, then the findings of the study and the researcher's analysis, along with recommendations, need to be laid out in a presentable form which then is readied for the client. There are two aspects to a presentation:

(i) the writing of the document (i.e., presentation-making)
(ii) verbalizing it in front of the client (i.e., presentation-giving)

Writing the presentation

In order, to make an impressionable presentation, certain critical guidelines should be kept in mind.

When making the format, one needs to follow the steps given below.

1. The research logistics have to be detailed first, for example, research background coming from the initial research brief, the research objectives, the methodology, the sampling plan, etc.
2. Then comes the 'findings' section which will state 'what came out' from the consumers; this section must follow the discussion guide because it has to state the findings as per the sections of the discussion guide.
3. Once the findings have been stated, the derivation of the implications from these findings should be stated in the 'conclusions' section which then has to adhere to the research objectives of the study.
4. Finally, comes the 'recommendations' section which contains the 'way forward' based on what the consumers said and how the researcher has analysed; these recommendations must adhere to the deliverables of the study, that is, the interpreted research insights must have application value in the context of the client's brand-related needs and issues. In short, the recommendations should have marketing relevance for the client.

Post the format, certain basic pointers for making the presentation are also important. These have been listed below.

- The look of the presentation needs to be neat, consistent, and should appropriately alternate between verbosity and graphics.
- The language used has to be very lucid, easy to understand, but, at the same time, it should be clear and precise.
- Only relevant data should be put in the document; it should not just be 'filled' with irrelevant findings.

Verbalizing the presentation

The presentation reaches its last stage when the researcher has to stand in front of the client's team and verbalise the content of the reported document. When doing so in order to make an impressionable presentation the researcher should adhere to the following guidelines:

- Do not read from the screen, but from the laptop—this helps maintain eye contact with the audience.
- Have closer eye contact with your audience and orient your body towards them; one should not *sway* from the screen to the audience and vice versa.
- Do not read the slide; explain only if required or read only the moot points.
- Do not read quotes except maybe one or two which are the critical ones.
- Body language needs to indicate that the researcher is confident about the data that she/he is presenting.
- The tone should be clear (not hesitant) and firm; bring in tone variations, for example, read a quote in a 'colloquial tone'.

- Keep value-adding to slide data by telling what happened 'on-the-spot' to give a feel of consumer behaviour during the qualitative probing sessions.

SUMMARY

The core of qualitative research is concerned with understanding human behaviour and the mindset underlying this behaviour. This approach is more into experiencing the consumers, as they reveal themselves in their language, understanding their world through their eyes. The skills of the researcher lie in optimally balancing creativity and objectivity in data collection methodology and analysis. Qualitative research is conducted when the client seeks to find out and understand the reasons underlying consumer behaviour, that is, when the client wants to know why the consumers behave in the manner that they do. Thus, the key words that would help recognize the need for qualitative research, when faced with an information dilemma, are 'explore', 'understand', 'generate', and 'explain'. The applications of qualitative research are in understanding consumer mindset, needs, expectations (what more and what new), and barriers. It is also used when the clients need directions vis-à-vis communication and positioning of brands, and when they need to know what is 'going wrong' and 'how to set it right'. Thus, the hallmarks of qualitative research are flexibility and depth. The qualitative researcher needs to have skills that bring out optimally both these features of this research approach. Qualitative research has its own specific deliverables, which are distinct from those of quantitative research. Both these methods are different in their approaches and objectives and provide conclusions with different data. Some areas where qualitative research is used most effectively are product opportunity identification, new products/services idea generation, product development, product positioning (i.e., advertising) concept testing, diagnostic research, exploratory research, and strategic research. Though qualitative research probes deep into the respondent's psyche and provides actionable answers to the question 'why', it suffers from some major limitations as it usually works with smaller sample sizes, is open to subjective interpretation of the data obtained, and the validity of findings is dependent on the researcher's skills. While there are limitations involved in conducting qualitative research and analysing the data, the art lies in the researchers working around these shortcomings and deriving maximum output from the study to meet the research objectives to their fullest. Hence, the key to getting the most value out of any research methods is to, first, assess the marketing objective on hand; and, secondly, to study what data output will be required from the chosen research method and then compare these two to see if the data output would meet the marketing objective. Apart from the understanding of the fundamentals of qualitative research, it is also imperative to get an inner view of what are the steps involved in its execution— right from taking a research brief from the client, converting the same into an elaborate research proposal, followed by preparing the research instruments (essentially of two types: one, for recruiting the consumers for the qualitative sessions, and, two, for conducting the probing process in such sessions). The last step (post data analysis) is that of presentation-making and verbalizing the same to the client. Meticulous preparation at each stage contributes significantly to the success of any qualitative study.

KEY WORDS

Human behaviour refers to anything that an individual does, overtly or covertly, that can be observed and recorded in some way.

Human perception is an individual's immediate experience of the world, thus incorporating not just what she/he sees visually, but also what she/he feels, thinks, emotes, and interprets.

Attitude is an evaluation; a learned predisposition (tendency, habit) to think and behave in a consistent evaluative manner toward a person, a group of people, an object, or a group of objects.

Mindset is based on the idea that the human mind comprises of thoughts and emotions which then form the bases for needs, barriers, fears, desires, aspirations, and expectations—all this put together becomes the human mindset.

Motivation refers to the driving and pulling forces that result in persistent behaviour directed towards certain goals; the need/drive to get/do something.

Phenomena, the plural form of 'phenomenon', refers to any occurrence, happening, or event in the consumer's world.

Need gap is the gulf that emerges when the consumer expects certain needs to be fulfilled but certain others get fulfilled or the needs get fulfilled but not in the manner in which expected.

Brainstorming is a term coined by Alex Osborn (1957), an advertising person, for referring to the activity of a group of individuals getting together and bringing out view points and/or solutions vis-à-vis a particular issue and/or a problem; there is a free-wheeling discussion where the main instruction is to generate ideas and thoughts and to build upon the ones generated by the others, with no 'buts' and no criticisms. It is more like a free-flow of ideas.

Creative problem-solving as a process has more focus then a brainstorming session. Mostly, the creative problem-solving session is preceded by the brainstorming session. A problem is attempted to be sorted out through the generation of creative solutions through a series of individual and group activities rather than just simple talking.

Verbatim refers to the quote/direct speech of the consumer; what was said and the way it was said.

Personality refers to a group of traits that become the thinking and behaving pattern of an individual and which, over a period of time, became the patent and habitual way of responding to situations and people.

Frame of reference is based on the idea that every human perceives and reacts to a situation from a personal point of view; this frame of reference gets built from the interaction between two sources—nature (i.e., inherited genes) and nurture (i.e., the environment a person is exposed to).

Mnemonic is a symbolic representation of a thought, idea, or message and is mostly graphic.

Data refers to recorded observations, usually in numeric or textual form.

Deductive logic is a form of reasoning in which conclusions are formulated about particulars from general or universal premises.

Inductive logic is a form of reasoning in which a generalized conclusion is formulated from particular instances.

Research brief is a client's detailing of what is needed from a research study and how the research findings will be used vis-à-vis the brand and related marketing strategies.

CONCEPT REVIEW QUESTIONS

1. What is the value of qualitative research in the entire schema of a marketing research exercise?

2. What can qualitative research deliver with utmost efficacy and what can it not deliver optimally?

3. What kind of problems, issues, and questions should be a part of the qualitative research brief given by the client to the research agency?

4. What kind of an approach (work and attitude related) should a qualitative researcher develop vis-à-vis the research task, the business, and the client?

5. What are the moot points that a qualitative researcher needs to avoid if a research modus operandi needs to deliver value to the client?

6. How do qualitative and quantitative researches differ in terms of approaches, objectives, and data?

7. In what specific areas of marketing inquiry can we apply qualitative research most effectively? Give reasons for your answer.

8. What are the strengths and limitations of qualitative research? How should one try to minimize the shortcomings of qualitative research to get the best out of a research study?

9. What are the challenges that need to be overcome in using qualitative research?

10. What are the key 'dos and donts' of a qualitative research brief?

11. What are the key sections of a qualitative research proposal?

12. What are the key fundamentals to be kept in mind when preparing a discussion guide?

13. What are the cornerstones of a good presentation-making?

CRITICAL THINKING EXERCISES

1. A marketer puts forward a problem by saying, 'I want to connect with my adult consumer; so far my brand was more for the child consumer'. Ladder this broad problem to specific marketing issues and make a list of issues that need inputs from research which will help get answers to the core problem.

2. A company in the restaurant business wants inputs for the training modus operandi for the HR department, based on some qualitative studies conducted regarding their brand and consumers. Are they justified in asking for this from the qualitative studies conducted? Make your decision and work out the reasons for your answer. In both cases, state what the study data can give (if possible) as inputs for the training process and what would be the limitations, if any, in extending the research data from the brand context to the human resource context.

3. A consumer durables manufacturing company wishes to understand where their ten-year old brand stands today with respect to the competition and how to communicate a new positioning to the brand audience. What are the various kinds of research that should be undertaken?

4. A cellular service provider wishes to know how the latest communication will fare in terms of strengthening the brand perceptions of the target audience? What kind of research is appropriate and what all should be checked?

5. A researcher has been given an assignment by a client wishing to diversify from industrial chemicals to condoms. The client wants to understand women's attitudes towards male contraceptives. What is the best way to obtain this information?

6. A new entrant into the banking sector wishes to test out the ability of its new communication to create strong positive perceptions. The company has so far been a well-known NBFC (non-banking finance company). What methods should they use to test their new communication?

7. A consumer durables manufacturing company that was the market leader for over three decades, suddenly finds itself fighting MNCs and local players, resulting in the loss of market share. What are the various kinds of research that they can undertake in their quest for a marketing strategy that will help understand the market and fight competition?

PROJECT ASSIGNMENTS

1. A company called IDTA, a media concern that has been more active in the television industry events, now wants to launch a magazine related to this industry. Would qualitative research be relevant here? If yes, then at what stages? What would be the core research tasks for this study? Draw up a research brief and a research modus operandi plan.

2. Assume you have been retained as a consultant to an organization that wishes to diversify from tractors and automobiles into travel tourism. Design a project to define the target consumer, and plan and execute research that will identify the expectations of these consumers and their perceptions of the organization's ability to deliver value in this new market.

3. A research brief from the client states: 'I have a fast food chain catering to non-Indian cuisine and my main target consumes are children and families; I now want to appeal to the young adult (18–28 yrs) and, therefore, I want to understand how I

can connect with them and their needs better'. Find out what is missing in this brief and how can it be made complete and comprehensive for the researcher. Also list out the questions that the researcher needs to ask in order to work out the appropriate research approach. Finally, work out a research proposal based on this research brief; the main components of the proposal are: (a) how the researcher understands the client's research brief, (b) how the research design will be formulated, (c) the methodology that will be used, and (d) the appropriate sample coverage.

CASE STUDY

Shoppers' Stop

The case study discussed here elaborates on the diagnostic-exploratory type of qualitative research. It also explains in detail how a qualitative approach helps to answer the 'whys' behind the consumers' preferences, choices, and behaviour, and its connections with the product/service and the brands. It will also been seen how the insights from the qualitative research helped the client to take the necessary action that helped them move towards a higher sales revenue. Shoppers' Stop is a chain of stores that has a nation-wide presence in the key metros and mini-metros and mainly offers apparels, accessories, and home products across age-groups and genders.

Project brief given to the researcher

The client has two stores in Kolkata , one at Salt Lake City, and the other in the heart of the town. It was observed that even a year after the opening of the Salt Lake City outlet, it did not pick up the desired sales inspite of all the marketing efforts although the other outlets and stores in Salt Lake City were doing phenomenally well.

Thus, the client wanted to know

- why this store has not met the expectations of the client, and
- what is required to be done to increase the saliency of and preference for this store for the customer.

Research issues at hand

Perceptions about the Salt Lake City outlet of Shoppers' Stop were to be comprehensively studied with respect to other outlets (including the older Shoppers' Stop outlet) on the basis of

- tangible dimensions such as product quality (type and range—width and depth), product display, pricing, promotions and discounts, and other options in the store,
- intangible dimensions such as ambience and service inside the store, and
- the key strengths and weaknesses of the Shoppers' Stop Salt Lake City outlet in relation to competition, which will help in identifying drivers and barriers for the respective outlet.

Thus, the key questions that needed to be answered through qualitative research were as follows:

- Why did the consumer purchase/not purchase from Shoppers' Stop (Salt Lake) vis-à-vis other stores?

- Why did the consumer not go at all to Shoppers' Stop (Salt Lake) versus other stores?

- Why did the consumer prefer to go to the older Shoppers' Stop store?

The research plan

The research approach adopted was qualitative because the task here was to diagnose the reasons behind the existing problem and thus deliver the 'whys' behind the behaviour of the respective set of consumers and thus provide inputs for the client's marketing and communication strategies. The qualitative approach was further divided into exploratory and diagnostic. In the exploratory phase, the research focused on understanding the overall customer needs and mindset of a Kolkata consumer, his/her shopping habits, etc. Having understood these habits and needs, a diagnostic study was then conducted to evaluate the customers' perception of Shoppers' Stop (Salt Lake City) on various dimensions and needs.

Sampling

The sample profile coverage was of adults (men/women) belonging to an age group of 18–45 years, married and unmarried. This group comprised people who had shopped at an outlet at least once during the last three months in the current year, but had not shopped in Shoppers' Stop (Salt Lake City) this year (though he/she may have shopped there last year). Instead, they may have shopped in other competition outlets, including the older Shoppers' Stop outlet (quota was taken to include coverage of all competition stores). Importantly, one sampling criterion was that the selected consumers who were aware of the Salt Lake Shoppers' Stop outlet, would not have shopped there because they did not want to, and not because they were unable to do so. This criterion was important in order to ensure that there were no dead-end reasons for not shopping at the respective stores—in fact significant insights were the need of the hour.

Methodology adopted

In-depth interviews were conducted (at the residence of the customers) and these consumers were from a catchment area around the Shoppers' Stop, Salt lake outlet (within a 8–10 km radius around the outlet).

Recommendations of the study

The recommendations of the research as per the findings from the exploratory and the diagnostic phases are as discussed below.

- The need is to connect the store and its marketing efforts to certain hooks in the earlier stated mental models of a Kolkata-ite vis-à-vis shopping . For a Kolkata-based consumer, festival shopping is a very important activity, the critical months for this being March–April and September–October. Bulk purchases are usually made during Durga puja, *Poila baishakh,* and *Jamai sashti* festivals. Thus, the need is to make the best use of these periods for promotions and sales, especially because,

- during this time, basics as well as fineries are bought, fulfilling two key needs— celebration needs, and the need to flaunt and let others know that the person concerned has bought so much;

- when shopping during festive times in a shopping outlet, one expects traditional/ ethnic apparel, traditional gift items, and attractive packaging. During such times, one does not expect exemplary service at the outlet; however, at other times, feelings of comfort and familiarity with a retail outlet mainly comes through the service provided there.

• During festive times, there should be discounts to increase sales of segments such as apparel (especially ethnic), handloom, jewellery, gift items (jute, ivory, and sandalwood items), and gift packaging. The association of one distinct attribute with a respective store is a great allegiance-inducing factor for the store. For example, sarees are always associated with Gariahat. Also, cotton is the preferred fabric, even for festivals and marriages other preferences are silk, cotton-silk, tussar, and handloom products. Jute and ivory items are also popular. Therefore the cotton range should be expanded with respect to the types, colours, and designs of fabric available in the market. In fact, Shoppers' Stop (Salt lake) could position itself as a 'cotton world' in apparel, which would be its USP.

• Significantly, even during non-festive times, people enjoy a festive spirit, therefore, theme-based 'shopping festivals' (e.g., cotton festival, handloom festival, trousseau festival, apparel and accessories festival) should be conducted on a regular basis. All these events can be conducted as 'in-store events' with cultural overtones of Bengali music, décor, etc.

• During non-festive times, women tend to patronise shopping outlets amongst friends and relatives. So, more displays and schemes/promotional offers are needed to attract them. Importantly, shopping decisions are usually taken by women, who may have limited fluency in English. So, it is essential to have Bengali-speaking staff who are proactive in their approach.

• The Shoppers' Stop Salt Lake outlet should be evaluated on four important parameters—perceptual halo, service, merchandise, and advertising and promotions.

Perceptual halo It is perceived as a contemporary, expensive, modern, western, and trendy store meant for non-festive shopping aimed at young and sophisticated persons. Thus, it is perceived as more suitable for sightseeing and less for shopping, because it has a beautiful ambience, but its products are expensive.

Service Its service is considered to be formal, distant, not-warm, very Westernized, and aloof, implying a sense of alienation and a 'place not for me'/'does not want me' feeling.

Merchandise It is considered to have limited and monotonous designs, a 'not-good' range of cottons, and higher range products that are good for gifting. Its product range is not considered to be 'exclusive. Thus, its products are expensive but there's nothing exclusive; they do not have much ethnic wear either.

Advertising   Adverstising is perceived to be infrequent, aloof, not prominent, especially in-store. Thus, it breeds a perception that 'not much is happening in the store', and that it is not a very inviting place; there are no sales, discounts, or promotional schemes.

- Why has this store not met the expectations of the customer?

  The reasons are multifold—there is no single, exclusive reason for this; and in the understanding of the researchers, it is more like a self-reinforcing circuit of perceptions that is creating hesitancy in the customer in patronising the store frequently. To start with, the store is perceived as being too sophisticated and unreasonably expensive.

- Where does this perception of it being 'expensive' come from?

  It was felt that at the base of this perception there may be a sense of alienation, and a feeling that the store is 'out of my league, expensive, and has nothing exclusive'.

- Where does the perception of 'not-for-me' come from?

  It comes from the experiences of the customer, for example, the people manning the store have not given a hospitable feel, and the behaviour and speech of the staff gives it a very Western feel. English is the predominant language, there is no feel of familiarity in the store, and no proactive hand holding.

- Where does this feeling of 'no familiarity and not feeling comfortable there' come from?

  The merchandise is completely Western, there is nothing ethnic, everything is very glamourous without touching tradition at the core—either in merchandise and/or in the behaviour of the personnel.

- There is a need to enhance the 'outside buzz'. For this, the following steps can be taken:

1. Advertising communication can be used to bring about an association of the store with its USPs. Some examples are listed below.

   - Apparel: It can promote its unique fabrics, combinations, and cuts and styles, etc.

   - Gifts: It can talk about 'small to big'/'less to more' gifts.

   - Change effect: There should be regular introductions of styles and cuts to emphasise 'movements' in variety, thus breaking the perception of monotony and no exclusivity in apparel stock.

2. Advertising communication is required to make the customer realise that the store is within his/her reach in terms of pricing, is not alienating, and one can 'walk in anytime—for anything'. As some customers rightly said, 'Have an ad that says Shoppers' Stop is open for all'—wherein 'open for all' needs to imply a store for all classes.

3. It was noted that there are many residents in Salt lake staying on their own, especially the older generation whose kids have settled abroad. So, it should have promotions and schemes for such segments, for example, exchange offers such as 'old for new' clothes, special apparel offers—winter wear, summer wear, 'send-a-gift' scheme—

wherein a tie-up with a courier agency can be made, through whom they can send gifts to loved ones all over the world. 'Dida-Dadu festival/promotions' can also be launched for the elders of the family.

4. It was suggested that the *young* image association be converted into that of being *youthful*, to connect better with the young and the old. And, of course, this should be done by making available an appropriate range of merchandise and through advertising by communicating the right USPs of the store, relevant in-store promotions and sales. 'Young' can be alienating but 'youthful' is aspiring to all.

Most of the above recommendations were incorporated in the Salt Lake City outlet and the client observed a positive impact of the same. Thus, the qualitative research approach, given its open-ended and deeper probing, helped the client to gain pertinent and actionable insights.

Questions

1. What value did a qualitative research approach to the client's problems provide to the store?

2. What did a qualitative research approach deliver in the context of the client's problem which a quantitative research approach would not have been able to deliver?

3. The sample for the study comprised 'people who had shopped at an outlet at least once during the last three months in the current year, but had not shopped in Shoppers' Stop (Salt lake city) this year (though he/she may have shopped there last year). Instead, they may have shopped in other competition outlets, including, the older Shoppers' Stop outlet (quota was taken to include coverage of all competition stores).'—Why did the sampling consider these criteria in the consumer?

4. In retrospect , what value did the methodology of in-depth interview bring in that a focus group discussion would not deliver in the context of the current study?

5. What were the key insights that were the outcome of the richness of a qualitative research approach?

REFERENCES

Boone, L.E. and D.L. Kurtz 1999, *Contemporary Marketing*, 11th edition, The Dryden Press Series in Marketing, South-Western College Publications.

Boyd, Harper W. 1966, *Marketing Research: Texts and Cases*, 3rd edn, Richard D Irwin, Illinois pp. 589, 590.

Casebeer, A.L. and Marja J. Verhoef 'Combining Qualitative and Quantitative Research Methods: Considering the Possibilities for Enhancing the Study of Chronic Diseases'. *www.phac-aspc.gc.ca/publicat/cdic-mcc/18-3/de.htm*, Accessed on 8 June 2005.

Chappelle, Camille 'The Nature of Quantitative Research', *www.2.gsu. edu/~mstswh/courses/it7000/papers/the1.htm*, Accessed on 8 June 2005.

Coleman, J. 1976, *Abnormal Psychology and Modern Life*, 5th edition, Scott, Foresman and Co.

Gay, L.R. and P.W. Airasian 1999, *Educational Research: Competencies for Analysis and Application*, 6th edn, Upper Saddle River, New Jersey, Merrill.

Green, P.E. and D.S. Tull 1978, *Research for Marketing Decisions*, 6th edition, Prentice Hall, New Jersey.

Huysamen, G.K. 1997, '*Parallels Between Qualitative Research and Sequentially Performed Quantitative Research*', South African Journal of Psychology, vol. 27, pp. 1–8.

Luck, D.J. and R.S. Rubin 1987, *Marketing Research*, 7th edition, Prentice Hall, New Jersey.

ANNEXURE 15.1

Research Proposal for an Eatery

The following is a research proposal for exploring the product and store perception of clients vis-à-vis Brand X, an eatery.

Research Brief

- The client has a two-fold research need:

  - Part I—to simplify the decision-making process through ease in the comprehension of menu boards, product offerings, value perception through the pricing structure, etc.

  - Part II—to understand the value perceptions of the offerings in order to increase the saliency of the brand vis-à-vis the consumers' preference options for eateries and, thus, increase their patronization of the brand.

Our understanding of the client's brief

- Since the information needs of the client focus more on the 'whys' of consumer perceptions and preferences, we recommend a qualitative research approach

- In order to meet the objectives of the client, the information that we need to unearth is as follows:

  - *Part I* : Menu offering and menu board analysis (visual layout)

    (i) Is the consumer able to decode the menu with ease?

    (ii) Is she/he more comfortable with pictures, or with words? What should be the ideal combination of both?

    (iii) Is she/he able to perceive value in this pricing structure?

    (iv) What in the menu (and other factors) arrests/negates affordability perception?

(v) After decision-making, does she/he face any issue vis-à-vis placing the order or paying the bill?

■ *Part II* : Mapping the mindset, value perception, the brand's menu preferences, and price perceptions

    ❏   What is value for the consumer in the store offering?

    ❏   What is the definition of a 'value-for-money' meal?

    ❏   What made her/him come to the store, and what will make her/him a patron of this place?

    ❏   What are the reactions to the price points for the core products?

    ❏   What is an ideal menu perception?

    ❏   How much, on an average, does she/he spend on eating out per day, per week? Would she/he spend this amount on the eatery under study? Why? For what items?

    ❏   What is her/his perception of 'filling' vis-à-vis the food available in this eatery? How can such a perception be induced? What gives a sense of filling?

Research Deliverables

- Consumer insights thus generated will be inputs for working out strategies vis-à-vis

  ■ corrections required—meal offerings, menu board layouts—to ease comprehension and decision-making

  ■ Solving confusion in communicating price, communicating meal options

  ■ Reviewing of meal options vis-à-vis consumer needs

  ■ Identify the factors that will help in increasing the loyalty of the consumers towards this brand of eatery

Methodology

On the basis of our understanding, we suggest the following:

Part I:

- In-store interviews—with customers, randomly selected at the branded eatery outlet. Some of the customers will be interviewed before they've placed their order and interviewed after they've ordered and after the meal was served.

  ■ The second methodology recommendation for Part I of the study is to constitute a 'panel of 8 sensitive customers' from diverse backgrounds (mainly to bring in lateral thinking for working out the corrective measures required). The group will be a mixed group of males and females. The data obtained from the exit interviews will be sifted through by this panel. In addition, the panel's own reactions will also be taken into account. This will help us generate concrete solutions for the corrective measures to be taken in-store. This probing of this panel will be through paired interviews—i.e., two individuals at one time will be interviewed in the store premises.

- The rationale for this methodology is as follows:

  - A panel group of sensitive customers recommended because, very often the average set of customers are unable to give us the 'creative/innovative' insight vis-à-vis the problem at hand. Therefore, talking to individuals with a diverse mindset, a more creative mindset will enable us to supplement our findings from the main segment with more insights of value and relevance. The perception insights will mainly come from the exit interviews.

  - The 'what to do about this issue' insights will mainly come from the Panel group

Part II :

- In-store interviews—with customers selected at and interviewed within the store premises (recruitment to happen Monday and Thursday)—some of these consumers will be pre-selected, invited to the store mainly to ensure that we get the right set of consumers that fit the definitions (to be given by the client)

- For these interviews the following 'types' of customers will be recruited at the store:

  - Sets of friends

  - Individual persons

Research Centres

The client's presence is in Kanpur, Surat, Coimbatore—therefore all these centres will need to be covered in the study.

Sample Size

- Total 6 stores (2 per city)

Interviews per store—

  - Part I : 6 In-store interviews

  - Part II : 8 In-store interviews

Total—84 interviews

Then come the cost and time details along with the terms of the research study/agency.

ANNEXURE 15.2 ▬▬▬▬▬▬▬▬▬▬▬

Recruitment Questionnaire

Date	Time	
Venue		

Project Style	Recruitment Questionnaire	Mode

CENTRE : Bangalore		
RESPONDENTS	:	Segment 1 Loyalists of Brand X Eatery
NAME OF RESPONDENT	:	
ADDRESS OF RESPONDENT	:	
PHONE NO.	:	
INTERVIEWER'S NAME	:	

FIELD CONTROL INFO.		DATE OF INTERVIEW :						
FO/FE CODE		TEAM CODE		SUPV CODE	INV CODE		SCRUT CODE	CHKE CODE
ACCOMPANIED CAL			SPOT/BACK CHECK			SCRUTINY		
Y–1 By N–2 CD		Sg	Y–1 By N–2 CD		Sg	Y–1 By N–2 CD		Sg
ANALYSIS OBS : EXTENT OF PROBLEM			NO/MINOR – 1			MILD – 2		SEVERE – 3

SECTION I	:	SCREENING

Speak to Any Adult:

Good .... I am from .... We meet various people and collect their views and opinions about various products, issues, and services. I would be grateful if you could spare some time to answer a few questions. Thank you.

1. Can you tell me whether you or anyone in your household works in any of the organizations/jobs listed on this card? (SHOW PLACE OF WORK CARD)

Advertising agency	:	1
Market research company	:	2
Company manufacturing food products	:	3
Shop selling food products, restaurants, etc.	:	4
Stockists for personal care products such as talcum powder, soaps, creams, shampoos, cosmetics, etc.	:	5

– TERMINATE

Banks	:	6
Insurance companies	:	7
Others	:	8

– CONTINUE

Continue only if 6–8 coded or else terminate.

2a. I would now like to ask you a few questions about the Chief Wage Earner of your household. By Chief Wage Earner, I mean the person who contributes the most

Occupation		Illiterate	EDUCATION					
			School upto 4 years	School 5–9 years	SSC/ HSC	Some College but not Graduate	Graduate/ Post-graduate- General	Graduate/ Post-graduate Professional
Unskilled workers	1	X	X	X	X	X	X	X
Skilled workers	2	X	X	X	X	X	B2	B2
Petty workers	3	X	X	X	X	X	B2	B2
Shop owners	4	X	X	X	B2	B1	A2	A2
Businessmen/Industrialists With no. of employees:								
• None	5	X	X	B2	B1	A2	A2	A1
• 1–9	6	X	B2	B2	B1	A2	A1	A1
• 10+	7	B1	B1	A2	A2	A1	A1	A1
Self-employed professionals	8	X	X	X	B2	B1	A2	A1
Clerical/Salesmen	9	X	X	X	X	B2	B1	B1
Supervisory level	M	X	X	X	X	B2	B1	A2
Officers/Executives— Junior	N	X	X	X	B2	B1	A2	A2
Officers/Executives— Middle/Senior	O	B1	B1	B1	B1	A2	A1	A1

tcwards the household budget. Could you please tell me her/his name? (NAME OF CWE).

....

Please note: For the Young Adults group ensure that the respondent is the CWE

2b. Can you please tell me what is the occupation of the Chief Wage Earner?

If retired, seek the Last Occupation and Code accordingly

OCCUPATION : ....

2c. Please tell me what is the education level of the Chief Wage Earner?.

EDUCATION : ....

Continue only if Sec A1 or B1 else terminate.

2d. Can you please tell me which of these restaurants have you visited in the last six months?

Brand C	1
Brand Y	2
Brand Z	3
Brand A	4
Brand X	5

Repondent must code 5 to continue or else terminate

2e. Can you please tell me how many times have you visited Brand X in the last six months?

		Action
Never	1	TERMINATE
Once	2	TERMINATE
More than twice	3	RECRUIT

.... Times

Please note how many times the person has gone to Brand X

2f. Could you please tell me what you mostly eat when you go to Brand X?

Pizza	1
Only Chips	2
Chips, Coke and Sandwich	3
Burgers	4
Indian meal	5
Desserts	6
Any other	7

Repondent must code 2 or 3 to continue or else terminate

2g. In the last 3 times you visited Brand X what did you eat at the restaurant and how many times?

	Only once	Action	More than once	Action
Segment 1				
Product Q	1	TERMINATE	2	RECRUIT
Product S	1	TERMINATE	2	RECRUIT

Repondent must code 2 to be recruited or else terminate

* Please ensure an equal mix of Vegetarians and Non-Vegetarians

From time to time we conduct studies on various products among people like you. We would be grateful if you could kindly participate in the same and spare us 45 minutes now.

Hand Over the Invitation

Willing   :   1   Not Willing   :   2

Self Filled Questionnaire

1. Which newspapers do you read on a daily basis? How much time do you spend reading each newspaper?

Name of Newspaper	Amount of Time Spent

2. Which magazines do you read on a regular basis? How much time do you spend each magazine?

Name of Magazines	Amount of Time Spent

3. Which TV channels do you view regularly? Which serials do you like to see on each of these channels?

Name of TV Channel	Name of Serial

4. Which advertisement do you recall having seen in the newspaper in the last 15 days?

- ....
- ....
- ....
- ....
- ....
- ....

5. Which advertisement do you recall having seen on television in the last 15 days?

- ....
- ....
- ....
- ....
- ....
- ....

6. Which hoarding do you recall having seen in the last 15 days?

- ....
- ....
- ....
- ....
- ....
- ....

ANNEXURE 15.3

Discussion Guide: Moderator Instructions

Tone of moderator:

- Moderators should express extreme politeness in their manner of talking.
- Must make the consumer feel that her/his perspective vis-à-vis our topic is imperative to making our project/endeavour a success.

- Need to keep in check that the consumer's voice is louder than the moderator's– i.e., the moderator must ensure that the consumer is heard out properly and only at appropriate junctures should she/he intervene with relevant questions.

Attitude towards consumer:

- Moderator should not come across as 'knowing-it-all'.

- Need to communicate non-verbally that 'I am here to learn from you and not to teach you'.

Mode of questioning

- Moderator to put forth questions in the third person—mostly as— 'what do most consumers prefer?'—rather than asking—'what do you prefer?'.

- Need to know the 'why' of every response given by the consumer—however, this 'why' should be cloaked when asked (in due course of time) and should not be thrown to the consumer each time she/he makes a point.

- Instead of asking 'why' as'why'—ask—'Could you explain the reason for this?' Or 'How come this is done/believed/practiced?' Or 'I am sure…..only I don't understand it too well…..', etc.

- Moderator to note all important points and leads on show cards for future reference.

Self introduction:

'I come from a Market research company and we go into the market and talk to consumers, get their opinions on various topics, products, etc.—basically try to understand those topics from their eyes. We do not belong to any manufacturing or marketing company. Our job is to gather information from the market and sell our reports—so that a consumer can get better products and services.'

Process introduction:

'We do not "run a courtroom" in our sessions where we adjudge what is right and what is wrong—we are talking to you knowing that you have the knowledge and expertise which we could learn immensely from and which is not to be evaluated by us but only to be understood and learnt from.'

'I would like to audio-tape this session for my convenience because I will not be able to write down our entire conversation….and everything you say is important for us.'

'Importantly, we promise you complete confidentiality of your name.'

Task/Topic introduction:

'Today our topic of discussion is eating out. As we move forward you will learn more about it.'

When concluding:

'At this point we will conclude....thank you very much for being so helpful and talking so well.'

Sample segments:

In-store interviews—with customers randomly selected at Brand X eatery.

Some of the customers will be interviewed before they've placed their order and as well as after they've ordered and taken their order.

Core research objective:

To simplify the decision-making process through ease in comprehension of the menu boards, product offerings, value perception through the pricing structure.

The core session (post warm-up):

- From the time you enter, till you leave, just trace your journey for me and tell me where you face any kind of problem and where it is absolutely convenient and easy? Please explain all of this to me in detail.

- When you stand at the counter and look up at the menu—what are the first points that strike you?

- Why do these points strike you first?

- What other points do you notice?

We will take each area and discuss it in detail—

- First look at this menu board....What do you like about it? Why do you say that?

- What is it that attracts you the most?

- What on the menu board is most relevant for you?

- Now tell me what is it that you don't like about this menu?

- Which part of the menu puts you off?

- Which part of it is not relevant to you?

- Briefly, tell me two positives about this menu (the way it is written) and two negatives. What makes you say that?

Let's focus on the prices here.......

- What is your reaction to the way the prices are written here? I don't want reactions such as 'Brand X is expensive' or 'Reduce the price'. Instead I want to know what you feel are the issues/problems with this pricing structure?

- What is the positive aspect of this? What is the negative? Why?

- Does it suit you? Why?

- Does this pricing structure make sense, indicate value? Why do you say that?

- What do you understand by these names? Are you ok with this or do you feel that there should be another system? Why so?

- The moment you look at this menu, what do you feel—that it is just right, or does it look as if only expensive stuff is available here, or do you feel that this is a value-for-money place, or what? Why do you say that?

- Now—If you had to redo this, how would you do it?

- Here is a paper and pen—please explain to me by writing how you would redo this? What all would you add, remove, modify? What makes you do that?

- Would you be more comfortable with only pictures or with only words, or do you want both?—How? What combination?

- Next, tell me about the meal combinations that you see here—what do you feel regarding these? Adequate, inadequate? Appropriate or not? Or what else?

- What are your suggestions in this context? How else would you make these combinations, and then, how should these be communicated to the consumer so that she/he can understand things easily and without any difficulty? What makes you say that?

- After you decide what you want to order, what next?

- You place your order—any issues, inconvenience felt here? What makes you say that? Think and tell me about each step in detail

  - Order placing
  - Bill (paying and understanding), etc.

- Any communication in each of these steps?

- What would be your suggestions for each of these areas such that the consumer feels more comfortable and at ease? Please explain to me in detail—however small a change that you feel will make a difference in the following:

  - Order placing
  - Bill (paying and understanding), etc.

Conclude with thanks.

16

Qualitative Research Methodology

INTRODUCTION

After having understood the fundamentals of the qualitative research approach, the current chapter builds upon it in order to give an in-depth understanding of what happens in a qualitative research study, i.e., its application, methodological frameworks, techniques, and researcher skills required. It is imperative to get an understanding of how the data should be collected in order to ensure that the data has depth and relevance and is free from any bias. Therefore, it is not enough to understand that the consumer is asked open-ended questions, it is more important to get a grip of how to ask, how to sequence one's line of questioning, how to 'handle' the consumer in order to get the best and most out of her/him. Therefore, this chapter discusses the key methods of qualitative research, viz focus group discussion and in-depth interview. A significant feature of the qualitative methods is that they have the ability to provide a holistic view of a situation. The focus group discussion and in-depth interview detail the modalities involved in each respective methodology—how to organize a focus group, how to talk to the consumer, what factors need to be kept in mind in order to have maximum facilitation and minimum inhibition in the consumer's articulation, what are the pitfalls that researchers must be wary of in order not to 'goof-up' their session. The chapter goes on to discuss the projective methodology, which is the crux of qualitative methodology. Projective techniques are a disguised mode of questioning that allow for deeper probing of the human mind in terms of reaching to the latent thoughts, feelings, and motives that underlie the overt behaviour manifested by the consumer. The chapter details the nature of projective techniques, their advantages and disadvantages, and the specific exercises. Finally, the chapter ends with a discussion on innovations in qualitative research, which have only added value and depth to the approach and deliverables of this mode of research. In this context the chapter discusses three key research approaches, viz, semiotics, observational-ethnographic research, and synectics.

METHODOLOGICAL FRAMEWORKS OF QUALITATIVE RESEARCH

Qualitative methods allow us to know people personally and to know them as they develop their own view of the world. The researcher has the opportunity to experience meaning in the form in which people feel it, to understand naturally occurring phenomena in their naturally occurring states.

When a question is asked in any qualitative methodology, it is mostly in an open-ended format. For example, 'Do you like Shoppers' Stop because it displays a lot of products of different brands and it is very spacious?' It is not a question that is asked in a qualitative methodology. Instead, the question should be framed and put forth as: 'What do you like about Shoppers' Stop?' Thus, for the answer that the latter question will yield, the options are not with the consumer. Therefore, consumers will need to use their own thoughts and vocabulary to work out an answer. In this way, they are left with a wide canvas to look into their own mind to bring out a reaction and one gets to know the consumers' world better through their own eyes and in their own words.

Broadly speaking, there are two main methodological frameworks in qualitative research—group situation, termed as focus group discussion and one-to-one situation, termed as in-depth interview (Fig. 16.1). In both these frameworks, the moderator plays a key role. It is the moderator who facilitates the session and ensures that the objectives of the session are met by asking relevant questions and leading the discussion as per the discussion guide.

FOCUS GROUP DISCUSSIONS

A focus group discussion is a group methodology, which has a prefixed quorum of consumers—the minimum number is eight and maximum is twelve, depending upon

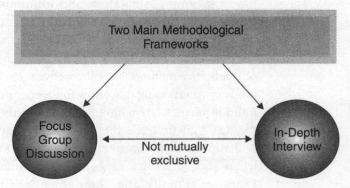

Fig. 16.1 Qualitative Research Frameworks: Focus Group Discussion and In-depth Interview

the nature of discussion required, objectives of research, and comfort level of the moderator.

This framework of a focus group discussion is appropriate in case of the following types of research study:

- Studies for idea generation for communication and/or new product development ideas, concept exploration for advertising communication and/or product, brand name testing, etc. The important objective here is to 'generate' and for this purpose a group setting helps wherein each consumer in the group acts as a catalyst to the other's thoughts and builds upon her/his thoughts based on the stimulation from other people's thoughts and ideas.
- Establishment of consumer vocabulary as a preliminary step in questionnaire development: Expression of language is required. Therefore, when such is the requirement, then a group generates a wider spectrum of language expressions.
- Exploratory studies: When the need is to generate spectrum of perceptions, attitudes, and behaviours then a group setting facilitates this objective to the fullest.

However, a key factor that should be kept in sight is the nature of the topic/issue under study. If the topic/issue under study is sensitive and/or embarrassing then a group session will be more hindering than generative, e.g., condoms, financial issues, mapping of sexual habits, and preferences, etc.

Advantages and Disadvantages

As true with all things, there are both advantages and disadvantages with the methodology of focus group discussion. Certain pros and cons are inherent in the methodology itself whereas some pros and cons come about due to moderation-related issues.

Advantages A group discussion is generally more exciting and offers more stimulation to the participants and hence the thoughts of one become stimulating to the other, thus bringing out latent thoughts.

Also, the 'security' of being in a crowd encourages some members to speak out when they otherwise would not – because any questions raised by the moderator are to the group as a whole rather than to individuals. Due to this, the answers contain a degree of 'spontaneity' not produced by other techniques.

Another important fact of this methodology is that it is time saving and cost-effective because at least 8-10 consumers are spoken to in the same setting at the same point in time—in this way larger number of consumers can be covered during a shorter span of time.

Disadvantages The inherent problems of the methodology are that consumers may 'play games', and go along with the group rather than express their own opinions.

Also the group may go haywire and not give appropriate responses to meet the objectives of the research.

Moreover, being in a group setting, individuals are more concerned that the responses they give are intelligent and socially acceptable.

ORGANIZATION IN FOCUS GROUP DISCUSSIONS

Researchers have to keep in mind two aspects when they think of a focus group discussion: How to moderate it well i.e., how to conduct a focus group discussion and what are the key logistics that need attention.

Conducting a focus group discussion

The most important aspect in understanding the methodology of focus group discussion is the modalities of moderation. The discussion is led by a researcher-moderator who attempts to progress through three key stages:

- Establish rapport with the group, structure the rules of group interaction, and put the agenda in place
- Facilitate, and at times, provoke intense discussion in the relevant areas
- Summarize the group's responses to determine common thoughts and significant thinking patterns.

Getting started   The initial part of each session should be devoted to an introduction. The objective of this task is to familiarize everyone with everyone else and to 'loosen up' the group. Most people may not have previously attended a group interview session and, consequently, they may be anxious about the procedure and expectations. All members can be asked to give their names, occupation, hobbies, etc. This familiarization stage should also be used to set the tone for group.

For example, the moderator can address everyone by their first name and make casual remarks such as: 'It is really hot these days…must be very strenuous to work in this heat'. Such an approach would signal to the respondents that the session is to be informal and free wheeling.

Next, a general explanation as to the nature and norms of group interviewing needs to be given:

- Introduction of the moderator/research company
- Nature of market research
- Not for promoting sales, strictly research oriented
- Advantages of a group session
- Acceptance of all answers since there are no right or wrong answers, rather points of view, so nobody would be adjudged

- The importance of everyone's contribution, and therefore, everybody's voice needs to be heard
- Justification of the recording devices, i.e., session is being recorded/monitored for purpose of the research
- Speak one at a time to avoid garbled recording of the session
- Anonymity of the client and respondents with no one held accountable for comments made
- And, finally, it is advisable to give the respondents some idea of the scope of the interview and the general topics to be covered. This brief outline should allay their 'fear of the unknown' as well as create a task-oriented atmosphere.

There is a tendency for the moderator to get stale with the instructions and to ramble about them by rote. What must be remembered is that while it may be the moderator's umpteenth group session, it is the first for most of the members. The initial stage of the group discussion must never be rushed through in order to get to what may be perceived as the 'more' important tasks at hand.

Deciding on style   The moderator should be conscious of the overall manner or style and pace at which the interview is conducted. The style adopted by the moderator will influence the interaction of the group and the nature of the resulting data. The chart of moderator styles (Fig. 16.2) is a useful organization of the major approaches available.

Along the horizontal axis is the directive/non-directive level of involvement. The directive portion describes a situation in which the moderator maintains strict control of the discussion. This high-involvement approach is an effort to keep the discussion orderly by closely following the moderator's discussion guide.

In contrast, the non-directive approach is a hands-off approach. The emphasis is on the group and the interaction between the group members. The moderator becomes involved only when the group wanders too far a field or hits a sticking point. The approach is much like that of a psychoanalyst who encourages the group members to continue their 'self-exploration of an experience until some measure of clarity is attained.'

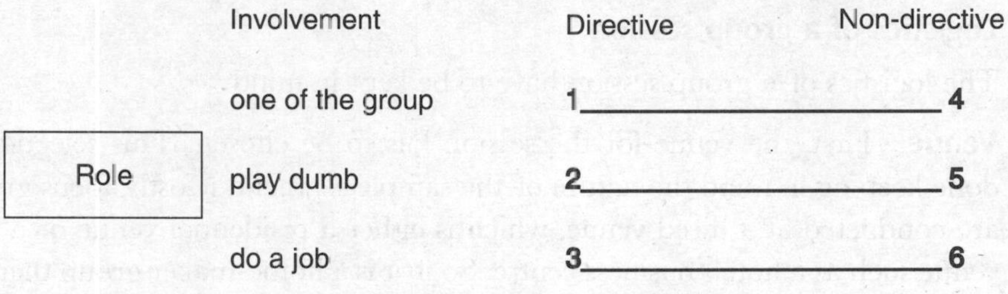

	Involvement	Directive		Non-directive
	one of the group	1_____	_____	4
Role	play dumb	2_____	_____	5
	do a job	3_____	_____	6

Fig. 16.2 Moderator's Style Chart

The other axis represents different types of roles that a moderator can create:

- The 'one of the group' role is established when moderators attempt to identify with the group and remove themselves from an overt leadership role. The democratic approach creates an atmosphere in which everyone feels comfortable in expressing their opinions. It is an appropriate climate when attempting to generate hypotheses or describe a set of attitudes towards common objects.
- The 'play dumb' role is indicative of a situation in which moderators allude to the fact that they are 'ignorant about the area and want to learn more'. It works well with professional people or when discussing complex issues.
- The 'do a job' role befits a formal and serious session. It is useful when there are hard choices to be made—a new advertisement concept to evaluate or questionnaire to design.

Each of these roles can be conducted at either a directive or non-directive level of involvement; hence the style also differs. For example, a moderator who adopts a play dumb role can take a high level (directive) of involvement by asking such questions:

'I need you to explain that point a little more clearly for me'

'I'm not sure, but I think we should move along to…'

At a non-directive level, a play dumb role question might be: 'Perhaps you could help me to understand the way in which you…?'

A key point to be noted is that any moderator who approaches every group session with the same style will never be successful. The moderator style sets an important atmosphere in which the data are collected. It must change according to

- the nature of the research objectives,
- the sample profile, and
- the 'personality' of the group.

The moderators who adopt a middle-of-the-road approach and do not waiver from it will do well. However, it is the 'true expert' of group dynamics who can overtly adapt her/his style to reflect the conditions at hand.

Logistics of a group session

The logistics of a group session have to be kept in mind.

Venue First, the venue for the session has to be chosen. This selection has to be done keeping in mind the nature of the sample segment. Mostly, focus group sessions are conducted at a hired venue, which is either a residential venue or a commercial venue such as a hotel/business centre. So if it is a home-maker group then mostly it is a residential location than a commercial one. For example, a trucker segment will not be comfortable in an affluent hotel. Therefore, it is imperative that the kind of venue chosen has to be in sync with the profile of the consumer group.

Sitting arrangement   It is also important to ensure that the consumers are seated comfortably because any kind of discomfort for them could make them edgy and impatient. Therefore, the ventilation of the room, the temperature in the room, etc., should ensure optimal comfort of the consumers.

Eye contact   Another aspect related to the seating arrangement of the consumers is to ensure that the moderator is able to make eye contact with everyone.

For instance, if the consumers are not seated properly, the ones sitting at elbow-distance from the moderator on either side will be quiet. This is because they are sitting too close to the moderator to make meaningful eye contact. The other logistics that need a final check is whether the recording apparatus is in order, it could be the CD player, the audio sound recording system, etc.

Miscellaneous   Also, minor details such as checks whether the phones in the venue are off the hook, refreshments are served on time, etc., contribute significantly to the smooth functioning of the group session.

Lastly, attention has to be paid to the dress code of the researcher, which has to be in sync with the nature of the consumer profile of the group session. For example, for a session with children, the researcher should be dressed informally, however, a formal dress code is recommended in a session with the trade consumers, CEOs of companies, etc. The dress code of the researcher, subconsciously, fosters and/or hinders the establishment of an amicable and comfortable rapport between the researcher and consumers. This rapport is extremely essential for the successful articulation of the consumers' ideas.

Levels of group discussion

Conducting a group discussion interview necessitates that the moderator operates on at least seven different levels of communication simultaneously. These are as follows:

1.   cover the discussion guide
2.   involve all of the group members
3.   introduce related points to stimulate and motivate discussion
4.   probe to get beyond the guide into the group's thoughts and feelings
5.   constantly think ahead about the next area of the guide
6.   set an emotional tone
7.   constantly needs to weigh the importance of what is being said

Discussion guide   Regardless of whether the moderator chooses a directive or non-directive level of involvement, the moderator is still responsible for generating information on all aspects of the discussion guide.

In a directive situation, the topic areas are covered sequentially with the moderator questioning the members until the first topic is exhausted; the moderator then proceeds to the next topic. Any off-the-immediate-track topics are discouraged and the efforts are devoted to keep the conversation focused. In non-directive situations, the moderator's guide is much less rigid and the moderator usually lets the discussion wander. If it jumps forward, the moderator does not interrupt, but simply makes a mental note of those issues that are missed (and returns to them later). This will make sure that the topic areas are covered, irrespective of the direction taken by the group.

The moderator must assign an implicit weight and time to each question and move on, even if the discussion is not over, when the question has taken as much time as it is worth. An ideal interview should get over at the stipulated time.

Participation of all group members   While it is not necessary for each respondent to participate with equal frequency, the objective is to promote an active exchange of ideas and attitudes amongst group members.

One technique to facilitate such an interaction is the 'ping-pong' method. The moderator simply interjects: 'And what is your opinion on what this person has said?' If the moderator does this early in the session, the members usually pick up the idea that they are encouraged to react to one another's comments. In many instances, such natural interaction does not occur; there is no easy interchange of ideas. One reason for this is that some people feel a lack of expertise in an area, or are shy about articulating an opinion. They seem to sink back into the couch, pull back their chairs, or simply give monosyllabic responses. Shy persons need encouragement and reassurance that their views are of value to the moderator and are acceptable to the group as a whole.

Once an opinion has been elicited from a non-participant, it is extremely important that the moderator reinforces or rewards the effort. Such comments as: 'that's very interesting' or 'that's an important point', will bolster the members' confidence in his articulation and encourage them for actively participating.

At times, there is an 'expert' in the group who unconsciously relegates everyone else to the position of 'non-experts'. Usually experts of this kind can be induced to refrain from group domination by such comments: 'we'd like to get some other opinions on this matter', or, by addressing another group member by name 'Rita, tell me how you feel about this advertisement?'

Such negative reinforcement will normally induce the expert to be somewhat less vocal. At times the 'know-it-all' require some drastic actions:

- interviewer can cut them off in mid-phrase,
- ask pointedly if there are others who want to express an opinion,
- avoid eye contact with the problem maker,
- change the subject immediately but politely the moment the person has stopped talking, and
- display other signs of disinterest.

Most trouble makers can be controlled by such tactics but, there may be a few stubborn ones who will not refrain from speaking, in such cases, it is best to ignore them or politely ask them to leave the room.

Stimulation of thought and discussion   With the directive level of involvement, it is much easier for moderators to interject a different line of reasoning or stimulating a new idea. For example, they can ask: 'Perhaps we should discuss the area of nutrition', or 'Let's try to think of as many different uses of this product as we can.'

When operating on a non-directive level, however, new ideas should emerge spontaneously. Such natural inclinations presumably get minimized under moderator prompting. Therefore, if any stimulation or motivation is to be done in such a situation it must be done with extreme subtlety or none at all. In fact, prompting may result in just mechanical answers to questions.

Probe group thought process   The moderator must probe to get beyond the discussion guide into the group's thoughts and feelings. This 'getting beyond' can happen if the following guidelines are adhered to:

- The kind of question that is asked
- The laddering of 'whys' that is done to get to the deeper layers of mind
- How it is phrased
- When it is asked
- The tone in which it is asked

All this can affect the kind of response generated.

Usually, structured questions will result in standardized and socially acceptable responses. The question: 'Do you think nutrition is important in a breakfast cereal?' will evoke a positive reply. But such direct frontal questions rarely uncover true feelings. The responses that come forth more likely to be 'socially appropriate' answers with little information value. If, however, we juxtapose a structured question next to an unstructured one, we can see the potential value of coming at the issue indirectly:

- Structured question: 'From your personal knowledge of the candidates, do you think that Minister X is more qualified in the area of foreign policy than Minister Y?'
- Unstructured question: 'What impresses you most about any of the candidates for the prime ministership?'

With the structured question, moderators assume almost total control. They are able to single out the candidates to compare and think of attributes on which to compare them.

The unstructured question, in contrast, is '… one that does not fix attention on any specific aspect of the response; it is, so to speak, a blank page to be filled in by the interviewee.' One of the best unstructured questions may be the simple follow-up question, 'Why?'

With this the respondent is being forced to analyse his or her own rationalizations or explanations for an expressed attitude, belief, or behaviour. Such questions then become almost automatic: 'How did you arrive at that conclusion?' 'Why did you say that?'. By continuing this probing, the moderator may be able to uncover feelings that are either not evident to the respondent and/or suppressed.

Jump ahead of the discussion guide   There may be the need to jump ahead of the guide if someone opens up a new topic. This is a matter of contingency planning. The moderator must map out where the conversation is heading and be in a position to anticipate problems and accordingly, work out new areas of enquiry in her/his mind.

Set an emotional tone   The moderator must be able to set an emotional tone that coincides with the makeup of the group members and the topic under investigation. The emotional tone of the group contributes to the context in which interaction takes place. The moderator should be able to set the appropriate emotional tone in the group in order to generate appropriate responses as per the articulation requirement of the research objectives of the study:

- Some groups are reticent, delicate, and fragile, therefore, wooing and encouragement is needed
- In other instances, the chemistry is not there, the liveliest response is apathy, and the situation may be unproductive. This can be rescued by 'blasting', i.e., raising the most dramatic or controversial aspect, shifting gears and calling for a break, or confronting the problem by exploring why the group seems to be uninterested
- Some groups require emotional responses far more than rational ones. Accordingly, the emotional tone will need to be set by the moderator. However, certain other groups (e.g., for finance-related isses) may be cued for a more rational discussion.

Evaluation of the group discussion   For the entire duration of a group session, the moderator continually makes intuitive judgments about the relative merits of continuing on or changing directions. If a judgment is made to continue, it is with the belief that some additional under-standing will take place; that any additional mileage of information is worth the time and energy it will take to generate it. In contrast, by moving on to another topic area, the belief is that either no additional information is available or that the value of the information is not worth the effort to extract it.

IN-DEPTH INTERVIEW

The second important methodological framework in qualitative research is that of in-depth interviews. This is a one-on-one interview session between one consumer and a moderator. Such an interview session has its application when:

- Detailed probing of an individual's behaviour, attitudes or needs, processes such as decision-making is required
- Subject matter under discussion is highly confidential in nature (e.g., personal investments), or of an emotionally charged or embarrassing nature
- Certain strong, socially acceptable norms exist (e.g., breast feeding) and the need to conform in a group discussion may influence responses
- Interviews are with professional people with whom availability and time are major constraints

Advantages and disadvantages

Once again, as discussed earlier in the context of the focus group discussion, this methodology of in-depth interview has its pros and cons and the skill lies in optimizing upon its advantages while overcoming its disadvantages.

Advantages In an in-depth interview, being a situation wherein there is an interaction between one consumer and a moderator, there tends to be a higher level of intimacy and mental comfort between the moderator and the interviewee. Therefore, there is a marked lowering of defenses due to lack of presence of 'others' and there is expression of more deep and honest reactions. All this results in a better articulation from the interviewee as a result of this level of intimacy and comfort.

Importantly, there is reduction of such influences that can bias the interviewee since there are no other opinions coming forth. Thus, in this process one can get a lot of depth in the information, and be able to penetrate deep into the subconscious mind of the interviewee.

Disadvantages However, absence of other members in an in-depth interview session can have its set of drawbacks. Therefore, there will be a lack of 'peer' influence that is critical in 'normal/day-to-day' situations experienced, decision-making, and purchase, etc. Importantly, there is lack of a catalyst-like stimulation of latent thoughts and needs that may not get uncovered due to the absence of the thoughts and feelings of 'others'.

Also, there is a higher probability of getting irrelevant, atypical reactions that may not hold true in a real-like setting. Finally, in-depth interviews are time-consuming and therefore less cost-effective.

FLOW OF COMMUNICATION IN IN-DEPTH INTERVIEWS

In obvious contrast to the focus group session, the in-depth interview is a one-to-one interaction. The atmosphere consequently is very simple, with the interviewee responding to the moderator's questions and the moderator reacting to the interviewee's answers. A major function that the moderator performs is to increase the flow of relevant communications. Within this role, the moderator can increase the flow of relevant information by employing various tactics to minimize the 'inhibitors' of communication and enhance the use of 'facilitators'.

Inhibitors

The inhibitor categories discussed below act to prevent the communication flow. The first three tend to make the interviewee unwilling to give information, while the final two tend to make the interviewee unable to give information even though willing.

- time constraint
- personal inhibitors
- culture
- difficulty in recollection
- unconscious behaviour

The detailed description of the above mentioned five inhibitors is given below.

Time constraint An in-depth interview may take between half an hour and several hours to complete. This is time the interviewee could use to do other things and, therefore, the interview competes with other activities of the interviewee. First, the moderator must sell the idea of being interviewed in order to gain individual's initial cooperation. And while this may prove to be somewhat easy to do with individuals with flexible schedules, it may require innovative interviewing approaches with a busy executive. The moderator should also be concerned with trying to get the interviewee to set aside an appropriate amount of time so that interruptions or other pressing commitments do not interfere. The moderator must aim for the interviewee's full concentration.

Personal inhibitors Interviewees may withhold information because of a psychological block due to the increased intimacy which is related to in-depth interviewing. For example, they may not admit to the use of some consumer products (e.g., perfume, clothing) in a sexual manner because of social taboo attached to it. At other times, the interviewee hesitates to communicate honestly because of fears of eliciting the disapproval of the moderator. And finally, while the interviewee may not be concerned about the moderator, he or she may be fearful of public disclosure of their personal feelings. The moderator can overcome many of these personal threats of the interviewee

- indirect questioning and probing,
- expressing a sympathetic and non-judgmental attitude, and
- giving assurance of anonymity.
- continuous positive reinforcement as in, 'Go on ... I am listening ... I am with you ...'

Culture There is a set of do's and don'ts that are imposed on individuals via their 'cultural' environment. It has been noted, e.g., that 'it is accepted' that there are

- things that men do not discuss in front of women and vice versa,
- things that married couples do not discuss in front of unmarried people,
- things students do not tell teachers,
- things doctors do not tell patients, and
- things people do not tell preachers.

Additionally, there is a desire to respond to questions within a range of cultural acceptance, avoiding any embarrassment, shock, or threats. The best way to minimize this communication block is to 'match' moderator and interviewee, which can be achieved in the following ways:

- manner of dressing—clothes, hair, jewellery, etc.
- manner of sitting
- language used for communication
- overall demeanour—facial expressions, gestures, verbal expressions, etc.
- verbal stressing of the fears, worries, concerns of the interviewee by the moderator in order to appear as close and 'humane' to the interviewee as possible

Difficulty in recollection At times, the interviewee is unable to report relevant information because of an inability to recall it. In marketing and advertising, we are continually asking people to reconstruct what they did or why they did it. Most people in an interview situation are trying to help, but their ability to give truthful answers is compromised by the passage of time since the event and the relative importance of the event.

Unconscious behaviour When using the in-depth interview technique, we are often interested in probing attitudes. Some activities such as using a particular brand of shampoo or choosing a wine are repetitive behaviours and do not have clearly defined elaborations. They have become so ingrained in most people that they cannot articulate specific reasons.

The moderator must avoid prompting and cueing the interviewee (e.g., 'Do you think you use this shampoo because you like the feeling of being clean all over?') and instead must use indirect questions and at times, be willing to accept an 'I don't know' answer.

Facilitators

While the moderator should make every effort to overcome or minimize the communication inhibitors, attention should also be given to a set of facilitators, the objective being to increase the flow of relevant information and create a good reationship between the interviewer and interviewee. There are three major communication facilitators:

- instill a sense of purpose
- recognition
- catharsis and empathy

The above mentioned major communication facilitators have been discussed below in detail.

Instill a sense of purpose   The moderator must develop an environment in which it becomes apparent to the interviewee that cooperation is necessary. When the interviewee gets an understanding that the interview session has relevance to her/his needs and that the session could eventually accrue benefits to her/him, then it would get motivating for her/him, to talk with clarity and sense. Therefore, the moderator could say something like, 'whatever you tell me ... will help the manufacturing company behind such products to give you better products and services ...'.

Recognition   It must be remembered that the in-depth interview is a social interaction and, as such, there is a social exchange. The moderator receives information through this interaction. But what does the interviewee receive in return? Therefore, praise, approval, and esteem are sources of personal gratification, which should be conveyed to the interviewee. All people like to be appreciated, and experimental studies of interviewing have shown that praising the interviewee's cooperation results in positive returns from the interview. The skilful moderator, therefore, should take every opportunity to recognize the importance of whatever the interviewee is contributing.

Catharsis and empathy   Everyone needs to vent frustrations or, at the very best, they require a medium for expressing their opinions. An interview can provide this function by encouraging the interviewee to verbalize hostility, guilt, frustration, hopes, and fears. Moderators, therefore, should provide a service akin to that of a psychoanalyst when probing sensitive issues. The listening skills of the interviewer are her/his strength. The very fact that they do not argue or criticize, make no demands, and just listen makes the interviewee free to talk without any fear of the consequences.

The basic reward that an interviewee can receive is the fact that someone is there to listen to them. Teenagers appreciate anyone who tries to understand them. Older people often complain that no one spares time to listen to them.

Moderators who can convey the notion that they are really interested in understanding what the interviewee (consumer) has to say, will go a long way in facilitating good communication.

The inhibitors and facilitators are, therefore, the factors that impact the communication flow between the moderator and the interviewee.

VARIATIONS IN QUALITATIVE RESEARCH METHODOLOGY

Even though there are two main methodological frameworks, i.e., group session and one-to-one interaction, depending upon the research objectives and the nature of the target sample, certain variations within these two basic frameworks may be more relevant in certain situations. For example, in the case of an in-depth interview, instead of the moderator interviewing one person, interviews two persons at the time and this is called a dyad or a paired interview.

In addition, three persons can be spoken to at the same time, and this is termed as a triad.

Therefore, the next key point for discussion is 'which variation to use in which case'. When the research objectives are more to unearth barriers and key loyalty sustainers, a dyad would be more apt because, typically, in a dyad we will have two different users. For example, a Shoppers' Stop loyalist customer versus a Shoppers' Stop non-loyalist customer—the two users, in a dyad, need to be on a par with demographic parameters such as age, gender, socio-economic status, income level, etc. But they will be different on a key parameter such a brand usership; thus the two customers will be pitted against each other to interact and understand why is the store being preferred versus why not being preferred. For example, what are the key barriers and motivators behind visits/no visits to the store.

During the course of such a dyad session, the whys and why nots of brands preferred and/or not preferred come out more clearly and in depth.

A triad is normally a mid-way between an in-depth interview session (with one person) and a focus group discussion (with 8–10 persons). In a triad there are three consumers, once again, demographically on a par, but different on one key parameter, as mentioned earlier in the context of a dyad. A triad can also be homogeneous in nature, i.e., all consumers are on par all key profile parameters. In this case, a triad variation is selected in order to avoid the inhibiting and influencing bias of the presence of a larger number of persons (as in a focus group). However, in this triad the catalyst effect of a group discussion can still be attained, which is absent in an in-depth interview session. For example, if the research product/topic is sensitive, then ideally one should opt for an in-depth interview approach. However, if the research objective is to generate cues for communication, generation and development, then a group session is required, in this case a triad is more advisable. In this manner, the disadvantages of a group session as well as in-depth interviews will get minimized and controlled to a large extent.

In another situation such as above, another variation of a dyad can be utilized, e.g., a friendship paired interview wherein the two consumers are not only equal on key demographic parameters but are also known to each other; this familiarity ensures a comfort level necessary for discussing a sensitive topic, such as attitude related to sex, preferences, condoms, etc., or finance/investment related topics. In such cases, each consumer does not feel 'threatened' because of the presence of another known person.

Along with the variation of numbers, there are marginal moderation differences in the three methodological variations:

In-depth interview (1 interviewee)

- More parity between the moderator and the interviewee
- More interaction between moderator and interviewee
- More of a question and answer session

Dyad (2 interviewees)/triad (3 interviewees)

- More interaction amongst interviewees
- More of a confrontation/debate like exchange
- More of a self-reinforcing discussion rather than a question and answer session

ROLE, DEMEANOUR, AND SKILLS OF A MODERATOR

Be it a focus group discussion session or an in-depth interview session, there are certain norms that moderators need to adhere to in order to ensure that their sessions yield rich and relevant data. Moderators have a role to play and within the scope of this role, their appearance, body language, behaviour, and bonding with the consumer play a key role in enhancing their efficiency in order to have a successful session. Therefore, moderators must take care of the following aspects of their personality and behaviour.

Behavioural skills

- Are they sensitive to what the group members will be comfortable with? Moderators must be very alert, all their senses need to be working well and in tandem, i.e., they need to pick-up the key leads from the consumer speak and further lead those into asking more relevant questions. So, they need to listen, see, and observe the respondents to the fullest.
- Are they able to pitch themselves right to strike the right chord and build bonds of empathy? Moderators need to establish a rapport between themselves and the consumer. This rapport is essential in order to relax the consumers such that their defenses get lowered to enable them to talk uninhibitedly. Once the introductions are over and the warm-up phase is through, the group should talk spontaneously and feel motivated to articulate well.
- Is the moderator sensitive to body language and group dynamics? Moderators must understand and recognize the emotions of their consumers by their body language. For example, if the consumers are sitting on the edge of the chair, then this is an indication that the group/consumer is uncomfortable for some reason. Moreover, if the group/consumer talks aggressively then the moderators need to pick-up this and accordingly tailor their approach.

Listening skills

In order to make consumers talk, moderators need to listen well. A moderator with good listening skills will motivate the consumers appropriately to think and express themselves. In order to have good listening skills, certain basic norms need to be kept in mind:

- Are the moderators adept at making all the respondents talk, including the timid and shy ones?
- Are they secure enough to tolerate silence in the group or do they panic when sometimes the group does not answer?
- Do they have the patience to let group members express themselves in their own natural style, without interrupting them every now and then?
- At the end of the group, are people surprised that they had so much to say about soft drinks or paints that they could keep going on and on for an hour and a half?
- When a moderator is heard less and more animated participation from the respondents takes place, it is certain that there is a good group.
- In a good group discussion, there would be a clear beginning, middle and an end. Therefore, the moderator has to ensure a start with a warm-up, then move through the discussion guide to cover the main topics and conclude with an expression of gratitude.

GUIDELINES FOR EFFECTIVE MODERATION

Be it an in-depth interview session or a focus group session, moderation norms have many commonalities. The manner in which moderators behave, articulate their questions, and encourage their consumers is more or less the same be it a one-on-one session or a group session.

Effective Formulation of Questions

Importantly, the words and phrases used in a question are the smallest controllable elements of the in-depth interviewing process. The moderators have their choice of every word that is used to interact with the interviewee. But how important can such decision be—whether to use this word or that word?

Thus, some major concerns which the moderator should have in mind while formulating questions are as follows:

- framing the question
- open-ended vs closed questions
- relevance of antecedents
- ambiguity and misperception
- leading questions
- loaded questions
- sequencing

Grilled but not Broiled

In a comparative advertisement, one fast food joint claimed that their *flame broiling* was preferred over *frying* (done by another competitive fast food joint) by a margin of three to one. The key question was: 'Do you prefer your hamburgers *flame-broiled or fried*?' To a question put forth like this, the answer of the majority of the consumers was that they preferred it flame-broiled. However, the question was asked in another way: 'Do you prefer a hamburger that is grilled on a hot stainless steel grill (referring to the frying method) or cooked by passing the raw meat through an open gas flame (referring to the flame-broiled method)?' The results to this question revealed that the majority of the consumers preferred the former grilling process!

Framing the question   A temptation that besets moderator is to translate the research objective into questions too directly. If an objective of the research is to find out something about the determinants of a given attitude or behaviour, the moderator may ask:

- 'Why did you do that?'
- 'Why do you feel like that?'

Simply asking the interviewees to provide insights about the determinants of their own behaviour may be more than a moderator can hope for. Asking in the form of very direct questions will tend to generate typical or defensive answers.

Therefore, innovative ways of asking 'why' are required. For example, if one is in the process of introducing a new medical product, then a moderator might do a series of in-depth interviews with doctors. At some point in the interview a logical question might be developed along the lines of:

- 'What product do you currently use to treat depression?'

The obvious follow-up question would be to ask:

- 'Why that?'

However, it may not be immediately apparent to the doctor why he/she prescribes that particular product versus some other. Consequently, it may be a more rewarding beginning to ask:

- 'How long have you been prescribing that product?'
- 'Are there circumstances in which you would not prescribe that specific product?'

Open-ended vs closed questions   Questions, regardless of their length or subject matter, contain expectations of the length of response necessary for adequate coverage. Open questions elicit longer, more elaborate answers, which call for an explanation.

Compare these open versus closed questions and then contrast the nature of the responses:

- 'How did you feel after visiting Shoppers' Stop?'
- 'You felt great after visiting Shoppers' Stop, didn't you?'
- 'What's the matter with the advertisement?'
- 'You don't seem to like the advertisement. Is it not acceptable?'

An open-ended question allows the interviewee full scope to stay what she/he wants to; a close-ended question limits the interviewee to a specific answer. Moreover, an open question solicits views, opinions, motivations, feelings, etc., whereas a closed question usually demands only cold facts.

Relevance of antecedents The antecedent of a question is something that the moderator infers from a previous question or comment by the interviewee. However, not every question has an antecedent. The opening question of the interview does not contain an antecedent, nor does any subsequent question that enters a new subject area unconnected with any previous discussion. Antecedents are important in question construction for two major reasons:

- First, they link together the questions in a continuous, logical process, e.g.,
  Q: *We've discussed the style of the car, now what do you think of its price?*
  The antecedent is the previous 'style' issue. The moderator appears to be following a cohesive outline.
- Second, the antecedent can be important to reinforce the interviewee's statement, e.g.,
  Q: *Earlier you said you liked cars with very sleek lines. What's your opinion of this car?*

By linking questions to what the interviewee has said, the moderator demonstrates that he or she has been listening carefully to the interviewee and is concerned with the answers, not just rushing through a series of questions.

Ambiguity and misperception The language in the question must conform to the vocabulary level of the interviewee. Using words that are unknown or unclear to the interviewee will result in invalid responses and alienation of the interviewee. The ambiguity of words or a sentence can result in the moderator asking one question and the interviewee answering quite a different question. The moderator must be constantly aware of the alternative meanings given to words and the possibility of misinterpretation.

For example, a classic case was reported by McNemar in 1946 when he asked rural southerners if they favoured 'government control of profits'. Feelings were overwhelmingly negative, since most of the interviewees felt that 'prophets' should be regulated only by the Lord!

Leading questions   The term 'leading question' refers to any question that is worded or phrased so that it appears to the interviewee that the interviewer desires or expects a certain answer. For example, questions designed to elicit general attitudes towards advertisements directed towards children might read: 'How do you feel about children's advertisements?' Different forms of the same question that are leading are: 'You wouldn't say that you were in favour of children's advertisements, would you?' And: 'Would you say that you are in favour of advertising directed towards children?' The result being that the responses will have a tendency to reflect the views of the moderator rather than the unbiased opinions of the interviewee.

Loaded questions   Emotionally charged words or stereotypes will influence the interviewee's view of the situation. Words such as 'wealthy', 'elderly', and 'luxury' are value-laden terms.

Sequencing   Within the interview session, it is important for the questions to be properly ordered. In general, the sequence should be planned to make the interview as meaningful as possible; to give it a beginning, a middle, and an end. The initial questions should serve to engage the interviewees' interest without threatening or taxing them before the interview begins. The most demanding or sensitive questions should be asked later in the interview. The body of the interview can follow two general procedures, the first being referred to as the 'funnel sequence'. The term describes a method of asking the most general or unrestricted questions at the beginning of a topic area and following that with successively more narrow or specific questions.

The purpose is to prevent early questions from conditioning or biasing the interviewee's later responses and to establish a context within which specific facts are related. If the moderator was concerned with relating peoples' lifestyles to the magazines they read, he/she could 'funnel' in the following manner:

Q. What kind of leisure activities do you engage in, and why?

Q. Of all these activities, which one is the most important or enjoyable for you?

Q. Do you read a lot?

Q. How about magazines?

Q. Do you read *Femina* and *Savvy*?

In the first question, the moderator has established total freedom in the discussion of the topic area. There are no antecedents or clues as to what is an 'appropriate' answer. The second question requires the interviewee to rank mentally all these activities. While the third question is concerned with one specific activity, the fourth and fifth questions are even more narrow.

The 'inverted funnel' is a pattern of narrower questions followed by broader ones. It is especially helpful for topics in which the interviewee has low involvement and, therefore, may not have an established general opinion. It is also helpful in studies where a stimulus evaluation is required to be done. For example, when advertising or packaging or product concepts are to be tested it will lead to minimal bias in evaluation if the concepts are probed upon first and then any exploratory exercise is done. Yes, it can be counter-argued that this in such a case, exploratory research could get biased because the test concepts are discussed first; thus to nullify such biases, the probing order should be rotated, i.e., in some sessions the concept evaluation should precede the exploratory probing, and in some others, vice versa.

Providing Encouragement and Direction

An effective moderator makes use of several verbal and non-verbal techniques to encourage the interviewee and to move the conversation forward. Some of these are discussed below.

Encouragement is necessary to maintain communication and move the conversation in a direction which will satisfy the research objectives. It also expresses the empathic understanding of the moderator and reinforces the notion that the moderator is indeed 'listening' to the interviewee.

Verbal and non-verbal techniques of interviewing

Let us look at some specific verbal and non-verbal techniques used in interviewing.

Verbal remarks   These include such interjections: 'I see', 'Really?', 'Is that so!' Even the seemingly inane 'Hmm' can convey to the interviewee 'Go on, continue, I'm listening and following you'.

Non-verbal communication   This technique is also important: a nod of the head or an expectant facial expression are communication cues that will reinforce the verbal reactions of the moderator.

Mirroring   A more specific non-verbal technique is the process of *mirroring*. The moderator can slowly adopt the physical mannerisms of the interviewees by mirroring the way they sit in their chairs, move their hands, and so on. Such subtle moves can significantly reduce the psychological barrier between the moderator and the interviewee, and result in an atmosphere more conducive to communication flow.

This mirroring should not get exaggerated as to come across as blatant imitation of the interviewee by the interviewer. Therefore, it should be done as naturally and subtly as possible.

Encouraging elaboration   The most logical way of encouraging elaboration would be to ask the simple question, 'Why?' It is quick, efficient and gets at once the basic facts that are necessary for truly understanding a phenomenon.

The term 'why' symbolizes the moderator's inquiry into the reasons that motivate a particular attitude or behaviour. However, even though the moderator wants the interviewee to explain a point by self-analysis (Why do I behave this way?), it is generally agreed that the question 'Why?' should be avoided. The reasons are two fold. First, it tends to make interviewees feel as though they are undergoing a police interrogation.

Therefore, the word 'why' can connote disapproval, and displeasure as there are overtones of accusation that infer that you should account for your behaviour. Second, Paul Lazarfeld in his classic article, 'The Art of Asking Why?' has shown the amount of ambiguity involved in the word 'Why'. When asked why they bought a certain product, interviewees may reply in terms of a product characteristic, or they may explain that they just happened to see it on the shelf, or may refer to a friend who had used it in the past. The interpretations are numerous.

Probably the most direct alternative to 'Why' is to begin the question with the word 'How'. 'How' did this happen or come about?' is less antagonistic and, therefore, more likely to elicit an informative response. If it is necessary to ask a 'why' question, the moderator should avoid asking it in a monosyllabic manner. The moderator can tone it down by adding other words:

- Why do you feel that way?
- Why do you think that is so?
- I wonder why would you see it that way?
- Why would you say that?

While the 'why-type' question is the most obvious question to ask in order to get an interviewee to elaborate, there are other effective and more subtle tricks of the trade.

Silent probes   The most unobtrusive and neutral technique is silence (since it neither designates the area of discussion nor structures the answer in any way). Inexperienced moderators have a difficult time in using the silent probe because they are overly concerned with maintaining a continuous flow of verbal interchange.

The interviewee is bombarded with a host of questions: 'Why is that important to you? How do you suppose such attitudes came about? Why? How many times? Why?'

Psychoanalysts have been very successful in using silent probes in therapy sessions. It conveys a relaxed mood and reinforces the notion that the researcher is not 'imposing' anything on the interviewee. It communicates: 'Yes, I'm with you, go on' or 'I'm waiting, sensing that you haven't finished' or 'That's good, but what else do you think?'

Echo technique   Another elaboration technique widely used in psychotherapeutic counselling is the 'Echo', an exact or almost exact repetition of the interviewee's words by the moderator. For instance, if an interviewee were to offer the following: 'My experience with that brand of cosmetic was very upsetting', the moderator may echo 'You were upset?' The echo, or 'verbatim playback', does not exhibit the same intrusive qualities of a 'Why?'

It is an indirect way of saying: 'I am listening carefully and I want you to continue; to explain yourself in greater detail'. It offers sympathy and encouragement while cueing the interviewee to refocus his or her attention on the research question.

The following is an illustration of the echo technique in an in-depth interview on toilet soap:

Q: What's the best toilet soap you've ever used?

A: Glow Shine, definitely. I always use it when I go out in the evening.

Q: You always use it when you go out in the evening?

A: Well, I often go dancing…there are always masses of people there, but I feel more at ease if I've used it.

Paraphrasing A more difficult form of echoing is the *paraphrase*. This involves summarizing what the interviewees have said in order to assist them in examining attitudes as a basis for self-insight. The moderator is attempting to function as a mirror for interviewees' attitudes so that they can see themselves better. The use of analogies and metaphors are particularly useful in capturing the interviewees' emotions:

Q: Could you describe the factors that influenced your decision to buy a house?

A: Well, there were so many things…it was so confusing.

Q: Hmm…

A: Of course, price was the most important factor since this was our first house. We didn't have enough money to shell out. However, we were also concerned about the location because of the proximity of the school the kids would be in. We needed a good enough backyard, too.

Q: It sounds as though you had very little options.

A: Yes! We were also concerned about the commute for my husband. Several houses that we looked were almost an hour away from his office.

Clarification The problem relative to clarification is somewhat more straightforward. It is not a matter of attempting to figure out how to probe deeper or cover new territory, the moderator should simply try to define fully what territory has already been covered:

Q: You mentioned you were part of the system. What did you mean by that?

Q: Could you clarify something for me…?

Q: What did you mean when you said…?

Discouraging Excessive/Irrelevant Communication

At times, the interviewee could be

- wandering off the topic,
- covering ground which was already covered, or
- going into a level of detail which is not appropriate given the research question.

At all such times, the moderator has to utilize certain tools in the form of questions, exclamatory reactions, non-verbal messages, etc.

Ways of interceding An effective method of shortening responses is when the moderator waits until the interviewee finishes a sentence, and then forcefully intercedes. The key, of course, is to put a halt to the topic under discussion, but at the same time to avoid alienating the interviewee. Several of the more subtle approaches can be:

- 'We don't have a great deal of time, so perhaps we should move along...'
- 'Let's move to a related topic...'
- 'I think we have said enough on this. Now let's talk about...'

Checks on the Moderator

Moderators should not do anything that would distract the members from expressing themselves.

They should not draw attention to themselves in a way that affects the process. However, often one comes across moderators

- playing with their pendants,
- fiddling with a pen in hand, and
- chewing at something.

Moderators should abstain from doing any of the above mentioned activities while conducting an interview or group session. It is important for the moderators to ensure a warm yet neutral demeanour towards the interviewee, however, moderators cannot transfer their own emotions and opinions on to the interviewees. Therefore, when any comment comes from the interviewees, moderators have to look interested but not judgemental. If they display a judgemental attitude then they would be biasing the interviewee into giving reactions that 'suit them' and not what the interviewee really wants to say.

MODERATION OF FOCUS GROUP DISCUSSIONS

As group interviewing has increasingly become a popular and familiar consumer research technique, more and more analysts, managers, and directors have decided to 'peer through the looking glass.' The result can be a rather heady experience—real people expressing their thoughts about an advertising concept or a new package design. The strengths of the technique are quickly obvious to the observers.

On the other side of the mirror are consumers who are willing to speak out their own experience. Group dynamics can create insightful exchanges and a skilful moderator can probe for meaningful explanations. The unique aspect of most group discussions is that this rich flow of data can be directly observed by decision-makers as it happens.

However, observation of the proceedings should not be viewed as a comfortable spectator sport. Some observation skills need to be detailed in order to make sense of the information.

In the same way, the following points by the Advertising Research Foundation need to be enumerated for moderators in order to help them know exactly what to look for in a group discussion:

- Moderators should not expect every moment of the discussion to be meaningful, every question to work, or every response to be salient and quotable. Participants will be real people responding spontaneously

- Moderators should not expect a consensus within a group or among groups. Qualitative research is designed to generate a range of response, develop hypotheses, and deepen understanding

- It is important for moderators to listen carefully to what is being said. In other words, they should avoid selective listening to support a preconceived point of view and avoid projecting personal meaning and values to what is being said. For listening, it is important to be alert to the shades of meaning and to word selection

- Moderators should try to watch as well as listen. Non-verbal cues can sometimes be more meaningful than verbal responses

- During the discussion, moderators should make notes of key impressions for discussion during the debriefing after the focus group

- Moderators may want to ask for additional probes or to insert new questions during the discussions, or at the end of the session. Some moderators come to the viewing room before the session ends for such additional question areas. Other moderators prefer to have a note brought to them in the discussion room

PROJECTIVE TECHNIQUES

Projective methods are most useful for generating information at the most repressed level. Such projective methods are necessary because they enable the researcher to begin to understand the basic motivations underlying attitudes and behaviours. By getting people to talk about themselves in this way, they may disclose information that they may not normally reveal. The advantage of such an 'indirect' method of assessment is that it conceals from the individual the intent of the questioning.

It is interesting to note that people project some part of themselves into everything they do, watch a person walk, watch someone drive a car, listen to a woman talk to her husband, examine an artist's paintings, study a professor's lecture style, observe a child play with other children, or with toys and dolls, and so on.

Through all these activities human beings express their needs, drives, styles of living, attitude to life/self, etc. Projective techniques are not finite. They can be applied with flexibility, imagination, ingenuity, and flair. Four important fundamentals of projective techniques are as follows:

- the type/nature of the stimulus
- the manner in which the technique is articulated to the respondents by the moderator
- the kind of support questions asked
- the extent of leeway given to allow for spontaneous reactions before support questions are asked

A projective technique has the following characteristics:

- It is especially sensitive to covert or unconscious aspects of behaviour.
- It permits or encourages a wide variety of subjective responses.
- It is highly multidimensional, and it evokes unusually rich data with a minimum of subjective awareness concerning the purpose of the test/technique.

Further, the following facts are also true of projective techniques:

- The stimulus material presented by the projective test is ambiguous.
- Interpretations of the data depends upon holistic analysis.
- The techniques can evoke fantasy responses.
- There are neither correct nor incorrect responses to the test.

Advantages and disadvantages

The projective approach to questioning is a complex one because by nature its stimulus is vague and ambiguous. In addition, there could be an experience of failure due to heavy reliance upon the consumer's ability to articulate. Further, there is a subjective interpretation of the consumer's responses, therefore it is difficult to measure without error. Thus, it is often accused of being unscientific, subjective, and lacking precision.

Nevertheless, it has certain justified advantages as well. The insights attained are into non-rational, unconscious, and latent realms of the human mind, which give tremendous depth to the information as to why a consumer tends to behave in a particular way. These insights are often in the realm of brand imagery related insights. Then, these further ladder to give insights into the 'relationship/bond' that a consumer shares with a respective brand/product.

TYPES OF PROJECTIVE TECHNIQUES

There are four broad categories of projective techniques, which are not mutually exclusive because, at any point in time, a completion technique can become a construction technique and vice versa. However, the projective techniques can be broadly categorized into:

- association technique
- completion technique
- construction technique
- expression technique

Association technique

The association technique requires responses to the presentation of a stimulus with the first thing(s) that come to mind. For example, the word association technique is useful in testing potential brand names for measuring attitudes about particular products, product attributes, brands packages, advertisements, etc. This method can be used for naming a new product to make sure that the name has the correct connotations. In a classic study, the stimulus words were 'Doeskin' and 'Kleenex', the former drew a large number of replies such as soft, softness, downy suggesting—the concept of softness is built into the Doeskin brand name—an important characteristic of a cleansing tissue.

Following are some common types of word association techniques:

Free word association   Only the first word/thought is required, e.g., here the instruction of the moderator will be: 'Tell me what comes to your mind when you think of cooking oil? Whatever comes to your mind, just speak it out…'

Focussed word association   A series of words/thoughts are required, e.g., the moderator would ask: 'Give me the names of feelings that come to your mind on hearing the name Shoppers' Stop', or, 'Give me the names of animals that come to your mind…' or '…the adjectives that come to your mind', etc.

Benefit chain   The purpose is to uncover the 'network of meanings' associated with the product, brand, or concept. A product or brand is shown to the interviewees and asked to give all benefits that possession/use of that product might provide. Then for each benefit said, one is asked to name two more benefits, e.g., 'less fatigue'—a benefit of taking a daily vitamin… One might say:

- 'More efficiency at work'
- 'More energy'
- 'More fun'
- 'Fewer problems in dating'

Personification   This can be done for a brand or the user of a brand in order to establish how people feel about a brand. Word association (through personification) can be used to enumerate the human characteristics that people link to the brand. For example, the moderator's instruction would be: 'Just imagine that Shoppers' Stop turns into a human figure…tell me what will this 'Shoppers' Stop person' be like in terms of age, occupation, lifestyle, hobbies, temperament, attitude, etc.' Or, the same can be asked in the context of the customer of Shoppers' Stop: 'Suppose there are two persons, one is a customer of Shoppers' Stop, and the other is not a customer of Shoppers' Stop. Now, describe each of these in terms of age, occupation, lifestyle, hobbies, temperament, attitude to life, brand preferences, etc.'

Completion technique

The stimulus given to consumers is 'half complete' and the consumers are required to complete this stimulus as per their imagination, understanding, and judgement. This incomplete stimulus can be in any form; two such forms are sentence completion and story completion.

Sentence completion   This technique to some extent, rephrases an open-ended question. For example, the sentences that can be given to the consumer would be:

- I like Shoppers' Stop because…
- Shopping in Shoppers' Stop, to me, feels like…

Story completion   Let us understand this technique through an example. A story is given that includes a visit to a furniture store and a disagreement between husband and wife as to which brand to purchase... This story needs to be completed on the basis of the following instruction: 'You will need to complete this story by saying what made them come to this store, what did they say to each other and to the shopkeeper after entering the store, what is their disagreement all about, what will happen after they leave the store…'

The presumption here is that because one does not know how the people in the story will react, they will tend to give inputs based on their own experiences and attitudes, thus projecting their own thoughts, needs, and issues.

Construction technique

The construction technique requires one to produce or construct something, generally a story, dialogue, or description.

For example, the moderator will provide the consumers with a description of a set of an individual's possessions, purchases, activities and ask them to describe the individual's personality: The consumer's feelings towards the items will be reflected in the description of the owner's imagination scenarios, which requires one to make-up a fantasy about the product/brand.

Expression technique

The expression technique involves role playing and play techniques.

Role playing   Consumer is asked to 'assume the role/behaviour of an object or another person'. In this state the consumer is asked to be the product and talk 'from the point of view of the product'. For example, the moderator asks the consumer to become a brand of soap and convince the other consumers to 'interact' with this 'product'. The observations here will comprise of

- what kind of words are being used to describe the respective brand of soap,
- in what kind of tone is this soap brand being talked about, and
- what positive aspects of this soap brand are being highlighted.

Play techniques   Play techniques are used especially for children. It analyses how children play rather than just what they say. For example, such a technique will be of use for product development for the toy industry, for developing child-related educational equipment and so on.

Thus, the emphasis in expressive techniques is on the manner in which construction occurs. The end product, or what is constructed, is less important than the process of activity.

SPECIFIC PROJECTIVE TECHNIQUES

Let us now discuss some specific projective techniques, such as photo sorts, conviction technique, etc., used to explore the consumer's psyche.

Photo sorts

Photo sorts are useful for brand or product explorations and theoretically allow people to project themselves into the brand or product. Market researchers tend to use photo sorts to identify lovers (motivations) of brands of product as well as haters (barriers). The contrast between lovers and haters can be used to uncover more information. Here, the moderator will expose products or brand stimulus to the consumer. For example, the moderator would instruct: 'We have here some pictures of people. Whilst we don't know these people, we have some impressions of them, their personality, lifestyles, likes and dislikes. What you need to do is tell me:

Which person would use/love which product/brand (straight sort procedure, reverse for not use/hate) and then explain to me:

- What is it about the product/brand that attracts this person
- What is unattractive about the other products (brands) for this person (treat other products/brands as a generic group, not as specific items)
- How does this person feel about this product
- How does this person feel about their family/household/partner/best friend using that product/brand
- How would the person use/prepare product/brand
- What would the person expect from the product/brand
- What expectations would the person have of the product/brand

Importantly, the objective here is to find out about the consumer's thoughts and feelings, attitudes, needs, along with an understanding of the brand/product:

- Motivations/barriers to purchase/use
- Attributes
- Need states
- Relative market positioning

However, this is a complex procedure; huge amount of information come forth that has to be analysed intricately. Moreover, it is time consuming, therefore pertinent questions should be asked along with having a proper set of photos to sort from.

Exploring a brand name

A great deal of qualitative research studies require brand name perceptions and first-level sifting out from a list of names, which then should ideally be shifted to quantitative research for the final selection of the appropriate brand name. In such an exercise, various modes can be adopted. One such mode is to expose the brand and the moderator to give the following instructions:

'Let's pretend that this brand is a descriptive name'

- What does it tell us?
- Why is it called that?
- What is it?

Alternatively, the moderator can read out each name option and ask for word associations (discussed earlier) for each name and check for its emerging connotations and imagery and then probe to understand the consonance/dissonance of the respective name with the brand/product.

Conviction technique

This technique works best with two respondents. For example, the moderator explains that one consumer is going to be the user of brand X and the other consumer will be the user of brand Y. The task is for each to convince the other that their brand is better. Here, the important task of the moderator is to note the terms used to describe the respective brand and then at a later stage the moderator needs to do a benefit ladder to understand the link of perceptions. Through such an exercise, brand perceptions as well as the needs that they are able to satisfy and/or dissatisfy come forth very clearly.

Family ties

In this exercise, the moderator's instructions are: 'I'd like you to imagine that these products/brands are all members of a family. You know how families differ from house to house, family to family, but they all have people in them who have certain roles and attitudes (i.e., black sheep, and so on)…' Each 'family member' is then probed upon in order to understand its relationship with the brand and the consumer's sense of affinity with the respective products/brands through his/her projections in the form of family ties.

Improving/creating an ideal

The moderator here attempts to understand brand perceptions along with needs and expectations from it, by adopting an 'ideal' approach. Therefore, the moderator will instruct as:

'Let's imagine that there exists an ideal cooking oil. It's the best that you will ever be able to find. Please tell me what it will be like in terms…'

- What are its important and different attributes
- How does it cost
- How does it taste
- How does it perform
- How is it made
- What is in it
- What will its packaging be like
- What would be the ideal situation in which to consume the product (probe for pleasure/enjoyment factors)

Once, this 'ideal' description has got formulated, the moderator will then present existing products to be compared with the ideal, and then probed as:

- How is it similar
- How is it different
- Do existing products fall short when compared to this 'ideal' product
- Could the ideal be better? Is anything missing
- What do they have that matches the ideal
- What do they not have to match with the ideal
- What do they need in order to match with the ideal

Deprivation/withdrawal technique

In this technique, the moderator attempts to understand the consumer–brand relationship by mentally taking away the respective brand from the consumer's life and then asks the consumer to describe 'a life without this brand'. Ideally, this technique can be successfully applied to users and preferably lovers of a respective brand/product.

During the course of questioning, the moderator, after pointing out that 'what if such a brand/product is not in the market any more…', asks the consumers to articulate:

- What would be missed by them
- How would they feel
- How would they substitute the absence of this product/brand
- What would they lose out on permanently by substituting it with another brand/product
- What would be the additional gains by the substitute product/brand

One variation of the deprivation format of questioning is to ask the consumers to write an epitaph or letter on the death of a brand/product, the content of which should reflect their feelings, loss, fears vis-à-vis the respective brand/product.

Planets/world view technique

In this projective technique the consumer is asked to imagine each brand as a planet in the universe and then to describe this planet in terms of:

- The kind of landscape
- The kind of people
- The lifestyle of the people
- Their dress code
- Their houses
- Their likes/dislikes when it comes to entertainment, food
- The kind of colours that dominate this planet
- The beliefs of the people of this planet, etc.

This technique brings out brand perceptions with a lot of depth and dimensions. For example, the consumer can be asked to give a 'world view' of a brand of tea and its leading competition brands.

Collage

This is an interesting projective exercise wherein consumers are asked to explain their perception of a brand through an analogous approach, i.e., through pictures. For example, there could be two key competition airlines and the client would want to know how the two are similar or different from their brand. Therefore, the moderator will ask the consumer to make collages for each brand from magazines, by cutting out any words, pictures, or images that represent the way the customer sees the respective brand.

The symbolic representation through pictures, which the consumers associate with each brand, will then give a clear idea about what a brand means to them and their relationship with the brand in the context of competition brands.

Within the context of collage-making, some proportion of the exercise can be devoted to projective drawing, in which the moderator asks the consumers to draw their impressions of what a respective brand/product should look like (i.e., its physical dimensions, packaging, etc. It will be important to communicate to the consumers that they are not expected to draw in the mould of a great artist, however, what is important is to portray it the way the brand/product is perceived by the consumer.

Use of projective technique in advertising

An interesting approach to doing advertising research is to take the 'behind the scenes approach'. Therefore, the moderator exposes the advertising stimulus and asks questions such as:

- What do you think the person who designed this advertisement had in mind?
- What do you think he/she meant to say?

Also, the consumer could be asked to be a part of the scene:

- What would it be like to be there?
- What else happened?

Or, imagine meeting (main character in TVC)

- How might they get on?
- What do they have in common (brand fit)?
- How are they different (brand fit)?
- What would be admired most about the main character?
- What would be dislike most about the main character?

Also, if there are more than one advertising stimuli then moderators can continue their probing on the following lines:

- In which of the advertisements would you get along best with the main character?
- In which of the advertisements the message of the advertiser is coming out most clearly?

THE INNOVATIVE METHODOLOGIES OF QUALITATIVE RESEARCH

Although, the two main methodological frameworks of the qualitative methodology remain the same, over time, different processes within these two frameworks have got developed. These innovative approaches have brought out newer dimensions to exploring and analysing the consumer speak. At the end of the day, qualitative research has one commitment to its output and to the client, i.e., of delivering depth and reasons why vis-à-vis any consumer behaviour under study.

In this section three innovations have been discussed, namely:

- semiotics research
- observational-ethnographic research
- synectics research

Semiotics Research

Typically, researchers interpret consumer responses in order to understand the drives behind them, sometimes on the basis of theory (predominantly psychology) but, more often, as inspired guesswork. Semiotics is different. First, it looks at things through the other end of the marketing telescope—the cultural end. Secondly, it bases the interpretation of what it sees firmly on the theory of consumers and culture. The fundamental premise being that consumers are made not born.

In semiotic theory, consumers are not independent spirits, articulating their own original opinions and making their own individual buying decisions. By and large, consumers are products of the popular culture in which they live. They are constructed by the communications of that culture. As a result, they are not prime causes; they are cultural effects. So to find out what is really going on in the market place, in semiotics, one begins by looking beyond the consumers into the cultural context that surrounds and informs them.

Stages in semiotic analysis

Semiotic analysis is a form of focused desk research, which comprises of the following stages:

First, it examines the marketing communications of both the client company and its competitors—products, packaging, advertising, retail environments, promotions, PR, etc., historical and current. The analysis shows the cultural 'body language' unconsciously coded into brand messages.

Second, it reviews relevant areas of the popular culture of the day—TV, press, music, clothes, attitudes, design, humour, folklore, etc.

Third, the analysis relates the marketing communication material to these surrounding cultural contexts. Marketing communications tend to work effectively if they can be made relevant in some way to the contemporary popular culture of their target audiences.

Fourth, it identifies and tracks the communication codes of the brand (and those of the competition) across the real time frame of the surrounding cultures in order to project future market developments that the brand can tap into.

These are the emergent codes of the product field. The findings from this comparative analysis (which is both wide-ranging in scope and rigorous in its method) enable us to develop hypotheses concerning the dynamics of the marketplace and help us to understand how these hypotheses influence the specific problem under consideration. These hypotheses structure and guide the second stage of the programme—consulting the consumer. This allows us to see how consumers (consciously and unconsciously) use contexts, codes, myths, and metaphors to make the important cultural connections with the brand and its spectrum of marketing messages.

The final results of both stages produce guidelines for cultural creativity in advertising, packaging, retail design, promotions, NPD - and all other aspects of creative development. These guidelines will help to locate the brand at the heart of the contemporary popular culture of its target audiences.

Strategically, by virtue of its holistic approach, a full semiotic research programme is clearly valuable in the development of communications strategy when employed at the beginning of the process:

- Before any other research (qualitative or quantitative)
- Before any creative planning or the development of ideas
- Before any form of new product development

When properly used, the semiotic research then provides a ground plan, from which to structure and orchestrate all these other activities. Tactically, semiotic research is focused on precisely how brand communications work. So, specially designed programmes have also been found to have tremendous value for all forms of tactical creative development.

Tools of semiotic research

Some tools of semiotic research are described below.

Mood boards These are generally used to explore product propositions, brand attributes, and possible positioning. Over twenty images are chosen to stretch the imaginative boundaries of any given theme, enabling respondents to exercise their own imaginations in discussion.

Positioning and concept boards These come in a variety of shapes and sizes. Some are more textural than graphic, while others need more innovative layout and high production values to fully express the mood and tone of the idea. The more elaborate pieces bridge between animatic and storyboard, using objects, textures and collaging to produce 'virtual advertising'.

Lifestyle boards These are used extensively to illustrate group lifestyles and current cultural trends, such as 'cocooning', these boards are invaluable presentation aids. Whether briefing for creatives or debriefing clients, lifestyle boards ensure that everyone is thinking along the same lines.

Texture board It is an increasingly popular form of semi-abstract stimulus, invaluable for exploring brand promises such as 'softness' or sensory-related attributes like 'mouth feel'. The texture board is now widely used in New Product Design (NPD), brain-storming sessions, and children's research studies.

Typology boards It explores who uses which brand, when and how? What type of house does X live in? What type of car would Y drive? These questions and more can be answered by using the typology board—a selection of types of things—for brand mapping exercises, and for discussing style and usage patterns.

Observational-Ethnographic Research

Observations, apart from direct talking, are a necessary activity in order to get a sense of the real. In most cases with consumers, the 'stated' and the 'real' could be two different things. Observations enable us to bridge this gap and give in a 'sunk-in' experience of consumers and their lifestyle. This then adds depth to the researcher's understanding of the consumer. Therefore, along with the main methodology of a study, a module of observation should be carried out as a supplementary exercise. For example, observation at the home level will give a holistic perspective on the person under observation in order to understand where this person 'comes' from and what his/her roots are given the research context. The below-stated points of observation will help understand better the consumers' background, nature and attitude, and an overall feel of what they experience on a regular basis.

Home-level observation

- type of house
- the manner in which it has been kept
- number of family members
- the manner in which they interact and behave with each other
- the manner in which every one interacts with moderator

Some more details about the living style of the consumer can be observed, such as the aspects mentioned below.

Room

- arrangement – neat, tidy, ruffled or stuffy
- what kind of furniture is kept

Grooming

- the way he/she is dressed
- the type of colours, brands (if any), shoes, etc., chosen
- the manner in which he/she carries himself/herself

Attitude

- his/her mood (excited, nervous, thrilled)
- his/her manner of coordination
- find out which is the spot they have decided to meet and how

Lifestyle and preferences

In the context of another consumer segment such as teenagers, one observational space could be a hangout joint when attempting to understand a teenager's lifestyle and preferences. This will help generate rich information on attitudes and values in choosing a place and explicate the concept of togetherness and fun. So, if a teenage group is observed, the focus needs to be upon:

- type of place
- kind of crowd
- kind of food available and what they prefer to eat
- do they order the same thing or each one for themselves
- the extent of bonding that is taking place
- service demands and expectations
- nature of interaction in the group and overall group dynamics (to gain a sense of the group values such as approval, conformity, reinforcement, reasons for sticking together, etc.)
- type of friends the consumer hangs out with, etc.

Interaction

- friendly, warm, sharing, serious
- close/bonded or strained
- unifying criteria
- subgroups within groups

Type of conversation

- cracking jokes, whispering secret jokes, eve teasing, or exchange of information

Attitude

- towards each other in the gang
- towards other girls/boys in the gang
- towards passers-by
- shelling out money
- liking some objects/items in the respective place, etc.

Observation of Gestures

Another interesting observation is of gestures (be it a group session or an interview), which gives an indication of what is going on in the mind when interacting.

Finger pointing   While talking to other members of the family, always indicating what has to be done, appears as if talking down with a 'I told you so' attitude, gives cues to the most domineering among the lot.

Mock fights signals   Such gestures between siblings in the family enable to measure the bonding or domination of one over the other, establishing hierarchy between the elder child and the younger, and intensity of aggression between the children.

Impatient signals   For example, such gestures between a mother-in-law and daughter-in-law where the mother-in-law is explaining and giving detailed instructions to her while she is actually smiling and lowering her head down and nodding as if submissive and listening, but her tapping toe is signalling impatience with her mother-in-law and desire to somehow finish this talk.

Disinterestedness signals These include staring elsewhere, looking here and there when father talks to the child. Or, staring at the TV and not responding to the child's queries, indication of not mentally present in the scene.

Superiority signals Husband raising his head and lifting his chin up every time his wife speaks to him—depicting a superiority, strong male domination. It is a reflection of how the husband looks down upon his wife and the fabric of their relationship is not rooted in togetherness or bonding. He is the authority in all decision-making and she has to abide by what he says.

Teenagers with certain attitudes reflect values ingrained in them by their parents. They may hurl insults, draw superiority lines with high-mindedness, or throw their heads back indicating exaggeration, high status display, and pompousness.

Rejection signal During conversational exchange, child rejects mother's view, shrugs shoulders, and depicts discontent or non acceptance of mother's or father's perspective.

Guidelines for Moderation in Rural India (and Lower SECs)

Tips regarding dressing and overall demeanor

1. Never tuck in one's shirt (men) or wear a T-shirt as this is perceived as being 'modern' or 'hero-like'

2. Always remove your shoes outside a room–shows a sign of respect

3. It is preferable not to wear sneakers as it is perceived as 'filmy' or 'something teenagers do for style'

4. An unshaven look helps male moderators as it gives a more earthy and down-to-earth look which the respondents are comfortable with; a smooth look is perceived as being sophisticated and suavé

5. The women must always wear 'Indian clothes' with minimum jewellery

6. Never try and become a rural consumer as this alienates these consumers more

7. Always greet by saying *namaste* and then by shaking hands as this is perceived to be polite as well as 'modern', and they often aspire to be 'modern'.

8. Never park the vehicle at the door of the consumer; walk up to their house as cars are associated with officials and thus rural consumers tend to close up once they see the moderator emerge from a car

9. Never refuse water, tea, or food offered by the consumers as they see it as an insult

Tips regarding mode-of-questioning

1. 'Don't be a villager as you are not one'–be natural but empathetic

2. Spend a large amount of time in the warm-up session as this helps in lowering of defence amongst the respondents

3. Never come across as being surprised about the way of life in a village as the consumers then close themselves up, as they perceive themselves as being inferior to 'city-folk'

4. Talk to them about the similarities of the problems they are having and the ones faced by themselves(moderator)

5. Never glamourize city life

6. Keep nodding when the respondent is talking as it shows the consumer that you are interested

7. Never keep asking 'why' as, unlike a 'city-consumer' whose behaviour is influenced by media, in rural India, behaviour is dictated by 'tradition' and hence questioning the tenets of tradition is perceived as insulting

8. The mode-of questioning should not be interrogative but more of 'understanding', thus, instead of asking 'why' one must ask 'what makes you say this?', 'how does this happen?'

Synectics

The term 'synectics' is derived from the Greek word 'synetikos' meaning 'understanding together something which is apparently different' (Gunter, Estes, and Schwab 2003). William Gordon, the developer of Synectics, has devised ways to connect dramatically different ideas, thus providing new insights into old problems. It has been rightly said by Max Ernst, 'Creativity is the marvelous capacity to grasp distinct realities and draw a spark from their juxtaposition.'

The approach, in this methodology, is a structured one to create understanding by relating new information to prior knowledge. This understanding is built by using metaphors, which allows to create a unique meaning, build a new concept or idea through association with the familiar. In fact, synectics is also known for popularizing the power of metaphor, which includes figures of speech that join together different and apparently irrelevant elements through the use of analogy, which could be in the form of simile, personification, or oxymoron.

Analogies

The use of analogies is a significant 'process tool' of the synectics process. Analogies (in other words, symbolic comparisons) can be of various types. Some of these are:

Direct analogy   It is a direct comparison between two objects, ideas, or concepts. For example, 'How is a classroom like an anthill?'

Personal analogy   In this type of analogy the group participants are invited to become part of the problem to be solved or the image being explored and the goal is empathy. For example, 'How would you feel if you were a tree that had been attacked by acid rain?'

Symbolic analogy or compressed conflict   It involves descriptions that appear to be contradictory but are actually creatively insightful. For example, 'Why is an unmarried person like a married person?'

Oxymoron   It is derived from the Greek word 'oxys', meaning sharp or keen, and 'moros', meaning foolish. In ancient Greek, the word 'oxymoros' meant 'pointedly foolish' (Gunter, Estes and Schwab, 2003). For example, thunderous silence, deliberate speed, open secret, cruel kindness, deafening silence, etc.

Observation Case Studies

Following are examples of interpretations and take-outs from observations made during an interactive session.

Jewellery

'Here are my ornaments. Some of these are Mom's but her's are too heavy to wear, however, the designs are beautiful... I bought this new set, which has the same kind of design but it looks more contemporary and is less heavy to wear... I have decided to wear this one... I love the traditional look, I am also borrowing Mom's sari, it will match well with this'.

Take-out—traditional jewellery has sentiments attached to it, however what is required is a contemporary feel by a younger generation consumer. It has to look expensive and different but feel light; the non-verbal gestures indicated

that the 'rich look' of the jewellery was desired more for the earrings than the necklace by this consumer; the necklace was preferred to be lighter in look and weight.

Refrigerators

'If I buy a fridge, where will I keep it? you can see that my house is so small... there is hardly any room'.

Take-out—an embarrassing factor not revealed in focus groups.

'It's too hot to offer you tea, I shall ask my son to go and get a cold drink for you ... it will take a few minutes. There is no fridge in my house so I can't offer cold water.'

Take-out—simulation of embarrassment faced at the arrival of strangers.

Process of synectics

The composition of synectics is a group session with about 8–10 participants who are higher on the creativity score. The process of synectics is based on the spectrum policy wherein the assumption is that any idea, however ridiculous and absurd, has a spectrum of possibilities. For example, the bright speck in a very dark landscape can become a brilliant star when you look at it closely. Thus, in synectics groups, members are asked to follow the spectrum policy and to participate without criticism. A particularly 'silly' idea becomes an opportunity to find that scintillating speck.

The spectrum policy, the participants are taken through the following processes:

Defining the problem   First, the problem is defined in complete detail. Participants continue to question the person presenting the problem until everyone understands all aspects of the problem. No brainstorming or solution gathering occurs at this time.

Mental vacation   Second, the participants are asked to 'leave the problem' entirely, i.e., take a mental vacation.

One member suggests a fantasy or a place to go, mentally, emotionally, or spiritually, e.g. to a beach in Goa, Himalayan peaks, outer space, a rock concert, an imaginary tour through the valves of the heart, etc. The idea is to move away from the original problem. All group members contribute to the fantasy, just as they do to the problem definition. Someone takes notes of the proceedings.

Using an analogy   Third, take the elements and aspects of the vacation, and use them as an analogy to the problem solution. The members practice the spectrum policy and 'force fit' the vacation analogy as a metaphoric solution to the problem.

For instance, what clues can a beach in Goa give us about making a soap mould? The obvious clue can be to use sea shells as the container to press the soap into. Or, instead of a press, how about a clam-like mould? Such fragrances and shapes of the soap can be promoted that will remind buyers of their favourite vacation place. The soap can be advertised as an exotic Goan tradition of soap-making, etc.

Trigger questions   Fourth, after defining the problem, the instruction to the group is to transform it using some or all of these processes.

Subtract   Remove certain parts or elements. What can be reduced or disposed of? How to simplify?

Add   Extend or expand. Develop your reference subject, magnify, and make it bigger. What else can be added to your idea?

Transfer   Move the subject to a new situation, adapt it to a different frame of reference or move the subject out of its normal environment, move it to a different historical, social, or geographical setting.

Empathize   More than sympathize with the subject—'put yourself in its shoes'. 'What if the subject has human qualities?'

Symbolize   Design a visual symbol for your idea. How can your idea be imbued with symbolic qualities?

Fantasize   Fantasize your subject. How far out can you extend your imagination? E.g. What if automobiles were made of bricks?, What if alligators played pool? What if insects grew larger than humans? What if night and day occurred simultaneously?

Combine   Bring things together—Connect, arrange, link, unify, mix, merge, and rearrange. Combine ideas, materials, and techniques. Bring dissimilar things together. What else can you connect to your subject? Connect different senses, frames of reference, or disciplines.

At the end of this creative process, the group has to give a hierarchy for the creative solutions/ideas generated and this is then taken by the researcher through a process of analysis and interpretation in order to arrive at relevant data output, as in bringing forth creative solutions for the client's marketing/business problem being researched upon.

SUMMARY

In qualitative research, the researcher's estimation is of key importance. Most often than not, on the basis of this experienced-based estimation, the researcher decides what methodology to use for a given set of objectives. However, there are certain norms which guide this estimation of the researcher and enable them to take a decision that is not arbitrary and vague. These norms come into play in the context of the two main methodologies of qualitative research, i.e., the focus group discussion and in-depth interview. Organizing a session is an important aspect of planning and of even more importance is the art of moderation—speaking rightfully, what to ask, how to ask, when to ask, whom to ask. All these aspects make the effort of the moderator more of a skilful art. A key value that is expected out of qualitative research is the depth of information by reaching out to the sub-conscious layers in human mind. This is attained by the use of a disguised mode of questioning, which is termed as projective methodology—which is the soul of qualitative research. The projective techniques are important tools by which deeper penetration into the consumer mindset becomes possible and the emerging insights become rich and meaningful. Thus, both the knowledge and the application of the projective techniques are important for a researcher who wants to understand and master qualitative research.

KEY WORDS

Discussion guide is a written blueprint that includes guidelines for the content, language, and sequence of the questioning process followed in a focus group discussion and/or an in-depth interview.

New product development Brands, from time to time, need to re-invent themselves and therefore they need to be developed—horizontally and/or vertically; Alternatively, ideas for new products are also required; both these tasks then need research exercises, in order to generate new product development ideas.

Advertising communication is either audio/print/audio-visual communication that introduces the brand to the consumer.

Moderator/Interviewer is the person who facilitates the discussion either in a group session and/or in an interview session.

Interviewee/consumer/respondent is the person who is interviewed either in a group session and/or in an interview session.

Rapport is the relationship between the moderator and his/her consumer/interviewee.

Defenses are the mental blocks that inhibit honest articulation of thoughts and feelings.

Empathy is the close bond between a consumer and a brand/advertising/moderator.

CONCEPT REVIEW QUESTIONS

1. What is the core rationale, each, for using the methods of focus group discussion and in-depth interview?

2. What are key aspects that one needs to keep in mind when it comes to moderating a focus group versus an in-depth interview?

3. What are common tenets of moderation, irrespective of whether it is a focus group session or an in-depth interview situation?

4. What is the need to use the projective methodology, i.e., what is its value in qualitative research?

5. For what kind of information tasks would projective techniques work well?

6. What are the pros and cons of projective methods?

7. What is difference in the approach and output of synectics and semiotics?

PROJECT ASSIGNMENTS

1. An airline company wants to understand its brand image and attain perspectives on repositioning its brand; its key consumer segment is the corporate traveller for both the Business class as well as Economy class. The client wants to know the kind of research methodology that needs to be adopted:

   (a) What is the target sample that one needs to cover for this study?

   (b) What methodological approach to adopt?

   (c) What is the rationale for the suggested approach?

   (d) What could be the disadvantage of the suggested approach?

2. In the context of chickenpox vaccine, a client wants to understand where his/her brand X stands in relation to two other competition brands (Y and Z) in the mind of the doctor.

   (a) What kind of information will give the right answers to the client about his/her brand?

   (b) Is projective methodology required? Why?

   (c) If yes, then which projective techniques would be apt to generate relevant information?

3. A fast food joint mostly patronized by children and teenagers wants an answer to its marketing plan for: 'How should they connect with their adult consumer?'

   (a) How should this research be planned? What method to utilize for this and why?

   (b) What will this methodology yield, which any other approach would not?

   (c) Who should be the target consumer for this research exercise?

   (d) What will be the requirements for this research study? What preparations need to be done?

CASE STUDY

Mahindra and Mahindra Tractors

The following is an example of a qualitative research study conducted for a tractor giant, Mahindra and Mahindra, for understanding the key consumer perceptions regarding its tractors. The case explores the principles of effective moderation.

Research brief for the researcher

The tractor industry is undergoing change and there is intense competition both from national and international manufacturers. The national manufacturers include Mahindra and Mahindra, Punjab Tractors Ltd., among others.

Through this research the client wanted a complete understanding of the consumers of various brands so that they could understand the key touch points of brand for the consumer.

Research deliverables

For the client the key research deliverable were as follows:

1. Understanding how the respective brands have seeped into consumers' lives along with getting insights into their life and in what way does Mahindra and Mahindra connect/disconnect with these respective brand-consumers.

2. For a consumer of a rival brand what is the equity of Mahindra and Mahindra brand, encompassing all aspects—image, product, service, etc. This knowledge would provide a direction for a rival brand-consumer to be pulled towards becoming a Mahindra and Mahindra consumer.

Methodology

DiL: Day-in-Life (ethnographic observation plus an individual dialogue)

This was a one-on-one interaction with the consumer in an environment that was 'his'—work, home, leisure. A portion of the day (at least 3–4 hours) was spent with the consumer across varying time periods.

The Value derived from the DiL methodology is listed below:

- DiL helped the moderator to get an in-depth understanding of the consumer in his environment, time and space; and, importantly, it made the moderator understand issues and feelings beyond the 'good-to-say things'. Spending more time with the consumer helped the researcher get the consumer's defenses lowered and hence he could speak about his life with a great deal of openness and intimacy.

- Secondly, by going to the consumer's fields and travelling on his tractor helped the researcher to move him beyond his house, which was a place where he was looked up for everything, so here he behaved in a rational way; on the other hand, in his fields he was on his own and hence opened up and spoke 'more from his heart'.

- Lastly, through such a methodology, the researcher not only heard the consumer talk but shared his feelings, thoughts etc., while he spoke.

Customer Interaction

- When in the first couple of interviews the moderator travelled in a car to the respondent's house, the neighbours and the consumer's family got curious and surrounded the respondent. This further made him uncomfortable as he became the centre of attention. Thus when he was talking to the moderator the words chosen by him were 'carefully thought and chosen' and not 'spontaneous'

- Once having understood this behaviour, the moderator parked the car on the highway and walked up to the respondent's house thus taking away the attention of the neighbours, this helped the respondent relax for the process

- At a second level, to help the respondent open up more to the whole process, the moderator asked him to take him to his fields on his tractor. This helped him articulate better, as being in his fields the respondents felt more in control of the situation and thus opened more and was more receptive to moderator's questioning. Importantly, being in the fields besides his tractor aided him in explaining his points better

Key Responses of Consumers

- 'It's gear is very strong' ('*Gear iske bade sakth hain*')—From a competition brand of tractor owner. This information did not come forth in direct questioning but came forth when we observed the respective tractor owner struggling to change gears and grunted every time he changed gears.

- 'This is a common man's tractor' ('*Yeh ek aam aadmi ka tractor hai*')—From a tractor owner of a competition brand.

Key nuggets of information derived

The aforementioned learnings came from understanding over a period of time, based on the way the questions were put forth.

1. When in the first couple of interviews, in a bid to become more empathic the moderator tried to use an accent like that of the villager, he was seen as mocking. Thus, although the moderator had to completely avoid using English words, speaking the local dialect helped the moderator in avoiding being seen as mocking.

2. The warm-up is the most important aspect of any interview (urban or rural), especially in rural India. Hence in the warm-up session it is important to note that questions should be asked in third person.

   - For example, instead of asking 'What problems are faced by you?' one should ask, 'In the farming community today what are the problems faced?'

   - This helps take away the onus of responsibility from oneself to more generic problems faced by all and in the process lowers the respondent's defenses

3. Although understanding the 'why' is an important tenet of qualitative research, by constantly asking too many 'whys' the whole process is transformed into an interrogative one, leading to a respondent getting defensive, suspicious, and uncomfortable.

   - Thus, instead of asking 'why', one should throw the question as 'what are the reasons behind this', 'how does this occur', giving the entire process an exploratory feel. The following examples will illustrate the difference between, first person and third person in direct questioning.

First person

M: What are the problems, faced by you, with the Mahindra brand?

R: None, it is the best tractor.

M: Anything related to fuel, spare parts, etc.?

R: No, not at all.

Third person

M: I met this person who is the owner of a Mahindra tractor and he told me that there were a few issues with the tractor, which ones do you think are the prominent ones he must have said?

R: There are not any significant ones but sometimes one does feel that it cannot take weight of the trolley uphill.

M: And …?

Hence, by employing indirect/third-person questioning method, the key insights derived were:

• Mahindra tractors sometimes have a product-related problem vis-à-vis the pulling capacity

Important inputs in projective techniques

Consumers in rural India and lower SECs find it difficult to articulate when a projective technique is employed as most are not used to lateral thinking and associations, therefore, there is need to:

1. Give lot of examples or analogies prior to executing projective techniques to aid the respondent to start thinking laterally

2. Be patient, as in time, they will respond to the projective technique

3. Not look for associations that are city specific, even the ones that are local in nature will suffice

Applying a projective technique

The key to successfully using projective techniques lies in familiarizing the consumers to the technique, first, by giving a number of examples of how to do them rather than just giving an academic explanation. Importantly, the key to success of any projective technique, is patience as respondents normally are not creative and articulate to get it right the first time.

Thus the key insights generated here, through the use of projective techniques such as word association, brand personification were:

• The Mahindra brand was perceived as one that was low on running costs

• The Mahindra brand has an image of being simple, hard-working, efficient, and modest

Questions

1. Why was a focus group discussion not suggested for the respective study?

2. Why was a projective methodology required in the context of the current study?

3. What were the key differences between the 'right' and 'wrong' ways of putting forth the projective technique of personification?

4. What did body language/non-verbal communication tend to convey to a qualitative researcher, which the verbal speak did not?

5. Why was it so important to keep in check the demeanour and dressing of the moderator?

Some related aspects

Wrong Application of a Projective Technique (Personification)

M: Let us now play a game, imagine, in case the Mahindra tractor was to become a person, what kind of a person would he be, what would be his personality, his age... please think and tell me?

R: How can a tractor become a person?

M: This is an imaginary exercise...please think and tell me...

R: I don't know, how is it possible to think of a tractor as a human being?

M: What about a film star, can you associate any of them with the Mahindra tractor?

R: I don't understand your question...

Right Application of a Projective Technique (Personification)

M: Let us now play a game, I must tell you that it takes a little time to understand but after that it is a lot of fun... are you ready?

R: Is it my age to play games?

M: Why, don't you like playing cards, it's just like that... don't worry I am there to help...

M: Let me explain how this works, one rule is that don't think this is silly, so relax and think with both your head and heart...suppose a wrestler becomes a building, try to decribe that building to me...probably you would say 'this building will be big, tall, strong...' and this you would say keeping in mind what you think of a wrestler...in the same manner I will now ask you about the tractor.

M: If Mahindra tractor was to become a person, who would it be? If not a person, you can also think of an animal...

R: Mahindra is like an ox...

M: Very good. But tell me why is it like an ox?

R: Because just like an ox, Mahindra tractor works for long hours, consumes less fuel, and is always there for its owner when hard work is required...

M: And what else about an ox resembles the Mahindra tractor?

R: Simple and not flashy...does its work well and diligently...

M: Any negative traits associated with an ox?

R: None...really...

REFERENCES

Aaker, D.A., V. Kumar, G.S. Day 1995, *Marketing Research*, Fifth Edition, John Wiley & Sons, Inc.

Crask, M., R.J. Fox 1997, *Marketing Research: Principles and Applications*, Prentice Hall, Englewood Cliffs, New Jersey.

Gordon, William J.J. 1961, *Synectics*, Harper and Row, New York.

Gunter, A., T. Estes, and J. Schwab 2003, *Instruction: A Models Approach*, 4th edn, Allyn & Bacon, Boston.

Holbrook, M.B. 1995, *Consumer Research: Introspective Essays on the Study of Consumption*, Sage Publications.

Malhotra, N.K. 1999, *Marketing Research: An Applied Orientation*, Third Edition, Prentice Hall.

Sherry, J.F. 1995, *Contemporary Marketing and Consumer Behaviour*: *An Anthropological Sourcebook*, Sage Publications.

www.creativerealities.com

www.davidgoldsmith.com

www.synecticsworld.com

www.voipreal.com

www.wikipedia.org

17 Analysis and Interpretation of Qualitative Research Data

OBJECTIVES

After reading this chapter, the readers will be able to understand:

- how to make sense of the collected data, i.e., data analysis
- the process of qualitative research analysis and the various stages involved in it
- how the data should be differentially analysed and interpreted, depending upon the nature and objectives of the research study
- in the interpretation of the research study, what should be the focus points and what should be avoided in order to minimize researcher bias
- guidelines for making a presentation of the research findings
- the dos and don'ts of qualitative research data emerging out of the analysis and interpretation processes

INTRODUCTION

In the previous chapters, we understood the process of data collection, including various probing techniques (projectives, laddering, cognitive maps, etc.) to be used within the two main methodologies of qualitative research, i.e., in-depth interview and focus group discussion. Moving ahead from here we will now understand how the data collected, through any methodology, should be analysed and interpreted in order to make sense and provide relevant insights in the context of the research objectives of a respective study.

When doing the data analysis, no doubt one can segregate the data into certain typical heads (e.g., perceptions, needs, motivators, barriers, attitudes, expectations, etc.) for all qualitative research studies. However, such a universal approach will only lead to a rather superficial analysis wherein there will be a mechanical churning out of the data minus relevance and 'insightful' insights. Qualitative research is often accused of being a subjective process of analysis because it is felt that there are no set norms for analysing the data. However, it can be confidently argued that although there may not be any formula and/or tables in qualitative analysis, the researcher develops the skill and expertise to follow a process and pattern in order to analyse with depth and thus be able to read between the lines. Also, when doing the analysis, the researcher has to strictly keep in view two aspects—the type of the study and the deliverables of the respective research study, i.e., the expected use of the research findings. The nature of the study spells out to the researcher how to approach the analysis and what the draw-outs should be, and, the deliverables of the study ensure that the researcher's draw-outs are relevant and have marketing value.

Thus, in this chapter, we will understand the system and processes of qualitative analysis. The chapter details out the fundamentals of qualitative analysis, be it any type of study, these are certain common tenets that need to be adhered to in order to do a meaningful analysis of the data. Further, the chapter breaks down the analysis process into specific components to give an understanding of what the process of analysis should be step by step. The chapter goes on to offer a detailing of variables bases as to which data should be looked at and segmented—mainly to ensure that there is relevance and depth in the analysis. It is truly a microscopic way of looking at the data. Further to this, is given a perspective on how different types of studies and data need a differential analytical approach. This perspective, then, makes the take-outs of the study be in sync with the research objectives and deliverables of the respective research study. Finally, the second but crucial part of qualitative analysis, which is data interpretation and the presentation of the findings, respectively, is discussed. Once the process of analysis is complete, the data has to be carefully looked into in order to elicit the deeper and not-so-obvious insights. As it has been rightly said for qualitative research, 'its raison d'etre is to read between the lines', therefore, the data needs to be interpreted in order to attain relevant marketing insights so as to resolve client's business and/or brand-related issues. Interestingly, analysis is done from an elementalist perspective and interpretation is done from a holistic perspective. Finally, this analysed and interpreted data needs to be given a shape and form in order to present it to the client. This entails presenting the details of the research process and the findings to the client in the form of a presentation.

QUALITATIVE RESEARCH ANALYSIS

When a qualitative research problem is framed by the client, it typically reads as 'I want to know reasons why the brand is not connecting with its consumers; I need to understand what is happening in the consumer's mindset; I want to explore the decision-making process of the consumer when it comes to selecting one brand over the others; I need to formulate hypotheses in order to test them further for complete validation in the quantitative research module; I want to develop the communication for my brand and so I need to weave out a way forward for my brand', etc.

Key Tasks of Qualitative Research Analysis

Thus the key tasks mentioned above, i.e., probing for reasons why, understanding, exploring, generating, developing, and weaving out a way forward not only translate into research objectives at the beginning of a study but also set a precedent vis-à-vis how the data will be analysed and what it will need to deliver at the end of it all.

Therefore, when the data analysis is to be planned out for a qualitative research exercise, the following tasks are undertaken.

- The task is to look for 'benefit ladders', e.g., 'If a soap gives me the benefit of cleanliness then what does cleanliness in turn give me and/or make me feel, and then with that feeling how in turn am I impacted in my thinking and behaviour'. In this manner the attempt is to penetrate deeper (i.e., beyond the rational and towards the emotive) into the layers of the consumer's thinking in order to identify the core reasons behind usage and loyalty vis-à-vis the respective soap brand.

- Also, another task is that of weaving out hypotheses, i.e., generating insights vis-à-vis what may be working/not working in the favour of a brand, what the consumer perceptions vis-à-vis needs and barriers in the context of a brand are, etc.

- Importantly, a key task of qualitative analysis is to 'look ahead', i.e., it is important to understand the current brand status, i.e., perceptions, barriers, expectations, etc. vis-à-vis a respective brand. However, also required is a directional perspective on what next so as to move the brand from one realm in the marketing scenario to another, which will forge a better connection between the consumer and the respective brand especially in terms of increasing brand saliency, evoking brand preference, bettering overall brand perception, and enhancing brand loyalty. Since the approach in the qualitative research data collection process is that of asking open-ended questions, consumers are free to talk about their world in their own language and in the way they see and experience this world, with no boundaries in their thinking. Therefore, such a process tends to yield creative insights that have a lot of value in offering inputs for charting out the way forward for the brand and its communication and marketing.

Value of Qualitative Research Analysis

Very often clients are confused regarding what kind of answers they need in order to resolve their marketing issues. Therefore, at this point, it becomes relevant to explain what insights and solutions qualitative research can deliver.

For example, there is need to *measure and identify* how many doctors prefer to prescribe a brand of antibiotic over the other competition brands and which types of indications/ailments this respective brand best used for. In this case, the research analysis needs to indicate two things—the number of doctors who prefer and prescribe this brand of antibiotic, and, a correlation between this brand and the type of indications for which this brand is used. Therefore, a quantitative approach and analysis will give the appropriate results. Whereas, if the client's need is to understand how a doctor perceives this brand of antibiotic versus the competition brands, and how to take this brand forward in terms of developing more appealing visual aids for the doctors, enhancing its image, the research analysis will need to indicate two things, namely, the doctors' perceptions of the core strengths and weaknesses of the respective brand—where and why is the brand being prescribed/not prescribed, what connects well with a doctor in promoting an antibiotic—what information he requires, what is his perception of an ideal antibiotic, his needs, concerns, barriers vis-à-vis antibiotics in general and the respective brand under study, in particular. Thus, a qualitative approach and analysis can do justice to these information arenas.

The forte of qualitative research is not to do market estimation, price-sensitivity tests, and consumer profiling. Its value comes in strong when the marketers steer into the realm of exploring creative development of their brand-related strategies. The insights derived through the qualitative research analysis is rich data because it gives insights into human psychic patterns, which are critical for identifying the key vulnerabilities and sensitivities of the consumer to capitalize upon in the marketing and communication strategies of a brand.

In other words, qualitative analysis yields layers of reasons and perceptions that lie beneath a respective thought and/or behaviour. Once the gamut of the layers of reasons and perceptions are understood and identified, quantitative research zeroes down on the key and core ones through the process of validation.

Traits of a Qualitative Researcher

The qualitative researchers need to have a flexible and creative approach in the manner in which they look at the data. The crucial task is to rise above the obvious and the rational in order to deliver that learning about human psyche and behaviour, which is either unknown or not understood.

Therefore, it is imperative that qualitative researchers have to first develop the following traits in their thinking pattern:

- To learn to think out of the box, i.e., not look at the data in a stereotypical manner

---

Megamart

If a departmental retail outlet, Megamart, wants to know why a shopper prefers a competitive outlet such as T-mart over Megamart, qualitative research will be of no meaning if the researcher comes back and tells the client that the shopper prefers T-mart because its price is low, it has good variety of products and of good quality. These features of T-mart would not be of much relevance from a reporting point of view simply because the Megamart client would know about these features given their obvious nature. Therefore, it is critical for research to delve for deeper reasons behind a shopper's preference for T-mart over Megamart. To get to know that T-mart is being preferred over Megamart because the former makes the shoppers feel at ease in the store; there is no negative attitude shown towards them when they shop there; they do not get a feeling of being 'watched and upon with suspicion' when they move around in the store, is more relevant and meaningful, along with the knowledge that all these feelings for the consumer are absent when they shop in Megamart. Thus, such insights will bring out the reasons in depth, which most clients would not be aware of as these feelings are not the first layer of reaction. In fact, such perceptions, in qualitative research, come forth with a lot of probing and emanate more from the consumer's heart than head! In sum, the unearthing of such consumer speak is the forte of qualitative research and its analysis and interpretation.

Tangible and Intangible Perceptions

In a study on a café outlet, the consumers said that when they think of this name and place what strikes them is that it is international, premium, for upper class people, and teenagers. Now, if the researchers, in their analysis, stopped at the take-outs such as core perceptions of this café, then although they would be correct, the take-outs would still be the more rational ones. Therefore, what is of critical importance is to check whether there are any underlying barriers emanating from these core perceptions, which then become the flip side of these apparently positive perceptions. Here, the researchers, in their probing at the time of the interview or group session, would need to ask, 'So what?' for each of the perceptions stated, and then, at the analysis stage, move into working out the layers behind each perception, i.e., if 'premium', then what does that make them feel, what restricts them from going there, how is the perception of being 'premium' affecting their behaviour towards this brand of café, etc. In this manner, the researchers will be able to uncover the tangibles and achieve more relevant insights into the consumers' mind vis-à-vis their perception of the brand.

- To think creatively because they have to uncover intangible/emotive factors from the data apart from the rational tangibles.

  Thus, it is imperative that qualitative researchers should be able to think and look beyond the data and not get restricted to what is being said by the consumer. More often than not, situations where consumers hesitate to articulate a particular issue, get contradictory in their responses, or simply say less but imply more through their non-verbal reactions, provide leads into what the consumers are actually feeling and thinking.

- To have the skill of looking at the data by first dissecting it into parts and understanding each part in depth, and being able to piece the parts of the data together and look at it holistically. In this way they will be able to read between the lines better, and this reading between the lines is the main deliverable of qualitative research.

It has been correctly said that, in this kind of research, the researchers read the two things that have been overtly said by the consumer. However, at the same time they have to understand what is not being said overtly.

In analysing the data, reactions can neither be taken at face value nor in isolation. Though, at the start, one dissects the data, but when interpreting it, it should be looked at as a whole in order to derive valid insights, which may not be present in the data at a superficial rational level.

One interesting view about qualitative research analysis is that its analysis is the invisible part of the job that actually begins from the moment one gets the research brief!

The analysis of qualitative research starts with the enquiry from the client and finishes with the writing of the final report. It is not a discrete part of the process and does not take place only after fieldwork. In fact, it is an ongoing process; only if the analysis is approached in this manner, will it yield the right results.

Researcher Question Thyself!

In a study on a packaging test for a dishwashing soap bar, at the start of the focus group session the homemaker consumers uninhibitedly spoke about the household chores that they disliked tremendously, one being washing dishes. Also, in explaining their usage process, they said that they rip off the packaging and put the bar in a case for regular usage. Later when the new packaging of the dishwashing soap bar was exposed, the consumers first reaction was: 'Oh, how nice...now we will enjoy washing the dishes'. At the time of the analysis of the data, the researcher must weigh all the reactions and statements holistically to arrive at the true reactions to the new packaging. The questions he has to ask himself are how important is packaging in dishwashing per se as well as in the dishwashing bar? If important, then what does it influence? What role does packaging play in making the chore of dishwashing enjoyable?

The researcher's job is to elicit structure, describe and interpret, i.e., to go beyond the obvious and the superficial. If that does not happen, it is not qualitative analysis.

Although, there are some basic common tenets for analysis, there is not one analytical process that is appropriate for all types of research likely to be encountered. The ideal is to develop a repertoire of approaches, and be able to choose one that is appropriate in the given set of research objectives and deliverables.

Tenets of Qualitative Research Analysis

Success and value of qualitative research analysis depends upon the following key factors:

- depth of insights
- applicability of insights

Depth of insights

Clients know so much about their brand and market—what they are grim about is the consumer psyche; the understanding of this with its deeper emotive layers, the connection between the rational and the emotive, all these constitute the forte of qualitative research and its analytical approach. As has been explained earlier, clients come to researchers because they do not know about the consumers' thinking underlying their behaviour. Therefore, it is imperative for researchers to tell clients more than what is apparent in consumers' behaviour. Once the underlying emotional aspects of thinking and behaviour get identified, clients have to be given 'key hooks' from this emotional sphere to peg upon the hat of their brand such that the consumer–brand connect gets maximized.

For example, in the study on a café outlet, the core perceptions that emerged were that the place and name evoked connotations of being international, premium, sophisticated, modern, and for youngsters. So, in probing and analysis, the endeavour has to be towards finding out what feelings each of these perceptions are linked to, e.g., it could be that the connotation of being 'for youngsters' is linked to gaiety, fun, light-hearted feeling, evokes romanticism, etc. If this linking is done in the analysis, then the value of the rational perceptions will come out better and there will be a meaningful link between the rational and emotive layers in the perceptions of the brand—thus offering insights to the client which have great potential for developing the communication of the brand.

Importantly, in finding this depth, the first crucial step is to uncover (mind you, there are no inventions, only discoveries of the vagaries of the human psyche) the 'why' behind any thought, process, behaviour, etc. However, the unearthing of the 'why' behind these is not enough; there has to be a further penetration (through the technique of laddering) to unearth the deeper whys behind the first-level why. Only in this way depth will come into the data; width in the data is important but the core is the depth in the data. This striving for depth begins during the interview sessions and gets continued during the analysis and interpretation stages as well, or else, the analysis and resultant output would be shallow and meaningless.

Marsh vs Exotica

Marsh, a chocolate manufacturing and marketing company, was in the business for over five decades. At one stage, they wanted to get into manufacturing and marketing of premium fine chocolates especially for gifting. Therefore, they developed a premium brand in the name of Exotica and set up a retail outlet within their office premises. Two years after the launch, the brand sales indicated that it was not doing well. Therefore the client conducted a qualitative research to get an understanding of the reasons 'why' behind the lack of sales. Some of the findings of the study revealed that the consumers were unhappy with the attitude of the staff of the retail outlet; parking was not available and therefore it was inconvenient to go there, etc.

However, such reasons did not seem to be reason enough to explain the lack of growth in the sales of Exotica. Here again, the researcher's striving was for more depth in data in order to reach to the core reasons behind the low sales of the brand. Therefore, with the use of some projective techniques, the more insightful answer that came forth was that Marsh's brand colour was purple, which was also the colour of its premium brand, Exotica. During the interview sessions, the consumers living in the vicinity of Marsh revealed that they could see the Marsh and Exotica boards from their homes. The researcher went on with his probe and asked, 'So what?' The consumers said, 'We can see the purple... 'So what?' Purple is Marsh...Marsh is ordinary chocolates, available even at a general store...Exotica is also purple...so Exotica is also ordinary...in that case how can Exotica be something exclusive and for gifting?'

Thus the unearthing of this chain of thoughts in the consumer mindset gave depth to the data that Exotica was not being accepted by the consumers as an exclusive brand of chocolates. To the consumer, this brand, having the strongly associated purple colour of Marsh, the mass brand of chocolates, was as ordinary as Marsh. Therefore, there was nothing exclusive about Exotica, and so, it was perceived as not meant for gifting.

The above probing was done in order to elicit a deeper understanding about why the consumer was not going for the brand Exotica. And, at the time of the analysis, the perceptual connection (or the lack of it) between Marsh, Exotica and premium and gifting was step-by-step delineated and explained. The clear finding was that Exotica was not being accepted as a premium and exclusive brand of chocolates by the consumer because of its association with Marsh, the name behind mass chocolates.

Melting Moments

In a research study conducted for Melting Moments, a chocolate manufacturing client, to understand gifting habits and needs of individuals, an insight such as the fact that a customer enjoys gifting even during non-festive times is good to know. However, it is not of much use to the client unless it is followed by the insight that gifting during non-festive occasions is mostly done amongst friends, and the preferred gifts are chocolates, flowers, cards, etc. and, during non-festive times, packaging is not as important as it is for festive gifting.

Thus, with these insights, the client was able to develop advertising communication for non-festive times accordingly and emphasize on how chocolates are fit for gifting especially during these times.

In this way, depth in the data was sought at both stages, viz. during the time of data collection as well as at the time of the analysis.

Applicability of insights

Once the attempt to arrive at the depth in the data is successful, relevance of the findings will automatically fall into place. However, it should be kept in mind that during the course of the research a lot of data can emerge, which is good to know but is really of no use if no relevant marketing insight can be drawn from it. No doubt, the client wants to understand human behaviour, but this understanding is not required to write a book on human psychology! What is required from this understanding is how this insight can become a relevant input into the client's marketing strategy.

Therefore, insight that is just 'good information' is not enough; what is really of value is how can the respective insight be used to forward the client's marketing plan.

PROCESS OF QUALITATIVE RESEARCH ANALYSIS

Qualitative research analysis is done as a process and there are a number of stages involved it. Critically, it starts from sifting out data and putting it into slots and sections as per the key sample profile variables, i.e., if at the start of the study, the key focus is to find out regional differences in data then the analysis will be as per this focus. However, if the key information required is connected to gender and age then the data will be keenly sifted out as per these two sample variables of gender and age.

Thus, the qualitative research analysis involves the following stages:

- transcripts
- content analysis
- data interpretation
- presentation of findings

The analysis process of qualitative data is presented in Figure 17.1.

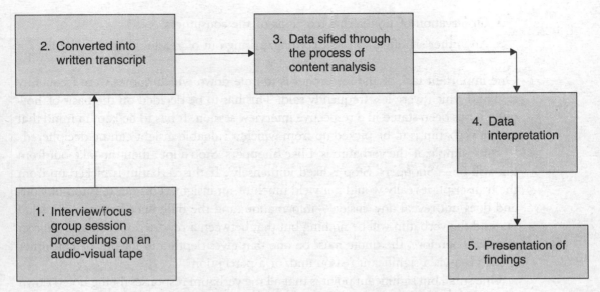

Fig. 17.1 Qualitative Research Analysis Process

CONTENT ANALYSIS OF THE TRANSCRIPTS AND VIDEO TAPES

This part of the research analysis is the foundation on which the eventual take-out of insights will be made. Therefore, the stronger this part/base is, the more valid will be the interpretations made from it.

This part of the analysis starts with:

- Reading transcripts (these are verbatim written reports—decoded from an audio recording format—of an interview and a focus group session between the consumer and the moderator.)
- Viewing video tapes (which contain happenings of the interview/group sessions)
- Working out content analysis sections as per the discussion guide, which provides guidelines for the moderation of an interview session
- In literal terms, a content analysis can be worked out on paper and/or as an electronic file—this will contain section heads and columns
- Picking relevant consumer quotes from transcripts and slotting these quotes under respective section-heads of the content analysis

Insights from the transcripts

From the transcripts (and also a brief from the moderator of the sessions), the following have to be picked up and slotted under the respective section heads of the content analysis:

- Verbatim, i.e., all quotes/direct speak of the consumer connected to the respective section head

- Observation of non-verbal reactions of the consumers
- Any other significant insight coming/arising out of reading between the lines

One important task of the researcher is to note down which quotes were frequently said and which were less frequently said. This has to be decided on the basis of how often it has been stated in a respective interview session. It has to be kept in mind that such a verbatim is to be picked up from which a valuable insight can be deciphered.

For example, if the verbatim is 'I like Shoppers' Stop a lot', then the take-out from this will be—'Shoppers' Stop is liked immensely'. If this verbatim is picked up from the transcript, it really would not yield much of an insight. This quote is too obvious and does not reveal any 'inside'—information, and the difference between the take-out and the verbatim will be nothing but that between a reported speech and a direct speech. Therefore, the quote must be one that gives depth and flavour of consumer speak vis-à-vis a significant reason and/or a perception.

One small but significant point is that all the verbatim responses (being noted down from the transcripts into the content analysis sheets) must be put into italics and double inverted comma with the right punctuations. This will tell the researcher, at one glance, which one is the quote and which one is a deciphered insight in the content analysis sheet, as the latter will not be in italics. Also, the researcher will understand well, with the presence of the punctuations, in what tone the comment/quote was made.

- 'Do I feel….??!!' vs 'What do I feel?'
- The former verbatim implies indignation, surprise whereas the latter is a simple question

A last point to be remembered is in the context of a task that the qualitative researcher should keep in sight when doing the content analysis, that of being alert about which parts of the consumer speak should be included and which ones to be ignored. The choice of which aspect of the consumer utterance is to be picked up, as well as how it is to be coded influences the rest of the analysis.

For example, suppose in an exploratory study of shampoo, a woman consumer says:

I buy the shampoo for our family. Sometimes I call the shop and they deliver it at home. My neighbour always wants to know which shampoo we use. In her family, they use four different types of shampoo. They always buy their shampoo from one shop, which is near our building. We all love to shampoo our hair…it makes us look and feel good. I get the green one…I forget the name. It's got a conditioner in it, which is good for me because I have long hair. But my husband's hair is short and not too thick, and he has dandruff, so he uses another shampoo, which I buy only for him.

Consumers, like everybody else, rarely speak in complete sentences that make sense. Therefore, from such consumer speak, the researcher will need to sift out the relevant hypotheses and insights from the not-so-relevant ones.

In this example, the relevant ones will be:

- Woman buys for husband and other members of the family
- Shampoo usage gives a 'feel good' feeling apart from good looks to the person
- Recognition of brand by colour
- Has conditioner in it
- Conditioner linked to long hair
- One shampoo not suitable for all types of hair, so different types of hair linked to different types of shampoo

The not-so-relevant ones will be:

- We all love to shampoo our hair
- Sometimes I call the shop and they deliver it at home
- My neighbour always wants to know which shampoo we use
- In her family they use four different types of shampoo (however, this point will be relevant if these different types of shampoo are associated with different ages, different types of hair, etc., because then this quote would imply what is preferred as per age and type of hair)
- They always buy their shampoo from one shop, which is near their building

Also, this sifting out from the data gives some idea of what areas are the most important, based on the theory that wherever people have most to say is likely to be an area of importance to them (an 'energy' centre) and therefore of significance for the client as well as the researcher.

Content Analysis Process

Content analysis is a very critical stage in the process of qualitative analysis because on the basis of this the draw-outs of insights are made. It is nothing but gathering of quotes/verbatim that will help the researcher understand consumer speak in terms of

- what was spoken by the consumer, and
- how it was spoken—the tone, emphasis, hesitations, etc.

The key to a good content analysis is that it is done as per the sections of the discussion guide.

Content analysis format

The discussion guide of a research study is a blueprint of how an interview session is moderated. Therefore, it contains most of the information and probing arenas of the

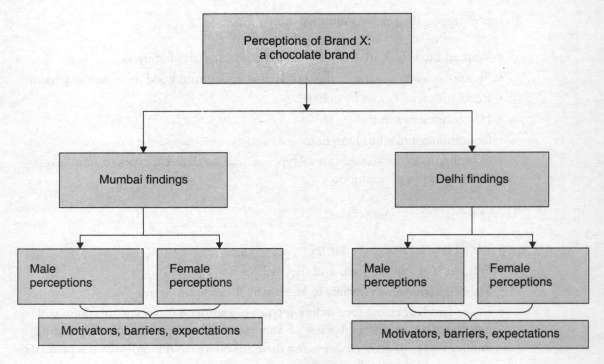

Fig. 17.2   Content Analysis Format

interview/group session. So, by adhering to the sections of the discussion guide, the analysis gets comprehensive and complete. For example, for a study on a chocolate brand's image perception, the content analysis section heads should be made as follows:

- Perceptions about the respective brand
  - Positive; negative
- Perception of this brand vs competition brand
  - Positive; negative
- Reasons for consuming the respective brand
  - Positive; negative
- Reasons for not consuming the respective brand
  - Positive; negative
- Expectations vis-à-vis the respective brand
  - Positive; negative

Fig. 17.2 shows the content analysis format for a brand of chocolate X

Variables in the content analysis format   Every research study will have important variables in its sampling, in the selection of research locations, therefore, the content analysis of the data should also have its sections worked out on the bases of these variables. For example, some most commonly used variables for analysis are:

- Gender
- Socio-economic classification (SEC)[1]
- Region
- Age
- Usership, etc.

In a study for a fast food chain of restaurants on palate preferences, the sampling was done as per the following variables: male, female, SEC A and B; and the research locations were two urban cities each in north and south India. Therefore, in this study the key analysis variables were—gender, SEC, and region.

Also, within this, one can prioritize as per the client's specifications. It could be that for the client the most critical parameter is region when it comes to understanding palate preferences, followed by SEC; age may not of be much relevance. Thus, as per these priorities, the researcher can work out the analysis.

Value-adds for the content analysis

When working out the content analysis, some sections may get added on from what emerges during the course of the fieldwork, which may not have been a part of the probing in the discussion guide.

To cite an example, in carrying out research on a chain of fast food restaurants, it became clear that the brand's 'competitive set' (those brands with which it competes for the consumer's money) also included Udupi (south Indian fast food restaurants) and *chaat* (spicy, snacky items) joints, apart from other types of fast food and fine dining restaurants. Therefore, the content analysis for this research had to include a section on Udupi and *chaat* joints as this was an important part of research since the consumers patronized these places as well when making a choice of eating out. Initially, such eating out places were not a part of the discussion guide but had to be included in the content analysis.

Atypically, qualitative research analysis approach has a method in its madness! Every researcher does this analysis as per his/her conditioning and his/her approach to their work. There are no fixed norms and formulae to work out this analysis, but what remains consistent along all qualitative research is a framework of viewing the data, i.e., a framework of logic, intuition, and creative thinking. All these then form the basic framework for searching insights that go beyond those the stated in the data, thus looking for the deeper layers in the consumer's thought process.

In qualitative research, the approach to analysis and interpretation has to be in consonance with the research deliverables of a respective study. Therefore, every study should not be analysed in a universal manner. Or else, the analysis will lose its relevance. Therefore, a customized approach for analysis and interpretation will aid in making relevant inferences given the framework of the information needs of the client. It is

---

[1] SEC is a valid and standardized classification based on education and profession, followed by the market research industry.

only when a differential analytical approach as per the type of research study is adopted that the true value of the qualitative analysis will emerge.

ANALYSIS APPROACH FOR QUALITATIVE RESEARCH

In this context, we will discuss the analysis approach for four types of qualitative research studies, which are, broadly speaking:

- exploratory research
- explanatory/diagnostic research
- evaluative research
- communication development research

In the subsequent sections, it has been discussed in detail how data analysis should be approached given that differing answers would be required by the each of these above-stated respective studies.

Exploratory research

This research is used to mostly explore those arenas that are relatively ill-defined and need more depth in understanding its dynamics, example, a new sector of the market, or an emotional or psychological state of the consumer, etc.

Typical jobs in this sort of arena are when the client asks a research agency to report on a new market, or says, 'We know nothing about the condensed milk sector but are interested to get into it'.

In other words, the client is asking the researcher, 'Tell me what this market is all about and how it operates'. To provide an answer to this requires the aggregation of data to reveal the patterns of attitudes and behaviour of the respective market.

The objective is to create a conceptual framework as to how this market (sector) operates. Therefore, in qualitative research analysis, it involves creating a map of attitudes, behaviours, need gaps, brand values, retail needs and practices, usage pattern.

Explanatory/diagnostic research

This is, in essence, problem solving, and calls for a mix of logic, intuition, and lateral thinking in the analysis approach. The client demand in such a type of a study is 'Explain to me why this has happened…' Therefore, it requires close examination of the problem and its specific ingredients. All aspects of this type of research are more focused than in exploratory research and often the mood surrounding it (just because it is a problem-solving situation) is tense and demanding. For such a study, the analysis needs to seek out 'explanations' behind the occurrence of the problem. Therefore, the researcher has to determine motives, issues of dissatisfaction, barriers, strengths, and weaknesses vis-à-vis the brand. For example, in a qualitative research of a pharmaceutical brand, the client wanted to know why their brand of antibiotic was not being preferred by doctors and why it had a lesser number of prescriptions in comparison to its nearest competition brand.

When working out the analysis of this research, the following answers were sought:

1. What were the core strengths and weaknesses of the client's brand vs the competition brand?
2. What were those aspects on which the competition brand scored over the client's brand?
3. What were the core reasons for preferring the competition brand over the client's brand?
4. What were the core reasons because of which the doctors dropped the client's brand?

Evaluative research

In this type of research, it is crucial to test out hypotheses against criteria that have already been identified and agreed upon. Typically, this kind of research is used to evaluate new advertising ideas, or existing advertising, new packaging, line extension concepts, etc.

In this type of research, interviewing is often brief and convergent in style, for, the objective is to check issues off the list so there is little need to linger or explore.

Moreover, likewise, the analysis is brief, often taking the form of going through the data and setting them against the evaluative criteria, and reporting where there are discrepancies.

To illustrate the nature of analysis for evaluative research: In a study on the evaluation of packaging options for a brand of dishwashing bar, the client's brief to the research agency was that a winner packaging option was to be identified on the bases of two parameters: the 'eye-catching' appeal of the option, and the sync of the pack graphics, colour, and image of the pack with the brand image.

Thus, in analysis, the packaging options were weighed against the two above-stated parameters.

Communication development research

When a client develops advertising or any sort of communication for his brand, it is an expensive proposition and, therefore, in order to be sure whether the communication is able to meet its objective, the client undertakes a qualitative research exercise. This is the research for evaluating and developing the existing communication; the latter through the generation of creative thoughts from the consumers.

This developmental research exercise is a process that encourages consumers to work with the advertisers or manufacturers to develop new ideas or modifications to the existing ideas.

Therefore, in such situations, the client demand is: 'Help develop these advertising concepts', where the researcher is asked to work with consumers to create new advertising, new packaging, new product variants (brand extensions), and is looking for 'solutions' to problems or opportunities that have yet to be defined.

Here the structure of analysis is even less structured as compared to the one required in the other three types of researches; for such research the analytical approach of the researcher has to be creative, getting more into extrapolation and extension from the stated data.

Sometimes the concepts tested are baseline (i.e., single statements and/or one paragraph, not in a story or any other graphic format), mostly in a written format. At other times, an idea is converted into story boards (i.e., pictorial representation of the idea in a story format, which would eventually get converted into an advertising commercial) and this is tested out on parameters such as comprehension, appeal, credibility, relevance, uniqueness, etc. and a key deliverable is also developed to refine the respective story board.

In the current scenario, this is an important arena for research because the approach of most companies is to tread cautiously in their spends and, moreover, to ensure that the brand gets built up relevantly to occupy a significant niche in the consumer's perception. Especially companies manufacturing personal care products are currently a lot into communication development research.

Socio-economic Consumers

A fast food joint had the need to bring into its customer base lower SEC consumers as well, apart from higher SEC consumers, and so a two-fold research was envisaged. In the first part, the lower SEC consumers' perceptions, barriers, needs, etc., vis-à-vis eating out and this fast food joint per se were understood. Then, from this understanding, communication concepts were developed, which were then tested for fleshing them out better in a way that they would lower the barriers to this lower SEC consumer vis-à-vis entry into this food joint and thus be able to forge a better connection between the brand and the consumer.

Advertising Concepts: Cosmetics

In a study on a brand of lipstick, the exposure was of two advertising concepts—the researcher needed to identify a winning concept; one concept took the rational route in explaining the benefit of the product and the other concept took the fear route for the same. In the analysis of this research, the researcher dissected both concepts on a pre-defined set of parameters and knocked out both concepts from the race because the two concepts were not up to the mark when adjudged in the respective parameters. However, the researcher went one step ahead and worked out a third concept (as the more appropriate winner concept) from his end, which incorporated the relevant learnings of both the concepts based on consumer feedback. Thus came into play the researcher's creativity and led to the adoption of processes of extrapolation and extension from the stated data.

CUSTOMIZED ANALYSIS OF QUALITATIVE DATA

Every research study has its distinct research objectives and deliverables. Therefore, when analysing the data for a respective study, the analysis should be approached in a manner suitable to that study. If the analysis of data from all types of studies was treated as a unilateral approach then the researcher would be committing a grave folly, resulting in data interpretation that would not meet the requirements of the client. A communication development study needs derivation of creative insights and way forward; whereas the usage and attitude studies require the derivation of trends and practices. Therefore, there is need to have a customized approach to the analysis of qualitative data. In the next section, such a differential approach has been detailed in the context of different types of studies.

Analysis of Projective Data

There is often a great deal of anxiety about how to analyse the content of projective or enabling techniques. In general, the key to this is to get consumers themselves to analyse what they have pulled out of their sub-conscious. Four crucial analysis perspectives (which, though, are not mutually exclusive) need to be the bases of analysing projective data:

- the niche/space occupied by the brand in the mindset and lifestyle of its consumers
- the nature of relationship shared between the brand and its consumers
- the impact of the usage/non-usage of the respective brand on its consumers/non-consumers
- what needs (especially the intangible ones) it fulfils for its consumers

For example, an international brand of chocolate bars, most often when personified in research, has emerged quite often (and not surprisingly) as a 'big black man'. However, what is important is the relationship the consumer has with the brand.

- Men/boys often identify with it and want nourishment as well as pleasure.
- Women/girls respond to it and want pleasure from it, and often eat it in a playful way.

Analysis of Communication Development Research

As explained in an earlier section on communication development research, in this kind of a research study the core objective can be of creatively enhancing a thought and/or perspective vis-à-vis a brand as well as that of evaluating a communication concept (also referred to as advertising concept) in order to ensure that the communication meets its intended objective optimally.

In that case, when advertising concepts have to be tested out, parameters need to be adhered to for testing the effectiveness of a concept in solus as well as on a comparative level. Thus, the evaluation of these parameters will help understand the impact the concept has had on the consumer as well as help identify a winner concept from amongst a set of concepts (if more than one concept is to be evaluated).

The first step is to understand which are the parameters that hold relevance for the client, e.g., for one client it is important that the concept be relevant to the consumer's needs and habits, but it is, not important that the concept stands out on the parameter of appeal. Whereas, for another set of objectives, emotional content of the concept maybe more important than the uniqueness of the advertisement.

Evaluative parameters

Overall, the following evaluative parameters are critical for adjudging the efficacy of a concept.

Decoding of the intended communication (i.e., semantic take-out) as per:

Manner/language of decoding and expressing Very often the advertiser has a message to be communicated—the decoding of this message happens entirely at the end of the consumers, given their frames of reference and in their language. It is important to understand how well the intended message has been understood and interpreted by the consumer. If, between the intended message and the consumer decoding, there are major gaps, then these can get rectified before the advertisement goes into the final production, which is a high-cost proposition.

Content in terms of core message, impressionable mnemonics In the interpretation of the advertising stimuli, a lot of messages may have got decoded by the consumer, but the crucial question is, was the core message understood with clarity. In this understanding, certain words, print graphics, or even a signature tune of an audio-visual advertisement get registered well in the consumer mindset. This helps in the easy recall of the advertisement.

Understanding connectivity (link) between sequences—story and meaning If it is an audio-visual advertisement then it is important that the consumer decodes the meaning of the advertising stimulus by understanding the link between the scenes of the advertisement—if these links are inappropriate then the intended communication will not be correctly decoded.

Intelligent vs dormant advertisement The main function of an advertisement is to provoke thinking and to generate inquiry. Therefore, if an advertisement is able to achieve this then it justifies its making. Thus, there is need to check whether the advertisement is intelligent, i.e., thought provoking or not.

Clarity of brand message The consumer may have understood the core message only after repeated exposures of the advertising stimulus. However, such multiple exposures may not always happen; therefore, it is imperative that the advertising clearly communicates the brand message at the first exposure.

Brand proposition

Relevance and distinctiveness: The evaluation of this parameter reveals the following:

- Is the advertising stimulus projecting the brand as different from the competition basket?
- Is the advertising stimulus making the brand feel relevant to the needs of its target consumer?

Brand attributes/benefits: The evaluation of this parameter reveals the following:

- What kind of brand features are getting communicated to the consumer?
- Which of these are tangible ones and which ones intangible?
- Which attribute is being perceived as connecting the most with the consumer needs?

Brand image: The evaluation of this parameter reveals the following:

- The brand values that constitute the perception of the consumer about the brand.
- The relationship that a brand shares/can share with a consumer.
- How clearly and effectively the advertising communication has been able to etch out this brand image in the consumer's mind

These parameters would then be used as comparative parameters in deciding upon the winner concept from amongst a set of advertising stimuli. For example, let us explain the above stated analysis for communication development/advertising from the context of a non-sticky hair oil, offering benefit of strong hair through nourishment. However, the client developed a TV commercial with the intended communication that 'this brand is a nourishing oil that is also light', key broad parameters of evaluation of the advertisement being the clarity of comprehension of above message (i.e., key take-out), credibility, relevance, and appeal.

Consumer perspective on evaluation

The evaluation of the communication from the consumer perspective included:

Comprehension Decoding of the intended communication (i.e., semantic take-out): On showing the TV advertisement, most consumers picked up the 'nourishment' property of the oil in the test advertisement. They attributed the same to the key ingredients in the product.

So, in sum, what got comprehended was: 'It is an advertisement for a new hair oil that will provide nourishment to hair'. What got additionally comprehended (due the presence of some additional ingredients) that was not intended but was favorable to the brand's image was: 'This oil would take care of hair problems such as those of hair loss and dandruff'.

What got completely missed out was 'It is a light hair oil, i.e., non-sticky'.

Content in terms of core message, impressionable mnemonics In the interpretation of the advertising stimulus, a lot of messages may have got decoded by the consumer, but the crucial question is whether the core message is understood with complete clarity. Generally speaking, in this understanding, certain words, print graphics, and maybe even a signature tune of an audio-visual advertisement could get registered well in the consumer mindset. This then helps the advertising communication to get a better space in the consumer mind set and thus the respective advertisement gets recalled well and spontaneously by the consumer.

Interestingly, in the tested advertisement, there were many mnemonics that were intended to communicate the 'light' aspect of the oil—such as the music, words such as 'swish-swish' and swaying of the hair, the playful mood of the protagonist playing with her hair, etc. However, none of these got picked up immediately, nor did they contribute to the product/brand being translated as a 'lighter' hair oil. However, on repeated exposure, the consumers did pay attention to the above mnemonics as well as to the jingle (song of the advertisement). These were interpreted as: 'Oil in the advertisement seems to be a non-sticky one ... as hair is flying with the breeze, they are using certain words'.

Understanding connectivity (link) between sequences   Interestingly, even on repeated exposure there was a confusion amongst most consumers whether there is one protagonist or more than one (in reality, there were three different characters being shown). However, they were unable to distinguish one character from the other …all seemed to be alike. Another mismatch in the communication was that there was a series of visuals of various ingredients. However, the voice-over mentioning the ingredients was not really matching the visuals; this further added to the confusion regarding what each product was. This was essential since some ingredients were not very popular across India for giving hair-related benefits. Also, there were no immediate—tangible or intangible—benefits that were shown to be achieved by using the brand in the commercial. Thus, the communication was not alluring enough to the viewers.

Intelligent vs dormant advertisement   Lack of any story in the commercial and disjointed scenes that did not match with the jingle, which was not felt to be very catchy, made it a boring and slow advertisement. Moreover, it was not very thought provoking in any way, in terms of evoking curiosity and intrigue to know more about the product or its ingredients. Thus, overall, it was a dormant advertisement.

Clarity of brand message   It was observed that the consumers actually noticed and recalled many visuals/mnemonics only on repeated exposures, which then helped them in interpreting one of the key elements of the intended message, i.e., 'This was a light oil'.

Brand proposition

Importantly, the consumer completely missed out on the brand name. Further, the communication advertisement did address the relevant needs of the consumer—nourishment and non-stickiness. However, the consumers doubted the co-existence of the above two in the same hair oil—'How can a hair oil be nourishing as well as light?' Moreover, what was lacking in the communication was that it failed to address and explain this aspect. Thus, although the TV commercial spoke of the relevant benefits, the brand proposition was not found to be very credible because it did not connect logically with the consumer.

Brand image

No significant brand image was formed on the basis of the tested communication. Prior to the exposure to the advertisement, most consumers were not aware of the brand name.

Thus, on the overall basis of the consumer evaluation, the communication did not create any distinct image of the brand in the consumer's mind. It was seen to be communicating the message that 'The brand is a nourishing oil that is also a lighter oil'. However, keeping in mind the intended communication objectives, the communication was doing its job although, at a broader level, the brand having a very low recognition, required a much more creative approach so as to leave a mark in the consumers' mind by conveying the brand more distinctively.

Analysis of Usage and Attitude Data

A usage and attitude study is exploratory in nature and is conducted in order to understand and map consumer usage habits, practices, needs, perceptions, satisfaction/dissatisfaction vis-à-vis a product category and/or brands.

For example, such a study was undertaken by a client to understand hair care in general and the hair oiling practices and needs in particular. Within the scope of this study, the probing focused on what hair oil users and non-users do for hair care. Therefore, the products used, manner of usage, quantity used, frequency of usage, types of packs preferred, how it was stored, usage as per seasons, gender-specific usage, age-specific usage, and region-specific usage, etc. were identified. And, within this framework, perceptions and evaluations were sought for national and regional brands.

Typically, data analysis for a usage and attitude study is expected to yield the following:

Patterns/process in usage, purchase

- For example, in the context of hair oiling, the patterns in usage could be something like:
  - hair oiled once a week—pre-wash (more by women)
  - hair oiled twice a week—post-wash (more by women)
  - hair oil bought once in six weeks
- Correlation of consumer's tangible and intangible needs with brand attributes
  - For example, in the context of hair care, one finding could be that a consumer wants to feel beautiful (an intangible need), therefore wants a product that gives sheen and shine to the hair post wash.
  - Also, a consumer wants both a non-sticky and traditional look (tangible needs), therefore, wants a product that is non-sticky and light.

- Issues of satisfaction/dissatisfaction with the respective brand/product category. For example, consumers may feel that hair oil is not effective because their hair fall is still heavy inspite of usage, therefore, they become lapsed users when it comes to the frequency as well the manner of oiling of hair.

- Time-tested and potential barriers blocking re-entry into respective brand/product category. For example, the key emerging barriers to hair oil could be—it is no longer efficacious, it is not a solution to hair-related problems such as dandruff and hair fall.

- Potential triggers for re-entry into a respective brand/product category. For example, the key trigger for a lapsed user to return to using hair oil could be an addition of an exotic ingredient in the hair oil, a new format of hair oil, a credible promise of efficacy through a quality seal, celebrity endorsement, etc.

In most usage and attitude studies, the qualitative output is for providing inputs into the quantitative phase, since every significant emerging pattern needs to be validated through measurement in order to ensure its strength as a 'usage attitude' amongst the consumers.

A Final Perspective on Content Analysis

Once the content analysis sheets are made it is always better to go through a check-list procedure in order to give full allegiance to the two key tenets of the analysis of qualitative research, namely, bringing depth and application-value to the insights. Therefore, the following check-list will make the content analysis process complete and comprehensive:

- Does the researcher feel that there is enough information to give a satisfactory (i.e., relevant and useful) answer to the problem stated in the research objectives of the study?

- Was the sample correctly recruited? If not, is there any bias in the sample that needs to be accommodated in assessing the information?

- Was the problem correctly conceived or did it emerge as being a slightly different problem than the client had thought? If so, why had it been incorrectly perceived? And what is the solution for the new problem?

- Did any stimulus material that was used work well, or did the researcher have to compensate for it in some way? What was the problem? What was the learning to be carried forward for the next project?

- Were there any peculiarities about the groups/interviews that didn't reveal themselves in what they said but in the type of people they appeared to be (the way they were dressed, the way they spoke etc.)?

- Does a re-reading of the proposal reveal any further understanding of the market background, which in turn helps to give meaning to the data?

DATA INTERPRETATION IN QUALITATIVE RESEARCH ANALYSIS

After the content analysis has been done, the researcher will need to keep in mind the following points for working upon the interpretation of the findings:

Per section

- What is the main take-out in terms of implications and insights from the verbatim?
- What are differences in reactions, as per the main analysis variables, be it those of sampling profile, centre-related ones, etc.

Interpretation consists of two stages:

- consumers' own analysis
- researcher's interpretation of the data

Thus there are two dimensions of Interpretation

It is imperative to interpret what consumers said (or did not say) and to discover what it all means at two levels (both these levels of interpretation are required and have to be done in conjunction and not in isolation):

- Basic level interpretation (i.e., consumer's own analysis): Making sense of the content of the qualitative interviewing process, i.e., what do people mean (as opposed to what they say).
- Deeper level interpretation (i.e., researcher's interpretation of the data): What conclusions does the researcher draw about what people really meant in what they said.

However, as stated earlier, data must be interpreted holistically, although analysed element by element, bit by bit.

Also, a question that researchers need to ask is: 'What should I go for in the data—consensus versus significance?'.

Most of the times, the data from the interviews and group sessions may not have consensus on a respective point. This is where the researchers' skills and experiences need to come into play. Given their holistic interpretation of the data and allegiance to the research deliverables, the research should be able to resolve this issue, keeping one thing in mind—sometimes significance of a finding is more valuable than complete consensus on it, i.e., some point of view may be far more relevant and insightful than all points of view.

Finally, it is important to note that in qualitative research, the focus is not just on how to go into the field, which questions to ask, which consumers to pick, which marketing stimuli to show, etc., rather on how to think, how to observe, and how to interpret, and think about 'What's going on?'

It is important to understand that 'subjectivity is not a dirty word, but an integral part of the qualitative analysis process', and qualitative research, being an amalgamation of art and science, has its own set of norms and processes in order to minimize the research bias creeping into the analysis and interpretation of the data.

When working on the presentation for a qualitative study, after the data has been fed into a powerpoint presentation, the researcher has to mull over the data over and over again and attempt to read between the line, deeper into the overt data, in order to decipher latent insights, which are not very apparent. What always works is interpreting with a sense of logic and asking oneself: is this possible? does this really happen? The answers one gets to such questions only help the researcher to do a higher level of interpretation as in what the consumers really meant and not just what they said and/or thought they meant. Also, it is imperative to look beyond the data and capitalise on one's experience rather than look at the data with blinkers on.

In the example of the fast food eatery discussed in the exhibit, at the basic level the interpretation was acceptable. However, at a higher level, the researcher's endeavour should have been to understand how this description affected these consumers who belonged to a lower SEC. Therefore, if the researcher thought hard to understand what the consumers really meant when they gave such a description, only then would he able to decipher that the preconceived image of this fast food joint was possibly a deterrent for them in patronizing this place for eating out. These were the strong barriers that the communication would need to overcome.

Consumer's Own Analysis

At the end of a projective technique, one must ask consumers to indicate the meaning of what they have done, what they have said. Firstly, they have to describe what they have done/said (so that one does not make incorrect assumptions), and, second, to explain what they said meant to them, i.e., its significance. Third, where do they feel that this idea comes from? Gross misunderstanding can arise without asking consumers to analyse their own feelings, once these have been elicited.

Then comes, for example, if the consumer says: 'I like it, because of it's blue-like packaging', they need to check further what does that mean to him? What is the significance (a peaceful colour, a colour suggesting serenity)? Where does 'that' association come from? So on and so forth.

User Profile: Fast Food

In a study on a fast food eatery (at the time of its launch), the consumers (married couples) when asked to personify the typical consumer of such an eatery described the person as being modern, sophisticated, driving a sedan, living in posh localities, etc. When the consumers were asked for the reasons for giving such a description, they explained themselves by saying that in their perception this eatery was of international standards, a premium place that served non-Indian food. Therefore, the given description was that of its typical user.

Thus, the projective material should:

- be described and explained in the consumer's own words,
- given its significance by the consumer, and
- identified in terms of its origin, how it came to be associated with the brand by the consumer herself/himself.

Researcher's Interpretation of the Data

Most of the interpretation should, in fact, be provided by the consumers themselves, but there are times when knowledge of psychological theories can help to give substance as well as a fundamental framework of understanding to a specific response.

There are many ways in which a psychological theory can help interpret consumer behaviour. Given the common cultural context for a segment of consumers, a number of universalities develop in the perceptions and behaviour and, therefore, time-tested theories aid us in understanding these universalities better.

Some important theories are:

- Maslow's hierarchy of needs is a construct that researchers make use of to explain the difference between people in terms of their underlying needs and motives. This theory assumes that individuals have to fulfil their basic physical needs before they can progress to the more self-expressive and intellectual aspirations.

- Learning theories of psychology such as classical conditioning, operant conditioning, etc. are helpful in decoding influencing factors and how thinking and behaviour patterns get formed.

- American psychologist Louis Cheskin related colours to different psychological status, red for example, is seen as making a dynamic emotional impact, while blue and grey are calming, even depressing.

- Berlin and Kay, two anthropologists, noted in a global study that in the development of a colour language, there always originated in all cultures the triad of black, white, and red. These are the 'primary' colours that humans respond to, and is one reason why they said that the psychological significance of colour varied from one culture to another. Thus, black is used in the West for mourning, but white is

---

Meaningful Interpretation

If a consumer chooses a picture of the sea in a picture-sort to represent a specific brand, it would be easy to imagine that the choice was based on association with the symbolism of the sea—great emotional forces, mother nature, etc.—However, the consumer may have used that picture for its colour ('the package is this sort of blue') or for the flock of birds in the sky ('it gives a sense of freedom to use it'), or for personal associations ('I lived near the sea in my childhood and this brand is a long-established brand') etc.

the colour of mourning in India. Moreover, in Islamic culture, green has a special religious significance, but is usually associated with nature and tranquility in Christian societies.

PRESENTATION OF QUALITATIVE ANALYSIS FINDINGS

Once the data has been analysed and interpreted, it needs to be delivered to the client—the ultimate destination from the researcher's point of view. The delivery of the findings is done in the form of a presentation, which is mostly done in PowerPoint and can also comprise of the audio-visual clippings of interview sessions, if required. This presentation has typically four broad sections:

- Research logistics: It contains the research background (with details of the client's brief), research design, methodology, and sampling
- Findings section: It contains the consumer speak as discovered during the fieldwork. This section must adhere to the sections of the discussion guide, in this way the findings section will be comprehensive
- Conclusions section: It contains a summation of the core research findings and the researcher's interpretation (with insights) of the data. This section must adhere to the objectives of the research study.
- Recommendations section: It contains a build-up on the insights from the consumer speak in terms of way forward on the client's objectives and issues. This section needs to adhere to the deliverables of the research study.

Thus, the the presentation of findings with clarity and precision is a piece of art—this should be the ideal thought and approach of the researcher when working on the presentation of the research findings.

Some Guidelines for Making a Presentation

The hallmark of a good presentation is two-fold in order to make an impact on the clients and be of use to them. This will happen in two ways:

One, by giving the client relevant in-depth insights, which are actionable and have marketing relevance.

Two, the manner in which is the presentation is worded and written, it is not only what is said that is important but also how it is put forth that makes a difference. Therefore, the data presented:

- Should be put forth with precision and be directional in nature
- Should be graphic wherever possible as this drives home the message with greater clarity. A qualitative researcher is often accused of making presentations that tend to be verbose and which then become monotonous to read. A graphic

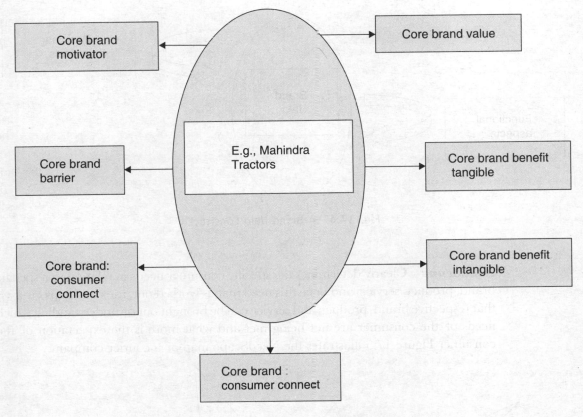

Fig. 17.3 A Brand Mirror Output

representation of the data helps break this monotony apart from succinctly but precisely putting forward the research findings. For example, Brand Mirror, Brand Halo, NeedScape, etc. can be used.

Brand Mirror It succinctly determines the core perceptions of a brand and/or product. A graphic presentation of this format is given in Fig. 17.3.

Brand Halo It is a perceptual aura surrounding a brand that has two components—one is the functional aspect of the brand and the other is the persona aspect, and the amalgamation of both these aspects gives the brand halo for a respective brand:

Functional Refers to the tangible attributes of a brand, e.g., in the case of a water purifier the functional aspects would be convenient, pure, high quality, justified price, etc.

Persona Refers to the image aspects of the brand, e.g., for the same water purifier the persona aspects would be efficient, simple, value-for-money, etc.

Thus the Brand Halo for this water purifier will be hard working, committed, etc. Fig. 17.4 illustrates the functional and persona aspects of a brand.

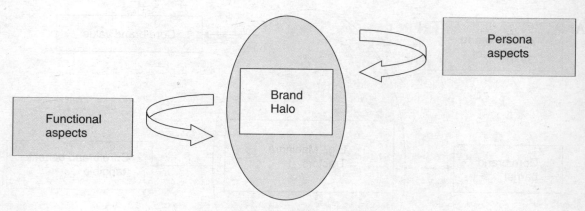

Fig. 17.4   A Brand Halo Construct

NeedScape   Clearly determines the specific consumer needs in relation to a specific brand, product, service, and once this need map is worked out, the need gaps vis-à-vis that respective brand, product, and service can be brought out by understanding which needs of the consumer are not being met and what more is the expectation of the consumer Figure 17.5 illustrates the NeedScape map of a courier company.

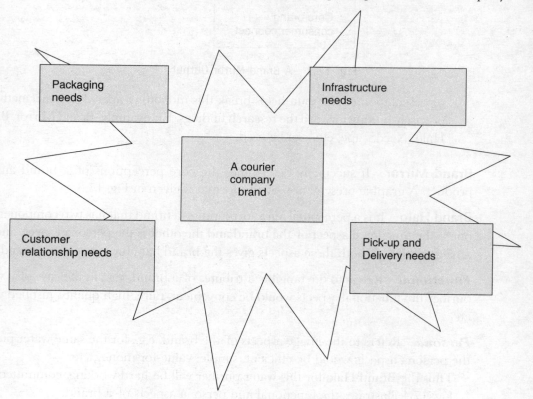

Fig. 17.5   NeedScape Map

ANALYSIS AND INTERPRETATION

In sum, it can be reiterated that the forte of a qualitative research study is to deliver depth and dimensions behind a thought, process, and behaviour. So, it has the capacity to bring meaningful answers to the following information arenas:

- psychographic description of studied consumer segments
- belief/need/attitudinal clusters
- brand values
- determining of:
  - need gaps
  - expectations
  - barriers
  - triggers/motivators
  - influencers
  - product/brand-attribute matrix
  - ladder of brand satisfiers/dissatisfiers
  - advertising/communication evaluations
  - actionable directives vis-à-vis communication, marketing, new product development derived in the form of baseline perspectives, cues, and needs expressed

In the analysis and interpretation of the qualitative data, there are few do's and don'ts for qualitative researchers, which they must not lose sight of or else their body of work will become larger than the scope of the study and also irrelevant, thus reducing their work to being an overconfident (and unnecessary) aggregation of pages and slides! Therefore, some cautions, when handling qualitative data and while making a qualitative presentation, that need to be kept in check are:

- It cannot state conclusions—only trends/patterns/perspectives/directions/cues.
  - Therefore, it cannot make categorical, strong statements. Reporting has to be in probability terms, e.g., 'The consumers do not go to Foodplace, a restaurant, because they don't like the taste of its food.'—such a statement is a strong statement for qualitative research and conclusive statements are more the prerogative of the quantitative research. At most, in qualitative research, on the basis of the claim of depth. one can state clear findings in a language such as 'Mostly the consumers do not like to go to Foodplace because of the taste of its food,' simply because the sampling of qualitative research, although representative in nature, is smaller in size as compared to quantitative research. Hence, qualitative research data are more of pointers and cues, and not conclusive statements.

- Therefore, one should not quantify the qualitative research output in numerical terms. However, it can be graded as per degree of universality, viz. minority vs significant, more or less, greater ro lesser, stronger or weaker.
- It cannot state a researcher's personal point of view, thus:
  - Insights and inferences can be drawn as per the researcher's interpretation; however, using only the collected data as the basis for drawing out these insights and inferences
- One cannot state data in the language of the researcher, there has to be reporting of the consumer language
  - Verbatim cannot be reported in the form of interpretations of the researcher, they need to be stated as they had been said.

SUMMARY

The hallmark of qualitative research analysis is to be able to blend precision and depth with creative thinking. When analysing and interpreting the data, researchers have to keep the facts in sight, but at the same time work with their sense of intuition and experience and give the ultimate test of logic when deriving insights from the analysed data.

Qualitative analysis is an organized process that moves forward in stages. Therefore, each part of the data is thoroughly looked at in isolation, and after the completion of this task, the data is to be reviewed holistically in order to do justice to the raison d'etre of qualitative research, which is that of delivering depth in understanding by reading between the lines and going beyond the stated data. It is important to note that after the analysis of the data, comes interpretation which happens at two levels—one, at the level of the consumer, and two, at the level of the researcher. That is, the consumers must explain why they are saying what they are saying and then the researcher must go beyond the stated data to make complete sense out of it to be able to derive insights of value for resolving client needs and issues.

KEY WORDS

Classical conditioning is a theory of learning in psychology, formulated by the Russian Physiologist, Ivan Pavlov. In classical conditioning, learning happens through association of events that come close in time and space.

Operant conditioning is a theory of learning in psychology, its main proponent is B.F. Skinner. In operant conditioning, learning is contingent upon reinforcement where an overt reaction is followed by feedback and reward, leading to the reaction being repeated.

Attitudinal cluster attitude is an evaluation; attitudinal cluster is an aggregation of related evaluations that, by virtue of their common threads, can be clubbed together. Hence, it is referred to as a cluster.

Barrier refers to a hindering thought, feeling that pulls away from a brand.

Motivator is a deep-set feeling or thought that pushes and pulls towards a brand.

Trigger is an immediate feeling or thought, which pushes and pulls towards a brand.

Brand proposition refers to the package of a brand consisting of its attributes (both tangible and intangible), image, etc.

Brand image is the impression that a brand leaves on the consumer mindset. This image is composed of two aspects—what the brand is and how the consumer interprets the brand to be.

Brand value is the glue that binds the consumer to the brand. This must be linked to the brand's attributes.

Projective technique is an instrument of research probing that reveals something about self, which one may not be able to express explicitly and/or be even aware of.

Lateral thinking relates to the thinking which is not uni-directional but is more multi-dimensional and hence richer and more creative.

CONCEPT REVIEW QUESTIONS

1. What are the key tenets of qualitative research analysis and should the analysis be kept standard or customized as per the research study?

2. What are the components of qualitative analysis?

3. What are the key do's and don'ts of qualitative analysis?

4. Is there a difference between analysis and interpretation?

5. What perspectives should be adhered to when doing data interpretation?

6. What are the guiding principles of a good research presentation?

PROJECT ASSIGNMENTS

1. An FMCG company got a research conducted for its brand of hair oil, covering four regions of India— north, south, east, west—in metro and mini metro centres, amongst men and women aged between 25 and 40 years, belonging to SEC B and C. These consumers are current users of hair oil as well as lapsed users who have moved out of the category. The key objectives of the research were to understand hair oil usage, purchase decision-making, and brand perceptions along with reasons for preferring/not preferring the brand potion vis-à-vis competition brands.

   (a) What should be the key approach of analysis for this study?

   (b) What will be the answers that will be sought from the research analysis?

   (c) What will be the primary and secondary analysis variables of this study?

   (d) What will be the key do's and don'ts in this research analysis?

   (e) Which graphic interpretation formats can be utilized here to represent the interpreted data?

2. From the interview sessions, the following data were collected from doctors through the use of the projective technique called personification for the clients' brand of antibiotic vs its key competition brand:

   (a) '... like Amitabh Bachchan'

   (b) ' ... like a rose ... also reserved but classy'

   (c) ' ... premium and distant'

   (d) ' ... resembles a fox'

   (e) ' ... I am not sure whether this is my friend or acquaintance'

   From this consumer speak, take out what the image of the brand is in the consumer mindset and what is the relationship shared by the consumer with this brand.

3. In a research analysis for understanding the perception and customer satisfaction for an airline, work out a brand-attribute-benefit matrix and list out factors that could be potential barriers and motivators for patronizing the respective airline; following which, make a ladder of customer expectations.

CASE STUDY

Glaxo Smithkline

This was a qualitative research study conducted to check the acceptance of the Hepatitis A vaccine among adults for the pharmaceutical giant Glaxo SmithKline (GSK). The purpose of this case study here is to explain the process of interpretation of the data collected.

Research Brief

There are a set of 'compulsory' vaccines and 'optional' vaccines, while vaccines for diseases, such as mumps, measles, polio, rubella, smallpox, etc. are compulsory, those for hepatitis A come under the optional category. It was observed that this optional category of vaccines was normally avoided by most children and adults.

The client wanted to know the reasons for this mental block.

Research Deliverables

How can GSK increase the acceptability and importance of the hepatitis A vaccine amongst adults? Thus

- Identifying the Achilles' heel (vulnerabilities and issues) vis-à-vis vaccination

- Identifying needs that can be exploited to create receptivity towards and acceptance of adult vaccination, especially the client's vaccine

Research Objectives

Understand the thinking pattern vis-à-vis the relevance and efficacy of vaccination for adults from the point of view of each sample segment covered

- To understand the motivators and barriers (doubts, concerns, myths, etc.) vis-à-vis vaccination for adults

- To identify the influencers affecting the decision to go for vaccination in each sample segment covered

- To gauge the receptivity (and/or the lack of it, with reasons) for the test concept of hepatitis A vaccine in terms of need and relevance

The sample coverage was of end users as well as the doctors and the methodology employed was in-depth interviews.

Findings From Consumer Segment

When spoken about the vaccination, the consumers gave correct and diplomatic answers such as:

'Vaccines are a useful means to stay healthy.'

'Yes, vaccines help in maintaining better health as they provide protection against targeted diseases ... it is like prevention of a disease'.

However, as the researcher explored further, it was discovered that there were some other myths/beliefs vis-à-vis vaccines, which acted as barriers against the vaccination:

- Vaccines are meant for kids, not for adults

- Vaccines are to be taken at the time of epidemic only

- There may be side effects, such as fever, post vaccination

Some other responses were:

- 'We have been vaccinated against important and fatal diseases in childhood'.

- 'Jaundice is not a fatal disease ... it is a common one ... I know of many persons who have suffered and recovered from jaundice'.

- 'Hepatitis B is a fatal disease to be vaccinated against'.

- 'Isn't hepatitis A taken care of once we get vaccinated against hepatitis B?'

- 'One may get jaundice only if a person stays in unclean surroundings, we stay in a very clean locality, and drink clean and filtered water, so there is no risk of jaundice'

- 'No vaccine is foolproof.'

- 'People have survived without vaccination till date, so why now?'

- 'Indian climatic conditions have toughened the immune system of an average Indian!'

Many consumers also suffered from certain attitudinal barriers such as:

- 'I don't need it because I am fit and healthy.'

- 'Nothing will happen to me'...

- 'When it happens we shall see to it then'...

Thus, while interpreting the data it was observed that:

- There was a low level of awareness among consumers about hepatitis A

- The sources of catching infection of hepatitis A were unknown

- Hepatitis A was not considered as a serious disease and seriousness was evaluated on the basis of fatality or mortality of the disease

- The need to get vaccinated for any disease was not felt as most believed that 'I will not get any infection'

- Most believed that physical fitness and proper diet can well take care of such infections well

Thus, there was a *low perceived need* for Hepatitis A vaccine

Findings From the Doctors' Segment

The doctors felt that the consumers exhibited resistance when advised about any preventive approach, be it vaccination, healthy lifestyle, physical exercise, and so on.

Very few patients voluntarily asked for information, the others had to be educated, which meant precious time off their practice.

Thus, doctors pushed only those vaccines which had easy acceptability such as those meant for fatal diseases (hepatitis B, etc.), or those causing epidemics (cholera, typhoid, etc.).

The doctor also 'advised' those who voluntarily sought information on prevention. Thus, the main barrier that emerged at the first level against hepatitis A vaccine was the low awareness of the disease/vaccine, low demand, and low acceptance of a preventive approach among most patients. However, when delved deeper, the researcher discovered there were other barriers, which emerged at the doctors' end.

Doctors feared losing the patient

'There is no point pushing it down the patient beyond a point, they think the doctor wants to make money and is hence pushing it ... they sometimes become unhappy with the doctor and may want to try out someone else ... '

Doctors question the vaccine cost

'It is difficult to justify the cost of the vaccine, the patients think we are making money in the process...the vaccines are so expensive nowadays...Moreover, it just prevents from hepatitis A, which is not a very serious disease.'

Doctors saw less value in convincing for Hepatitis A vaccine

'The hepatitis A vaccine costs Rs. 1,500 while the hepatitis B vaccine costs just Rs. 500...patients are definitely more open to the cheaper option....moreover, Hepatitis B is a fatal disease ...'

In doctors' perception, their skills as doctors do not get utilized when they advocate a vaccination for their patients—in this scenario they are more of a middleman since there is no diagnosis involved, no discussion involved, no prescription given and so on.

' Patients need not really come to me for knowing about vaccination per se...if they are interested they can get the information from anywhere...it is just a prevention not a cure...'

Thus the researcher's interpretation from the above insights are:

- Doctors seem to 'believe' in vaccination only as much as the patient does and vice versa

- However, the onus of disbelief rests a little more on doctors—their attitude towards vaccination is contagious

- They associated recommending vaccine as a task that did not require expertise

- Vaccination symbolizes the following for:
  - Patient—an unnecessary medical expense
  - Doctor—fatal disease, epidemic

Interestingly, when it comes to vaccination, it is the patient's word which matters, not the doctor's. The apathy (towards vaccination) is among the doctors, hence the inertia among the patients.

Vaccination has not much saliency for the doctor and the same holds true for the patient. For both, vaccination is a pain—for doctors it is a 'pain' because they find it difficult to convince a patient to go for it, knowing that there it does not come with 100%; it is a pain for the patient because it is an injection and that too a very expensive one that treats an invisible disease, which one is not sure of getting even with no vaccination.

Also, there are certain attitudinal barriers amongst doctors, which translate into behaviour that resist their push for hepatitis A:

- They are unable to justify the cost of the vaccination

- They are not convinced themselves about the 'guarantee' of a vaccine and do not consider it a complete preventive measure

- They are not talking (to the patient) about the intangible benefits of taking a vaccination

- They convince up to a point—'Take it...it will save your life from a fatal disease'.

- They do not talk about what one gains—day-to-day, better quality of life, and so on.

- They do not talk about savings—time, future medical expenses, hassles of personal and professional discomfort, etc.

- They do not talk about the relevance of the 'habit' of vaccination vis-à-vis preventive healthcare

Thus, the doctors' motivation comes more from the patient, i.e., 'If you ask, I will give it to you'. It is the patient's initiative, which makes the doctors even talk about it.

Thus, the key findings from the research are that there is a need to motivate the doctors to push the hepatitis A vaccination, additionally, there is a need to educate the patients in order to create a pull in the market.

Questions

1. From what part of information was the researcher able to make the following interpretation:

    (a) Doctors seem to be 'believing' in vaccination only as much as the patients do and vice versa

    (b) Vaccination symbolizes the following for:

        (i) Patient—an unnecessary medical expense

        (ii) Doctor—fatal disease, epidemic

2. In the current set of findings, apart from the above stated issues what were the key findings and what were the interpretations of these findings?

3. What was the 'common truth' from the interpretation of the end-consumers' and doctors' findings?

4. What were the key attitudinal barriers amongst doctors, which translated into behaviour that resisted their push for Hepatitis A vaccination?

    (a) From these attitudinal barriers, do a benefit laddering and take-out related attitudinal stances, which may be further reinforcing this resistance in some way.

5. What were the key attitudinal barriers amongst end-consumers, which translated into behaviour that made them resist vaccination for Hepatitis A?

    (a) From these attitudinal barriers, do a benefit laddering and take-out related attitudinal stances that may be further reinforcing this resistance in some way.

REFERENCES

Britt, S.H. 1966, *Consumer Behaviour and the Behavioural Sciences; Theories and Applications*, Wiley, New York.

Coulson-Thomas, C.J. 1990, *Marketing Communication*, Heinemann Professional Publishing, Oxford, UK.

Gordon, W. and R. Langmaid 1988, *Qualitative Market Research: A Practitioner's & Buyer's Guide*, Gower, London.

Kassarjian, H.H. and T.S. Robertson (eds) 1991, *Perspectives in Consumer Behaviour*, 4th edn, Prentice-Hall.

Luck, D.J. and R.S. Rubin 2001, *Marketing Research*, 7th Edn, Prentice Hall of India, New Delhi.

Morgan C.T., R.A. King, J.R. Weisz, J. Schopler 1986, *Introduction to Psychology* (7th edition)

PART FIVE

Getting Meaning Out of Data and its Applications

- Report Writing and Presentation
- Interpretation of Marketing Research Reports
- Applications of Marketing Research

18

Report Writing and Presentation

After reading this chapter, the readers will be able to understand:

- how to write a marketing research report and relate it to the various objectives of the study
- some ethical issues in preparing the report
- how to prepare and make the oral presentation of a report

INTRODUCTION

The basic purpose of all marketing research, we have seen, is to help managers take informed decisions in the area of marketing. This obviously implies that the process of understanding the manager's requirements, the genesis of the issue, and the process of finding answers, must all culminate in some communication from the researcher that would help the manager in such a decision. In other words, a final marketing research report is an essential part of the research process, without which marketing research is meaningless. Such a report, which is the final tangible product of the research project should, to be optimally effective, be best presented in a written form, ideally followed by an oral presentation to the concerned managers. As we discussed in the initial chapters, the best report is one that understands and answers the major concerns of the managers. The consideration that every manager who is likely to be involved in the final marketing decision is not necessarily involved in the commissioning and the administration of the research project, and will depend upon the report for these decisions, further enhances the importance of the research report. This chapter defines the scope, structure and flow of a marketing research report and discusses some ethical issues in preparing the report. Finally, the chapter provides some guidelines regarding the oral presentation of the report.

A MARKETING RESEARCH REPORT

Some of the most important points to keep in mind while writing the marketing research report are:

- As mentioned in the introduction, the fact that most of the managers involved in the decisions based on the report will not be involved with the project on a day-to-day basis
- Each manager will approach the issue necessitating the research from the standpoint of his or her functional responsibility, and will therefore examine the report differently
- Departmental heads, divisional heads, and similar other senior managers will usually not be interested in the details but rather in a review of the issues examined in the report, the major conclusions reached, and the recommendations made by the researcher
- The client is concerned with taking decisions on the basis of the report. Recommendations made by the researcher should therefore suggest definite action points rather than adopting a speculative approach, and be actionable.

Scope and Structure

These considerations determine the scope and structure of a marketing research report and also of the oral presentation. At the same time, the researcher must bear in mind that one marketing research study usually examines one or at best a limited number of issues. It should not therefore purport to be a solution to all marketing problems that the client organization may be facing in various areas of marketing activity. For example, a brand perception study may find that the brand's penetration and availability are perceived as inadequate. If the client is already operating at optimal market coverage per sales representative, then this problem is linked to the size of the organization's sales force, and the researcher's recommendation for filling this gap between the current and the optimal coverage cannot be acted upon unless the client is in a position to increase the size of its sales force.

Writing a Marketing Research Report

The steps required to be followed in writing a marketing research report are discussed below.

Title of the report

The title page of the report should carry four distinct items of information—the subject of the study, the name of the organization for whom the report has been prepared, the name of the organization carrying out the study, and the date of submission. The topic of the study should be defined in specific, self-explanatory terms and the title should not be too long. Some authors recommend inclusion of the letter of authorization from the client to the researcher immediately after the title page. Figure 18.1 outlines the steps to be followed in writing a marketing research report.

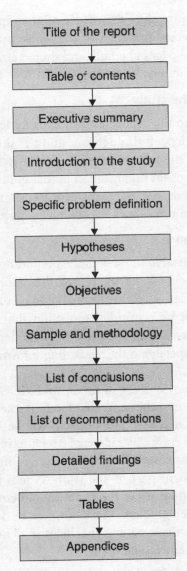

Fig. 18.1 Steps in Marketing Research Report-Writing

Table of contents

It should be exhaustive and should indicate section titles as well as the corresponding page numbers. Section headings should refer to the various stages in report presentation, such as executive summary, introduction to the report, and so on.

Executive summary

This is the summary of the entire project report, beginning with a brief description of the relevant environment, and the rationale of the issue under study. The executive summary aims at providing the reader of the report with an overview of the entire project, and is directed primarily at the senior management. It should therefore not exceed two to three pages in length and should emphasize the problem definition, the conclusions, and the recommendations.

Introduction to the study

The introduction to the report aims at explaining to the reader the rationale of the problem being addressed through the study. It should essentially provide some brief information about the relevant environment, e.g., the trends in the relevant industry, the position of the client organization in that industry, the importance of the product category to the client, major competitive trends, and the purpose of the study. The introduction should usually not exceed half a page or one page at most.

Problem definition

This is the most crucial initial step in the preparation of the report, since it determines the structure and coverage of the rest of the report. The definition of the marketing research problem derives from the marketing issue being addressed. Inexperienced researchers cannot be reminded too often that while the marketing problem is concerned with a marketing decision, the definition of a marketing research problem is concerned with specifying the marketing information required for arriving at that marketing decision.

For example, if the client organization, an FMCG company, is interested in exploring the opportunity to enter the processed foods market, the decision involved is 'whether or not to enter the market'. The decision will be based on the attractiveness of the opportunity and the company's internal strengths in that area. The marketing research problem then is only to assess the attractiveness of the opportunity. The client's internal strengths will not form part of the study. Nor is the researcher required to take a decision about whether or not the client should enter the market.

Marketing research problems must, however, be defined in specific terms, delineating parameters that are measurable. This helps in delimiting the scope of the study and identifying the measures to be used.

Defining hypotheses

All descriptive and causal studies in marketing research establish conclusions by testing hypotheses for validity. These hypotheses have to be defined in quantifiable terms. They should emerge from discussions with the client. As discussed in earlier chapter, the marketing research problem must be further divided into sub-problems, each addressing a unique dimension of the problem. Each sub-problem is translated into one or more hypotheses. The final report must list all the hypotheses the study aims at testing.

Listing objectives

Research objectives are the first of the three stages of research design, which includes, apart from objectives (what), the sample (from whom), and the methodology (how). Once the hypotheses have been defined, the objectives of the study must be specified.

We have discussed in an earlier chapter that objectives or areas of enquiry emanating from the hypotheses can be divided into primary and secondary objectives. Objectives must be defined in terms of specific, measurable parameters, and the list should ideally not exceed eight or ten objectives. These objectives must be listed separately in the report in the section following the list of hypotheses.

Sample and methodology

The second part of the research design is the sample, describing whom the data is to be collected from. In the final report, a summary of the sample design must be provided. This should include the sampling method, the population and the size of the sample—total as well as in each market segment—and the sampling element. It is a good idea to present the planned as well as the achieved sample size and explain reasons for the discrepancy.

Methodology includes the methodology of data collection as well as the methodology of data analysis.

- The section relating to data collection methodology should specify the method used for collecting data— secondary research, observation, experimentation, or interviews. Again, the kind of interviews—structured, group interviews, group discussions, in-depth, or projective techniques—if employed, should be specified. The data collection procedures such as face to face interviews, mail or internet surveys, or telephonic interviews must be indicated and the reasons for choice of these procedures must be explained.
- The methodology of data analysis must also be explained in some detail. This should include the specific techniques employed for data analysis, the reasons for choice of these techniques, and briefly, the conclusions arrived at using them.

Conclusions

The section on sample and methodology must be followed by summary conclusions arrived at in the study. Conclusions are not mere summary findings. Findings state facts; conclusions draw inferences. Findings can therefore not be treated as substitutes for conclusions. Sometimes, especially if the findings are extensive and complex, there is a temptation not to put in a separate section for conclusions. Such a temptation must always be resisted for reasons stated earlier in this paragraph.

The reason behind placing the conclusions before the section on findings rather than at the end relates to an issue touched upon earlier—every manager involved in decisions based on the study will not be concerned with or interested in the details of the report, and senior members of the organization will usually be concerned only with the conclusions and recommendations of the study.

Conclusions should be listed in the decreasing order of priority, and should not exceed a maximum of three pages. It is not necessary to include a great deal of numerical data in conclusions; usually reporting of results reached on the basis of data-based analysis should suffice. This is particularly important if the client does not have a technical background, and is interested in results more than in methodology or numbers.

Recommendations

This section, along with conclusions, is based on detailed findings arrived at from analysis of the data obtained in the study, and the two should form the essential substance of the entire report. Recommendations, like conclusions, should not exceed three to four pages in length.

Management students and inexperienced researchers sometimes tend to leave out the recommendations section from their reports on fact-finding studies. It is important to remember that marketing research studies are commissioned to derive direction in taking marketing decisions, and must therefore provide pointers to these decisions. Let us for example consider a descriptive study conducted by a readymade garments retail chain, such as Pantaloons, catering primarily to the mass market. The company wants to determine the profile and purchase pattern of its current customers. The researcher must obtain, as part of the research brief, the assumed profile and purchase pattern. The findings of the study will help determine the actual profile and purchase pattern, which may be compared with the expected pattern. The conclusions of the study will then include the inferences drawn from this difference between the assumed and the real profile and purchase pattern. A useful study should recommend ways of narrowing the disparity, thus providing directions for corrective action.

Findings

This is usually the longest section in any marketing research report. The purpose of findings is to explain the data, rather than draw inferences from it. Findings should provide information on the objectives of the study, and each finding should be related to one objective. Ideally, they should be presented in the same sequence as the objectives, and each finding should provide reference to the table(s) whose data it aims at explaining. It is useful to include graphs and charts explaining the table in the main body of the findings.

Figure 18.2 provides an illustration of a hypothetical finding relating to the Pantaloons Customer Profile study. Consider the purchase pattern demonstrated in Table 18.1.

Table 18.1 Purchase Pattern of Trousers

Frequency of Purchase	No. of Buyers	No. of Trousers Bought per Occasion	No. of Buyers
Once a month	10	1	30
Once in 2–3 months	58	2–3	45
Once in 3–6 months	27	3–5	22
Once in 6–12 months	5	More than 5	3
Total	100		100
Average Frequency	3.68	Average no. of trousers per occasion	2.49

Table 18.2 Age Distribution of Buyers

Age (in years)	No. of Buyers
Up to 25	10
25–40	23
40–60	47
Above 60	20
Total	100
Average Age	46.23

Table 18.3 Income Distribution of Buyers

Monthly Household Income	No. of Buyers
Up to Rs. 20,000	14
Rs. 20,000–40,000	26
Rs. 40,000–60,000	35
Rs. 60,000–80,000	15
Above Rs. 80,000	10
Total	100
Average income	44,940

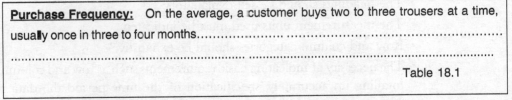

> **Purchase Frequency:** On the average, a customer buys two to three trousers at a time, usually once in three to four months...
> ....
>
> Table 18.1

Fig. 18.2 Findings of the Study on Pantaloons Consumer Profile

It will be noted that the finding relates to the objective 'purchase frequency' and explains the information captured in Table 18.1.

Sometimes the information pertaining to one objective is spread over more than one table. In that case, all the relevant tables must be listed at the end of the finding pertaining to that objective (e.g., Tables 18.1 – 18.3 instead of Table 18.1 in Fig. 18.2 above). For example, let us assume that Tables 18.2 and 18.3 provide details about the age and income category of the buyers

The findings related to 'purchase profile' (Fig. 18.3) would read as:

> **Purchase Profile:** On the average, a customer buys two to three trousers at a time, usually once in three months. The average age of the buyer is about 46 years, and he is likely to be in the income category of Rs. 40,000–60,000 per month.............................
>
> Table 18.1–18.3

Fig. 18.3 Findings of the Study on Pantaloons Consumer Profile

Tables

Tables are an important part of the report, since they present data in a concise, efficient way and facilitate quantitative comparisons in a detailed, easy-to-understand manner. General, long tables provide opportunities for complex analysis that can help draw significant inferences. They derive most of their utility from the variety of cross-tabulations they present, making the study of a large number of interrelationships between variables possible. Such tables should normally be placed at the end of the report in a separate section. If the number of such tables is large, it might even be a good idea to present them as a separate volume.

Short or summary tables may sometimes be included in the main body of the report to lend statistical support to research findings, though many readers find them rather unacceptable as they have to be interpreted and tend to break the flow of the text. It is better in such cases to substitute them by graphs, charts, and other visual representations of information. Apart from breaking the monotony of the text, they are easier to understand and interpret.

Whatever the size and complexity of a table, it must adhere to some basic rules of easy and accurate interpretation. For example:

- All tables should be numbered
- The headings should be self-explanatory
- The measurement units used must be indicated
- Row and column categories should be exhaustive
- The necessity of indicating basic requirements such as row and column frequencies totalling up accurately, specification of the time period the data relates to (if necessary), and mention of the base of percentages can never be overemphasized
- If a table lists categories where multiple responses are possible, this information should be noted at the bottom of the table
- In fact, all needed explanation should be given in footnotes
- Similarly, if a table lists frequencies corresponding to a rating scale, the verbal equivalent of all ratings should be specified
- If the data in a table is from a source other than the field survey, as in the case of secondary research, the source must be quoted

Appendices

All reference material used in the study should be included in the appendices. This includes questionnaires (or interview guides in case of unstructured interviews), show cards, pictures, or any other aids used for administering projective techniques. Sometimes published material such as newspaper or magazine articles related to the subject of study or advertisements used in the survey may be included in the appendix.

While writing the report, it is essential to keep the reader(s) in mind—their technical background, familiarity with jargon, and the amount of time they will be able to spend on reading the report. The purpose of the report is to provide a solution to the clients' marketing problems and help them take a decision, and not to impress them with one's erudition. Moreover, as we have discussed earlier, in an organization the report will be read by a large number of managers, most of whom will approach it from different backgrounds and different points of view. Usually, the report will be read in the researcher's absence. If the presentation of the report is not logical in sequence, the language too terse, or the appearance too unprepossessing, very few managers are likely to revert to it, but merely file the report instead. It is therefore essential that the written report is easy to read and follow, and inviting enough in appearance to draw the reader in.

PRESENTATION OF A MARKETING RESEARCH REPORT

Often, the client goes through the written report and then asks the researcher to make a presentation. If such a request from the client is not forthcoming, the researcher should take the initiative and volunteer to make a presentation. An oral presentation has many advantages:

- An oral (and visual) presentation is made to a captive audience and therefore usually has a greater impact on a group compared to a written report
- It ensures that the client is actually exposed to the results of the study instead of merely filing the report as a window dressing
- It involves managers from various functional areas and often from different levels, and therefore makes for greater acceptability
- It usually generates discussion and thus provides an opportunity to the researcher to clear any doubts the client's representatives may have about the results arrived at
- The discussion also increases the possibility of decisions being taken

Some guidelines for the oral presentation of the report are given below:

- The presentation should usually be made by a senior member of the research organization. This serves to convey to the client that the study is treated seriously by the researchers
- It is important to circulate copies of the summary report to each member of the audience before the presentation is started
- Though the decision about who should attend lies with the client, to the extent possible the researcher should request the presence of executives from various functional areas
- Use of aids such as a power-point presentation help to enhance the air of professionalism, make it easier for the discussion that follows to be more focused as it is possible to go back and forth with the slides, improve aesthetics, and break the monotony of a presentation made without any aids
- The presentation should follow a three-step process—the introduction that explains to the audience what is going to be presented including the problem, the actual presentation including recommendations for action, and the summary of the presentation
- It is important to provide the background and outline the research problem in some detail. Adequate amount of time should be spent explaining the research design

- It helps to tell the audience in advance that the presenter will answer questions at the end of the presentation, unless some clarifications are sought about the terminology
- The researcher must try to get a 'buy-in' from the manager who commissioned the study by discussing the report with him/her in advance of the presentation
- The client's representatives will often have questions regarding the analysis related to certain conclusions. The researcher must be prepared to do so without lapsing into jargon or technicalities. Nothing reduces the chances of a report being accepted more than the impression created that the researcher has been trying to show off or talk down to the client's representatives. Equally, it is important not to get on the defensive about the findings

ETHICAL ISSUES IN A MARKETING RESEARCH REPORT WRITING

Apart from the accuracy and actionability of the results, ethics is a major consideration in writing and presenting a report. The reporting of research results to the client should be honest, accurate, and complete. Ethical considerations govern issues such as the kind of data collected or reported and the manner of data reporting. Some examples of these issues are mentioned below.

Kind of data collected or reported

- If the researcher has at any time conducted studies for the client's competitors and thus has access to proprietary confidential data, such competitive information must never be quoted or used in arriving at findings
- Presenting secondary data without quoting the source is also to be included in the same category
- Researchers are at times guilty of reporting false or inaccurate data. This includes presenting data from incomplete fieldwork or inaccurate fieldwork, or even not collecting data at all
- Compromising the research design in other ways such as asking leading questions in a questionnaire or deliberately interviewing wrong respondents is also equally unethical

Manner of data reporting

- Biased reporting in order to justify or disprove one point of view. This is especially likely in internal marketing research
- Misusing statistics and twisting data to support preconceived notions
- Deliberate misinterpretation of results
- Presenting the results in a manner likely to lead to confused or wrong results, such as presenting only percentages when the base is small and percentages are likely to give an inflated result

- Deliberately withholding information that is not likely to support the corporate view
- 'Sitting on the fence', i.e., not recommending any definite action on the basis of the study, but presenting the results in such a manner that either of the two opposing conclusions can be justified.

Other issues relating to ethics in research are concerned primarily with dissemination of research results to people or organizations not authorized to receive them. For example, publishing data from proprietary research in an article without the client's permission is a definite breach of ethics.

SUMMARY

A marketing research report is the final tangible product of a research project. An ideal report should answer the major concerns of the client and offer suggestions to help the client take informed decisions in the area of marketing. Written reports must follow a definite structure in order to optimize their utility and acceptability. Beginning with the title of the report, this structure includes the index, executive summary, problem definition, and research design including list of hypotheses, objectives of the study, sample definition, methodology of data collection, and methodology of data analysis. Next come the sections concerned with conclusions of the study, recommendations based on the results, and detailed findings. It must be remembered that findings and conclusions are not substitutes for each other. Detailed data tables must be included at the end of the report and may, if necessary, be presented in a separate volume. Appendices must include all material used in the study.

Apart from the accuracy and actionability of the results, ethics is a major consideration in writing and presenting a report. The reporting of research results to the client should be honest, accurate, and complete and results of the study must not be disseminated without the client's permission.

Oral presentations have the advantage of involving other executives in the organization besides the manager commissioning the study and are likely to help spur decisions. It is best to use visual aids for this purpose. The presentation should be a three-step process, including the introduction to the problem, the results, and finally, a summary of what has been presented. The presentation should be kept simple and free of jargon, and questions relating to research design must be answered clearly and in detail.

KEY WORDS

Biased reporting is a written or orally presented report that is based on inadequate or erroneous data collection or data analysis.

Conclusions are inferences drawn from the data collected and analysed as part of the research study.

Executive summary refers to the summary of the study, including the rationale for the study, the research problem, sample definition, conclusions, and recommendations, aimed primarily at senior management.

Findings are explanation of facts culled from the data collected for the study.

Proprietary research is the research commissioned by and conducted for a client organization.

CONCEPT REVIEW QUESTIONS

1. List and discuss the steps in writing a research report.

2. List the guidelines for preparing tables. Why should detailed tables not be part of the main body of the report.

3. What are the internal ethical issues a researcher must keep in mind while preparing a research report?

4. Research reports, if they contain poorly presented though useful data, tend to be ignored. What are the ways of including statistical presentation in the report that will enhance the readability and utility of the report?

5. What are the advantages of oral presentation of a research report? What are the points the researcher must keep in mind in order to make an impactful presentation?

PROJECT ASSIGNMENTS

1. Assume that Asian Paints are exploring the possibility of setting up a specialized mall for all material related to building and construction. They have hired you as a consultant to establish the chances of their success in entering this market. If you decide to undertake a market research study for this purpose, how will you define the marketing research problem? Design a detailed format of the marketing research report you will submit.

2. 'Oral presentations, in spite of all their advantages, run the risk that all those present will take up definite positions for or against the issue studied merely on the basis of the presentation, and the net result will be a delay in the implementation of the project.' Discuss in groups.

3. Take up a marketing research report submitted by one of your classmates or seniors. Critically evaluate the report.

4. Take up a marketing research report prepared by one of your seniors. Develop a detailed plan for oral presentation of the report. How would you ensure that it is not seen as biased?

REFERENCES

Cooper, D.R. and P.S. Schindler 1999, *Business Research Methods*, Tata McGraw–Hill, New Delhi, pp. 417–419.

Malhotra, N. 2004, *Marketing Research: An Applied Orientation*, fourth edn, Pearson Education.

19

Interpretation of Marketing Research Reports

OBJECTIVES

After reading this chapter, the readers will be able to understand:

- the role of marketing research in reducing uncertainty and errors in a marketing research report
- the role of the researcher and the client in using marketing research reports
- how to link information to decision-making
- strategic and tactical levels of decision-making using marketing research
- the functions of strategic research and its contribution in helping the client take long-term marketing decisions

INTRODUCTION

There is an old story about two shoe salespersons who were sent by their company to a country in Africa to determine the possibilities of selling their brand of shoes. Both of them toured the country extensively for a week. At the end of the week, one salesperson wired his boss, 'No market here. Nobody wears shoes.' The other salesperson also sent a wire to the boss, 'Fantastic opportunity. Virgin market. Nobody wears shoes.'

The moral of the story is, it is not the information that is of any use by itself. It is the way an information is interpreted that makes a difference to its utility in decision-making. That is where the role of the client becomes crucial in putting marketing research information to productive use. While the researcher has to collect data, analyse it, and provide information, it is the client's responsibility to interpret that information, analyse it, if necessary, beyond the analysis provided by the researcher, and take decisions on the basis of this analysis and interpretation, keeping in view the other realities within the organization. These realities will usually not be accessible to the researcher even in the most open client organization.

THE MARKETING RESEARCH REPORT

The important role played by a marketing research report and its correct interpretation and use have been discussed in this section.

Reducing Uncertainty Errors

Marketing decisions are almost invariably taken under conditions of uncertainty and could be based on a variety of errors in the marketing research report. According to Cornell (1980), there may be numerous reasons for these errors:

- Poor problem formulation
- Inflexibility in considering new information
- Communication failure
- Not asking the right questions
- Insistence on examining the issue from the narrow focus of one model
- Ignoring the limitations of information obtained
- Inadequate attention to uncertainties inherent in the situation

As we have noted earlier, the role of marketing research is to reduce uncertainty in marketing decisions. The level of uncertainty and its impact varies with the kind of marketing issues for which marketing research is used, broadly divided into problem identification research and problem solution research. Research provides the customer driven or market driven perspective, and thereby defines the more acceptable and less risky options in a decision situation.

Green and Tull (1978) have quoted a list prepared by D.W. Twedt (1973) of the kind of marketing research studies conducted or commissioned by more than 1,300 companies in USA. A large proportion of these include studies to determine market potential, market share, and market characteristics, as well as market analysis to determine the acceptability of sales performance.

Role of the Researcher and the Client

The involvement of the client in marketing research studies varies with the problem area, though the final interpretation and decision-making is certainly within the domain of the client's responsibility. The importance of marketing research is therefore dependent on (a) the amount of information delivered by the researcher, (b) the speed with which this information is delivered, and (c) the value that the client may derive from such research. The value derived is thus contributed by both the researcher's effort and the client's effort.

Researcher's contribution

The researcher can contribute to the quality of the report in the following areas:

- Understanding of the client's problem
- Quantity of information provided
- The rigour of analysis and interpretation by the researcher

Client's contribution

The client plays an important role in the formulation of the research report and in interpretation in the following areas:

- The formulation of the marketing problem and sub problems

- The clarity and detail of the requirement and the research brief given to the researcher
- The interpretation of the information by the client in the broader context of the market, the marketing-mix and non-marketing variables in the internal and external environment. This interpretation links the information to the final decision. In most quantitative research, a measure of the value of research is provided using decision theory, as we have discussed in earlier chapters.

The client's interpretation and implementation of the marketing research report needs to be made in the context of the following.

The immediate marketing issue   At the initial level, the marketing research report is expected to provide an answer to the marketing issue being investigated through the study—should the client organization enter the new market being considered? Should the current market segment be changed or expanded? Does the product require any actual or perceptual change? How is the brand perceived by the consumer? What are the consumer's expectations from the brand? A good marketing research report should be able to provide answers to such queries.

The internal environment   Recommendations of the marketing research report, even if acceptable within the context of the immediate issue, must be examined from the perspective of the non-marketing variables within the organization, such as organizational strengths, weaknesses, and resources. For example, if the research report recommends a change in the product-mix, how will its implementation influence the raw material inventories, the manufacturing process, the response of the trade, the sales training process, the sales process, and the communication? What will be the costs involved? Will it affect the brand image?

How much time will this changeover (in the product-mix) take? Will the competitors take advantage of the time required for change? Will the returns be worth the cost, immediately and in future? Does the company have the monetary and skill resources to enter the new market recommended by the marketing research report from the point of view of attractiveness of the opportunity? How long will it take to acquire such resources? How difficult will it be? If this involves buying out another company, how feasible will it be? What about the cultures of the two organizations? All such questions may need to be examined before a decision is taken to implement the marketing research recommendations.

The external environment   The recommendations also need to be examined in the context of the realities of the external environment such as competition, socio-economic trends, and government policies. For example, a market research study commissioned by Wal-Mart might indicate that the potential for organized retailing in India is huge, but that information is not actionable as long as the Government of India continues with its policy of not permitting FDI (Foreign Direct Investment) in multi-brand retailing. Similarly, the market potential for geriatric medicine and special toilet soaps for the 30-plus women have to be studied keeping in mind that people are living longer now, and attitudes and lifestyles have changed so that a 30-plus woman does not hesitate to take care of her special requirements.

These environmental factors have long-term impact on the actionability of marketing research reports. Competition impacts marketing decision-making in the short-term as well as the long-term. Sales promotion strategies will influence the turnover of a competitor's brand in the short-term, while market clutter will influence the decision to enter or not enter a market.

Strategic requirements   The key to business success in a competitive environment is planning, which in turn is dependent on accurate, timely, and reliable information, since the more competitive the environment, the more uncertain it is. The decision on the implementation of marketing research findings is also influenced by the planning orientation of the client organization—where the organization wants to be, how it wants to position itself or its brands in the short-term and in the long-term. For example, a market research study for a baby lotion may provide opportunity for the company's brand to offer moisturizing for older women as well as protection for the baby's skin in winter months. The company will, however, have to choose between these two market segments depending on its long-term strategy.

Awareness of limitations of research   Most marketing research, even if meticulously planned, carried out, and interpreted, suffer from three sets of limitations, which the manager must bear in mind before deciding on the implementation of its results:

- Most research is concerned with tests of certain hypotheses. If these hypotheses change or cease to be valid because of environmental or organizational changes, the relevance of research based on them will also decline.
- Research is usually based on data related to a specific time period, and is therefore valid only for a certain time period. This is especially true of quantitative research. Beyond this time frame, environmental changes detract from the validity of the findings. For example, the consumer purchase decision process for a high involvement product, goes through various stages as depicted in Figure 19.1.

The research required at each of these stages is different, and the results of research conducted for one stage will not be valid once the consumer has moved on to the next stage. Again, the findings keep changing with geography and with time; findings of research conducted ten years earlier may not be valid now. Similarly research conducted in rural areas will not be relevant in urban areas.

- The utility of a research result varies at different levels of the organization. The evaluation of success of a sales promotion scheme may be of great relevance to the concerned brand manager. At more senior levels of the organizational

Fig. 19.1 The Consumer Purchase Decision Process

hierarchy, the response to a single sales promotion scheme will usually be of limited value, except to the extent, it effects the brand's promotion budget. The exception would be the kind of sales promotion scheme that is innovative enough to serve as a model for future schemes of the same kind.

USING MARKETING RESEARCH

The utility of research will be extremely limited if its results cannot be applied to planning the future. In an organization, therefore, research is used at two levels—tactical and strategic.

Tactical Research

Most of the marketing research in organizations have traditionally been related to tactical decisions. One major use of research has been in *post facto* evaluation of decisions, such as was the market segment selected appropriate? Was the positioning right? Was the pricing right? Were the various other marketing-mix variables adequate and appropriate? To what extent has the marketing response to the major competitor's promotion been successful? And so on. Most tactical research are concerned with pre-launch, post-launch, and other ad hoc studies of the various marketing-mix variables relevant at different stages of the brand's life cycle. Research responses to such questions help in assessing the extent to which short-term marketing objectives have been attained. For the most part marketing research is employed for answering such questions, or to evaluate the possible impact of such marketing decisions in the immediate foreseeable future.

Strategic Research

With the business environment getting increasingly competitive, it is however no longer enough to restrict the use of research to verify the achievement of short-term objectives. As the environment gets increasingly dynamic, extension of strategies that are relevant today to tomorrow is not necessarily useful or profitable. Competitors and their strategies change, the business and Product-Life Cycles (PLC) become shorter and the response of consumers to competitive activity also become different. Planning for the future then becomes essential to an organization's survival and growth.

Future planning must thus consider the changing environment and its impact on current and future activities, on the basis of the impact current decisions will have on future activities. Since the future is more uncertain than ever, this planning involves building scenarios likely to occur, given different inputs. This scenario-building exercise thus depends on comprehensive and accurate information obtained on the basis of the strategic research.

Defining strategic research

What is strategic research? Stevens et al. (2004) have defined it as 'the integration of the tools and techniques of research, competitive analysis and forecasting as integral parts of the planning and decision process.' Other interpretations of strategic research are concerned with its long-term and organization-wide perspective. These are research related to identifying the appropriate target segment, identifying market gaps or consumer need gaps that the organization has the expertise to exploit profitably, and assessing indirect competition from different product categories for satisfying a need. Further, strategic research is concerned with predicting and forecasting long-term market growth and market shares to help determine whether new markets or new marketing-mix would be a more profitable proposition (prediction must be treated as separate from forecasting; prediction is announcing the likelihood or otherwise of the occurrence of an event by examining the cause–effect relationship between two variables; forecasting is concerned with a more rigorous measure of the exact probability of the occurrence of the event) and identifying new opportunities, and so on.

Functions of strategic research

In this sense, strategic research is concerned with:

- Defining organizational goals and objectives: 'we will try to be among the first three in any market we enter, or we will not enter it'
  'we will aim at the largest share of the consumer's wallet'
  'we will diversify into this market where our actual expertise is matched by consumer perception of our expertise'
  'we will position ourselves as an Indian company promoting Indian values'
  'we will identify brands/businesses that are not contributing either to our image or to the bottom line and jettison them; instead we will concentrate on a few select brands/businesses, etc.

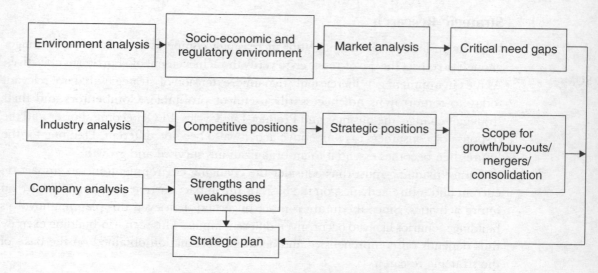

Fig. 19.2 Functions of Strategic Research

- Providing information to help plan strategies for achieving these goals and objectives. It is thus also concerned with identifying current and desirable market positions for the organization to occupy—market leader, challenger, follower or nicher—and with how to achieve them. In this sense, it is different from research into product or brand strategy, and has a broader horizon, arrived at through analysis and prediction of the environment, the industry and the company's current and future position. This is depicted in Figure 19.2.

Difference Between Tactical and Strategic Research

The differences between tactical and strategic research that influence marketing decisions can therefore be summarized in Table 19.1.

It is thus apparent that questions of tactical and strategic research engage different time frames, objectives and often, managers at different levels. As the decisions based on research move from the tactical to the strategic level, the sphere of involvement of managers from non-marketing areas also widens, since decisions regarding what will

Table 19.1 Differences Between Tactical and Strategic Research

Dimensions	Tactical Research	Strategic Research
Decision Area	Setting and evaluation of current marketing mix, brand strategies, short-term brand objectives, and consumer perceptions	Setting and assessment of the organization's marketing directions and long-term goals
Time orientation	Short-term to medium-term	Long-term
People mainly involved in implementation	Brand managers, functional area managers	Senior managers

constitute competitive advantage have to be made taking into account organization-wide repercussions.

SUMMARY

The role of marketing research is to reduce the uncertainty and errors in marketing decision-making. These errors can arise because of a variety of reasons, and uncertainty levels also vary with the kind of marketing issues in question. Marketing research is therefore divided into problem identification research and problem definition research. The involvement of the client in such studies varies with the problem area, though the final interpretation and decision-making is within the domain of the client's responsibility. The value derived by the client from marketing research is owing to both the researcher's effort and the client's effort.

The client has to interpret and implement a marketing research report keeping in mind the immediate marketing issue, the external environment, the internal environment of the company, and its strategic requirements. The client must also be aware of the limitations of the research, viz. its dependence on the validity of the hypotheses, the time frame during which the results may be valid, and the managerial level to whom the report is addressed. From the point of view of the reach of marketing decisions, marketing research can be divided into two groups—tactical and strategic. Tactical research, which accounts for the major part of marketing research in most organizations, is primarily concerned with day-to-day decisions, usually related to the marketing mix and brand strategies. Strategic research, on the other hand, helps set directions and goals and evaluates them as well. Major strands of the strategic research are environment analysis, industry analysis, and company analysis. These three kinds of analyses together help the manager take long-term marketing decisions.

KEY WORDS

Marketing issue is the marketing problem or marketing question on which the decision has to be taken and which is being explored in the study.

Internal environment is the environment within the company, in the marketing as well as non-marketing functions, which impact the decision on the marketing issue.

External environment refers to the environment around the company, including the government, regulatory, socio-economic, industrial, and competitive environments, which impact the marketing issue.

Strategic requirements are the long-term information requirements on which planning and decisions regarding the company's future strategies will be based.

Tactical research relates to setting and evaluation of current marketing-mix, brand strategies, shortterm brand objectives, and consumer perceptions.

Strategic research relates to the setting and assessment of the organization's marketing directions and long-term goals.

Prediction concerns announcing the likelihood or otherwise of the occurrence of an event by examining the cause–effect relationship between two variables.

Forecasting is concerned with a rigorous, quantitative measure of the exact probability of the occurrence of an event.

CONCEPT REVIEW QUESTIONS

1. What is the difference between tactical and strategic research? Give two examples of each.

2. How do the client and the researcher both contribute to the value the client may derive from research?

3. How does the internal environment influence implementation of research reports? Is this influence more significant in case of tactical research than for strategic research?

4. How do the assumptions made by the client about the external environment influence the marketing research study? Support your argument with two examples.

CRITICAL THINKING EXERCISES

1. Your company is experiencing a sudden drop in the sales of one of your major products A. A research proposal to examine the possible causes suggests investigating competitive activity. Another suggests studying environmental variables including government policies that could have adversely influenced the sale of A. Which of these proposals would you consider? Why? If you are likely to consider both the options inadequate, give your reasons. How would you want the proposals modified in this case?

2. Your team works for a company marketing mobile phones. As a team member, you are commissioning a study on the penetration and use of mobile phones in a metro. One of your teammates has been entrusted with the responsibility of a similar study in a large village adjacent to this metro, and a third teammate has been asked to conduct the same study in a class III town. How will the three proposals differ in structure and content? What similarities and differences would you expect in the results?

PROJECT ASSIGNMENTS

1. Take up the report of any live marketing research project you may have conducted as part of your MBA programme, and discuss its implementation with the manager who commissioned it. What are the limitations in the implementation of all the findings? Under what assumptions would they be fully applicable? Discuss these with the manager and report his/her response.

2. Working in small groups, examine a marketing research report that some members of your group may have prepared. Get them to play the role of a researcher, defining the research brief given to them by the client, including the marketing problem, the

marketing research problem, and the major data from their study. How will the rest of you, in the role of managers from various functional areas in the company, interpret that data? What conclusions would you draw from it? To what extent do they differ from the conclusions drawn by the researcher? If the members of the group play the role of non-marketing managers in the company, what will be their response to the information and the impact it will have on the functioning of their department?

REFERENCES

Cornell, A. 1980, *The Decision Maker's Handbook*, Prentice Hall, quoted in Stevens et al., 2004.

Green, P.E. and D.S. Tull 1978, *Research for Marketing Decisions*, Prentice Hall, New Jersey.

Stevens, R.E., B. Wrenn, M.E. Ruddick, and P.K. Sherwood 2004, *The Marketing Research Guide*, Viva Books, New Delhi.

Twedt, D.W. 1973, *A Survey of Marketing Research*, American Marketing Association, Chicago, quoted in Green and Tull 1978

20 Applications of Marketing Research

After reading this chapter, the readers will be able to understand:

- the use of marketing research in determining market attractiveness and market potential for a new market offering
- the relevance of researching the various marketing mix elements at different stages of the product life cycle
- various market research models for an effective marketing mix
- the utility of marketing research in brand positioning and developing and measuring brand equity
- the application of marketing research in market segmentation and forecasting
- the use of research in developing and evaluating marketing strategies

INTRODUCTION

The preceding chapters of this book examined the theory of marketing research, the risk inherent in various marketing decisions because of the uncertainty under which they are taken, and the role of marketing research in reducing this risk by providing relevant information. The extent of uncertainty regarding a marketing situation determines the nature as well as the degree of this risk, which in turn influences the importance of research. The relevance of marketing research thus begins at the stage an organization begins to examine a marketing situation, though the kind of questions it seeks to answer vary across marketing situations.

This chapter discusses some of the specific marketing situations requiring research, and the kind of research that helps reduce uncertainty. It examines an organization in the context of its marketing environment and the opportunity that environment offers for entry and growth in a specific field. At this stage, marketing research defines the contours of that opportunity in terms of the potential it holds for the organization's growth. The chapter further explains the research processes for marketing mix at various stages of the product life cycle and discusses the risk involved and the kind of research required at each stage to reduce that risk.

A specific kind of risk is concerned with the way a market offering is interpreted in the consumer's mind—the extent of its relevance and uniqueness compared to other similar market offerings as perceived by the consumer. Planning and defining this positioning accurately makes for the success of a market offering or a brand. The role of research in positioning the market offering has been discussed in the chapter, along with research into brand equity. Identification through research of the kind of consumer to whom the brand would be relevant, i.e., definition of the appropriate market segment and its size has also been discussed. The chapter goes on to define the role of research in quantifying the size of the opportunity through various formal and informal market forecasting techniques. Finally, the chapter discusses the long-term role of research in developing and evaluating marketing strategies.

MARKETING RESEARCH FOR SPECIFIC MARKET SITUATIONS

As part of the continual process of evolution and growth, organizations routinely examine the markets for opportunities. Once opportunities have been assessed, specific ideas may be generated to tap the potential of these markets, usually through new products. New products are essential to the survival and growth of an organization, whether it is in order to take advantage of an opportunity that others, including sometimes the consumers, have not yet identified to enter a market that is growing, or even to keep the sales force interested and motivated. Opportunities, to be actionable, have to be defined in tangible terms of needs that they aim at, products that provide the means of need satisfaction, and the scope, size and growth possibilities of these means of need satisfaction. Urban and Hauser (1981) have listed a number of desirable characteristics that an attractive market must possess, and have also provided measures of these characteristics that can be quantified through research (Table 20.1). This approach assumes that the market is already well defined.

Marketing textbooks tell us that new market offerings may be new in a variety of ways, ranging from 'new-to-the-world' product concepts to new packaging. The degree of novelty influences the risk involved in exploring a new market, since the history of consumer experience on the basis of which product acceptance may be predicted is minimal at best. The information required for reducing this risk also varies in degree and content.

New-to-the-world Product

Every new way of satisfying a need starts out as a new-to-the-world concept, whether it is the household pressure cooker or a complex computer system. Such new concepts

Table 20.1 Desirable Characteristics of Markets

General Characteristics	Measures
Potential	• Size of market • Sales growth rate
Penetration	• Vulnerability of competitors
Scale	• Share of market • Cumulative sales volume
Input	• Investment in money and technology
Reward	• Profits
Risk	• Stability • Probability of losses

do not have a defined market, and have their origin in identification by the researcher of defined or latent dissatisfactions with existing means of need satisfaction. Research skills required are the most complex and most critical in identifying needs here, and exploratory research plays the most crucial role. The information required to be obtained through research may be grouped under several heads. Some of these are listed here.

Identification of dissatisfaction   Identification of dissatisfaction with the accepted ways of need satisfaction is an important step.

Research moves from the familiar to the unfamiliar here, identifying established ways of satisfying a need, defining the contours of that need, establishing areas where the established ways do not satisfy that need fully, the reasons why that happens, and how the need could possibly be satisfied better. This serves to develop the concept of the new product or service. *Perceptual mapping* is an effective technique for identifying gaps between the desired and the provided, especially if the measurement identifies the ideal. Another technique for measuring this gap, developed in the late seventies, is the *benefit structure analysis* (Meyers 1976), which operates by assessing on a four-point scale how much of a benefit customers want, and how much benefit they get (also measured on a four-point scale). The matrix of differences between the wanted and the received levels provides a measure of the gap size.

Prodegy (Urban et al. 1979) is another robust and popular model available for defining the market at this stage by dividing products into direct and indirect competition. It operates by assigning product entities to mutually exclusive branches based on product type, form, or brand name (e.g., instant vs ground coffee, single malt vs blended whiskey, soap vs detergent, etc.). The data collected is observed to ascertain product choices and relative preferences—respondents are asked for their first preferences and grouped into the branch where their first preferences are included. They are then asked to indicate the brand/product they would opt for if their first preference in a branch was not available. The average probability P of a consumer buying into the same branch if his/her first preference is not available is then calculated. One minus P provides the switching probability out of the branch, and can be used to estimate market shares vis-à-vis indirect competition.

Assessment of acceptability of the new concept   The purpose of research here is to determine the degree to which the consumer is likely to find the new concept satisfactory, convenient to adapt to, and providing a significant advance over the existing means of need satisfaction. Since the concept is intangible, it should be well defined and clearly communicable. Its test requires substantial research skills. Only if a concept is perceived through research to offer a significant advantage should it be developed further. Apart from the general acceptability of the concept, the major objectives of research at this stage are to determine if there are any major flaws in the concept that can be corrected, which consumer segments will find it especially acceptable, and why will they find it acceptable.

Product design and evaluation As mentioned earlier, there are many techniques available in marketing research for identifying gaps in the existing market that can be filled through a new product.

Conjoint analysis It is an effective tool for identifying attribute combinations that can optimize the utility and value of a product to the consumer. If the concept is found sufficiently acceptable to render its development as a possibility, and some prototypes are developed, research moves to the role of product evaluation.

Placement test The traditional research at this stage is concerned with 'placement test'—the prototype is distributed to a sample of consumers who are users or potential users of the product category, and they are requested to try it for a period long enough to be able to assess its benefits. The research aims at determining

- the frequency with which the prototype was used, and the reasons for any change from the usual frequency;
- who used it most often;
- situations and pattern of use;
- post-use experience;
- perception of the prototype compared with the usual means of need satisfaction; and
- future-use intent, which often helps in predicting trial purchase.

This kind of research is particularly useful for frequently purchased consumer goods and for many services, but is not easily adapted to durables or industrial goods. It provides the opportunity for product modification if significant flaws in the prototype are reported by the consumer at this stage.

The perceptor model A somewhat similar model is the perceptor by Urban (1975), mainly aimed at determining long-term market share of frequently purchased consumer durables. The model uses pre-trial and post-trial perceptions, awareness, and availability of data for the prediction. It is a two-stage model:

1. In the first stage, the pre-test market model based on the concept use test (CUT), personal interviews of respondents provide data on brand perceptions, perceived brand similarities, and brand preferences within their evoked brand set. They are then asked to buy the most liked brand concept in a simulated sales situation. The selected brand concept is given to the respondents for actual trial, and post-usage perceptions are obtained.
2. In the second stage, the Markov process is used to determine the market share m of the new brand, defined as
   $m = ts = qwv$ where t = % of ever triers of the new brand in the long run
   s = % of purchases among triers
   q = long-term probability of trial

w = long-term awareness

v = long-term availability

s is obtained from the steady state two-stage Markov process, measuring purchase probability.

Test marketing Once the product has been tested and found acceptable, marketing research should be employed to test the other elements of the marketing mix individually and as a composite market offering. This provides an opportunity for testing out the marketing programme in a real life situation rather than the artificial conditions employed in testing the concept and the product, as well as for predicting the outcome of the product launch in the total market. A test-market, of course, presumes that other elements of the marketing mix have been developed and are ready for testing. The elements tested with the consumers during the test-market are as follows:

- awareness, trial, and perception of the product
- repeat purchase and future-purchase intent
- brand switching—extent and pattern
- availability
- price perceptions
- response to promotion and merchandising

Another important area of research during the test-market is the dealer response—stocking, placing (where in the outlet are the product and promotional materials displayed), satisfaction with margins, company policies and consumer off take, perceptions of consumer response, active support to promotion of the product, and future-purchase intent. For both these segments, panels are set up to collect marketing research data in the test-market, and information from the panels is collected and analysed with regular periodicity in order to determine trends relating to these parameters. Estimates of trial, repeat, and usage rates are established from panel data.

The Parfitt-Collins model The Parfitt-Collins (1968) model is a popular means of predicting market share using panel data in a test-market. It defines ultimate brand share S as

$$S = prb$$

where p = ultimate or equilibrium level penetration rate of the brand (i.e., percentage of new buyers of the product who try this brand)

r = ultimate repeat purchase rate of the brand (i.e., the level at which the repeat purchase rate stabilizes)

b = buyer rate index of repeat purchase of this brand (average buyer =1)

Pre-test market evaluation Pre-test market or simulated test-market methods are sometimes used instead of the test-marketing technique. These have the advantage of being cheaper, quicker, and do not run the risk of interference by competitors. However, at the same time, they suffer from the limitation of being conducted in artificial laboratory conditions, and are therefore less reliable.

The assessor model One well known pre-test market model is the assessor model, developed by Silk and Urban (1978). The model is summarized in Table 20.2.

According to Zhao (2006), 'It predicts long-run market share and sales using two models: trial/repeat and preference, and is designed for branded, low-price packaged goods. It provides actionable diagnostics for improving product and marketing materials—trial and repeat rates, perceptions, preferences'. Though it is a very popularly used model and the success rate in test-market after the use of assessor has been 66% compared to 35.5% for products that did not have a formal pre-test market model analysis, it does suffer from some limitations (Zhao 2006):

- It is targeted at established product categories.
- It assumes a stable competitive environment.
- It assumes that customers learn about new brands quickly.
- It assumes that advertising influences consumers quickly.
- It assumes that preference for new brands stabilizes quickly.

Table 20.2 The Assessor Model

Design	Procedure	Measurement
O_1	Respondent screening and selection (personal interview)	Criteria for target group identification (e.g., product-class usage)
O_2	Pre-measurement for established brands (self-administered questionnaire)	Composition of 'relevant set' of established brands, attribute weights and ratings, and preferences
X_1	Exposure to advertising for established brands and new brand	
O_3	Measurement of reaction to the advertising materials (self-administered questionnaire)	Optional (e.g., likeability and believability ratings of advertising materials)
X_2	Simulated shopping trip and exposure to display of new and established brands	
O_4	Purchase opportunity (choice recorded by research personnel)	Brands purchased
X_3	Home use/consumption of new brand	
O_5	Post usage measurement (telephone interview)	New brand usage rate, satisfaction ratings, and repeat purchase propensity. Attribute ratings and preferences for relevant set of established brands plus the new brand

Source: Adapted from Silk and Urban (1978).

Entry into Defined Markets

A decision that marketing is frequently faced with is the possibility of entry into markets where the company is not the first entrant. The market is well defined in such cases, and competition is usually well entrenched. Consumer expectations are also usually formed, and new entrants are measured for acceptability against these expectations. Though most research is similar to that in case of the new-to-the-world concept discussed earlier, competition is confined to other brands and forms.

There are some popular models to predict chances of success in established markets.

Strategic cube analysis model   Sethi and Chandrasekhar (1993) have suggested a model called 'strategic cube analysis for brand equity leverage' for selecting the most suitable market to diversify into. The model develops an index by examining three parameters—consumer perceptions of the company, consumer perceptions of competitors, and the motivating power of the attribute/benefit sought to be highlighted. The three parameters are measured on 5-point 'desirability' scales. The model has been found to be of special use in choosing between markets that are all highly cluttered, so that no 'ostensible competitive advantage or ease of entry' may be expected by choosing one product field over the other.

Apart from identifying the most appropriate marketing mix, marketing research is called upon to provide information on the following issues in defined markets:

Brand positioning and brand perceptions   Scaling techniques, discussed in earlier chapters, including multidimensional scaling and perceptual mapping are useful for developing brand positioning as well as for determining consumer perceptions of established and new brands. A variety of qualitative research methods such as focus groups, in-depth interviews and projective techniques can also be used effectively for determining consumer perceptions of brands.

Identification of appropriate segments   There are many methods of segmentation available in marketing, such as the VALS 2 (values lifestyles) framework given by the Stanford Research Institute (SRI) and the AIO (attitudes, interests, and opinions) framework given by Plummer (1974). Both these methods require marketing research for collection of data and analysis. The VALS 2 framework is also available on the SRI website, www.future.sri.com, as a self-administered questionnaire. The most frequently used method, and the one rated among the most effective, is cluster analysis. This is useful not only for dividing the market into internally homogeneous, distinct groups, but is also used extensively for identifying test-markets.

Brand-switch   Market share is one measure of the rate of acceptance of a new brand in a defined market. However, growth in market share results from adoption of the brand by new users of the product category, as well as from transfer of preference and purchase from other brands. It is therefore important to keep track of brand-switch into and out of a brand on a continuous basis. Consumer panel data as well as ad hoc market surveys to determine changes in brand usage patterns provide such information. Markov chain analysis is a technique frequently employed for predicting market share using brand-switch data collected over a period of time (Kapferer 1992).

Product/Service Modification

A product or a service usually needs to be modified or repositioned when drawbacks in the product lead to consumer dissatisfaction, resulting in decline in sales, consumer preferences undergo a change, so that the market in which the product is participating stops growing, or the product acquires an outdated image, or new market opportunities develop that could profitably be taken advantage of by the product.

MARKETING RESEARCH DURING VARIOUS PRODUCT LIFE CYCLE STAGES

Once the new market offering has been successfully test-marketed and launched in the market, information is continuously required about qualitative and quantitative aspects of its acceptance among consumers and trade channels, and about its growth. The importance of data on the various elements of the marketing mix differs with the product life cycle (PLC) stage. According to Lilien et al (1992), 'the concept of the life cycle is an attempt to recognize distinct phases in the sales history of the product and to develop strategies appropriate to those stages.' Researchers have made significant efforts to forecast the duration of various product life cycle phases and the transition from one phase to the other.

Everett Rogers (1962) has segmented the total consumer market into five groups on the basis of the speed with which consumers adopt an innovation—*innovators* (2.5%), *early adopters* (13.5%), *early majority*, whose percentages are fairly stable across product categories (34%), *late majority* (34%), and *laggards* (16%). The five groups together thus form a bell curve. According to him, these category sizes are fairly stable across product categories, though for an individual, the speed of adoption will vary from product to product, depending on the consumer's personal characteristics, occupation, and involvement level with the product. Research based on panel data or ad hoc longitudinal studies is needed to verify the extent to which a new product follows this pattern of diffusion of innovations.

Again, Rogers maintains that consumers belonging to any one adopter category display significantly different characteristics from other categories. For example, the innovators are the most media savvy and rely much more than any other group on media for information about new products, are less integrated into the society in the sense that they neither seek approval of their choices from the other groups, nor are they likely to share their opinions about new products with the early adopters. Laggards may belong to relatively lower socio-economic classes, be cautious about adopting new products, and be very dependent on the other categories like the early or late majority for obtaining information and forming their product perceptions. Or, at the other extreme, they may be relatively older and from higher socio-economic classes,

Table 20.3 Marketing Research for New Products

Marketing Element	Status	Research requirement
Product	Basic	Determining product awareness, acceptability among innovators and early adopters, trial, repeat purchase, conversion; pre-use and post-use perception; response to packaging; future-purchase intent
Price	Skimming or penetration, depending on marketing objective	Determining price acceptability using either the 'Gabor and Grainger Method' of determining 'buy-response' curves at different prices, or the multi-brand method comparing the new brand with competing brands; value perceptions
Availability	Limited	Perceived and actual availability; consumer perception of channels and outlets, dealer perception of and satisfaction with the product; support provided to the product; opportunities for expansion of distribution; distribution equity
Promotion	Aimed at building product awareness among early adopters and dealers	Pre-launch and post-launch copy research and media research to determine initial response to advertising—levels of awareness, recall, comprehension and perceptions of advertising, acceptability of copy, media reach, coverage and image; brand image created; brand positioning; suitability of non-advertising means of promotion
Competition	Indirect; limited	Identification of major competitors and their response to the introduction of the new brand; tracking competitive activity
Consumer	Innovators and early adopters	Socio-economic and personality characteristics, communication behaviour, needs satisfied through the new market offering

and be so set in their ways that they may not want to easily adopt a new product regardless of current trends, unless it fits in with their lifestyle. Using Rogers' model of diffusion of innovations, it is possible for product managers to identify the characteristics of their consumers, and also to develop future strategies for their brand.

Introductory Stage

Table 20.3 specifies the status of the various marketing mix elements and the research required at the introductory stage.

The Rogers' model also specifies characteristics of an innovation that would influence its rate of adoption:

- relative advantage over existing means of satisfying the same need
- compatibility with the consumer's lifestyle, attitudes, and values
- complexity

- trialability in terms of pack sizes, pack forms, and price
- observability of benefits

Consumer research into these characteristics will help predict the rate at which the adoption of an innovation or a new market offering is likely to proceed. Lilien, Kotler, and Moorthy (1992) have discussed a large number of models that relate to various aspects of research required for new products and services. These models have been discusssed in a latter section of this chapter.

Growth Stage

If the strategies adopted at the introductory stage result in the growth of the market offering, in its growth stage it displays the characteristics and information requirements described in Table 20.4.

At the growth stage, a large part of the potential market is yet unexplored. While competition begins to emerge, brand awareness and attitudes towards the brand are in early stages of development. Marketing-mix elements that need to be emphasized at this stage are therefore the product and the promotion, and research has to concentrate chiefly on these two elements.

Table 20.4 Marketing Research for Growing Products

Marketing Element	Status	Research requirement
Product	Product extensions	Reasons for non-adoption among category users and need for product modification; perceived brand differentiation among consumers; differentiating product attributes and benefits; brand preference; acceptance of extensions; extent of market extension; brand positioning
Price	Stable	Determining price acceptability and price perceptions among new users; influence of price on brand adoption and brand image; influence of short-term price modifications on brand adoption and brand image
Distribution	Increased availability; intensive distribution	Determine opportunities for expanding distribution; new channels; dealer satisfaction and support; consumer perception of channels and outlets
Promotion	Aimed at increasing awareness and interest; 'talking' brand	Determine awareness and interest among consumers; consumer awareness and acceptance of brand differentiation; relative efficacy of various means of promotion day-after-recall studies
Competition	Increasing, new and established players	Determining competitive strategies; market shares and growth; brand-switch
Consumer	Early majority	New consumer segments—size, characteristics and profitability; stages in consumer decision process; product involvement levels; product attitudes; choice process; brand behaviour

Table 20.5 Marketing Research for Mature Products

Marketing Element	Status	Research requirements
Product	Many forms, models, and brand extensions	Product modifications, evaluation of brand equity; identification of most suitable brand extensions, repositioning opportunities, new markets; brand valuation
Price	(1) Price to match or beat competitors (2) Exclusive market niches created through high prices	Determining consumer's price sensitivity and importance of price in brand choice; influence on brand perception, competitive pricing strategies; opportunity for segment-wise pricing; impact of short-term variations in pricing (pricing as a promotional tool)
Distribution	Extended intensive distribution	Determining channel design constraints, relative effectiveness of channel alternatives, choice of locations, potential of markets, channels and outlets, site selection, dealer research, retail research, logistics and supply chain research
Promotion	Stress brand differentiation and benefits	Research for setting promotion goals, pre-tests and post-tests of message, copy and media; short-term and long-term consumer response to promotion; research to assess relative impact of advertising and promotion; determining suitability of advertising appeals, DARs
Competition	Stable, beginning to decline; consolidation; emergence of niches and sub-segments	Determining direct and indirect competition: competitive strategies and marketing mix; consumer perception of competition; positioning, brand equity and distribution equity
Consumer	Loyal; late majority as well as laggards	Consumer segments and their socio-economic, communication and product usage characteristics, trends in product usage and brand adoption; brand associations, brand perceptions and brand loyalty, research related to Customer Relationship Management 'CRM'

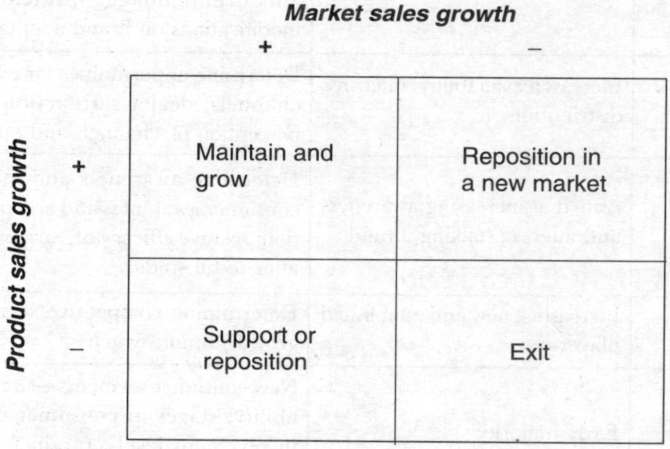

Fig. 20.1 Product Sales Growth vis-à-vis Market Sales Growth

Maturity Stage

The product or service stays at this stage for the longest period in its life. The market is most cluttered at this stage, with the largest number of competitors. Towards the end of the maturity stage, some of the weaker competitors begin to move out, opening up the market for the bigger players and reducing competition in the short-term as consolidation takes place.

The market reaches its maximum potential in the maturity stage. Profitability peaks as costs decline. All potential buyers would have already tried out the product, so that future growth becomes dependent on market development, repositioning, product and brand extensions, and finally diversification. Research becomes a crucial means of risk reduction and aims at answering tactical problems as much as at planning and evaluating long-term strategy.

As markets are commoditized, brand positioning becomes difficult to sustain, and price based competition becomes dominant. Brand equity at this stage is dependent more on brand and corporate perceptions rather than on real brand differences. Distribution and distribution equity become major planks of competition, as the emphasis shifts from new customers to customer loyalty and customer retention. Research requirements in the maturity stage of the PLC are discussed in Table 20.5.

The need for repositioning a mature brand is dependent on data regarding its growth vis-à-vis the growth of the market, as depicted in Figure 20.1.

Repositioning is required if the brand is participating in a fast-growing market but registers poor growth, or if a strong brand is participating in a slow growing market. In other words, repositioning strategies are needed if there is a mismatch between the growth rates of the market and the brand. Research data based on retail audit would provide the required information. However, in the first case, the retail audit indicates good market potential, but since the brand is not doing well, we need to determine if the brand requires greater support in terms of product modification, positioning change, additional promotional inputs, or modifications in distribution strategy. Price modification in a mature, fast growing market is likely to provide temporary benefits, if any. Market research should be employed to identify the cause.

In the second case, where the brand is growing well, but the market is weak, it is necessary to shift the brand to another market, since a weak market does not provide potential for future growth in the long term. Choice of the most suitable market will have to depend on marketing research findings.

MARKET RESEARCH MODELS FOR EFFECTIVE MARKETING MIX

There are many research based models available for measuring the success of the marketing mix strategies.

Defender Model

Lilien, Kotler, and Moorthy (1992) discuss the defender model (Rogers 1962), which suggests how a brand should adjust its marketing efforts, pricing, and positioning in a competitive environment. The model assumes that

- existing brands can be positioned in a multi-attribute space, where brands are ratio-scaled,
- consumers choose their utility-maximizing brands,
- consumer's utility functions are linear or linearizable, and
- awareness and distribution are concave functions of advertising and distribution spending, respectively, i.e., they increase with increased advertising and distribution spending up to a point and then start declining with every additional unit of expenditure.

Given the information about a brand's price, rating on specific attributes and importance attached by the individual respondent to the various attributes, the utility of the brand to the individual (sum of brand's attribute ratings multiplied by the importance attached to the attribute), and the 'preference angle' for an individual, the market share m of a brand j is defined as

$$m_j = \sum m_{j/l} \times s_l$$

where $m_{j/l}$ is the market share of brand j belonging to the subset A_l of evoked brands from the set of all brands, and s_l is the probability of a randomly selected customer choosing a brand from subset A_l. Depending on the perceptual proximity of the new brand to the other established brands and the efficiency with which it enters the market, the model shows that the profit of the brand under study will come down, and with advertising and distribution costs fixed, the optimal response to the new brand's entry will be a price decrease.

Fishbein's Model

Another marketing research based model that defines consumer attitudes towards an object (brand) on the basis of attribute ratings is proposed by Fishbein (1967):

$$A_o = \sum b_i a_i$$

where A_o = attitude towards object o
b_i = belief that object o possesses attribute i, and
a_i = evaluation of attribute i

Both b_i and a_i are measured through personal interviews.

Hierarchy of Effects Model

While developing an advertising programme, the purpose of advertising in terms of its impact on consumer attitudes—creating, strengthening, or correcting attitudes—has to be kept in mind. Creation of attitudes through advertising is a multi-stage process, defined by a variety of hierarchy of effects models. One such model, proposed by Lavidge and Steiner (1961), takes the consumer through the effects of advertising at the different stages shown in Fig. 20.2

Distributed Lag Model

The distributed lag model, another model of the effect of advertising on sales, proposed by Rao and Miller (1975), has been discussed by Lilien et al (1992). The model is defined as:

$$S_t = a_o + a A(t) + a\lambda A(t-1) + a\lambda^2 A(t-2) + \ldots + u(t)$$

where S_t = market share at time t

a_0 = minimal sales value that may be expected in the absence of any advertising

a = impact of advertising at time t

$A(t)$ = advertising expenditure at time t

λ = decay rate of advertising

$u(t)$ = error term that reflects the effect of variables not explicitly included in the model

In the long run, the steady-state market share Se is

$$Se = (1 - \lambda)\, a_o + a\, A(t)$$

Hierarchy of Advertising Effect from Awareness to Purchase	Type of Related Research
Creating awareness	Measures of creating awareness
↓ Knowledge	exposure and awareness
↓ Liking	image and attitude studies
↓ Preference	brand preference measures
↓ Conviction	brand purchase intent
↓ Purchase	intent versus purchase

Fig. 20.2 Hierarchy of Advertising Effects

Both λ and a are measured through research.

Market research is also used extensively in advertising planning for identifying the most suitable advertising appeals. A variety of techniques are used for this purpose, but the most popular one is the method of experimental design. Using the randomized block design, a random sample of consumers is divided into matched subsamples, and each subsample is presented with advertising copy using a distinct appeal. The appeal generating the highest response is used in the final copy.

OTHER APPLICATIONS OF MARKETING RESEARCH

Let us now discuss some other areas where marketing research plays an important role.

Customer Relationship Management

A major area of application of marketing research in mature markets that has developed in recent years is customer relationship management (CRM). The scope for adding new customers is limited in such markets, and the cost of new customers acquisition is also much higher than the cost of retaining existing customers. Customer relationship management therefore aims at organizational growth through identification of loyal customers, maintaining a special relationship with them in order to retain them, and developing strategies for loyal customers to increase their offtake. In the early stages of its development, CRM operated by collecting and maintaining customer data on the following areas:

- *Recency of purchases made by the customer*: When did the customer last purchase from you?
- *Frequency of purchases made by the customer*: How often does the customer buy something from you?
- *Monetary value of purchase*: How much does the customer spend on a typical transaction?

On the basis of this information collected through research, organizations are able to estimate the *lifetime value* of customers (the average value of purchases made by the customer over the estimated period during which the customer will keep buying from the organization) and use it for segmenting the customer group by profitability.

Database Marketing

A related concept is *database marketing*. Databases are marketing-research-based lists of customers and potential customers, with additional information about customer characteristics of relevance to the organization. They also provide details of transactions made by customers—products, the amount of expenditure, frequency of purchase, enquiries about other products.

Databases are useful to both customers and marketers since they help focus on a customer, match customer wants and needs with products and services, improve customer interaction, pinpoint ideal time and occasions for sales promotion, and measure customer response regularly. They help to group customers into three categories:

- active customers
- inactive customers
- enquiries

Such a classification helps the marketer to devise appropriate marketing strategies for different groups of customers.

MARKETING RESEARCH AND BRAND POSITIONING

Branding is another major decision area in marketing where marketing research plays a significant role. Though research permeates the entire brand process, its contribution is of particular value in the following areas:

- identification of branding opportunity
- brand positioning
- brand extensions
- developing and measuring brand equity

Opportunity for Branding

Most product categories, even in the established categories, start life as commodities. Consumers often do not differentiate between market offerings, and use them because of the basic tangible attributes that differentiate them from other means of satisfying some need. Consumer choice at this stage is based on price and availability of the product. As markets evolve, the process of branding begins and develops through various stages of sophistication, which are discussed below:

Brand as a reference

In the initial stages of development of the process of branding, consumers begin to base their choice on non-price attributes and differentiate between market offerings from different marketers on the basis of attributes such as convenience, tangible quality, and company image. A brand thus starts life at this stage as a 'reference'. It is chosen because identifying a brand in the store saves time for the consumer as well as the retailer, provides stability of attributes from one purchase occasion to the other, and earlier experience with the brand as well as the manufacturer's reputation provide the consumer with some confidence in it. The potential for branding at this early stage depends largely on factors such as increase in the consumer's purchasing power and education, exposure to sophisticated markets, and change in consumer attitudes that improve consumer willingness to consider non-price attributes as a basis of choice. Research provides information at this stage on whether the consumers are ready to upgrade their requirements for possibly higher priced product options providing these additional advantages.

Brand persona

As consumer expectations continue to evolve, brands begin to acquire a persona, a relevance other than merely acting as a means of satisfying physical needs. Research is needed to determine if the consumer has evolved to this stage. Questions such as 'whom is the brand meant for?', 'what is it about?', 'what is its parentage?', and 'how is it different from and superior to others?' need to be answered through research as a basis for brand differentiation in a competitive market. At this stage, the brand acquires a personality and differentiation is no longer restricted to physical attributes, but transcends the functional associations to develop emotional linkage with the consumer. As we will discuss later in this section, the brand now acquires a positioning in the consumer's mind.

Brand as an icon

As brands continue to grow and develop, some of them succeed in reaching a stage where their emotional link with the consumer acquires an unquestioned status—it is adopted for reasons that surpass definable physical or emotional benefits. Rather, the consumers seek to define themselves through the adoption and use of such brands. A classic example of an icon brand is Coca-Cola. A brand that has managed to reach this stage does not have to fight competition from other brands.

Research is crucial at each stage to determine whether the market has evolved to a particular stage, the potential of individual brands to reach that stage, and later, to verify the success it may have attained.

Brand Positioning

We discussed earlier that in the second stage of evolution, a brand acquires a positioning in the consumer's mind, the exclusive space in the consumer's perception that differentiates it from competition and emphasizes its special attributes and benefits. Ries and Trout (1985), the founding fathers of the concept of brand positioning, explain that while positioning begins with a product, the concept really is about positioning that product in the mind of the customer. They opine, 'Positioning is not what you do to a product; positioning is what you do to the mind of the prospect.'

The positioning of a brand, which is based on consumer perceptions, may not always be what the marketer intended it to be. In order to ensure that this gap does not exist, the positioning exercise requires communication of a consistent message to the consumer about what the brand is and where it fits into the market. The promotion, packaging, brand name, and market segments aimed at for a brand must communicate the same message.

As marketing textbooks tell us, a brand can be positioned in a variety of ways. The marketer must choose the one that is not occupied by any other brand, is significant to the consumer, and provides the maximum competitive advantage to the marketer. Effective positioning thus requires research to address the following questions:

What is the desired positioning Are there any unmet or inadequately met consumer needs that the brand could effectively satisfy? Does the brand have any unique and significant strengths that could be projected? Can consumer usage patterns be modified to include special uses for the brand? Are there any consumer segments that are best suited to the brand?

What is the current positioning For an established brand desiring a repositioning, research is required to identify the major consumer segments; the most important product dimensions the consumer considers for the product category; the gaps, if any, between consumer requirement and those met by other brands; projected growth rates for the current market and the market being considered; and consumer perception of the brand in the current and the desired market. As mentioned earlier, perceptual mapping is an effective research technique for identifying the positioning of a brand and the dimensions which are considered important by the consumer in evaluating the product category.

What is the best means of creating a positioning? Should tangible differences or image differences be used as the basis for positioning?

Brand Extensions

According to Keller (2003), 'a brand extension is when a firm uses an established brand name to introduce a new product.' It could be either a line extension or a category extension. Extensions are a popular means of brand growth, but not every brand may gain from brand extension. Some issues that must be borne in mind while contemplating an extension are discussed below.

Strength of the parent brand

A weak brand cannot be revived or strengthened by introducing an extension; an extension has the advantage over a new product as the image of the parent brand rubs off on it, thereby facilitating an early acceptance of the extension. A weak brand will not achieve this purpose, and an extension may cannibalize its sales.

Fit between the parent and extension brand

The extension will gain and contribute to the parent if it is seen to belong to the area of expertise of the parent brand.

Life cycle stage of the parent brand

An extension introduced too early in the PLC of a brand, before the parent has had time to establish a definite image for itself, will only detract from that image. If, on the other hand, it is introduced when the parent brand is in the decline stage, the negative traits ascribed to the parent brand will get attached to the extension brand as well.

Brand extensions have advantages as well as disadvantages, which might help or harm the parent brand. Research is required to determine whether a brand can be safely and profitably extended, and whether a planned extension will reinforce or harm the brand.

Developing and Measuring Brand Equity

Keller (2003) defines *brand equity* as 'the differential effect that brand knowledge has on consumer response to the marketing of that brand'. Aaker (1991) has defined it as the 'set of five categories of brand assets and liabilities linked to a brand, its name, and symbol that add to or subtract from the value provided by a product or service to a firm or to that firm's customers, or both.' These five assets are as follows:

- brand loyalty
- brand awareness
- perceived quality
- brand associations
- other proprietary brand assets, such as brand name, logo, jingles, etc.

Brand equity has been defined in various ways by other authors. One popular example is Kapferer's (1992) *brand identity prism*, which measures brand identity along six brand dimensions—brand personality, culture, self-image, reflection, relationship, and physique. Building brand equity requires regular research along these dimensions in order to identify brand elements on which to base it. Tracking studies help in identifying changes at an early stage so that a corrective action can be taken.

The concept of brand equity occupies such a significant place in marketing today that many organizations have considered including the 'brand' on their balance sheet. According to Keller (2003), 'brand value (or brand equity) creation begins with marketing activity by the firm that influences customers in a way affecting how the brand performs in the marketplace and thus how it is valued by the financial community.' In broad terms, the equity of a brand can be measured by the price premium consumers are willing to pay for acquiring the brand, compared to other brands in the product category. Other financial methods of measuring brand equity, as mentioned by Aaker et al. (1998) are as follows:

Trade-off (conjoint) analysis

The method of conjoint analysis, which has been discussed in detail in Chapter 14, is also used for measuring brand equity.

Replacement cost approach

This approach recommends the cost of establishing a similar product that would bring in comparable amount of business. If it is assumed that a similar product will cost Rs 25 crore to develop and market and the chances of its success are 25%, we will need to develop at least four such products, costing Rs 100 crore, to ensure one winner. A company would therefore be willing to pay Rs 100 crore for a comparable established brand. Its brand equity may thus be valued at Rs 100 crore.

Stock price approach

This approach uses stock price as a basis for evaluating brand equity. For a single-brand firm, the approach is based on market capitalization. Replacement costs of tangible assets are deducted from the market cap value. The balance, which represents intangible assets, is divided into three components—the value of brand equity, the value of non-brand factors such as R&D, and the value of industry related factors such as regulation and concentration. Brand equity is then measured as a function of the age of the brand and its order of entry into the market, its cumulative advertising, and its current share of industry advertising.

Future earnings approach

One of the most popular methods is the calculation of the discounted present value of future earnings attributable to brand equity assets.

RESEARCH FOR MARKET SEGMENTATION

Market segmentation is an early, crucial step in planning the marketing programme. It aims to divide the market into groups that are internally homogeneous and as distinct as possible from other groups. The objective of segmentation is to improve the efficiency of marketing strategies. In a segmented market, it is possible to address a group of consumers who share some significant characteristics that influence their response to marketing variables and strategies. It is therefore possible to fashion marketing strategies to optimize consumer response.

Market Segmentation Methods

Segmentation methods can be divided into two broad groups, which have been discussed here.

A priori segmentation

A priori segmentation is one where the basis for grouping the respondents is chosen in advance, e.g., the frequency of usage of a product or brand. Respondents can then be grouped into heavy, medium, and light users, and non-users, and some of their other characteristics such as demographics can be studied within the group. It is then possible to identify the characteristics on which the groups differ significantly, and to study the manner in which these characteristics influence brand behaviour. Techniques such as discriminant analysis are used for this kind of segmentation.

Post hoc segmentation

In this kind of segmentation, the respondents are classified into groups on the basis of their profiles relating to brand behaviour, and then other characteristics are studied for inter-group differences. Cluster analysis is one of the most popular techniques for this kind of segmentation. Respondents can be grouped into clusters with respect to individual characteristics, and the brand behaviour of individuals in each cluster studied. Multidimensional scaling is also used frequently for market segmentation: brands and consumers can be positioned in the same space and thus groups of consumers with similar brand perceptions can be identified. The choice of the most suitable approach is based on research.

The second issue in segmentation is to choose the basis or criterion for segmentation. A variety of such bases have been identified in marketing, which can be broadly characterized as individual-characteristics-based segmentation and brand-/product-behaviour-related segmentation, as indicated in Table 20.6.

Brand positioning generally follows the market segment selection—usually, the market is segmented, segment characteristics (size, growth, brand behaviour, etc.) identified, and the most suitable segment is targeted. The brand is then positioned to fit in with the perceptions and expectations of the target segment. However, sometimes market offerings may be clustered first on the basis of perceived similarity/dissimilarity, or similarity of usage profile, and the characteristics of users of similar brands can be identified.

RESEARCH FOR MARKET FORECASTING

Market segments can usually be expected to be dynamic in terms of size and growth, therefore, marketing research is required to select and target the initial market segments and position the brand in the most suitable segment. Marketing research is also needed

Table 20.6 Criteria for Segmentation

Individual characteristics based segmentation	Brand/product behaviour related segmentation
• *Demographic characteristics*: age, income, occupation, location, education, stage in life cycle	• *Product-related characteristics*: benefits sought, attribute trade-offs
• *Social class*	• *Brand-attitude-related characteristics*: awareness, knowledge, beliefs, perceptions, and preferences
• *Lifestyle*	
• *Psychographic characteristics*: attitudes, opinions, motivations, values and beliefs, personality and self-concept	• *Brand-usage-related characteristics*: usage rate, other brands used, duration of use, loyalty levels
• *Decision-making process*: deciders, *influences* and influencers	
• *Adoption process*: innovators, early adopters, early majority, late majority, laggards	

on a regular, continuous basis to keep monitoring the growth of the segment and the continued fit between the segment requirements and brand delivery. In addition to the continuous evaluation of the marketing strategy adopted, marketing research also involves forecasting the sales and growth of the segment and the brand.

We have stated earlier that market forecasting, as different from prediction, is a precise procedure for estimating quantifiable variables such as future sales, market share, consumption levels, production, and demographic and economic variables such as population, GDP, and per capita income. In short, forecasting deals with any variable that can be quantified and there is some uncertainty about the direction and degree of its future development.

Market forecasting is required in order to identify and solve marketing problems. If sales for a product or a region do not match the forecast, a problem is identified, and an investigation into the reasons can be initiated. If many alternative actions are considered for solving the problem, they need to be evaluated for suitability and desirability through a forecast of their results.

Market Forecasting Techniques

Forecasting procedures vary on the basis of the duration for which forecasts are required, the assumption of stability of the environment, and the number of variables whose interrelationships are taken into account in developing the forecast. We shall now examine some forecasting techniques in marketing that take these factors into account.

Extrapolation Techniques

These techniques assume that the environment will remain stable in the period for which forecasts are required. Such techniques can be used for the short-term in a volatile market but in a reasonably stable environment, they can be used for long-term forecasts.

Moving averages model

This is the simplest of forecasting models and ideally is suited only for short-term forecasts. Given the data for t periods, a moving average M of a variable X over m ($m<t$) most recent periods is calculated as the forecast for the $(t+1)$th period:

$$M_t = (X_t + X_{t-1} + \ldots X_{t-m+1})/m$$

This is the forecast for period $t+1$. The average M_{t+1} for the next m periods is calculated similarly by adding X_{t+1} and dropping X_{t-m+1}, and provides the forecast for the period $t+2$. The assumption obviously is that the conditions prevailing in any m periods will remain stable so that the average values during those periods will provide a reasonable estimate for the next period.

Exponential smoothing

This is an improvement on the moving averages model, in that it works on the assumption that the pattern in the recent periods will most influence the immediate future, and accordingly assigns increasing weights to the most recent values of the variable being forecast. The moving averages can therefore be treated as a special case of exponential smoothing, where all variable values are assigned equal weight. The exponential smoothing model is defined as

$$S_t = \alpha X_t + (1-\alpha) S_{t-1}$$

where S_t is the forecast for period t of the sales variable S, X_t is the sales value in the period $t-1$, and $\alpha \, (0 \le \alpha \le 1)$ is the weight assigned to X_t. In a volatile environment, α may be assigned a large value, in order for the forecast to be responsive to the change.

Time series analysis

A time series is the record of movement of a variable or a set of variables over time. They operate on the assumption that data measured over time is influenced by four components—a trend (T), a seasonal component (S), a cyclical component (C), and an 'irregular' or random component (I), and the relationship between these components is multiplicative. The data can be expressed as

$$D = T \times S \times C \times I$$

Methods are available for decomposing each of the four components, and long-term forecasts based on time series analysis are then made using this model. As can be noticed, this method also assumes a steady, predictable environment, so that it is possible to extrapolate current patterns to the future.

Regression Techniques

Regression techniques, when applied to forecasting, take into account the relationship between the variables being forecast, i.e., the dependent variable, and other independent variables that can be expected to influence its performance. The value of the dependent variable is then forecast by fitting time series data values in the equation. This method can thus be regarded as a special case of time series analysis. It has the advantage over time series analysis in that taking changes in other variables into account provides a more realistic picture of the actual situation, so forecasts that are more accurate can be made.

Polling Techniques

Another set of forecasting techniques is based on consumer polls and expert polls. Though not formal systems of forecasting, these have usually been found to be reasonably accurate. One of these methods is the Delphi technique.

Delphi technique

This method uses an iterative procedure. A panel of experts is given basic information about the product and asked to indicate their estimate of the sales the product is likely

Table 20.7 Average Probability of Purchase

Rating	Probability of Purchase	Frequency of response (No. of respondents)
Very likely	0.8	40
Rather likely	0.4	45
Neither likely nor unlikely	0.1	30
Rather unlikely	0	20
Very unlikely	0	15
Total		150

Average probability of purchase = $(0.8 \times 40 + 0.4 \times 45 + 0.1 \times 30 + 0 \times 20 + 0 \times 15)/150 = 35.33\%$

to achieve. These estimates are then circulated to the entire panel and each member is asked if they would like to revise their earlier estimates in light of the response of the rest of the panel. The process is continued till a consensus is achieved, or some experts decline to make any further changes in their estimates. The technique has been used extensively in forecasting new product sales successfully.

Consumers are often asked to indicate their future purchase intent towards a new product. This data is usually collected on a rating scale varying from 'very likely' (or equivalent rating) to 'very unlikely'. Each of these scale values is assigned a weight, which is used to develop a 'purchase intent index'.

Alternatively, some probabilities can be assigned to each response, and the average probability of purchase can be calculated on that basis, as in Table 20.7.

A rule of thumb for this technique is to regard the product as having low potential of success if the probability of purchase at this stage averages to less than 40%. Similar processes can be administered to company employees and dealers.

Experimental Techniques

These techniques base their results on data collected from field experiments or simulations. Panel data from test markets is one example of application of this forecasting technique. We have discussed the results of models based on this method of data collection earlier in the chapter.

RESEARCH FOR DEVELOPING AND EVALUATING MARKETING STRATEGIES

Strategies are defined as road maps for getting from the current situation to the planned situation. In other words, they specify the link between the current situation and the goals. Marketing research plays different roles at each stage of developing marketing strategies. Most of these roles have been discussed in various sections of this book, and are summarized in Table 20.8.

Ansoff's classical product–market grid is one of the frequently used techniques that provide the basis for strategy development, as shown in Figure 20.3.

This grid discusses the strategies available to the company in four marketing situations, where either the market or the product, or both are new.

Table 20.8 Role of Marketing Research in Developing Market Strategies

Decision Stage	Information Requirement	Information Tools and Techniques
Current situation analysis	1. Identification of market position—leader, challenger, follower, nicher 2. Market segments available and participated in; segment attractiveness; performance in segment 3. PLC and brand life cycle	Market share data, consumer and dealer perception studies; distribution and market reach; competitive advantage; consumer loyalty studies Secondary (retail audit/industry) data on market size, growth, clutter; government regulations; major competitors; market shares, market studies to determine competitive strategies; consumer perception of performance; positioning studies; attitude-and-usage studies; customer satisfaction surveys
Objective/goal setting	1. Potential of current markets and current products; new growth opportunities—markets, products, consumer segments, competition 2. Opportunity—company capability match 3. Growth, sales, market share, distribution reach and penetration; consumer segment participated in; consumer/dealer image of company and brand	Forecasts of markets and products; secondary data on socio-economic trends; studies on competitive position; survey of consumer perceptions of company expertise in various opportunity areas; consumer perception of competition; competitive advantage
Strategy development and evaluation	1. Potential and suitability of the four quadrants of Ansoff's matrix 2. Most suitable markets/products—product–market fit 3. Most suitable element of marketing mix for strategy development 4. Consumer's stage in hierarchy of communication effects 5. Consumer attitudes, positioning, major competition, competitive strategies and competitive position, extent and direction of brand switch, scope for brand extension/new product introduction 6. Brand equity of the company and its market-offerings	1. Research to determine scope for increasing penetration—market growth, size and loyalty of user segment, opportunities for brand switch, increasing frequency of use, acceptability of new uses 2. Market development opportunities—research to assess size and growth of new user category, identification of needs, consumer perception of need–product fit 3. Consumer/dealer acceptability of new product, product forecast, likely rate of diffusion, positioning studies 4. Surveys to determine consumer communication needs—awareness, knowledge, interest, preference, purchase intent 5. Studies to identify major dimensions forming basis of brand equity 6. Measurement of brand equity

Figure 20.3 Product–Market Grid

Research for marketing strategy development helps set benchmarks against which measurements are made for evaluating the success of strategy. The measurements are both quantitative and qualitative in nature.

SUMMARY

As part of the continual process of evolution and growth, organizations routinely examine the markets for opportunities. These opportunities include new market offerings, which may be new in a variety of ways, ranging from new-to-the-world product concepts to new packaging. The risk involved, and so also the need for research, varies with the degree of newness of the market offering. Research in such cases goes through many stages, from identification of the dissatisfaction with the current means of satisfying a need to the acceptability of the new market offering for the same need and development and test-marketing of the new product or service. Many models and techniques have been developed for researching each of these stages. In case of late entry in a defined market, research is required to provide answers to somewhat different questions. Apart from identifying the most appropriate marketing mix, marketing research is called upon to provide information on issues such as brand positioning, consumer perception of the new brand, identification of appropriate segments, and the rate and extent of switch into the new brand. Specific techniques have been developed for segmenting markets as well. The rate of adoption of innovations by different consumer groups varies by product category, and Everett Rogers' model of diffusion of innovations provides a well-accepted guideline for this. Research requirements change as the product or service goes through various stages of its life cycle, and the emphasis on various elements of the marketing mix shifts. There are many research-based models available for measuring the success of the marketing efforts.

As markets evolve, the concept of branding comes into its own. The emphasis in marketing shifts from the product to the brand and its positioning. At this stage, research is required mainly to develop and verify competitive strategies. As the brand and the market mature, the positioning of the brand may at times have to be changed. Repositioning is required if the brand is participating in a fast-growing market but registers poor growth, or if a strong brand is participating in a slow growing market. Brand extensions are an effective way of reviving and growing a mature market, however, research is required to determine whether a brand may safely and profitably be extended.

In a competitive market, brand acceptance and growth is not dependent merely on physical attributes, but also on the equity of the brand. Marketing research is needed for the development as well as measurement of brand equity. Research is also needed for the measurement of brand equity. Market forecasting is a precise procedure for estimating future values of quantifiable variables such as sales, market share, consumption levels, production, or demographic and economic variables such as population, GDP, and per capita income. Various techniques of forecasting are employed in marketing research. Forecasting is particularly important for identifying and solving marketing problems related to future growth. It helps in setting objectives for the brand and for the firm, following which the most suitable marketing strategies can be set. Research plays a major role in identifying the current situation of a firm or an SBU, in setting objectives, developing strategies, and evaluating these strategies.

KEY WORDS

Market potential is the size and growth rate of a market, which determines the opportunity for successful performance of a market offering.

Market penetration is the extent of coverage of a market by a firm, measured by market share.

Scale is the size of operations of a firm.

Benefit structure analysis is a marketing research technique that measures, using a four-point rating scale, the extent to which a product benefit is desired and the extent to which it is perceived as being delivered.

Concept use test (CUT) is a method of testing the acceptability of a new market offering, in which the prototypes of a product are placed with a sample of respondents for in-use tests over a period of time.

Markov process is a process of market forecasting in which the previous states are irrelevant for predicting the subsequent states, given the knowledge of the current state.

Distribution equity is defined as the ability of a firm to have its products accepted widely by dealers because of the brand acceptance it enjoys among the consumers.

Preference angle is the opposite of the 'indifference curve', indicating graphically the extent to which a brand is preferred by consumers.

A priori **segmentation** is a method of market segmentation where the basis for grouping the respondents is chosen in advance.

Post hoc **segmentation** is a method of market segmentation in which the respondents are classified into groups on the basis of their profiles relating to brand behaviour.

Moving averages is a market forecasting method in which the variable value in time '$t+1$' is estimated to be the average of the values in the first t periods.

Exponential smoothing is a market forecasting method, similar to moving averages, where the variable value in time '$t+1$' is estimated to be the weighted average of the values in the first t periods, with more recent periods being assigned greater weight.

Time series analysis is a market forecasting model where the estimate of the variable to be forecast is decomposed into four time based components—the trend (T), a seasonal component (S), a cyclical component (C), and an 'irregular' or random component (I), and the relationship between these components is multiplicative.

Delphi technique is a polling based method of market forecasting where the forecast is obtained by iteratively obtaining estimates of the variable or event under study from a sample of experts.

Purchase intent index is a polling based method of forecasting where potential consumers are asked to rate their chances of buying the brand on a rating scale and the purchase index is then calculated as a weighted average of the responses.

CONCEPT REVIEW QUESTIONS

1. What criteria should be used in evaluating a new product concept? What role does marketing research play in the process?

2. How would research conducted for testing the potential for a new-to-the-world product differ from research for a new product in a defined market? Why?

3. How practical is the concept of brand equity? What role, if any, does research play in developing brand equity for a brand?

4. What are the advantages of regression-based techniques of market forecasting? How can they be used for forecasting sales of a new product?

5. How can marketers use information about their customers to identify prospects?

PROJECT ASSIGNMENTS

1. Assume that a major domestic airline in the country is planning to launch a holiday travel plan to be available during the off-peak season at discounted prices. The plan will cover visits to five destinations in any geographical region, east, west, north, or south, which are currently on the airline's route as well as stay at a 2-star hotel at subsidized rates. Interested tourists will have to book at least one month in advance and there will be no refund on cancellation. Develop a research plan including the hypotheses, objectives, data collection instrument, sampling plan, and analysis plan to test the market potential of the scheme. Conduct the study with an appropriate sample in your city; analyse the data, and prepare a report.

2. Compare the positioning of Indian (previously Indian Airlines), Jet Airways, Kingfisher, and Air Deccan on the basis of a field survey. To what extent do these positionings match the image the airlines are trying to build up for themselves?

3. What kind of market segmentation strategy does the retail chain Pantaloons appear to be following? What advantages and disadvantages does it have for its future growth?

4. What kind of data do you need to maintain in order to build long-term relationships with your customers if you are (a) a retail chemist, (b) a large department store, (c) a consumer products company, (d) a hospital, and (e) an industrial products company?

5. A large company manufacturing and marketing two-wheelers and three-wheelers in the country is examining growth options. The company is currently the second largest manufacturer of two-wheelers. Using Ansoff's matrix, which growth strategy would you recommend to the company? Why? What data would you need for making your recommendation?

REFERENCES

Aaker, D. 1991, *Managing Brand Equity*, Free Press.

Aaker, D., V. Kumar and G.S. Day 1998, *Marketing Research;* sixth edn, Wiley, Singapore.

Fishbein, M. 1967, 'A Behavioural Theory Approach to the Relations between Beliefs about an Object and the Attitude toward the Object', in *Readings in Attitude Theory and Measurement, Wiley, pp. 389–400, quoted in* Green, P.E. and D.S. Tull 1978, *Research for Marketing Decisions,* Prentice Hall, New Jersey.

Hauser, J.R. and S.M. Shugan 1983, 'Intensity Measures of Consumer Preferences,' *Operations Research,* vol. 28, no. 2, quoted in Urban and Hauser 1975, 'Perceptor: A Model for Product Positioning', *Management Science*, vol. 21, no. 8, pp. 858–71.

Kapferer, Jean-Noel 1992, *Strategic Brand Management*, Kogan Page, London.

Keller, K.L. 2003, *Strategic Brand Management,* second edn, Prentice Hall.

Lavidge, R.C. and G.A. Steiner 1961, 'A Model for Predictive Measurements of Advertising Effectiveness', *Journal of Marketing,* vol. 25, pp. 59–62.

Lilien, G., P. Kotler, and S. Moorthy 1992, *Marketing Models*, Prentice Hall.

Meyers, J.H. 1976, 'Benefit Structure Analysis: A New Tool for Product Planning', *Journal of Marketing,* 40, pp. 23–32.

Parfitt, J.H. and B.J.K. Collins 1968, 'Use of Consumer Panels for Brand Share Prediction,' *Journal of Marketing Research*, vol. 5, no. 2, pp. 131–46.

Plummer, J. 1974, 'The Concept and Application of Life-Style Segmentation,' *Journal of Marketing*, vol. 38, no. 1, pp. 33–37.

Rao, A.G. and P.B. Miller 1975, 'Advertising/Sales Response Functions,' *Journal of Advertising Research*, vol. 15, no. 2, pp. 7–15, quoted in Urban and Hauser 1975, 'Perceptor: A Model for Product Positioning', *Management Science*, vol. 21, no. 8, pp. 858–71.

Ries, Al and J. Trout 1985, *Positioning: The Battle for Your Mind*, McGraw-Hill, New York.

Rogers, E. 1962, *Diffusion of Innovations* Free Press, New York.

Sethi, A. and V. Chandrasekhar 1993, 'Strategic Cube Analysis for Brand Leverage', Proceedings of the Annual Conference of Market Research Society of India.

Silk, A.J. and G.L. Urban 1978, 'Pre-Test Market Evaluation of New Packaged Goods: A Model and Measurement Methodology,' *Journal of Marketing Research,* vol. 15, no. 2, pp. 171–191.

SRI consulting Business Intelligence 2003, Understanding U.S. Consumers, http:www.sricbi.com/VALS?USConsumers; www.future.sri.com.

Urban, G.L. 1975, 'Perceptor': A Model for Product Positioning,' *Management Science,* vol. 21, no. 8, pp. 858–71.

Urban, G.L. and J.R. Hauser 1981, *Design and Marketing of New Products,* Prentice Hall.

Urban, G.L., P. Johnson and R. Brudnick 1979, 'Market Entry Strategy Formulation: A Hierarchical Model and Consumer Measurement Approach,' working paper, Sloan School of Management, MIT, Cambridge, Massachusetts, quoted in Urban and Hauser 1975, 'Perceptor: A Model for Product Positioning', *Management Science*, vol. 21, no. 8, pp. 858–71.

http://en.wikipedia.org/wiki/Markov_chain.

Zhao, Y. 2006, chs. 15, 16, and 17 in *Market Testing (PPT)*, road.uww.edu/zhaoy/ Marketing, UW, Whitewater.

Index

A

analysis of covariance 273
analysis of data 291
  techniques 291
analysis of variance 270
association 256
  bivariate regression 265
  chi-square (X^2) statistic 256
  contingency coefficient 260
  correlation 262
  Cramer's V 260
  lambda coefficient 260
  multiple regression 267
  phi coefficient 260
  stepwise regression 268
attitude scales 197
  types of 197

C

causal relationship 79
  asymmetrical 80
  reciprocal 80
  symmetrical 79
causality 111
  conditions of 112
  deterministic causation 79, 111
  probabilistic causation 79, 111
choice of respondents 131
client–researcher relationship 428
cluster analysis 331
  SPSS commands for 341
  the process of 334
coding of data 245
commencement of the qualitative
research study 437
  presentation of findings 441
  qualitative research brief 438
  qualitative research proposal 439
  research instruments 440
computer based techniques of data analysis 314

D

data 6, 91
  classification of 91
  types and sources of 91
data collection 93
  errors in 97
  methods of 93
decision-making perspective 34
  Bayesian decision theory 35
designing a questionnaire 172
  errors in 176
  for telephone and Internet surveys 182
discriminant analysis 316
  multiple discriminant analysis 322
  SPSS commands 322
  two-group discriminant analysis 318

E

editing data 247
  statistical adjustment of data 248
experimental designs 115
  types of 115
experiments 112
  factors affecting the results of 113
  in marketing research 112
  limitations of 126
  validity in 113

F

factor analysis 325
  SPSS commands for principal components
analysis 330
  the process of 325
fieldwork 239
  process of 240

conjoint analysis 360
  stages in conducting 361
content analysis 519
  final perspective on 532
  process 521

focus group discussions 464
  advantages and disadvantages 465
  moderation of 486
  organization in 466

G

generalizability 217
guidelines for effective moderation 479
  discouraging excessive/irrelevant
  communication 485
  formulation of questions 479
  providing encouragement and direction 483

H

hypotheses generation 63

I

in-depth interview 472
  advantages and disadvantages 473
  flow of communication in 473
information 6
interview method 138
  cognitive maps 141
  critical incident technique 140
  focus group interviews 142
  laddering 141
  projective techniques 140
interview techniques 130

L

levels of uncertainty 27
  external risk 27
  factors influencing uncertainty 28
  internal risk 27

M

managerial dilemma 29
market research models 583
  defender model 584
  distributed lag model 585
  Fishbein's model 584
  hierarchy of effects model 585
marketing decision-making 8
  levels of complexity 9
marketing problem 61

marketing research 3, 59, 573
  and brand positioning 587
  applications of 572, 586
  during various product life cycle stages 579
  entry into defined markets 578
  for developing and evaluating marketing
  strategies 595
  for market forecasting 592
  for market segmentation 591
  nature and scope of 3
  need for 5
  new-to-the-world product 573
  product/service modification 579
  role of 8
  scope of 10
  stages in 59
  strategic decision-making 13
marketing research brief 59
marketing research problem 61
  sub-problems 62
marketing research proposal 66
  data collection and analysis 69
  limitations and scope 69
  research objectives 67
  the sample 68
  time and cost estimates 69
marketing research report 549, 562
  ethical issues in 558
  interpretation of 562
  presentation of 557
  reducing uncertainty errors 562
  role of the researcher and the client 563
  scope and structure 550
  writing a 550
measurement of data 192
  attitude measurement 196
  methods of 192
methodological frameworks of qualitative
  research 464
mode of interview 138
moderation of focus group discussion 486
multicollinearity 269
multidimensional scaling 346
  models of 354
  SPSS commands for 356
  the process of 348

N

non-parametric tests 300
   multiple-sample tests 303
   one-sample tests 300
   related samples 306

P

parametric tests 293
   hypothesis testing and confidence intervals 299
   matched samples 298
   one-sample tests 293
   two independent samples 297
post-introductory studies 86
pre-introductory decisions 82
preliminary analysis of data 253
   univariate, bivariate, and multivariate
   analysis 254
projective techniques 487
   advantages and disadvantages 488
   specific projective techniques 491
   types of 488
projective techniques and interview guides 183

Q

qualitative research 415, 416
   correct usage 421
   forte of 429
   in application 419
   observational-ethnographic research 498
   semiotics research 496
   some words of caution 425
   strengths and limitations of 434
   synectics 501
   the right application of 436
qualitative research analysis 512
   analysis and interpretation 539
   analysis of communication development
   research 527
   analysis of projective data 527
   analysis of usage and attitude data 531
   approach for 524
   data interpretation in 533
   findings 536
   key tasks 512
   presentation of 536

   process of 518
   tenets of 516
   value of 513
qualitative research methodology 463
   variations in 477
qualitative research vs quantitative research 429
qualitative researcher 426
   skills required in a 426
quality of research 31

R

reduction and grouping of data 314
   canonical correlations 316
relationship between qualitative and quantitative
research 431
reliability of scales 214
research 6
research approaches 74
   causal or diagnostic 78
   descriptive 77
   exploratory 74
role, demeanour, and skills of a moderator 478
   behavioural skills 478
   listening skills 478
role of research in marketing 26
   opportunity definition research 27
   problem-solving 27

S

sample selection 150
   the process of 150
sample size 161
   ad hoc methods 162
   the Bayesian approach 166
   the Neyman–Pearson approach 162
sampling 148
   major benefits 149
   stages 149
sampling techniques 154
   choice of 154
   non-probability sampling 160
   probability sampling 155
scale construction 218
   considerations in 218
SPSS commands 274

analysis of variance 278
    correlation 281
    cross-tabulations and chi-square test 276
    factorial experiment with interactions 280
    frequency tables 274
    randomized block design 280
    regression 282
strategy-related studies 86
survey techniques 132
    direct and indirect interviews 134
    structured and unstructured interviews 134
survey environment 133

T

tabulation of data 249
    data mining 252
tips for researchers 46

actionable research 53
    boundaries of marketing research 50
    manager–researcher dialogue 47
    marketing intelligence and marketing research 52
traits of a qualitative researcher 514

U

univariate techniques of data analysis 254
using marketing research 566
    strategic research 567
    tactical research 566

V

validity of scales 216